ALMOST TO THE PRESIDENCY

THE PIPER COMPANY

Executive Offices
120 North Main Street
Blue Earth, Minn. 56013

West Coast Offices
P.O. 26274, U.S. Custom House
San Francisco, California 94126

ALMOST

TO

THE

PRESIDENCY

A Biography of Two American Politicians

ALBERT EISELE

Manufactured in the United States of America

International Standard Book Number: 0-87832-005-9

Library of Congress Catalog Card Number: 76-187432

First Edition, First Printing

To Susan Frawley Eisele,
who cares about her writing.

CONTENTS

BOOK FOUR: CROSSROADS, 1968

BOOK FIVE: TWO TRANSITIONAL MEN, 1969–1972

FOREWORD

*I hold that man is in the right who is most
closely in league with the future.*
> Henrik Ibsen, "Letter to George Brandes":
> January 3, 1882.

The thought of what might have happened if Hubert Humphrey and Eugene McCarthy somehow had reconciled their twin drives to political power, and the question it raises of why they were unable to, is what led to the writing of this book. As its title implies, this is a book about their failure to achieve the office of ultimate power in the American political system. However, it does not deal with what might have been or what might be, since speculation about what kind of a president Hubert Humphrey or Eugene McCarthy would have made serves no useful historical purpose. It is, rather, simply a book about two proud, gifted and flawed men whose vanities and ambitions, triumphs and defeats, strengths and weaknesses make them representative American politicians. Hopefully, it sheds some light on how and why they moved from their common origins to a point of confrontation that changed them, the Democratic party and the course of American history.

The idea for this book came as a natural consequence of observing these two men for the past seven years from the vantage point of a Washington correspondent for the St. Paul *Dispatch & Pioneer Press,* the Duluth *Herald & News Tribune* and other Ridder newspapers. Often, my writing about these men dealt with their involvement in events that were of little interest beyond the borders of Minnesota. Nevertheless, my vantage point offered the opportunities for close observation that are helpful for any biographer in understanding the origins, evolution and achievements of those he writes about. I have been given no special access to the private papers or lives of either of of my subjects, nor have I asked for any, and most of the raw material from which this book is constructed, except for my first-hand observations, was available to any researcher willing to struggle through the voluminous public record compiled by these two men during careers that link four decades of American history. I am naturally indebted to those friends, aides, advisers, colleagues and antagonists of both men who spoke so freely of their associations with them, particularly those who knew them in the years before I began to report on their activities.

Hubert Humphrey and Eugene McCarthy are, above all, products of a state that has a well deserved reputation as an exporter of political talent, and not to view them in the context of their Minnesota origins is to miss much of that which makes them what they are. It was my original intention to examine more closely the contemporary political character of Minnesota, but that task is beyond the scope of this book. I have necessarily limited my treatment of Minnesota politics to the early years of the party that shaped and was shaped by Humphrey and McCarthy, devoting less attention to it in more recent years as their preoccupation has become almost exclusively the national arena.

I will not attempt to single out any individuals among the more than 125 persons who granted me interviews and shared their knowledge of my two subjects. Their contributions are evident in the book. There are, however, others whose contributions are too great to go unacknowledged. The first of these are my employers, Walter T. Ridder and Bernard H. Ridder, Jr., whose generosity in granting me time to write this book went well beyond that which I had any right to expect. William Broom, the Washington bureau chief of Ridder Publications, Inc., made my task easier by his patience and understanding, as did the various editors of the Ridder papers, particularly William Sumner, John Finnegan, Harry Burnham, Donald O'Grady and Lew Parlin at St. Paul and Orville Lomoe at Duluth. I am also indebted to Robert O'Keefe, political editor of the St. Paul *Dispatch & Pioneer Press*, for his knowledgeable and thorough coverage of Minnesota politics, which made that newspaper's files a rich source of material for me. Special thanks also are in order for my colleague on the Washington bureau of Ridder Publications, Ed Zuckerman, and for former colleagues Baxter Omohundro and Ernie Hernandez, as well as Karen Matthiesen, an extraordinarily able secretary who helped in many ways.

Of all the people who had a hand in shaping this book, none was more important or valuable to me than Lou Cannon, my former Washington bureau colleague now with the Washington *Post*. He shared unselfishly and without any limits his time, his own experience as an author of two excellent political biographies, his insights as a political reporter, and his talents as an editor and literary stylist. It is no exaggeration to say that this book could not have been written without his help and that of his equally astute and generous wife, Virginia.

I also wish to thank a number of my colleagues in the Washington press corps for their help and encouragement. In this category are Charles Bailey II and Frank Wright of the Minneapolis *Tribune*, both respected competitors and friends; Jules Witcover of the Los Angeles *Times*; James Doyle and Paul Hope of the Washington *Star*; David Broder of the Washington *Post*; Paul Weick of the *New Republic* and the Albuquerque *Journal*; Alan Otten of the *Wall Street Journal*; James Dickenson of the *National Observer*; John Farmer of the Philadelphia *Bulletin*; Ned Kenworthy of the New York *Times*; Jack Kole of the Milwaukee *Journal*; Richard Stout of *Newsweek*; William Prochnau of the Seattle *Times*; William Eaton of the Chicago *Daily News*; Marty Nolan of the Boston *Globe*; David Schoumacher of CBS; Nick Thimmesch of *Newsday*; Philip Potter of the Baltimore *Sun*; Ernest Cuneo of the North American Newspaper Alliance; Frank Cormier of the *Associated Press*; Jack Germond and Peter Behr of Garnett News Service and Peter Barnes, West Coast editor of the *New Republic*. Mercer Cross and Wayne Kelley of the *Congressional Quarterly* also kindly made their files available to me.

Special thanks must be given to my able researcher, Stephanie Eller, who spent her summer mining dusty files at the Library of Congress, Washington *Post*, Washington *Star*, New York *Times*, *Wall Street Journal*, *Congressional Quarterly*, the McCarthy Historical Project at Georgetown University and my own office, as well as transcribing tape-recorded interviews and performing other valuable chores. Barbara Hunter provided competent help as my researcher in Minnesota, Joyce Abbell was helpful as a volunteer researcher, and Ruth Darmstadter, Margo Kline and Barbara Willette were effective in transcribing interviews. Donald Picard of Webb Publishing Co., a former colleague on the St. Paul *Dispatch & Pioneer Press,* and Denis Gordon, a friend and neighbor, also helped in the final preparation of the manuscript.

Another person who deserves special mention is my publisher and long-time friend, Paul Piper of The Piper Company. His conviction that this would be a valuable book and his steadfast moral and financial support have made this dual biography possible. I am also thankful for the technical assistance provided by John M. Sullivan, Jr., in the editing of my manuscript.

Finally, I express my profound gratitude to my wife, Moira, for her long, painstaking hours of editorial assistance, personal advice and loving understanding, and to the members of the Nova Community and the Community of the Word for their friendship. Without them and all of the others, this book would not have been possible.

Falls Church, Virginia   *Albert Eisele*
April, 1972

*A brother offended is harder to be won than a strong city;
and their contentions are like the bars of a castle.*

Proverbs 18:19

BOOK ONE
TWO MEN FROM MINNESOTA

CHAPTER I

ORIGINS OF A PRAIRIE POPULIST

*I must say that the Depression left a lasting
impression on me. Much of my politics
has been conditioned by it.*
                    Hubert Humphrey in a 1971 interview.

The flat windswept prairie country of eastern South Dakota where Hubert Humphrey was born and grew to manhood was settled by people who never forgot that they lived in the shadow of forces beyond their control. Spring tornadoes, summer drought and winter blizzards made hardship and heroism commonplace occurrences on the primitive frontier of nineteenth-century South Dakota.

Norwegian-American Author Ole Rolvaag, whose son Karl would one day figure prominently in Humphrey's life, captured the essence of this land and its people in his epic narrative of immigrant pioneer life, *Giants in the Earth*. Rolvaag, who left Norway as a young man in 1896 to work as a farmhand in South Dakota, took his title from the Book of Genesis. His pioneers, like their Old Testament namesakes and real life counterparts, were a proud, confident people who were willing to pay an immense physical and psychological toll to conquer an untamed land. They were tragic figures whose lives dramatized the conflict between the practical philosophy of the New World and the idealistic values of the Old, but they were also figures throbbing with vitality and determined to make the American dream come true. They were Hubert Humphrey's spiritual ancestors and they left him the legacy of an indomitable spirit and an unshakeable optimism.

Humphrey was born on the sunny spring morning of May 27, 1911, in the bedroom of a three-room apartment over his father's drugstore in the tiny crossroads community of Wallace, South Dakota. Word spread quickly among the town's 181 residents that Hubert and Christine Humphrey had a second son and that both mother and baby were fine. "He was a beauti-

11

ful baby, dark-haired and very healthy," recalls Mrs. Olga Burge, Mrs. Humphrey's then teenage sister who later lived with the family.

The baby was christened Hubert Horatio Humphrey, Jr., an alliterative name that had first shown up in the family in the inverted form of Horatio Hubert back in 1843. Mrs. Frances Howard, the first of two sisters to follow Hubert, thinks her mother chose the name because she sensed something unusual about the baby. "My mother always thought Hubert was special from the day he was born," Mrs. Howard said more than a half a century later. "Her father was a Norwegian sea captain and maybe it was the sense of mysticism she inherited from him, that comes from the sea, but she had an absolute conviction that Hubert was a child of destiny. This was accepted unquestioningly by all of us."

Her mother's attitude toward Hubert later would manifest itself when strangers came to visit the Humphrey home, Mrs. Howard remembers. "She would introduce us children and say, 'This is my daughter, Fern, my daughter Frances, my son Ralph — and *this* is Hubert.' "

The child soon demonstrated an irresistible attraction to the limelight. At age three, he disappeared during a Norwegian Independence Day celebration. When his worried parents found him, he was proudly marching down the main street of Wallace helping lead the town band.

That the Humphrey family tree should one day bear such special fruit is hardly surprising. Its branches are heavily laden with remarkable figures on both sides of the family. The maternal side of Humphrey's genealogy has been traced all the way back to fifteenth-century Norway. His mother, Christine Sandnes, was born in 1883 in Kristiansand, a southern Norwegian seaport where her father, like Ole Rolvaag and generations of adventurous Norsemen before him, followed a life at sea.[1]

Andrew Sandnes worked on Norwegian merchant ships that plied the trade routes of Europe, Africa and Asia, and was captain of one of the first ships to pass through the new Suez Canal. But in the late 1880's, driven from the sea by the competition of steamships and a restless urge to find a new life for his family of twelve children, he crossed the Atlantic to the undulating sea of the South Dakota prairie and settled in a sod hut on three hundred acres of virgin land near Lily, South Dakota.

Humphrey's paternal ancestors came to America even earlier. Family records show that Humphrey forebears emigrated from the British Isles in pre-Revolutionary War days, almost three centuries before one of their descendants would join the ruling class of the yet unformed nation. The roots of the Humphrey family tree go back to medieval Scandinavia, where the name had its origin in the words *holm frid,* meaning "peaceful island."

One of Hubert's ancestors, Elijah Humphrey of Dudley, Massachusetts, served with distinction in the Revolutionary Army while another, Harry

---

[1] The name was later Americanized to Sannes.

Mark Humphrey, a great-grandfather, married a cousin of Henry Wadsworth Longfellow and moved to Minnesota in 1855, linking the state with the Humphrey name for the first time. The last of his nine children was John Wadsworth Humphrey, who grew up on the family homestead near Union Lakes in southern Minnesota, married a Quaker school teacher and set out on the Oregon Trail. Hubert Horatio Humphrey, Sr., was born, in 1882, near Albany, Oregon, the fourth of five children, and shortly afterwards the family moved back to Minnesota.

John Wadsworth Humphrey settled on a farm on the bank of the Mississippi River near Elk River, just north of the twin cities of Minneapolis and St. Paul, and became a prosperous farmer. He sold his dairy products in the Twin Cities, became active in the National Grange, the agrarian protest movement founded in 1867, and set out to make his farm one of the best in the state. But his wife, Adeline, described in family histories as a strong woman of "pronounced intellectual tastes," urged her daughter and four sons toward scholarly pursuits.[2]

The Humphrey and Sannes families were joined, much to the delight of Andrew Sannes, in 1907 when Hubert Horatio, Sr., and Christine Sannes were married at Lily, South Dakota. Christine's father was the happiest man in Codington County, relatives said, because most Norwegian girls in the area married Swedes, whom he considered second-rate citizens.

Young Hubert's parents met at a church social in Lily, where his father came to work in a drugstore after graduating from the Drew School of Pharmacy in Minneapolis. After their marriage, they moved a short distance across the Minnesota border to Granite Falls, where the senior Humphrey went into partnership in a drugstore. Their first son, Ralph Wadsworth, was born shortly thereafter in 1908. Late in 1910, the Humphreys moved to Wallace, South Dakota, where they bought their first drugstore. A few months later, in May, 1911, Hubert Horatio, Jr., was born. (The timing of the move prompted Hubert to claim while running for the Senate in Minnesota that "I may have been born in South Dakota but I was conceived in Minnesota.")

Wallace, a name oddly to be repeated in two future maverick political foes of young Humphrey, proved too small to support the growing Humphrey family (Frances was born in 1914). So a year later, the Humphreys bought a drugstore in Doland, a community of about 550 persons, 35 miles to the

---

[2] That she succeeded is evident from the fact that none of the sons followed in the family tradition of farming. The eldest, Harry Baker, took his Ph.D. at Stanford, became chief plant pathologist for the U.S. Department of Agriculture and would later take young Hubert on his first tour of Washington, D.C. The next son, John Wadsworth, Jr., invented the first mechanical potato digger and later became chairman of the Department of Economics at the University of Kentucky. Hubert Horatio became a pharmacist and the fourth son, Robert Ford, was an accomplished artist. Even the lone girl in the family, Frances Estella, produced a son who became an internationally famous plant botanist.

southwest in neighboring Spink County. Young Hubert was conceived in
Minnesota and born in Wallace, but he was shaped in Doland. The thirteen
years he lived there were among the happiest of his life and they provided him
with a childhood as secure as any boy could ask for.

Doland was a one-horse town, not unlike a thousand other placid enclaves
of civilization scattered over the Great Plains. It stretched only a few blocks
in each direction, a tiny encroachment on the vast prairie equidistant from
its larger neighbors of Aberdeen, Huron and Watertown and exactly 1,342
miles from Washington, D.C., according to a sign on the edge of town. But
it had two banks, three churches, an independent elementary and high school,
and even a hotel, built when the senior Humphrey got the town to float a bond
issue. The town's name was emblazoned on the Peavey grain elevators, the
municipal water tower and the Chicago and Northwestern Railroad depot.
And of course there was the Humphrey drugstore, one of a dozen or so business establishments on Main Street.

The Humphreys lived in one of the best houses in Doland, a large white
frame structure with four bedrooms, two bathrooms, a huge kitchen with
big cupboards where presents were hidden at Christmas, a large living room
and dining room, and a screened front porch. In the front was a spacious
lawn with fruit and shade trees where the children romped with an Airedale
named Rex, and in the back was a rabbit hutch and garage where the family's
green Model T Ford was kept. The house was equal to any other in town,
although Mrs. Humphrey was secretly envious of the mirrored French doors
in the home of Doland's other druggist, a luxury she attributed to the fact
that he sold liquor in his store.

Books were almost as important as meals to Humphrey, Sr. He compiled a superb collection of volumes covering the great thought of the
Western world. His library got a shaky start, however. Shortly after they
were married and living in Granite Falls, his wife sent him to the store for
household supplies and he returned home loaded down with books instead.
Distressed at her husband's impracticality, Mrs. Humphrey angrily dumped
the books into the nearby Minnesota River. After that he was more discreet
in buying books. He hid them in the children's bedrooms, bringing them
out one at a time.

"My father was an intellectual prober, more interested in books and
ideas, while my mother wanted more practical things like rugs or dresses
or pots and pans," Frances recalls. "She was a strict Lutheran and I don't
think she approved of a lot of books like Darwin, Kierkegaard and Kant.
But she had an absolute devotion to Dad and she'd say, 'I don't understand
your father. He's different, but he's brilliant.' "

Frances remembers her father as "sort of an agnostic" as a result of his
having been influenced by Robert Ingersoll's book, *The Great Agnostic*.
He refused to be baptized until he was forty, the same day Ralph and

Hubert, Jr., were baptized, and even then agreed only when it was done not in church but in Doc Sherwood's office. But he soon became a leading layman in the Doland Methodist Church, which the family joined because there weren't enough Lutherans to support a church in Doland.

The senior Humphrey, one of five Democrats in Doland, was more puzzled by his wife's views on politics than her religion. He told people he became a Democrat after hearing William Jennings Bryan speak in Minneapolis, and he couldn't understand how his wife could vote for Warren Harding and Calvin Coolidge. People in Doland were both religious and Republican, and it was hard to tell where religion stopped and Republicanism began. But Humphrey cautioned his children to treat their mother with respect. He told them, "Don't argue with her and don't ever speak harshly to her, because she's my sweetheart," Hubert later recalled. But he also cautioned the boys that while their mother was a lovely woman, "Sometimes she's politically unreliable."

Almost every night after closing up the drugstore, usually after 10:00 or 11:00 P.M., the children gathered in the library in their flannel nightgowns to hear their father read to them while their mother pleaded unsuccessfully for their father to send them to bed. "You go to bed for all of us," the father told her. "We're gonna talk politics." For bedtime stories, instead of Peter Rabbit, the children would hear about their father's heroes. "He would read about the lives of the men who were his favorites — Jefferson, Lincoln, Woodrow Wilson — he read a lot of Wilson, he was a great Wilsonian Democrat," Humphrey said years later. "He read Elbert Hubbard's *Little Journeys to the Home of the Great;* he read a great deal of Emerson; he would read a great deal of poetry — most American poetry, nothing too sophisticated, I suppose. Longfellow, I remember, Whittier, Tennyson, and of course, you couldn't live in South Dakota without hearing from Edgar Guest." Along with his books, the senior Humphrey had an outstanding collection of classical records, which he carefully listed in his will to be divided among his children.

About twice a year, he would bring out a copy of Bryan's immortal "Cross of Gold" speech of 1896 and read it to the family after dinner. Young Hubert had heard it and Wilson's "Fourteen Points" so often that by the time he was ten, he could recite them from memory.

The events in the world outside South Dakota came to the Humphrey home through newspapers, magazines and the radio. The very first newspaper young Hubert read was the *Christian Science Monitor.* His father also subscribed to the New York *Herald-Tribune* and kept bound copies of the newspaper along with the *National Geographic,* sent by Uncle Harry as a gift. Often, when reading a news story about some national or world event, the father would say, "You should know this, Hubert, it might affect your life someday." The exposure to these men and ideas greatly expanded the universe of the Humphrey children, Frances notes. "We lived out in the middle of South Dakota, but we were in touch with all these great people, intellectually, all our lives."

Years later, Humphrey talked of the big house he grew up in and Doland during a television program in which he and Author James Baldwin discussed their childhoods. The interview provided a dramatic contrast between the extremes of American culture, with Baldwin describing a childhood in the Harlem ghetto and Humphrey recounting "those very happy and exciting growing-up years" in Doland. "I just loved that town," reminisced Humphrey. "You knew everybody and everybody knew everything about you. It was a community of warmth . . . it was a very intimate, close relationship. It was simply wonderful. Yes, Doland was just like a family."

One of Humphrey's most vivid memories was listening to the outside world beckon in the lonesome whistle of trains passing through Doland. "I can remember standing and looking down that track . . . it was so flat that you could see the tracks just fade away in the distance and out of existence. I can remember wanting to get on a train and travel long distances. I remember very well watching the trains and thinking about the state capital, thinking about Washington, and dreaming about that kind of thing."

The dreams of the young son of the Doland druggist would not become a reality for many years. Tagged with the nickname "Pinky" by his mother because of his fair complexion, the boy was a model son. Like his brother Ralph, he began working in the drugstore at age six by sweeping floors and uncrating merchandise. At seven, he was checking invoices and standing on a wooden crate in the store's Bluebird ice cream parlor making root beer floats and ice cream sodas.

He also showed evidence of his latent leadership qualities. Once, when his mother left him in charge of Frances at the Spink County Fair, he called some friends together and organized a game of "Napoleon," leaving several "soldiers" in charge of his "prisoner of war" sister while he went off to see the sights of the fair. He swore Frances to secrecy but his mother found out anyway and the budding Napoleon met his Waterloo.

Another incident, now part of the family lore, foreshadowed one of the boy's most singular future talents. "Hubert was always the mediator," says Frances. "He'd do it not so much with great pontifical words, but with a sense of coming up with something so clever. For example, he had been very naughty and my mother called my father at the drugstore and told him to come home 'because this boy is really out of hand.' So Dad switched Hubert and hadn't finished the job when Hubert crawled under the big front porch. When Dad bent down to look under the porch, Hubert's comment was, 'Come on in, Dad. Is Mother after you, too?' Papa laughed so hard he couldn't finish the job." When he was nine, Hubert admonished his six year old sister for volunteering her age to a train conductor so that her father had to pay full fare for her. "That should teach you a lesson, Franny," he declared. "You shouldn't lie, but you don't have to open your mouth."

Hardly anybody in Doland today admits to having seen Hubert walk anywhere. Townspeople called him "Hurrying Hubert" because he was always running along the street delivering the St. Paul *Dispatch* and jogging to the four-room school or taking a prescription to his father's customers. "When he stood out there on Main Street in front of the drugstore selling an armload of papers, you could hear him all over town," says Frances. She also remembers that at football or basketball games, "Everybody sort of looked at Hubert's face to see how the game was coming, like watching the scoreboard."

Mrs. Olive Doty, one of Hubert's teachers at the red-brick Doland grade school, was one of the few people able to slow Hubert down. She once stopped a skinny fifth grader who was bounding up the stairs and demanded, "Hubert Humphrey, go right back down those stairs and come up again, one step at a time, not three." The embarrassed boy complied, explaining that he was hurrying to the library to sign out a new book before somone beat him to it.

Tragedy only occasionally intruded into the healthy, happy years of Hubert's childhood. His closest brush with serious trouble came in the winter of 1918 when a nationwide influenza epidemic reached the South Dakota prairie. The disease infected the entire Humphrey family, but with young Hubert it developed into pneumonia and he almost died.

He remembers lying in bed delirious with fever, afraid that he was going to die. He dreamed of an old deserted barn outside of town where the older boys would frighten younger ones by hanging the bleached skull of a cow in the doorway. Several people had already died, and Doc Sherwood was pessimistic about the boy's chances for recovery, but Hubert's father had heard of an experimental drug available in Minneapolis. Too sick to make the trip himself, he asked a friend, Herb Gilbey, to go. Gilbey drove all night, completing the five hundred mile round trip in a snowstorm. The drug he brought back broke the fever and the boy recovered. His father and Doc Sherwood credited the medicine with saving the boy, but his Aunt Olga and his mother were sure he was cured by the dose of whiskey they secretly gave him.

The Humphrey drugstore was the social center of Doland as Humphrey, Sr., sold pills and ideas in equal measure. The mid-morning coffee hour was a time of political free-for-all attended by the local Republican bankers and businessmen, and young Hubert drank in the stimulating atmosphere like a thirsty boy swigging soda pop. "In that ice cream parlor I heard things that shaped my life and my attitude toward people and ideas," he said later. "I've attended two or three good universities, and I've heard some of the great parliamentary debates of our time, but I don't think I have ever heard better discussions of basic issues than I did as a boy standing on a wooden platform behind my father's soda fountain."

Hubert also received some on-the-job training in the art of practical politics from his dad, who served as a councilman and later mayor of Doland and was opposed to selling the municipally-owned power plant to a private utility. "He was a city councilman then and he fought the idea tooth and nail," Humphrey remembers. "I was only twelve years old, but he would take me to the evening meetings of the council, put me in a chair by a corner window, and then he'd do battle, hour after hour. Toward the latter part of the evening, I'd doze off, but I'd wake up when Dad hit another climax. He lost that fight, but his independence, his outspokenness, his spirit never interfered with the mutual respect he and the town had for each other. He was a Democrat and a rebel in a politically orthodox town, but they elected him mayor."

Nearly a half a century later, the astonishing influence of his father would still be fresh in Humphrey's memory. "Dad set high standards for me and all my life I've tried to live up to what he taught me. As a boy I was more concerned that I would fail the standards that he set for me than anything else," Humphrey wrote after becoming vice president of the United States. "My father was a passionate believer in this country, in democracy, and in social justice, a man who was interested in ideas but related them to his love for human beings, a man to whom hard work was a way of life not for its own sake but because it was part of the action and passion of his time." He added, in an interview in 1971, "One thing I learned more than anything else from my father was respect for another man's point of view. I must say that today I don't have much respect for people who don't have respect for another man's point of view."

From his father, young Hubert also acquired a lifelong habit of herculean work and a disdain for inactivity. His father thought vacations were a waste of time and Hubert once confessed, almost plaintively, "Sometimes I used to wonder why I didn't get a vacation occasionally like the other kids — a regular vacation. But my father wasn't very strong on vacations; he was strong on work." His father often told the boy, "You've got to work be-cause you're never as smart as you think you are. You're going to have to depend a lot on just out-working the other fellow."

As far as sleep was concerned, the elder Humphrey regarded it as little more than an interruption in the work day. He contended that by proper living and supplementing one's diet with vitamin pills, a person could get along with an absolute minimum of sleep. "I can never remember going to bed before midnight since I was twelve years old, except when I was sick," his son says. "He told me once, 'Never go to bed. Stay out of bed as long as you can. Ninety percent of all people die in bed.' "

Having inherited his father's awesome work habits and his hunger for learning, Hubert found little challenge in Doland High School. He memorized most of his lessons with a single reading and whizzed through his courses with all A's except for a B in Latin and a B+ in music. Mrs. Lulu Herther, who taught him as a sophomore, can remember Hubert telling his class that he wanted to be president someday, but everybody laughed and he took it back. Nevertheless, there was little question he was destined for some kind of leadership.

He was senior class valedictorian, captain of the debating team, a Life Scout, played the lead in the senior class play, *Captain Applejack,* sang in the operetta, played in the school band, and won letters in football, basketball and track. Although too light to excel as an athlete, his coach, Irven Herther, remembers that Hubert often pulled teams out of a slump with a halftime pep talk.

Humphrey's most avid extracurricular interest seemed to be debate. Doland oldtimers still talk about the "four aitches" — Humphrey, Julian Hartt, Alvin Hahn and Earl Hansen — who made up one of the best debate teams in the state and filled the school's trophy case.[3] Hubert was so able a teacher that he helped Frances win a state declamation championship, patiently coaching her by having her do scenes from *Quo Vadis,* explaining her mistakes to her and sometimes challenging the judges when she lost.

Guy Cook, Doland's high school superintendent from 1923 to 1942, later pinpointed one of the qualities that would serve Humphrey well in political life. He remembers that the Doland coach asked the judges in a debate at Brookings to rate each of his debaters individually. "Our instructor had rated Julian Hartt a little better than Hubert. We were surprised when the judges rated Hubert first. But here's the difference. When Hubert got his material lined up, he went out like he was preaching a holy crusade. He was arguing for something for which he had a dedicated feeling . . . it made him more effective."[4]

One of Humphrey's classmates, Mrs. Ann Decker, also recalled Hubert's knack for placating people. One day, during a community sale, she and Hubert opened several crates containing live chickens, and townspeople scurried after the birds and the youngsters. "We hid for hours to keep away from everybody," she said. "But no matter what trouble Hubert got himself into, he always talked his way out of it . . . and he didn't have an enemy in the world."

By the time Humphrey graduated from Doland High School in 1929, the

[3] Hartt, whose father was the Methodist minister and the only man in Doland with a degree from Harvard, went on to become professor of theology at Yale, while Hahn became an attorney in Seattle and Hansen settled down on a farm near Doland.

[4] One of the judges was Karl Mundt, who was elected to the U.S. Senate from South Dakota in 1948, the same year Humphrey was elected in Minnesota.

school news notes column in the Doland *Times-Record* noted that the slogan of the thirteen member class was "We're Out to Win!" and that valedictorian Humphrey "spoke the farewells of the class" in a "sincere and convincing manner." But the happy days of Hubert Humphrey's boyhood were about to come to an end as South Dakota began to feel the first pangs of what was to be a decade of depression and drought.

The first serious duststorm hit eastern South Dakota on Armistice Day, 1932, and Humphrey, who was hunting pheasants at the time, has the day and many like it that followed imprinted on his mind: "The sun was blackened out and all you could see was a small, shining disk. The heat was terrible and the dust was everywhere. It came in under the doors, through the cracks and it covered everything. People walked around with wet handkerchiefs on their faces. The wells ran dry and people bought bottled water. Then the grasshoppers came, hordes of them — they even ate the paint off our houses. I thought it was the end of the world."

For some people, it was. "They lost their land, they lost their property and many of them even lost their lives," he remembers. "You could see it in their faces — great fright. This look of despair, of uncertainty, of unpredictability. Hopelessness."

Humphrey learned the meaning of the Depression in one traumatic moment when he found out that the family's home would have to be sold to cover his father's debts. It was the first time he'd ever seen his father cry, and it was a major turning point in his life, an incident that more than any other single experience would color his political philosophy. He once called it "probably the most profound experience of my early years . . . the moment I ceased being a child, when I began to have an adult's awareness of the pain and tragedy in life."

Humphrey later described that day in language straight out of *Giants in the Earth:* "I recall vividly coming home from school one day late [in the] afternoon. I found my mother and father together . . . standing in the orchard. And there was another man there. And my mother was weeping. And Dad, too, had tears in his eyes. I asked my father what had happened. He told me we simply had to sell the house. This was the only way he could cover and pay his bills. And I seemed to learn then, that no matter how competent my father may have been, or how good my mother, or how fine my community, that it could be wrecked by forces over which we had no control. That this little secure world of my hometown just wasn't strong enough to fight off the powerful forces that seemed to be crowding in on us."

And in words that were almost prophetic in their description of his own reaction to losing the presidency in 1968, Humphrey told how his father overcame his worst defeat:

"Through the years, I carried with me from that scene not just the picture of this masterful man in tears, but the fact that after this terrible loss he carried not an ounce of bitterness, of apology or defeatism. He continued to do what he had always done — plunge into life without protecting himself with suspicion, reserve or emotional caution. People like that enjoy the sunshine of life to the full. But many of them are unprepared for the storms, and when they are shocked or hurt, they withdraw and cover up. Not Dad. The same sensitivity to things he cared for that made him weep carried him beyond this wound into the future. Right up to the time he died, in November of 1949, he had an undiminished appetite for life, the bitter and the sweet, with nothing held back."

The Depression soon struck full force in Doland and the rest of South Dakota. Shortly after young Hubert joined Ralph at the University of Minnesota in September, 1929, both of Doland's banks failed, bankrupt farmers were bringing in milk, eggs and meat to barter for drugs, and the credit books in the Humphrey drugstore were filling up with unpaid debts. Since there wasn't enough money to keep both boys in college, Ralph stayed and Hubert gave up his dreams of a college education and came home in the middle of his sophomore year. His father, meanwhile, had obtained five thousand dollars worth of merchandise on credit from a Minneapolis drug wholesaler and moved the drugstore and family to the nearby larger city of Huron.

Hubert, Jr., would complete his college education many years later and the experience of the Depression years would forge in him a mental toughness and habit of self-discipline that would never leave him. But it would leave some permanent scars on his psyche as well, as one of his biographers, Winthrop Griffith, noted in 1965. "Beneath his buoyant optimism is a small but hard seed of fatalism. Under his ebullient confidence runs a streak of insecurity, a fear that forces outside his control might, at any moment, darken his world, destroy his achievements, and depress his spirit."[5]

A more critical observer, conservative columnist John Chamberlain, argued at about the same time that Humphrey had drawn the wrong conclusions about what was essentially a cyclical natural disaster. "Logic should tell anyone that 'economics' and 'catastrophe,' though they may coincide when nature howls, are not always the same subject," Chamberlain wrote in the September, 1964, *National Review*. "But as the supposedly mature Humphrey preaches his Liberalism up and down the nation today, everything is a 'catastrophe' requiring government aid. Life itself is a catastrophe, and everyone should get crutches for free."

Humphrey himself makes it clear that he is still first and foremost a child of the Depression. "I must say that the Depression left a lasting impression on me," Humphrey said in an interview in 1971. "Much of my politics has been conditioned by it. When I see bankers raise interest rates, I don't

[5] Griffith's book, *Humphrey — A Candid Biography*, has been unfairly discounted because he once worked for Humphrey, but it remains one of the best studies of Humphrey in his pre-vice presidental years.

look upon it theoretically. I studied a lot of economics at the University . . .
but I want to tell you, I learned more about economics from one South
Dakota duststorm than I learned in seven years at the University."

The Depression also confirmed the deep distrust of money manipulators
in Washington and on Wall Street that Humphrey learned from the family's
household prophet of Populism, William Jennings Bryan. "I saw what
happens when there's no money and no crops and then the drought hits.
You see what happens to people. I think that to this day, this is what affects
me more than anything else. Even now . . . when I see tight money, and
when I see the Federal Reserve Bank raising that discount rate, and the
prime rate, I remember my daddy telling me what happened in 1922, and
I remember 1926, and I remember 1928, and I am rightly suspicious of
the manipulators of money.

"It's a damn good thing to remember — it's as true as there's twenty-four
hours in a day. I'm suspicious and I'm fearful of them. One of the reasons
I thought so much of Franklin Roosevelt is because I thought he was the
first president in my lifetime to challenge the power of these money-changers.
I think he humanized the banking institutions too. I think we're prone to
depend too much on monetary policy; I don't think it's fair to ask the banking structure to take on that much responsibility for the economy.

"I've undoubtedly altered some of my views. I think I'm less emotional
about it. I've lived long enough to know that you can't expect a banking
system to be able to be the total regulator of an economy. It has a role to
play, but there's a natural reaction — the child who has burned his hands
on the stove is afraid of the heat."

Humphrey gave himself heart and soul to Roosevelt's New Deal philosophy in the seven years he spent in Huron from 1930 to 1937. These were
years when the fundamental liberalism he inherited from his father blossomed
into a deep yearning to transform his opinions into action through the political forum. But there was little time for anything but the grueling work necessary to keep the family business going.

With five other drugstores in Huron, competition was fierce, and Humphrey's father expanded the soda fountain into a restaurant and added
veterinary services — and a pig to the storefront sign — in a bid for the trade
of farmers in the area. The entire family pitched in to help, with Mrs.
Humphrey and the girls cooking blue plate luncheons that sold for twenty-
five cents and sandwiches that sold first for ten cents and then for eight
cents to beat the competition, whose prices the children went out to check
on Saturday nights. Ralph returned from college and he and Hubert took
turns making the rounds of the Beadle County farms with their father
to inoculate hogs and cattle and to stuff pills down chickens' throats.

Although the senior Humphrey was bitterly opposed to chain stores, he
could see the inevitable. When he heard that Walgreen's was thinking of

opening a drugstore in Huron, he went to Chicago to see the head of the company and talked him into making his store the local Walgreen outlet. But when the company attempted to put a large "Walgreen Agency" sign on the store, he refused to permit it. "My dad said that the big sign out there was going to say 'Humphrey and Sons,' " Hubert remembers. "And it did. We put the 'Walgreen Agency' on a little sign below."

The elder Humphrey's competitors remember him as a shrewd business-man but one who was never obsessed with getting rich. He practiced a form of pragmatic philanthropy during the Depression years that paid off when times got better, sending out notices to people who owed him money, in-forming them that their accounts were paid. "These are proud people and they're not going to come in as long as they owe us money," he explained to Ralph and Hubert. "People would come in with a prescription and they'd say 'Charge it,' and Dad would say, 'No, we don't charge it,' " Hubert recounts. " 'Here's what we'll do. Here's a slip, here's how much it is. You keep it. If you can pay it sometime later, pay it. If you can't, forget it.' "

"And I remember Dad saying to me, 'Son, you know we're no better off than they are. If they're broke, we're going to be broke in due time. When they come around to foreclose on us, those half-empty prescription bottles back there that have the seals broken on them won't be worth anything anyway. So we might just as well give it to them and a lot of them might come back.' And so help me God, after the Depression was over, these people came back — I would say that two-thirds of all the people came back and paid their bills and in the meantime, we got their cash trade. Today, we're the only independent drugstore in that town; there were six of them fifteen years ago. Every other one is a discount house, but Humphrey's store is still there."

When his father died in 1949, people came from all over South Dakota to his funeral, Humphrey recalled twenty-two years later in a voice full of emotion. "I can hardly talk about it, I get so sentimental . . . I found people there who came and I hadn't seen them for years. I said, 'What are you doing here?' They said, 'Oh, your dad put me through college.' I said, 'What are you talking about?' And they said, 'Oh yes, he helped me.' "

But in the mid-1930's, as the country struggled to find its way out of the Depression, the continuing frustrations of what looked like a deadend job in a small town drugstore began to gnaw at the young man who once dreamed of riding a train out of Doland to the big city. There were stomach pains and fainting spells but doctors could find nothing wrong with Hubert. When his father refused to let him hitchhike to the World's Fair in Chicago, a shouting match ensued between father and son with the young Humphrey threatening to leave home for good and then taking his frustration out by smashing some glasses behind the store's lunch counter.

Also, Hubert was nursing his own private heartache. A girl he'd become engaged to who was studying music in Minneapolis broke the engagement and never returned the diamond ring he'd given her. "He thought it was the greatest and most tragic of all love affairs," says Frances. "He swore he would never fall in love again."

However, as the New Deal policies took hold and relief checks started to trickle into Huron, Humphrey's father scraped together two hundred dollars and sent his son to the Denver College of Pharmacy. He finished the two-year course in six months and demonstrated his phenomenal memory by learning the English and Latin names and prescribed dosages of all the drugs listed in the druggists' *Pharmacopoeia*.

Frances believes that experience changed her brother in a profound way. "Some of the emotional and spiritual things he went through that year to physically and spiritually survive shaped him. I remember him telling me that he became very faint right before the exam, and when he came to, a lot seemed very clear to him. He'd been working under such pressure, there were things that bothered him so much, and when he went in and took the exam, he passed, I think, second highest. From then on, he used to have what we call a nervous stomach."

Back in Huron in 1933, young Humphrey became something of a man about town. He was scoutmaster for the Methodist church troop, became active in the local Young Democrats organization, and pretty much ran the drugstore as his father took to the road selling pig serum and veterinary supplies to area farmers.

He even got some experience in radio work, interviewing people on the street for a program his father sponsored on a local radio station. But his father used the time mostly to play good music. "He said people needed to hear good music and he'd play classical records and read poetry," Humphrey recalls. "I'd say, 'Dad, nobody listens to that stuff.' And he'd say, 'Well, I'm buying it and it's my right to read it. I believe in the First Amendment and I'm going to read it.' "

One day in 1934, a woman who worked for his father introduced the twenty-three year old Humphrey to two girls who came into the store for Cokes. One of the girls was Muriel Fay Buck, the pretty twenty-two year old daughter of a Huron butter and egg dealer. She had met Humphrey casually at a dance in 1931 and had seen him around town, but wasn't overly impressed. She once said of their initial meeting, "He was a skinny boy, and he kidded and joked so much I thought he was kind of childish." But now they began to see each other regularly, going to dances at Lampe's Pavilion to listen to touring bands like Lawrence Welk and Wayne King, and taking long drives in the country with Humphrey's father after the store closed.

By the summer of 1935, the young couple had decided to get married. At the same time, in August, Humphrey finally took the trip he'd been dreaming about since his childhood. He accompanied Huron's Boy Scout troop on a bus trip to Washington, D.C. The trip crystallized his future ambitions.

The skinny 127-pound Humphrey was more enthralled than any of his young charges by the nation's capital. He gazed at the marble monuments erected to honor the men of history whom he'd first learned of in his father's library, and looked with fascination from the Senate visitors gallery at more contemporary figures of history like Louisiana's Senator Huey "Kingfish" Long. He spent the night with his Uncle Harry, who was working at the Department of Agriculture and had taken him to see the place he wanted to visit first, the Jefferson Memorial. After talking late into the night with his uncle and his sister Frances, who was studying at George Washington University, Humphrey sat down and wrote an airmail letter to his fiancée back in Huron.

In the handwritten "Dear Bucky" letter, which was to become the prime exhibit in the Humphrey memorabilia, he gave full expression to his frustrated yearning for a life in politics and signaled his determination to achieve it:

> Maybe I seem foolish to have such vain hopes and plans, but, Bucky, I can see how someday, if you and I just apply ourselves and make up our minds to work for bigger things, we can live here in Washington and probably be in government politics or service. I intend to set my aim at Congress. Don't laugh at me, Muriel. Maybe it does sound rather egotistical and beyond reason, but, Muriel, I know others have succeeded. Why haven't I a chance?

Humphrey also revealed in the letter a dazed excitement with Washington and an awed reverence for his new hero, President Roosevelt, that was matched only by his ungrammatical disdain for the opposition party:

> Washington, D.C., thrills me to my very finger tips. I simply revel and beam with delight in this realm of politics and government. Oh Gosh, I hope my dream comes true — I'm going to try anyhow, but first I shall prepare myself for the task by reading and thinking always as a liberal. Roosevelt is a super-man. His speech last nite surely baffled the republicans, in fact they are lost in a sea of uncertainty as to how to attack him.

If Muriel had any doubts about what her husband-to-be wanted, the letter dispelled them. When Humphrey returned to Huron, she urged him to go back to the University and complete his education. By the time they were married in September, 1936, she had made it possible by saving six hundred dollars from her pay as a billing clerk for a local utility company. Humphrey later jokingly said that "I married her for her money." Friends say he definitely was receptive to Muriel's gentle pushing to get him back in school.

It was a big wedding, and the church was filled with relatives and friends. Frances came home from Washington and caused Hubert embarrassment by

losing her garter and delaying the ceremony. Then she added the ultimate in-
dignity by hitching a ride in the backseat of the newlyweds' Model A Ford to
Minneapolis to catch a train back to Washington. As they headed for their
honeymoon in northern Minnesota, a relieved Humphrey stopped in Duluth
and used part of his father's wedding present of fifty dollars for a bottle
of whiskey to celebrate a future full of promise and his deliverance from
relatives.

When the couple returned to Huron, however, the past still clung tenaci-
ously to them. Arriving home behind a tow truck after hitting a cow thirty
miles from Huron, Hubert had to pay for the damage to his father's car as
well as reimburse an irate farmer for his cow. His stomach pains returned
and he again suffered from fainting spells as he clashed with his father over
the young man's desire to return to school and the father's own hopes for
political office.

The senior Humphrey now had time to devote to politics with Hubert
running the store at a salary of fifteen dollars a week. The one-time mayor
of Doland had won a seat in the South Dakota legislature and was being
urged by party leaders to run for governor or the U.S. Senate. The situation
became a hotly-debated topic within the family councils, according to Frances.

"Like all daughters, I worshipped my father, and as much as I admired
Hubert, when it came to a showdown, I was on my father's side. My mother
was on Hubert's side. I can remember this exchange going on in our house
at that time. Either Hubert would have to come to the drugstore to permit
Dad to run or Dad would have to stay in the drugstore to permit Hubert to
go back to school. You couldn't have both."

In August, 1937, the issue was resolved. The elder Humphrey offered
his son a full partnership in the store if he'd stay. Hubert gently but firmly
refused, explaining that he and Muriel had made up their minds to pursue
their own dream. Humphrey's father, even though he knew it meant the end
of his political ambitions, gave his son his blessing.

A month later, the young Humphrey left his native state for the last time
to resume his quest for the university education that had been cut short six
years earlier. The dry grass from a decade of drought and depression grated
on the baked earth as he drove with Muriel and his father and mother into
Minnesota where, like the giants in the earth he descended from, he answered
the call to a new destiny.

CHAPTER II

GENESIS OF AN ENIGMA

The motto of the Benedictine order is
"Keep death daily before your eyes,"
which is a very good motto for politicians.
Eugene McCarthy in a 1969 interview.

One hundred and fifty miles due east of Hubert Humphrey's birthplace, the grey slate-covered spire of St. Anthony's Catholic Church thrusts its stout cross high into the central Minnesota sky over the village of Watkins. Here, in the gently undulating, lake-dotted terminal moraine that marks the furthest advance of a prehistoric glacier, Eugene Joseph McCarthy was born on March 29, 1916.

McCarthy grew up in the shadow of the gothic spire of St. Anthony's in a house on a street with no name. He spent hours playing in a backyard sandpile with his younger brother, Austin, building imaginary farms and buying and selling toy horses in emulation of his father, a livestock buyer. McCarthy's rural origins were reflected in his first word — "cow" — uttered at age two when he picked up a letter sent to his father by a South St. Paul livestock company and identified the picture on the envelope.

In November, 1918, the little boy who would make a historic protest against another American war a half-century later, joined the rest of Watkins in a parade celebrating the end of the World War I. Like his future antiwar dissent, McCarthy's first appearance in the public spotlight was a solitary venture, and it caused his mother some anxious moments before she found him toddling down Main Street behind the Watkins village band.

And just like another mother in Wallace, South Dakota, McCarthy's mother had an instinctive feeling about her son. "My mother always sensed that Gene had something of greatness in him," recalls Mrs. Marian Enright, one of McCarthy's two older sisters. "We could always tell — there were certain ways it showed up. For instance, if she was sick or there was a crisis, she always wanted Gene to be with her."

It was McCarthy's mother, a quiet, gentle, deeply religious woman, who was the dominant influence on him during his formative years. She raised him, his two sisters, and his brother, while her husband, Michael McCarthy, was absent for long periods of time buying livestock in the West. "Mother was the one who really raised us," recalls Austin, now a surgeon in nearby Willmar, Minnesota. "Dad would be on the road six and eight weeks at a time buying cattle and horses and then he'd be home four or five days and go again. Mother was always there."

Mrs. McCarthy also was a very religious person, her children recall. Even on the most bitterly cold winter mornings, she would walk the two and a half blocks to St. Anthony's Church to Mass, and she regularly led her children in prayer at home. "She didn't do this just to set an example for us," says Austin. "She really believed in it. I'd say she was a saintly person."

Austin, who was born two years after Eugene, remembers his mother as a "very diligent, hard worker who was very conscious of not offending anybody by word or deed." But his father, now ninety-seven and living in a nursing home in Willmar, was a feisty, rugged individualist with a short temper. "Dad would flare up and shake you by the back of the neck when he got mad."

Austin believes that his mother's gentle nature made a deep impression on all her children. "We respected her for the fact that she didn't become excited and angry with us. I think this had the effect — I don't know about Gene but this was certainly true of me — of teaching us not to react in anger and with words that we'd regret later. I think this has been a real factor in the way Gene has reacted to things."

The influence of Anna McCarthy would rub off on Gene in many ways as he grew older. "Eugene was always so good," says Marian. "Sometimes you almost would wish he'd do something naughty so the rest of us wouldn't look so bad. I can remember one time when somebody was drunk at a dance and fell down and Gene helped him up. You know how these things get around a little town, so the next day, somebody was telling me about it and said, 'Didn't Gene tell you?' But he hadn't told any of us."

Anna Baden McCarthy, like her husband, was born to immigrant parents ten miles south of Watkins at Forest City, a tiny settlement in Meeker County about seventy miles northwest of Minneapolis and St. Paul. Her parents were a Bavarian couple who were part of the great surge of German Catholic settlers attracted to Minnesota after the Civil War by the promise of rich farmlands, a healthy climate and freedom from religious or political oppression. Anna's oldest sister had been born in Germany, but most of her eleven brothers and sisters were born in this country. Her mother died giving birth to her last child, a boy, and Anna's father sold his blacksmith business and moved the family to a farm near Forest City where she helped raise the family.

Michael McCarthy was born in 1875, a year earlier than his wife. His mother, Mary Harbinson, came to Quebec as a baby from County Antrim in northern Ireland. There she met Michael's father (also named Michael) who was born in Canada to parents from County Cork, Ireland. They were married and had the first of their eleven children in Canada, then moved to Chicago, where Anna Baden's family also first lived after coming to this country. In the 1870's, for reasons unknown to present day descendants, both families moved to the sparsely populated Minnesota frontier and settled in Forest City.

Watkins and Forest City were semi-isolated farming villages like hundreds throughout Minnesota when Eugene McCarthy was growing up. But Watkins had its own railroad — the Soo Line — and a good east-west highway that skirted the edge of town. The Soo Line tracks still slice through Watkins at the north end of Main Street near the Werner Elevator, where the McCarthy boys once dueled with wooden snow fence slats among sacks of grain, placed pennies on the tracks to be flattened by speeding trains and watched tractors and horse-drawn wagons unload rich bounties harvested from the surrounding small grain farms.

The two-story cream-colored house that Mike McCarthy's father built for him when he was married in 1902 and which he lived in until the 1960's still stands, although it is now painted green and the barn in back where he kept horses is gone. Visitors to Watkins can still see the Watkins Creamery that was and is the town's major industry, the baseball field and the site of the hockey rink where Eugene and Austin spent a large part of their free time, and even the hotel where the elder McCarthy lived for a few years, although it now serves as a liquor store. Motorists driving past Watkins on the Floyd B. Olson Memorial Highway can still see the sign put up a few years ago which announces Watkins' population ("760 Friendly People Plus a Few Grouches"), and proclaims it to be "A Town of Free Enterprise."

A smaller sign attached in 1968 notifies passersby that this is the "Hometown of Senator Eugene McCarthy," but the sign is badly faded now. Towering over everything except the village's silver mushroom water tower is St. Anthony's Church. Next door is the red-brick school building where the McCarthy children went to school under the strict German nuns.

St. Anthony's Church is a surprisingly large church for such a small town, but is not unlike the other big Roman Catholic houses of worship in the surrounding communities settled by devout German immigrants. On a hot summer day it is pleasantly dark and cool inside and even more imposing than it appears from the outside. A large stained-glass window showing a haloed saint kneeling at prayer with face uplifted was donated by the McCarthy family and the large altar where young Eugene served as an altar boy is now only an ornate backdrop for a small table-like altar installed several years ago to permit the priest to face the people.

Watkins was a good place to grow up, and the McCarthy boys were well-behaved but typically combative brothers. They fought often, Austin remembers. "I guess I had my dad's temper and didn't need much provocation. I used to chase Gene with anything I could find, but he was pretty tricky. He could anticipate what I was going to do and I didn't catch him very often."

The boys were good workers. They spent their summers pulling weeds on their father's farm four miles south of Watkins, peddling handbills around town for J. H. (Pep) Weber's general store, and working in a lumber yard across the street from the McCarthy house. Gene enjoyed driving Weber's 1927 Hudson while doing errands for Mrs. Weber. "He was a very clean-cut boy, didn't smoke, drink, chase around," says Weber, who managed Watkins' baseball team in the Great Soo league. "There aren't many like that anymore."

Young Gene McCarthy was obviously a bright student. From the moment he entered St. Anthony's grade school he excelled in his studies. Austin remembers the frustration of trying to match his older brother's scholastic record. "It was kind of an unfortunate thing that I had to follow in his footsteps from grade school on into college. Gene didn't have any problems — he spent all his time studying — and his grades were always excellent. Then I would come along and have to plug along just to get acceptable grades."

The boys' oldest sister, Mildred now married to a retired oil company executive in Scarsdale, New York, was away at college and teaching school when they were growing up. But the second oldest girl, Marian, was at home. She helped the boys with their studies and would read them the comics from the Minneapolis *Sunday Tribune*, the only newspaper that came regularly to the McCarthy home other than a South St. Paul stock dealers' digest. Marian, now married to a newspaper linotypist and living in St. Paul, traces Eugene's scholarly bent to the set of Harvard Classics owned by her mother's oldest sister, Mrs. Mary Becker, who lived next door. These volumes were McCarthy's introduction to Aristotle, Plato, Thomas Aquinas, and other great thinkers whose ideas would influence him deeply.

Marian also recalls something that in the context of her brother's later life seems almost prophetic. "He always seemed to like little kids and they were always attracted to him. He was nicer to them, I guess, than most older boys would be. Usually boys that are ten or twelve years old can't be bothered with little kids. He used to do a lot of walking. Even just walking down the street, Gene would have a younger child walking with him, talking to him."

Gene kept pretty much to himself, says Austin, who went to northern Minnesota one summer to play semi-professional baseball but suffered a ruptured appendix and had to come home to recuperate. "I would be sitting in bed out on the screened front porch and Gene was supposed to be sort of babysitting for me," he recalls. "Well, I had trouble reading the Katzenjammer kids but he'd go next door to Aunt Mary's house to borrow the Harvard Classics and sit there reading them for three or four hours without saying a word. Then all of a sudden, he'd decide he was going to baseball practice and he'd just get up and go and I probably hadn't gotten two words out of him all day. I guess he had to sit somewhere to do his reading and figured he might as well sit with me. He liked his privacy even then."

McCarthy's grandmother lived with the family until her death at the age of ninety-six, after Gene was out of college. "She had such a brogue you'd think she just came over on the last boat, and she could sing all the Irish songs and dance the jig after she was ninety," says Marian. However, there were relatively few Irish living in Watkins when McCarthy was growing up. In fact, Watkins and the area north into the next county — Stearns — contains the heaviest concentration of German-Americans in the state. The nuns at St. Anthony's still spoke German occasionally when Gene and Austin first went there and the brothers picked up enough of the language to pray in German and to understand the players on the ball teams from nearby towns who spoke German on the ballfield.

The family often remarked, however, that Gene was a lot like his Grandfather McCarthy, whom the children called "Carty Pa." The old Irish-Canadian carpenter died at eighty-eight when Eugene was very young, and even Marian, who was a young girl at the time, has only a hazy recollection of him. "I just remember that he was a little old stooped man with a beard who used to sit in the corner of our kitchen by the stove. But he was always real interested in politics, and in reading the newspapers and finding out what was going on. People who knew him used to say Eugene was just like Carty Pa."

In ways that wouldn't show up until much later, Eugene was also much like his plain-spoken father. Those who knew Mike McCarthy agree that he was not the easiest man in the world to live with. "Mike was a strong Irishman and quite domineering," says Pep Weber, who lived across the street from the McCarthys. "He wasn't near as pleasant as Mrs. McCarthy. We used to call her 'Aunt Annie' and if ever there was a saint, she was one. But Mike could be ornery as hell when he wanted to."

Mike McCarthy was a staunch Republican who served as postmaster in Watkins from 1900 until Woodrow Wilson's Democratic administration took over in 1913. Then he turned to the livestock business for a living. He was moderately successful, keeping the family solvent during the lean Depression years, and sending all four children to college. He wasn't particularly close to his boys and was unenthusiastic at first about them playing baseball. "He said, 'All you kids have ever done is go to school and play baseball,' "

Austin recalls. But eventually, he grew to like the game and became an avid fan.

Mike McCarthy was known throughout Meeker County for his outspoken honesty and earthy wit, which Gene inherited. "Gene's wit is just like my father's, except in a more educated way," says Marian. "My father never had more than a grade school education and some business courses, although he was really sharp in mathematics. He had a great sense of humor. Even now, he can't see or hear very well, and can't read the paper or listen to the radio or T.V. and he prays the rosary most of the time. Once Austin went to see him and said, 'Well, Dad, you've prayed so many rosaries that you must have whatever you ever prayed for. Are you starting to thank the Lord?' and Dad said, 'Yeah, I can't see and I can't hear. I say thanks for nothing.' " On another occasion, her father came home one day after visiting a nearby farm and remarked to the family that the farmer's wife was getting so fat "you can't tell if she's standing up or sitting down," Marian recalls. "Gene was there, and he said, 'You mean she's shaped like a barrel, Dad?' Dad said, 'Yeah, with half the hoops busted.' "

Political adversaries of Michael McCarthy's son would discover one day that the sense of humor passed on to him by his father was an effective, if not always gentle, weapon. While the younger McCarthy's humor would become more sophisticated, he would lose none of his father's ability to deflate pomposity. For instance, Marian remembers going with her family to the St. Paul Cathedral one hot summer day to see her father's brother ordained as a priest. As they waited for the elaborate ordination rites to begin and watched Archbishop John Murray put on his ecclesiastical garb, the elder McCarthy grew restive.

"The archbishop was a little man and he had about six assistants helping him put on his vestments," Marian recalls. "After they finally put on his miter and gave him his staff, my father leaned over and said to the rest of us, 'They forgot his overshoes.' We just about exploded trying not to laugh."

Mike McCarthy's wit was employed with equal effectiveness against his own family and national origins. When his son later ran for office as a Democrat, he said, "Gene is a good boy but he's in the wrong party." After Gene went to Congress and Austin graduated from medical school, the elder McCarthy remarked, "Doctors and Democrats are good people to stay away from and now I've got both of them in the family." Of his fellow Irishmen, he once said, "They're the worst class of people there is. Scandinavians are the best. But the Irish, doggone, you just want to stay away from them. When I was buying cattle, I'd come to a town and I'd ask, 'What's the nationality here?' and if they said, 'Irish' I'd ask, 'When's the next train out?' All the Irish are good for is drinking and singing and dancing."

Because there were only eleven grades at St. Anthony's, Gene left home at age fifteen and enrolled for his senior year at St. John's Preparatory School at Collegeville, twenty-five miles north of Watkins. The school was run by the Benedictine monks of St. John's Abbey and was an adjunct of St. John's University where McCarthy enrolled a year later. It was the middle of the Depression and his father didn't feel he could afford to send the boy to college on a salary of about $150 a month plus a few commissions. Marian, teaching school in a nearby community, insisted that her brothers should be given a college education and offered to help pay Gene's tuition, as she would when Austin followed him to St. John's two years later. Even though St. John's was not an expensive school — room, board and tuition for both boys the one year they were at St. John's together was only $750 — they probably couldn't have gone without their sister's help and the aid of a $1,000 windfall willed to the family by an uncle.

St. John's and the Benedictines would have an enormous influence on McCarthy, greatly expanding and refining his spiritual and intellectual development during the seven years he would spend there as a student, Benedictine novice and teacher. Situated in the midst of 2,400 acres of woods and 2 jewel-like lakes, St. John's is reminiscent of the ancient Bavarian abbey of Metten, which sent 5 monks to found the school and abbey on the Minnesota frontier in 1857. The University is the oldest institution of higher learning in continuous existence in Minnesota, while the St. John's Benedictines have roots extending even further back into history, to the year 529, when Saint Benedict founded the order. As part of the oldest religious order in the Western world, the St. John's Benedictines have been careful to preserve tradition. Yet they also have been among the most progressive forces in American Catholicism, remaining open to new thinking and innovative approaches to dealing with contemporary social and economic ferment.

During the time McCarthy was at St. John's, he was exposed to the thinking of the Reverend Virgil Michel, who charted the original course in the United States for the liturgical and social reform which was already going on in Europe and which later found its ultimate expression in the Second Vatican Council. "He knew where it was, you know," McCarthy later said of the world renowned priest, who died in 1938 but who strongly influenced McCarthy's social thought.

Virgil Michel was a formidable figure in the American Catholic Church as well as at St. John's, according to the Reverend Ernest Kilzer, who succeeded Virgil after his death.[1] Virgil tried to get people to understand that a renewal in the prayer life of the Church had already started in Europe and was very much needed here. And when he began to look deeper into the matter, he began to see that there were social implications as well. So he connected these two things — the renovation of the prayer life of the Church and the renovation of the social philosophy.

---

[1] The Benedictines use their religious name rather than their surname when addressing or referring to each other.

Father Ernest believes that Virgil's emphasis on the papal encyclicals, *Rerum Novarum* (1897), which dealt chiefly with the twentieth-century adaptation of Thomas Aquinas' ideas on the rights of the workingman, and *Quadragesimo Anno*, a refinement of *Rerum Novarum* published forty years later, was important to McCarthy's thinking. Virgil's explanations of the two encyclicals, which asserted the right of workers to organize themselves, was published in book form under the title, *On the Reconstruction of the Social Order*, which McCarthy read as a student. "McCarthy and Emerson Hynes [a fellow student who later taught with and worked for McCarthy] were both very much under the influence of Virgil Michel's ideas," says Father Ernest. "I had them as students and I continued inculcating them with the same ideas."

McCarthy's entry into this formidable religious and intellectual climate was not an auspicious one. Raphael Thuente, who was a year ahead of McCarthy, remembers meeting him in the first week of school in September, 1931. McCarthy and his best friend, Louis Lundemo, the son of Watkins' pharmacist, came to Thuente's room one evening shortly before the freshmen had to go to a 7:30 P.M. study hall. "McCarthy came to the room with Louie and didn't say a word," Thuente recalls. "He was sitting on the bed and when the bell rang at 7:25, they got up to leave. Just as they were going out the door, I said to Louie, 'Who's that tall, skinny kid in the grey suit?' And Louie said, 'His name is Gene McCarthy. Smart, but quiet as hell.' "

Thuente, whom McCarthy would meet again during two critical junctures in his life, remembers that the quiet youth fit his friend's description perfectly. On Saturday nights, when most students went to St. John's nearby sister school, St. Benedict's, to visit the "Bennies," or into the neighboring city of St. Cloud, McCarthy remained in his room studying. "We'd walk down the highway and look back at Benet Hall and all you'd see was a row of four lights — these were the washrooms — and then you'd see a light on the first floor — that was the room of the head prefect, Father Walter — and one on the second floor — that was Gene McCarthy's," says Thuente. "And those were the only six lights on in Benet Hall."

Austin McCarthy followed his brother to St. John's in 1933 and immediately found out that competing with him in the classroom was still an impossible task. "They put me in an English class, a book analysis type of thing, and Gene was in the same class. There were only twelve or fourteen of us and it got to be just a discussion between Father Dunstan, the teacher, and Gene. Most of the rest of us just sat there wondering why we were there."

Father Dunstan Tucker, who taught English literature and coached baseball, remembers Gene McCarthy as an intense competitor in the classroom and on the athletic field, despite his quiet manner. "He enjoyed it when someone made a fool of himself in class," he says. Another monk remembers McCarthy as "an exceptionally independent-minded young man."

McCarthy may have been learning the ideals of Christian charity and brotherhood in the classroom but he didn't show any evidence of it on the school's pine-fringed playing fields. Austin remembers that Gene showed little mercy to opponents either on the baseball field or the hockey rink. "Certain melees would get started in our hockey games and he would come out unscathed while the fist were flying and the blood was flowing. I think he usually had something to do with starting them, like a little trip here and a little nudge there." McCarthy was captain of the conference championship hockey team in 1935 and scored the only goal in a 9 to 1 loss to a team on northern Minnesota's Iron Range, the center of U. S. amateur hockey. On the baseball field, Gene was known as a slick-fielding first baseman who hit the ball far but infrequently. "He was an excellent glove man, and when he hit the ball, he was a long hitter, but I think I was a better hitter than he was," says Austin.

The McCarthy boys played most of their baseball for the Watkins team in the Great Soo league, a collection of bush-league teams that took its name from two nearby parallel east-west railroads, the Great Northern and the Soo Line. The Great Soo would achieve a measure of immortality when McCarthy reminisced about it while covering the 1968 World Series for *Life* magazine. Many of his favorite stories about the Great Soo league would turn up later in other articles and in his conversation, including the tale about the cemetery beyond left field in New Munich where outfielders were reluctant to chase a ball as it caromed off the tombstones of their ancestors. "In the Great Soo, that was considered place-hitting," McCarthy wrote in a 1971 article in *Sport* magazine.

McCarthy, who advertised "Stamen's Cafe" on the back of his uniform, recalled other favorite tales in the article, such as the erratic left-handed pitcher whose favorite pitch was a "side-hill gouger," the local moonshine liquor which took its name from a hybrid corn called "Minnesota 13" and Danny Manuel, the deaf-mute scorekeeper from Watkins who refuted complaints about his judgment with emphatic hand signals. "He was like Zacharias in the Bible," McCarthy recalled. "It was written, and there it is: An error or a hit — forever." Some people saw a parallel with McCarthy's later behavior when he wrote that sportsmanlike gestures such as picking up the catcher's mask when he threw it off to chase a foul ball "were considered a sign of weakness in the Great Soo. What you did was kick the mask out of the batter's box and let the catcher pick it up himself."

When McCarthy graduated from St. John's in 1935, he had compiled a scholastic record that was to become almost as famous as "the loaf that became a legend," the coarse brown bread sold by the monastery. Earning A's in every course but trigonometry, he graduated *cum laude* with a major in English and 362 honor points, 234 more than needed for a degree. It remains the most brilliant record ever achieved by a St. John's student, and

causes some people to wonder whether he may have been more of an influence on St. John's than it was on him. "It was a good place to go to school
if you wanted to learn by yourself," says McCarthy of his alma mater.

The 1935 yearbook accurately predicted that McCarthy's "really breath-
taking accomplishment is yet to be recorded," and observed that "the Watkins Wonder leans toward the serious side of life." It also noted that he
was president of the "Scribblers Union," whose sole criterion for membership
was a "capacity for writing and undergoing the initiation exercises which
some of the more waggish charter members devised."

McCarthy would return to St. John's five years later as an instructor of
economics and then as a Benedictine novice, but when he graduated, the
Depression was still on and there were few jobs available for a nineteen year
old with a Bachelor of Arts degree and an English major, no matter how brilliant his record. "When September came around, he still didn't have a job
and he was real unhappy," Marian remembers. "So I told him, 'Why don't
you go to the University of Minnesota and get started on your master's degree
and if something comes up in the spring, you can quit and take it.' "

McCarthy followed his sister's advice, and in early 1936 when one of his
St. John's classmates who was a principal of the high school at Tintah, Minnesota, became ill and died, he was offered the job and took it. He became
probably the only nineteen year old high school principal in the country,
remaining for another year and then taking a job at Kimball, Minnesota, in
September, 1936, while continuing to work on a master's degree in sociology
and economics.[2] Then, in what was to be another milestone in his life,
McCarthy accepted an offer to teach at the public high school in Mandan,
North Dakota.

Again, it was a priest from St. John's, Father Hildebrand Eickhoff, who
was instrumental in turning McCarthy's life in a new direction. Father Hildebrand had a parish and grade school at Mandan, and felt the students in his
school, many of whom were children of German and Russian immigrants
who had brought the hardy Ukranian wheat to the Dakota plains, weren't
getting a proper education at Mandan's public high school. Naturally he
turned to St. John's for teaching recruits, and in September, 1938, Eugene
McCarthy arrived in Mandan.

When Raphael Thuente, who had come to Mandan a week earlier to
become principal of Father Hildebrand's grade school, heard that McCarthy
was coming to teach at the public school, he wrote him a letter. "I told him
he'd better be prepared because this was still the Wild West and the town

  [2] While McCarthy was teaching at Kimball, Hubert Humphrey passed within a
few miles on his way back from South Dakota to the University of Minnesota to
complete his interrupted college education. It was the first remote crossing of paths
of the two men whose unyielding confrontation would change the course of history
in 1968.

was full of Indians," Thuente recalls. "Actually, there were some Sioux Indians dressed up in their tribal regalia who met the train as sort of a tourist attraction. And when Gene got off the train, he said, 'Gee, there really *are* Indians here.' "

McCarthy's arrival and his installment as head of the high school English Department didn't sit well at first with a pretty young teacher from Wabasha, Minnesota, named Abigail Quigley. A year older than McCarthy, she had come to Mandan two years earlier to teach German and English, and she hoped to become head of the English Department. She had attended the College of St. Catherine, a Catholic women's college in St. Paul, where she wrote prize-winning fiction and graduated Phi Beta Kappa in 1936.

When Miss Quigley heard that the young teacher from St. John's was taking over the English Department, she remembers she "was pretty mad about it because it meant I had to go on teaching German." But she changed her mind when she got her first look at him. "I thought he was too handsome to be true," she later confided.

Her opinion was soon verified, according to Thuente. "We were walking down Mandan's Main Street one day when we passed two teenage girls," he says. "Just as we passed, one of the girls said to the other, 'He's *more* handsome than Robert Taylor!' All Gene did was mutter under his breath to me, 'Goldanged girls.' "

McCarthy didn't seem much more interested in Miss Quigley at first. As the teachers congregated in her room after the first faculty meeting, she remembers, "He came wandering in with someone and just sort of sat there. We all thought he was sort of stand-offish." On the first Sunday he was there, he and Thuente went to Mass together and then to breakfast at the Northern Pacific Railroad depot restaurant which the teachers affectionately dubbed "the Beanery." Thuente's future wife, Margaret Fahey, and some other women teachers were sitting nearby when McCarthy suggested to Thuente that they visit the nearby frontier army post of Fort Lincoln. "I said 'Fine, and I'd like to take that girl with the Irish name who's sitting over there,' " Thuente recalls. "But Gene said, 'Why do you always want to take a girl along?' "

The two men soon became close friends and Thuente moved into McCarthy's rooming house. Often Thuente would wake up in the middle of the night to see McCarthy's light still burning, but McCarthy rarely failed to get up every morning to attend the 6:15 A.M. Mass in Father Hildebrand's nearby church. "He would slip some trousers over his pajamas, and a sweatshirt to go to Mass," says Thuente. "One morning there was a shotgun wedding with no best man, so Father Hildebrand called him up to be best man. He came back and said it was probably the first time in the history of the Church that the best man served in his sweatshirt and pajamas."

McCarthy showed little interest in material things or in having a good time, although he asked Thuente to help him buy a car. Thuente found a green 1937 Chevrolet with 4,000 miles on it in Bismarck, across the Missouri River from Mandan, and after some difficulty, persuaded McCarthy that it was a good buy at $350. (Ten years later when he and Thuente would be teaching college in St. Paul, McCarthy was still driving the same car.)

Another teacher remembers McCarthy as a serious, introspective loner who "kept very much to himself." Thuente says he also sensed a vague restlessness in McCarthy, "a certain dissatisfaction with life" which he expressed by running his hand through his hair and saying "Pshaw." "I think he could see through the imperfections of society at that point. He used to make remarks about how conditions were changing, how the old order had passed. He was talking about the social order, not the Church."

McCarthy was also at least occasionally dissatisfied with his teaching job, Thuente remembers. "One day I went over to the public school and as I was walking down the hall, here was Gene and I thought he was demented. I said, 'Gene, what's wrong?' The first thing I got out of him was, 'Oh these damn kids.' So I asked him to tell me about it. Well, he was trying to teach poetry — probably 'Ode to a Waterfall' or something — and those German-Russian kids didn't understand it and he had walked out of the room."

Before long, however, Abigail Quigley's charms finally caught McCarthy's eye, and he asked for a date. They went to a movie in Bismarck but left fifteen minutes after it began. "I found out that he wanted to leave because he was afraid I'd think the picture stupid," she later said. "I left because I thought he'd think I was stupid. I still wonder how that movie came out." Instead of movies, the two young teachers had long visits with Father Hildebrand, discussing his ideas on the organization of rural cooperatives and borrowing books from his extensive library.

"We were engaged just after Christmas," says Abigail. "I was so impressed, he was the only one I knew who went to Mass every morning . . . I thought he must be some kind of a saint, very handsome and intelligent." McCarthy announced the engagement to his roommate about two o'clock on a Sunday morning. "Somebody was shaking my shoulder and I woke up and recognized Gene," Thuente recalls. "He said, 'We're engaged,' and I said, 'Who the hell is engaged?' and he said, 'Abigail and I.' "

But the young teachers didn't have enough money to get married, and spent most of what they did have traveling back and forth between Mandan and Litchfield, Minnesota, where Abigail went to teach the following year. In the fall of 1940, McCarthy returned to St. John's to teach economics, but a year later, he told Abigail he'd decided to enter the monastery at St. John's, a decision he had been pondering for several years. "I guess I thought it was the will of God and I accepted it that way, but I was sad," she said later. They broke their engagement, although McCarthy gave her his car and they still saw each other until he entered the novitiate at St. John's in the fall of

1942. Abigail went back to St. Paul to teach at the College of St. Catherine, and to work on her master's degree at the University of Minnesota.

McCarthy spent nine months at St. John's Abbey as a Benedictine novice, taking a new religious name, Frater Conan, and following the rigorous monastic discipline expressed in the order's Latin motto, *Ora et Labora* — worship and work. However, he gave up his plans for the priesthood the following year — after spending another month at St. Francis' diocesan seminary in Milwaukee. McCarthy later described this period of his life as "a mixed sort of case" in which he wanted to test his vocation for the priesthood, saying "If it didn't prove out, it doesn't really hurt to spend nine or ten months drawn away from it all." It was clear that McCarthy was still torn between the vocations of the priesthood and marriage, as was evident from the fact that the abbot at St. John's permitted him to continue to correspond with Abigail.

A priest who knew McCarthy then also thinks he was discouraged by the tough German novice master, Father Basil Stegmann, who was suspicious of the Irish intellectual pride he saw in McCarthy. "Basil wanted dumb, simple souls who could be taught a little St. Thomas Aquinas and become good monks or parish priests and not question the organization," says the priest, who also was subject to Father Basil's discipline. "But here was this smart Irishman, the brightest student ever to hit St. John's, a guy who'd been a high school principal at nineteen, a golden boy who was not only a good athlete but an intellectual. Basil attacked him head-on. He'd say, 'If you came here to write books or be a great professor, you'd better leave.'

"These were very deep influences on a guy and I think that year cut very deeply into McCarthy. It was probably the first time he was forced to really look deeply into himself and his own motivation. I think his idealism was shattered very quickly by Basil. If Basil had been sympathetic to him, he would have sailed through and been a great success as a monk, maybe another Thomas Merton."

Others who knew McCarthy discount the theory that Basil was responsible for McCarthy leaving the monastery. "That's an oversimplification," says Father Colman Barry, a member of McCarthy's novice class who later became president of St. John's University. "Basil was a very strong personality and he and McCarthy never hit it off, but as I observed it, Gene paid no attention to him. Basil wanted to be the novice master, but Gene never in any way allowed Basil to master him."

The Benedictine training stressed prayer, manual labor and study, but McCarthy clearly preferred the latter, says Father Colman. "Gene always hung loose. He would take copies of *Orate Fratres* [a liturgical review started by Father Virgil Michel] with him to choir and read the whole thing for his meditation. Basil really resented that. To him, that was intellectual pride."

Father Colman remembers the day that he learned McCarthy was going to leave the monastery. It was May 19, 1943, and the two novices were taking their daily walk by the lake behind the monastery. "He just said to me, 'I'm going to go,' " Father Colman recounts. "I wasn't shocked. Gene was never very happy anyway." McCarthy's departure came as a shock to many others in the monastery, however. One priest who was there says, "It was like losing a twenty-game winner."

McCarthy left the monastery, but in many ways, the monastery never left him. His intimate acquaintance with the contemplative life and the rule for monks written 1,400 years ago by Saint Benedict left an indelible mark on him. Father Walter Reger, who spent fifty-four years at St. John's before his death in 1971, later said the Benedictine principles "are the key to Gene perhaps without his realizing it. He has absorbed them. He talks about moral issues and he is conscious of moral and spiritual values. He wants to achieve these values. He conceives of them for others as well as for himself."

McCarthy also learned at St. John's to view events as part of the broader sweep of history, a trait that would become much more evident in later years and one that is very familiar to the Benedictines. When St. John's announced in 1954 that it had commissioned Architect Marcel Breuer to design a comprehensive building plan that would take one hundred years to complete, the abbot of St. John's remarked, "After all, what are a few generations to the Benedictines?" McCarthy henceforth would reflect the Benedictine approach of combining utopian ideals with the realization that utopia will never come, a practice best expressed in the Benedictine admonition, "Be kind to people, but lock your doors at night."

Abigail, meanwhile, was studying at the University of Chicago when McCarthy was in Milwaukee that summer, and they saw each other on weekends. "I could tell he wasn't happy, but I thought it was just the adjustment from St. John's to St. Francis," she said. But one day that fall, he showed up at her apartment in Minneapolis and announced he had quit the seminary. Although Abigail says "It was hard to just pick up again," they began going together once more.

Because he left the monastery, McCarthy was no longer exempt from the draft, but the Meeker County Draft Board classified him 4-F because of an acute case of bursitis in his feet, a condition that would plague him the rest of his life.[3] Instead of going into the service, McCarthy volunteered to work for the War Department in Washington, D.C. in the fall of 1944. He deciphered Japanese codes for the Army Signal Corps and took weekend bus trips to Virginia's Shenandoah Valley to view the fall scenery and "just to

[3] Questions about his draft status would be raised by several of McCarthy's opponents in his early House campaigns, but unlike Humphrey, McCarthy's lack of a military record never became a major issue.

see the horizon again." In early 1945, he returned to Minnesota and taught briefly at a high school on Minnesota's Iron Range.

In June, he and Abigail were finally married at her parish church in Minneapolis by a priest who was McCarthy's cousin, with Emerson Hynes acting as best man and Abigail wearing something borrowed — Margaret Thuente's veil.

The couple then bought eighty acres of land kitty-corner from Mike McCarthy's farm south of Watkins and moved there to begin a rural life cooperative where they could put into practice Father Virgil's ideas on religious and social reform. Also, St. Anthony's High School in Watkins had been closed because the nuns couldn't staff it and the McCarthys "wanted to reopen it with lay teachers with sort of 'one-foot-on-the-land,' " according to Abigail.

They moved into an old farmhouse on the land, remodeled it and planted crops. But McCarthy "just wasn't cut out for farming," says a friend from those days. "They had two horses. Well, he couldn't harness those damn horses. They had some chickens. That lasted about a year. They had mostly clover, I think —which the bees took care of. Then Gene got a little hungry and started looking for a teaching job."

Austin remembers visiting his brother and sister-in-law in their home. "There was a long passageway from the kitchen into the living room that was lined with books and two typewriters and desks on each side. I don't think Gene really did much farming." The McCarthys stayed on the farm until the fall of 1946, after they had lost their first child — a stillborn boy — and it had become clear that their plans for reviving the school with lay teachers would not be approved by Church authorities.

While they were trying to decide what to do that summer, Raphael Thuente came home from the service and was hired as a teacher by the College of St. Thomas in St. Paul for the 1946-47 school year. The McCarthys invited him and his wife and two children to stay with them at the farm while their house was being painted, Thuente remembers. "One day the four of us were having lunch in the shade of the house when a car pulled up. There were two gentlemen in it and because I'm a nosy guy, I asked Abby who they were. She said they were the principal and superintendent of the high school at Eden Valley and they wanted Gene to teach there that fall.

"Gene was talking to them in the car, and just at that point, Abby said to me, 'What are you going to do next year, Rafe?' I said, 'Well, I've signed a contract to teach English at St. Thomas.' Abby hesitated for about ten seconds, and then she got up and called Gene and they spoke briefly and Gene went back to the car. Then he came back to our group and said, 'I'm going to change clothes. I'm going into town for a while. I'll be back later this evening.' When he came back, he said, 'I talked to Father Flynn and I'm going to teach at St. Thomas this fall.' That's the way it happened."

CHAPTER III

MINNESOTA — NORTH STAR
OF LIBERALISM

Minnesota is a state spectacularly varied,
proud, handsome and progressive. . . .
It is a state pulled toward East and West
both, and one always eager to turn
the world upside down.
                    John Gunther: *Inside U.S.A.*

The spirit of reform and renewal that Author John Gunther described a quarter of a century ago was deeply ingrained in Minnesota's political life long before the state became the matrix for the intertwined destinies of Hubert Humphrey and Eugene McCarthy.

Flames of political protest, ignited by social and economic frustrations that couldn't be satisfied by existing political parties or governmental structures, have swept across the North Star State with periodic regularity ever since she entered the Union in 1858. Minnesota's political landscape is littered with the vestiges of once-potent third party protest movements that flourished in the late nineteenth and early twentieth centuries as farmers and workers expressed their resentment of the financial leviathans that controlled their lives. Such colorful and influential third party movements as the Anti-Monopolists, the Greenbackers, the Farmers' Alliance, the Populists, the Non-Partisan League and the Farmer Labor party kept a continuous pressure on Minnesota's political system, forcing it to protect the public interest from private privilege.

By the time the Democratic Farmer Labor party — the party that was to serve as the vehicle for the political ambitions of Humphrey and McCarthy — was created in 1944, Minnesota's third party protesters had caused dozens of major economic and social reforms to be written into state law. The first significant protest party, the Minnesota Grange, was founded in 1868, exactly one century before Humphrey and McCarthy were to battle each other for control of the Democratic Farmer Labor party and its national parent party. Although the Grange was only moderately successful in reforming the economic system that left the fate of farmers in the hands of Eastern banking, merchandising and railroad interests, it served as the first important political forum for farmers and helped establish a fundamental doctrine in the history of political protest — that industries "clothed with public interest" are subject to government control.

A direct descendant of the Grange and a more effective political force was the Anti-Monopoly party, found in 1873 by the celebrated congressman, land speculator, orator and writer, Ignatius Donnelly. One of the first Minnesota political leaders to argue for a fusion of farm and labor forces, Donnelly wrote a radical platform that attracted so much support that Republicans — the dominant party through the state's early history — nominated a progressive, Cushman K. Davis, for governor. Davis was easily elected, and his successful efforts to be responsive to political grievances by keeping radical reform within the confines of existing party structures were seen as similar to those which Harold Stassen would make some sixty-five years later. "Davis, like Stassen, presented himself as an enlightened Republican in tune with the needs of the times but opposed to radical excesses," wrote Arthur Naftalin, an ally of Humphrey's and later mayor of Minneapolis, in a 1948 study of the Farmer Labor party.[1] Naftalin's words illustrated the classic pattern of agrarian protest which forced the state to take greater responsibility for economic justice but fell far short of reformers' utopian goals. They would be equally applicable to the roles played by Humphrey and McCarthy (and Naftalin in ridding the Democratic Farmer Labor party of extremist influences in the 1940's.

The remaining years of Minnesota's nineteenth-century politics were dominated by the pugnacious and tireless Donnelly, whose organizational talents led to formation of the powerful Farmers' Alliance in the 1880's and the Populist party in the 1890's. Although defeated as the Populist candidate for governor in 1892, Donnelly set the philosophical tone for William Jennings Bryan and the explosive Populist revolt that burst upon the nation in the late 1890's when he declared, "The fruits of toil of millions are boldly stolen to build up colossal fortunes for a few . . . and the possessors of these, in turn, despise the republic and endanger liberty. From the same prolific womb of governmental injustice we breed the two great classes — tramps and millionaires."[2]

---

[1] Naftalin's unpublished doctoral thesis, "A History of the Farmer Labor Party in Minnesota," remains the best study of Minnesota politics through the 1930's. Naftalin was studying under Dr. Evron Kirkpatrick, another Humphrey ally, at the University of Minnesota at the time he wrote his thesis.

[2] Donnelly was not always the champion of the little man that he became in later life. He took railroad stock in exchange for supporting federal land grants to rail-

Although the Populists joined with Democrats and Republicans opposed to the gold standard to elect the state's first Democratic governor in 1898, the Populist prairie fire had burned itself out as Minnesota entered the twentieth century. But many of its leaders would be active in the next cycles of Minnesota's third party protest — the Non-Partisan League and the Farmer Labor party. Minnesota's modern political history began with the election of 1918. Three years earlier, A. C. Townley, a Minnesota native who was inspired by the LaFollette progressive program in Wisconsin, organized the Non-Partisan League in North Dakota to seek public ownership of grain elevators and other agricultural processing facilities. The League spread quickly to western Minnesota, which provided a fertile seedbed for the flowering of its mildly socialistic goals, and it became a powerful political force in Minnesota almost overnight. However, the outbreak of the World War I unleashed a climate of repression and strong-arm tactics against the League, many of whose members were of German origin and opposed to U.S. participation in the war. The League-backed gubernatorial candidate, isolationist former Congressman Charles A. Lindbergh, Sr., father of the "Lone Eagle" aviator whose 1927 transatlantic solo flight would make him a national hero, was defeated but showed remarkable strength.

The 1918 election permanently rearranged Minnesota's political spectrum as the League's leaders, recognizing that they would also need the state's urban vote to win elections, forged an alliance with labor groups and, after a futile attempt to merge with the Democratic party, became the Farmer Labor party in 1922. Republicans kept control of the state government through the rest of the 1920's, assisted by public charges of Communist infiltration of the Farmer Labor party, but by the time the Depression arrived, Minnesotans were looking for a political messiah. They found him in 1930 in Floyd B. Olson.

Olson, the most radical, beloved and controversial governor in Minnesota history, was a poor Norwegian-Swedish boy from Minneapolis who dropped out of the University of Minnesota in 1911 to become a roustabout worker in Alaskan gold fields and Western wheat fields. Returning to Minneapolis, he put himself through night law school, got elected Hennepin County attorney and ran as the Farmer Labor candidate for governor in 1924. He was defeated but kept his political fences mended and was ready when his chance came six years later. A flamboyant, powerful personality who thrived on controversy, Olson was elected governor three times by voters who were willing to overlook his friendship with Twin Cities underworld figures and his own flexible personal morals. (When a woman complained to him, "Gov-

roads and sold speculators information about government commodities dealings while in Congress. But he later stood by his principles in an unusually unprincipled era and became, in his own words, "one man proclaiming truth year after year." Called a "country crank" and "a fat brute" by his detractors, Donnelly is, with William Jennings Bryan, a prototype of the rural reformer.

ernor, I hear you lead an immoral life," he reportedly answered, "That's a cross I got to bear. Pray for me.")

The Farmer Labor party that Olson headed was unique in American political history. Similar to the British Labor party in structure and ideology, it was a frankly radical party headed by a self-proclaimed radical, and its 1934 platform still stands as probably the most far-reaching blueprint for change ever put forth by a major American party. The platform stated:

> We . . . declare that capitalism has failed and immediate steps must be taken by the people to abolish capitalism in a peaceful and lawful manner and then a new sane and just society must be established; a system where all the natural resources, machinery of production, transportation and communication shall be owned by the government and operated democratically for the benefit of all the people and not for the benefit of the few.

The platform was even too much for Olson, who pushed for New Dealish reforms rather than the frankly socialistic planks of the platform as he won reelection for a third time in 1934. He worked hard to translate his reform rhetoric into public policy and won passage of landmark laws in the social welfare and economic fields, including legislation that forbade foreclosure of farm mortgages and the use of injunctions against striking workers.

Olson's successes in Minnesota attracted nationwide attention. By 1936, he was being urged to lead a national third party ticket patterned after the Farmer Labor party. But his friendship with President Franklin Roosevelt prevailed and instead, he was planning to run for the U.S. Senate when he died of cancer at the age of forty-five. (Ironically, another Minnesota governor with a background remarkably similar to Olson's, John Johnson, was serving his third term thirty years earlier and was also being boosted for the presidency when he too died of cancer.) Had Olson been elected to the Senate, there are those in Minnesota and Washington who are convinced he would have been a serious candidate for the presidency in the 1940's.

Olson was succeeded in 1937 by another Farmer Laborite whom he had appointed to the U.S. Senate, Elmer Benson. Benson and the Farmer Labor ticket swept into office on a wave of sympathy for Olson, but it was the beginning of the end for the Farmer Labor party's power and for the party itself. Benson's term was marked by an upsurge of labor violence and public unrest and he was accused of corruption, administrative incompetence, and blindness to Communist infiltration in a primary fight that was one of the most bitter in Minnesota's history. Benson was, if anything, even more radical than Olson. Shortly after he took office, an associate came away from a meeting with shaking his head. "Olson said all these things," he declared, "but this son of a bitch believes them." In 1938, Benson was defeated in a turn-around of nearly a half million votes by the man who would become Minnesota's next aspirant to the presidency, Harold Stassen.

Stassen, who along with Olson and Humphrey must be considered among the founding fathers of Minnesota's modern political system, was a thirty-one year old county attorney from South St. Paul when he was elected as the nation's youngest governor. Of German, Czech, and Norwegian descent, he grew up on a farm and worked his way through the University of Minnesota. A liberal Republican who promised to rid the state of corruption and Communists, Stassen soon made good on his promises by starting another cycle of reform. He sent several Benson holdovers to jail, reorganized state government, and successfully sought enactment of well-financed programs in welfare, conservation and mental health.

His election was the beginning of a sixteen-year reign of moderate-liberal Republicanism in Minnesota, and he quickly burst upon the national political scene as the keynoter of the 1940 Republican National Convention and floor manager for Wendell Willkie.[3] Stassen resigned in 1943 to join the Navy, then served on the U.S. delegation to the 1945 San Francisco conference at which the United Nations was formed. By 1948, he was ready for his first serious bid for the presidency, and John Gunther was so impressed that he devoted a whole chapter of *Inside* U.S.A. to him, entitled, "Stassen — Young Man Going Somewhere."[4]

Stassen went somewhere, but not to live in the White House as he hoped. He lost the 1948 Oregon primary and with it the Republican nomination to Thomas Dewey. In 1952, he tried again, but lost to Dwight Eisenhower after Minnesota voters overwhelmingly expressed their preference for Eisenhower on a write-in ballot. Stassen finally made it in the back door of the White House, as a disarmament advisor to Eisenhower. He also served as president — of the University of Pennsylvania — and he was a leading proponent of world peace, but his increasingly futile campaigns for the presidency and other public offices in the 1950's and 1960's overshadowed his considerable achievements and made his name a synonym for insatiable and unrealistic political ambition.[5]

The Republican domination of state government that began with the Stassen era would last for sixteen years, and, as had happened so often in the past, it left the two remaining political parties competing for survival.

[3] Eight years later, in the same Philadelphia auditorium, the thirty-seven year old Humphrey would give a dramatic speech at the Democratic National Convention that also would send him on a lifelong quest for the presidency.

[4] Gunther also was impressed with Humphrey, declaring him "one of the best mayors in the nation." However, he failed to get Humphrey's name right, calling him "H.J. Humphrey, Jr."

[5] Stassen's most lasting monument to Minnesota was the corruption-free civil service system which he instituted and which removed any taint of patronage or "bossism" from state politics. Also, in what was to become a pattern in Minnesota politics, he attracted large numbers of bright young people into government, including two fellow South St. Paul natives, Warren Burger and Harold LeVander, who would become chief justice of the United States and governor of Minnesota, respectively.

The Farmer Labor party had been mortally wounded by the 1938 primary struggle and was now indisputably infiltrated by Communists and other extreme left-wing elements. It was, as its name implied, largely a party of farmers and workers, with strong Scandinavian and Protestant coloration, and its members were strongly individualistic and idealistic as befitted the party's radical origins. Democrats, on the other hand, were essentially an urban party, with strong Irish and Catholic representation. Numerically inferior to the Farmer Laborites, tightly organized and led by uninspired men with conservative inclinations, the Democratic party was little more than a patronage dispensing arm of the Democratic National Committee, which was grateful that Minnesota carried for Roosevelt every time he ran.

However, the 1940 election made it clear to Roosevelt and his political advisers that he could no longer take Minnesota for granted. Roosevelt had carried the state by wide margins in 1932 and 1936, but in 1940 he carried it against Wendell Willkie by only 3.8 percent of the vote. There was now good reason to believe that unless the state's badly divided liberal forces were united behind him, it was unlikely Minnesota would help him in his quest for an unprecedented fourth term.

The same realization on a smaller scale — that no liberal could win a statewide election in Minnesota as long as the Democratic and Farmer Labor parties were separate — would occur at about the same time to Hubert Humphrey. It marked the beginning of another era of Minnesota political history that would eventually launch two more Minnesotans on a quest for political power ending only at the door of the White House, and provide the North Star State with the latest in a long line of native sons who would make it almost to the presidency.

CHAPTER IV

THE FIGHTING MAYOR

The time has arrived for the Democratic
party to get out of the shadow of states'
rights and walk forthrightly into the bright
sunshine of human rights.

Hubert Humphrey at the 1948
Democratic National Convention.

Hubert Humphrey left South Dakota in 1937 with a passionate will to succeed. In his newly adopted state of Minnesota, he began the long climb up the ladder of success.

Humphrey was twenty-six years old, married and almost broke, but he was now on his own, doing what he wanted to do. "My whole world opened up then," Humphrey said later as he looked back on the climate of intellectual challenge and political ferment that he found at the University of Minnesota's sprawling campus overlooking the Mississippi River in Minneapolis.

With Muriel providing the couple's main income from a fifty-five dollar a month bookkeeping job with a Minneapolis investment firm, they rented a third-floor apartment near the University of Minnesota and Humphrey plunged into his studies. He found time to work part-time as a pharmacist, win a Big Ten conference debating championship and membership in Phi Beta Kappa, and compile a straight A record as a political science major. With credit for the courses he had taken six years earlier, Humphrey satisfied the requirements for a bachelor's degree in only two years and graduated *magna cum laude* in June, 1939.

Humphrey was only one of several prize pupils in the University's excellent Department of Political Science, remembers Dr. Evron Kirkpatrick, one of his professors who was to become the most important influence on Humphrey during his college years. In the same class were Orville Freeman, a

49

future governor of Minnesota and secretary of agriculture, and Arthur
Naftalin, who would become one of Humphrey's closest advisers and would
eventually succeed him as mayor of Minneapolis.

Kirkpatrick, now the executive director of the American Political Science Association in Washington, taught Humphrey and Freeman in a course
called "American Constitutional Development." "One thing you became
immediately aware of with Humphrey was that he was very bright, very
articulate and a very willing talker. I've never seen such a photographic
memory. We could talk fifteen minutes about something and Hubert could
go out and speak an hour on it and make it interesting."

Humphrey met Freeman and Naftalin in one of Kirkpatrick's classes
and, although he wouldn't become close to Naftalin until later, he and Freeman quickly became intimate friends. "We both felt that it wasn't enough
just to talk," says Freeman, who joined Humphrey on the debate team and
later babysat for Humphreys' first child, Nancy. "In our academic way,
we made plans to act in the field of politics."

But first, Humphrey had his eye on a Ph.D. and a possible teaching career.
He applied for a fellowship for the 1939–40 school year at several schools
and received one from Louisiana State University after Kirkpatrick wrote
a letter of recommendation to a friend who was chairman of the department
there. The year in Baton Rouge was a difficult one for the Humphreys.
Muriel made sandwiches which Hubert sold to fellow students for a dime
apiece. One month they had to sell their refrigerator to pay the rent. But
they survived and Humphrey won his master's degree with a well-researched
thesis entitled "The Political Philosophy of the New Deal," a glowing appraisal of the first six months of Franklin Roosevelt's new administration.

Humphrey also won a place on the LSU debating team, where he met
Russell Long, son of Louisiana's flamboyant governor and senator, Huey
Long. The younger Long, who would become Humphrey's Senate colleague
and Washington neighbor ten years later and help him gain acceptance
among Southern senators, teamed with Humphrey to successfully argue
the negative side of the question, "Should the U.S. go to the aid of Great
Britain in the war in Europe?" with a team from Oxford University.

The young graduate student from Minnesota also saw something in Louisiana that would influence him in an important way. For the first time in his
life, as he watched the treatment of Negroes in the South, Humphrey became
aware that a large group of Americans was being denied the constitutional
rights he'd been studying the year before. The memory of their treatment
was indelibly imprinted on Humphrey's mind and would dramatically manifest itself in later years.

In June, 1940, Humphrey eagerly returned to Minnesota so he could
begin work on his doctoral degree. Muriel went back to her old job and
Freeman, flush with money from two summer jobs, loaned Humphrey

enough to buy his first car. Kirkpatrick helped by getting Humphrey a summer job conducting a political science seminar for Minnesota teachers sponsored by the Work Projects Administration. In the fall, Humphrey was back at the University of Minnesota taking graduate courses and teaching full-time. But in 1941, his student days ended permanently when he took his first full-time job, as a $150 a month teaching supervisor for the WPA's Workers Education Service.[1]

Kirkpatrick explains how Humphrey made the critical decision that turned him from a teaching career to a life in politics. "He'd done such a damned good job teaching for the WPA the previous summer that they offered him this full-time job. He took the job, partly because he just needed the money. He'd virtually completed the course work for his Ph.D. and thought he'd write his thesis and finish up in his spare time and still become a teacher. But, of course, he never did. He would have made a great teacher."

Once again, Humphrey found the need to make a living upsetting his plans. His struggle to make a living and get an education, like the struggle to survive the dark days of the Depression, left its mark on him. Henceforth, he would always be slightly envious of those who acquired their wealth easily and scornful of those who were not willing to work hard to succeed. "That's why I have so little time today for people who whine and don't want to buckle down," Humphrey said years later. "I hear people say, 'I don't like that kind of work.' Well, who the hell does? I used to swab out the toilets when I went to college and we were caretakers for a fourplex. I repaired the roof, fixed the plumbing, cleaned the sewers, shoveled the snow, and besides that worked six hours a day in a drugstore for twenty cents an hour. So when I hear people say 'I don't like that kind of work,' I say, 'Well, isn't that too bad.'"

Humphrey had an unseen ally in landing his first job. Mrs. Dorothy Jacobson, one of the group of remarkable people he met during his college days who would become lifelong friends and advisers, was working part-time with the Minnesota Department of Education when she was asked to recommend someone to head the WPA's adult education program. She called the chairman of the Political Science Department at the University and said she needed someone "who was very bright, very able, who could speak and write, who knew what the current problems were and who would be willing to work with the kind of people we had." The chairman told her he had a young graduate student who would fit the bill perfectly and needed a job. "His name is Hubert Humphrey," he said.

Humphrey got the job, which made it necessary for him to travel through-

---

[1] One of Humphrey's classmates in graduate school was Malcolm Moos, later a speechwriter for President Eisenhower and now president of the University of Minnesota. Humphrey and Moos once debated the relative merits of Franklin Roosevelt and Wendell Willkie in a radio debate, with Humphrey reluctantly giving up the microphone only after he had extolled Roosevelt's merits for twenty-eight minutes of the thirty-minute program.

out Minnesota, and he soon began to acquire an intimate knowledge of the state.

"He developed, without any sense of the political implication of it, a view that here you have these people in classes in communities around the state trying to improve themselves, but they had nothing to show for it," says Kirkpatrick, who traveled a good deal with Humphrey. "He thought it would be a good idea if those people got a certificate showing they'd completed their courses. So he developed a certificate. I don't know if he signed all of them but he sure signed a lot of them. Later, when we were getting involved in politics, I can't tell you how many meetings I was at where people came up to him and would bring out one of those goddamned certificates signed by him. Lots of people framed those things — it was a symbol of their having accomplished something."

Just as Humphrey's year at LSU was important because it brought him his first real contact with Negroes, his WPA job introduced him to the workingman. The effect was immediate and long-lasting as Humphrey saw firsthand the often grim living conditions and economic exploitation of miners on the Iron Range and lumberjacks in the forests of northern Minnesota, and the militant unionism of workers in the slaughterhouses and manufacturing plants of the Twin Cities. The WPA experience and the year in Louisiana implanted in him a fervor for social justice and economic opportunity that, combined with his innate sympathy for farmers and small-town merchants, would tie him irrevocably to the New Deal political philosophy that was the subject of his master's thesis.

By late 1942, Humphrey had progressed through a series of jobs with wartime agencies in Minnesota to become regional director of the War Manpower Commission. He had also been making a name for himself by speaking to fraternal groups and social clubs in Minneapolis, and soon there was talk that the skinny thirty-two year old professor who was bubbling over with raw energy and passionately held ideas would make a good candidate for mayor of Minneapolis.

One of those who first encouraged Humphrey to run was Naftalin, who was a classmate of Humphrey's at the University but knew him only slightly until he quit his job as a reporter for the Minneapolis *Tribune* and returned to the University to study under Kirkpatrick, who introduced them in early 1942.

But the key person in getting Humphrey to run for mayor was the late Vincent Day, a Hennepin County judge who had been the top aide to the late Governor Floyd B. Olson and was the closest thing to a boss in Minneapolis courthouse politics. Judge Day had heard Humphrey speak at meetings of the Saturday Club, a group of old Farmer Laborites and other Day cronies who met regularly for lunch, and at a University student gathering. Impressed by the young man's potential, Day suggested he run as labor's candidate.

Naftalin remembers Humphrey coming to him in December, 1942, and saying, "Gee, they're really hot for me to run for mayor. Do you think I should?"

One of the things holding Humphrey back was Minneapolis' unsavory reputation as a haven for racketeers and criminals. The city had witnessed several violent labor strikes in the late 1930's, still had a series of unsolved murders involving underworld figures, and there was evidence that City Hall was riddled with corruption. Naftalin, who knew something of the underworld influence from his days as a reporter, told Humphrey his concern about the crime problem was justified.

Humphrey vacillated for several months but finally decided to run. On April 17, just nineteen days before the primary election, he went to City Hall and paid his ten-dollar filing fee and became a candidate for public office for the first time. He was as indefatigable in his first campaign as he would be later, Kirkpatrick recalls. "Hubert would wind up a series of speeches about 1:00 A.M. and Art and I would be exhausted. He'd look around and see some campaign literature on the table and drag us out into the night to distribute it in apartment houses on the fringe of the downtown area."

Humphrey surprised everyone, including himself, by coming in second among nine candidates in the primary and qualifying for the final election against incumbent Mayor Marvin Kline. After an amateurish and under-financed campaign, Humphrey claimed a moral victory by losing the June election by only 4,900 votes.

Although he drew mostly Democratic and Farmer Labor support in the non-partisan election, Humphrey was able to capitalize on the fact that he was relatively unknown by Minneapolis voters. "He was not so strongly identified in the partisan sense that he couldn't play cute about being independent," Naftalin says. "I remember one of our campaign pictures had Humphrey reading Wendell Willkie's *One World* — it was a pitch to the little Republicans."

The near-win clearly identified Humphrey as a political comer but it left him heavily in debt. With a bank account of only $7.00 and a $1,300 printing bill to be paid, Humphrey took a variety of jobs. He became a news commentator for a local radio station, continued working as a part-time pharmacist, and joined Kirkpatrick and Naftalin in a small public relations firm that was mainly a front for the trio's preparation for the next mayor's race.

Humphrey also did some hard thinking about his future. He decided he would have little chance of winning statewide elections — his ultimate goal — while the Farmer Labor and Democratic parties continued to divide the non-Republican vote. The realization that a successful candidate has to have a strong, unified party behind him was a fundamental lesson in practical politics that Humphrey would never forget, and it caused him to write a twelve-page letter in July, 1943, to Frank Walker, then postmaster general and chairman of the Democratic National Committee. In it, Humphrey analyzed Minnesota voting statistics and argued that the Republicans were "a plurality party and that if we could bring together the Democratic and Farmer Labor parties, we could win elections." Unless this were done, Humphrey asserted, the state would remain virtually the private reserve of the Republican party and be extremely difficult for President Roosevelt to carry in 1944.

Undaunted when he received a noncommittal reply from an aide to Walker, Humphrey decided to go to Washington and talk to Walker personally. He put together what little money he had — seventy-seven dollars — and bought a bus ticket to the nation's capital. But he never got beyond the front door of the national committee's Mayflower Hotel headquarters, Humphrey recalls. "I talked to the man who answered my letter — he was sort of an assistant to the chairman — but I never got to see the chairman or deputy chairman. And one time I saw all these other people getting in and I said to him, 'You know what's wrong with this party? It's politics on crutches. This is like an old peoples' home. I'm the only young guy who ever comes in here, and I got more votes by losing in Minneapolis than a lot of these people did by winning.' "

Humphrey stayed for four days before he finally gave up and went to catch a bus to Minneapolis. But he remembered at the last moment that his father had told him to call a family friend from Huron, former Assistant Postmaster General W. W. Howes, Humphrey called Howes from the Willard Hotel and, after exchanging pleasantries, explained his unfulfilled mission. Howes told him to wait there and he'd be right over.

Humphrey spent his last fifty cents on a scotch and soda in the hotel bar, then hastily chewed some mints to cover the smell of liquor on his breath. Howes arrived in half an hour and after hearing Humphrey's tale of frustration, called Walker and urged him to see Humphrey. "By God, inside of five minutes, a limousine that made my eyes pop out parked right in front of the Willard, picked me up and took me to the postmaster general's office," Humphrey remembers. "I had never seen an office so big in my life and I was scared to death. But I went in and told him my story and he said, 'All right, this is a good idea. I'll send a man out to work with you.' "

An elated Humphrey returned to Minnesota to prepare for his new teaching job at Macalester College in St. Paul and to await the arrival of Oscar Ewing, a hard-nosed Wall Street lawyer who was executive vice-chairman of the national committee. Ewing arrived in August and since Humphrey had taken the Macalester job with the understanding he would not be openly involved in politics, the meeting was quietly held in the St. Paul Hotel with Humphrey, State Democratic Chairman Elmer Kelm and about a dozen Democratic party officials present.

Ewing made it clear that President Roosevelt wanted the two parties to merge and agreed to help organize the merger. A merger committee of eighteen persons — nine Democrats and nine Farmer Laborites — was appointed with Humphrey designated as a liaison person to work with both sides. More than a hundred meetings were held over the next seven months before the complex, tedious negotiations finally produced a merger plan agreeable to the Democrats, who controlled federal patronage, and the Farmer Laborites, who were the stronger politically.

In April, 1944, the two parties held simultaneous but separate conventions at nearby hotels in Minneapolis, with Humphrey keynoting the Democratic convention. When the report came to the Democratic convention that the Farmer Laborites had voted to change their name to the "Fellowship party" — a necessary move because state law restricted the use of a party name to the party that first used it — the Democratic convention promptly changed the party's name to "Democratic Farmer Labor party," thus ushering in the new era in Minnesota politics. (Although Humphrey had been present for the birth of the new party, he missed the birth of his first son, Robert, who arrived the same night. "I called Muriel when she was practically in labor and she said, 'You stay there and take care of politics,' " Humphrey recalls.)

The merger brought the two parties together but it failed to do the same for their leaders. Bitter arguments still rage over Humphrey's role in the merger, with former governor Elmer Benson, a leader of the Farmer Laborites on the fusion committee, and others disputing the widely-held notion that Humphrey was the chief architect. Benson has claimed that President Roosevelt first discussed the merger with him, and has even publicly stated that Humphrey not only had no part in the merger but was actually opposed to it.[2]

Naftalin, who spent so much time working on the merger with Humphrey and Kirkpatrick that friends began referring to them as "Faith, Hope and Charity," calls such claims "an inexplicably curious distortion of history . . . like eerie props in an Orwellian play." He asserts that the merger talks were often on the verge of collapsing because of the deep ideological conflicts and controversy over distribution of leadership positions, and adds that they "were held together by Humphrey's skill as a moderator."

Less partisan observers believe Humphrey's role has been both exaggerated and downgraded. The possibility of a merger had been talked about for at least twenty years and Roosevelt was undoubtedly aware that it would

[2] Benson's claims are colored by his later battles with Humphrey over control of the merged party as well as his bitter disappointment over his defeat by Harold Stassen in the 1938 gubernatorial election and his loss to Joseph Ball in the 1942 Senate race. After the latter defeat, he charged that Roosevelt and the Democratic National Committee had actively supported his Republican opponents in both elections. He supported the 1944 merger only after advisers persuaded him that a split liberal vote could help elect a Republican president and possibly delay a speedy end to World War II.

improve his chances of carrying Minnesota in 1944. Most historians accept the view that Humphrey served as a catalyst for the merger, but that others, particularly Kelm — who served as first chairman of the merged party — and Ewing were equally important figures in actually hammering out the details of the merger agreement.

Humphrey himself called Kelm "a principal architect" of the merger at the time of Kelm's death in 1947, although he later added, "I'll throw modesty aside and take credit for a large part of the success of the merger." Kelm's son Douglas, now chairman of the Twin Cities Metropolitan Transit Commission, says, "My dad and Humphrey complemented each other beautifully. Dad was an excellent political mechanic who knew what levers to pull and what buttons to push. Humphrey was a brilliant and extremely articulate strategist."

Almost everyone connected with the merger agrees, however, that it could only have been accomplished when it was because of the widespread desire among both parties to reelect Roosevelt or whoever was the Democratic candidate for president, and thus assure continued U.S.-Soviet military pressure against the Nazis. Humphrey is emphatic on this point. "I'll just lay it on the line to you," he said. "The only reason they allowed this [merger] to happen was because of the spirit of Soviet-American friendship at the time. . . . I'll never forget Mike Dillon, the chairman of the Fifth District Democratic party, telling me, 'They'll never do this, they're left wingers,' And I said, 'That's exactly why they'll do it . . . as long as it helped the war effort, that was it.' As I said to Mike, "We'll never ever get another chance. We either do it now, or we'll never get it.' "

The 1944 convention that launched the Democratic Farmer Labor party and touched off the controversy over Humphrey's role in creating it also highlighted another problem that was to plague Humphrey throughout his career. Deciding to stop a move to draft him as the party's first candidate for governor, Humphrey withdrew with the melodramatic statement, "I want to go in the armed services if I am acceptable. I want to be with those other young men and women in the armed forces and you can't deny me that privilege."[3]

But Humphrey never did enter military service. He tried to enlist in the Naval Reserve Officer program several times, but was rejected because of color blindness and a double hernia (which he had repaired in 1950). First classified 3-A in 1940 because he was married and a father, Humphrey was later reclassified 2-A as an essential civilian because he was teaching Army Air Corps cadets at Macalester. In July, 1944, he was reclassified 1-A and called up for induction, but was rejected because of the hernia and a minor lung calcification caused by his childhood pneumonia.

Humphrey's war record was to become a major issue in later campaigns,

[3] Minneapolis *Star Journal,* April 15, 1944.

especially the 1960 West Virginia primary. The clerk of his Hennepin County
Draft Board, Clinton Norton, said in 1960 that he had received telephone
calls from people interested in seeing Humphrey elected mayor of Minneapolis, but added, "At no time did Humphrey fail to comply with the requests
of the board. It is unfair to imply that he tried to dodge the draft." [4] Ramsey County draft board officials said Macalester President Charles Turck
asked deferment for Humphrey and several other faculty members "for oc-
cupational reasons" but added, "At no time did Mr. Humphrey ever ask
deferment of us." [5]

With the merger successfully accomplished, Humphrey continued to follow the advice he'd given his students in the spring of 1944. After a five-
hour and forty-minute class in American government that was the longest
in Macalester's sixty-two year history, he said, "Whatever your views are,
don't just sit there jeering from the bleachers. Get in there and clean it up.
Yes, study history, fine. But above all, make it."

Setting out to make some history of his own, Humphrey left Macalester
and turned full-time to politics in 1944. (He would return to the St. Paul
school twenty-five years later to teach and to recover from the most crushing
defeat of his life.) He became director of Roosevelt's campaign in Minnesota, helping him carry the state handily. He toyed with the idea of running for governor or Congress, but gave it up in favor of running for mayor
again. He filed against Kline in the spring of 1945 and launched his campaign with a promise to "clean up this town and make it a decent city in
which to raise our children." The campaign theme proved fortuitous when a
gangland slaying occurred. The murder of a small-time weekly newspaper
publisher and former convict named Arthur Kasherman who had attacked
Kline in print as a "hypocrite and a liar" was never solved, but it highlighted
the concern of Minneapolis citizens about criminal elements in the city
and undoubtedly helped Humphrey. He carried 11 of the city's 13 wards and
beat Kline by 31,114 votes, the greatest majority in the city's history. "Humphrey probably would have won the election no matter what happened,"
Ed Ryan (the police chief he named to help him clean up the city) recalled,
"but the Kasherman murder helped."

In August, 1945, the thirty-four year old Humphrey took office as mayor
of the fourteenth largest city in America — the youngest mayor the city
ever had — and pledged immediate action to clean up the crime problem.
"I considered my first job to clean up the city, to give it honest administration," Humphrey later said. "And we did it."

Humphrey "did it" by bringing in Freeman to head the Civil Service
Commission and by instituting the toughest "law and order" program the
city of a half-million persons had ever seen. Although handicapped by a

[4] Minneapolis *Tribune*, May 10, 1960.
[5] St. Paul *Dispatch*, May 7, 1960.

weak-mayor form of government which left most of the power in the hands of the city council, Humphrey took advantage of what little power he had. He named Ryan, a tough FBI-trained Irish cop, to head up the police department, and gave him carte blanche authority to crack down on crime. It was a controversial appointment. Union officials who supported Humphrey's election wanted to pick the new police chief because of their bitter memories of the vicious anti-labor police tactics during a bloody 1934 Minneapolis truck strike. The business community wanted an incorruptible professional who would not favor any one group. And some less respectable business interests wanted a police chief who would allow their liquor, gambling and prostitution activities to continue to flourish.

Humphrey and Ryan carried out their anti-crime drive with a vengeance, closing down dozens of after-hours bars, ordering a grand jury investigation of underworld activities centering around syndicate-controlled liquor traffic, and at times resorting to hard-line tactics that made civil libertarians wince. But the crime drive succeeded — with a healthy boost from federal law enforcement agencies — and Humphrey gained a reputation as a crime-busting reformer who ran a "clean" city.

Humphrey quickly discovered ways to exercise the power that was denied him by the city's charter. He built a government within a government by setting up dozens of citizens' committees and advisory commissions, and used the power of his own personality to institute a series of innovative reform measures. When school board members refused to close or repair a school building he considered unsafe, Humphrey focused public attention on the situation by personally boarding up the entrance to the building.

He attacked the city's festering problem of racial prejudice, which had caused Writer Carey McWilliams to brand Minneapolis "the capital of anti-Semitism in the United States" in August, 1946. He established a Mayor's Council on Human Relations and initiated a "community self-survey" by Fisk University that highlighted previously-ignored areas of discrimination. He fought for and won passage of the nation's first Fair Employment Practices ordinance, became a self-appointed arbitrator of labor-management disputes and helped settle more than two dozen threatened strikes, dramatized the need for additional housing for veterans and low-income persons and got the city council to approve a two million dollar program for more housing, and battled unsuccessfully with the twenty-six member council for reform of the city's antiquated charter and revision of the city's haphazard fiscal practices.

Humphrey's energetic brand of leadership went over well with Minneapolis voters. In the next election in 1947, they returned him to office with a record 52,000 vote majority and, by the end of his second term, many community leaders called him the best mayor the city ever had. Humphrey's two terms as mayor were summed up in June, 1948, by Editor Bradley Morrison of the Minneapolis *Times* in language that pinpointed his flaws as well as his achievements:

> Humphrey has not transformed Minneapolis into Utopia, by any means. The city's archaic weak-mayor charter would prevent that. And it can be said that he scatters his energies over too wide an area; that he talks too much; that he often jumps to superficial judgments and conclusions which he afterwards regrets; and that he is sometimes guilty of political double talk which distresses even his most ardent admirers.
>
> But when the evidence is impartially weighed, the scales tip far toward Humphrey as an honest, progressive and efficient mayor. He has given the city a first-rate police administration; he had made Minneapolis soberly conscious of its human relations problems as it had never been before; and he has sweated more earnestly over the city's bad financial situation and impoverished schools than half a dozen previous mayors. Perhaps his most important contribution has been the great popular interest he has created in city government and his success in dramatizing the charter fight. Humphrey has aroused Minneapolis from a great lethargy. . . . He has enlisted hundreds of previously dormant citizens in his fight for a new deal in city government.

Such accolades weren't necessary to start Humphrey thinking about higher office. As he told a group of journalism students at the University of Minnesota in 1948, he had wanted to be a United States Senator ever since he was four years old, and there was little doubt that he was looking ahead to challenging Republican Senator Joseph Ball in the 1948 election.

At least a few of Humphrey's supporters were looking ahead to something else too. Max Kampelman, a political science teacher at the University who was to become a lifelong Humphrey confidant, says the Political Science Department "saw Humphrey's potential and encouraged him to run very early on. I don't know what he had in mind for 1948 but most of the fellows thought that he might run for the president someday. We talked about it and many said he could run for president from the governor's seat more easily than from the Senate."

The Humphrey-for-Senator boom actually got its start at the 1947 American Federation of Labor convention in San Francisco, where the AFL's late president, William Green, heard Humphrey speak and immediately tabbed him as labor's candidate against Ball. Humphrey remembers returning from that trip and being greeted by a newspaper editorial entitled "Humphrey — Ambitious?" A short time later he told a group of Minneapolis supporters who wanted him to run for a third term, "What's so un-American about being ambitious? Of course I'm ambitious." He told them he thought he was going to seek national office.

Humphrey had learned some important lessons about political leadership as mayor, and he was anxious to put them into practice at a higher level. "I found that my job as mayor of Minneapolis gave me the chance to talk to everybody who came to town," he said later. "I never missed a conven-

tion that came to Minneapolis — the turkey growers, the honeybee association, the PTA's — I was there at every meeting. I loved my job as mayor
and the people knew it and I think we did a good job. I think that was the
most rewarding period in many ways in my public life."

Humphrey had been warned before he ran for mayor that it was a deadend street for anyone with political ambitions. But as mayor he found "that
if you have a job and a title, you can do most anything with it. I guess the
lesson that I learned was that by being creative, innovative and daring, you
can break out of a mold. You don't have to let the constraints of office
determine what you're doing. . . ." Humphrey says he also learned the
need for a political base. "I never took for granted for a single day that
I had political support. I kept working at it all the time. And I never let
the party be my whole political support. I always moved out beyond the
party, because the party always has so many people within it who are seeking to take your place. . . ."

His City Hall experience also taught him something that was to become
the hallmark of his political philosophy. As his official biographer, Michael
Amrine, wrote in a 1960 book, *This Is Humphrey:*

> He began to sense, through all the antennae he had developed as a sensitive
> politician, that the American public fundamentally prefers constructive
> criticism. Humphrey, even while a young mayor, began to see how things
> could be done by compromise and conciliation, through middle-of-the-road
> policies, and seldom through rigid programs conceived by social theorists
> and executed by efficient administrators.

Probably no single experience of his early political career, however, did
more to mold Humphrey as a man and a politician than the savage struggle
over control of the Democratic Farmer Labor party that ensued after the
1944 merger and came to the surface in 1946–48. Just as the merger had
marked a watershed in Minnesota politics and Humphrey's career, so would
the latter period be remembered as the time when the future of the party —
and of Humphrey — was determined.

Yet Humphrey, preoccupied with his mayor's duties and his own desire
to make 1948 his year of golden opportunity, almost failed to respond to
the crisis before it was on him. Shortly after he was elected mayor in 1945,
Freeman, Naftalin and others warned him that the party was being taken over
by left-wing radicals, including a small but vociferous group of Communists.

"An important point to make about Humphrey is that he has never really
paid a lot of attention to organizational politics," Naftalin, his executive
secretary through most of the mayor years, said later. "We pleaded with him
to pay attention to the party. We tried to explain that people unfriendly to
him were going to take over the party and he'd be in one hell of a lot of
trouble, that he'd be running in a party dominated by the Communist line.
And he'd say, 'Yeah, well okay,' but he was busy making speeches, run-

ning around, building his fences as far as the mayor's office was concerned. So by 1946, our dire predictions were borne out; because of lack of attention the party was lost. But . . . we were still having trouble getting him to pay attention to the party."

The struggle for control of the DFL actually began during the months of intense negotiations that led to the merger as both sides jockeyed for key leadership positions. Due to failing health, Elmer Kelm stepped down as chairman in 1946 and, soon afterwards, extreme left-wing elements took control of the party. By now it had become split into two bitterly feuding factions, the extreme left-wing group headed by former Governor Benson which supported Henry Wallace as a presidential candidate of the newly formed Progressive party, and a more moderate reform group headed by Humphrey which supported President Truman or another potential Democratic candidate.

The hostility which the Benson left wing felt for Humphrey — who supported Wallace for vice president in 1944 but broke with him in 1946 because of his denunciation of Truman's foreign policy — boiled to the surface at the 1946 DFL state convention.[6] Humphrey, the party's most prominent office holder, was jeered at and spat upon when he arrived to give the keynote address. Cries of "fascist" and "warmonger" greeted him from an audience that was heavily weighted with Benson and Wallace supporters, and he was unable to complete his speech. The convention elected a slate of extreme left wing party officers, mostly ex-Farmer Laborites, who took almost complete control despite some behind-the-scenes maneuvering by Kelm, wearing dark glasses with his coat collar turned up because he had a federal appointment pending.

However, the Humphrey forces salvaged one strategically important leadership position as the convention elected Freeman party secretary.

"We were totally naive and stupid," Freeman later recalled. "They outmanuevered us on all the points and issues. We had enough people but didn't know what to do with them." But because the left wing wanted a semblance of unity, they asked Freeman, an ex-Marine and wounded war hero, to be party treasurer. "Humphrey insisted they make me not treasurer but secretary," says Freeman. "They didn't want to, but Bob Sheran [a former Minnesota Supreme Court justice now practicing law in the Twin Cities] got up and made an impassioned speech and the result was I became secretary."

Humphrey and Freeman and a small band of liberal, anti-Communist friends used Freeman's new position to loosen the Benson faction's grip

[6] On April 12, 1945, minutes after hearing of President Roosevelt's death, Humphrey wrote to Wallace, "If ever we needed men of courage, it is now. I simply can't conceal my emotions. How I wish you were at the helm. I know Mr. Truman will rise to the heights of statesmanship. . . . But, we need you as you have never been needed before."

on the party and frustrate the plan by Benson — who was national campaign chairman for Wallace — to make Wallace the DFL presidential nominee in Minnesota and force Truman to run as an independent. The Humphrey-Freeman forces carefully organized themselves and moved with military precision to take over the 1948 precinct caucuses, the first step of the process leading to the selection of the state and national convention delegates, and, in fact, control of the party. (It was almost exactly the same way that insurgent supporters of Eugene McCarthy's presidential candidacy would try to take control of the party from Humphrey supporters twenty years later.)

A major part of the Humphrey-Freeman strategy in 1948 was based on the contention that Communists and fellow-travelers had gained control of the DFL. Benson and other critics of Humphrey vigorously denied the charge, while accusing Humphrey in turn of using "red-baiting" tactics to take over the party. Few people involved in the fight dispute the assertion that Communists and Communist supporters were active in the party. In fact, there is reason to believe that for a brief period in 1947 and 1948, the Minnesota DFL became the only major American party ever to be controlled by Communists.

"There's absolutely no doubt in my mind that there were hard-core Communists in the party then," Freeman says. "I confronted a number of these people and I knew where they came from — I had ways of getting information — and I knew they were Communist party members. There's no question about it — of course they took over the party. There was just a handful of them, from a couple of labor unions, from the old Farmer Labor party, but they controlled it."

No quarter was asked and none given as the competing factions fought for survival, Freeman recalls. "There are still some people who resent how rough we were. I drew the line very, very tough with some old friends. I said if you didn't go with us in this fight, you were on the other side and you were out, and that was too bad. We paid a price for it, but we wouldn't have won otherwise." [7]

Another key Humphrey ally was Mrs. Eugenie Anderson, later to become America's first woman ambassador and a lifelong Humphrey adviser. She remembers that Kirkpatrick and Naftalin had worked out a scenario for the 1946 state convention just as they had two years earlier. "It worked in

---

[7] Among those "on the other side" was Freeman's father-in-law, James M. Shields, who joined the Benson forces after resigning his job as regional director of the National Labor Relations Board in 1947. Shields wrote a favorable biography of Benson (*Mr. Progressive*, T. S. Denison & Company, Inc., Minneapolis) in 1971, in which he quotes Benson's assessment of the effect of Freeman's election as party secretary in 1946: "Thus the door was held open to the termites, and once in they never left." Shields gives most of the credit for the DFL merger to Benson and to Oscar Ewing, who, he wrote, arrived at a critical time — "somewhat inebriated, true, but still swinging a big stick to compel local Democrat functionaries, including Humphrey, to abide by agreements."

1944, but in 1946 it didn't, primarily because there were so few people who understood what was going on. There were only a handful, as I recall, of real Communists, and there was a larger circle of sort of fellow-travelers, and there was still a larger circle of confused people and a larger mass who didn't understand what was going on. It was impossible for us to succeed. It was a very good demonstration of how a minority can control a majority, if the minority knows what it wants and is willing to use almost any tactics."

Not everyone allied with Humphrey in the fight for control of the DFL shared his assessment of Communist and extreme left-wing strength in the party in the late 1940's. John Blatnik, elected to Congress in 1946 from the northeastern Minnesota district that was one of the centers of Farmer Labor-ite strength in the state, said in a 1971 interview, "That's one place I dif-fered with Humphrey. We had a small core of what you would call the 'hard left' in Duluth and on the Iron Range, but I never believed they were that strong. They were resourceful and effective, but the issues they raised were the issues of the Farmer Laborites. The Farmer Laborites were real militant liberals and activists but they weren't Communists or revolutionaries at all." [8] However, Blatnik concedes there was considerable Communist strength in the labor movement in Minneapolis at the time.

In the convention which elected Freeman secretary, Mrs. Anderson was named second vice-chairman of the party's executive committee. About a week after the convention, she and Freeman and other Humphrey sup-porters who felt the party had been taken over by the extreme left seriously considered starting another party. "But we decided that would not be the best way to deal with it. We decided that if we stayed in the party, and worked within it, and worked to build, that there was a potential majority — in fact, we were sure there was. The people had just not understood the issues. We believed if we made the issues clear, and could build an organiza-tion within the next two years, we could win back control of the party."

The battle with the Benson-Wallace wing was a rude awakening for many of the young idealists around Humphrey, and even for Humphrey himself, who at least had some exposure to rough and tumble City Hall politics. It also produced, almost overnight, a cadre of hardnosed semi-professional politicians who would be able to hold their own in almost any future fight. "If you hadn't been through that kind of a serious defeat at the hands of a ruthless minority, it's difficult to understand the tactics of any kind of a totalitarian group," says Mrs. Anderson. "We really were burned. I had never understood this kind of tactics before." [9]

[8] Gus Hall, head of the American Communist party, was born in Blatnik's district in the small Iron Range community of Cherry, but according to Blatnik, never con-centrated his activity in his home state.

[9] Mrs. Anderson also remembers the first time she heard Humphrey speak, at the 1944 state convention. "I remember particularly that he quoted Thomas Jefferson and Woodrow Wilson quite a lot. I thought that not only was he an eloquent speaker, but

Dorothy Jacobson, who had helped Humphrey land his first job back in 1941, tells how the battle was carried on. "You had to learn, as I learned, to beat them at their own game because they used all these clever techniques. For example, in the middle of page two in a three-page resolution, there would be one line giving the [Communist] party line. I remember one long resolution that was in opposition to Walter Judd [a conservative Republican congressman from Minneapolis]. All of us wanted to defeat Walter Judd, of course, but buried in the resolution was one of these lines and unless you caught that, you'd have the party line written into your platform."

Years later, after Mrs. Jacobson was named U.S. assistant secretary of agriculture for international affairs under Freeman, she headed a U.S. delegation to a United Nations conference in Rome. She was called back to Washington for an emergency meeting and when she returned to Rome, she learned that Communist Cuba had passed several resolutions at the conference containing hidden language embarrassing to the U.S. She was able to get the resolutions rephrased to remove the objectionable parts and passed over Cuba's opposition, and later explained to the State Department how she was able to do it. "You know, I learned this back in the Twelfth Ward in Minneapolis. The Communists fight the same way whether they speak in Spanish or with a Swedish accent."

The Communists in the DFL were dedicated and well-organized, and could control a meeting of several hundred people with only a handful of members. Lee Loevinger, whose father was a founder of the Farmer Labor party and Floyd Olson's first judicial nominee, was legal counsel for the DFL during the 1946–48 period. Loevinger, who later served on the Minnesota Supreme Court, and was an assistant U.S. attorney general and member of the Federal Communications Commission, remembers how it was:

"These bastards were hard-line Commies and their strategy was to pack the meetings and out-sit everybody else. Our idea was to get enough of our friends and not get tired, not let them out-wait us. I can remember some meetings dragging on until 1:00 and 2:00 A.M. and I thought, 'For Chrissakes, isn't anybody ever going to go home?' "

As Humphrey and his supporters moved toward a showdown with the Benson wing, they began to look for help outside Minnesota. In January, 1947, Humphrey, Freeman, Naftalin, Kirkpatrick and Mrs. Anderson went to Washington for the organizing meeting of the Americans for Democratic Action, a liberal anti-Communist organization created, as its founders said, to keep the Democratic party, "with all its faults," on liberal paths.

Back in Minnesota, they quickly formed a state ADA chapter, with the idea of using it as a caucus in organizing to recapture grassroots control of the party. With Humphrey as president and Mrs. Anderson and Naftalin as

---

I sensed that he had the qualities of leadership. I remember turning to the county chairman sitting next to me and saying, 'That man will be president some day.' "

top officers, they roamed over the state organizing local support and demonstrating techniques for taking over the precinct caucuses.[10] In March, 1947, the St. Paul *Dispatch* reported that Humphrey,

> after many months of polite undercover sparring with Communists and party-line followers of the DFL, is out in the open as leader of a definite anti-Communist drive. At a meeting of the Americans for Democratic Action in Minneapolis, he urged 'true liberals' to join him in 'wresting control' of the DFL from Communists and their supporters.

Others remember that the group used copies of FBI files obtained by Humphrey to identify suspected or known Communists, who were quickly eliminated as prospective allies.

One of the people to join the ADA organizing effort was a young college teacher from St. Paul who showed up at Humphrey's office one day in early 1947 and agreed to begin a similar drive in St. Paul and Ramsey County. "Gene McCarthy was recognized early as one of our best leaders," says Mrs. Anderson who, like Humphrey, was destined to clash with McCarthy in the years ahead.

At about the same time, a related effort was being organized by younger Humphrey supporters, mostly ex-G.I.'s and local college students, to take over the Young DFL that was being organized by the senior party in the fall of 1947. Doug Kelm was just out of the Navy and was in graduate school at the University of Minnesota, where he roomed with a Minneapolis law student named Donald Fraser (later elected to Congress). Using Freeman's party secretary office to give themselves an aura of legitimacy, they contacted other young people in the Twin Cities and Duluth — mostly college students — and brought enough supporters to the YDFL organizing convention so that they completely controlled it.

"We set up an office in downtown Minneapolis and financed it by selling our blood to the Veterans Administration hospital," Kelm remembers. "In those days you could get twenty-five dollars a pint and fifty dollars if it was a negative type. We sent them back as often as we could."

One of the people involved in the YDFL effort was Joseph Dillon, a St. Paul law student who later became mayor of St. Paul. He remembers that Fraser was the group's expert on parliamentary questions, a talent that would be recognized in 1970 when Fraser was named chairman of the Democratic National Committee's top reform commission. "We learned parliamentary law because we had to," says Dillon. "The Communists knew it so well that we had to learn it in self defense. They knew the liberals prob-

---

[10] After the 1948 elections, the Humphrey faction decided that the ADA had served its purpose, according to Mrs. Anderson. "The ADA was really the vehicle for getting back control of the party. Once we got control [of the party], we felt that there wasn't much need for ADA in the state any more. We not only lost interest, but it was a conscious decision. We felt that it had served its purpose. We felt we had achieved what the ADA was trying to achieve — political power."

ably would go to a meeting and leave early so they could get a couple of beers before they went home. Our toughest job was to get enough guys who would come and just out-wait them."

The multi-level organizational effort paid off handsomely for the Humphrey forces as they gained a clear numerical majority over left-wing supporters in the April, 1948, precinct caucuses throughout the state, and in the subsequent county and district conventions. At the state convention in June, the Humphrey faction finally won the long, bitter struggle for control of the party and Humphrey was endorsed for the Senate. Benson's followers angrily accused Humphrey of "Tammany-like tactics" and walked out, calling a rump convention and forming a separate "Progressive party" which filed a list of Wallace-pledged presidential electors as the official DFL ballot. However, the Minnesota Supreme Court ruled that the "right wing" Truman-pledged electors were entitled to the party label, which in effect sounded the death knell for the Benson "left wing." [11]

Ironically, supporters at the 1948 DFL convention provided a foretaste of the rhetoric that would be used against Humphrey a month later at the Democratic National Convention in Philadelphia.[12] DFL Vice-chairman Byron (Barney) Allen, in his keynote speech, urged Henry Wallace — an old friend of Allen's — to renounce his third party movement and work for party unity and the election of Truman. "While there is still time, I call on [Wallace] to abandon the mad course which can only lead to his own destruction and the destruction of our president."

Nevertheless, the state convention avoided pledging Minnesota's delegates to Truman, mostly at the urging of Humphrey, who in previous months had been a leader of the ADA's stop-Truman movement and had even talked about the possibility of dumping Truman in favor of General Dwight D. Eisenhower or Minnesota-born Supreme Court Justice William O. Douglas. Humphrey did not announce he would support Truman's renomination until July 11, three days before the national convention opened in Philadelphia. By then, Truman's renomination was virtually assured and the major concern of party leaders was to avoid a fight over the civil rights plank that could hurt Truman in the South and damage his already-dim election prospects.

Humphrey quickly made it clear that he wouldn't accept an innocuous civil rights plank. When the platform committee — of which Humphrey was a member — came out with a plank that was little more than a rewritten

[11] Although the Humphrey supporters were identified at the time as the DFL's "right wing" and the Benson supporters the "left wing," the terms are misleading in the context of their modern meaning. Humphrey's supporters were "right wingers" only in relation to Benson's radical "left wing," but they bore no resemblance to the militantly conservative philosophy connoted by the "right wing" appellation today.

[12] Humphrey's followers would use similar language twenty years later against Eugene McCarthy as well.

version of the 1944 plank, he denounced it as a "sellout to states' rights over human rights," causing Truman's chief spokesman, Senate Majority Leader Scott Lucas of Illinois, to brand him a "pipsqueak." Humphrey then joined with former Wisconsin Congressman Andrew Biemiller (now an official of the AFL-CIO in Washington) in preparing a minority report with a strong civil rights plank, and on the evening of the second day of the convention, met with Biemiller and leaders of the ADA in a college fraternity house rented by the ADA to decide whether they should take their fight to the convention floor.

Orville Freeman, a member of the Minnesota delegation, recalls the impassioned arguments that lasted until 5:00 A.M. while Humphrey and the others debated the warnings of party elders that a civil rights fight would "split the party wide open" and cost Truman the election.

"Humphrey didn't think he could win the fight and neither did I," says Freeman. "I counselled him not to do this. I was for it in principle all the way but as a matter of practical politics, I was afraid we were going to lose and be laughed out of the hall and told to go home. But Humphrey finally said, 'If there is one thing I believe in in this crazy business, it's civil rights. Regardless of what happens, we're going to do it. Now get the hell out of here and let me write a speech and get some sleep.'"

The room was cleared by Frederic J. (Freddie) Gates, a Minneapolis penny arcade owner who was Humphrey's all-round handyman and devoted friend. "He's gotta get some sleep before making this speech," Gates declared as he shooed everyone out.

Humphrey also was aware of the very real threat the Wallace Progressives posed to his own election hopes in Minnesota, and some people feel that his efforts on behalf of a strong civil rights plank were at least partially motivated by a desire to blunt left wing attacks against him in Minnesota.

However, the overriding factor in Humphrey's decision to give the speech was a long conversation he had that night with his father, a member of the South Dakota delegation. The two men talked for several hours, with the father cautioning his son that what he planned to do would split the party. "Then he said, 'You believe strongly in this, don't you Hubert?'" Humphrey recalls. "And I said, 'Yes, I do.' Then he told me, 'There's only one thing that you ought to put ahead of trying to keep this party united, and that is your principles. If you believe strongly enough in it, you have an obligation to go in and battle it out. But you'll most likely be defeated.'"

Ten hours later, as a nervous, perspiring Humphrey waited in the sweltering convention hall putting the final touches on his speech, he was approached by an old-time party boss from the Bronx, Ed Flynn, who asked to see Humphrey's speech. Afraid that Flynn would object to it, Humphrey said apologetically, "It's not extreme. All we've got here are some of the features of

the president's commission on civil rights. I don't want to divide the party —
I'm a good Democrat, a solid Democrat."

Humphrey recalls that he was startled when Flynn read the speech and
declared, "Young man, that's just what this party needs." When Humphrey
reminded him of the Southerners' threat to walk out, Flynn said, "Let them.
Some of them should have been out of the party a long time ago." Flynn
assured Humphrey that the minority plank would win and promised to line
up the ninety-eight votes of the New York delegation and the other populous
Northern states to support it.

His confidence bolstered by Flynn's promise of support, Humphrey, with
a yellow "Truman" button in his lapel, stepped to the platform and in a
high-pitched earnest voice, gave what many people felt was the most elec-
trifying convention speech since William Jennings Bryan's celebrated "Cross
of Gold" speech in 1896. "It was the greatest speech I ever heard," Illinois
delegate Paul Douglas — who would soon join Humphrey in the Senate —
later declared. "He was on fire, just like the Bible speaks of Moses. His face
was glowing and his sentiments were marvelous."

Unlike many of Humphrey's later speeches, this one lasted less than ten
minutes. But it was as powerful, dramatic and eloquent as any he would
ever give and he spoke with a fervor that brought sweat pouring from his
face and spattering on the pages of his speech. He began by expressing his
"respect and admiration" for those who felt differently than he did on the
emotionally-charged civil rights issue, and then delivered a fervent plea
for equality for all Americans, capped by a twenty-seven word sentence that
would become the most-quoted line he ever uttered:

> The time has arrived for the Democratic party to get out of the shadow
> of states' rights and walk forthrightly into the bright sunshine of human
> rights.

Humphrey was interrupted more than twenty times by applause, and
when he concluded, the convention hall erupted into a wild demonstration
that lasted almost as long as the speech. When the demonstration subsided,
the delegates voted down a Southern-sponsored states' rights minority report
and the convention chairman, Speaker of the House Sam Rayburn, called
for a vote on Biemiller's resolution to adopt the minority plank which Humphrey spoke in support of.

But Douglas and Jake Arvey, the Democratic party boss from Chicago,
thought that Rayburn, a Southerner, was trying to confuse the delegates by
identifying the minority plank as "the Biemiller resolution." Douglas, a big
hulking man standing over six feet tall, boosted the smaller Arvey onto his
shoulders and demanded to be recognized.

Douglas recalled the climactic scene in a 1971 interview. "Arvey was a
little fellow, only about a hundred pounds, and he stood on my shoulders

and said to Rayburn, 'Is this the Humphrey resolution?' Rayburn said, 'This is the Biemiller resolution.' Now, Jake got mad and said, 'Don't give us any of that stuff. Is this the resolution Mayor Humphrey voted for in committee and spoke for?' Rayburn said, 'I believe it is,' and this went out over the microphones so we had it identified."

When the roll was called, Freeman sat on the convention floor with a tally sheet, convinced there was no chance of getting the necessary 617 votes for a majority. As he heard Hubert Humphrey, Sr., report South Dakota's eight votes for the resolution, he knew it would be close, and when Biemiller's Wisconsin delegation cast its twenty-four votes to assure a majority, Freeman and almost everybody else was stunned. "I was certain we'd be blown out of the water," Freeman said in 1971. "I didn't think we'd get more than 150 votes and when we won it going away, I couldn't believe it. It was a great piece of courageous judgment and risk-taking on a moral issue."

The final vote was 651½ for the liberal substitute plank and 582½ against, causing Humphrey to leap to his feet with joy, and South Carolina's Governor J. Strom Thurmond — who would serve with Humphrey in the Senate and live in the same apartment building — to lead a walkout of thirty-five Southern delegates, who later held a rump convention and formed a new States' Rights party, just as Henry Wallace's supporters had formed a splinter party on the left.

Humphrey never forgot the support given him by the party bosses at Philadelphia. "The man who gave me the courage and the man who stood up when I was scared to death was Boss Flynn," Humphrey said after he returned to the Senate in 1971. "Most of the good things that have been done in this country happened because somebody had the guts to do them, and generally it's a 'boss.' One of the things that's wrong with the Democratic party today is that it doesn't have any more 'bosses.' It's like trying to run a family on the basis of polling it. When the chips were down in our family, the old man called the shots — we got a chance for our arguments, we all had our say — but somebody had to be in charge. I've never forgotten old Boss Flynn."

Humphrey's speech at the 1948 national convention would be remembered by millions of Americans as one of the most stirring moments of their lives. People all over the nation clustered around radio sets — the convention was the first to be televised but relatively few people saw it on television — and read about it in their newspapers, and he became a nationally recognized figure overnight.[13] When he returned to Minnesota, he was greeted by a

[13] In retrospect, Humphrey's decision to give his 1948 civil rights speech was no less unthinkable than Eugene McCarthy's decision to challenge an incumbent president of his own party twenty years later, particularly in view of the fact that the Democratic party was already threatened on the left by the Wallace progressives when Humphrey made his speech, and when one remembers that virtually no major

tumultuous demonstration and was hailed by one political expert as "the nearest thing to a liberal meteor this state has seen since Floyd B. Olson flashed across its political sky in the Thirties."

He easily won the Democratic Senate primary and turned his attention to his campaign against Republican Senator Joseph Ball, in whom Humphrey had the perfect opponent. Ball's rocklike conservatism and blunt, slow-moving manner (by actual count, Humphrey could speak three times as fast as Ball) contrasted sharply with Humphrey's liberal philosophy and whirlwind campaign style. Zeroing in on Ball's key role in passing the Taft-Hartley bill and his vote against the Marshall Plan, and capitalizing on the publicity from the Philadelphia convention, Humphrey carried on a campaign the likes of which Minnesota had never seen before. He made an estimated 700 speeches and traveled more than 31,000 miles, traversing the state in a 1946 Buick driven by Freddie Gates, who kept a wheel of Longhorn cheese and a loaf of bread in the back seat so Humphrey wouldn't have to waste time stopping for meals. In November, he defeated Ball by 243,693 votes to become Minnesota's first Democratic Farmer Labor Senator and helped send McCarthy and three other DFL candidates to Congress. Meanwhile, the fears that Humphrey had endangered Truman's reelection by his Philadelphia speech proved unfounded as Truman defeated Republican Thomas Dewey by more than two million votes despite the splinter party candidacies of Progressive Henry Wallace and Dixiecrat Strom Thurmond.

Clearly, Humphrey was now on his way up the ladder of political success, and he would take many people with him, including one who would one day help thwart his dream of the presidency. "Gene McCarthy or any of the rest of us could never have gotten anywhere in politics without Humphrey," Freeman declared years later. "The guy who put it all together, the symbol, the figurehead, the guy with the charisma was Humphrey. He couldn't have done it alone, but certainly until some of us could fly alone, he was the leader."

Humphrey had led the struggle for control of his own state party and had proved, in the words of Minnesota Political Scientist G. Theodore Mitau, "that the will of the majority can be made to prevail over the concerted efforts of even a better disciplined, numerically small, but closely knit party segment." He had also led the battle over the soul of the national Democratic party and he had won.

---

civil rights legislation had been passed at the time. Humphrey still considers his 1948 stand on what he calls "the basic issue of all time, human rights," the supreme achievement of his career.

CHAPTER V

PROFESSOR McCARTHY AND THE NEW POLITICS

*My first real participation in politics
began almost by accident or default in 1946.*
Eugene McCarthy, explaining how
he got started in politics.

Eugene McCarthy learned the facts of political life in a city once described by his fellow Minnesotan and critic, Sinclair Lewis, as the Boston of the Midwest. F. Scott Fitzgerald, who grew up in St. Paul and did some of his best writing in the garret of a brownstone Victorian rowhouse on once-elegant Summit Avenue, called it the last city of the East. And a later writer characterized St. Paul as a Boston that never quite made it out to San Francisco.

All of them were right to a degree, although St. Paulites favor Lewis' phrase since he is said to have used St. Paul's bigger and more aggressive twin, Minneapolis, as the model for the crassly commercial Zenith City of his novel, *Babbitt*. Certainly no other city in the Midwest, and probably in the nation, combined so many elements of Boston's rich ethnic mix, instinct for politics, intellectual atmosphere, straight-laced morals, continental flavor, unimaginative wealth, love of the past and provincial outlook as St. Paul did when McCarthy arrived there as a college teacher in 1946.

For McCarthy, who later would move with equal ease through labor halls in South Boston and the Harvard Club in Cambridge, St. Paul was the perfect place and 1946 the perfect year to plant the seeds of a political career. The city was an historic stronghold of Democratic strength in Minnesota. Along with the Great Lakes seaport city of Duluth, it consistently supplied the bulk of the statewide Democratic vote both before and after the 1944 merger of the Democratic and Farmer Labor parties.

Heavily unionized and predominantly Catholic, St. Paul was a prosperous, pleasant city that was trying hard to forget its well-earned reputation as one of the nation's most congenial gangster hideouts in Prohibition days.[1] Ironically, a reform mayor elected in 1932 began an anti-crime campaign that drove many of St. Paul's criminals across the river to Minneapolis, where they flourished until Hubert Humphrey was elected mayor in 1945.

St. Paul was slowly starting to awaken to the problems and promise of the postwar boom in 1946 when McCarthy took a $2,750 a year job at the College of St. Thomas as an instructor of economics and sociology. Within a few months, two Republicans whom McCarthy would later defeat were elected to Congress — Edward Thye to the Senate and Edward Devitt to the House of Representatives from the Fourth Congressional District. Devitt won in the solidly Democratic district that included St. Paul and Ramsey County largely because he was a handsome Irish Catholic and his opponent was plagued by personal problems. But the future was dim for any Republican in St. Paul and it was clearly a good time for the thirty-two year old McCarthy to get into politics.

Gene McCarthy met the man who steered him to politics on registration day at St. Thomas in September, 1946. Both he and Marshall Smelser were new faculty members who were helping some eighteen hundred students register for the fall semester at the small Catholic men's college run by the Archdiocese of St. Paul. Smelser had spent the war years working in Washington, but had not known McCarthy, who was working as a civilian intelligence analyst for the War Department in 1944–45. "On registration day, he came up and introduced himself, saying that a mutual friend in Washington had told him I was coming here and he should look me up," Smelser later recounted.

The two young teachers became close friends as they shared cramped office space in the small college that was jammed to overflowing with serious-minded veterans who wanted to trade in their G.I. benefits for a Catholic liberal arts education, providing it showed them how to make a good living as well. "Our desks were right next to each other and we soon found out that we felt the same way about Washington," Smelser recalls. "We both felt like we'd been riding on a roller coaster and had no control over our lives because we were deprived of our vote in the District of Columbia. And we agreed that now that we were in a place where we could exercise our vote, we would."

Smelser, whom McCarthy credits with being the first person to urge him

[1] Perhaps the most notorious criminal to find shelter in St. Paul in the 1930's was Alvin Karpis of the infamous Karpis-Barker Gang. Karpis was sentenced to life imprisonment in 1936 for his part in the kidnapping of William Hamm, Jr., a wealthy St. Paul brewer. He was personally escorted to his trial in St. Paul from New Orleans, where he was arrested, by J. Edgar Hoover, the FBI director whom McCarthy would seek to have replaced in 1968.

to become actively involved in politics, suggested a few months later that they seriously consider trying to reform the patronage-encrusted left wing dominated Democratic Farmer Labor party in St. Paul. McCarthy suggested that they get some advice on how to get started by talking to a state legislator from St. Paul named William Carlson, whom McCarthy had gotten to know because their wives had been close friends in college. "So we went to Bill's house, and although he didn't wish to get directly involved, he advised us as an elder statesman — he was about a year older — to go over and see Hubert Humphrey in Minneapolis and get in on his action," says Smelser.

They took Carlson's advice and went to see Humphrey in his office in the Minneapolis City Hall early in 1947. "Humphrey and Art Naftalin and a lot of other people from around the state were gathered there for a meeting to see what they could do about organizing to take over the precinct caucuses in 1948," Smelser remembers. "They were making plans to see what could be done to advance Humphrey, who was presented as a symbolic figure, and others in taking control of the DFL."

Smelser, who now teaches American history at Notre Dame, recalls that Humphrey talked to him and McCarthy briefly ("You don't talk much when Humphrey's talking," he says). Humphrey advised them to go back to Ramsey County where he felt the party organization was very weak and try to take it over. So they returned to St. Thomas and began to recruit as many like-minded friends as they could. "They proved to be scarce in 1947," Smelser adds.

However, they were able to enlist a number of Smelser's and McCarthy's faculty colleagues in the reform effort, including Raphael Thuente, who had known McCarthy as a student at St. John's and as a teacher in Mandan, North Dakota. "I remember that Gene came to me one day and said there was a precinct caucus that night and I should come," Thuente says. "There were about fifteen people present and we were sitting in a circle. One gentleman was about fifty-five or sixty years old but the rest of us were in our twenties or early thirties. The purpose of the meeting, as I recall, was to find delegates to go to the county convention. And I've often thought of it — Gene simply took over the meeting. He just moved his chair in, put his long legs out and got himself appointed to be a delegate to the county convention. I would say that was the start of his political career."

McCarthy's new career was temporarily nipped in the bud at the 1947 Ramsey County convention (held annually then but only in even-numbered years now). Smelser nominated McCarthy in the pre-convention maneuvering as the leader of the "right-wing" faction that was trying to control the convention and choose party officers. He described his spirited nominating speech in a 1964 article which appeared in *Harper's* magazine and was prophetically subtitled, "How to Succeed by Ignoring Your Well-Wishers."

I hit the Irish Catholic Democrats with McCarthy's still hush-hush career in Army Signals (Patriotism), and harvested the flinty-eyed Farmer Labor types by offering them a plain candidate who owns a walking plow (Populism). We had only one opponent, and a lady nominated him with the peroration, 'I haven't got anything against professors, but I think we ought to have a man who works for a living.'

McCarthy won easily, Smelser wrote, but McCarthy and his supporters were "massacred" on the convention floor a few days later and went home in abject defeat without winning a single party office. "But Gene McCarthy had emerged as our leader against all who booed the Truman Doctrine and attacked Humphrey as a reactionary lackey of the interests," he added.

By now, McCarthy had been named acting head of the Sociology Department at St. Thomas and had plenty of time to ponder what went wrong and to plan another attempt to take over the party the following year. The subject was discussed at length in meetings in "Tom Town," the village of two-family Navy quonset huts on the St. Thomas campus where the McCarthys lived with other faculty members and married veterans. The discussions often included faculty members and students from other nearby private colleges like Macalester and Hamline who had become interested in the party reform effort.

Life in Tom Town was short on comforts but long on community spirit and helpful neighbors. The McCarthys lived in Hut 8A, which they shared with Raphael and Margaret Thuente. "I remember in the spring of 1947 when I took Margaret to the hospital to have a baby boy," says Thuente. "I just knocked on the wall and Gene came over and crawled into our bed so there'd be somebody with our two other children. I was back in two hours and I said, 'Get out. Nice boy.' And he went back to his hut."

Another resident of Tom Town was J. Herman Schauinger, an American history professor, who came home from the hospital one day to find McCarthy tacking up weather stripping around the front door and windows of the Schauinger hut. Schauinger remembers that each morning during his convalescence, McCarthy, just like the milkman, would leave a five-gallon can of fuel oil at his door to keep Schauinger's stove going in the cruel Minnesota winter. Schauinger, who later dedicated a book about Catholics in American political life to McCarthy, recalls that Gene went to Mass every day, cooked meals when Abigail was pregnant with their first daughter, Ellen, and helped him organize the village council. McCarthy and Schauinger often talked about the role of the Christian in government in the office they shared. Once, after reading the pope's Christmas message urging Christian involvement in politics, McCarthy declared, "Herman, the pope says we should get into politics. Instead of griping, we should act."

But it was another new colleague on the St. Thomas faculty who was to exert an even greater influence on the young McCarthy. Heinrich Rommen, who lived in the hut next to the McCarthys, was a refugee from Nazi Germany, which he fled in 1938 after refusing to write an article favorable to the Hitler government. A brilliant man and internationally recognized political scientist, Rommen taught first at a small college in Connecticut before moving to St. Paul at the same time McCarthy did. Just before coming to St. Thomas, Rommen had completed his third book, a massive study of the development of Catholic political thought entitled *The State in Catholic Thought.*

In the book, Rommen analyzed the development of the relationship between Church and state from the earliest days of Western civilization, and concluded, in words that would echo throughout McCarthy's political career:

> Man's end transcends the state. Man's end is the other world; the state's end is in this world. The state ceases to be the omnipotent, absolute pedagogue of man; it and its end become a relative value, a subordinated end in the new hierarchy of ends and values. The individual person is no longer bound to the state. . . . What before was an absolute ethics established by civil law, is now put under the direction of the superior morality of love of God and neighbor.

Rommen's influence on McCarthy was "very great," according to Mrs. McCarthy, who had returned to teach at the College of St. Catherine, the nearby sister school of St. Thomas, and had translated some of Rommen's works into English. "I think he opened up for both of us a whole new group of thinkers and writers," she said later as she talked of theologians and political theoreticians who had been involved personally in struggles with totalitarian governments as Rommen had in Hitler's Germany.

Rommen had written his doctoral thesis at the University of Bonn on Francisco Saurez, the seventeenth-century Spanish Jesuit theologian whose political doctrine based on the equality of all men and the repudiation of the divine right of kings heavily influenced subsequent Catholic teachings on democracy. Rommen introduced the McCarthys to writings that were "quite liberated thinking compared to most [American] Catholic thought," says Mrs. McCarthy. "John Courtney Murray [a leading American Jesuit theologian of the time] was still struggling to reach a formula that would be acceptable about Church and state. Whereas in the thought of Saurez, it was all there already."

Mrs. McCarthy and others believe Rommen's influence came at a critical time, welding thought and action in McCarthy and refining the social and political theories he learned from Father Virgil Michel and others at St. John's University.

"McCarthy was in awe of Rommen in the early days," recalls Lawrence Merthan, a suave Washington lobbyist and former McCarthy aide who taught part-time at St. Thomas and shared an office with Rommen. "Rommen was like a godfather to him. Here was this great international scholar, the first political theorist he'd been exposed to in person, and McCarthy devoured it all. We used to sit at Rommen's feet and talk about how social problems in Germany related to the U.S. and how we should guard against the rise of militarism here. He was a great influence on McCarthy."

Rommen apparently saw exciting potential in his young disciple. "He took a great liking to Gene and really encouraged and pushed him," says Joseph Gabler, who taught English at St. Thomas and later clandestinely used the school's mimeograph machines to turn out McCarthy campaign leaflets. "Rommen had gotten into fights with leftists before and had a lot of experience in practical politics, and I think he saw that Gene combined a helluva mind with great practical ability to get along with people."[2]

Rommen also proved to be a valuable ally when McCarthy led the successful drive to capture control of the DFL party machinery in St. Paul and Ramsey County (Fourth Congressional District) during the winter of 1947–48. "Here was a guy who was both a great historian of political theory and a good precinct worker," Smelser remembers. "He found voters in precincts that nobody even knew about. He was a pretty formidable figure."

The intense loyalties that McCarthy attracted during his 1968 presidential campaign were present twenty years earlier among the cadre of professors, students, housewives, businessmen, and workers who helped McCarthy take over the party, Merthan recalls. "We went out and began organizing, going from precinct to precinct and telling people how to participate in the caucuses. McCarthy would get up and tell people this is what we have to do and this is how we do it, and people would come up to me afterwards and say, 'I don't understand what he's saying, but when he talks I'd follow him anywhere.' "

Part of the reason that they didn't understand McCarthy was that his talks were larded with scholarly allusions and professorial rhetoric that was more suited to the classroom than the soapbox. Joseph Dillon, the St. Thomas graduate who later became mayor of St. Paul, remembers that he, McCarthy, Merthan and a St. Thomas teacher named Philip Desmarais, belonged to a Confraternity of Christian Doctrine lecture team that discussed the Catholic faith at church gatherings around St. Paul. McCarthy often drew comparisons between the contrasting views of Aristotle and Plato concerning the ideal ruler. "He said Plato was really the rule to follow rather than Aristotle," says Dillon. "I always thought he figured he was Plato, that he felt the elite should rule, that they're entitled to rule by virtue of sheer intelligence."

[2] Rommen, who was teaching political science at Georgetown University in Washington, D.C., when he died in 1967, later expressed disappointment with McCarthy's performance in the Senate. According to associates of Rommen, he felt that McCarthy's 1962 book, *The Crescent Dictionary of American Politics,* was a shoddy, staff-produced work, and that McCarthy had not worked hard enough on civil rights and other legislation in the Senate.

Although McCarthy would soon find himself strongly opposed by most of organized labor in St. Paul, he made some important allies among leaders of the young, less powerful Congress of Industrial Organizations. Robert Hess, who had helped organize the CIO local at the 3M Company on St. Paul's East Side, recalls his impressions the first time he met McCarthy at a meeting at the Lowry Hotel in early 1947. "I hate to use a trite phrase, but he was kind of a natural born leader. He had that kind of something that all good leaders have."

The meeting, which fit into the statewide strategy being developed by Humphrey to oust the DFL's left-wing leadership, was called by a man named Darrell Smith, a CIO organizer from Washington who was sent to Minnesota to help the Humphrey forces. There were about fourteen people present, including several who were destined to play major roles in Minnesota and U.S. public life in later years. In addition to McCarthy, Dillon, Bill Carlson and Larry Merthan, there was Hess, who later became executive vice president of the Minnesota AFL-CIO and a member of the University of Minnesota's Board of Regents; his brother Bart, who became a federal labor conciliator; Walter Mondale, a Macalester student who was to serve as Minnesota's attorney general and a U.S. senator; Joseph Karth, a 3M employee and fellow CIO organizer with the Hesses who would succeed McCarthy in the House, and G. Theodore Mitau, a political science professor at Macalester who would become chancellor of the Minnesota state college system.

At the meeting, they agreed to join the Humphrey effort to take over the party by controlling the April, 1948, precinct caucuses, and continued to meet from time to time in a rathskeller on St. Paul's West Seventh Street. In that and subsequent meetings, Hess recalls that McCarthy was the leader as they set out first to take over the newly-organized Young DFL and then to capture control of the precinct caucuses from the left-wing Wallace progressives who dominated the Ramsey County DFL.

The murky issue of Communist infiltration of the DFL was present in St. Paul and Ramsey County as it was in Minneapolis and other parts of the state, and there is no doubt in the minds of Hess and Dillon and other people who supported McCarthy then — but not in 1968 — that the Communists were active and powerful adversaries. "These weren't left-wing liberals," says Dillon. "These were Communists and they controlled the DFL from 1944–48, especially in St. Paul, Minneapolis and on the Iron Range." Hess, who battled Communists in the St. Paul CIO, adds, "There wasn't any fooling around then — they were tough, well-trained union organizers and they controlled the CIO in the Twin Cities and Duluth. There were more extreme left wingers per square foot in Duluth than any town I've ever been in."

The tactics of the McCarthy-led group in taking over the party at the grassroots level provides some obvious comparisons with the methods employed by his supporters twenty years later. Merthan, whose technique was more family-oriented than most, describes the process that was the latest manifestation of Minnesota's protest-politics syndrome: "For my precinct caucus, I took my eighty year old father, my brother, his girl friend, my sister, her boy friend and several neighbors. When we walked in, we had a 3 to 1 majority and I had my sister nominate me as precinct chairman. That's the new politics."

The successful battle for control of the party in St. Paul was a heady experience for many of the young political neophytes, and the experience produced, just as it did in Minneapolis, some seasoned political veterans overnight. "It was a great beginning, a marvelous education," says Martin Haley, a St. Thomas student who helped organize the takeover of the Young DFL and his own precinct. "You really don't know politics until you've carried your own precinct," adds Merthan.

McCarthy's success at party organization set him thinking about his own prospects as a candidate for Congress from the Fourth District. Although he had been a resident of St. Paul for only about eighteen months and had not yet voted there, he decided in early 1948 to seek the DFL nomination.

McCarthy made the decision after discussing it with several people, including Orville Freeman, then the state secretary of the DFL and a leading Humphrey ally in Minneapolis. According to Freeman, McCarthy's decision to run was made one night in early 1948 in the kitchen of Freeman's house. "They put their first child to bed in a basket on the porch and we talked about it and decided it was worth a try, even though it looked tough," Freeman said later. "He carried out an effective and courageous campaign in St. Paul."

Nevertheless, McCarthy's decision came as a surprise to many people, including his wife. "I just thought he was interested in the philosophical problem of the caucuses and getting control of the party and all that," Mrs. McCarthy said later. No one was more surprised, however, than the McCarthys' friend, Bill Carlson. Carlson, considered by some DFL party people as a promising young liberal after his first term in the legislature, thought he had the inside track for the party's endorsement to run against the Fourth District's freshman Republican congressman, Edward Devitt. He also thought he had McCarthy's support, and was shocked when McCarthy sent word to him through an emissary that he was planning to run.

Adrian Winkel, a fellow St. Thomas faculty member who was to become McCarthy's first administrative assistant in the House of Representatives, was given the job of telling Carlson. "Bill didn't believe it — he just didn't think his friend would do this to him," says a friend of Carlson and McCarthy.

Few party people had envisioned McCarthy as a candidate for Congress. "The guy who was out in front and who had the nominal support of labor was Carlson," Bob Hess recalls. "Bill was an East Sider [a blue collar neighborhood] and he was around our CIO local office all the time. Then all of a sudden, McCarthy was running for Congress." But when the powerful AFL Trades and Labor Assembly, the major unit of organized labor in St. Paul and the one with the most political muscle, supported Carlson for Congress, its smaller counterpart, the St. Paul CIO Council, decided to back McCarthy. In doing so, the CIO was challenging the long standing custom of allowing the city's dominant labor organization to pick the liberal candidates for major offices.

"There was as much or more competition between the AFL and the CIO than between the DFL and the Republicans," Karth explained long after he replaced McCarthy in the House of Representatives. "The CIO was relatively new and inexperienced, but we were gung-ho and more idealistic because we were newer and fresher in the labor movement. So this bright young professor really appealed to us."

The issue came to a head in May at the Ramsey County and Fourth District DFL conventions (the geographical boundaries were the same so the conventions were held simultaneously). On the day of the convention, after Carlson indicated that he wouldn't run in a primary if he failed to get the convention's endorsement, the Trades and Labor Assembly announced that it was backing John Barrett, a law school graduate and former state legislator friendly to the union.[3]

Ray Devine, a member of an AFL union, gave the nominating speech for McCarthy and, as he was talking, the AFL leaders took seats in front of the microphone and harassed him. "Frank Thill [a rough-hewn AFL boss who won ten thousand dollars by betting 10 to 1 odds on Harry Truman that fall] kept saying the worst thing you can tell a labor man — he kept mumbling, 'Ray, you've lived off the union all your life and now you're selling labor down the river,'" says Devine. But Devine, who was picked to give the speech because of his union ties, stuck to his guns and urged the convention to endorse McCarthy. "I told them he practically single-handedly reorganized the party in Ramsey County and I didn't think that a few people in the labor unions could make the decision for the people."

When the convention failed to give a two-thirds majority to any of the four candidates (McCarthy, Carlson, Barrett and Frank Starkey, a former St. Paul congressman), a screening committee was named to recommend one of them. Meeting in the nearby Ryan Hotel, the committee recommended McCarthy by a one-vote margin, and Barrett promptly announced he would oppose him in the primary election.

[3] Barrett, now retired and living in Phoenix, Arizona, would seek McCarthy's help in October, 1967, in getting federal funds for a migrant laborers' job training program for the Arizona Ecumenical Council. The two men met in Phoenix on the day before McCarthy made a speech in Berkeley, California, urging that the issue of the Vietnam War be put to a political test by opposing President Johnson in the 1968 primaries.

The steering committee's razor-slim vote for McCarthy was partly due to McCarthy's personal appeal and partly to the heavy-handed tactics of Carlson's and Barrett's AFL supporters. "All the CIO guys left Carlson and voted for McCarthy," recalls Bob Hess, one of several CIO members of the committee. "It was tough for us because we knew Bill better. Why did we do it? I don't know — I guess it was just because we sensed something about McCarthy."

Carlson, now the Ramsey County assessor, says he was "kind of surprised" when he found out about McCarthy's plans to run. "I really hadn't felt he was seriously thinking about running himself. He was doing quite a bit of party work and I had just assumed he was working on my behalf. I think Gene at the time said he was disappointed with me, that he thought I should have worked more with the party. And I know some people felt Gene double-crossed me, but I never really felt that way. We had a temporary falling out, but I don't think we stayed mad long."

The same thing couldn't be said, however, of their wives, Carlson relates. "There were a few sharp letters exchanged between Virginia and Abigail. Women play this game a little harder than men and they get madder. The longer I stay in politics, I've learned to just assume you're supposed to get screwed in the end. Actually, I was kind of relieved because I had a fairly safe seat in the legislature and I wasn't sure I could beat Devitt."

Ray Devine soon learned from Abigail that he'd done her husband no great favor by helping him win the DFL endorsement and get elected county and district chairman. "Abigail wasn't exactly tickled," Devine recalls. "Gene was head of the Sociology Department at St. Thomas and I. A. O'Shaughnessy [a wealthy St. Paul oilman and major benefactor of St. Thomas] was a Republican and she figured I put Gene's job in jeopardy. She raised hell with me, frankly. I was pretty shook when I walked out of their place. I can still see her by that round table and she was furious."

Even with the DFL endorsement, McCarthy still faced a formidable task in winning the primary, since the DFL endorsement without the support of the Trades and Labor Assembly was almost meaningless. But McCarthy, running his campaign on a shoestring with a battalion of eager volunteers, defeated Barrett by a sparse 550 votes.

The night after the primary, the labor movement united behind McCarthy. Bob Hess remembers that he, McCarthy, Devine, Winkel and Frank Wanzong, a brewery worker active in the campaign, were meeting in a classroom at St. Thomas when Jerry O'Donnell, chairman of the Trades and Labor Assembly, called to tell McCarthy the Assembly would support him. "It was our biggest and sweetest victory because it was the first," says Hess.

"It was a characteristic McCarthy campaign," Haley said after a similar McCarthy campaign in 1968. "Nothing much has changed — loose structured, campus oriented, full of professors and a large number of ad hoc committees." Winkel recalls that McCarthy "put things together like he does now — out of his head and hip pocket — and not by a table of organization."

The first of many McCarthy election-night victory parties almost turned into an Irish wake. The McCarthys were waiting for the primary returns at Ray Devine's house when there was a report that Barrett had won. "We thought it was all over with," says Devine. "I think the radio said Barrett had about a five thousand vote lead with only about three thousand votes to be counted, and Gene had been leading him until them. We had a group of people there who had worked hard for Gene — he called them 'the Twelve Apostles' — and one of them was Mrs. Elizabeth Dunn. When we got the radio report, she wanted to pray the rosary.

"Since everybody there was Catholic, we all knelt down and started to say the rosary. We were into a couple of decades when the phone rang and it was our man at the courthouse, Tony Blaha, and somehow I sensed that there'd been a mistake. He said, 'I've got good news,' and I said, 'Don't tell it to me, tell it to Gene.' Gene was tickled when he took the call — it seemed they had a mix-up in the Eleventh Ward and they counted Barrett's vote twice. I can still remember him answering the phone and grinning with his big dog right alongside of him."

Devine adds that they finished the rosary ("Mrs. Dunn always said we won because of the rosary") and he and the McCarthys drove to the Lowry Hotel to visit the county DFL headquarters. "On the way down, we picked up a paper saying Barrett had won and on the next corner, we picked up one that said McCarthy won."

McCarthy's successful challenge of St. Paul's dominant labor organization offered a preview of his later campaign style and technique. Depending almost exclusively on volunteers rather than professionals, he attracted people into politics who had never set foot in a union hall or precinct caucus before. And while he showed a flair for organizational strategy, he seemed to have little taste for administrative detail. He also played his cards very, very close to his vest, according to a woman who worked with him at that time. "He made a lot of decisions on his own that he wouldn't let his co-workers in on. You sometimes wondered what your role was." The woman's husband, also involved in the McCarthy campaign, sensed something else about McCarthy: "There was always an element of uncertainty, because within Gene there is a strong authoritarian, almost Thomistic, sense of rightness, of righteousness. He had a strong sense of what he wanted to do at a critical moment."

The husband remembers that he was impressed by the progressive nature of McCarthy's Catholicism and how he linked his religion with politics. "Ideologically, he was a Jacques Maritain Catholic with a strong sense of mission. He was charismatic from the very beginning — charming, sophisticated, very bright, a superior person quickly recognized by the independent voter as a man of quite unusual stance."

If McCarthy had any of his later wit or eloquence in 1948, it didn't show up in his campaign speeches, several supporters recall. "Martin Haley and I would go listen to Gene's speeches and he was so awful we'd put our heads in our hands," Dillon says. Karth, who actually went to sleep during several McCarthy speeches, adds, "They were probably as dry as any speaker I'd ever heard. He was a professor and his whole approach was professional, without any humor. He just wasn't a fire-eater on the stump."

McCarthy's crowds were so small at the beginning of his campaign that Karth, Bob and Bart Hess and others attended just to increase the audience. "We went to listen to McCarthy to swell the crowd. Later on, of course, we went to listen because he was so good," Hess remembers.

In the general election campaign against Devitt, McCarthy's dry speeches became such a subject of concern that several supporters decided something had to be done about it. Ray Devine was assigned to tell him. "Tom O'Neil [one of the Twelve Apostles] knew that Gene came to my house almost every night to plan strategy," Devine says. "He kept telling me, 'Ray, you've got to tell that guy he's going over everybody's head.' Well, Gene never sat on the davenport — he half laid on it — and when I told him, he sat up and asked how I got that impression. I told him a great many people told me he spoke like a teacher and that he should be more dynamic. He gradually changed, started using more humor, and I thought his speeches got better."

Despite his unexciting oratory, McCarthy was a good campaigner, according to Devine, although it took a push from Devine to get him to go to all the places the votes were. One night Devine was driving McCarthy home from a meeting when he stopped his car at a bar on University Avenue and reached into the glove compartment for several dozen of McCarthy's cards. "I told him I was going to get some cigarettes and said, 'I'm going to pass out cards and tell them you're coming right behind me.' He didn't want to do it, but he came in and with his good looks, he was a big attraction. He got to like the idea, but when we got back to his house and told Abigail what we'd done, she was mad again. She told me in no uncertain terms, 'You don't win elections in beer joints.' "

As in the primary, McCarthy had little money but plenty of willing helpers. Humphrey, who was preoccupied with his own campaign, helped out by lending a sound truck that announced McCarthy's imminent arrival in the rickety 1937 Chevy that he'd bought nine years earlier in North Dakota. At other times, McCarthy would drive down the street, passing mimeographed copies of a campaign leaflet and a newspaper called "The People's Voice" to helpers on either side of the car who then distributed it to homes. "I can still see him driving up Charles Street," says Merthan. "He had a window out on the right side, and when it snowed he had to brush the snow off the seat."

But the biggest asset McCarthy had was Devitt's vote for the Taft-Hartley bill, which helped drive most of the still-divided labor organizations into McCarthy's camp. McCarthy also benefited from the heavy outpouring of Democratic votes for the state ticket headed by Humphrey and President Truman. By 9:30 P.M. on election day, it was clear that McCarthy had defeated Devitt. "The night before the election, we figured I might win by about 5,000 votes," said McCarthy later, whose final margin of victory was 24,902 votes.

Many people felt Devitt would have defeated McCarthy if it hadn't been for Devitt's Taft-Hartley vote, but Devitt doubts whether he could have won under any conditions. "I'd say any candidate could have knocked me out," says Devitt, who was a student at St. John's with McCarthy. "I was a Republican and I'd voted for Taft-Hartley, which was enough, I guess, in a district that was about 70 percent Democratic."

The campaign, as Devitt remembers it, was rather routine, with his Taft-Hartley vote the central issue. Devitt, who was named a federal district judge in 1954 and now often interprets the controversial labor law he voted for, says the Senate race between Humphrey and Republican incumbent Joseph Ball drew more interest in St. Paul than his contest with McCarthy.

On election night, in what was to become a custom for McCarthy, he listened to early returns at Ray Devine's home until it became clear he'd won. Then he paid a brief visit to party headquarters in St. Paul and drove to Humphrey's home in Minneapolis to wait for the outcome of the Humphrey-Ball election. "We stayed until five in the morning," says Devine. "We were all interested in how Humphrey was doing and nobody was paying much attention to Truman because we figured he couldn't win. On the way back to St. Paul, we heard on the car radio he was winning."

Afterwards, McCarthy estimated he'd made one hundred speeches and spent five thousand dollars on his campaign. He didn't really campaign hard until the final two weeks, he said. "I didn't have too much money and I wasn't relieved from my teaching duties until then," he told a reporter for the St. Paul *Dispatch* the next day. He also confided that his classes at St. Thomas were rather poorly attended on election day, adding, "I guess they were all out voting."

McCarthy capitalized on his new job and $12,500 salary shortly after the election by taking out a loan for a new car to drive to Washington. He "sold" his trusty 1937 Chevy to Devine, telling him, "Never mind paying me." Later, when Russ Laub, a St. Paul CIO official who had worked in the campaign, went to pick up the new Nash he'd ordered several months earlier, the dealer told him, "You'll have to wait a while because I just sold it to the new congressman to drive to Washington."

Just as he later carefully explained his reasons for challenging an incumbent president, McCarthy explained why he challenged Devitt and offered a preview of his own concept of public leadership in an interview with a pretty young girl reporter from the Minneapolis *Tribune* shortly before he went to Washington.

The reporter was Miss Geri Hoffner, who as Mrs. Burton Joseph later became the DFL national committeewoman from Minnesota and served as vice chairman of the Democratic National Committee and a top strategist in Hubert Humphrey's 1968 presidential campaign. "I remember thinking, how can he be a politician?" Mrs. Joseph recalls. "He was much too open, much too apolitical, and I wondered why he wanted to be a politician. He was also one of the most engaging, witty, attractive people I'd ever seen, and an absolute delight to interview."

The newly-elected congressman told the young reporter that he decided to run for two reasons: the need to make the Minnesota DFL a party for the independent liberal as well as for the workingman, and the conviction that a man backed only by organized labor could not beat Devitt. He said his major legislative interests would be in the fields of labor and civil rights.

In her article, Mrs. Joseph described McCarthy with adjectives that would cling to him through the years like iron filings to a magnet. "Calm — almost to the point of appearing detached — McCarthy has none of the quick temper for which the Irish are famous in story and song." Then she quoted the words that summed up McCarthy's political philosophy and his view of the new life he was about to begin.

"There are altogether too many technicians in Washington now," said McCarthy with a grin. "I guess I agree with Plato that it's the philosopher who should rule."

BOOK TWO
CONFEDERATES BUT NEVER CONFIDANTS
1949–1964

CHAPTER VI

LEARNING TO LOVE
THE ESTABLISHMENT

*We can have disagreements without being
disagreeable.*
>   Hubert Humphrey in a 1958 interview.

On January 3, 1949, thirteen years after writing the "Dear Bucky" letter
that declared his intention to "set my aim at Congress," a somber Hubert
Humphrey was sworn in as the new junior United States senator from
Minnesota.

The thirty-seven year old Humphrey stood fourteenth in line among other
such extraordinary freshmen as Clinton Anderson of New Mexico, Paul
Douglas of Illinois, Lyndon Johnson of Texas, Robert Kerr of Oklahoma,
Estes Kefauver of Tennessee and Russell Long of Louisiana as he took
the oath of office from the out-going president *pro tempore*, Michigan's
Arthur Vandenburg.[1] Walking back to his desk in the rear of the Senate
chamber, Humphrey looked up at the visitors' gallery at his proud wife,
parents and family. "The looks on their faces, especially on Dad's, was
one of my greatest thrills," Humphrey confided afterwards. "So many people
expecting so much of you . . . it puts goose pimples on you just to think
about it."

Humphrey had reason to feel that much was expected of him. His fiery
civil rights speech at the 1948 Democratic National Convention, his decisive upset of Republican Joseph Ball in Minnesota and his outspoken
espousal of New Deal liberalism marked him as a potential star as the

---

[1] Anderson and Long were the only Democrats remaining from the Class of '48 when
Humphrey returned to the Senate in 1971. Two Republicans, Karl Mundt of South
Dakota and Margaret Chase Smith of Maine also remained, although Mundt was inca-
pacitated by a stroke in 1969.

Democrats took control of the Eighty-first Congress. Humphrey, who soon became acting national chairman of the liberal anti-Communist Americans for Democratic Action, personified the new liberalism whose theme he had sounded repeatedly during his Senate campaign as the keynote of his own political philosophy: "The purpose of government in this country is to benefit the people."

Life in the nation's capital was a big disappointment to Humphrey at first. He had resigned his mayor's job shortly after the election, sold his house and come to Washington to go house-hunting and prepare for his new career. He looked at 125 houses in 8 days, finally buying one for $28,000 in suburban Chevy Chase, Maryland. He used the money from the sale of his Minneapolis home for the down payment but, still broke from his Senate campaign, had to borrow $1,100 from his father to pay the moving company after his furniture sat in a van on a Washington street for 2 days. Denied the usual courtesy of an interim office for senators-elect because of a brief recess scheduled in January by the Eightieth Congress, he had to use the offices of Washington Attorney Paul Porter as a temporary headquarters.

During the week before Christmas, Humphrey was buoyed by the arrival of Muriel and the four children they now had — Nancy, nine; Hubert (Skipper), six; Bobby, four; and Douglas, eleven months. But the highlight of Humphrey's first days in Washington came on the afternoon of New Year's Eve as he ushered Muriel and his parents into President Truman's office. Truman put his arm around Humphrey's awed mother and assured her, "Oh, we're just folks here," and then gave them a half-hour tour of the White House.

Humphrey didn't find the red-carpet treatment awaiting him in the Senate, however. The senator-elect was sitting in the visitors gallery during the recess session when Alabama's Lister Hill noticed him and brought him to the floor to be introduced with other freshmen. "Ed Thye [Minnesota's Republican senior senator] didn't bring me in and Joe Ball didn't bring me in," Humphrey later complained to a friend. "But Lister Hill did."

Humphrey at first carefully obeyed the unspoken Senate rule that requires newcomers to keep their eyes and ears open and their mouths shut. However, he served notice on the world's most exclusive club that he didn't intend to remain silent for long. Sitting behind his glass-topped mahogany desk and an eight-ball paperweight, he told a reporter in his first week in office, "I'll speak when the time comes." [2]

---

[2] The reporter was Miss Evelyn Petersen, an editor of the now-defunct *Pathfinder News* magazine and the daughter of Minnesota's last Farmer Labor Governor Hjalmar Petersen, successor to Floyd B. Olson. She is now Mrs. Evelyn Metzger, and as Washington editor for Doubleday, Inc., was responsible for her company's publication of the 1965 Humphrey biography, *Humphrey — A Candid Biography*, and Eugene McCarthy's 1968 campaign memoir, *The Year of the People*.

Washington had been alerted that Humphrey was not just another freshman senator. *Time* magazine singled him out as "the most articulate spokesman of the Fair Deal among the newcomers to the Eighty-first Congress." The magazine described him as a "brash, bustling . . . hard-working, fast-talking fireball from the Midwest," and for good measure, called him a "glib, jaunty spellbinder with a 'listen-you-guys' approach."

It was nice to get all the attention, but the article had the doubly harmful effect of making some other senators jealous and carving in granite an unfavorable image that Humphrey would never succeed in shaking off. Another observer, Washington Correspondent Joseph Driscoll of the St. Louis *Post-Dispatch*, predicted Humphrey would become known as "The Voice," and added, "A voice like Humphrey's does not come often to Congress any more than a voice like Enrico Caruso's always is to be had at the Met." Driscoll also noted that Humphrey was already being mentioned as a presidential possibility for 1952.

For his first two and a half months in the Senate, Humphrey appeared to be keeping a pledge he made a few days after his election to spend his first year in Congress "talking less and studying more." But on March 14, 1949, in his maiden speech — a brief argument for a bill to establish a Missouri Valley Authority similar to the TVA — Humphrey chided his colleagues for doing too much talking and too little acting. "What the people want is for the Senate to function," he declared. "Sometimes I think we become so cozy — we feel so secure in our six-year term — we forget that the people want things done."

From then on, Humphrey was off and running — usually at the mouth, his critics sneered. He attacked the seniority system, calling it "the most sacred cow in the legislative zoo," advised the Senate establishment to "give the spirit of youth a larger place in our legislative halls," and, in general, tried to tell his elders how to run the Senate. His cocky attitude caused Republican William Jenner of Indiana to whisper to a colleague during a Humphrey speech that the brash Minnesotan reminded him of some tomatoes he once planted "too early in the spring and the frost got them."

By June, there were signs that Humphrey was no ordinary debater. He spoke for seven hours and forty-six minutes against an amendment to the Taft-Hartley labor reform bill, causing Ohio's Robert Taft to charge him with conducting a filibuster. Humphrey retorted, "It takes time to discuss and analyze the one hundred mistakes of the Taft-Hartley Act." Paul Douglas remembers another debate with Republican isolationists over the Marshall Plan in which Humphrey impressed him. "Styles Bridges [of New Hampshire] was attacking the administration for giving aid to Great Britain and he was shouting, 'What have the British got that we haven't got?' Well, he didn't even get the last words out of his mouth before Humphrey interrupted, 'Westminister Abbey!' It was the quickest coordination of brain and tongue I ever saw."

Humphrey was clearly one of the most liberal members of the Senate's freshman class, along with Douglas and New York's Herbert Lehman. The first bill he introduced was, like many of his early legislative proposals, years ahead of its time. It called for the establishment of a program of medical care for the aged through Social Security (Congress finally passed it in 1965 as the Medicare program). He also headed a labor and public welfare subcommittee that reported out the first "impacted areas" school aid bill and other federal aid to education proposals enacted in the 1950's.

Testifying before the House Education and Labor Committee in May, 1949, on an administration bill to create a national fair employment practices commission which he had done locally in Minneapolis, Humphrey foretold the civil rights attitude of an administration that would come to power twenty years later. "If this bill is beaten," he warned, "it will not be our Southern colleagues who will be to blame. It will be the indifference, apathy and, at times, the politics of our Northern, Western and Eastern brethren." Among the committee members who agreed with Humphrey was Congressman Richard Nixon of California. The bill was beaten and Truman refused Humphrey's advice that he create a fair employment practices commission by executive order. (The FEPC legislation finally was approved by Congress in 1964 after Humphrey led the first successful fight against a Southern civil rights filibuster.)

Humphrey used his influence at the White House to push another idea that was ahead of its time — the acceptance of women in high public office. In October, Truman named Mrs. Eugenie Anderson, Humphrey's political ally from Minnesota and fellow organizer of the ADA, as America's first woman ambassador. She was only the first of many Minnesotans who would follow Humphrey into government service to form a "Minnesota Mafia" that pervaded official Washington in later years.

In November, the death of his father left Humphrey severely shaken. The elder Humphrey had told his son in January he had a premonition that he wouldn't live out the year and, when he suffered a cerebral hemorrhage and died three weeks later, Humphrey was shattered. After the funeral, Muriel's father urged them to take a vacation and gave them five hundred dollars to help pay for it. The Humphreys took a boat to Europe, their first trip overseas, but when they returned for the second session of the Eighty-first Congress in January, 1950, Humphrey still missed the counsel of his father.

His shaky first year in the Senate and the grief over his father's death contributed to what Humphrey still regards as the worst mistake of his Senate career. On February 24, he took the Senate floor to call for the abolition of the Joint Committee on Reduction of Nonessential Federal

Expenditures. The nine year old committee was an obscure panel that mostly duplicated the work of one that Humphrey belonged to that was created by a Congressional reorganization plan two years earlier, the Committee on Expenditures in the Executive Department.

But the chairman of the Committee on Nonessential Expenditures definitely was not obscure. Virginia's ultraconservative Democrat Harry F. Byrd was the patriarch of the Senate's Southern-dominated establishment and a symbol of the institution of the Senate itself.

Humphrey went after Byrd's committee as though he was chasing another crook out of Minneapolis. He charged that the very existence of the committee was a "wanton waste and extravagance," that it violated not only the "spirit of the Legislative Reorganization Act" but also wasted more than a million dollars during its brief existence, and that its regular statements criticizing the growth of the federal bureaucracy were "undocumented." He called it a "nonessential committee on nonessential expenditures" and, in what many of his colleagues regarded as a classic case of the pot calling the kettle black, charged that the committee "is merely used as a publicity medium."

Humphrey was not aware of it but he had committed a grievous error of protocol by raising the issue when Byrd was absent from the floor visiting his seriously ill mother. He was simply delivering, with his customary intensity, a speech prepared for him by friends in the ADA who, like Humphrey, were unhappy with Byrd's recent attacks on Truman's fiscal and foreign policies.

Six days later, on March 2, Byrd took the floor to answer Humphrey's charges. Armed with a carefully prepared speech and the support of a phalanx of loyal Southern Democrats and conservative Republicans, Byrd fired the initial salvo of a verbal barrage that has seldom been equalled in modern Senate history. Byrd declared that Humphrey had been guilty of "nine misstatements in two thousand words" and added, "this is an average misstatement in every 250 words, and the senator speaks like the wind." Byrd claimed his committee had saved several billion dollars for the government at a minimal cost, sarcastically pointing out at the same time that Humphrey had sought a $250,000 appropriation to investigate the coal industry only the day before attacking Byrd.

Then Byrd delivered his *coup de grace*. "As the senator from Minnesota is a publicity expert himself, his statement, although not intended as such, could be regarded as a compliment from one who welcomes and has been signally successful in creating publicity for himself and his objectives. If he has ever hid his light under a bushel, I am unaware of it. And I have not observed any indication that he is of the shrinking violet type evading publicity."

Byrd's remarks were the beginning of an anti-Humphrey demonstration that lasted almost four hours. One by one, Byrd's allies — including nearly all the patriarchs of both parties — got up to defend Byrd and excoriate Humphrey, who sat slumped in his chair after vainly seeking recognition from the presiding officer. Typical of the accusations against Humphrey was the one made by Georgia's Walter George, Finance Committee chairman and member of the Byrd committee. Looking directly at the glowering Humphrey, George thundered that it was the "height of reckless irresponsibility for any man to suggest" the Byrd committee was nonessential.

When the triumphant Byrd finally yielded the floor, an unrepentant Humphrey compounded his error by tactlessly bouncing up and down to show that he was still alive and kicking. "The senator from Minnesota is no shrinking violet, and before this debate is over he will not be an apple blossom either," he said in reference to Byrd's apple orchards in Virginia's Shenandoah Valley. Then, mixing his metaphors, Humphrey added, "When I introduced the bill, I knew that I would set loose a hornet's nest, and I was advised that I'd be mowed down. There has been some lawn mowing going on today, but the shrinking violet has not been clipped."

Before Humphrey could finish, Byrd and his supporters turned their backs on Humphrey and walked out of the chamber, leaving Humphrey alone with Douglas, Lehman and a few silent onlookers. Humphrey ended the session in a less than contrite manner by lecturing to the nearly empty chamber, ". . . while it is a part of our code of ethics as gentlemen to be friendly and congenial one with another, our major responsibility is not the art of making friends — Dale Carnegie tells us how to do that; our major responsibility is to legislate."

But even the vehemence of Byrd's counterattack left Humphrey undaunted at first. He stubbornly kept on denouncing the committee and even challenged Byrd to a debate. On March 20, he wrote a long letter to the New York *Times* calling Byrd's committee "a violation of the intent and purpose of the Legislative Reorganization Act and . . . a brazen example of the continuance of overlapping functions and duplications of activities in the legislative branch." Byrd, however, ignored him and the committee continued as before.

Gradually, Humphrey realized that he was wrong on two counts. First, he had neither mastered his subject nor gotten his facts straight when he challenged Byrd. More importantly, he had failed to understand a fundamental precept of Senate protocol — that what someone says is often less important than how he says it. (Humphrey would wisely counsel his successor Walter Mondale in 1964 to "do as I say, not as I did.")

In retrospect, Humphrey sees the Byrd affair as a humiliating but isolated incident in "the most miserable period of my life. I was a Truman Democrat," Humphrey recalled in an interview many years later. "I liked the president and I believe in supporting people I like. It's stood me very well in politics. Well, I just couldn't understand how a man like Harry Byrd could be so strong in the Senate. Here he was, this big conservative power; people almost kissed his ring, so to speak. He had this committee and every damn month there was this blast against Truman for budget deficits and for this and for that and God, it was just bitter toward the president. Well I just figured Harry Byrd was a phony on this business, so I got up and made my speech, which was one of the better speeches of my public career in terms of facts, in terms of principles, sincerity and integrity. And the next thing I knew, the roof fell in on me. This was like attacking the basic theory of the revolution in the Soviet Union or the basic tenets of Christianity. . . . I was very much surprised at the vehemence of their attack. I guess they thought this was their chance to finish me off. The only guy who stood up for me was Millard Tydings of Maryland. I never forgot it and always was grateful to him for it."[3]

The incident made Humphrey determined to win the friendship and respect of his peers. "I really felt uncomfortable," he later recalled. "I think it's fair to say I'd been a very popular mayor with a lot of friends, and I'd always been able to have political battles with people and still like them. When I first came to Washington, I sensed right away it was kind of a foreign city. I didn't feel any comradeship, any friendship, partly because of the '48 convention and also partly because we just didn't have any contacts. Nobody showed us around, not like today when they have a welcoming committee out to greet you and make you feel at home. Mrs. Humphrey and I were very young, we had a young family, and we weren't very social. We didn't go to a lot of parties and the few we went to weren't very helpful." He was, Humphrey admitted on another occasion, "lonely, broke and bitter" after the first few months in Washington, and he envied other freshmen like Johnson, Kerr, Kefauver and Long. "They had friends in the South," says Humphrey. "That's all you needed. I had nothing. Absolutely nothing. No friends anyplace."

The going was unquestionably rough at first. In April, 1951, Humphrey tangled — verbally and physically — with Indiana Republican Homer Capehart after a radio debate over General Douglas MacArthur's plea to Congress to allow United Nations forces in Korea to bomb supply bases in Manchuria. In the debate, Humphrey reiterated charges he made two weeks earlier in St. Paul that the Senate Republican leadership was guilty of "political and military stupidity" in pushing for military action against Communist China. Capehart responded by calling him a Communist sympathizer and a supporter of Red China.

According to newspaper accounts of the incident, the fifty-one year old

---

[3] Humphrey felt Truman should have come to his defense. Afterward, he called the White House and complained bitterly to a Truman aide: "Every time I have been to the White House, President Truman has spent part of the time telling me what a menace Byrd is to a liberal government. But where were my liberal friends when I took on Byrd?"

Capehart pushed Humphrey out of the studio in the basement of the Senate Office Building — which Capehart said had the same initials as what Humphrey called him. Humphrey denied he used profanity but both men agreed there had been pushing and shoving. The New York *Times* described the affair as "a rough and bloodless battle of clinches and cliches" and declared it a draw between "Slugger" Capehart and "The Lip" Humphrey.

The incident ruffled Senatorial dignity and caused Senate elders to ridicule Humphrey behind his back. A former Humphrey aide remembers hearing Vice President Alben Barkley grousing in the Senate cloakroom shortly afterwards. "That Minnesota is a great state," said Barkley. "First they sent us their Ball, then they sent us their Thye, and now they've sent us their goddamn hindend."

Nevertheless, Humphrey was taking his first tentative steps toward Senate acceptance. In August, 1950, he had introduced a series of twelve amendments to an omnibus tax bill aimed at removing loopholes in the tax law which he said were costing the government billions of dollars. Georgia's Walter George, chairman of the Finance Committee, and Colorado's Eugene Millikin, senior Republican on the committee, gave him a rough going-over, but he spent five hours defending his amendments on the floor — humbly conceding he possessed little expertise on the subject — before the Senate voted all of them down.

Convinced he was on the right track and obsessed with mastering Senate procedure, Humphrey called in outside tax experts during the next year to brief him on the intricacies of tax legislation. He told them, "I'm *magna cum laude*. I'll learn. Teach me." They taught and he learned, and when the time came for consideration of the next omnibus tax bill in September, 1951, Humphrey had twenty well-researched, anti-loophole amendments ready. He was able to answer detailed technical questions about his amendments during a week-long debate over the tax bill, and although his amendments were all defeated, he won the grudging respect of George and Millikin and other senior members by his skill in debate, his mastery of the subject and his deferential attitude.

The 1951 tax bill debate clearly marked the beginning of Humphrey's acceptance by the Senate establishment. "That was the real turning point," says Max Kampelman, a University of Minnesota political science professor who followed his student to Washington and became his first legislative counsel. "No one had ever challenged the Finance Committee's recommendations on a tax bill before, and Humphrey won the respect of the Senate for the way he did it. They treated him like dirt at first, but he responded with a smile and humor and he demonstrated his competence. Before it was over, George and Millikin were congratulating him."

Another Humphrey confidant, Arthur Naftalin, came to Washington in the summer of 1951 to work on Humphrey's staff for about six weeks, and was surprised to find him acting like "sort of a beaten man." But this soon changed as his relations with the Senate elders improved, and Naftalin thinks that experience had an important effect on Humphrey. "From then on, I think Humphrey no longer regarded himself as a maverick," Naftalin said many years later. "Humphrey never really wanted to be the marginal spokesman for reform. He always felt more comfortable working as a moderator, a mediator, that sort of thing, and I think that when he got to the Senate, he didn't quite appreciate the range of the political spectrum."

The lesson wasn't lost on Humphrey. Two months after the tax bill debate, he offered an olive branch to the South in a two-thousand word letter to twenty prominent Southern newspaper editors. He appealed for "more understanding" of the objectives of the Senate civil rights bloc and, without making any specific concession, said he realized that legislation alone wouldn't solve the civil rights problem.

Ironically, it was a Southerner, Russell Long — his old debating partner from LSU — who was most helpful in showing Humphrey how to get his foot in the door of the Senate establishment. Humphrey tells how it happened: "Russell was my neighbor and we used to go walking together late at night. Russell said to me one night, 'You know, Hubert, you've been going into that public Senate dining room, but if you really want to get acquainted, you should go into that little private dining room in the back where the senators eat.' Well, he took me in there the next day and it worked. They were all there — Walter George, Harry Byrd, John Sparkman, Lister Hill, Bernie Maybank — the fellows who ran things in the Senate. And Russell Long's taking me in there and introducing me to some of his friends and getting me to spend more time with the senators was a turning point."

The young fire-breathing champion of civil rights actually sat down to lunch late in 1951 with a group of leading Southern senators at Long's invitation, and to everyone's surprise, the meeting was completely cordial. Humphrey said later, "We got to know each other as humans." It was another important breakthrough in the Senate for Humphrey and one that would pay rich dividends in the form of choice committee assignments, the translation of many of his ideas into legislation, and a place on the escalator to Senate acceptance and leadership.

Humphrey, who has a habit of occasionally speaking of himself in the third person, told an interviewer in 1964 that "Humphrey was a young man. He learned that you accomplish things in the Senate through good manners. It's not necessary to sacrifice convictions for manners, but you cannot operate on those convictions without manners." Later, reverting to the first person, he explained how his awkward entry into the Senate helped him. "I was one of these eager-beaver young liberal Democratic progressives who didn't quite understand that the way to get legislation through is not merely to have a good idea. You have to nourish and nurse it through the Congress. You have to know the system, which I learned, and may I say that I think I'm one of the few liberals who learned how to use the system."

While Humphrey was battering down the doors of the Senate's Inner Sanctum, he wasn't neglecting his political fences at home. He pushed his staff unmercifully to take care of constituent needs, insisting that every letter or telegram be answered the day it was received, and sending congratulatory letters for practically every birth, graduation, marriage and wedding anniversary in Minnesota. "If we read in the Caledonia *Argus* that some farmer's horse died, he'd get a letter from Humphrey," says a former staff member with a slight bit of exaggeration. (Humphrey ended all his letters by asking constituents' prayers for divine guidance in his Senate work.)

Humphrey also kept a sharp eye out for the interests of Minnesota farmers, workers and businessmen. He fought for higher farm price supports and battled the oleomargarine industry on behalf of the state's dairy farmers, pushed for repeal of the Taft-Hartley Act and for adoption of favorable labor laws, helped lead efforts to establish the St. Lawrence Seaway and improve Duluth's port facilities, and promoted Minnesota's burgeoning agribusiness industry.

If there was any doubt Humphrey was learning to use the system to his political advantage, it was removed in 1951 when Humphrey wrangled a federal judgeship for Minnesota's highly popular three-term Republican governor, Luther Youngdahl, thereby removing the man who was considered his likely opponent in 1954. Humphrey had been tipped off by a mutual friend of his and Youngdahl's, Minneapolis businessman Ray Ewald, that the fifty-five year old Youngdahl was suffering from high blood pressure and was not anxious to run for a fourth term in 1952 and then take on Humphrey.

Ewald had told Humphrey that Youngdahl might consider a federal judicial appointment, so when Humphrey picked up the Washington *Post* a few weeks later and read of the death of Federal Judge T. Alan Goldsborough from the District of Columbia, he immediately asked Truman to appoint Youngdahl to the post.

Truman, who remembered that Youngdahl was a thirty-second degree Mason and one of the few Republican governors who had backed him on the firing of General Douglas MacArthur, agreed and Humphrey relayed the offer to Youngdahl, who accepted. Humphrey had Youngdahl flown to Washington on July 4 and registered him at the Statler Hitlon Hotel under the unimaginative name of Smith. The next morning, he took Youngdahl through the back door of the White House for an unannounced meeting with Truman and then stood by triumphantly while the appointment was announced to reporters whom he had alerted.

Youngdahl later recalled that when Humphrey called his home and told Mrs. Youngdahl of the judgeship offer, ex-Governor Harold Stassen was in Youngdahl's office at the state capitol urging him to run for a fourth term and to nominate Stassen for president at the 1954 Republican National Convention. Of Humphrey's reaction when he accepted the offer, Youngdahl says with considerable understatement, "He was somewhat relieved that I would not be around to run for the Senate against him." [4]

The Youngdahl appointment highlighted Humphrey's close ties with Truman and stirred speculation — some of it started by Humphrey — that Truman was eyeing Humphrey as a Democratic vice presidential candidate in 1952. Humphrey entered the Minnesota presidential primary that year at Truman's request and won easily. After Truman decided against running again, Humphrey considered seeking the presidential nomination, but declined because he said he didn't want to become "another Harold Stassen."

Humphrey's name was placed in nomination as a favorite son candidate at the 1952 national convention by Congressman Eugene McCarthy, who praised him as "a man close to the heart of the people of America" who "does not support or offer a watered-down, bargain basement variety of democracy." Humphrey released his delegation after the first ballot and threw his support to Adlai Stevenson. (The 1952 convention also featured Humphrey in the familiar role of a civil rights strategist. He led an unsuccessful effort to use a "loyalty oath" to block the seating of several Southern delegations.)

Humphrey campaigned in eighteen states in Stevenson's losing campaign and after Dwight Eisenhower's election, called for the organization of a liberal caucus in the Senate. Washington's Henry "Scoop" Jackson, Montana's Mike Mansfield and Missouri's Stuart Symington were among the Democratic newcomers whom Humphrey sought to enlist in an effort to persuade Eisenhower to follow "an internationalist, responsible foreign policy which will seek to bring peace with honor [in Korea], but which will also stand forthrightly against Communist aggression."

Humphrey's unflagging opposition to Communism was a natural consequence of his struggles with the extreme left in Minnesota in the 1940's but he was also influenced by the virulent climate of McCarthyism in the early 1950's. Despite his gilt-edged credentials as an ardent foe of Communism, he still found himself coming under attack by followers of Republican Senator Joseph McCarthy of Wisconsin because of his ultra-liberal image and his close ties to the ADA. Humphrey feared that the soft-on-Communism issue and McCarthy smear tactics that had been freely used against Democrats in 1952 would be employed against him when he ran for reelection in Minnesota two years later, and he was anxious to nullify such tactics. "There

---

[4] Youngdahl went on to a distinguished career on the bench before becoming a senior judge in 1966. He dismissed the politically-motivated perjury charges against State Department official Owen Lattimore in 1954, an act that was the first significant pronouncement by the courts against Senator Joseph McCarthy's red-hunting tactics and an important factor in the eventual decline of McCarthyism.

probably isn't a Democrat in the Senate who the Republicans would prefer to unseat — for to them Senator Humphrey is the epitome of the New Deal-Fair Deal party which they insist is leading the country down the path of socialism," Columnist Gould Lincoln observed at the time.

Humphrey's anti-Communist zeal was behind two actions that in retrospect can only be interpreted as efforts to protect himself from soft-on-Communism charges. In 1952, he chaired the Labor-Management Relations Subcommittee that conducted an investigation of Communist infiltration of labor unions. Humphrey said he was starting the investigation with "only one preconception" — that "there are certain Communist-dominated unions in the United States operating in defense industries, and we must face up to what this fact means for our national security." There was no doubt in his mind, Humphrey declared, "that Communists seek to use the unions as systems of power to promote Soviet Russia's foreign policies. . . ."

The subcommittee held ten days of hearings between March and July and Humphrey suggested in interviews at the time that Communist-dominated unions be excluded from the privileges of collective bargaining, although he later denied that he ever seriously considered such a drastic step. The investigation attracted little attention and produced even less evidence of any conspiratorial activity by Communists in labor unions, and Humphrey allowed the probe to end quietly without proposing any legislation.

Then, on August 11, 1954, with the dark five year old era of McCarthyism still potent but nearing its end (the Senate's censure of Joseph McCarthy would come four months later), Humphrey introduced a bill more extreme than anything McCarthy ever proposed. Rising on the Senate floor during consideration of a Republican-sponsored bill strengthening the existing law against Communist-dominated labor unions, Humphrey offered a substitute amendment outlawing the Communist party and providing criminal penalties for membership. "I am tired of having people play the Communist issue," he declared. "I want to come to grips with the Communist issue. I want senators to stand up and to answer whether they are for the Communist party or against it."

The Senate combined the two bills and passed them by an 84–0 vote after a confused debate about the Humphrey bill's legality and effect. The House softened the bill by knocking out the Humphrey proposal but it was restored by the Senate and then partially deleted in conference. Signed into law by President Eisenhower on August 24, the Communist Control Act of 1954 was a jumbled patchwork of doubtful constitutionality and uncertain phraseology that was never enforced.

Columnists Joseph and Stewart Alsop hailed Humphrey for his "theft of anti-Communist thunder" from the White House and the Republican Congressional leadership, calling his action "the most cleverly conceived, ruthlessly executed and politically adroit of all the sudden Democratic raids that have been such a feature of this session of Congress." However, there were others who saw Humphrey's action as an inexcusable departure from principle. Republican John Sherman Cooper of Kentucky, the lone senator to openly oppose the bill on the floor, warned that the measure would "depart from precedents and principles held since the adoption of the Constitution." He termed Humphrey's action "shameful" and said that if McCarthy or his leading ally, Indiana's William Jenner, had sponsored the bill, "They would have been attacked all over the country."

Humphrey's liberal friends were no less incensed, and some still remember it as the only time they were ever ashamed of Humphrey. Joseph Rauh, a Washington civil rights attorney and longtime friend of Humphrey, spoke for many liberals when he called the bill "a superpolitical ploy."

Humphrey says he introduced the bill after deciding to "give the back-row red-hunters on the other side some real legislation to chew on." Actually, the basic idea of the bill, that the Communist party is not a political party but "an instrument of a conspiracy to overthrow the United States government," was conceived by Max Kampelman. Kampelman sold Humphrey on the bill, arguing that it would accelerate the demise of McCarthyism, destroy the Communist party and defuse an issue that undoubtedly would be used against Humphrey and other liberal candidates in the fall.

While Humphrey was active on the anti-Communist legislative front during the McCarthy era, his record in opposing McCarthy was neither much better nor much worse than that of most senators. As a member of McCarthy's Government Operations Committee, Humphrey was reluctant to condemn or even strongly criticize McCarthy, particularly after McCarthy became chairman in 1953. However, he was not silent on the issue either. In February, 1951, just one year after McCarthy unleashed his anti-Communist crusade in a speech at Wheeling, West Virginia, Humphrey joined in a Senate discussion of McCarthy's tactics and deplored the "psychosis of fear" he saw developing in the country. In 1952, he rose on the Senate floor to join several other members in defending a Senate Rules Committee employee accused of pro-Communist tendencies by McCarthy. "Something terrible has happened to us," Humphrey said. "We go around accusing people day after day and demanding they prove their innocence. That is totalitarian law, not democratic law. I think it is time we stated that we are not going to let people be ruined, their reputations destroyed, and their names defiled because we happen to be in the great game of American politics. If that is what politics is coming to, I am getting out."

Humphrey made his strongest statement against McCarthy in April, 1954, in a speech delivered not on the Senate floor but to a receptive audience at an ADA convention. He described McCarthyism as "this madness of know-nothingness" and attacked McCarthy and his followers as people who "pretend to be the leaders of anti-Communism and the saviors of our liberty."

But by the end of 1954, the McCarthy era was on the wane as the Senate voted to censure him. Humphrey, who spoke only once during the Senate debate on the censure motion to ask for a ruling on a point of procedure, voted for censure.

In retrospect, Humphrey says the bill "is not one of the things I'm proudest of." Nor is he proud of his behavior during the McCarthy era, Humphrey told television interviewer David Frost in 1968. "I felt that America was going through a very unwholesome, degrading experience, and sometimes I feel that I should have stood up more strongly against [McCarthy], but I was literally fighting for political survival and even though I voted against him and I took my knocks from him and his supporters, I think I could have been a little braver during that time."

Humphrey may have felt his political future was at stake, but most political experts didn't. He was considered almost unbeatable after Luther Youngdahl's removal as a possible opponent, a judgment borne out in November, 1954, when Humphrey won reelection for the first time by a respectable margin of 162,000 votes over Republican State Treasurer Val Bjornson. His coattails also helped elect his old babysitter Orville Freeman as governor, as well as Minnesota's first woman in Congress, Mrs. Coya Knutson.

Humphrey's own intelligence from Minnesota had told him that the soft-on-Communism issue probably wouldn't be the overriding issue in his 1954 campaign. He sent an aide, Herbert Waters, to the state to take political soundings in late 1953, and after a three-month tour of the state, Waters reported that farm unrest, not Communism, would be the paramount campaign issue. But he warned Humphrey that unless he "raised a little hell" with Agriculture Secretary Ezra Taft Benson, Minnesota's independent-minded voters might vote against him just as they voted against Joseph Ball in 1948.

Waters passed on his assessment of the Minnesota situation to Humphrey and Orville Freeman in a meeting at Freeman's house in December, 1953, saying that Humphrey could pretty well count on holding his support in the populous Twin Cities and on the heavily Democratic Iron Range in northern Minnesota, and that if he concentrated on the rural areas, he could win by a large enough margin to carry a DFL governor into office on his coattails. (Freeman, who had been defeated as an attorney general candidate in 1950 and a gubernatorial candidate in 1952, decided to run again for governor on the basis of that estimate, according to Waters.)

Humphrey's 1954 campaign illustrates weaknesses that would be magnified in Humphrey's later national campaigns. Waters, who ran the campaign, remembers that the two most frequent complaints about Humphrey were that he talked too long and was always late. "When we were planning the campaign, he started complaining about how we were setting it up, and I said, 'I want you to do something for me. Write down the four or five main things you think your opponent will use against you.' Well, he struggled around but he wrote it, and the first thing he put down was, 'He talks too much.' For him to recognize this himself was really what I was trying to get at, so we designed the whole campaign around the idea of a guy who gets things done, to contrast the idea of Humphrey as a talker. And by God, we made him stay on schedule. In fact, people were so used to his being late that when he was on time, hardly anybody would be there."

Waters also found a way to harness Humphrey's spontaneous speaking style. He developed a format — used extensively in later campaigns — of preparing a brief press release for major speeches and showing the release to him just before he spoke. "You can't control everything Humphrey says, but he would very religiously cover the part in the press release and then take off from there. That way we had some control over what he said and could build a sequence of themes along the way. I think it helped Humphrey learn you can't just freewheel once you get into a national campaign."

An interesting feature of Humphrey's campaign was a letter of support from Senator George, whom Humphrey now counted among his friends. Another was the appearance in Minnesota of Senate Minority Leader Lyndon Johnson, who was running for reelection himself in Texas and trying to elect Democrats to take control of the Senate and make himself majority leader the next year. "Not many places in the North wanted him because they were all kind of scared of a Southerner," says Waters. "We sent him out in the western part of the state in the more conservative areas along the South Dakota border where those farmers liked his style, and just brought him into Minneapolis for a private dinner.[5] He never forgot the fact that Humphrey helped him prove he could campaign in a liberal Northern state."

Humphrey's friendship with Johnson, dating back to their simultaneous arrival in the Senate in 1949, would become the most important alliance of his political career. Johnson had gone out of his way to greet Humphrey at the first Democratic caucus, Humphrey recalls, and they established a working relationship during their first two years in the Senate. But they were not particularly close until Johnson became minority leader in 1953 and saw in Humphrey a potential bridge to the Senate's liberal bloc. Johnson was responsible for getting Humphrey his most important committee assignment — Foreign Relations — in January, 1953.

After both men were reelected in 1954 and Johnson became majority leader, their friendship deepened and Humphrey became Johnson's unofficial ambassador to the liberal-intellectual circles where Johnson, liberal only by Texas standards, was looked on with suspicion.

[5] The private dinner wasn't without incident, however. Waters remembers that Johnson caused a minor scene at a plush Minneapolis restaurant by demanding an extra well-done thin steak. "Everybody in Minnesota likes those big thick juicy steaks, but Johnson wanted his done Texas style — thin and burn the hell out of it. It almost broke up the dinner."

Humphrey recalls that about this time, Johnson fell into the habit of telephoning him after adjournment almost every evening. "What you doin', Hubert?", Johnson would inquire. "Come on around — got some things I want to talk about." The two men would relax over drinks and talk about "liberalism or legislation or some editorial that got under Lyndon's skin," says Humphrey.

Herb Waters also remembers many an evening when Humphrey — always a late worker — would receive a call from Johnson. "We'd go over and sit in the majority leader's office and he'd say, 'Goddammit, Hubert, Dick Russell's breathing down my neck. He wants to raise hell with me if you can't hold your bombthrowers down on this one.' Then, of course, he'd go to Russell and say, 'Goddammit, Dick, you've got to make your old bastards give in a little. Hubert's bombthrowers are getting restless and they're going to raise Cain.' He played them against each other to drive things toward the center, and it was a pretty good process of compromise."

As Humphrey began his second six-year term, he began to follow earnestly the maxim often quoted by his old political science mentor, Evron Kirkpatrick: "Power goes to those who seek it." Humphrey knew he had excellent credentials as a civil rights leader and a staunch friend of organized labor and he had reestablished his ties with farmers and small businessmen in his 1954 campaign. Now, with an eye toward winning a spot on the 1956 Democratic ticket, he began to devote more of his attention to international affairs.

Always an international-minded senator, Humphrey had been actively interested in foreign policy during his first term, especially after joining the Foreign Relations Committee in 1953. But in 1955, he persuaded the Senate to create a Foreign Relations Disarmament Subcommittee and name him chairman. The subcommittee allowed him to specialize in the field of disarmament and arms control, a specialty that would later provide the vehicle for his most important contribution in the Senate.

Humphrey had discovered during his first term an issue that allowed him to relate American foreign policy to the productive power of American agriculture. That issue was, he said in a 1954 speech, "development of an international program for making . . . food supplies available to avert famine and combat Communism." Humphrey had been the chief sponsor of emergency grain shipments to famine-stricken India in 1951 and was instrumental in winning approval in 1954 of Public Law 480, the landmark law which authorized the sale of surplus farm commodities to friendly nations for foreign currencies and the gift of surplus food for famine relief abroad. This was a kind of internationalism that Minnesota's farmers and businessmen could understand, and Humphrey later parlayed the idea into the Food for Peace program in 1959.

But Humphrey's principal interest as he began his second term was in joining his liberal hero Adlai Stevenson on the 1956 Democratic presidential ticket. In November, 1955, Humphrey endorsed Stevenson for president and invited him to enter the Minnesota presidential primary the following March. Stevenson did, with disastrous results for Humphrey's political prestige. Stevenson was soundly trounced by Senator Estes Kefauver despite all-out support from Humphrey, Freeman and most of the DFL party apparatus. The upset was only a temporary setback for Stevenson, but it was a stinging rebuke to Humphrey and caused the first of a series of bitter intra-party squabbles that would plague the DFL until the present.

When Humphrey picked up the New York *Times* the day after the Minnesota primary, he was able to read one story crediting him with swinging the Senate vote on restoring high price supports in a farm bill and another story detailing Kefauver's upset victory and pointing out that Humphrey had been defeated as a convention delegate.[6] The defeat forced Humphrey to spend months trying to patch party wounds, an effort that didn't set well with him. "Old Humphrey had to go around that state for a whole year kissing asses," he told Senator Gaylord Nelson of Wisconsin.[7]

Despite the Minnesota defeat, Humphrey still had high hopes of becoming Stevenson's vice presidential running mate. His hopes were reinforced when Stevenson asked Humphrey to come to his room following a party honoring Senator George at Washington's Mayflower Hotel on July 20, six weeks before the convention. Humphrey recalls that they began discussing possible running mates for Stevenson, when Stevenson asked Humphrey why he didn't speak for himself. "He said,' If I had my choice, I'd rather have you,' " Humphrey recalls. "He said in substance, 'You've got to get some support for yourself and if you get that support, I'll pick you.' "

Humphrey was on top of the world when he went home to wake up Muriel at 4:00 A.M. and tell her about Stevenson's comments. His supporters quickly began a campaign to stir up support all over the country and, on July 29, Humphrey became one of the first men to campaign openly for the vice presidential nomination. He announced his decision in a letter to Minnesota's Representative Eugene McCarthy, saying that after "considerable soul-searching," he was now "willing for my friends to work actively in my behalf."[8]

Humphrey came to the August 15 Democratic National Convention in

[6] Another Minnesota Democrat who backed Stevenson and wound up without a seat in Minnesota's delegation to the national convention was Congressman Eugene McCarthy.

[7] Humphrey also took a lot of ribbing about the Minnesota primary in Washington. He was introduced at a Women's National Press Club dinner as "the man who holds Minnesota in his — whoops!"

[8] On the same day Humphrey announced his candidacy, another Minnesotan, former Governor Harold Stassen, began a futile drive to replace Vice President Richard Nixon as Eisenhower's running mate.

Chicago — the same city where he would receive his party's presidential nomination twelve years later — convinced that he was going to be Stevenson's running mate. But just like the later Chicago convention, it turned out to be one of the worst fiascos in Humphrey's career. Humphrey, who had been rebuffed in his attempts to be keynote speaker at the convention, was devastated when Stevenson announced he had decided to "depart from the precedents of the past" and let the convention pick his running mate.

Totally unprepared to wage the necessary floor fight, a confused and angry Humphrey stood by helplessly while his support melted away — he ran fifth on the first ballot. Finally, on the second ballot, he threw his support to Kefauver and watched with tears rolling down his cheeks as Kefauver narrowly defeated John F. Kennedy for the vice presidential nomination.

Humphrey later said he felt Stevenson acted as he did because Kefauver had too much support to overlook and because of pressures from Southern delegates, who found Humphrey unacceptable. Although bitterly disappointed, Humphrey made up with Stevenson and campaigned vigorously for the Democratic ticket that fall, helping to heal some of the frictions between the Stevenson and Kefauver factions in Minnesota at the same time. "I always was of the opinion that I may have over-interpreted what Adlai said," Humphrey later commented.

But his humiliating experience at Chicago made Humphrey determined never again to go into a national convention unprepared for a bruising battle. "I know exactly where the pressure points in a convention are now," he declared afterwards. Humphrey immediately began looking toward the 1960 convention after Stevenson's defeat. Three days after the election, before departing for New York to serve as a delegate to the United Nations General Assembly, Humphrey disclosed his blueprint for winning back the White House for the Democratic party. In language almost exactly the opposite of that he would use after his own presidential defeat in 1968, Humphrey called for a renewed "liberalism" to replace the "centrist" philosophy that he said characterized the Democratic Congressional leadership. "I don't think a party can win by running on 'trouble' — on economic difficulty," Humphrey declared. "We must design a new liberal program."

Humphrey joined with Stevenson, Mrs. Eleanor Roosevelt and other liberals on a policy-making Democratic Advisory Committee to draw up a sixteen-point program of action for the Democratic party, with particular emphasis on civil rights legislation. Majority Leader Johnson and House Speaker Sam Rayburn were asked to join but refused because they considered the committee an infringement on the Congressional leadership's policy-making function. Johnson resented Humphrey's participation in the committee and gave him the cold shoulder treatment when the Eighty-fifth Congress opened in January, 1957. "You broke faith with me," Johnson complained when he saw Humphrey. "Now, Lyndon," replied Humphrey soothingly, "you know I wouldn't do that. You can get more votes out of this body than anyone else. You are a good leader, Lyndon. You are a great, great leader. . . . I was simply trying to make you an even better leader."

Humphrey and Johnson soon made up, however, and by July Humphrey was huddling daily with Johnson to help him win Senate passage of the Civil Rights Act of 1957, the first major civil rights legislation of the twentieth century.

At the same time, Humphrey was building a reputation as a leading Democratic foreign policy spokesman. At the United Nations, he had been an articulate and indefatigable lobbyist for the United States, and now found himself consulted with surprising frequency by foreign diplomats. During the Turkish-Syrian-Soviet crisis in 1957, the Syrian foreign minister desperately summoned him from Minnesota to the U.N. to mediate between Soviet and Turkish officials. In the Senate, he called for a broad investigation of U.S. foreign policy and aggressively pursued his international interests on the Foreign Relations Committee, spending a month on a wide-ranging tour of the Middle East and meeting with Prime Minister David Ben-Gurion of Israel and President Gamal Abdel Nassar of Egypt.

Humphrey had to do some intensive lobbying to keep his disarmament subcommittee, however. The Foreign Relations Committee normally created such special purpose subcommittees with the understanding that they would be disbanded at the end of a Congress, but Humphrey refused to let his subcommittee expire. A Foreign Relations Committee aide remembers a heated debate about extending the subcommittee's life for another two years that was settled when the ranking Republican, Iowa's Bourke Hickenlooper, grumbled, "We might as well let Hubert keep that goddamn subcommittee until he finds out whether he's going to get the nomination."

Humphrey parlayed his longtime interest in international affairs into a highly visible forum from which he continued to pursue his presidential ambitions. In November, 1958, after a sweeping Democratic victory in the Congressional elections that sent Eugene McCarthy to join him in the Senate Humphrey was aboard the S.S. *Liberte* on his way to a UNESCO conference in Paris and a nuclear test suspension conference in Geneva. Interviewed by a reporter, Humphrey made it clear he hoped to be the candidate of Democratic liberals in 1960. But not too liberal, he emphasized. "There is no radical movement in America today, and no call for one," he said. "It's a progressive party, an adventurous and international one, with vigor, not just vivacity, that is called for."

Humphrey was in Geneva when he ran into an extraordinary stroke of luck that would project him into the middle of the 1960 presidential picture. Scheduled to visit the Soviet Union after his Geneva stop to explore the possibilities of further cooperation between U.S. and Soviet scientists on health problems, Humphrey met a Soviet official in Geneva whom he'd known at the United Nations and told him he was going to Moscow and would like to see Premier Nikita Khrushchev. With little hope that his request would be granted, Humphrey went to Moscow and was astounded when he was called to the Kremlin on the afternoon of December 1 with only a half-hour notice. At 3:00 P.M. he was ushered into Khrushchev's office and began a marathon talk that lasted for eight hours and twenty-five minutes and provided the world with the most intimate glimpse it had ever been given of the Soviet premier.

With only one other person present, interpreter Oleg Troyanovsky, Khrushchev and Humphrey posed for pictures and exchanged pleasantries, then talked about the need for an exchange of medical and scientific information between the two countries. "Khrushchev was as uninterested in those things as if I were talking to a fence post," Humphrey recalled many years later. "We just sort of visited lethargically and uninterestingly for about an hour, and when it looked to me like my time was running out, I said, 'Mr. Chairman, it looks like I've taken more of your time than I should.' And he said 'No, let's visit, let's talk.' "

Humphrey took him at his word. The two men relaxed and began a frank discussion that covered every conceivable aspect of U.S.-Soviet relations and foreign policy, including trade, disarmament, peaceful coexistence, NATO, Berlin, the Middle East, China and the personalities of American and Russian leaders. Humphrey received permission to take notes and, when he was through, he had twenty-three pages of notes. The conversation continued without interruption for four hours, when Khrushchev got up to go to the toilet. When he returned, Humphrey apologized for taking so much of his time, but Khrushchev suggested they continue their discussion over dinner.

"It was delicious food," Humphrey recalls. "First, we had some caviar. Then they brought in pheasant, chicken, beef, fish, fruit and so on. He had mineral water on the table, and he said, 'We have mineral water from the North or the South. Which do you want?' I told him that I was a Northerner and I'd better have the mineral water from the North."

After dinner, they began talking about foreign trade, and Khrushchev said, "I don't know much about that. I'll call up my Persian rug peddler." Minutes later, Anastas Mikoyan arrived and the three men talked for another two and a half hours. Humphrey recalls that Mikoyan noticed a bottle of brandy on the table and offered to pour some for Humphrey. "I said no, I had already had my brandy with the chairman. But Mikoyan was very insistent about it. He said, 'No, you take some brandy.' Then Khrushchev said to him, 'You drink the brandy. My friend from Minnesota and I have had our brandy. You drink three brandies.' And by golly, Mikoyan belted down three brandies, one after the other."

At 11:00 P.M., remembering that Khrushchev said he had an appointment at 7:00 A.M. the next day, Humphrey got up to leave, saying as an after-thought, " 'But there's surely a lot of things I would have liked to ask you.' He asked me what I meant, and I said, 'I was going to ask some things about China.' He said, '*Nyet, nyet,* no questions about our good ally China.' And I said, 'I wasn't going to ask about defense matters. I just wanted to ask you about those communes.'

"Well, he just leaned right back and sat down again and started talking about China. He kept downplaying China and said the communes wouldn't work. He asked me, 'Do you know what principle those communes are based on? They're based on the principle that from each according to his ability, to each according to his need. You know that won't work. It takes incentive to make production.' I said, 'Well, Mr. Chairman, what you said sounds rather capitalistic.' He said, 'Call it what you will, but it works, doesn't it?' "

Khrushchev's remarks to Humphrey were the first indication of the deep ideological split that would surface between Russia and China four years later, even though Khrushchev, soon after their conversation, denounced Humphrey as a "Baron Munchausen" who told "fairy tales." Humphrey's Kremlin visit made worldwide headlines for weeks as Humphrey held air-port interviews and news conferences from Oslo to New York. When he returned to Washington, he told two hundred waiting reporters that he had a special message to deliver to President Eisenhower from Khrushchev, in-cluding two important "secrets." The next day, Humphrey met with Eisen-hower for eighty minutes and then flew to Minneapolis for another press conference and a rally that featured banners proclaiming, "Humphrey in 1960."

Humphrey's presidential boom had been launched and it didn't matter that his "secrets" turned out to be something less than advertised — that Russia had a missile of 8,700 mile range and that the Soviets had a proposal for settling the Berlin crisis. Neither was particularly surprising to U.S. officials, nor were they startled by Khrushchev's special message — that he would accept an invitation to visit Washington. "You've been in the lion's den and described the lion for us, Hubert," a State Department official told him. "But we already knew there was a lion in there."

Nevertheless, Humphrey was now off and running on his first serious bid for the White House. The brash newcomer who had fallen flat on his face in 1949 had become a bona fide member of the Senate's Inner Club and one of the most influential men in Congress. He had discovered and he now illustrated what Author-Columnist William S. White pronounced as one of the ultimate truths of the Senate: ". . . that one cannot forever refuse there to make any compromise at all and remain a good, effective member."

CHAPTER VII

McCARTHY'S MAVERICKS

*I'm more interested in legislation than in
administrative office.*
> Eugene McCarthy in a 1955 interview.

Shortly before the 1948 election that sent him to Congress, Eugene McCarthy offered the voters of Minnesota's Fourth Congressional District a preview of what his behavior would be as their elected representative in the nation's capital.

In words that would set the seal upon his public life, the thirty-two year old college professor declared, "I make no pretense of being acceptable in all respects to each and to all persons and groups of persons who support my candidacy. I have promised them only one certainty, that I will judge and act on this principle: That the proper ordering of society depends upon a recognition of the dignity of the human person as an intelligent, responsible, creative being . . . and of the acceptance that it is the function of government and of other social institutions to serve the person."

McCarthy's campaign oratory foretold the paradoxical blend of humility and arrogance, of idealism and pragmatism, of detachment and involvement that would characterize his political career. But on January 3, 1949, McCarthy was merely one of sixty newly-elected Democrats sworn in for the first session of the Eighty-first Congress, an event he was almost late for after he got tied up in Washington traffic on the way to the Capitol.

McCarthy settled into a first floor suite in the Cannon House Office Building to begin a "learning and building term," according to Adrian Winkel, a fellow teacher at St. Thomas College who became his first administrative assistant.[1] "Gene was more or less feeling his way the first year or two," says

---

[1] Winkel remained on McCarthy's staff until 1954, when he returned to St. Paul to run unsuccessfully for mayor. ("There was no friction between us," says Winkel. "It was just that it was a kind of dull existence.") He held several federal jobs before

Winkel. McCarthy was disappointed when he failed to get his first choice of a committee assignment — Foreign Affairs — and had to settle for the less glamorous Post Office and Civil Service Committee.

McCarthy's colleagues remember him as an easy-going person with a good sense of humor. "He made friends very easily," recalls Fred Marshall, one of three new Minnesota Democrats elected with McCarthy. "His sense of humor stood him in good stead. I don't know of any man in the House who made as many friends as McCarthy did at first." John Blatnik, another Minnesota Democrat who was elected two years earlier and who introduced McCarthy at the Democratic caucus, remembers that McCarthy was "quiet, low-key and very friendly. He was an intellectual, or at least I thought so. We called him the moral conscience or spiritual adviser of the Minnesota delegation."

McCarthy's tall good looks, scholarly appearance and genial manner helped single him out of the mass of obscure freshmen, while his proclivity for deflating wisecracks soon earned him the nickname, "The Needle." "He'd kind of sidle up to you and make a few clever comments about somebody or something going on on the floor," says Blatnik. "He was always funny as hell."

Marshall, a lanky, laconic farmer from western Minnesota who had accomplished the unprecedented feat of unseating the chairman of the Ways and Means Committee — Republican Harold Knutson — was probably closer to McCarthy than anyone in the House. He recalls that both he and McCarthy were awed by their new surroundings at first, but that McCarthy didn't stay awed for long. "He had a certain amount of cynicism even then," says Marshall. "He just didn't seem to be quite ready to accept the traditional way of doing things. He didn't feel any of the committee chairmen were as high and mighty as they felt they were." Marshall also recalls that McCarthy was "extremely close" to the states's new junior Democratic senator, Hubert Humphrey. "At that time, I'd say Humphrey was somewhat of an idol of McCarthy's."

Although McCarthy was well-liked by most of his colleagues, he had few close friends, according to Ohio Democrat Wayne Hays, another freshman. "Gene was always kind of a loner," says Hays, something of a loner himself. "If he had any close friends, I don't know who they were. On the floor, he was always restless. He'd sit with somebody three or four minutes and then move somewhere else. And he always had this dry sense of humor. Somebody would be speaking and he'd say to me, 'Why don't you say something?' Once or twice I did, and I immediately got into hot water. I found out then that Gene was a great guy who, as my father would say, would mold the bullets and get somebody else to shoot them." Hays, like McCarthy a former

---

returning to Washington — and the Cannon House Office Building — to become administrative assistant to California Democrat Phillip Burton in 1971.

school teacher, recalls that once, during a droning floor speech, McCarthy turned to him and commented, "This is a hell of a way to make a living, isn't it? — But it sure beats teaching."

McCarthy's first term set the pattern for the liberal voting record that he would follow throughout his twenty-two years in Congress as he consistently supported the Truman administration on domestic and foreign policy.[2] While serving on the Post Office and Civil Service Committee, McCarthy became interested in the problems of federal employees and was instrumental in pushing through an amendment giving government employees fired as security risks the right to be hired in non-sensitive jobs.

The latter measure became a minor issue in his first campaign for reelection in 1950 when McCarthy's opponent charged that it was a "bad amendment." But McCarthy, relying on his strong pro-labor, pro-administration voting record and pointing out that he had promised in his first campaign to see that civil rights were "courageously promoted," was easily reelected to a second term in the heavily Democratic district.

Still failing to get his preferred committee assignments, McCarthy switched to the Agriculture Committee in 1951, where he was one of the few members representing an urban district. When a colleague kidded him about representing the "farmers of Ramsey County," McCarthy pointed out that widespread truck farming and fruit gardening produced an average return of $99.56 per acre of farms in Ramsey County, or $30.00 higher than anywhere else in the state. His position on the Agriculture Committee also enabled McCarthy to launch a long campaign to improve the working and living conditions of Mexican-American migrant farmworkers.

McCarthy's infrequent floor speeches were larded with scholarly and literary references. Speaking against a proposed 350 million dollar cut in economic aid to Europe in August, 1951, McCarthy quoted Edmund Burke to buttress his argument that "our ties of blood and belief bind us to Western Europe." On another occasion, he chided Republicans for contradictory statements on U.S. foreign policy, saying that their comments reminded him of the race in *Alice in Wonderland*. "When the race was over," said McCarthy, "the Dodo announced that everybody has won and all must have prizes."

Party leaders soon took notice of the St. Paul congressman. House Majority Leader John McCormack, always glad to promote a bright young Irish Catholic, hailed McCarthy as one of the outstanding young members in 1953.[3] Wilbur Elston of the Minneapolis *Star's* Washington bureau, noted

[2] Unlike his later position on U.S. military involvement in Asia, McCarthy defended America's entry into the Korean War. "We as a nation moved to the point where we accepted responsibility for people who couldn't do anything for us," he later said of the U.S. action. "We tried to save them from tyranny."

[3] McCormack didn't feel the same way about his fellow Boston Democrat, John F. Kennedy, according to Fred Marshall. "McCormack had no love for Jack Kennedy

that McCarthy "has been getting the little extra attentions which the party leadership usually reserves for a political 'comer.' " He reported that McCarthy was "invited to an evening at Blair House with President Truman" (Truman was living there while the White House was being renovated). Elston also wrote that McCarthy was tapped by the Democratic National Committee in 1951 for speaking dates in New York, Milwaukee and Columbus, "where his professorial approach and his tall, dark and handsome appearance are best appreciated."

According to Fred Marshall, McCarthy was impressed by another young Irish Catholic congressman who was elected two years before him, John F. Kennedy of Boston. "I think a lot of things attracted them to each other, and I remember that Gene was more or less enamored of Jack Kennedy and his family at first," Marshall recalls. However, Marshall says McCarthy came to feel — as he did — that Kennedy "wasn't very serious about his work as a congressman" and that during the second term they served in the House together (Kennedy was elected to the Senate in 1952), McCarthy felt Kennedy "pulled the rug out from under him" during a floor debate. Nevertheless, the McCarthys were among the few non-Massachusetts House members invited to Kennedy's wedding to Jacqueline Bouvier in 1953.

At the same time, McCarthy was turning his attention to the broad issue of religion and morality in public life. In a speech to the National Catholic Education Association in Cleveland in March, 1951, McCarthy warned that governmental interference in matters of personal morality is a greater threat to human freedom than interference at the material level. Writing in the *Commonweal* magazine in December, 1951, McCarthy declared:

> We must take immediate action to develop in the United States a code of ethics for men in public office, and to lay the foundation upon which we can build a tradition of the high honor and responsibility of government office.

McCarthy was soon called upon to defend himself against an attack on his own integrity. When he ran for a third term in the fall of 1952, his Republican opponent, a twenty-six year old St. Paul law student named Roger Kennedy, cited McCarthy's 1950 security risk amendment as proof that he "does not understand the danger of subversion." Kennedy also charged that McCarthy lied about his voting record "in order to justify his unholy proposal."

The charges were particularly grating to McCarthy, who only three months earlier, in one of the most courageous acts of his career, had stepped forth as the first member of Congress to oppose Senator Joseph McCarthy of Wisconsin in a public debate. The decision to appear in the debate was not taken lightly by the thirty-five year old sophomore congressman. Joseph 'McCarthy's cries of treason in high places had touched a sensitive nerve in America,

then," says Marshall. "They had a sort of Irish feud going, and I think McCarthy may have enjoyed that feud a little bit."

and to oppose him was to risk being destroyed personally and politically. Several senators had declined to debate the Wisconsin senator before his namesake and fellow Catholic from Minnesota agreed to meet him on the half-hour nationally televised "American Forum of the Air" on June 22, 1952.

The debate was sponsored by the Bohn Aluminum and Brass Corporation, which set the tone of the evening with commercials warning that "to keep America the way it is, freedom must be protected from the seeds of socialism." Senator McCarthy was at his demagogic best, using up about two-thirds of the time, butting in frequently ("I don't like to interrupt, but . . .") and flinging charges of traitorous conduct at the makers of American foreign policy. Much of the debate centered around what both men agreed would be the big issue of the coming campaign — foreign policy, and although the younger McCarthy was a member of the House Agriculture Committee and supposedly not well-versed in foreign policy, he was surprisingly well-informed on the subject. Some of the things he said were strikingly similar to the language he would use fifteen years later in criticizing U.S. policies in Asia.

> SENATOR McCARTHY: We know we have lost an average of 100 million people a year to Communism since the shooting part of World War II ended. Not 100 thousand, 100 million. Since the shooting part of World War II ended, the total lost has been about 700 million people. Right, Gene?
> CONGRESSMAN McCARTHY: Senator, I don't think you can say that we have lost them. We never had them. Of course, it is not our policy to have people. I think that we can say that we have saved much of the world from Communism through the sound foreign policy which the Democratic administration did initiate, and which was given bipartisan support by the Republicans as long as it seemed to be going along very well.
> SENATOR McCARTHY: You said we never had these people. We have had the Chinese people, 450 million of them, as our friends for over a hundred years. This present administration has betrayed China.
> CONGRESSMAN McCARTHY: . . . I don't think we have betrayed anyone. If we look back at the American foreign policy it becomes clear that we have not had a consistent foreign policy since 1920.
> SENATOR McCARTHY: Since 1930.
> CONGRESSMAN McCARTHY: Since 1920. . . . Let us go back and reexamine our Far Eastern policy for a minute. The U.S. did support the "Most Favored Nation" treatment in the Orient, and that was the basis of our policy until about the year 1900. Actually all this meant was that if anybody was exploiting the Chinese and Orientals, we insisted that we have the same right to exploit them. After 1900 we began to talk about the "Open Door" policy. This meant we were willing to exploit them in greater degree than anyone else if we could get the advantage.
> SENATOR McCARTHY: Let us bring it down to date, if we may. As of tonight there exists one of the most treasonable, traitorous orders that has ever been issued by any nation in war or peacetime. I am sure you will agree, Gene.
> CONGRESSMAN McCARTHY: I am *not* sure.
> SENATOR McCARTHY: There exists as of tonight an order to our

Seventh Fleet, which says that if our friends on Formosa, if they try to stop the Communist shipping, our Seventh Fleet will sink our friends, and shoot their planes. . . . If that is not treason, I ask you what is treason?
CONGRESSMAN McCARTHY: I would deny it is treason unless the words "conspiracy" and "conspirator" and "treason" have been redefined. You have to look at it in relation to the whole problem of the Far East. The question is one of whether we are going to be involved in an all-out war in that area or not. . . .

While there is no evidence to suggest that the debate marked the beginning of Joseph McCarthy's eventual decline, at least one observer felt it was the first time anyone had shown that the Wisconsin senator could be successfully debated. "The fallacy of Senator McCarthy's invincibility in debate was exploded on Ted Granik's 'American Forum of the Air.' " Harry MacArthur, television critic for the Washington *Evening Star* wrote afterwards. "The technique for dealing with him in T.V. discussion — or maybe any other discussion for that matter — was demonstrated by another and different McCarthy, Representative Eugene McCarthy of Minnesota." MacArthur said the younger McCarthy "emerged unruffled and unscarred," and added "that is tantamount to victory in this league." Says John Blatnik, "That's when the strong Gene McCarthy, the man with real depth, started to emerge."

While the debate boosted the younger McCarthy's stock among liberals, it also caused some amusing incidents when people confused him with the Wisconsin senator. Once, when the Minnesota McCarthy stood in for Senator Hubert Humphrey at a trade union convention in Baltimore, a member of the Amalgamated Clothing Workers of America shook his hand and said, "Ah, McCarthy, I'm glad you're here. I knew you didn't have horns. Lots of us in the Amalgamated are for you!" Congressman McCarthy got so many telephone calls and letters intended for Senator McCarthy that he issued a statement to the press pointing out that he was not related to Senator McCarthy, was a member of a different party, came from a different state and held different views.

But there was nothing amusing about Congressman McCarthy's 1952 campaign. Roger Kennedy's attacks produced the kind of response from McCarthy that would occur whenever anyone attempted to distort his voting record or question his integrity.

"His reaction was very similar to what it was twenty years later to what he felt were low blows," recalls Adrian Winkel. "It was calm, deliberate and deep." The McCarthy-Kennedy contest grew more bitter as charges and countercharges dominated radio and newspaper coverage of the campaign. Kennedy's supporters continued the soft-on-Communism attack against McCarthy. In an unprecedented action, a panel of thirty-six attorneys supporting Kennedy charged that McCarthy had falsely claimed that his amendment was incorporated into law. Twenty-eight pro-McCarthy attorneys responded with a letter from the Republican chief counsel of the House Post

Office and Civil Service Committee pointing out that the law "in effect" contained McCarthy's amendment. Humphrey also went on the radio to defend McCarthy and denounce the tactics of his opponent.

McCarthy's deep feelings about the type of campaign waged against him were evident in the single debate he had with Kennedy. Joseph Karth, who succeeded McCarthy in the House in 1958, recalls that encounter, which occurred at a meeting of the White Bear Lake League of Women Voters. "McCarthy got so mad he walked out on Kennedy," says Karth. "He made some comment like, 'I'm just not going to take part in this kind of a low level campaign.' "

McCarthy's intense feelings about the 1952 campaign were exacerbated by the effect of the soft-on-Communisim charges on his family. When his daughter Ellen came home from kindergarten in St. Paul one day, she asked her mother, "Mama, what's a Communist?" Mrs. McCarthy was aghast because "I just knew some child had asked her why her father was a Communist."

However, McCarthy reserved his deepest resentment for a prominent Republican St. Paul attorney named Warren E. Burger. Burger, the future chief justice of the United States, was one of the signers of the attorneys' statement attacking McCarthy. McCarthy was — and is — convinced that Burger masterminded the smear campaign against him. The genesis of McCarthy's unforgiving attitude — manifested when he voted against Burger's confirmation as chief justice in 1969 — can be traced back to a debate between the two men on October 21, 1952, at Hamline University in St. Paul.[4] With Burger standing in for Kennedy, the debate before several hundred listeners quickly turned to the question of McCarthy's security risk amendment. The arguments went like this:

McCARTHY: I have supported every basic piece of legislation against insecurity, including the so-called security bill. The thing that makes me dangerous in the eyes of my Republican opponent is my amendment giving the right to appeal. A loyalty case [considered more serious] does have a right to outside appeal.
BURGER: Congressman McCarthy's approach is using a feather duster when he ought to be using a pick ax. A bad security risk shouldn't be employed by the government anywhere, and the congressman is still for a proposal to give job preference to people dismissed as security risks.
McCARTHY: Veterans still come first. And keep in mind that these people must be cleared by a board before being eligible for other jobs. Without the

[4] McCarthy made it clear he held Burger at least partially responsible for the tone of the 1952 campaign as he explained his reasons for voting against Burger's confirmation on June 9, 1969. McCarthy said his reasons were "somewhat personal and political." He described Burger as "a most active participant" in the campaign, and added, "It is my opinion that the manner in which the issues were presented to the people of my district that year first of all misrepresented my position, but more significantly than that, they were designed to elicit an emotional, if not prejudiced, response."

amendment, when a security risk was discharged — that was the end of the road for him. Yet the loyalty risk had an appeal.

BURGER: I don't agree with Congress that there are sensitive and non-sensitive agencies. Our civil service procedures don't provide protection against Communism.[5]

The debate with Burger was apparently the straw that broke the camel's back as far as McCarthy was concerned. A future governor of Minnesota, Karl Rolvaag, then Minnesota DFL chairman and a candidate for Congress from Minneapolis, was at McCarthy's house when he returned from his debate with Burger. "Gene was as emotional that night as I have ever seen him," Rolvaag recalled years later. "His face was ashen grey. I can't remember all the details, but he was very, very upset. He never forgave Burger for that."

Burger has a different recollection of the debate. "I was invited to give the Republican point of view and we had what I thought was a very pleasant discussion," Burger said shortly after McCarthy opposed his confirmation. "It always baffled me why he carried 1952 as something of a grudge. I can't imagine what's sticking in his craw." Burger also pointed out that he had been deeply involved that summer and fall in Dwight Eisenhower's campaign. (Burger was instrumental in shifting the Minnesota delegation from "favorite son" Harold Stassen to Eisenhower to give him the presidential nomination on the first ballot at the 1952 Republican National Convention and had been asked by Herbert Brownell to join Eisenhower's campaign team.) "I declined because I'd taken too much time off for the convention, but I told him I would help with position papers and analyses and so on," Burger recalled in 1969. "I was deeply involved at that level, and obviously I didn't have much time to work for a nice young man who didn't have much chance in a congressional campaign."

Kennedy, a former St. Paul banker who is now vice president of the Ford Foundation in New York City, discussed his memories of the campaign in a 1971 interview. As Kennedy remembers it, Burger had no part in putting together the lawyers' statement attacking McCarthy. "My recollection is that Burger, like a lot of other senior lawyers who mostly happened to be Republicans, looked at the statement and concluded that Gene had made an error, that he was wrong in what he had proposed and that his interpretation of what this amendment would have done was not correct. As a lawyer, I think my lawyers were right and his lawyers were wrong, but that isn't really the point."

Kennedy, who became Burger's assistant when Burger was named assistant U. S. attorney general in 1953, says McCarthy "probably thought I was a whippersnapper who had no business contesting someone of his stature, and he probably was right, but I didn't think so at the time. I suspect

[5] St. Paul *Pioneer Press,* October 22, 1952.

that it's possible that he might have begun to worry about the outcome and that any pressure from someone as distinguished as Warren Burger was unwelcome. And I would suspect further that in no other Congressional election did he have that anxiety and that's why it stands out for him. Warren and I were both very much surprised that his very limited role in that campaign loomed so large in Gene's memory. Something may have happened in that debate which particularly addled Gene. It's conceivable that Warren, who's a very, very articulate courtroom antagonist, was successful in making his point."

Kennedy now says that "If I were ten years older, I probably would have said to myself that this issue is so inflamed that I don't want any part of it; that whether he was right or wrong, let's talk about other things and make it clear that we aren't in the Joe McCarthy bag. I also think a lot of decent, liberal people including many Democrats, who supported us on the basis that we were young and bouncy and full of idealism, dropped away because Gene and his supporters were very successful in associating us with the Republican right, which we didn't belong to. It rather suprises me that if he does think about that election, he isn't rubbing his hands with glee, saying, 'Boy, they certainly walked into that one!' "

Another view of Burger's role contrary to McCarthy's is offered by Stassen. The former Minnesota governor and perennially unsuccessful presidential candidate is now a wealthy Philadelphia lawyer, and has known Burger as a close personal friend and political associate since he worked in Stassen's first campaign for governor in 1938. Stassen thought so highly of Burger that he almost appointed him to the U.S. Senate in 1940 instead of Joseph Ball.[6] "Although I was extensively involved in Eisenhower's national campaign that year and not in very close touch with the Minnesota scene, from what I know of Warren Burger, I would be very surprised if he was responsible for anything negative or not constructive in that campaign," Stassen said in 1971. "He was always on the side of constructive campaigning, an intelligent facing of the issues and the forward thrust of solutions."

McCarthy's supporters wanted to reply in kind to Kennedy's charges but McCarthy refused to, according to Theologian Robert McAfee Brown, then a Presbyterian minister at Macalester College in St. Paul who supported McCarthy in 1952 as he would again in 1968. Writing in the magazine, *Christianity and Crisis,* in 1953, the Reverend Brown told of a group of

[6] Stassen astounded most Minnesotans when he picked Ball, a relatively unknown St. Paul political reporter, to succeed Ernest Lundeen, who was killed in a plane crash. Stassen says he chose Ball over Burger and several other more prominent Republicans largely because of his internationalist views on foreign policy and "his ability to phrase the issues for moving the Republican party in the direction I wanted to see it go in the international field." (It is interesting to contemplate whether Humphrey would have fared as well against Burger as he did against Ball in 1948.) Reaction to Ball's appointment ranged from surprise to outrage. Exclaimed the Fairmont *Daily Sentinel,* "Joe Ball for Senator? Good God!"

McCarthy supporters who raised $1,100 for a "smear sheet" to attack Kennedy. "It was a high moment in my understanding of democracy to see a man whose political life was being threatened . . . say 'no.' It might have cost him the election. At that point, no one knew. But, as Eugene McCarthy said later, 'It is not worth winning to have to win in that fashion.' "

Despite the bitterness of the 1952 campaign, it had little effect on the outcome of the election. McCarthy got 61.7 percent of the vote and won a third term by a 38,000 vote majority, the largest margin he'd ever gotten. At the same time, Eisenhower was carrying Minnesota against Adlai Stevenson with 55.3 percent of the vote. McCarthy wasn't overly concerned about his election, according to William Carlson, the man he nudged aside in winning the DFL endorsement for Congress in 1948. Carlson, who ran unsuccessfully for the U.S. Senate that year against Republican Edward Thye, recalls that McCarthy "was so bored with his own campaign he took off with me and campaigned all over the state. He was smart enough to know 1952 was not a good year to run against Thye because Ike was running and farmers were prosperous." [7]

Back in the House, McCarthy continued to build on the liberal voting record he'd established during his first two terms. He changed his committee assignment for the third straight Congress, moving from Agriculture to Banking and Currency and Interior, and generally supported the Eisenhower administration on foreign policy while opposing it on domestic programs. In fact, he supported Eisenhower so much (55 percent during the Eighty-third Congress) that he preempted his 1954 opponent's "back Ike" campaign platform. "About half of his program was the Democratic program anyway," said McCarthy. "I'm for Ike when he's right." [8] (McCarthy's St. Paul-born opponent also raised the carpetbagger issue against him, and when a local newspaper printed a cartoon showing McCarthy asking directions in St. Paul, he quipped, "As soon as I learned about St. Paul, I came here.")

Easily reelected to a fourth term by a 34,000 vote majority, McCarthy offered some "Election Year Lessons for Our Children" in the *National Parent-Teacher* magazine in December, 1954. In words that foreshadowed his 1968 presidential campaign, he wrote:

Truth will prove the best antidote for cynicism, which is an especially dangerous attitude when it prevails among young people. Not only does it

[7] McCarthy seriously considered running against Thye. He also allowed friends to float a trial balloon for him for governor in 1954, and even asked a DFL official to line up out-state speaking engagements for him. The official recalls that he scheduled McCarthy to speak at Warroad, a remote community on the Canadian border. "It was an all-night trip by train and car and when he got back, he told me he'd decided against running for governor," says the official.

[8] However, McCarthy called for the resignation of Eisenhower's Attorney General, Herbert Brownell, whom Warren Burger was now working for. He said Brownell used his public office for personal advancement and that he "misled" Eisenhower on the issue of Communists in the government. Brownell had "asked the president for a hunting license without telling him what he was going to shoot," McCarthy said.

destroy confidence and hope, some of the most precious assets of youth, but it also eats away the will to attack difficult political problems — as it does problems in other fields.

McCarthy's high-minded prose may have sounded a bit overblown to hard-boiled politicians but it was consistent with his longtime concern with reconciling politics and religion. That concern was summarized in an article entitled "The Christian in Politics" which he wrote for *Commonweal* magazine in 1954. "The calling of a Christian is not to judge the world, but to save it," McCarthy wrote in language reminiscent of Thomas Aquinas. "In the conflict between good and evil, in which great advantage is given to evil by neglect, the Christian cannot be indifferent to so important an area of conflict as that of politics."

In the same article, McCarthy expressed the attitude that was to become the hallmark of his political style: "The Christian in politics should shun the devices of the demagogue at all times, but especially in a time when anxiety is great, when tension is high, when uncertainty prevails, and when emotion tends to be in the ascendancy."

McCarthy articulated yet another cardinal principle of his approach to politics when he wrote that the Christian in politics should be judged by the standard of whether "he has advanced the cause of justice, and helped, at least, to achieve the highest degree of perfection possible in the temporal order."

The rather pedantic tone of McCarthy's public utterances was explained by his wife, Abigail, in a 1955 interview. "He is . . . taking seriously the obligation of the educative function of his office — writing and speaking to groups he thinks ought to know more about government." Mrs. McCarthy, a former teacher and writer herself, found little time for either interest, however, as she concentrated on keeping up the two homes the McCarthys kept in Washington and St. Paul and raising the couple's three children, Ellen, seven; Mary, five; and Michael, four. (A fourth child, Margaret, would arrive a year later.)

McCarthy's career was given an important boost when the Eighty-fourth Congress convened in January, 1955. He was named to the prestigious Ways and Means Committee, an assignment that would give him an understanding of tax and fiscal policy and international trade legislation that would serve him well in later years.[9] Unlike Humphrey, McCarthy moved easily through the Southern orbit from his first days in Congress. He was well-liked by Chairman Jere Cooper of Tennessee and ranking Democrat Wilbur Mills of Arkansas (Mills became chairman in 1958) as well as by House Speaker Sam Rayburn.

Rayburn came to know the young Minnesota Congressman well as the

[9] Joseph Karth, who took McCarthy's House seat in 1958, also followed him on the Ways and Means Committee in 1971.

result of McCarthy's friendship with two members of the Texas delegation, Homer Thornberry and Frank Ikard. McCarthy often joined them at the Texas table in the House dining room, where Rayburn held forth each day. (McCarthy's Texas ties would pay off handsomely when he went to the Senate, as Rayburn's warm endorsement of him assured his kind treatment by Rayburn's fellow Texan, Senate Majority Leader Lyndon Johnson.)

"Gene was clearly identified as a comer," says Ikard, now president of the American Petroleum Institute. "He had one of the most scintillating minds I've ever been exposed to and a wonderful sense of humor." Ikard says the Texans' regard for McCarthy was so high that they helped raise campaign funds for him in 1952. "A number of us talked to people around the country and told them we thought it was important that Gene McCarthy be reelected."

A colleague on the Ways and Means Committee remembers McCarthy as "the only intelligent liberal" on the committee, while a former staff member describes him as "a competent guy who understood the issues, particularly when we got into technical things." The staff member recalls that McCarthy "had a willingness to sit back and make jokes, particularly if he saw the cards were stacked against him, as opposed to Tom Curtis [Missouri Republican], who raved and ranted that the cards *were* stacked against him."

Once, when the committee was considering a bill sponsored by Brooklyn Democrat Eugene Keogh involving favorable tax treatment for the Minneapolis-based Investors Diversified Services and another bill sponsored by McCarthy that would provide tax exemption for children's phonograph records, a colleague asked McCarthy why he hadn't introduced the bill involving the Minnesota company. "He said, 'There's big money in the IDS bill and they wouldn't trust me,' " the colleague recalls. "He said, 'The only thing they trust me with is children's records.' " Later, when the House passed the children's records bill along with bills to repeal taxes on cabarets and the breath freshener Sen-Sen, McCarthy observed that the House had made the entire family happy. "Parents could have a night out at a tax-free cabaret, buy some tax-free Sen-Sen to mask their alcoholic breath and go home to children playing tax-free records."

McCarthy's reputation as a kind of Greek chorus observer of the House grew with each passing year. When a Republican colleague told the House that a television play about Joan of Arc reminded him of the political persecution of the controversial Secretary of Agriculture Ezra Taft Benson, McCarthy rose to his feet and declared, "If I remember my theology and history, Joan of Arc was never canonized for advocating flexible farm price supports." Of Secretary of Labor James Mitchell, McCarthy said his policies were overruled by the White House so often that when he testified before Congress, "He wears a red tie on days he is talking for the administration and a blue tie for days when he is just talking for himself." McCarthy said he quit criticizing Secretary of State John Foster Dulles "because all I have to do is wait two weeks and he changes his position."

Some of McCarthy's constituents back in St. Paul didn't find anything funny about the way he handled their requests for help on local matters. Former St. Paul Mayor Joseph Dillon recalls that when city and county officials came to Washington, they would pay a protocol visit on McCarthy and then go see Humphrey, John Blatnik or August Andresen, the senior Republican in the Minnesota House delegation for help on local projects. "We had a long struggle to get a federal flood control project for St. Paul and we got more help out of Blatnik and Andresen than McCarthy," Dillon says. "We used to say we realized that a congressman was expected to represent the United States of America, but we also expected him to represent the Fourth Congressional District. He was a good congressman for the country, but not for St. Paul." Another constituent, M. W. Thatcher, head of the Farmers Union Grain Terminal Association, said he never bothered to see McCarthy in Washington. "I felt he would be informed, that he would do what he thought was right, and there was no use trying to sway him."

McCarthy clearly didn't fit into the mold of the ordinary congressman, those who watched him in the House recall. "He always saw himself as a parliamentarian," says Charles Bailey II of the Minneapolis *Tribune's* Washington bureau. "He often talked in the frame of reference of the British Parliament and I think he wished that's the system we should have." But Bailey adds that McCarthy "worked very hard in the House. I guess I'd subscribe to the view that he was lazy or bored in the Senate, but he understood the House and was interested in how it worked."

McCarthy's plain-spoken friend, Fred Marshall, disagrees with Bailey's assessment. "To be blunt about it, Gene was a little on the lazy side," Marshall said after serving with McCarthy for ten years in the House. "I don't quite know how to say it, but he could get away with being lazy because of his intelligence and his sense of humor. He didn't have to work as hard as the rest of us to accomplish what he wanted."

McCarthy was also an unconventional liberal. He warned of "certain dangers" in the liberal approach in a speech to the Minnesota Association of Cooperatives in October, 1955, saying, "Because the future is not the past, the liberal is often led to underestimate and discount the lessons of the past; or to believe that there must be an absolute break between the past and the present, or the present and the future."

In 1955, McCarthy also began to voice doubts about the Central Intelligence Agency and other government intelligence units operating overseas. Concerned that they were operating without adequate Congressional supervision and in effect, making their own foreign policy, he introduced a bill to create a joint Congressional watchdog committee. The bill was designed to supplement a proposal offered in the Senate by Humphrey to create a bipartisan commission to investigate the nation's domestic intelligence system. A year later, after returning from a month-long NATO parliamentary conference in Paris, McCarthy called for a "new look" at U.S. intelligence operations in light of the Hungarian and Suez crises. It marked the first of many times that he would clash with a leading defender of the CIA, Senator Henry Jackson of Washington. "Gene got tired of hearing Scoop Jackson say, 'if you know what I know about the CIA,'" a McCarthy friend says. "That's what first got him interested in the CIA."

In what was becoming a pattern for McCarthy, he was again active in the 1956 presidential campaign. He backed Humphrey's futile bid for the vice presidential nomination and spent a half an hour trying to talk former President Truman into supporting Humphrey, but Truman declined. Active on behalf of the Stevenson-Kefauver ticket that fall, McCarthy called Vice President Nixon the "vital issue" in the campaign. He noted that newspaper stories reported that Nixon showed "great evidence of restraint and political maturity" during Eisenhower's recuperation from a heart attack, and quipped, "I don't know what they expected him to do. Certainly he didn't set off any firecrackers under the hospital bed."

McCarthy's own reelection to a fifth term was little more than a formality. He continued to receive strong backing from St. Paul's labor union members, who found little wrong with his voting record. (The AFL-CIO's *Machinist* magazine credited McCarthy with voting "right" from labor's point of view on every one of fifty-six key issues during his five House terms.)

Using his position on the steering committee that parceled out committee assignments to new members, McCarthy blocked Southerners' efforts to fill an important vacancy on the Education and Labor Committee with North Carolina's Alton Lennon, a strong segregationist, and helped give the seat to new Congressman George McGovern of South Dakota.

The former slick-fielding first baseman from the Great Soo League also demonstrated his prowess on the baseball field again in 1957. For the third straight year, he helped win the Congressional baseball game for the Democrats, pitching and hitting a single and triple in a 14 to 10 victory over the Republican team. (His exploits were recorded in a St. Paul newspaper under a photograph of McCarthy's head superimposed on Babe Ruth's body.)

The most impressive accomplishment of McCarthy's House career was not on the baseball diamond, however. It came during his last term as he welded together an informal coalition of Democrats to press the liberal viewpoint on major legislative issues. The coalition, later formally organized as the House Democratic Study Group, traces its origins back to the 1956 "Southern Manifesto," a denunciation of civil rights proposals signed by most Southern Democrats. McCarthy saw the need to counter the Southern statement as well as to improve on the poor legislative record of the previous

Congress, so he suggested to several colleagues that they draw up their own long-range legislative program.

One of those whom McCarthy approached was Frank Thompson, a freshman Democrat from New Jersey. "Gene said we're going to lose the presidential election this year but we'll keep control of the House and we ought to do some work in anticipation of what will probably be a mediocre Democratic platform," Thompson recalls. "So, at Gene's direction, a few of us got together during the election recess and after the election and put together a number of position papers. What we had amounted to a liberal legislative program which we called 'McCarthy's Manifesto.'"

When Missouri Democrat Richard Bolling heard of the document, he went to McCarthy and suggested it be shown to Speaker Rayburn as a courtesy before being released. Bolling, who was courting Rayburn's support for important pending civil rights legislation, says McCarthy gave him a copy which he then showed to Rayburn. "The old man looked it over and said he didn't disagree with anything in it," recalls Bolling. "But he said he couldn't possibly come out in support of it publicly because of the strong civil rights position it took."

Bolling went back to McCarthy. "I told him what Rayburn said and stressed that he absolutely didn't want anybody to know he supported it," Bolling recalled in 1971. "McCarthy made it very clear he understood. The very next day, one of Drew Pearson's legmen called me and had the story in detail. I called Pearson and asked him to do something I've never asked a newspaperman to do, to suppress a story. I explained that it could kill our chances of passing the civil rights bill and Pearson agreed not to print the story. I didn't ask Pearson how he got the story, but I didn't have to. There were only three people who knew about it — me, Rayburn and McCarthy. I've never forgiven McCarthy for that and I don't intend to. I never talked to him about anything serious after that because I never trusted him."

On January 8, 1957, twenty-eight Northern and Western Democrats led by McCarthy, Thompson and Lee Metcalf of Montana announced a liberal legislative program for the Eighty-fifth Congress. "The reaction to it was so spectacular," says Thompson, "that Gene began to get calls from other Democrats asking why the hell they weren't included." By the end of the month, eighty members from twenty-one states had signed a liberal "state of the union" message outlining major legislative goals. The group soon became known as "McCarthy's Mavericks," since most of its steering committee meetings were held in his office.[10] Operating on an informal basis during

[10] Some of the other popular nicknames applied to the group included "McCarthy's Marauders," "McCarthy's Mustangs" and the "McCarthy Group." There was a semblance of a formal liberal bloc in the House as early as 1935, founded by Texas Democrat Maury Maverick, grandson of the Texas rancher whose refusal to brand his cattle

1957 and 1958 the group developed a system of "whips" to alert members to be on the floor for important votes.

"Gene was an absolute goddamn genius at going in and making one-minute speeches that would articulate a complex issue or needle the bejeezus out of somebody," says Thompson. "His analysis of political situations, of parliamentary procedure, of motivations and tactics and issues and personalities was remarkable. I've never met anyone more brilliant and I've met a fantastic number of people."

The extreme informality and flexibility of "McCarthy's Mavericks" offers a good illustration of McCarthy's concept of political leadership. "We were trying to tighten up the group and to build around the edges of its strength," he said in explaining why he distributed a draft of the "Manifesto" for signatures. The steering committee consisted of anyone who attended the strategy sessions in McCarthy's office. Meetings were announced by word of mouth, and began whenever the chairman — usually McCarthy or whoever was best informed on the issue being discussed — felt there were enough people present. Decisions were never made on the basis of a vote but rather by getting a Quaker-like "sense of the meeting." It was an almost existential approach to political organization that McCarthy would follow throughout his later career and one which would baffle and dismay associates not familiar with it.

The Democratic Study Group would not be formally organized until 1959, the year after McCarthy went to the Senate, but he was instrumental in helping plan it, according to Metcalf, who served as first DSG chairman and followed McCarthy to the Senate two years later. "We all looked to Gene as our leader in those days," says Metcalf. Another DSG organizer, Wisconsin's Henry Reuss, took the floor to praise McCarthy when he announced his decision to run for the Senate. "Gene McCarthy has proved it is possible to have a vision without being a 'visionary'; to espouse sound doctrine without becoming doctrinaire, to be at the same time a thinker and a doer." (In the 1960's, the DSG would become an effective political force, leading an ultimately successful fight to reform the archaic rules and procedures of the House, and threatening the historic stranglehold of Southern conservatives on the levers of Congressional power.)

By late 1957, McCarthy found his attention being diverted increasingly from parliamentary intrigues to the upcoming Senate election in Minnesota the next fall. Republican incumbent Thye, a popular and respected former governor, was running for a third term and was considered a formidable opponent for any Democrat. In addition, there were several other possible candidates including Blatnik, Governor Freeman, Lieutenant Governor Rolvaag and Mrs. Eugenie Anderson, Minnesota's DFL national committee-

---

made the family name a synonym for anyone of outspoken independence. Maverick himself coined a colorful new word to describe unclear bureaucratic language — "gobbledygook." Maverick's liberals disbanded in 1938 after he was defeated for reelection.

woman who was appointed America's first woman ambassador in 1949. Finally, McCarthy was aware that Minnesota voters had never elected a Catholic to the Senate.[11] Nevertheless, he decided to run.

One of the first people to learn of McCarthy's decision was his old friend Raphael Thuente. Thuente remembers that McCarthy called him and asked him to accompany him to the southern Minnesota city of Albert Lea, where he was giving a speech in September of 1957. "We were driving along and suddenly he asked me if I had a subscription to *Time* magazine. I said, 'Yes, why?' He said, 'Did you ever hear of or see a representative being quoted?' I said I couldn't recall and he said, 'Do you recall reading the quotations of a senator?' And I said, 'Yes, senators are quite frequently quoted.' Then I looked at him and I said, 'Are you toying with the idea of running for the Senate, Gene?' And he said, 'I guess so, Rafe.' "

When other McCarthy friends heard he was thinking about running against Thye, they cautioned him against it. Joseph Gabler, who would manage his 1958 campaign, was typical of those who discouraged McCarthy from running. "He called me one night in the winter of 1957 to say he thought he was going to go," says Gabler. "I suppose it was one of the few times he ever asked me what I thought because he doesn't usually do that. If he does, you know he's made up his mind and he's using you to confirm the decision he's already made. Anyway, I sat down and wrote him a long letter explaining why he couldn't be elected. I told him religion was a terrible handicap, which it was, and that Thye was a hell of a man to fight — honest, a good solid Scandinavian ex-governor, and that Gene wasn't well known around the state. He kidded me about that later and I said, 'Well, good, after this I'll keep my opinions to myself.' I learned then that when he decides to do something, he generally knows more about it than anybody else." [12]

McCarthy had clearly had his eyes on the Senate for several years. He spoke enviously of the greater freedom senators enjoyed in a 1954 interview in which he was asked his opinion of Senator Joseph McCarthy. "After all, Joe McCarthy is a senator, and there isn't much you can do about the activities of an individual senator," he said. "There never has been any way to control

[11] Minnesota had a Catholic senator before, however. He was James Shields, a truly remarkable man who became the state's first senator when Minnesota was admitted to the Union in 1858. However, Shields was elected by the state legislature, a procedure followed until 1913, when the Seventeenth Amendment gave the election of senators to the people. The Irish-born Shields deserves a place as one of the most legendary figures in American history. He served as a senator from two other states — Illinois and California, was territorial governor of Oregon, a Supreme Court justice from Illinois, commissioner of the U.S. Land Office and once challenged Abraham Lincoln to a duel.

[12] McCarthy was encouraged by the election of Democrat William Proxmire in neighboring Wisconsin in August, 1957, to succeed the late Joseph McCarthy. Proxmire's victory was seen as a sign of a possible Democratic resurgence in the Midwest in 1958. Shortly after Proxmire's election, McCarthy told a friend, "The House is not a home. I will either go to the Senate or back to teaching."

them." He also discussed his concern over the decline of House prestige in a 1955 interview with John McDonald of the Minneapolis *Tribune,* noting that the Senate "has seized the leadership of foreign affairs . . . and has come to be accepted as a public forum."

That the forty-two year old McCarthy wanted a broader public forum for his views was borne out in an interview with Columnist Roscoe Drummond in early 1958. Asked by Drummond why a House member would give up a safe seat to run for the Senate, McCarthy said, "Great debates today are the Senate debates. As a result, public interest, at least as reflected in the press, is generally concentrated not on what is said in the House but simply on the outcome of the voting. To men who believe that an informed public is a necessary condition to effective democratic government, the fact that the Senate offers a forum in which what one says is likely to be heard or read not only by other senators but by people of one's own state, and in some measure by the people of the country, is also attractive." He also stressed the Senate's greater influence on domestic legislation, veto power over court nominees and other executive appointments and, above all, its role in formulating foreign policy.

McCarthy announced his plans to run for the Senate on February 1, 1958, causing the Washington *Evening Star* to comment, "There may be a new and different kind of McCarthy in the next session of Congress." In his ten years in the House, the *Star* added, "McCarthy has gained the reputation for serenely cleaving to his principles, no matter what the prevailing political winds."

But first, McCarthy had to get the DFL nomination, no easy feat considering the lineup of other likely candidates. He went first to the senior Democrat in the Minnesota delegation, John Blatnik, and told him he wanted to run but wouldn't if Blatnik did. "Gene made it perfectly clear that I had first crack at it," Blatnik recalls. "I wanted very much to run but all my friends said the same thing — 'We don't want to lose you,'" says Blatnik, who had twelve years of seniority in the House. "So Gene and I compared notes and I told him I just couldn't handle it. And I decided that because of his experience and his ability, that he ought to be a United States senator."

Blatnik's support proved to be crucially important in the May, 1958, state convention as Freeman and most state party leaders lined up behind Mrs. Anderson. In a fierce contest that left permanent scars on his relationship with Humphrey and Freeman, McCarthy was endorsed on the second ballot, with Blatnik and Gerald Heaney, the DFL national committeeman from Blatnik's district whom McCarthy would later recommend for a federal judgeship, instrumental in swinging uncommitted rural delegates behind McCarthy. McCarthy's victory, wrote one political reporter, "proved again that a good amateur rarely beats an old pro." Displaying a hitherto unsuspected knack for head-counting, McCarthy predicted he'd get 271½ of the required 300 votes on the first ballot. When the counting was finished, he had 271.2 votes, and went on to win on the next ballot.[13]

The 1958 endorsement fight also cleared up some other misconceptions arising from McCarthy's soft-spoken, professorial exterior. Angered because Mrs. Anderson's supporters raised the religion issue and suggested he was too lazy and not tough enough to be a good senator, McCarthy showed an element of ruthlessness that even some of his closest supporters hadn't been aware of. When a squabble developed over a picture-taking session at which Mrs. Anderson was present and McCarthy wasn't, Gabler called McCarthy at his hotel. "I told him the whole convention was in an uproar and that Eugenie was unhappy and hadn't meant to take advantage of him and that he should come over right away so they could take a picture of both of them," says Gabler. "He said, 'Let her wait. It's the first time she's heard the blood call of the Fourth District and it's good for her.' He didn't come down for an hour."

Gabler says that convention taught him that McCarthy is a dangerous opponent when backed into a corner or when he feels somebody has treated him unfairly. "I've told more than one guy, 'Don't ever put McCarthy in a position where he has to cut your throat, because he will and he'll do it without any compassion whatsoever.'"

Humphrey's neutrality during the endorsement fight irked McCarthy, and some people think the later split that occurred between the two men can be traced back to then. "I can't expect you to dislike anyone," McCarthy told Humphrey after the convention, "but can't you stay mad at them for at least two weeks?" Freeman says he and Humphrey were publicly neutral but he leaves little doubt that his personal choice was Mrs. Anderson. "I felt why take a chance of losing a sure House seat when we've got a good Senate candidate in a woman who was also a credit to the party." Bill Carlson has a more colorful and succinct comment on the role played by Humphrey and Freeman at the 1958 convention. "They both rode the fence so hard they've still got sores on their asses."

Nevertheless, once McCarthy was endorsed, Freeman got behind him. "Freeman did a hell of a job for McCarthy in 1958," says Robert Hess, the St. Paul labor union leader who was one of McCarthy's earliest supporters. Freeman is even more definite. "Frankly, McCarthy ran with me. I campaigned all over the state with him, I raised money for him, I got him entrée into Lutheran churches. I think I played a significant part in his winning."

---

[13] Mrs. Anderson was named U.S. representative on the United Nations Trusteeship Council in 1965 and resigned in 1968 to work in Humphrey's presidential campaign. It is doubtful that she would have been a peace candidate in 1968 had she been elected instead of McCarthy. Although she felt the U.S. was using the wrong tactics in Vietnam, she says she "agreed with the need to contain the Chinese Communists. I believed at that time that they were the aggressors. I believed that the U.S. had made a commitment and that it would be disastrous to walk away from it."

Humphrey loaned McCarthy staff and made several speaking tours for him. Also, because he was vice-chairman of the Senate Democratic Campaign Finance Committee, he saw to it that McCarthy received a generous campaign contribution.[14]

McCarthy ignored his own district to concentrate on areas where he was less well-known, and as a result gave minimal support to Joe Karth, who was running for his House seat. Karth has a vivid memory of what happened when he asked McCarthy to endorse him in the House race. "We asked Gene to make a strong endorsement statement and he finally gave us a statement to use on our campaign literature. I can remember every word of it: 'Looking forward to campaigning with you this fall.' "

Doubts about McCarthy's campaign zeal were expressed at the outset of his campaign. "Will he steel himself to the severe disciplines that drive the Freemans and Humphreys to shaking hands at 6:00 A.M. at factory gates and to talk on Main Street corners from dawn till dusk?" asked a Minnesota political reporter in June. "Will he find himself at home in muddy farmyards, and will his scholarly allusions and gentle satire fall on receptive ears in the rural areas?" McCarthy quickly put such doubts to rest, stumping the state tirelessly and disproving rural suspicions that he was an "egghead" professor who knew little about farm problems. Bob Hess says McCarthy was the best campaigner he ever saw. "He could see more people in less time than anyone I ever watched," Hess said in 1971. "He really came across to farmers and small town people. That's why I knew he'd do well in New Hampshire."

He overwhelmed his DFL opponent, former Governor Hjalmer Petersen, in the September primary, and went after the sixty-two year old Thye, who warned, "This young fellow is going to know he's been in a scrap." Thye decided the theme of the campaign by labeling McCarthy as a "big city congressman" who is a "johnny-come-lately" on farm issues. When Thye blasted him for belittling his bill to eradicate noxious weeds on farms, McCarthy promptly reminded voters of his own rural background, declaring, "I want him to know that I am opposed to noxious weeds and have been ever since I was a boy pulling mustard and cutting Canadian thistle with a hoe on my father's farm at Watkins in Meeker County." (McCarthy's fellow DSG organizer, Frank Thompson, later commented, "Gene used to say as near as he could understand, crab grass was the big issue that year.")

Actually, the big issue was not crab grass but crabby farmers. Rural discontent with Eisenhower farm policies was spelled out as the major issue in a pre-election survey by five New York *Times* reporters, and even though Thye tried to disassociate himself from those policies, McCarthy seldom

---

[14] According to Alwyn Matthews, an aide to Senator George Smathers, chairman of the Senate Democratic Campaign Finance Committee at the time, McCarthy received about $15,000 for his first Senate campaign, or "about what any good Senate prospect would get." However, Gabler believes that the figure was closer to $5,000.

missed a chance to remind voters that Thye had urged the Senate to confirm Eisenhower's highly unpopular Secretary of Agriculture Ezra Taft Benson.

A second and more indistinct issue which made the Thye–McCarthy contest a matter of national interest was religion. Many political experts doubted that a Catholic could win a statewide election in Minnesota, where 68 percent of the population was either Lutheran or other Protestant denominations. "If McCarthy can beat the able Senator Thye in Lutheran Minnesota, then it should be possible for a Catholic to be elected president," Columnist Drew Pearson wrote at the time, while another columnist, Doris Fleeson, observed that Senator John F. Kennedy of Massachusetts was among those "waiting hopefully in the wings while Minnesota counts its ballots." The election also was seen as important to Humphrey's prestige as a possible presidential candidate in 1960.

The religion issue was blunted somewhat by the fact that the Lutheran Thye was married to a Catholic. When a Lutheran minister wrote a letter to Twin Cities newspapers praising Thye as a humble man who always sat in the back pew of the church, McCarthy wisecracked, "He sits in the back pew so he can leave early to pick up his wife at the Catholic church." [15]

Minnesota Lutherans decided they liked McCarthy more than Thye and disliked Ezra Taft Benson more than Rome. McCarthy's good looks and witty style and his adroit use of the farm issue overcame any religious handicap as he defeated Thye, 608,847 votes to 535,629. His victory, observed St. Paul *Dispatch* Writer Fred Neumeier, "has eliminated religion as an issue in politics in Minnesota" and has paved the way for a Catholic to run for president in 1960 without fear that religion will be the main issue."

McCarthy's role in putting to rest the religious issue in Minnesota made him one of the state's "first effective political ecumenists," according to Walter Mondale, who would join McCarthy in the Senate in 1964. "It was difficult to put your finger on it, but there was always a profound gap — great suspicion, I thought — between Protestants and Catholics in the DFL," Mondale said in 1971. "It was a little bit like what divided the Farmer Labor Party and the Democrats. It seems like ancient history now because it isn't much of a problem anymore, but in those days it wasn't funny."

McCarthy took his seat in a Senate bristling with Democratic presidential hopefuls in January, 1959, as one of those hopefuls, senior Senator Humphrey, escorted him to the rostrum to be sworn in by Vice President Richard Nixon. McCarthy was looked on as one of the most promising of the fifteen new Democratic freshmen senators and, as Columnist Drew Pearson wrote,

[15] Polls taken before the election found that two-thirds of Minnesota's Catholics who planned to vote were on McCarthy's side while 54 percent of the non-Catholics favored Thye. However, the 1958 election followed almost the same pattern as the 1954 election when Catholics overwhelmingly voted for a non-Catholic Democrat, Humphrey, against a non-Catholic Republican. In general, religion yielded to party loyalty in both elections.

"a tough battle-seasoned House veteran who's sure to become a leader and wear no one's brand." But some people wondered if McCarthy made the right decision by giving up a bright future in the House to join a body notoriously slow to share its power with younger members. "His host of friends and admirers are holding their breath to see whether Eugene McCarthy will conquer the Senate or whether the Senate will engulf him," a *Wall Street Journal* reporter wrote at the time in an article entitled, "Will Success Spoil Gene McCarthy?" Columnist Charles Bartlett thought not. He wrote in March, "The new McCarthy is a man to watch . . . he is the sort of spokesman who can inject meaning and validity into a national climate that seems at times to be growing frivolous."

Named to the powerful Finance Committee — and to the less prestigious Public Works Committee as well — McCarthy was indeed conspicuous among the Senate's younger members. His leadership prospects were hailed in grandiose terms by Columnist William S. White, a close friend of Lyndon Johnson. White noted that McCarthy and two other junior members had gotten choice committee assignments — Idaho's Frank Church (Foreign Relations) and Wyoming's Gale McGee (Appropriations) — and declared, "No three men in history, so far as anybody can recall, have reached so much Senate power so soon. . . . Given normal life expectancy and political luck . . . these will be three names to reckon with in the Senate and in the country for decades to come."[16]

McCarthy's prospects became even brighter in September, 1959, when Johnson named him chairman of the newly-created Senate Special Committee on Unemployment Problems. The committee, while not empowered to draft legislation, was authorized to spend $100,000 to make a "full and complete investigation of unemployment conditions in the United States." Designating a first-year member as chairman was almost unheard of and caused some observers to ask what Johnson saw in the tall, reflective Minnesotan whose personal and political style were so different from his. "Lyndon thought that if he gave McCarthy Finance and then the chairmanship of his own committee that this would make Gene his friend for life," a person close to both men commented later.

That relationship started off on a sour note, thanks to McCarthy's unbridled wit. Campaigning in International Falls, Minnesota, shortly before the election, he told a labor union audience that the election of liberals like himself to the Senate would help steer Johnson along a more liberal path as majority leader. "Lyndon doesn't lean with the wind, he leans ahead of it," McCarthy wisecracked. The remark got into the newspapers and, after the

[16] Later events would place White's prediction in an ironic light. He himself bitterly attacked McCarthy for challenging Johnson as an antiwar candidate in 1967-68, while Church was one of those who declined to run against Johnson before McCarthy decided to. McGee, also one of Johnson's staunchest defenders, took McCarthy's seat on the Foreign Relations Committee when he resigned from the committee in 1969.

election, back to Johnson, who failed to see the humor in it. He called House Speaker Rayburn, who counted McCarthy among his protégés and had recommended him for the Finance Committee, and told him to advise McCarthy that such irreverent remarks would not help him in the Senate.

McCarthy also opposed Johnson on the first big fight of the Eighty-sixth Congress, the biennial liberal attempt to revise Senate Rule XXII to make it easier to invoke cloture (the forcible ending of debate) on civil rights bills. The vote came before the committee assignments were made, but McCarthy still got named to the Finance Committee even though several freshmen who opposed Johnson, including Maine's Edmund Muskie, were banished to lesser committees. (Indiana's Vance Hartke, the only other freshman Democrat named to Finance, voted with Johnson on cloture.)

Johnson's solicitous treatment of McCarthy on the matter of committee assignments later gave rise to the impression that McCarthy and Johnson were friendly from the beginning of McCarthy's Senate career. McCarthy would later come to have a grudging respect for Johnson's leadership abilities, but he wasn't particularly fond of the hard-driving Texan. "I don't think their relationship was ever very warm," says Clinton (Dick) Boo, McCarthy's administrative assistant at the time. "Gene never liked Lyndon's personal style, all those overwhelming mannerisms like sticking his face in yours when he talked to you. He thought Lyndon's passing out those gifts with 'LBJ' on them was sort of corny, too."

McCarthy learned another painful lesson soon after he arrived in the Senate. During the two-week debate on the House-passed Landrum-Griffin labor reform bill in April, he understood he had a commitment from the bill's floor manager, John Kennedy, and numerous other Democrats for their support on an amendment prohibiting the use of union funds for legal fees to defend union officials accused of violating the bill's provisions. But when the amendment came up for a vote, it was condemned by John McClellan of Arkansas, the chairman of the Labor Rackets Committee whose investigations of labor union mismanagement were largely responsible for the public indignation that led to passage of the Landrum-Griffin bill.

As the result of McClellan's attack on his amendment, McCarthy lost all the votes he'd lined up beforehand and was defeated by a humiliating 7–85 vote. It was the worst defeat McCarthy would ever suffer in Congress, and he never forgot that Kennedy and others had deserted him after giving their pledge of support. When McCarthy walked off the floor with his legislative assistant, Emerson Hynes, he met Kennedy standing outside the Senate chamber with Douglas and several other senators whose votes he'd counted on. Turning to Hynes, McCarthy said coldly and in a voice loud enough to be heard by Kennedy, "Well, I've learned one lesson about the Senate today. In the House, when you give your word, it's good. Over here, it means nothing."

The incident confirmed McCarthy's suspicion, which he'd held since serving with Kennedy in the House, that the Massachusetts Democrat would sacrifice principle for political expediency if necessary. It also marked the real starting point of the long feud with the Kennedy family that was to become an important fact of McCarthy's political life. Since that day, McCarthy later told a reporter, "I've had my guard up against the Kennedys."

The Senate's veto power over presidential appointments was one of the reasons he said he wanted to go to the Senate, and he quickly exercised that power by registering one of the first protests against the confirmation of Admiral Lewis Strauss as Secretary of Commerce. In his statement opposing Strauss, McCarthy revealed the concern with the balance of power among separate branches of the government that was to be a dominant theme of his Senate career. He charged that Strauss carried executive secrecy "beyond reasonable limits" while chairman of the Atomic Energy Commission and he questioned whether Strauss "recognizes the Congress as a policymaking branch of the government."

McCarthy also sounded a warning — that later would be repeated by President Eisenhower in his farewell address — when he told the Women's National Democratic Club in Washington that Strauss was typical of the high officials of the Eisenhower administration. "These are men with non-political backgrounds, and the procedures of the military and big business cannot be said to be wholly democratic. . . ." A year and a half later when Eisenhower warned of the dangers of a "military-industrial complex" in his farewell address and the Republican Congressional leadership failed to place the speech in the *Congressional Record,* McCarthy corrected the oversight, calling it "one of the most thoughtful and important speeches" of Eisenhower's career. (The famous phrase "military-industrial complex" was coined by Eisenhower speechwriter Malcolm Moos, now president of the University of Minnesota.)

When the Senate rejected Strauss' nomination in June, McCarthy was given a share of the credit for laying the philosophical base for the action. It was his first notable accomplishment in the Senate and emphasized his overriding concern for limiting the power of the executive branch, a concern that would lead him to a historic decision some eight and a half years later.

McCarthy's first year in the Senate was capped by his appointment as chairman of the nine-man Special Committee on Unemployment Problems in September. The committee was created by a resolution pushed through the Senate by Johnson as a favor to organized labor after the House failed to act on a similar bill approved by the Senate. McCarthy's selection as chairman was interpreted as both a reward for his longtime advocacy of organized labor and farmworkers and a not-too-subtle bid by Johnson for his support if it was needed at the 1960 Democratic National Convention.

The committee was a milestone in McCarthy's Senate career. From it would come some of his most positive contributions in the legislative field. It held hearings in 12 states and the District of Columbia in the fall of 1959 and winter of 1960 and took testimony from 538 witnesses. Its findings, contained in a 4,000-page report published in March, 1960, outlined the architectural blueprint for many of the economic development and social welfare programs of both the New Frontier and the Great Society. The report proposed a twelve-step plan to alleviate unemployment problems and warned that "after each of the last three recessions the rate of unemployment was higher than before the recession."

The committee's findings were cited by McCarthy and his supporters during his 1968 presidential campaign in reply to criticism that he had a lackluster legislative record. McCarthy told the *National Catholic Reporter* in March, 1968, that the committee's recommendations were "basic to the whole Great Society program." His claim was backed up in a letter to the same newspaper a month later by Francis X. Gannon, a Washington labor union official who followed the committee's hearings as research director for the Eastern Conference of the Teamsters Union.

"I have scant personal sympathy for the Senator's present position on Vietnam," Gannon concluded.

> Yet I believe we should not ignore his central contributions to our domestic well-being. If John F. Kennedy succeeded in 1960 in riveting attention on national unemployment and welfare problems, and if Lyndon B. Johnson pressured Congress in 1965–66 to act on these problems, we ought not to overlook that the Kennedy-Johnson contributions were made within a national framework which, if not fully created by, was dramatically developed and publicized by the McCarthy committee.

More objective observers point out that many of the committee's proposals were not original ideas and that McCarthy was not instrumental in securing their passage, but they admit that President Kennedy incorporated many of the recommendations — even using the same language in some cases — in his domestic legislative proposals. And they concede that the committee was responsible for establishing the permanent Senate Subcommittee on Manpower and Employment, which shaped the anti-poverty program sought by Kennedy and passed under Johnson.[17]

"The claims may be a little puffed up, but if you look beyond the political rhetoric, I think they're not too untoward," says Samuel Merrick, an official of the U.S. Conference of Mayors who served as counsel to the McCarthy committee and later as Congressional liaison officer for the Labor Department in the Kennedy-Johnson years. "Without question, the Subcommittee on Manpower and Employment and the 1962 Manpower Development and

---

[17] Now known as the Subcommittee on Employment, Manpower and Poverty, it is headed by Wisconsin Democrat Gaylord Nelson, who succeeded the first chairman, Pennsylvania Democrat Joseph Clark, after Clark's defeat in 1966.

Training Act came into existence because of that committee. Those two things by themselves are significant accomplishments."

Merrick, who traveled with the subcommittee on most of its out-of-town hearings, recalls that McCarthy "was a very hard-working chairman. He and certainly the major staff people involved wanted to show what the Democrats would do if they got into office." According to Merrick, McCarthy was both very careful and very pragmatic when it came to preparing the committee's report. He brought in academic experts in the unemployment field on a fee basis to analyze the committee's findings and help write the report. "At that time, this was an unusual procedure and as a result, we turned out a very high quality report." But McCarthy also was "pretty conservative in the arguments about what should go into the report. I think he was dealing strictly with what was possible rather than in terms of some high principle or trying to meet some liberal goals."

As his first year in the Senate drew to a close, McCarthy again found himself involved in Humphrey's presidential aspirations, as he had been in 1952 and 1956. He agreed to serve as co-chairman of a "Humphrey for President" committee and now was ready to help Humphrey make his bid for the 1960 Democratic presidential nomination against a field that included Kennedy, Johnson, Adlai Stevenson and Senator Stuart Symington of Missouri. However, McCarthy apparently felt the best-qualified candidate wasn't running.

"Why don't they just nominate me?" McCarthy was quoted in *Time* magazine in November, 1959. "I'm twice as liberal as Humphrey, twice as Catholic as Kennedy and twice as smart as Symington." McCarthy later wrote a letter to *Time* denying the quote, but it was a familiar line to his friends and members of his staff. "He was using that line around the office a long time before it appeared in *Time*," Dick Boo recalls. "He always enjoyed taking potshots at anybody who moved up in the limelight."

CHAPTER VIII

COLLABORATION — 1960

He is the best qualified candidate among the
leaders of our party.
> Eugene McCarthy announcing the
> formation of a "Humphrey for
> President" committee: July 13, 1959.

I am no longer a candidate for the Democratic
presidential nomination . . .
> Hubert Humphrey, after losing the
> West Virginia primary: May 11, 1960.

Hubert Humphrey had launched his first presidential campaign from the steps of the Kremlin in December, 1958, but he chose a more traditional setting to become the first formal candidate for president in 1960.

Standing before eighty reporters in the Appropriations Committee hearing room of the New Senate Office Building on December 30, 1959, the forty-eight year old Humphrey enthusiastically performed the time-honored ritual of throwing his hat in the ring. He proclaimed himself the candidate of the "plain people of the country," and willingly embraced the role of the underdog. In words intended to draw the contrast between himself and the wealthy John F. Kennedy — who announced his candidacy three days later — Humphrey said he would run as the candidate of people like himself who "are of modest origin and limited financial means — who lack the power or the influence to fully control their own destiny."

Humphrey, who had been campaigning ever since his marathon visit with Nikita Khrushchev suddenly projected him into the national limelight, announced his candidacy in an eight hundred word statement that he laboriously prepared himself. He clearly had no illusions about his quest for the nomination. "It will be an uphill fight," he declared — but he also left no

135

doubt that he relished the thought of that fight. "I like politics!" he exclaimed with characteristic exuberance as he answered questions about his candidacy for thirty-five minutes. "There's nothing that I enjoy more than campaigning — anywhere."

In the twelve months prior to his announcement, Humphrey had crisscrossed the country, answering speaking invitations that poured into his office at the rate of as many as a hundred a week after his return from Moscow. He had reorganized his staff, carefully charted the political terrain of a half-dozen states whose presidential primaries he considered important, and allowed his fellow Minnesotans, Senator Eugene McCarthy and Governor Orville Freeman, to form a 'Humphrey for President' committee to raise funds and generate support for his candidacy.

Humphrey's announcement was the logical culmination of his longtime pursuit of political power. Although he seemed genuinely awed by the thought of actually becoming president ("God no," he said when asked if he thought he should be president. "I should be back in Huron running the drugstore"), the White House had long fascinated him. Even as mayor of Minneapolis in the 1940's, Humphrey and his closest advisers thought it not preposterous to talk about whom they would have in a Humphrey Cabinet. In 1948, before he led the bitter civil rights fight at the Democratic National Convention, Humphrey had sent three associates — Mrs. Eugenie Anderson, James Loeb and Joseph Rauh Jr. — to Hyde Park, New York, to sound out Mrs. Eleanor Roosevelt about the possibility of his running for the vice presidential nomination. In 1952, he toyed with the idea of running for president and was briefly considered for the vice presidential nomination by Adlai Stevenson. And in 1956, Humphrey thought until the last minute that he was going to be Stevenson's running mate.

Now, however, Humphrey could point to twelve productive, and at times spectacular years in the Senate. His brilliant legislative record and powerful personality had made him a leading spokesmen among liberal Democratic senators, and unlike some of his unrealistically premature reaches for higher office in past years, he was now ready to make his move. Mrs. Roosevelt had recognized his new stature and future promise a year earlier when she said that Humphrey came closest among three potential Democratic candidates — Adlai Stevenson and Senator John Kennedy were the others — to having "the spark of greatness" needed in the White House.

Events, too, had moved in Humphrey's favor. His Khrushchev visit came on the heels of the defeat of Governor Averill Harriman of New York and a disappointingly narrow victory by Governor G. Mennen Williams of Michigan, both of whom were looked on as leaders who would promote the liberal viewpoint for the 1960 party platform and presidential nominee. Then there was the strong showing of liberal Democrats in the 1958 Congressional elections and the prospect of a further cyclical swing away from the Republican party in 1960. And finally, there was abundant evidence that many of Adlai Stevenson's supporters now looked on Humphrey as the heir apparent to the twice-defeated presidential nominee, although some politicians saw Humphrey as a stalking horse to keep anyone from sewing up the nomination and give Stevenson a third chance at it. Humphrey's advisers recognized this danger and accepted it as a necessary risk. "It's a question of who ends up using whom," one of his strategists said as Humphrey campaigned on the West Coast in April, 1959. "We just have to assume the Stevenson people will at some point give up waiting for Adlai and that they'll come to us then."

Humphrey occupied a position of strategic importance in the polite but deadly serious preliminary competition for the 1960 nomination. Of five major contenders, only he and John Kennedy were actively campaigning in the eighteen months prior to the convention. Therefore, the force of circumstance made Humphrey the agent of the other less active contenders — Stevenson, Senator Lyndon Johnson of Texas and Senator Stuart Symington of Missouri — in slowing the fast-running Kennedy and increasing the chances that the convention would require more than one ballot to select a nominee.[1] Clearly the most liberal of the Democratic hopefuls, he proudly called himself a "New Deal and a Fair Deal Democrat." He offered many Democrats the best hope of steering the party on a liberal path in 1960. "The Democrats must be a liberal party," he declared on one of his many exploratory trips in 1959. "If this is going to be a Tweedledum and Tweedledee affair, we are going to be Tweedledeed right out of a victory we richly deserve."

As events propelled Humphrey toward a showdown with Kennedy — the first of many of his battles with the family that would dominate American politics in the 1960's — the exposure that made Humphrey a serious contender also highlighted his liabilities. Although he sought to present a more serious face to counter his image as a glib radical, he still was unable to solve the problem of talking too much. He spoke for seventy-five minutes in Richland, Washington, one night and completely lost his audience. The next night in Eugene, Oregon, he promised his staff he would be brief and he was — he only spoke for forty-five minutes.

Hand-in-hand with the problem of talking too much was the more tangible problem of Humphrey's appearance. His high forehead, darting eyes, snapping month and slightly bulky figure made him look smaller than his 5' 11" height, and caused some political pundits to question whether he looked like a president, a question never directed toward the younger, taller and more handsome Kennedy. By coincidence, two national magazines hit the news-

[1] Humphrey also was the only non-millionaire among the five leading Democratic candidates, a fact that would be forcefully and painfully driven home for him during the 1960 primaries.

stands in May concerning Humphrey's physical stature. *Life* quoted former President Truman as saying Humphrey didn't have "the bearing of a presidential candidate," which prompted Eugene McCarthy to come to Humphrey's defense. "These are strange remarks for Mr. Truman to make," McCarthy said, "since exactly these points about his bearing . . . were made against Mr. Truman himself in the 1948 campaign." And when Humphrey saw an article written by Walter T. Ridder, Washington bureau chief of Ridder Publications, Inc., in the *Saturday Evening Post* saying that Humphrey "just doesn't look like a president," he snorted, "What can a guy mean by a statement like that? What a man does and what he thinks is more important than how he looks. The one who looked most like a president was Harding. And the man who looked least like one was Lincoln." [2]

Nevertheless, by mid-1959, it was becoming apparent that Humphrey was indeed a serious contender, whether he looked like one or not. His candidacy first began to take a definite shape after James Rowe, Jr., a Washington attorney and intimate of Lyndon Johnson, volunteered to help Humphrey. Rowe, a big, square-jawed man whose faithful adherence to the New Deal philosophy was matched by his understanding of the realities of power politics, was the first to analyze Humphrey's presidential prospects in cold, critical detail. He did it in a June 13 memorandum that served as the blueprint for Humphrey's 1960 campaign.

In the twenty-five page memorandum, entitled "The Strategy of Hubert Humphrey," Rowe pointed out that the only route open to Humphrey if he hoped to have even an outside chance at the nomination was through the presidential primaries. He warned that the primary path was politically risky, physically exhausting and exorbitantly expensive, and even if he did well, he still might not win the nomination. But, Rowe added, "He has *no* chance whatsoever if he does not take this stern and bloody path."

Only the primaries, Rowe argued, could give Humphrey the two essential things he needed — prolonged national exposure and the image of a winner. Without these, Humphrey could not possibly hope to compel the attention of the small group of power brokers who above all wanted a winner and regarded Humphrey as a divisive candidate who would be unacceptable to the South. Humphrey's strategy was then, in Rowe's view, to enter several carefully selected primaries, win them, and come into the Los Angeles convention with a minimum of 150 to 200 votes. This would be enough to at least establish a bargaining base with the power brokers, give him a major voice at the convention and possibly put him in serious contention for the nomination.

As for the crucial question of which primaries to enter, Rowe suggested

---

[2] When McCarthy saw Ridder's article describing Humphrey as "the last candidate in the tradition of the old frontier," he commented, "Hubert might have been on the frontier, but if he was, he'd have been selling axes instead of using them."

three where Humphrey's "secret weapon" — his own formidable campaign style — might be most effective. They were the District of Columbia, important largely because of its propaganda value with its large Negro vote, and Oregon and Wisconsin, two states whose social and political climate were not unlike Minnesota's. Several other primaries, including those in West Virginia and Humphrey's home state of South Dakota, were suggested to test Humphrey's voter appeal on a nationwide basis. But from the outset, it was clear to the Humphrey strategists that the first major battleground probably would be Minnesota's next-door neighbor Wisconsin, where the campaign could be waged at minimum expense, an important factor for Humphrey. "It is woefully apparent that the Humphrey forces will always be seriously under-financed right from the beginning [and] will be out-spent at least five-to-one by any other candidate who enters," Rowe stated. The Rowe memorandum can be considered an important document in Humphrey's political development, not only because of its coldly dispassionate analysis of his assets and liabilities, but also because it helped him understand for the first time the harsh realities of the process by which presidential nominees are chosen. The insights he gained from it and the lessons he would learn during the 1960 campaign would be evident eight years later in Humphrey's attitude toward the primaries and in his behavior during the convention that finally nominated him. As Rowe said:

> This memorandum holds no brief for presidential primaries. The truism is correct they have defeated many candidates and have never, by themselves, insured the winner the nomination.
> One of the most serious of the many strategic mistakes of Adlai Stevenson in 1956 was to enter any primaries at all since there was no real compulsion on him even though his advisers thought so at the time. He would have been nominated more easily without participation in them — by the same small group of professionals who may well make the nomination in 1960.
> Primaries are physically exhausting to everyone, just as they exhausted Stevenson and Kefauver and ruined them for intelligent post-convention campaigning. They are "chancy" and unrepresentative. . . . They are exorbitantly expensive. . . . Nothing is more risky, more uncontrollable by the candidate and his adherents, more uncertain.

Rowe's memorandum also left little doubt in Humphrey's mind whose support he had to win in the coming months. Rowe argued in effect that a handful of "organization professionals" controlling key states such as New York, New Jersey, Pennsylvania, Ohio, Michigan, Illinois, Texas and New Jersey would gather privately during the convention and decide on the nominee. These power brokers were generally more conservative than the voters and unfriendly to Humphrey, said Rowe. But he added:

> These men do not operate as individuals. They are essentially catalysts — catalysts who remain in power by reflecting accurately the moods and de-

sires of their constituents. Their constituents happen to be minor organization politicians but these in turn often reflect accurately the mood of the voters. These moods are, in turn, affected by the actions of the candidates. So the 'professionals' — like other politicians — are subject to political pressures from below.

Rowe's plan of strategy was translated into action for the first time on the afternoon and evening of June 11, when Humphrey met with several of his most trusted Minnesota advisers and friends in the aging Spaulding Hotel in Duluth. Humphrey, in the Lake Superior port for a ceremony marking the opening of the Saint Lawrence Seaway, was joined in his suite by his wife Muriel, Senator McCarthy, Governor Orville Freeman, Congressmen John Blatnik and Joseph Karth, DFL leaders Gerald Heaney, Ray Hemenway and William Kubicek, and Herbert Waters, Humphrey's top political aide and the only non-Minnesotan present.

Although there was a division of opinion between the Washington-based participants, who were reluctant to turn over control of the campaign to the state party, and Freeman and the DFL officials, who felt that Humphrey's campaign could be successfully waged as an expanded version of a Minnesota campaign, the group basically agreed it was necessary to begin immediately to raise money and round up support in neighboring states without forcing Humphrey to commit himself irrevocably to running.

Two days later, McCarthy held a news conference in his Senate office. Linked with Freeman by long distance telephone from St. Paul, he announced the formation of a "Humphrey for President" committee, with him and Freeman serving as co-chairmen and Lieutenant Governor Karl Rolvaag directing day-to-day operations from a St. Paul headquarters. McCarthy, who had sounded the strongest "stop Kennedy" sentiments at the Duluth meeting, denied that Humphrey's tentative campaign was a "stop Kennedy movement." However, he singled out Kennedy as Humphrey's principal opponent and managed to call attention to the advantage that Kennedy's family wealth gave him. "I might be mean," McCarthy replied when asked how Humphrey would finance his campaign, "and point out that it will not be financed by his father."

Humphrey immediately expressed surprise at the unveiling of his pre-campaign organization, but both the McCarthy-Freeman announcement and his own reaction were fully in accord with Rowe's advice that "the first foot forward in a quest for the presidency must always be from and by the candidate's home state" and "Humphrey should make no reply at this time . . . other than to say he is flattered." Said Humphrey, just back from two days of campaigning in California, "I'm pleased and grateful." Columnist Joseph Alsop saw the announcement in a different light. "With all the shy hesitation of a moose in the rutting season, the presidential candidacy of Hubert

Humphrey has now crashed out of the secret glades into the open glare of day."

Although the die had now been cast for Humphrey's candidacy, he still remained cautious and hesitant about officially entering the race. He recalled his humiliating experience with Stevenson in 1956, fretted about fund-raising problems, and worried that his involvement in the fight over the presidential nomination might endanger his Senate seat, which was also at stake in 1960. The night after his campaign committee was announced, Humphrey spoke at an NAACP dinner in New York City and was introduced as "the John the Baptist" of the civil rights movement. "You may recall what happened to John the Baptist," he quipped.

Humphrey was not inclined to play John the Baptist again to Stevenson, Kennedy or anyone else in 1960. He spent the rest of the year carefully testing his support around the country and scrupulously tending to his Senate duties, much to the dismay of Rowe, who threatened to quit unless Humphrey decided to run all-out. Finally, in December, Humphrey made up his mind. An important factor in his decision was a trip to Texas and an overnight visit with Johnson at the LBJ Ranch on December 4. Humphrey spoke to a Texas Farmers Union convention in Fort Worth in the afternoon and flew to the ranch for dinner, where he talked over his plans with Johnson. Johnson, whose own campaign committee had been announced in October, told Humphrey that his Senate majority leader's duties would prevent him from entering any of the primaries, but he indicated that he still hoped to win the nomination at the convention if no one was able to win on the first or second ballots.

Johnson's interest in the nomination was more obvious the next day, according to Patrick O'Connor, a Minneapolis attorney and fund raiser for Humphrey who accompanied him to the ranch. O'Connor recalls that Johnson woke everyone up at 5:00 A.M. for breakfast and an early morning deer hunt. "He came into the bedroom carrying coffee and orange juice and a big wet towel to wipe our faces. We went down to breakfast, and Johnson took great pride in the fact that the honey came from the Johnson bees and the ham from the Johnson hogs and the eggs from the Johnson chickens. He waited until Hubert had a big mouthful of eggs, and then he said, 'Hubert, you going to do me out of the nomination?' Well, Hubert sat there chewing and thinking all the time, and then he said, 'Lyndon, you have all this. Let me have the nomination.' This was the first time Humphrey found out Johnson was really serious about the presidency."

Humphrey came away encouraged by his reception in Texas' big-money circles. After shooting two deer, he flew with Johnson to Houston for a lunch arranged by Texas oilmen J. R. Partin and Marlin Sandlin at the posh Houston Club. About a hundred leading Texas businessmen turned out, largely as a courtesy to Johnson, and gave Humphrey a standing ovation after a rousing thirty-five minute speech. "I'm glad the election isn't to-morrow — I might vote for him," one oil magnate commented afterwards.

The Texas trip convinced Humphrey that it was now only Kennedy whom he had to worry about in the primaries and, if he could defeat Kennedy, he would go into the convention with a good chance of winning. Returning to Washington, he sat down in mid-December with Rowe, aides Herb Waters and William Connell (a public relations specialist from the University of Minnesota who joined his staff in 1955), two close friends from the ADA, James Loeb and Joe Rauh, and Max Kampelman, a Washington attorney who had been an adviser and aide to Humphrey since their student days together in Minnesota. "We decided to go then," Humphrey later said. "But to be totally blunt about it, we decided to do it with a completely inadequate organization and inadequate money."

When Humphrey announced on December 30, he disclosed his hopes to a friend for a convention miracle that would give him the nomination. "If I can win in Wisconsin and just stay alive until July, and if Kennedy hasn't won all the primaries and no one comes in with a big edge, the cold-eyed boys looking around for someone who is as tough and energetic and as mean — if need be — as Nixon, they might just try me."

On January 6, in his first speech as a candidate, Humphrey unveiled his pre-convention strategy while waiting for that miracle. He would attack the Eisenhower-Nixon record of the past eight years and zero in on Kennedy's wealth. Appearing before a full house at the National Press Club, Humphrey warned that America would become a second class power if the Eisenhower-Nixon "age of complacency" continues. And he highlighted Kennedy's wealth — and his own position as the poor man's candidate — by pointing out there were no limits to what Kennedy could spend of his own money in the primaries — "and I want to set the record straight on that right now," he declared.

Humphrey compared his campaign with "a corner grocer running against a chain store," but it was more than Kennedy's money that proved to be the decisive factor in Wisconsin. Humphrey had waited too long to build a campaign organization, and had to rely chiefly on an amateurish band of Minnesota volunteers who tried to run the campaign by telephone and weekend forays across the border.

The Humphrey organization was troubled by factionalism — just as it would be when he ran for president eight years later — with a conservative element headed by Rowe often disagreeing with liberals represented by former ADA chairman Joe Rauh. Humphrey himself was aware of his organizational difficulties. After the Wisconsin primary, he would comment, "What I need now more than anything is a good political boss. That's what I'm still looking for, somebody who could really run things and put every-thing together."

Humphrey also failed to capitalize on his image as Wisconsin's "third senator" and to draw a definite ideological line between himself and Kennedy, whose voting record was less appealing to Wisconsin's farmers and labor union members. Unable to entice Kennedy into a debate, Humphrey circulated pamphlets showing their respective voting records and called Kennedy "soft on Nixon." Waving a pamphlet at a March rally, he said, "I hate to do this, but I'm tired of hearing that there's no difference between the two candidates."

In another campaign speech, Humphrey declared, "I didn't come to Wisconsin to see if I could be the most pleasing man in the world. I came here to talk about public policy, public records and public purpose. We're in politics. We're not making love." He said if it was true that there wasn't any difference between him and Kennedy, "Then I ought to win because I'm older and have had more experience."

There were important differences between the two candidates, however, particularly in style. To many voters, Humphrey was "the embodiment of the New Deal" — as he was introduced at a Green Bay luncheon — while Kennedy symbolized the "new look" appeal and the promise of the new decade. Humphrey's physical appearance and strident oratory contrasted poorly with the youthful good looks and cultured Harvard accent of the forty-three year old Kennedy, whose glamorous family and Ivy League helpers swarmed over the state. The well-heeled, disciplined Kennedy organization had been preparing for the Wisconsin contest for months, and it succeeded in frustrating Humphrey's hopes of focusing on issues rather than personalities.

There was one issue that Kennedy couldn't avoid, however, and that was religion. It was an issue that would plague him throughout the year, and although both he and Humphrey sought to deemphasize it, the fact that about thirty-one percent of Wisconsin's population was Catholic like Kennedy made it too obvious to ignore. On an earlier trip to Wisconsin in 1959, Humphrey stressed that he had never made religion a campaign issue and he never would. "If you have to have campaigns based on bigotry, innuendo and smear, you can have your politics — I don't want any part of it," he told a press conference in Fond du Lac.

Humphrey had kept up a brave front through the closing days of the Wisconsin campaign, even though all the polls predicted that he probably would lose. He only hoped that he would not lose by an embarrassing margin, and when Kennedy won with 476,024 votes (56.5 percent) to his 336,753 (43.5 percent), he acted almost as if the figures were reversed. "The roof didn't fall in, the floor didn't collapse and we didn't make fools of ourselves," he said while pointing out that he'd won four of Wisconsin's ten Congressional districts and came close to winning a fifth. He claimed a "moral victory," and let it be known he felt a large crossover of Catholic Republicans to Kennedy had been responsible for his defeat.

Undaunted, Humphrey bounced into the lobby of his Milwaukee hotel after a round of television interviews on primary night and told well-wishers, "We're still in this fight." He had accurately read the results of the Wisconsin vote. He realized that the victory wasn't decisive enough to prove to the Democratic party's power brokers that Kennedy's Catholicism was no longer a handicap, and he knew Kennedy would have to face the issue head-on in the next primary on May 10 in West Virginia, a state with only a 5 percent Catholic population. Humphrey refused to quit, immediately announcing that he planned to carry on his campaign in West Virginia.

Although Humphrey's decision to contest the West Virginia primary would ultimately be a critically important factor in John Kennedy's drive to the nomination, the Kennedy camp interpreted it as a blatant stop-Kennedy move engineered by Johnson. Within a week after the Wisconsin primary, Humphrey was complaining of a Kennedy-backed pressure campaign to get him to withdraw. California's Governor Pat Brown telephoned Orville Freeman and asked him to persuade Humphrey not to go into West Virginia, and he was joined by Labor Leader Walter Reuther and other Kennedy supporters. When Robert Kennedy depicted Humphrey as a spoiler who could not be nominated or elected and whose only function was to create a deadlocked convention for Stevenson, Johnson or Symington, Humphrey's fighting instincts boiled over. "Jack will have plenty of chances to speak for himself without handouts through brother Bobby. Politics is a serious business, not a boys' game where you can pick up your ball and run home if things don't go according to your idea of who should win."

If, as Kennedy charged, Humphrey was acting in behalf of other presidential hopefuls, he was doing it without any visible help from them. He had spent an estimated $150,000 in Wisconsin, and when he went into West Virginia, his campaign was $17,000 in debt. "My cupboard is bare, my treasury is in the red and the only thing running good will be Hubert Humphrey himself," said Humphrey. "We are operating on Humphrey's energy and Humphrey's ability to campaign — and not on other people's money."[3]

Humphrey was confident he would do well in West Virginia. An economically depressed state with a heavy Protestant blue collar vote, West Virginia seemed ideally suited to Humphrey's folksy campaign style and solid record of support for federal social and economic aid programs. (He could point to an AFL-CIO study that showed he backed labor on 234 of 235 key votes in his Senate career.) The big Protestant vote seemed certain to work to his

[3] There definitely were some clandestine pro-Humphrey efforts by Johnson men in West Virginia, although Humphrey may have been unaware of them. Working through West Virginia Senator Robert Byrd, Johnson operatives were seen coming and going in Charleston in the final days of the campaign, and at least some Johnson money found its way into Humphrey's campaign coffers.

advantage and polls taken in April showed him well ahead of Kennedy. Although both candidates again tried to downplay the religion issue, the campaign soon degenerated into a bare-handed brawl against a backdrop of insinuation, innuendo and implication. The mud-slinging centered largely on the issues of Kennedy's spending and Humphrey's World War II draft record.

"I didn't expect it to become so bitter," Humphrey said after a Kennedy ally, Franklin Delano Roosevelt, Jr., came into the state and charged that Humphrey repeatedly sought deferment from military service while Kennedy was commanding a combat patrol boat in the South Pacific. "This is just cheap, lowdown, gutter politics." Kennedy was equally incensed by Humphrey's charges that he was "spending with wild abandon" and his statement at Kingwood, West Virginia, that "I can't afford to run throughout this state with a black suitcase and a checkbook." He had never been subjected to such personal abuse in fourteen years of public life, Kennedy complained two days before the election.

The bitterness of the exchanges even worried the two candidates' campaign managers. Humphrey's Herb Waters and Kennedy's Larry O'Brien held several late night meetings at the Charleston Press Club "to figure out how to keep our two tigers from tearing each other apart," says Waters. When Kennedy finally agreed to an hour-long televised debate on May 4, Waters and O'Brien got their candidates to agree not to attack each other. "We decided that the ground rules ought to be who could do a better job of nailing the Republicans to the mast instead of cutting each other up," Waters recalls. "Both principals agreed to this, but it was a rather tense moment when they came face to face because each didn't know if the other was going to break the rules." The debate came off pretty much as planned however, with the only personal note involving Kennedy's "stalking horse" charges against Humphrey. As a result, the debate was inconclusive and became a combined attack on the Republican administration. "The press was mad as hell because they lost the story of the conflict they expected, and the Republicans were screaming for equal time," Waters recalls.

That Kennedy's Catholicism remained a central issue was indisputable, however. He chose to attack it head-on through heavy use of television and even turned it into an advantage by making West Virginians think they could prove to the world that they were tolerant by voting for him. Humphrey, who had no desire to encourage intolerance, was powerless to discuss the religious issue without appearing intolerant himself, putting him in the ironic position of a victim of reverse bigotry.[4]

[4] Many of Humphrey's campaign helpers in West Virginia were Catholics, and they recall vividly the anti-Catholicism they ran into. St. Paul Mayor Joseph Dillon remembers going into one small town newspaper office and being introduced to the editor by Patrick O'Connor as "the St. Paul mayor who's here on behalf of Senator Hum-

Even more crippling to Humphrey was his lack of money. Deserted by organized labor, which wanted him out of the race, and heavily in debt from Wisconsin, he was forced to spend half his time calling friends to raise money to continue. But the Kennedy mercilessly cut off his flow of support, threatening Humphrey supporters with recriminations if they continued to contribute to his campaign.[5] A demoralized Humphrey gamely kept on barnstorming the state in a bus bearing the slogan, "Over the Hump with Humphrey," but the personal attacks, the exhausting schedule and the inability to raise money took a dreadful toll on him. A friend who had seen Humphrey in many times of crisis remembers the only time he ever saw Humphrey lose control of himself was in a Charleston hotel room several nights before the election. Humphrey needed several thousand dollars to purchase a half hour of statewide television for an election eve broadcast, and when Herb Waters told him flatly, "We don't have it and we can't get it," Humphrey blew up. "He said, 'Goddammit! We've got to get it!' " the friend recalls. "He chewed Herb out something awful. They were all so broken down with fatigue that Herb actually cried." Humphrey finally raised the money by dipping into his own bank account and making several desperation telephone calls to personal friends, but the program was poorly planned and the money was largely wasted.

West Virginia ended in a total, humiliating defeat for Humphrey. Two hours after the polls closed, it was obvious that Kennedy would sweep the state. Humphrey resisted the advice of Rowe — who undoubtedly wanted to help his old friend Lyndon Johnson — to put out a tough statement charging that Kennedy's victory had been achieved by extravagant expenditures, a claim for which there was ample justification. Instead, he put in a call to Donald Fraser, a young Minneapolis attorney whose cool, cerebral advice he valued and, after talking to Fraser for a few minutes, retired to the bedroom with Muriel to compose a gracious conciliatory statement of concession. When they came out, Humphrey walked through the rain to his headquarters a block and a half away and went before the waiting TV cameras to offer his congratulations to "my friend Jack Kennedy" for a "significant and clear-cut victory." Humphrey's voice broke momentarily and he stared hard at the paper in front of him, then continued to read: "I am no longer a candidate for the Democratic presidential nomination . . . ."

phrey." The editor, says Dillon, pointed to his head and his feet and said, "From the top of my head to the bottom of my feet, I'm a Protestant. You think I'm going to vote for that goddamn Catholic?"

[5] In *The Making of the President 1960*, Theodore H. White writes that Connecticut Governor Abraham Ribicoff, acting on John Kennedy's instructions, warned wealthy Stevenson liberals that if they continued to help Humphrey in West Virginia, Stevenson would not even be considered for secretary of state, a post he did not get anyway. White also says that Connecticut Democratic Party Chairman John Bailey threatened political retribution against one of Humphrey's top financial angels, former Connecticut Senator William Benton.

Humphrey offered no excuses for his loss. "When you're licked, you're licked," he told the Minneapolis *Tribune* in a telephone interview shortly after he conceded. "He got more votes than I did. I ought to be home. I'm going to be home for my daughter's wedding Saturday. I lost a primary and gained a son-in-law. I think I'm ahead."

Humphrey had lost much more than a primary, however. Kennedy's striking victory (he won 60.8 percent of the vote compared to Humphrey's 39.2 percent) shattered Humphrey's long-held hopes for the presidency, apparently eliminated him as a major influence at the 1960 Democratic convention and even cast his own reelection to the Senate in serious doubt. Nevertheless, after a few hours of sleep (a final woeful footnote was a parking ticket on his bus the next morning), Humphrey returned to the Senate and managed a tax bill through an all-afternoon debate. His remarkable display of resiliency prompted Estes Kefauver, who understood how it felt to have one's presidential ambitions dashed, to lead Humphrey's colleagues in a round of glowing tributes praising him as a gracious loser. "He lost the primary, but he has shown himself to be a man who can take defeat with grace and with a smile, and who can continue with his work in the Senate," Kefauver said.

Humphrey was indeed a gracious loser, but the West Virginia primary that had sent John Kennedy moving inexorably toward the presidency caused him to act in the next few months in a way that would have far-reaching consequences for the Democratic party and the nation. Humphrey's actions would pave the way for some of the most important decisions at the 1960 Democratic convention, project his old friends Gene McCarthy and Orville Freeman into overnight national prominence, and set Humphrey and McCarthy on an irrevocable course toward a later confrontation.

The motivating force behind Humphrey's post-primary actions lay in an uncharacteristic bitterness arising out of the West Virginia primary. The smear campaign based on his war record had cut so deeply into his normally all-forgiving nature — and Muriel's as well — that it forever colored his attitude toward the Kennedys. Although Humphrey later accepted John Kennedy's word that he had no prior knowledge of the personal attacks of Franklin Roosevelt, Jr., and would come to help and respect Kennedy as president, he never fully forgave either Roosevelt or Robert Kennedy, whom he held responsible for the attacks. Humphrey revealed the depth of his feelings about the draft issue in a 1971 interview with the author: [6]

HUMPHREY: It's a simple story — I simply wasn't accepted. Roosevelt knew that. I brought him into my office after the campaign and showed him those draft records. I said to him, "Frank, you know goddamn well that what you said isn't true." And Frank said, "I know that, but Bobby asked me to do it."

[6] For a more complete account of Humphrey's draft record, see chapter five.

Q: Did you forgive him for that?

HUMPHREY: Nope.

Q: That's the first time I've ever heard of someone whom you didn't forgive.

HUMPHREY: I did not forgive him for that because I thought it was unconscionable.

Q: Bobby or FDR, Jr.?

HUMPHREY: Both, but mostly FDR.

Q: He said Bobby asked him to do it?

HUMPHREY: Yes.

The West Virginia primary also helped make another enemy for the Kennedys who would embarrass them at the 1960 convention and become an adversary standing in the way of Robert Kennedy's presidential ambitions eight years later. Eugene McCarthy had never been an admirer of John Kennedy. He had served with him in the House and Senate, and was unimpressed with Kennedy's understanding of the legislative process and with his concept of the role of a Catholic in public office. But the ruthless tactics used against Humphrey in Wisconsin and West Virginia angered and deeply offended McCarthy and hardened his earlier disaffection with the Kennedys.

McCarthy first publicly took issue with Kennedy's views on religion and politics in 1959 when he wrote an article in the Catholic weekly magazine, *America.* He wrote it shortly after a national news magazine quoted Kennedy as saying, "Whatever one's religion in private life may be, for the officeholder nothing takes precedence over his oath to uphold the Constitution and all its parts — including the First Amendment and the strict separation of church and state."

McCarthy disagreed, writing:

> Although in a formal sense church and state can and should be kept separate, it is absurd to hold that religion and politics can be kept wholly apart when they meet in the consciousness of one man. If a man is religious — and if he is in politics — one fact will relate to the other if he is indeed a whole man.

McCarthy did not refer to Kennedy by name, but Kennedy saw the article and told a newsman he considered it a thinly disguised attack on him.

McCarthy definitely did not feel John Kennedy was the best presidential candidate the Democrats had to offer in 1960, as he would make clear to the nation at the convention. He publicly had indicated his feelings about Kennedy several times while campaigning for Humphrey in the primaries, and once, shortly before the Wisconsin primary, had a confrontation with Kennedy over Humphrey's criticism of Kennedy's farm voting record. Kennedy called McCarthy in his Senate office and asked if he could come to see him, but McCarthy suggested it would be less conspicuous if he came to Kennedy's office. When he returned, McCarthy described the meeting to an aide. "Do you know what he wanted?" asked McCarthy. "He told me to tell Hubert to 'lay off my farm voting record.' " McCarthy said he refused Kennedy's request and told him, "Jack, you've got looks, money and personality, and all Hubert's got is your voting record."

McCarthy's real feelings about Kennedy came to the surface most often in private. Mrs. Katie Louchheim, then vice-chairman of the Democratic National Committee, remembers sitting with McCarthy at a party dinner in Detroit, where he was standing in for Humphrey. Kennedy, sitting nearby, was being besieged by autograph seekers, causing McCarthy to comment, "Pay no attention. The meat is so bad they had to find something to distract them." Again, after hearing Kennedy quote history in an Albuquerque speech, McCarthy remarked, "All those years in the House, I never heard him quote history."

McCarthy made several appearances for Humphrey in Wisconsin, where his name was helpful among Catholic voters and those who confused him with the late Senator Joseph McCarthy. He found little reason for optimism, however, returning to Washington after one visit to tell a friend, "Every time I talk to a crowd, half the people are Kennedys or Kennedy relatives." McCarthy also compared Humphrey's low budget campaign with the Kennedys' lavishly financed operation. "I remember poor Hubert out there . . . running to catch the North Central DC-3 and then looking out on the field to see the *Caroline* waiting on the apron with the soup bubbling in the kitchen . . . ."

After Humphrey dropped out of contention, he made clear to John Kennedy that he felt he would win the nomination and said he would support him after the convention, but that because of his own reelection campaign coming up that fall, he could not afford to alienate Stevenson supporters in Minnesota by coming out for Kennedy before the convention. Kennedy, anxious to assure his nomination on the first ballot, then delegated his brother-in-law, Sargent Shriver, to find out whether McCarthy would help lead the Minnesota delegation into the Kennedy camp.

Shriver asked a mutual friend of Kennedy's and McCarthy's, Washington Newspaperman Walter T. Ridder, if he would sound out McCarthy for him.[7] Ridder recalls that McCarthy flatly refused to support Kennedy. "He didn't say why, but I gathered that he didn't think Kennedy had been a very good senator or a very good Catholic and that he just didn't like him personally," says Ridder. "So I went to Jack's office and told him he wasn't going to get any support from Gene. I was impressed by his totally practical response. He said, 'Well, you can't win 'em all.' From that point on, as far as I could see, Gene was dead with the Kennedys."

[7] Ridder, was until 1970, Washington bureau chief for Ridder Publications, Inc., which publishes fifteen daily newspapers in eight states, including McCarthy's hometown of St. Paul. He is one of the few newsmen who was personally close to Kennedy, McCarthy and Humphrey.

At about the same time, the Kennedys began to court Minnesota's Governor Freeman in hopes of persuading Humphrey to turn over Minnesota's 31 convention votes that were pledged to him as a favorite son, along with 36½ other votes Humphrey had picked up in the Wisconsin and District of Columbia primaries. Freeman, a blunt, brilliant, hard-driving ex-Marine, had molded the fractious Minnesota DFL into an effective political force during his six years as governor. But his prospects for a fourth term were dim in 1960, so he was receptive when Sargent Shriver and Theodore Sorenson came to Minneapolis to urge him to get on the Kennedy bandwagon early. Freeman talked with Shriver and Sorenson at his home until 4:00 A.M. following the DFL state convention in June and, although no promises were made by either side, it was clear that Freeman would reap rich political rewards if he delivered the Minnesota delegation to Kennedy.

Freeman had worked hard as co-chairman with McCarthy on the Humphrey campaign, but now that Humphrey was out of the race, he leaned toward supporting Stevenson, as he had in the two previous presidential campaigns. Freeman and his wife, Jane — an equally bright, tough-minded woman typical of Minnesota's activist political wives — went to see Stevenson one weekend at his Libertyville, Illinois, home. But dismayed by his indecisiveness, they decided that Kennedy should be the party's candidate. Freeman passed word to Kennedy that he would support him and do his best to swing the Minnesota delegation behind Kennedy.

Freeman's decision set the stage for a dazzling demonstration of Humphrey's political skills at the Democratic National Convention in Los Angeles. Humphrey felt Kennedy would win the nomination but he had never quite given up hope that Kennedy might be stopped. Humphrey also knew that there was strong support for Stevenson in the Minnesota delegation and any premature move away from Stevenson on his part could have disastrous consequences for party unity in Minnesota. Finally, Humphrey was determined to exert whatever influence he could on the convention and to gain some invaluable free publicity for his own reelection campaign and for Freeman's as well. "Orv wanted to come out early for Kennedy," a Humphrey aide relates, "but Hubert said, 'Once they've got you in their pocket, they'll ignore you. Let's keep Minnesota up in the air for a little while, and we might get some national attention for all of us.' "

Ironically, there is strong evidence that Humphrey's inability to overcome his bitterness from the West Virginia campaign cost him his chance to become Kennedy's vice president and, ultimately, president. Kennedy had been urged since West Virginia by several prominent liberals and leaders of organized labor to pick Humphrey as his running mate and had even discussed the subject at length with Humphrey shortly after West Virginia. "I wouldn't say Kennedy offered me the vice presidency," Humphrey recalled in 1971. "But he did come to my office and talk to me about it. My own view is that he was considering a lot of people. . . . It is a fact that both George Meany and Walter Reuther told me they were going to indicate to Kennedy that I ought to be his vice president. Particularly, Walter said this. And I think they did."

Whatever chance Humphrey had to be Kennedy's running mate was removed when Humphrey and his wife decided against it, however. "Muriel was still quite hurt by some of the things that had happened in the primaries," says Humphrey. "She's grown up on that since, but this was her first experience of this sort of thing and she was very upset. But that wasn't the sole reason for my decision. Frankly, I couldn't see the politics of it. I couldn't see why Kennedy would want me when we were both Northern liberals."

Nevertheless, the Kennedy camp did give serious consideration to inviting Humphrey on the ticket, even going so far as to designate Humphrey confidant Max Kampelman as a liaison to help plan a joint Kennedy-Humphrey staff session at Hyannisport after the convention. "There was no doubt in my mind or Humphrey's that Kennedy wanted him as his running mate," says Kampelman. Kampelman adds that when he met Humphrey's plane in Los Angeles three days before the convention opened on July 11, Humphrey took him aside and said, "Go back and tell our friends all signals are off — I'm not running for vice president."

"He never told me why, but my impression was it was because Muriel felt so hostile toward the Kennedys."

Even while Humphrey was passing the word that he didn't want to be Kennedy's running mate, Joseph Rauh, Jr., the ADA leader who had been one of Humphrey's most loyal supporters, was looking for Humphrey to persuade him to endorse Kennedy and make an all-out bid for the vice presidential nomination. Missing Humphrey at the Los Angeles airport because of the confusion, Rauh went to Humphrey's hotel, the Statler Hilton, and knocked on the door of his suite. There was no answer, but from inside he heard the unmistakeable sound of Humphrey's exuberant laughter. Just then, Pat O'Connor peeked out of the next doorway down the hall, and Rauh, recognizing him, started to walk through the door. Rauh was astounded when O'Connor tried to block him from entering and he swung at O'Connor. O'Connor swung back, hitting Rauh on the chin, and slammed the door in his face.

But Rauh had seen enough through the door to convince him that he had stumbled onto a secret stop-Kennedy meeting. Closeted with Humphrey were Lyndon Johnson, Texas Governor John Connally, and Jim Rowe, and Rauh immediately decided to drop his plan to put together a Kennedy-Humphrey ticket. "I think if Hubert wanted to, he could have been Kennedy's vice president," Rauh said later. "But he was too tied to Lyndon Johnson's coattails."

Some intriguing details on the two-hour secret meeting were supplied by Humphrey's old friend, Columnist Drew Pearson, the next day. Pearson quoted Humphrey as telling Johnson, "You're the only one who can beat Kennedy." He wrote that Humphrey expressed bitterness against Kennedy, reiterated his decision to concentrate on his Senate race ("Muriel is so fed up with all this that she'd divorce me if I ran for vice president"), and adamantly opposed any attempt by Freeman to swing the delegation to Kennedy even though Humphrey himself supported Kennedy's presidential bid. According to Pearson, Humphrey also gave Johnson some advice that would have untold consequences when he partially followed it four years later. "The man to run for vice president on your ticket is Gene McCarthy. He's the guy for you. But you've got to promote him. Tell some newspapermen about it. You've got to really publicize this."

Humphrey was just beginning to unfold his plan to make Kennedy pay the highest possible price for the support of the Minnesota delegation which, along with California's giant delegation (eighty-one votes) was the only major unknown in Kennedy's pre-balloting calculations. When Kennedy met with Freeman on Monday, the first day of the convention, and announced that Freeman was "very high" on his list of possible running mates, Freeman returned to the Minnesota delegation's caucus and begged Humphrey to help him deliver the delegation's votes to Kennedy. "I did everything you wanted," Freeman told Humphrey. "Now it's my turn." But privately, Freeman was disappointed because Kennedy had offered him only a seconding speech, and Humphrey counselled him to turn down Kennedy's offer. Humphrey did urge the delegation to endorse Freeman's vice presidential bid and released the delegates from their favorite son commitment, but he refused to ask them to vote for any one candidate.

That evening, Humphrey went to dinner with Pat O'Connor. "Muriel was tired so the two of us went alone," O'Connor remembers. "He said, 'Well, I guess I better give up the ghost and support Kennedy.' Herb Waters and I were fighting that and so was Gene so, afterwards, I got hold of Gene and told him Humphrey was starting to vacillate. The next morning, Gene came over to see Hubert and his approach was just beautiful. He said, 'Hubert, I understand you're going to throw in with the Kennedys. I think that's the right decision. I'll go to Kennedy with you and we'll kneel down and seek absolution together.' Then he said another thing. 'All those stories about Bobby bringing FDR, Jr., into West Virginia and calling you a slacker — they're totally unfounded.' Well, Humphrey really got upset and that swung him around completely. He never did give in."

Earlier, Humphrey had turned down a request to nominate Adlai Stevenson for president because he felt it would "look a little like sour grapes" and might also alienate the Kennedy supporters in the Minnesota delegation.

But when Freeman told him he'd been offered a seconding speech by Kennedy, he instructed aide Herb Waters to find Stevenson's three top strategists — Eleanor Roosevelt, Senator A. S. (Mike) Monroney of Oklahoma and Senator Herbert Lehman of New York — and tell them he wanted to see them.

Waters recalls that he brought the trio to a curtained-off room in the back of the convention hall, "and it very quickly got picked up by the Kennedy people. Humphrey was just using this for a cover, of course, and he told the Stevenson people, 'If you'll just hold out for a little while, I'll come out publicly for Stevenson, but I have one chore that has to be taken care of before that. I've got an idea about Stevenson's nomination.' And they agreed.

"While this was going on, Freeman got another call from Kennedy to come right on over. Kennedy had got reports that the Stevenson people were meeting with Humphrey, so he told Orv he'd offer him the nominating speech if Orv would get a commitment from Humphrey that he wouldn't nominate Stevenson. Orv came rushing back to Humphrey and he said, 'They've offered me the nominating speech. Will you promise not to nominate Stevenson?' God almighty, he was excited as hell! Humphrey says, 'Well, be careful now. They can still change their minds. You tell them that if they'll announce now that you have been selected to give the nominating speech, I will give my word that I will not nominate Stevenson. But I will not be bound by this pledge until I see on the news ticker that you're going to make the speech.'"

The next day (Tuesday) it was announced publicly that Freeman would nominate Kennedy, and Humphrey huddled with the three Stevenson leaders again that night. He said that since the Catholic Kennedy had picked a Minnesota Lutheran to nominate him, why didn't the Unitarian Stevenson pick a Minnesota Catholic to nominate him now that Stevenson had finally decided to run? "I told them that I thought Gene McCarthy was a good man to do it because I thought that Gene was fond of Adlai," Humphrey said later.

The Stevenson people were delighted with Humphrey's suggestion, even though McCarthy was not particularly close to Stevenson. McCarthy had spoken for Stevenson at a late night rally on the opening day of the convention and announced his support for him at the Minnesota caucus the next day. But he had permitted Senator Robert Kerr of Oklahoma — a powerful Johnson ally whom McCarthy had become friendly with — to announce at a news conference on the opening day of the convention that he was "all out for Lyndon Johnson." McCarthy said Kerr spoke without his clearance but he did not repudiate him. McCarthy later offered the lame explanation that he felt Johnson would make a better prime minister than president — meaning that there would be more restraints on his power under the British parliamentary system — and that he "doubted his ability to move the nation to new and different achievements." But not even his office staff knew which candidate he favored.[8]

When Monroney called McCarthy on Wednesday morning and asked him to make the Stevenson nominating speech — scheduled for only a few hours later — he asked for a brief time to consider. When Stevenson himself called a few minutes later, he accepted. McCarthy later said he felt there was little chance Stevenson could be nominated, but that the party owed it to Stevenson to round out his career with honor. He also was not unaware that this would be a rare opportunity for national exposure for himself.

McCarthy's decision to nominate Stevenson was also predicated, in part at least, on the fact that his fellow Minnesotan Freeman was scheduled to nominate Kennedy. When McCarthy encountered an aide, Miss Mary Naughton, in the lobby of his hotel Wednesday morning, he asked her if Freeman definitely was going to nominate Kennedy. "I said he was because I'd heard it on the radio," Miss Naughton recalls. "Then he said very quietly, and in a way that I knew he was serious, 'Find out for sure.'"

McCarthy was not entirely unprepared to make the Stevenson speech, according to Lawrence Merthan, his longtime friend from St. Paul who had left McCarthy's Senate staff earlier that year. Merthan, invited to McCarthy's hotel room while he worked on the speech, recalls that McCarthy said "he thought he just might be asked to give a speech so he brought his blue TV shirt. He wasn't a bit uptight. He said, 'We're going to have a lot of fun with this.'" Merthan sent McCarthy's suit — and Abigail's dress — out to be pressed and McCarthy, dressed in his tee shirt, socks and another pair of pants, discarded a speech that had been prepared for him and wrote the outline of a new speech on hotel stationery in about an hour.

When the clothes that had been sent out for pressing returned, McCarthy asked Merthan and Emerson Hynes, his legislative assistant, to accompany him and Abigail to the convention hall. Abigail and Hynes went inside while McCarthy retired with Merthan to Stevenson's trailer outside the hall to work over his speech. After an hour or so, McCarthy asked Merthan to get them something to eat, but all Merthan could find were several bottles of Coca Cola and some Chinese fortune cookies containing the message, "Stevenson will win."

When McCarthy finished typing his speech, he showed it to Merthan, who

---

[8] When an aide asked McCarthy before he left for Los Angeles whom he was supporting, he replied, "Hubert on the first ballot. That's for Minnesota. Stevenson on the second ballot. That's for the staff. And Jack Kennedy on the third ballot. That's for Joe." Stevenson wasn't spared from McCarthy's humor either. In 1956, when newspapers carried a photograph of Stevenson on a snowmobile that was stuck in an Oregon snowdrift, McCarthy told a friend, "If that isn't typical of Adlai — in the wrong place at the wrong time doing the wrong thing." In 1955 McCarhy showed little enthusiasm for a second Stevenson presidential candidacy. He told an interviewer, "There is a feeling that if Eisenhower runs again, there is no particular reason to name Stevenson to run against him again when he wasn't strong enough in 1952."

suggested only one change. "He'd written 'Do not turn your back on this man,' and I said that sounded too much like what Dean Acheson said about Alger Hiss," Merthan recalls. "I suggested he change it to 'Do not reject this man,' which he did. But the speech was pure McCarthy — he wrote it all. He kept working it over on the platform until he gave it, just like he does on all his speeches. When the press came to me for a text, I said, 'There is no text.'"

At 7:56 P.M., Kentucky's delegation yielded to McCarthy to put Stevenson's name in nomination. What followed was the most exciting convention oratory since Humphrey's civil rights speech of 1948. Although only about 1,200 words in length, the speech was packed with memorable phrases, all magnified by the ringing baritone of McCarthy's voice and the rare passion of his delivery. The man whose Senate speeches were so muted and scholarly that they could hardly be heard from the gallery was suddenly a man whose words were on fire, a velvet-tongued orator dramatically pleading with the convention to "strike off the fetters of instructed delegations" and to heed "this . . . man who talked sense to the American people."

The speech was unquestionably brilliant and moving, yet like the man who gave it, it was curiously restrained and even negative in thrust. It called on the delegates to nominate no one on the first ballot. It reminded them that Stevenson was one man who did not prophesy falsely, that he did not claim greatness or seek power for himself — an obvious reference to the Kennedys. Indeed, the climax of the speech was a crescendo of negative phrases, as though its emotional content or McCarthy's intellectual processes forced him to couch his praise of another man in a negative way: "And so I say to you Democrats here assembled: Do not turn away from this man . . . . Do not reject this man who made us all proud to be called Democrats. Do not reject this man who, his enemies said, spoke above the heads of the people, but they said it only because they didn't want the people to listen. He spoke to the people. He moved their minds and stirred their hearts, and this was what was objected to. Do not leave this prophet without honor in his own party. Do not reject this man."

The speech and the demonstration it touched were the high point of drama at the convention. It was a genuine display of emotion by Stevenson demonstrators who had packed the galleries and lasted twenty-five minutes.[9] But Stevenson's abortive bid for the nomination ended a few hours later as Kennedy won the nomination on the first ballot over his closest challenger, Johnson (Stevenson received only 79½ votes, far behind Kennedy's 806 and

[9] McCarthy received more than one thousand fan letters in the month following the speech, including a handwritten note from Switzerland from his chairman on the Senate Finance Committee, Harry F. Byrd, Sr., and another handwritten note from Supreme Court Justice William O. Douglas, who said, "I have never met you but I have long admired you. I thought your nominating speech tonight was one of the truly great public speeches of our age."

Johnson's 409). Leaving the hall after Kennedy's victory, McCarthy joked to an aide, "Pack your bags for Siberia," but he had become the new hero of the Stevensonians and a national figure overnight.[10]

Even though Humphrey released the Minnesota delegates from their favorite son commitment, they cast all their first ballot votes for him after an all night session of heated arguing. Even Freeman, who nominated Kennedy but was forced to ad-lib his speech when the Teleprompter stuck, voted for Humphrey, as did McCarthy. Don Fraser later summarized the confusion in the Minnesota delegation: "Our governor nominated Kennedy, our junior senator nominated Stevenson and the delegation voted for our senior senator, who wasn't even running."

When the vote for the presidential nomination was over, Senator John Stennis of Mississippi stood in the back of the hall, and shaking his head in wonderment, exclaimed, "You can never count that old Hubert out. Here he is, a defeated presidential candidate without a bit of power and the first thing you know, one of his boys nominates the winning candidate, another of his boys gives the best speech of the convention, and his delegation still votes for Hubert!"

Humphrey, however, had one more unexpected chore to perform at the convention. When Kennedy announced that Lyndon Johnson had agreed to become his running mate, Johnson asked Humphrey to help quell an incipient liberal revolt against his selection. Humphrey, who with McCarthy had been among the first to congratulate Johnson after his selection, worked furiously among the delegations where he had supporters, urging them to trust Kennedy's first major decision.

Humphrey almost didn't make it out of Los Angeles after the convention, according to Pat O'Connor. When it came time to check out of the Statler Hilton, none of the Humphrey people had enough money to pay the $3,500 hotel bill. O'Connor talked the hotel manager into letting him charge the entire amount to his Carte Blanche credit card, which had a $400 limit. "We grabbed our bags and ran," says O'Connor.

Two days later, O'Connor was in Las Vegas playing golf when he got a call from a Carte Blanche accountant. "He said, 'Mr. O'Connor, did you sign a $3,500 bill for Senator Humphrey at the Statler Hilton in Los Angeles?'" recalls O'Connor. "I thought, oh-oh, here it comes, and I said I did. The Carte Blanche guy says, 'That's all right. We just wanted to make sure because it was a large amount.'"

Humphrey left Los Angeles worried that he might be out of Kennedy's favor, says O'Connor. But a day later, he called O'Connor in Las Vegas and said excitedly, "Get hold of Herbie. Jack's been in touch and he wants us to

---

[10] Abigail McCarthy was so excited during her husband's speech that she held her "Win With Stevenson" sign upside down, prompting a friend to tell her, "Abigail, either you or your sign is upside down."

set up a farm rally in Des Moines. I want you and Herbie to get down there right away. We're right back in this ballgame!' "

Minnesota's Big Three of Humphrey, McCarthy and Freeman all left Los Angeles with new stature. Humphrey had won the gratitude of Kennedy and Johnson for pushing through the vice presidential nomination, and of Stevenson for contributing to his finest hour, while McCarthy had emerged as a new hero of the Stevensonians and Freeman was a rising Democratic star who would soon be named to Kennedy's Cabinet.

Freeman, however, had run out of political capital in Minnesota. While Humphrey easily won reelection to a third term in November by 235,000 votes over Minneapolis Mayor P. K. Peterson, Freeman lost his bid for a fourth term by 23,800 votes, almost the identical margin by which Kennedy carried Minnesota.[11] Even Humphrey's victory seemed in doubt as polls showed him holding a mere two-point margin the week before the election. The pessimistic polls triggered an outpouring of contributions into the Minnesota DFL headquarters in the closing days of the campaign that brought Humphrey the money he so desperately sought earlier in the year. "If you carried $5,000 into the DFL headquarters, you got a cup of coffee," state labor leader Robert Hess recalls. "For $10,000 you might get a doughnut."

McCarthy put the bitterness of the 1960 primary campaign behind him and campaigned extensively for his old rival Kennedy, helping him win a narrow victory over Richard Nixon, who would defeat Humphrey by an even closer margin eight years later after McCarthy refused to come to Humphrey's aid. Neither Humphrey nor McCarthy knew it, but 1960 marked the beginning of the end of the long collaboration between the two men from Minnesota.

[11] The events of 1960 would be weighted with bitter irony for Freeman. He had almost been named Kennedy's running mate, and thus barely missed becoming president instead of Lyndon Johnson. After Kennedy's assassination, Johnson told Freeman how close he had come to being the vice presidential candidate. Sitting by the swimming pool at Camp David, Maryland, in 1967, Freeman says Johnson said to him, "Jack Kennedy told me that if I had not taken the nomination, he was going to pick you." Freeman also feels he lost votes in Minnesota because he went on television to defend Kennedy on the religious issue. "But I feel it was one of the best things I ever did," he says.

CHAPTER IX

LEFT FIELD LIBERAL

*One thing is certain: Eugene McCarthy
will often take a position far out in left
field, but, stick around long enough and
you'll see left field rather crowded.*
> Jack Ludwig, *Holiday* magazine,
> June, 1962.

The speech that electrified the 1960 Democratic National Convention also heralded the appearance of a new hero for the perpetually restless liberal wing of the Democratic party. Eugene McCarthy's eloquent tribute to Adlai Stevenson earned him the gratitude of the small but influential group of reform-minded liberals who had tried vainly to nominate Stevenson for a third time and who now looked for a younger man to carry their banner in the decade of the 1960's.

In the forty-four year old McCarthy, they found him. A witty, reflective intellectual of practical bent like Stevenson, he stepped into the national spotlight for the first time at the Los Angeles convention and further impressed the Stevensonians as he sought their support for the Kennedy-Johnson ticket during the 1960 campaign. By the time Kennedy entered the White House, McCarthy was beginning his third year in the Senate and was being measured for Stevenson's mantle as a future spokesman for American liberals. "Gene McCarthy is an Adlai Stevenson with sex appeal," a Democratic professional commented after the campaign.

Yet at the same time, McCarthy found himself overshadowed in his party by Kennedy and in the Senate and Minnesota by Humphrey. McCarthy was secretly disappointed that it was Kennedy and not he who had become the first Catholic president and, although he later would change his mind, he doubted whether Kennedy was qualified to lead the nation. "I might not have seen his full potential," McCarthy admitted in an interview several

159

years after Kennedy's death, "though in his early years in Washington, he really fulfilled my impression that he was not ready."

Whatever his initial feelings were about Kennedy, McCarthy, like Humphrey, closed ranks behind the new Democratic standard bearer after the 1960 convention. Kennedy took the first step toward reconciliation with McCarthy when he invited him to breakfast the morning after his nomination and asked him to campaign in the areas of Stevenson's greatest strength. McCarthy responded by making sixty speeches in sixteen states for Kennedy and for liberal Democratic candidates for Congress. "We went where the Convairs and DC-3's fly," McCarthy commented after campaigning in out-of-the-way places like Luflin, Texas, and Albuquerque, New Mexico, as well as in Stevenson strongholds on the East and West Coasts. "I campaigned pretty hard for Jack after the '60 convention," said McCarthy. "I did everything they asked me to."

Much of McCarthy's campaign effort was made in conjunction with the National Committee for an Effective Congress, a Washington-based liberal lobby group that supported mostly Democrats. McCarthy sent out letters on behalf of the committee asking for contributions to seven Democratic Senate candidates, including Humphrey and Congressman George McGovern of South Dakota. He noted in the letter that "this year it is possible at last to break through the conservative barrier that frustrates so many hopeful efforts in Congress. The long uphill pull since 1954 is about to bear fruit. . . ."

Exhausted by his campaigning, McCarthy ended up in Washington's Georgetown Hospital after the election with a case of pneumonia. While he was hospitalized, Kennedy made a gesture which helped assure McCarthy's support for his new administration. During a Thanksgiving weekend visit to the hospital to see his wife and new baby son John, Jr., the president-elect made it a point to stop by McCarthy's room and thank him for his efforts and ask for his continued support. "That was a very smart thing for Kennedy to do," a friend of McCarthy commented afterwards. "He knew that's the way you have to treat McCarthy. You have to go to him and say, 'Gene, I need your help.' "

With the forty-three year old Kennedy installed in the White House in January, 1961, McCarthy gave up what ever hopes he had for the presidency and resumed his Senate duties. In his first two years in the Senate, McCarthy had been described as "the bright hope of the liberals," and it seemed at first that he was intent on fulfilling that prophecy. He had been named to the prestigious Finance Committee and had chaired the Special Committee on Unemployment Problems, whose landmark report foreshadowed many of the Kennedy administration's domestic proposals. In January, 1961, largely as the result of his brilliant espousal of Stevenson's lost cause at the 1960 convention, McCarthy was selected as the Democratic spokesman to oppose conservative Republican Barry Goldwater in a nationally-televised debate on the subject, "Does a Big Federal Government Threaten Our Freedom?" Taking the negative viewpoint, McCarthy again proved his debating skill against a right-wing leader just as he had done nine years earlier against the late Senator Joseph McCarthy.

But McCarthy's colleagues and friends sensed a subtle change in his personal and political style after he returned to the Senate in 1961, a change that was to become more pronounced in later years. Unlike his ten years in the House and his first two years in the Senate, McCarthy now seemed less concerned with the major business of the Senate. He concentrated instead on a few specialized legislative areas such as taxation, unemployment benefits, migratory labor and farm policy, and Congressional supervision of U.S. intelligence activities.

McCarthy's changing attitude toward the Senate was due in large part to the realization that the organizational skills he exercised in welding fragmented liberals together in the House weren't going to be welcomed in the Senate. This became clear to McCarthy soon after he came to the Senate, according to Representative Frank Thompson of New Jersey. "I don't think he was comfortable with the Senate's clubbiness," says Thompson, one of several Democratic Study Group leaders who continued to meet with McCarthy at irregular Friday lunches after he became a senator. "I think he saw he could never organize a Senate DSG."

McCarthy indicated his dissatisfaction with the Senate soon after he arrived there, Thompson recalls. "I had told him he'd be bored in the Senate, and sure enough, after a year or so, he called me and said, 'You're right, this is worse than the House.'"

McCarthy's hopes to foment a DSG-type liberal revolt in the Senate had caused a memorable run-in with then-Majority Leader Lyndon Johnson early in 1960. Johnson exploded when he picked up the January 6 Washington *Post* and read a Drew Pearson column saying that "more and more Northern and Western senators are lining up with Gene McCarthy in a close-knit group for an independent course of action this winter — regardless of Lyndon Johnson." A few days later, Johnson met McCarthy at a reception and said, in front of several witnesses, "I'll get even, Gene." According to the witnesses, McCarthy replied, "That's all right, Lyndon. You can get even, but don't go any further."

The liberal "revolt" never quite got off the ground in 1960, and died completely the following year despite the fact that McCarthy was joined in the Senate by Lee Metcalf of Montana, one of the other principal DSG organizers. Neither McCarthy nor Metcalf was anxious to embarrass or offend their senior senators, Humphrey and Mike Mansfield, who were elevated to assistant majority leader and majority leader, respectively, in January, 1961. "Gene had a senior colleague in a leadership position," Metcalf said later. "That made it hard to take a leadership role in the Senate." In addition,

Kennedy's ambitious legislative goals no longer made it necessary to organize liberals to push progressive legislation, which was the main purpose of the DSG-type operation.

At least one of McCarthy's longtime friends thinks 1961 marked the beginning of a pattern that would become apparent after McCarthy became successively more withdrawn and aloof after suffering disappointments in the presidential campaigns of 1964 and 1968. "The real trauma for McCarthy wasn't in 1964 [when he was rejected as Lyndon Johnson's running mate], but in 1960 with the election of John Kennedy as the first Catholic president," says Maurice Rosenblatt of the Committee for an Effective Congress.

McCarthy's attitude toward Kennedy manifested itself in his comments to his staff, Dick Boo, McCarthy's administrative assistant at the time, remembers. "He used to take Kennedy's speeches apart and ridicule them," says Boo, an ex-St. Thomas College teacher who was replaced in 1963 by Jerome Eller, who is still McCarthy's top aide. "There wasn't anything very bitter about it, it was just office sport and a lot of it was frequently just in fun. Somebody on the staff said if Kennedy had written the Sermon on the Mount, McCarthy would have taken it apart." (Describing one of Kennedy's speeches, McCarthy later said it "was like a meal at the Hot Shoppes. It wouldn't poison you, but it wouldn't nourish you either.")

Although McCarthy never would be the loyal ally and admirer of Kennedy that Humphrey later became, he at least achieved a state of peaceful coexistence with Kennedy that lasted until Kennedy's death in 1963. But McCarthy's conviction that Kennedy was not yet ready for the presidency was confirmed for him within three months after Kennedy took office. On April 17, a force of 1,200 Cuban refugees — recruited, trained and equipped by the U.S. Central Intelligence Agency — invaded Cuba's Bay of Pigs with the intention of overthrowing the Castro government. The invasion failed with disastrous results for American prestige and foreign policy, prompting McCarthy to tell a reporter, "The Kennedy administration is not going to make any little mistakes."

The highly publicized failure of the CIA-organized Bay of Pigs invasion in 1961 and the 1960 shooting down of the U-2 spy plane over Russia caused McCarthy to revive his earlier efforts to provide closer Congressional supervision of the CIA's activities. He had first introduced a bill in the House in 1955 to create a CIA watchdog committee modeled on the Joint Atomic Energy Committee, and called for creation of a similar Senate Select Committee on Foreign Information and Intelligence in 1961, and again in 1963, but without success. McCarthy said a watchdog committee was necessary because the CIA had "taken on the character of an invisible government answering only to itself," and was meddling in U.S. foreign policy. Writing in the *Saturday Evening Post* in January, 1964, he cited the CIA's role in helping bring about the downfall of the Diem regime in South Vietnam in 1963 and in overthrowing Prince Souvanna Phouma in Laos in 1960 as two recent examples of how the CIA was making foreign policy decisions that should be made by Congress and the president.

McCarthy would not become intimately involved in U.S. foreign policy issues until joining the Foreign Relations Committee in 1965. He had supported the overall U.S. foreign policy aims and national security programs throughout his Congressional career, but declared in his 1960 book, *Frontiers in American Democracy*, that the U.S. "often tries to direct the international policies of other nations — whether they be Communist or neutrals or allies of ours — as though their foreign policies were wholly unrelated to the internal politics and economies of those nations." He also warned against conducting foreign aid programs and cooperative ventures with non-Western countries "in the manner of the gospel mission," adding, "Our aid . . . should be principally at the economic level, because it is at this level that the peoples of these areas are willing to accept our help. It is at this level, too, that the great and most immediate needs of the peoples of Asia and Africa can be met."

McCarthy saw an even greater failure on the part of the new president in his treatment of the man to whom McCarthy had paid tribute in 1960 — Adlai Stevenson. McCarthy felt Stevenson should have been given the job he wanted — secretary of state — instead of being shunted off to the United Nations as U.S. ambassador. Worse still, in McCarthy's eyes, was the fact that Kennedy allowed Stevenson to unknowingly make a false denial to the UN that a preparatory air strike two days before the Cuban invasion was carried out with U.S. knowledge and assistance. Stevenson, who knew nothing of the U.S. role in the Bay of Pigs attack, was humiliated when it was learned that his denial was merely part of a futile attempt to conceal U.S. involvement in the Cuban fiasco.

McCarthy's memory of what happened to Stevenson during the Bay of Pigs invasion was to become a factor of monumental proportions in several later decisions that proved to be turning points in his life. Stevenson's fate would be on McCarthy's mind when he removed himself from consideration for the vice presidential nomination at the 1964 Democratic National Convention, when he refused to step aside for Robert Kennedy during the 1968 presidential primaries and when he turned down a similar offer from President Nixon in 1969. "I saw Adlai a few weeks before he died [in 1965]," McCarthy later said in an interview with the New York *Post's* Jerry Tallmer. "He was a sad fellow. I decided then that I wouldn't ever let myself be caught in that position, be turned into an expendable."

McCarthy said he advised Stevenson against accepting the UN post, warning him that he would be "locked in" if he did. "They [the Kennedy administration] didn't consult him, and lied to him — whereas Johnson consulted him but didn't listen. They're pretty tough fellows, you know." McCarthy made it clear in the interview that the lesson of Adlai Stevenson helped him make up his mind to go it alone in challenging Johnson on the war in 1967-68 after trying and failing to get Robert Kennedy to run. "Again, you see, I was determined not to put myself in a position where I could be expended, or expendable, on somebody else's determination."

McCarthy's estimation of John Kennedy as a president would increase as the result of Kennedy's handling of the 1962 Cuban missile crisis and his performance in the fields of civil rights legislation, economic policy and nuclear disarmament, even though he remained wary of Kennedy. However, McCarthy's reservations about President Kennedy didn't prevent him from performing two private diplomatic missions for him. In the summer of 1961, McCarthy, his wife, and aide Lawrence Merthan went to Santiago, Chile, to represent the Kennedy administration at an international conference of Christian Democrats. McCarthy explored Latin American reaction to Kennedy's new Alliance for Progress plan among Christian Democratic leaders at the conference, and gave Kennedy an assessment of Chile's Eduardo Frei, who later became president of Chile and one of the United States' best friends in Latin America.

The following year, McCarthy explored Vatican attitudes toward the Italian government's receptivity to the Left during a visit to the Vatican Council. McCarthy reported back that Pope John was "open to the Left and open to the Right and open to everyone."

McCarthy cooperated with the Kennedy administration in the domestic field as well. In June, 1961, he introduced a bill in the Finance Committee embodying Kennedy's proposal for major changes in the federal-state unemployment compensation system, an objective he and Kennedy had first cooperated on when they introduced companion bills in the House and Senate in 1958. The 1961 bill called for the most extensive overhaul of the jobless insurance plan since it was enacted in 1935, and included the imposition of minimum federal standards on state programs and increased federal responsibility for continuing payments to jobless workers. (McCarthy introduced the Kennedy administration bill again in 1962 and 1963 without success and was a leading advocate for revision of the unemployment compensation system until 1970, his last year in the Senate, when Congress finally passed a major unemployment compensation bill. However, McCarthy's amendment to set minimum federal standards in the 1970 bill was defeated on the Senate floor.)

Remaining on Finance but giving up his seat on the Public Works Committee at the outset of the Eighty-seventh Congress in 1961, McCarthy moved to the Agriculture Committee, replacing Humphrey. As the only Democrat on the Agriculture Committee from the Great Lakes states, McCarthy consistently backed high farm price supports and most of the Kennedy administration's farm programs pushed by his old DFL colleague, Secretary of Agriculture Orville Freeman. McCarthy's major efforts on the committee were on behalf of the administration's programs to raise farm income and reduce feed grain and dairy surpluses, while in the Finance Committee he sponsored bills to expand domestic acreage for sugar beet growers and to enlarge foreign trade of U.S. agricultural products.

McCarthy remained on the Agriculture Committee for four years, gladly passing it on to Walter Mondale when Mondale succeeded Humphrey in 1964. The committee was not high on McCarthy's priority list and his attitude reflected the general lack of interest in farm legislation in Congress. An aide to Freeman remembers Freeman and Agriculture Committee Chairman Allen Ellender of Louisiana discussing a bill which they both wanted but which they expected would have difficulty winning committee approval. "Ellender said, 'I'll have my people there,' and then he said to Freeman, 'See if you can get McCarthy there.' " Freeman often found he could not. "I went to McCarthy many times and asked him to cooperate [on farm legislation] and he said he would but he failed to do so," says Freeman. "He was totally unresponsive."

Nevertheless, the Agriculture Committee provided a forum for McCarthy to continue his long battle to improve the lot of Mexican-American farmworkers in the U.S. McCarthy had been one of the principal opponents in the House of the temporary program which authorized recruitment of low-priced Mexican workers for U.S. farms. He opposed the first extension of the program in 1953 and in subsequent years until 1961, when he led a Senate fight to reform the program. McCarthy's opposition was based on evidence that the availability of cheap imported labor resulted in lower wages and poorer working conditions for some 350,000 Mexican-American farmworkers and kept them in a state of perpetual impoverishment.[1]

The 1961 reform bill was introduced in the Senate by McCarthy and backed by the Kennedy administration and organized labor. It extended the existing program for two years but added amendments to a House-passed bill to protect U.S. migrant workers by prohibiting U.S. farmers from hiring Mexican *braceros* unless they first offered the same wages and working conditions to U.S. migrants. A central feature of the reform bill was McCarthy's amendment requiring U.S. farmers to pay Mexican farmworkers at least 90 percent of the prevailing wage rate in the area. The amendment was adopted by a 42–40 roll call vote and was included in the administration-supported bill that was passed by the Senate despite the active opposition of Vice

[1] The reform proposals also were based on recommendations issued in 1959 by a Labor Department study group that included the man McCarthy replaced in the Senate, Edward Thye. When McCarthy left the Agriculture Committee in 1965, Minnesota's new senator, Democrat Walter Mondale, succeeded him on the committee and continued his crusade for improving migrant workers' living conditions. In 1969, Mondale was named chairman of a Special Subcommittee on Migratory Labor.

President Lyndon Johnson. However, the amendment was dropped by a conference committee before Kennedy signed the bill despite the lack of what he called "provisions which I believe necessary to protect domestic farmworkers."

Two years later, after the House rejected another two-year extension of the Mexican farm labor program, the Senate approved a one-year extension after adopting a McCarthy amendment requiring protection for U.S. migrant workers similar to that which had been proposed in 1961. McCarthy also proposed that the program be terminated at the end of the one-year extension. McCarthy's amendment, favored by the administration, was adopted in August, 1963, by a 44–43 vote. Attempts to reverse the vote failed on a tie vote as Vice President Johnson declined to cast the deciding vote, apparently on orders from the White House. Again, McCarthy's amendment was dropped in conference but Senator Ellender promised he would not seek further extension of the program and it expired the following year.

McCarthy's interest in the migratory labor issue reflected his earlier preoccupation with social justice, a concern dating back to his days as a college teacher and one that would repeatedly manifest itself throughout his Congressional career. It also reflected the influence of McCarthy's closest aide throughout his Senate years, Legislative Assistant Emerson Hynes. Hynes was a former classmate and teaching colleague from St. John's, who, like McCarthy, had been active in the Catholic rural cooperative movement and had helped prepare many of McCarthy's speeches, articles and legislation on domestic issues. "The fundamental objective of politics is to bring about progressive change in keeping with the demands of social justice," McCarthy declared in *Frontiers in American Democracy,* the first of three books he wrote during his first term in the Senate.[2]

The book, which included portions of articles and essays published during his twelve years in Congress, was the first definitive exposition of McCarthy's political thought. It confirmed the assessment of McCarthy's friend, Joseph Gabler, that "Gene McCarthy probably is as pragmatic as anybody I've ever seen in the political field." McCarthy devoted an entire chapter to defending the necessity and inevitability of political compromise. "Compromise is the mark of human relations in almost every institution or social relationship involving two or more persons," McCarthy wrote. "Genuine compromise is not a violation of principle, not a compromise with principle but with reality." He added that a politician is seldom faced with a clear-cut choice between good

---

[2] The others were *The Crescent Dictionary of American Politics,* published by the Macmillan Company in 1962, and *A Liberal Answer to the Conservative Challenge,* published in paperback form by Macfadden Books in 1964. The latter book was written in anticipation of Senator Barry Goldwater's presidential candidacy while the former, a textbook supplement on American government and politics, was dedicated to the late speaker of the House, Sam Rayburn.

and evil, and often must tolerate "a measure of evil in order to prevent something worse, or to save the limited good."[3]

Nowhere in McCarthy's public life was his pragmatic view of compromise more vividly demonstrated than in his service on the Senate Finance Committee. The committee, with its control over tax and trade policy and other legislation of enormous importance to the American economy, was the only committee McCarthy would remain on throughout his twelve years as a senator. A natural extension of the legislation specialty he'd developed on the Ways and Means Committee — the Finance Committee's counterpart in the House — it was the focus of his legislative energies in his first term. Asked in 1964 what he considered his major contributions since coming to Congress, McCarthy cited his service on the Finance and Ways and Means Committees and his efforts to bring about "the reform of the tax structure of our country so that it would have the greatest possible effect by way of stimulating economic growth in the United States."

However, McCarthy's service on the Finance Committee would lead to harsh criticism in later years. The most persistent criticism was that he consistently supported legislation favoring the oil and gas industry because of his friendly relationship with the two men who controlled the committee, Chairman Harry F. Byrd of Virginia and ranking Democrat Robert Kerr of Oklahoma. The criticisms were fed by McCarthy's refusal to join fully with embattled liberal reformers on the committee like Paul Douglas of Illinois and Albert Gore of Tennessee in abolishing loophole provisions in the federal tax laws, particularly the 27½ percent depletion allowance which exempts oil and gas companies from paying any taxes on that percentage of their total oil income.

The first public attack on McCarthy's position on the oil depletion allowance was made by Columnist Drew Pearson in August, 1964, just before the Democratic National Convention at which McCarthy was a leading candidate for the vice presidential nomination along with Humphrey. Six months earlier, in February, McCarthy had voted against a Douglas amendment to reduce the oil depletion allowance from 27½ to 20 percent as the Senate defeated the amendment by a 33–61 vote. He had also missed a vote on reducing the depletion allowance in June, 1959, Pearson said, because he was drinking coffee in the Senate restaurant.

McCarthy, wrote Pearson, "happens to be the one Senate liberal who has consistently voted for the big oil companies" by opposing efforts to reduce

[3] *Frontiers in American Democracy,* published in 1960, enhanced McCarthy's reputation as one of the Senate's foremost intellectuals. A scholarly and far-ranging examination of the democratic system of government, it was hailed by Democrats of such diverse views as Lyndon Johnson ("one of the finest statements of the meaning of American democracy and the American political system I have read") and Harvard economist John Kenneth Galbraith ("Eugene McCarthy is the most literate and incisive writer now in public office").

the depletion allowance. Since he lined up with liberals on most other committee business, Pearson wrote, "it has long been assumed that he got his coveted place [the committee assignment] only after an advance pledge of loyalty to the oil and gas politicians."

McCarthy disputed the charges in a letter to Pearson, pointing out that in his first five years in the Senate, he voted four times in committee to reduce the depletion allowance and that he also supported Douglas the three times that he offered his amendment on the Senate floor in those years.

> On June 25, 1959, I was not present for the vote (I may have been having coffee, as you said), but I was listed as a co-sponsor of the four amendments offered that day, including the Douglas Amendment. . . . On June 20, 1960, I voted with Senator Douglas for his amendment. We lost, 30–56. On September 5, 1962, Senator Douglas again offered his amendment and I voted with him. We lost, 23–50.

McCarthy said his vote against reducing the depletion allowance during Senate consideration of the Revenue Act of 1964 was "another matter." He explained:

> The House bill, which was being considered by our committee, included changes in the law which, by changes in the oil depletion rules, would have brought an additional $40 million a year into the Treasury. It was my judgment that this was the best that could be done. This was the position taken by Secretary [of the Treasury] Dillon. . . . And it was, perhaps, as much as should have been done unless we were to have revised the whole Tax Code for depletion allowance for all minerals. I therefore voted against the Douglas Amendment in committee . . . and on the floor. . . . I also voted against the Douglas Oil Depletion Amendment to the excise tax extension bill in committee . . . as not being relevant to the tax provisions under considerations.

McCarthy's attitude toward the depletion allowance and similar tax loopholes was influenced, former colleagues and staff members of the Finance Committee believe, by the repeated failure of liberal attempts to close those loopholes. He quickly discovered how difficult this was when he joined Douglas and two other liberals in introducing four tax reform amendments in May, 1959. The amendments, including one by McCarthy to repeal the 4 percent stock dividend credit adopted in 1954 and one by Douglas to reduce the oil depletion allowance, failed to get the endorsement of the Finance Committee so the four senators took their fight to the floor.

On June 25, after a ten-hour debate, the Senate approved McCarthy's amendment by a 47–31 vote and rejected the other three — including the one by Douglas which McCarthy failed to vote on. A day later, however, his amendment perished when a House-Senate conference committee threw out most of the Senate changes. McCarthy, Humphrey and Russell Long of Louisiana then led a fight against adopting the conference report, but it was approved by a 57–35 vote. "From that day on, I think McCarthy saw the handwriting on the wall," says a former colleague. "He was smart enough to see that the oil depletion allowance was a sacred cow that couldn't be touched."

McCarthy expressed his feelings about that sacred cow in a 1961 radio interview.

> The oil depletion allowance [has] become kind of a rallying center, really. You're for or against it. If you're for it, why, you're said by some to be immoral and seeking special privilege; if you're against it, why, you're pure. I think a good study of this might serve to clear the air and my own feeling is that it would probably justify some reduction in the 27½ percent depletion allowance, but not the entire removal of it.

McCarthy's feelings about the depletion allowance were also colored, some people feel, by his friendship with Byrd and Kerr. There were ironic overtones to his friendship with Byrd, the courtly and conservative Southern oligarch whom Humphrey had tangled with during his awkward Senate debut in 1949. McCarthy defeated Byrd twice in floor fights in 1959, once in the repeal of the stock dividend credit and again on a special unemployment compensation program. Yet Byrd clearly liked the erstwhile leader of the rebellious House liberals and, later that year, publicly praised him as "one of the ablest, most experienced and best members of the [Finance] Committee." The two became even better friends in 1960 when McCarthy defended Byrd against an abortive liberal attempt to unseat him as chairman because he refused to endorse the Kennedy-Johnson ticket. In 1964, Byrd broke a long-standing policy against attending political fund raisers outside of Virginia and turned up at the head table of a McCarthy fund raiser.

McCarthy's friendship with Kerr was even more intriguing to many people. Kerr was one of the richest, most powerful and most feared men in the Senate. A brilliant, ruthless adversary in debate and an instinctively effective legislator, Kerr was de facto chairman of the Finance Committee until his death in 1963. He was also an unabashed champion of the oil and gas industry and Lyndon Johnson's mentor and confidant.

"McCarthy had an excellent relationship with Bob Kerr," recalls Larry Merthan, who worked with McCarthy on Finance Committee legislation. "Kerr had a summer home near Brainerd [a northern Minnesota resort town] and they used to see each other up there. Kerr said the oil people of Oklahoma sent him to the Senate to represent them and he was going to look out for their interests. McCarthy liked him because he was that honest and he liked McCarthy because the Minnesotan was the brightest guy on the committee. Their relationship had nothing to do with the way McCarthy voted on oil depletion or anything else."

Nevertheless, there were raised eyebrows when Kerr told a news conference at the 1960 Democratic National Convention that he was authorized to say that McCarthy was "all out for Lyndon Johnson," although McCarthy later denied that Kerr had gotten clearance from him before making the announcement. Questions about his relationship with Kerr and his position on the oil depletion allowance continued to plague McCarthy through his 1968 campaign. Asked about his oil depletion votes and about insinuations — by Drew Pearson — that Kerr had sent campaign contributions from the oil industry his way, McCarthy replied in a 1968 interview, "I'm on record against the allowances seven or eight times. Whenever the real test came up, I voted to cut the allowances. There were a couple of times when I considered the oil thing a mischievous and capricious attempt to clutter up a tax bill. I don't think anybody fought Bob Kerr better than I did. As for campaign contributions, Kerr died two years before I ran for the Senate the second time."

Kerr's death in early 1963 drew dozens of eulogies from his colleagues. One of the warmest came from McCarthy, who told the Senate on March 1 that Kerr was a man who "lived in the great tradition of the empire builders of America, a man who dealt with the physical and material structure of America. . . . His real goal and delight was to make and build things. He was concerned with cattle and with the land. He was concerned with rivers and with the minerals of his own state, and with the resources of this nation."

McCarthy denied that the respect given Kerr by his colleagues "was based more on fear than on affection and real understanding . . . . His basic strength was one which was based on loyalty and affection and respect for this intelligence, and on respect for his great effectiveness in the Senate." There were those who called Kerr a compromiser, said McCarthy, who might have been describing his own view of political compromise. "He would have been the first to admit it. However, his compromises were not compromises with principle, but rather, with the realities of the day or the day of history. He was a genuine realist in the best sense of that word. Indeed, he preferred some progress and some advance to a kind of perpetuation or a perfection of an issue without any achievement."

McCarthy's former colleague on the Finance Committee, Illinois' Paul Douglas, was one of those who was disappointed in McCarthy's behavior on the committee. "I don't think he could have been appointed to the committee without giving his pledge that he would go along with Johnson," the seventy-nine year old Douglas said in a 1971 interview. "He never voted for our progressive tax policies. That is, to me, the acid test of domestic liberalism; how they line up on who pays the bills, poor men or well-to-do-men. He was never with us. I think Johnson had it arranged when he put him on."

Douglas says there was no one he was more disappointed in than McCarthy. "In my naivete, I had expected that he'd be against the depletion allowance and against favoritism. We didn't have many hopes for Vance Hartke [an freshman Indiana Democrat named to the committee the same time as McCarthy], but we felt McCarthy had the brains and skill to help us. The disappointment was much greater because the expectations were much greater. I don't think he regarded taxation as a moral issue."

However, others who observed McCarthy at close range during his first term disagree with Douglas. "I saw no evidence that Bob Kerr or anybody had McCarthy in his pocket," says Donald Lubick, tax legislative counsel for the Treasury Department from 1961–64 and now a Buffalo, New York, attorney. Lubick, who worked closely with the Finance Committee, recalls that McCarthy often opposed Kerr in committee and on the floor. "There's nothing sinister or inexplicable about McCarthy's votes. They're all explicable in terms of getting reelected. Those of us on the Treasury side were often disappointed with him but he obviously had a tremendous amount of intelligence and a much greater understanding of legislation than most members of the committee. He was so far ahead of Byrd when it came to technical matters that he wasn't in the same league and he could hold his own with Kerr." [4]

Another close observer of McCarthy at the time was David Stern, an American Political Science Association fellow who worked on McCarthy's staff in 1962–63. Stern, now an associate professor of political science at Colgate University, recalls that McCarthy opposed Kerr on a major feature of the Revenue Act of 1962, the investment tax credit proposal. "I don't think there was a great deal of love lost between the two," says Stern.

Stern feels he can offer a fairly dispassionate assessment of McCarthy's service on the committee. "I think he had a better understanding of committee business than most members and, because of his innate intelligence was able to cut through a lot of the technical stuff. I was amazed at how much he understood about complex questions that I would have to study for hours. But he certainly was not a crusader who committed himself and was willing to die for a bill. He sort of drifted along and would make his opposition known if necessary. He wasn't like Douglas or [Senator Albert] Gore who laid down in the middle of the road all the time. Like the rest of the members, he had things he wanted, but he really had a broader view on the major issues on which he took a stand. Nobody really gave him any advice on a tax bill. He made up his own mind."

McCarthy was, however, careful to protect the interests of his Minnesota constituents while serving on the Finance Committee. He introduced several bills calling for favored tax treatment for northern Minnesota's iron ore processors and for the giant Minnesota-based mutual fund, Investors Diversified

[4] Lubick ran unsuccessfully as a delegate pledged to McCarthy in Hamilton, New York, in 1968, but he says he would not do so again. "I honestly thought he was about as good a man as there was in Washington between 1964–68, but I don't feel that way today," Lubick said in a 1971 interview.

Services, Inc. McCarthy expressed his attitude toward the Minnesota business community during hearings on the 1963 tax bill when Gore complained to an executive of the Minnesota-based 3M Company that its highway billboards were cluttering up the nation's roadsides. "Most of the ones I have seen advertise no products," said Gore. "It just seems to try to popularize a name, *3M*. What does *3M* stand for?" A grinning McCarthy interjected, "It stands for a lot in Minnesota."

The 1962 tax bill also included a McCarthy amendment entitled, "Income Tax Treatment of Certain Losses Sustained in Converting from Street Railway to Bus Operations." The bill was for the sole benefit of the Twin Cities Rapid Transit Company of Minneapolis-St. Paul, which McCarthy explained had made a too-rapid changeover from streetcars to buses "in order to complete [certain] fraudulent activities quickly, intentionally disregarding the income tax consequences." As a result, the company suffered losses so large that they could not be fully tax-deducted in the required amount of time and the new management was saddled with over five million dollars in losses for which it could get no tax advantages. The new management argued that it should not have to bear the consequences for the fraudulent activity by its predecessors, and McCarthy agreed to help.

The bill was not new; it had been passed by Congress in 1961 but was vetoed by President Kennedy. McCarthy made the measure veto-proof by tacking it on to the omnibus 1962 tax bill which the Kennedy administration urgently wanted passed and, when it was approved, so was McCarthy's streetcar bill.

"He threw it in at the last minute," says Stern of the streetcar bill. "He said, 'This is the kind of situation where when the ship leaves the harbor, everybody is trying to get his cargo on board.' " When Douglas objected to the amendment, McCarthy gently reminded him that "we passed a bill for the senator from Illinois" providing retroactive relief for a union pension fund.

McCarthy's approach to tax loopholes seemed to coincide with the general guide for a politician's behavior that he offered in *Frontiers in American Democracy*. The politician, he wrote, must try

> . . . to make his decisions in the hope that by these decisions an imperfect world may become somewhat more perfect; or that at least if he cannot make an imperfect world less imperfect, he can save it from becoming even less perfect or, finally, from becoming entirely evil and perverted. He can try to prevent degradation, prevent decline, and, if possible, to move things forward and upward toward right and justice. That is the purpose and the end of political action and of the compromises that go with that action.

In retrospect, the fights over tax loopholes have obscured the fact that McCarthy was also continuing the same strong liberal voting pattern that he had established in the House during his first term in the Senate. Many of his other Finance Committee efforts reflect his concern for the "social justice" principle he espoused in books, articles and speeches. He consistently supported other tax reform measures, particularly those affecting the elderly and the handicapped, introduced numerous bills to expand Social Security and other old age benefits, to abolish residency requirements for welfare recipients and to increase federal aid to education. (His strong support for expanded veterans' benefits and for creation of a Veterans Affairs Committee caused McCarthy to remark to his St. Paul friend Bill Carlson after a veterans organization attacked his Vietnam stand in 1968, "My veterans' record is so good I'm ashamed of it.") And he introduced legislation in 1962 to grant "head of household" tax relief to all single persons over the age of thirty-five. "We called it our 'Betty Beale and Mary McGrory' bill, "says an aide referring to two prominent unmarried Washington reporters.

McCarthy took an avowedly liberal attitude toward the broader subject of economic policy as he supported the expansionary economic goals of the Kennedy administration and his fellow Minnesotan Walter Heller, who was chairman of Kennedy's Council of Economic Advisers. McCarthy belittled conservative warnings against the dangers of deficit spending and inflation and outlined his own economic policy principles in a speech before the Economic Club of Detroit in March, 1963. He said the theory that federal deficits can be justified only to control recessions is "as outdated as Newton's theories in the world of physics." Balanced budgets are not necessarily good, McCarthy said. "Once the slogans are dismissed for what they are, we can proceed to objective judgments about the ways and means of achieving economic expansion here and now. . . ."

Despite his 100 percent rating from the ADA, McCarthy revealed himself in *Frontiers in American Democracy* as a liberal of a very non-doctrinaire stripe, something that came as a surprise to many of his supporters in later years.[5] The ideal liberal, he wrote,

> . . . is normally progressive . . . but he need not always advocate something wholly new; he can support elements of the status quo, or he may even advocate a return to conditions known in the past.

But perhaps the clearest insight into McCarthy's political philosophy and personal style was contained in the book's introduction, where he noted that the historic launching of the Russian Sputnik satellite in 1957 was viewed by some as the beginning of a new age that called for new ideas and institutions. Such views, McCarthy wrote,

> . . . represent the familiar startled reactions of man forced by history and new experience to an evaluation of belief. Change does not necessarily call for radical revision of philosophy and theology or for total recasting of social, economic and political organization and procedure. It demands only attentive re-examination of accepted beliefs, practices and institutions and adjustment or accommodation where necessary.

[5] McCarthy allowed his membership in ADA to lapse in 1960.

McCarthy's tendency to judge political issues and even crises by the yardstick of history was reflected in a somewhat leisurely attitude toward everyday Senate duties such as attendance at committee hearings and participation in floor debate. "The senator with the perfect attendance record is not always or necessarily the most conscientious and effective legislator," a statement put out by McCarthy's office declared defensively after he was criticized for missing several key votes in 1963.

McCarthy's lack of concern about the practical details of legislative and political procedure surfaced in his 1963 Detroit speech. Recalling G. K. Chesterton's observation that minds which deal in ideas and theory are just as important as practical minds in tracing the way out of a cultural muddle, McCarthy declared, "We need both practical minds and minds which deal in theory as we wrestle with the contemporary fiscal and economic policies."

McCarthy's detachment was, as a fellow alumnus of St. John's later noted, a legacy from the Benedictines. John "Blood" McNally, a former professional football star, once called McCarthy's Senate office and asked to speak to McCarthy. Told that no one knew where McCarthy was, what he was doing or when he would be back, McNally was not unduly disturbed. "The monks taught us that if a man believes himself to be engaged in a worthwhile endeavor, it is not necessary for him to alert any other parties to his whereabouts or the nature of his activity."

Actually, McCarthy's attendance record was not much better or worse than most of his colleagues during his first term in the Senate. He was recorded as participating in 84 percent of the 1,079 roll call votes from 1959–63, and he missed only 1 of 36 roll call votes on what the independent research publication, *Congressional Quarterly,* selected as significant issues during McCarthy's first term. The Americans for Democratic Action certified McCarthy's liberalism when it gave him a perfect rating for voting according to its views on key issues from 1959–63.

McCarthy's office staff, like the man it served, seemed to move at a slower pace than most other Senate offices, particularly Humphrey's. Although Humphrey and McCarthy worked together on legislation of major interest to Minnesota, there was little cooperation between the two staffs.[6] Dick Boo recalls, "There were passing attempts to try to mesh the offices in a lot of things, but we usually gave it up. Humphrey had too big an operation and McCarthy didn't think much of Humphrey's intense press operation. Humphrey would put out ten press releases a day but McCarthy felt it wasn't worth the effort."

[6] During the six years McCarthy served in the Senate with Humphrey, they had almost identical voting records. They disagreed only twice on major issues, once when McCarthy opposed reducing the oil depletion allowance and again when McCarthy voted to take away research powers from the new Arms Control and Disarmament Agency which Humphrey fathered. In 1963, they differed on only 3 percent of all Senate roll calls, making them the most "agreeing" pair of same-state senators.

Humphrey's staff, in turn, referred to the McCarthy office as "Sleepy Hollow," and complained about the staff's lack of interest in constituent problems. "It wasn't more than a couple of years after McCarthy came to the Senate that we gave up on his office for any kind of help," a Humphrey aide recalls. "Gene had his own style and his own way and his office didn't care about the nitty gritty stuff. It was kind of like we were working for different states. Humphrey would attend bureaucratic meetings to push Minnesota interests, but McCarthy usually would send somebody who didn't know anything about the problem."

McCarthy disliked roll calls, and resented it when anyone criticized him for missing one. "You get into this silly stuff about what your attendance record is, about the percentage of the roll calls you've missed, and stuff like that," he once said. ("Margaret Chase Smith had to get arthritis before she stopped answering roll calls," he would say years later when hip surgery stopped Mrs. Smith's consecutive roll calls at 2,941.) Mike Mansfield's egalitarian leadership style compared unfavorably with Lyndon Johnson's, McCarthy once told a lobbyist friend (he called lobbyists "rainmakers"), because Johnson at least "put on a good show by making all the animals jump through the hoop." Says a former colleague, who referred to McCarthy as "Eugene Cardinal McCarthy," "He preferred to sit in his office in his shirtsleeves honing a phrase and polishing a line than to come down and do the work he was supposed to be doing."

Adrian Winkel, McCarthy's friend and former administrative assistant, thinks much of the criticism of McCarthy stems from his tendency to search for universals rather than particulars. "He has this ability to detach himself and stand there and look at the whole, rather than be immersed in a situation. I guess this grew as time went on, whether it was caused by discontentment or personality, but he came more and more to feel that so much time was spent in the non-essentials and that really important things like the government and what this nation was and what it was going to be, the real questions, were being neglected.

In November, 1963, McCarthy was having lunch one day with Maurice Rosenblatt at the Plaza Hotel near the Senate when he was called to the telephone. He returned to the table and told Rosenblatt, "The president's just been shot in Dallas. He's in the hospital — it may be fatal. I'm going back to the floor of the Senate."

A short while later, McCarthy spoke a moving eulogy of the slain president. In words similar to those he would use when another Kennedy was killed who was running against him for president, McCarthy said the burden of the president's killing was too great to be borne by one person or nation. "Instead . . . the burden of guilt must be shared by all who through the years have excited and stirred the simple and the anxious, who have raised questions and turned them about until they became suspicious, who have nurtured doubt until it bore the fruit of accusation and false charges, who have spread themselves to make a shade for fear and to save it from the light of truth until it grew to be a despairing fear of fear; by all who stood in silent acquiescence or who protested softly, too little, and too late; by all who envied him or any man or wished them ill."

Kennedy had confidence in the future, McCarthy said, and the nation would survive after him. But, he added, "For some days, Americans will not walk as certainly or as straight as they did in the past. The quick step is gone. A strong heart has stopped. A mind that sought the truth, a will ready for commitment and a voice to challenge and to move are ended for this age and time of ours."

One month after Kennedy's death, Chairman Emanuel Celler of the House Judiciary Committee put McCarthy's name forth for the first time as a possible vice presidential running mate of the new president, Lyndon Johnson. Speaking in a radio interview, Celler called McCarthy "a scholarly gentleman, erudite and a real orator, who has carved out a remarkable career in the Senate." He would be, said Celler, "the best vice presidential candidate, and the strongest."

CHAPTER X

GIANT IN THE SENATE

*The name of Hubert Horatio Humphrey
must figure in any list of the dozen
most powerful and influential men in
the United States Congress.*
　　　The New York *Times* magazine,
　　　August 25, 1963.

With the inauguration of John F. Kennedy as president, Hubert Humphrey began the most satisfying and productive period of his life. The virus of presidential ambition that had infected him for so long had been cured — forever, he was convinced — and he looked forward to a third six-year term in the Senate and the prospect of working with the first Democratic president since Harry Truman.

When Humphrey was asked shortly after the election to become assistant majority leader of the Senate, he hesitated only briefly. He knew that he would be giving up the freedom that had enabled him to become an articulate spokesman for American liberals, to speak at length on any subject he chose and to stamp his imprint on nearly every major piece of legislation that passed through the Senate in the 1950's.[1] But he also knew that the job would give him a voice in the management of the Senate, place him only one step away from majority leader and give him an open door to the White House. "I have made mud pies and built dream houses long enough," the forty-nine year old Humphrey said as he dismissed his presidential ambitions and agreed to join the Kennedy administration team. "Now I want to do something."

Humphrey was thrilled with the prospect of once more having unrestricted

---

[1] Humphrey sponsored a total of 1,044 bills and joint resolutions in his first two terms, an incredible performance that prompted a fellow senator to comment, "He never seems to think what would happen if all the bills he introduces passed."

177

access to the White House. Not since his first four years in the Senate when Truman was president was Humphrey able to pick up the telephone and get an appointment with the president, and the idea of being so close to the center of power overwhelmed him. "I would now be having regular policy discussions, the privilege of sitting with the man who, more than anyone else, shapes the world today," he said after being elected majority whip. "It was a chance to speak my mind in his presence, and it was a chance no man could turn aside."

Humphrey was in New York City in December, 1960, trying to persuade another disappointed presidential aspirant, Adlai Stevenson, to become a New Frontier team player when he was asked to become whip. A disappointed Stevenson, who wanted to be secretary of state, was vacillating over his response to Kennedy's offer to become U.S. ambassador to the United Nations, and Humphrey was urging him to accept. Humphrey told Stevenson, "Adlai, you've got to take it, you don't have any choice. The president has asked you to do something and you may be responsible for this man's election. What makes you think that you can turn it down?"

While Humphrey and Stevenson were talking — ex-Senator William Benton of Connecticut was also present — Humphrey received a telephone call from Vice President-elect Lyndon Johnson. The former majority leader had hand-picked Mike Mansfield of Montana to succeed him and now wanted Humphrey to take Mansfield's place and he suggested that Humphrey return to Washington immediately to talk to him about it. Humphrey said he wanted to think it over and promised to get back to Johnson.

When he put down the phone, Humphrey turned to Stevenson and Benton and said, "That was Lyndon Johnson. He wants me to be majority whip." Both men argued against his taking the job, Humphrey says. "They told me, 'If you become majority whip, then you've got to become an administration man all the way and you won't have the independence that you need for a political future. Be a good senator and you'll be a good administration supporter, but don't get locked in.'"

But Humphrey felt he should apply the argument to himself that he'd been using with Stevenson. "I said, 'Well Adlai, I can't tell you one thing and tell myself another. Minnesota carried for Kennedy, and without Minnesota he might not have been president. I won Minnesota by 230,000 votes and Kennedy won it by 25,000.[2] I think that I've got the same obligation that I told you that you have. If they want me for majority whip, I'm going to be majority whip. We've got to make this administration the best one that we can.'"

Humphrey, of course, told Johnson he was interested, and Johnson

[2] Humphrey's winning margin over Republican P. Kenneth Peterson in the 1960 election was 235,582 votes, while Kennedy carried Minnesota over Richard Nixon by 22,018 votes.

paved the way for his election along with Mansfield by the Senate Democratic Conference on January 3, 1961. While Humphrey's election as whip would make him one of the Kennedy administration's most influential allies on Capitol Hill, it also marked the end of Johnson's vaunted power in the Senate. The Democratic caucus vociferously opposed a move by Mansfield and Humphrey to empower Johnson to preside over future caucuses and thus maintain his pervasive influence over the Senate even though the Constitution gave the vice president only very limited powers in the Senate. Johnson, who had been reelected to the Senate under a new Texas law that enabled him to run simultaneously for vice president and the Senate in 1960, resigned from the Senate after the caucus and never again exercised the power there that he once had.

Humphrey, meanwhile, plunged into his new duties in characteristic fast-moving, fast talking fashion. Operating out of a small whip's office on the third floor of the Capitol, just above the Senate chamber, he emerged in the first few months of the Eighty-seventh Congress as the Senate's most effective advocate of Kennedy's legislative program and in the eyes of many senators outshone the soft-spoken, easy-going Mansfield. "Mike Mansfield is a fine, sweet, lovable guy," a liberal Democratic senator said in April, 1961. "But when you want to get something done in the Senate nowadays, you go to Hubert."

Much of Humphrey's success in the whip's job stemmed from his vibrant personality, phenomenal energy, indefatigable hard work and exuberant love of politics and people. Although theoretically second in command to Mansfield, Humphrey capitalized on the ambiguous authority of his new post and Mansfield's distaste for senatorial arm-twisting and cloakroom cajolery to win a place at the epicenter of Senate power. He persuaded unyielding liberals to accept the administration's compromises, sweet-talked Southern conservatives into supporting New Frontier liberal schemes and pleased both sides by paying meticulous attention to each senator's ideological predilections and political situation.

He also showed that he had been an attentive pupil in Lyndon Johnson's School of Consensus Politics. "My task is primarily to cajole and to persuade," Humphrey said of his new job, "and to be a psychoanalyst of my colleagues in the hope that by understanding what is bothering them on a particular day, or what motivates them relating to a particular piece of legislation, I [can bring about] a consensus or majority to support a program . . . ."

"All in all, Senator Humphrey is making more out of the majority whip's job than anyone in recent memory," the *Wall Street Journal's* Robert Novak reported three months after Humphrey became whip. Novak, who later became one of the nation's most successful political columnists, listed some of Humphrey's accomplishments in his first days as whip. They included floor generalship of minimum wage and aid to education bills, engineering a compromise on the administration's farm bill, convincing liberals to drop their opposition to confirmation of Texas oilman John Connally as secretary of the navy and persuading Southerners not to block confirmation of a Negro Robert Weaver, as administrator of the Housing and Home Finance Agency.

Humphrey's decision to be a half-a-loaf pragmatist rather than an all-or-nothing martyr was illustrated by his handling of a squabble over the administration's top priority program for federal aid to economically depressed areas in February, 1961. The program, twice vetoed by President Eisenhower, was re-introduced by Illinois' Paul Douglas as the Senate's first piece of legislation in the new Congress, but ran into trouble when conservatives objected to direct funding by the Treasury because the Appropriations Committee would be bypassed. Humphrey advised the White House that the dispute over the method of financing might jeopardize the bill. Kennedy subsequently sent Congress his own bill providing that funds be appropriated rather than borrowed from the Treasury, and that the program be placed under the control of the business-oriented Commerce Department, both of which were opposed by Douglas.

Humphrey then privately suggested to Douglas that he do a little horse trading by offering to accept Commerce Department control in exchange for an agreement from conservatives to permit financing by Treasury loans rather than appropriations. When Douglas, whose snow-white hair matched the purity of his liberal ideals, refused to seek a compromise, Humphrey assured him, "I'll bargain for you. I'm not so pure." Humphrey did, the compromise was agreed to, and the Senate passed the bill on March 15. The House quickly followed suit and on May 1, Kennedy signed the bill creating the Area Redevelopment Administration.

Not everyone was happy with Humphrey's performance as whip, however. He failed to notify two administration supporters of a vote on a bill to temporarily continue unemployment compensation payments, Minnesota's Eugene McCarthy and Maine's Edmund Muskie, and left them enjoying a leisurely dinner at the nearby Carroll Arms Hotel while the bill barely survived a 44–42 vote. It was the old problem, critics said, of Humphrey trying to do too many things at once and rushing a vote before all his troops were ready to march.

Even more serious, however, were the growing signs of disaffection with Humphrey among the ranks of Democratic party liberals who had long regarded him as their champion. Even though Senate liberals liked the idea of finally having one of their own elevated to the Senate hierarchy, many others outside the Senate, particularly among Humphrey's friends in the Americans for Democratic Action, looked with distaste upon his involvement in the necessary compromises that lay at the heart of the legislative process.

His old ADA friends pointed to Humphrey's less than enthusiastic support for the biennial liberal fight to make it easier to override a Senate filibuster, his support of the Connally nomination and his vote for confirmation of an Alabama segregationist, Charles Meriwether, to be director of the Export-Import Bank as evidence that his commitment to liberal ideals was being diluted. "He can get away with a few things," an ADA leader warned as Humphrey demonstrated his willingness to accept accommodation for the sake of progress, "but it's going to catch up with Hubert if he keeps it up."

Humphrey dismissed the criticism of liberals who needled him about not playing a more militant role. "I don't have to prove I'm a liberal," he said the day after he was elected majority whip. "After twenty years of sincere and conscientious effort, there is nothing more I can do. I don't have to tell people I didn't sell out. I won't waste my time talking to them if they think that."

Humphrey quickly demonstrated that he knew how to capitalize on his new proximity to power. He used his entree to the White House to win administration support for the multitude of legislative proposals he'd pioneered during his earlier years and then employed his key position on Capitol Hill to press for Senate approval of them. The fact that many of these proposals, once condemned as visionary and even radical, neatly dovetailed with the innovative philosophy of the New Frontier enabled him to compile an incredible record of accomplishment during his whip years that has seldom been equalled in Senate history.

He was in large measure responsible for conceiving and guiding through Congress two of the Kennedy administration's first major achievements — creation of the Peace Corps and the U.S. Arms Control and Disarmament Agency — and played a pivotal role in Senate ratification of the 1963 Limited Nuclear Test Ban Treaty. In addition, the period 1961 to 1964 (the Eighty-seventh and Eighty-eighth Congresses) saw the flowering of a score of progressive measures in the fields of health, education, welfare, conservation, foreign aid and civil rights, all of which represented years of persistent effort by Humphrey.

For instance, the first bill he had introduced as a senator in 1949 called for a program of health care for the aged under Social Security. The bill died when the Eighty-first Congress adjourned without acting on it, and Humphrey introduced it in succeeding years without any results. In 1958, he got Senator Clinton Anderson of New Mexico, one of the powers of the Senate and a member of the Finance Committee, which would handle the bill, to introduce it. The measure, which had now become known as "Medicare," advanced slowly through the legislative channels until 1960, when it was sent to the Senate floor for a vote. But it was rejected. It was introduced again in 1961 but was again rejected by the Eighty-seventh Congress and was ignored by an election-minded Eighty-eighth Congress in 1963–64.

Humphrey, however, refused to give up. He noted that it now had widespread public support and predicted in 1964, "Its time will come." He was right. The bill was approved by Congress and signed into law in 1965, the year he became vice president and sixteen years after he first proposed the idea.

In 1950, his second year in the Senate, Humphrey took the lead in persuading the Truman administration to send surplus wheat to aid starving people in India and Pakistan. Two years later, in a speech to the Grain Terminal Association in St. Paul, he suggested that the U.S. use surplus farm commodities to aid famine-stricken and impoverished countries as part of our foreign policy. In 1954, he incorporated his suggestion in a bill that contained the framework of the Food for Peace program that was proposed by President Eisenhower in 1959, and he continued to push for expansion of the program — a popular cause with Minnesota farmers — in the early 1960's.

Humphrey was the first to propose a separate government agency to handle the Food for Peace program and was instrumental in getting ex-Congressman George McGovern of South Dakota named Food for Peace Director in 1961 after McGovern lost a Senate election in 1960. "Humphrey was the father of the Food for Peace program," says McGovern, who moved to the Senate and next door to the Humphreys in 1962 and was to contest Humphrey for the Democratic presidential nomination six years later.

Other major Humphrey proposals translated into legislative reality during his whip years included the Job Corps, which Humphrey proposed in 1959 as a "Youth Conservation Corps" and which was approved as a cornerstone of the 1964 War on Poverty program, and the National Wilderness Preservation System. He also was the original author of the 1958 National Defense Education Act, which provided funds to college students and which was expanded by Kennedy. Humphrey conceived the idea of linking education to the defense effort after the October, 1957, launching of the Soviet Sputnik.

But the two most lasting monuments to Humphrey's Senate career were those built on the foundation of his longtime concern for promoting international cooperation and reducing world tensions — the Peace Corps and nuclear disarmament.

Spurred by the ideas of a Minneapolis newspaperman and several other members of Congress (Wisconsin's Henry Reuss was among the first to push the idea in the House) who sought funds for a study of such a program, Humphrey introduced a bill in June, 1960, calling for a program to send young American volunteers overseas to teach and help carry out economic development programs. The bill got nowhere that year but the idea was pushed by Kennedy during his presidential campaign and he gave it top priority status when he took office.

Humphrey introduced the administration bill in mid-1961, and spearheaded the successful drive for Congressional approval after Kennedy first established the Peace Corps by executive order. Congress authorized an initial corps of 500 men and women in 1961, a figure that was boosted to 14,000 three years later.

Humphrey's outstanding achievement in the Senate, however, and perhaps the one which historians will judge his greatest single contribution in any area, came in the field of disarmament and arms control. He made his first formal statement on the subject in 1950, a month after President Truman announced that the U.S. was going ahead with plans to develop the hydrogen bomb. In a speech at the Washington National Cathedral entitled "God, Man and the Hydrogen Bomb," Humphrey pleaded for "universal disarmament" and "an unequivocal agreement to abolish war." His remarks, which showed the influence of Woodrow Wilson's "Fourteen Points" that Humphrey had memorized as a boy, received little attention as did similar Humphrey speeches promoting disarmament while the cold war intensified. By 1955, Humphrey had concluded universal disarmament was a hopeless dream, but that an effort had to be made to halt the arms race. "The United States," he told the Senate, as he sponsored a resolution to establish a Joint Congressional Disarmament Subcommittee, "must begin to seek progress in those areas — no matter how limited — in which there appears some chance of agreement and progress."

In 1956, the Senate approved his resolution, at the same time placing the disarmament subcommittee under the Senate Foreign Relations Committee and making him chairman. Humphrey used the position to generate support for a nuclear test ban agreement with the Soviet Union, but he found little interest in the Eisenhower administration (which had appointed former Minnesota Governor Harold Stassen as its disarmament advisor). Eisenhower, in fact, termed such a proposal "dangerous" and Vice President Richard Nixon called it "catastrophic nonsense" when Democratic presidential candidate Adlai Stevenson used testimony from the Humphrey subcommittee to urge a ban on unrestrained testing of nuclear weapons.[3] Humphrey struggled to keep the issue alive during Eisenhower's second term (he once made a four-hour Senate speech on the subject), and was encouraged when Eisenhower advocated a test ban agreement in 1958. But interest waned as U.S. and Soviet negotiators reached a stalemate, and Humphrey's February, 1960, bill to establish a "National Peace Agency" to coordinate scattered government disarmament studies got nowhere.

President Kennedy was more interested in the idea and when Humphrey

[3] Eugene McCarthy was referring to Nixon's comment in his 1960 nominating speech for Stevenson when he described Stevenson as "a man who talked sense to the American people" and added, "What did the scoffers say? The scoffers said: 'Nonsense. Catastrophic nonsense.' "

introduced a bill in June, 1961, to establish a United States Disarmament Agency, there was reason to believe Humphrey would succeed this time. However, the climate for a test ban suddenly deteriorated when the Soviet Union, in the wake of tensions caused by the building of the Berlin Wall, announced it was ending a three year old voluntary moratorium on testing nuclear weapons. Humphrey kept after Kennedy, though, arguing that he should couple a firm position against Communist aggression with an equally firm stand on disarmament. In early July, after returning from a trip to Berlin, Humphrey convinced Kennedy during a swim in the White House pool that he could drive the bill through Congress.

"We had hardly got dried off when the president asked, 'Do you really think that we have any chance on this?' " Humphrey later recalled. "I answered, 'Mr. President, I don't know, but I know that we can at least give it an honest effort. If we fail, we can try again.' "

Humphrey didn't fail. He mounted an intensive lobbying campaign, lined up an impressive list of witnesses to testify in support of the bill, and won Senate approval in August. The House quickly followed suit and on September 26, Kennedy signed the bill creating the U.S. Arms Control and Disarmament Agency, renamed because some senators objected to "Disarmament Agency." Two days later, Kennedy presented a new U.S. plan for general and complete disarmament to the United Nations, which was followed by two more years of unproductive test ban negotiations before Senator Thomas Dodd of Connecticut introduced a resolution suggesting a formal U.S. offer to negotiate a general nuclear test ban treaty. The resolution caught fire when Humphrey co-sponsored it, attracting thirty-two other Senators of both parties and making it clear to both Moscow and Washington that such a treaty would have a chance of Senate ratification.

Kennedy made the formal offer to negotiate on June 10, and negotiations were begun in Moscow two weeks later. They were successfully completed a month later and on July 25, Humphrey and other Senate leaders flew to Moscow and looked on as representatives of the U.S., Russia and Great Britain initialed the draft treaty suspending all aboveground nuclear weapons testing.

Humphrey returned to Washington to prepare for the Senate debate on ratification of the treaty, during which he unabashedly courted Republicans to gain the two-thirds majority needed for approval. His efforts paid off as Minority Leader Everett Dirksen of Illinois announced his support and called on his colleagues to vote for ratification. On September 24, 1963, the Senate approved ratification for the historic first treaty to restrict the use and development of nuclear weapons by a 80–19 vote.

After the White House ceremony at which President Kennedy signed the treaty, Humphrey filed out with the rest of the witnesses to the signing, but

Kennedy called him back. "Hubert," the President said with a smile, "this is your treaty — and it had better work."

A few months later, Senator Ernest Gruening of Alaska (who would become one of the first members of the Senate to oppose the escalation of the Vietnam War by the Johnson-Humphrey administration), hailed Humphrey's role in the signing of the test ban treaty, the creation of the Peace Corps, and the passage of other legislation credited to Kennedy. "These are major achievements, any one of which taken alone would cause Hubert Humphrey's service in public life to be rated as outstanding and unforgettable," Gruening said as he introduced into the *Congressional Record* an article entitled "Why Humphrey Gets Taken for Granted." The article, from the *New Republic* magazine, examined Humphrey's role in disarmament and the test ban treaty and concluded, "Men have won the Nobel Peace Prize for less."

Humphrey's push for disarmament accounted for only a small part of his overall activities during the whip years, however. Actually stepping up the exhausting pace of his earlier years, he spouted words, introduced bills, whirled in and out of meetings and ranged all over the Senate's legislative spectrum. His activities during his first year as whip (1961), for instance, filled thirty columns in the *Congressional Record Index*, including nearly three hundred amendments, resolutions and bills introduced.

In 1962, Humphrey explained, in a report to his Minnesota constituents, why it was impossible for him to take his friends' advice to slow down. In addition to his whip's duties, he pointed out that he was a member of four Senate committees — Foreign Relations, Appropriations, Government Operations and Small Business — and that his office each day received as many as a thousand letters, a hundred speaking invitations, more than five hundred telephone calls, and an average of a hundred visitors. To assure Minnesotans he was giving them their money's worth, Humphrey offered the log of one twenty-hour day which, while longer than his typical sixteen-hour workday, illustrates why he found time to read only one novel (*Seven Days in May*[4]) in the ten-year period from 1955–64:

> 6:30 A.M.: Out of bed for a drive to Capitol Hill and a breakfast meeting on federal aid to education legislation with Majority Leader Mike Mansfield, Health-Education-Welfare Secretary Ribicoff and White House Assistant Ted Sorenson.
>
> 9:30 A.M.: Checked into my office in the New Senate Office Building, read the important morning mail, dictated a dozen letters and placed five phone calls.
>
> 10 A.M.: Attended a meeting of the Senate Foreign Relations Committee to hear witnesses on the Educational and Cultural Exchange Act.
>
> 10:30 A.M.: Checked in at my Capitol Building office and returned several

[4] A fictional account of a U.S.-Soviet nuclear confrontation written by Fletcher Knebel and Charles Bailey II of the Cowles Publications' Washington bureau.

phone calls, including one to Agriculture Secretary Freeman to discuss farm legislation.

10:45 A.M.: Met with national officers of the Railroad Brotherhood to discuss pattern of railroad mergers and effects on employment.

11 A.M.: Another meeting with Majority Leader Mansfield and others to plan strategy for legislation to establish hospital and health care under Social Security.

11:40 A.M.: Met with Senator Eugene McCarthy and Representatives Joseph Karth and John Blatnik to discuss potential candidates for a Federal appointment in Minnesota.

Noon: Checked in for the opening of the Senate session and introduced four bills, including one to extend provisions of the Food for Peace program.

12:30 P.M.: Forced to cancel lunch with Senators McCarthy and Symington and Billy Graham because of a call from President Kennedy to a meeting at the White House.

12:45 P.M.: Arrived at White House for an hour-long conference and briefing by the President on developments in Southeast Asia.

2 P.M.: Returned to the Capitol, ate a sandwich for lunch, picked up a folder of reports to study and letters to sign and stepped into the Senate Chamber to act as Floor Leader in the absence of Senator Mansfield.

3 P.M.: Stepped into a room just off the Senate floor to address sixty-five visiting newsmen from Scandinavian nations for twenty minutes. (Left the Senate for brief periods several other times to greet visiting Minnesotans.)

4:15 P.M.: Spent a half hour in Capitol office near Senate Chamber, dictating another twenty-five letters and returning a dozen phone calls, including two to Administration officials on Area Redevelopment plans for Minnesota.

4:45 P.M.: Returned to the Senate until adjournment at 5:02 P.M., then took a half hour to get back to my office, with a dozen stops in the halls for impromptu conversations with other Senators and Capitol visitors.

5:45 P.M.: Checked with staff members, answered more phone calls and left Capitol Hill for the first of four downtown receptions, two honoring the independence of new African nations.

8 P.M.: Left final reception for a formal dinner at the Embassy of Denmark in honor of the Danish Under Secretary of State.

10:30 P.M.: Left the Danish Embassy to meet in a downtown hotel with officials of the Minnesota Farmers Union (Dwayne Andreas and M. W. Thatcher) to discuss their proposal to the president for expansion of cooperative movements in Latin America.

12:30 A.M.: Left meeting with Andreas and Thatcher.

1 A.M.: Arrived home, studied two committee reports, dictated another twenty letters.

2 A.M.: In bed and asleep.[5]

Humphrey's perpetual motion may have impressed his constituents, but it also raised questions in the minds of those close to him about where

[5] A more normal Humphrey day usually began at 7:00 A.M. with a cup of coffee, a few phone calls and a quick glance at the Washington *Post.* Humphrey read the New York *Times* on the way to work and skimmed Minnesota papers, marking them for articles he wanted clipped. He always carried a briefcase full of papers in his car or however he traveled and used every free minute working on them. Humphrey ne-

all that activity was taking him. "The question of how he spends his time is one that has always bothered me," says a former Humphrey legislative assistant. "He's a whirling dervish who absorbs things fantastically quick, but the idea of Humphrey reading a book or sitting down long enough to seriously think about the implications of what he was doing is hard to imagine. He was so active that I don't think he had time to think about the big things. I think also that it was impossible for Humphrey to think without speaking. As a physiological process, I doubt he's ever thought of anything that he never talked about, which is something of a liability."

The disarmament issue was important to Humphrey in addition to its obvious political value, the former aide feels, because "it was the one thing which captured his attention over a period of time and forced him to concentrate. He's a victim of the wide range of his own interests — there are no senators I can think of who really are experts on so many things. But even for him, there are only so many hours in a day. There's a question of how much is improvisation and how much is the result of steady application of self. This was a problem for anyone on his staff working on a particular subject or issue. You never knew for sure if Humphrey would give your speech or someone else's and you never knew for sure if the position he took this week was relevant to the one he took last week.

"He isn't shallow, it's just that the amount of time he could spend on one subject was never there in as concentrated form as the staff person would have liked and, over time, it became translated in the staff person's mind as an inability to focus in on an issue. I think disarmament was closest to being an exception to that over the years." Humphrey's reply to criticism that he was spreading himself too thin was, "I run a clinic in which I am the only general practitioner."

However, Humphrey's incurable optimism and frenetic activity caused some of his colleagues to look with scepticism upon even the nuclear test ban treaty. "Hubert personifies the kind of easy optimism which we, as a nation living in dangerous times, can't afford," one senator said in explaining his vote against ratification of the treaty. "It is fine to be buoyant and to hope for the best, as he always does, but sometimes it isn't realistic."

Humphrey may have been making some people uneasy, but he was winning new friends during his whip years among the ranks of his old archenemy, big business. His new, moderate image was recognized by *Business Week* magazine in June, 1963, in an article entitled, "Firebrand Senator Cools Down." The article approvingly noted Humphrey's efforts to pass a state constitutional amendment to give tax concessions to steel companies as an inducement to invest in low-grade iron ore processing plants on northern Minnesota's depleted Iron Range. It also lauded his work in passing the

---

glected to tell his constituents that he was chauffered around Washington during his whip years in a car that came with his leadership position.

Communications Satellite Act of 1962, which some liberals regarded as granting a monopoly in the space communications field to the American Telephone and Telegraph Company.

"I now think it's better for me to sit inside, at the seat of power," Humphrey told *Business Week,* "instead of waving banners outside. I'm fifteen years in the Senate. I don't think I should be making angry marches on the White House when I can just calmly walk inside."

Nor did Humphrey subscribe to the "all or nothing" doctrine of liberals who looked upon all compromise as an automatic betrayal of principle. "If I believe in something, I will fight for it with all I have," he said in another 1963 interview that summed up the lessons he had learned and signalled the new direction he was now moving in. "But I do not demand all or nothing. I would rather get something than nothing. . . . Professional liberals want the fiery debate. They glory in defeat. The hardest job for a politician today is to have the courage to be a moderate. It's easy to take an extreme position."

Hand in hand with Humphrey's friendlier attitude toward big business was a growing disenchantment with big government. When Norman Sherman, who would become one of Humphrey's top aides in later years, joined his staff in 1963, he recalls that Humphrey told him that " 'bureaucracy and big government are the enemy.' Humphrey said people don't know how to deal with big government and that any time a constituent complains, he is presumed right until proven wrong or mad." Sherman says he found this attitude "sort of fetching, since Humphrey always has been thought of as a big government guy, but on an operational level, he felt the opposite."

Humphrey's efforts on behalf of Minnesota business interests would later cause him some embarrassment as vice president, but in the early 1960's, he had a reputation as a man who could get things done for Minnesota businessmen regardless of their political views.[6] As a result, few Minnesota businessmen were surprised when Humphrey suggested to an American Management Association conference in New York City in 1964 that "we drop once and for all the myth of hostility toward business by government and by the Democratic Party and get on with a fruitful business-government partnership. . . . To make the promise of America a reality will take cooperation and respect between business and government . . . ."

Despite his close relationship to the White House, Humphrey occasionally grew weary of the administration's compromises with Southern Democrats and Republicans. He once complained to a White House aide, "It's hard for us down here to keep on defending the things we think the White House

---

[6] According to Columnist Drew Pearson, when Humphrey urged Kennedy to allow private U.S. companies to sell wheat to Russia, Minnesota Republicans attacked Humphrey as "soft on Communism" until executives of the Cargill Corporation, a large Minnesota-based grain company and a generous contributor to the GOP, passed the word to Republican officials to stop the attacks. They were stopped.

believes in, when the White House seems to spend its time saying nice things about the other side."

It was a minor gripe, however, and doesn't even register in Humphrey's memory now. "I would say that of all the years that I've had in politics," he reminisced in a 1971 interview, "none were more satisfying than the ones I had as majority whip. I got along well with Mansfield — I think in a sense we complemented each other — and I was close to Kennedy. I really was his ace-in-the-hole in many ways. I know that President Kennedy relied on me a great deal to do things that needed to be done in Congress, and I had total access to the White House."

Even though his next reelection campaign was still three years away, it was on Humphrey's mind when he extracted a pledge from Kennedy in late 1963 to locate two choice federal research facilities in Minnesota. One was a space research laboratory for the University of Minnesota and the other was a gigantic two hundred billion electron volt nuclear accelerator, which not only would provide a major boost to the Minnesota economy but would offset the drain of scientists and engineers from the Midwest to the East and West Coasts. Humphrey discussed the projects with Kennedy as they walked through the White House Rose Garden after Kennedy's last breakfast meeting with Democratic Congressional leaders on November 21. "These things were being worked out and he had given me his word on them, both of them," Humphrey recalls.[7]

Humphrey went from the White House breakfast to a downtown Washington hotel to speak to the National Association of Mental Health convention. He told the convention that the continued life of the world depends, fundamentally, on the mental health of the world's leaders. And he added, in a tragically prophetic footnote, "the emotional instability of a single man, if left untended, could impose monstrous penalties on our society."

The next day, Humphrey and his wife were having lunch at the Chilean Embassy in Washington when White House Aide Ralph Dungan telephoned him with news of an event that would turn him toward a new destiny. Humphrey remembers Dungan saying, " 'The president has been shot.' I said, 'What president?' He said, 'President Kennedy.' " Dungan told Humphrey it wasn't known whether Kennedy was dead and promised to call back as soon as he found out. "I hadn't more than hung up the phone when he called back and said, 'He's dead,' " Humphrey recalls.

Shocked and overwhelmed with grief, Humphrey wept as he told the luncheon guests what had happened and then went immediately to the White House. He sat in stunned silence with Dungan and another presidential aide, Kenneth O'Donnell, while they waited for the plane bearing Kennedy's body and the

---

[7] After Johnson became president, Humphrey told him of Kennedy's commitment, but Johnson refused to honor all of it. The space laboratory went to Minnesota but the giant atom smasher ended up in Illinois as a favor to Minority Leader Dirksen.

new president, Lyndon Johnson, to return from Dallas. "I remember they were fixing up the president's office while he was away," says Humphrey. "They were putting in a red rug, and I thought that damn red rug looked like it was covered with blood. It was really a terrible shock. I'd grown to have great affection for Kennedy. I think he was on his way to becoming a great president."

One of the first people Johnson saw when he returned to Washington was Humphrey, who was standing by as Kennedy's body was taken off the plane. Johnson passed word to Humphrey that he wanted to see him, Majority Leader Mansfield and Florida's George Smathers, one of Kennedy's closest personal friends and secretary of the Democratic Conference of Senators. The three men and Johnson met that evening in Johnson's vice presidential office next door to the White House. Johnson asked for their help in reassuring the nation and the world that there would be no abrupt changes in U.S. domestic and foreign policy. He also discussed with them his plans to appoint a blue-ribbon commission to investigate the tragedy in Dallas.

After the meeting ended, Johnson asked Humphrey to bring Muriel to the Johnson home in northwest Washington, where the two old Senate friends, their wives and the Johnsons' two daughters reviewed the unbelievable events of the tragic day that had just ended. "We sat out there until about two o'clock in the morning, just the four of us and his family, going through what had happened in Dallas and just talking," Humphrey recalls. "He didn't know what had happened."

Not surprisingly, Johnson relied heavily on the man with whom he'd had such a close relationship in the Senate to help smooth the transition to the new administration. Again, Humphrey played the familiar role of goodwill ambassador to the liberal-intellectual wing of the Democratic Party, providing reassurance of Johnson's intentions to build upon the New Frontier foundation and seeking pledges of support for the president's efforts to instill a sense of confidence and continuity in the grief-stricken nation. Humphrey also helped Johnson persuade many of the key Kennedy advisers to stay on in the new administration, including Minnesotan Walter Heller, the Council of Economic Advisers chairman whose "New Economics" set the tone of domestic policy for both Kennedy and Johnson.[8]

Johnson also relied on Humphrey's personal and political counsel during the difficult transition period. In his very first days in the White House, Johnson sought Humphrey's advice on the timing and format of his initial address to the nation. It was largely on Humphrey's advice — which was

[8] Unlike many Kennedy advisers, Heller had gone out of his way to be friendly to Johnson during his lonely vice presidential years. He made it a practice to give Johnson a copy of the economic briefing paper used by Kennedy to prepare for his press conferences, and as a result, Johnson felt more kindly toward Heller than perhaps any other Kennedy aide.

contrary to what most advisers urged — that Johnson decided to wait until January 8 and make the address in his natural habitat of Capitol Hill at the opening of the second session of the Eighty-eighth Congress. The night before the speech, Johnson summoned Humphrey and Abe Fortas to his home, The Elms, where they spent four hours polishing it. And it was Humphrey, in fact, who persuaded Johnson to make a short statement invoking Kennedy's memory with the exhortation that was to become the theme of Johnson's first year in office, "Let us continue." Humphrey and Fortas dictated the final version of the speech to Lynda Bird Johnson who finished typing it at 2:00 A.M., just ten hours before Johnson was due before the joint session of Congress.

However, Humphrey was to play a far more important role in the coming months in helping Johnson establish his image of leadership and of mastery over Congress.[9] It was Humphrey, in fact, who was instrumental in giving Johnson his first and most important symbolic victory on Capitol Hill just three days after Kennedy's death. Humphrey helped persuade nine Democrats to change their votes as the Senate defeated a bill by Republican Karl Mundt of South Dakota to block the sale of U.S. surplus wheat to the Soviet Union. Despite Kennedy's strong opposition to the measure, the Senate had failed to defeat it only two weeks earlier. When the bill was killed, the action was seen as a vote of confidence in the new administration and an important step toward thawing U.S.-Soviet relations. Johnson was so elated when Humphrey telephoned him with news of the victory that he impulsively invited the Humphreys to dinner that evening.

Humphrey also was an indefatigable lobbyist for Senate passage of the centerpiece of the administration's economic policy, the 1964 omnibus tax bill. The bill, which had been passed by the House in September, 1963, provided a huge reduction in both income taxes and government expenditures and was pushed through the Senate Finance Committee and the Senate itself with remarkable speed. Final Senate passage came after six days of debate in February, with Humphrey supplementing Johnson's own forceful lobbying on behalf of the bill. It was signed by Johnson on February 26, his first major Congressional victory.

Humphrey would prove an invaluable ally to Johnson in securing Congressional approval in 1964 of several other Kennedy proposals that had been written off as defeated, including the basic legislation for the anti-poverty program, federal aid to college students and for mass transit facilities, and a controversial farm bill that included an important wheat price support and a food stamp plan. Before the wheat price support bill came

[9] Humphrey plainly felt more at home with the folksy Johnson than with his elegant predecessor. Comparing their styles in 1964, he said, "It's like the difference between the court of Louis XIV and the early American republic under Andrew Jackson."

up for House action, Johnson handed Humphrey a list of twelve big city Democrats whose votes were doubtful and told him, "I want you to get these men." Eleven of the twelve voted for the bill.

But nowhere in Humphrey's long public career was there to be a greater moment of truth or a challenge with more meaning for his now-revived hopes for the presidency than his role in the battle over the historic Civil Rights Act of 1964.

The groundwork for what was to be the most spectacular civil rights breakthrough of the century was laid by President Kennedy on June 10, 1963, when he announced he was sending a comprehensive civil rights bill to Congress. His action was dramatically emphasized that same night when civil rights leader Medgar Evers was murdered in Mississippi, and again in September, when four Negro schoolgirls were killed when a bomb exploded in a Birmingham, Alabama, church. Within hours after Johnson took office, he told civil rights leaders he would allow no watering down of the Kennedy legislation, a promise he repeated when the House passed an even stronger civil rights bill in February, 1964, and he designated Humphrey to be the floor manager of the bill in the Senate.

"This is the most challenging assignment of my legislative career," Humphrey said as he contemplated the task of guiding the bill through the perils of a Southern filibuster. Humphrey also knew there was more riding on the outcome of the civil rights battle than just a major legislative victory for Johnson. He obviously was in the front ranks of Johnson's possible running mates and it was clear to everyone that just as the civil rights issue had catapulted him to national prominence in 1948, it could also give him the momentum to virtually guarantee his selection as Johnson's running mate at the Democratic convention in August.

However, Humphrey also recognized that even all his parliamentary skills and renowned persuasiveness wouldn't help unless he could somehow gain the necessary two-thirds majority vote to invoke the cloture rule that would shut off debate and end the Southern filibuster. Never in its history had the Senate succeeded in invoking cloture in a civil rights debate, but Humphrey was convinced it could be done.

After taking stock of the situation, he made three essential strategy decisions. First, the civil rights proponents would have to have bipartisan support, which above all else meant cultivating Minority Leader Dirksen. Second, they would have to be well organized, with bipartisan team captains appointed to discuss each major section of the bill and to make certain that fifty-one senators were always present to supply a quorum. Finally, the debate would have to be kept on a high level to avoid bitterness, and Humphrey would have to try to accommodate Southerners whenever possible in procedural matters.

Working closely with Majority Leader Mansfield and Minority Whip

Thomas Kuchel of California, Humphrey saw to it that all three strategy decisions were implemented. He maintained close contact with Dirksen, appealing to his sense of patriotism and duty and shamelessly praising him; joined with Kuchel in designating thirty-six Democrats and sixteen Republicans to be available on short notice for quorum calls and in publishing a daily "Bipartisan Civil Rights Newsletter" to keep civil rights supporters abreast of developments and stir up grass roots support, and he painstakingly strove to maintain a good working relationship with Senator Richard Russell of Georgia, the leader of the Southerners.

On March 9, the Senate began its discussion of the bill, and on March 26, formally took it up as the pending business of the Senate. On March 30, the day after Easter, the fifty-seven day filibuster began in earnest. In a major speech opening the formal debate, Humphrey issued a "friendly challenge" to the Southerners. "We will join with you in debating this bill; will you join with us in voting . . . after the debate has been concluded? Will you permit the Senate, and in a sense, the nation, to come to grips with these issues and decide them, one way or the other?" The offer to debate was unnecessary and the challenge to allow a vote was ignored by the Southerners, who taking their cue from Russell, argued that the bill was unconstitutional and that it would grant "dictatorial police powers" to the federal government. Russell called for defeat of the entire bill and adamantly opposed any compromises.

Humphrey's patience wore thin and the morale in the civil rights camp sagged as the debate dragged on week after week, with Humphrey at one point charging that the Senate was acting like "adult delinquents." But in the first week of May, Humphrey, Dirksen and Attorney General Robert Kennedy sat down in Dirksen's office to discuss Dirksen's objections to several key parts of the bill — sections prohibiting racial discrimination by employers and unions and in all public accommodations.

The negotiations were almost unprecedented in Senate history, with a kind of *ad hoc* committee taking the place of a regular legislative committee. Even some civil rights backers agreed with Russell when he charged that an unconstitutional "troika" of Humphrey, Dirksen and Kennedy were bypassing the Senate's legislative function. The negotiators were uncertain whether they could reach an agreement. Humphrey was stunned at the first meeting when Dirksen brought in some seventy amendments, but it soon became clear in a series of meetings which followed that Dirksen's main concern was to set some limits to the attorney general's enforcement powers. "It was like labor negotiations," a participant in the Humphrey-Dirksen-Kennedy meetings said later. "Everyone started out in adversary positions and overstated their cases. It took some time for it to become clear that they really weren't so very far apart."

Out of the negotiations came a substitute bill which provided that the

Justice Department could intervene only in areas where there was a "pattern or practice" of discrimination and otherwise only after an individual had taken his grievance to the newly-created Community Relations Service and Equal Employment Opportunity Commission or, as a last resort, to court. The substitute bill, designed to win over the needed Republican votes for cloture, was introduced on May 26, one day before Humphrey's fifty-third birthday. With Dirksen's support now assured, Humphrey set the date for the cloture vote for June 10. The night before the cloture vote, Johnson called Humphrey at the whip's office and asked him how many votes he had. Humphrey nervously admitted he had only sixty-six, one short of the required two-thirds majority but, later in the evening, he received word that two Republicans who had fought Dirksen, Bourke Hickenlooper of Iowa and John Williams of Delaware, would vote for cloture and he called Johnson with the good news.

At 11:10 A.M. the next day, three and a half months after debate began, exactly one year after Kennedy introduced his civil rights bill and almost sixteen years after Humphrey's historic civil rights speech at the 1948 Democratic National Convention, buzzers called senators to the floor for the cloture vote. With Humphrey sitting at a front row desk between Mansfield and Harry Byrd of Virginia, the longest filibuster in Senate history was ended by a 71–29 vote for cloture.

Humphrey's supreme moment of personal triumph came nine days later, on the evening of June 19, as the Senate approved the Civil Rights Act by a vote of 73–27, and he walked out of the Capitol into the soft summer twilight to be greeted by cries of "good job" and "God bless you" from several hundred people waiting to hear the outcome of the vote.

Humphrey's victory was tempered by the knowledge that his son Robert, twenty, was dangerously ill with cancer of the lymph glands. In the last week of the civil rights debate, his son was operated on at the Mayo Clinic in Rochester, Minnesota. After the operation he called his father, who was unable to leave Washington, and told him, "Dad, I guess I've had it." Humphrey, who'd been told by physicians that the boy's chances for recovery were good, tried to reassure him. "Don't be silly," he said. "I've talked to the doctors and everything is going to be all right." Then he hung up the phone and cried.

Humphrey returned to Minnesota the day after the historic vote to be with his son — who recovered — and came back to Washington on July 2 to witness the signing of the Civil Rights Act of 1964. Inscribed on the copy of President Johnson's remarks at the bill-signing ceremony were these words: "To Hubert Humphrey — without whom it couldn't have happened."

BOOK THREE
THE LIMITS OF LIBERALISM
1964–1967

CHAPTER XI

CONFRONTATION — 1964

*Nobody has to woo me. I'm old reliable,
available Hubert.*
      Hubert Humphrey in a July, 1964, interview.

*At no time in the recent history of any
political party has a party presented to its
convention and . . . to the people of
this country two men who are so alike in
energy, in ability, in experience, in dedication, and in compassion as the two men
whom the Democratic party will present
to this nation for approval in November. . . .*
      Eugene McCarthy, nominating Hubert
      Humphrey for vice president at the
      1964 Democratic National Convention.

One morning in January, 1964, Ted Van Dyk, a twenty-nine year old public affairs officer for the European Common Market, walked into Hubert Humphrey's Senate office and handed Administrative Assistant William Connell a three-page typewritten memorandum marked "Private." Although Van Dyk hardly knew Humphrey, he had long felt that the Minnesota senator would make a good president of the United States, and his memorandum was indirectly dedicated to that purpose. The thesis of the memo was that President Johnson had to be persuaded that Humphrey would be his strongest possible running mate in the 1964 election. "The best chance of doing this would be to convince President Johnson that American voters were more concerned with one thing than with all other considerations . . . that the 1964 Democratic vice presidential candidate *would be the best president in event of tragedy*," the memo declared.

The searing memory of the tragedy in Dallas that had made Johnson president only two months earlier dramatized the need for a strong, capable vice president, Van Dyk argued. He urged that a discreet but aggressive campaign be organized to change the public image of Humphrey from that of a man who seemed a "little too much like my neighbor down the street" to that of "an experienced leader in Congress . . . well versed in domestic and foreign affairs . . . a good family man . . . President Johnson's strong right arm . . . the sort of man to count on should, God forbid, anything happen to President Johnson." [1]

Van Dyk's unsolicited memo was hardly the first time that Connell or other top Humphrey aides and supporters pondered the question of what they could do to persuade Johnson to pick Humphrey as his running mate. Within days after Johnson was sworn in, the calls began pouring in from Humphrey backers in Minnesota and around the country asking what they could do to advance Humphrey's cause. The answer at first was simply, "Sit tight." Humphrey himself was too numbed with a sense of personal loss over John F. Kennedy's death and too involved in the intimate circle of advisers helping the new president through the difficult transitional period to give much thought to his own future. "The best thing I can do," he told his staff in the first weeks after Johnson's takeover, "is to be a good senator — and a good majority whip — and to be Johnson's friend and supporter."

A few Humphrey insiders began gathering quietly in early December for nighttime strategy sessions at the Washington home of Max Kampelman, Humphrey's longtime friend and closest political adviser, to discuss ways to promote Humphrey's selection as vice president. The group included Bill Connell; Dr. Evron Kirkpatrick, Humphrey's old University of Minnesota professor who was now director of the American Political Science Association; former Secretary of Defense Oscar Chapman; Joseph Rauh, Jr., vice chairman of the Americans for Democratic Action; and Charles Brown, manager of Missouri Senator Stuart Symington's 1960 presidential campaign. Operating on the premise that Humphrey was Johnson's personal choice, but also mindful of Humphrey's bitter experiences in presidential politics in 1956 and 1960 and of the fact that Attorney General Robert Kennedy was also a prospective contender, they decided they must move carefully and discreetly and not involve Humphrey directly. Humphrey's only orders were, "I don't want to be put in any kind of negative position, anti-Kennedy or anybody else. Keep it positive."

[1] Just in case anything *did* happen to Johnson before the November election, including further disclosures about escapades of Johnson protege Bobby Baker, the same strategy could be used to "advance Senator Humphrey's candidacy for another office," Van Dyk said in his memo.

Thus, Van Dyk's "best man" premise fit neatly into the soft-sell strategy being developed by the Humphrey inner circle. Connell invited Van Dyk back in the first week of February to meet with the Humphrey strategists, who authorized him to prepare a longer memorandum expanding on the idea that Johnson would be both a statesman and a smart politician by choosing Humphrey. Van Dyk drafted an eleven-page memorandum that was worked over by Kirkpatrick and Press Secretary Robert Jensen and anonymously circulated to two hundred columnists, publishers, businessmen and other opinion makers. Articles, polls, and opinions favorable to Humphrey were gleaned from newspapers and magazines and mailed to party officials, labor leaders and potential convention delegates with the knowledge that they found their way back to the White House.

By now, Humphrey himself fully approved of the vice presidential boom being built up on his behalf and, privately encouraged by Johnson to take confidential soundings around the country, he began making his first overt moves. He accepted bids for television and other interviews and made dozens of public appearances around the country, including an important trip in February to California, where he shuttled between Los Angeles and San Francisco for four days making news and building on a solid base of support he found there. When Humphrey discovered, as he was leaving for California, that his advisers had booked him to speak before the liberal California Democratic Council which was feuding with the official party organization, he exploded at Connell, "What the hell are you trying to do, demonstrate that I can walk through fire?" However, Humphrey emerged unscathed from the session and picked up some important allies during the California trip, including State Democratic Chairman Eugene Wyman, a Los Angeles attorney who would become Humphrey's most loyal supporter in California. "I proceeded on my own to advise the president that as far as California was concerned and as far as I was concerned, Hubert Humphrey would make a great vice president," Wyman later said.

Back in Washington, Humphrey was named floor manager of the civil rights bill, an assignment that would occupy most of his energy over the next three and a half months and would eventually help cement his claim for the vice presidential nomination.[2] Hoping to get some rest before the grueling civil rights filibuster began, he and Muriel planned a short vacation in late February in Bermuda. However, Connell and Kampelman persuaded Humphrey to go to Jamaica where, they said, "the sun is the same but there are other benefits." The other benefits were chiefly one, a chance to visit at length with U.S. Ambassador William Dougherty, a former president of the Postal Workers Union and a close friend of AFL-CIO President George Meany.

As a result of their talk, Dougherty arranged for Humphrey to stop in

[2] See chapter ten.

Miami Beach on his way home and see Meany, who was meeting with the AFL-CIO Executive Council in the Americana Hotel. Meany asked Humphrey to breakfast the next morning, "not in my suite but down in the coffee shop where we can be seen," and then invited him to one of the council's secret policy sessions, where Humphrey, the first politician ever to attend one of the meetings, discussed foreign and domestic problems for forty-five minutes.

Meany also took Humphrey down the hall to a meeting of the AFL-CIO's political arm, the Committee on Political Education (COPE), where COPE Director Al Barkan declared, "Maybe I'm speaking out of turn — and as you know the AFL-CIO does not officially take a position during a campaign — but I can say, speaking personally, what a great thing I think it would be to have you on the ticket." The obvious message that Meany was giving his blessing to Humphrey was not lost on the labor leaders or on the White House. When Johnson later asked Meany who his first three choices were for vice president Meany replied, "I have only one choice — Hubert Humphrey."

By spring, Humphrey clearly was a front-runner among the score of potential Johnson running mates most frequently mentioned by the political experts. All of Washington noticed when Johnson telephoned Humphrey on March 8, seconds after Humphrey appeared on a "Meet the Press" television interview, and congratulated him and Muriel. At the same time, Democratic leaders at the weekly White House legislative breakfasts noticed that Johnson went out of his way to praise Humphrey for a speech reported in the papers that day and for his work on Capitol Hill, and he often pulled polls out of his pocket showing Humphrey drawing strong support for vice president. At one of the legislative breakfasts, Humphrey drew a hearty laugh from the president by placing a facsimile Johnson-Humphrey campaign button under his orange juice glass.

Humphrey got a direct sign that he was Johnson's first choice in March when he discussed the subject of his own nomination with Johnson — the only time the matter was raised until he was actually picked. Johnson, who brought the subject up during a discussion of legislative business, told Humphrey that if there were no other political considerations, he would like to have Humphrey. "If I just had my choice, I'd like to have you as my vice president," Johnson said in language almost identical to that which Adlai Stevenson had spoken to Humphrey in 1956. But he made it clear it was not a promise and Humphrey said he understood. "He knows me well and knows how much I care for him," Humphrey said afterwards. "If it comes, it'll come."

However, there remained one other Democrat who showed even more strength than Humphrey in the leading public opinion surveys and whose presence represented a major obstacle to Humphrey's hopes — Robert Kennedy. After living under the Kennedys' domination when he was vice president, Johnson longed to be independent of them. Yet he dared not arbitrarily rule Kennedy off the ticket and risk losing support where he needed it most, among minority groups, Eastern liberals and Catholics.

Johnson had first tried to solve "The Bobby Problem" by promoting two surrogate Kennedys as possible running mates. He briefly considered Peace Corps Director Sargent Shriver, a Kennedy brother-in-law, a Catholic and a Midwesterner, but dropped the idea when Kennedy aides in the White House passed the word that if a Kennedy was going to be picked, it had to be Robert. In April, Johnson gave serious thought to putting Defense Secretary Robert McNamara on the ticket, and in fact all but asked him to run. Johnson was highly impressed with McNamara's executive abilities and felt the former Republican and Ford Motor Company president would help win the business community's support. More importantly, McNamara was Kennedy's closest friend in the Cabinet and thus would provide an easy answer to The Bobby Problem.

When the Humphrey camp learned of Johnson's interest in McNamara, it immediately spread the word. Van Dyk, by now a full-time staff member, prepared another anonymous memo emphasizing political unity on the presidential ticket and it was circulated by Connell at a Midwestern Democratic conference in Des Moines in May. As a result, Johnson was soon inundated with protests about putting a Republican on the ticket. However, McNamara ruled himself out of the running after talking to Kennedy, leaving Johnson to find another way to eliminate Kennedy.

Johnson now began to look for someone else who might appeal not only to Catholics and liberals as Kennedy did but also overcome Humphrey's two most glaring weaknesses, his unpopularity in the South and in the business community. Johnson didn't have to look far for a suggestion. Texas Governor John Connally, worried about both the effect of Humphrey on the ticket in Texas and a possible future Humphrey presidency, made several trips to the White House in early and mid-1964 to argue on behalf of Humphrey's fellow Minnesotan, Eugene McCarthy. Johnson's wife Lady Bird also was a close friend of Abigail McCarthy and was charmed by McCarthy's wit and intelligence, as were the two Johnson girls, Lynda and Luci.

Johnson was not unaware of McCarthy's strengths and weaknesses. He had spotted McCarthy as a comer when the tall, lanky Minnesotan arrived in the Senate in 1959, and had given him two choice committee assignments in his freshman year. Although never as close to McCarthy as he was to Humphrey, Johnson nevertheless relied on McCarthy's advice on a vital tax bill and on several foreign policy matters during his first weeks as president. In December, 1963, a few nights before he was to address the United Nations General Assembly, Johnson invited McCarthy, Foreign Relations Committee Chairman J. William Fulbright and four other Johnson friends to an informal White House dinner, and startled them by asking them to try to improve his speech. McCarthy and the others scribbled in the margins of the draft of the speech and Johnson delivered the talk as edited by his dinner guests.

Johnson gave an even more obvious sign of his regard for McCarthy in January, 1964, when he made a surprise appearance at a $100-a-person fund–raising dinner for McCarthy at a Washington hotel. Noting the presence of both McCarthy and Humphrey at the dinner, Johnson said "it took a lot of friendship" for McCarthy to draw him to a dinner where he would have to precede or follow the two Minnesotans as a speaker. "All my life I've wanted to be a speaker like Hubert or Gene," Johnson confessed to the overflow crowd of 550 persons. McCarthy reminded his audience that "all of us have an obligation to make decisions as easy as possible for this and all presidents."

The dinner drew a remarkable turnout. Almost the entire Cabinet was present (only Kennedy, McNamara and Secretary of State Dean Rusk were absent), as well as U.N. Ambassador Adlai Stevenson, twenty senators, several dozen House members, Supreme Court Justice Tom Clark and just about every well-heeled lobbyist in Washington. At the head table were Chairman Harry Byrd of the Senate Finance Committee and Treasury Secretary Douglas Dillon, both of whom rarely attended political gatherings.[3] Although Johnson's appearance was not, as McCarthy later noted, "the beginning of a vice presidential boom," it greatly boosted McCarthy's ranking among vice presidential hopefuls.

What really boosted McCarthy's chances, however, were two events beyond his control that happened almost at the same time Humphrey was enjoying his greatest triumph as mastermind of the Senate civil rights battle. The first came on July 15, when Senator Barry Goldwater became the Republican presidential nominee. With the conservative Goldwater as his opponent, Johnson no longer had to worry about losing the liberal Democratic vote, even if he did drop Kennedy. In addition, some of his advisers now argued that Humphrey added nothing to the ticket — and would even hurt it in the South — against Goldwater and his Catholic running mate Congressman William Miller of New York, but that McCarthy, with his good Southern contacts, less strident liberalism, and Catholicism, would be more of an asset. McCarthy had anticipated the conservative tide in the Republican party in 1964. Early in the year, he published a book entitled *The Liberal Answer to the Conservative Challenge*, in which he defended the liberal position from attacks made by Goldwater in his earlier book, *Conscience of a Conservative*.

---

[3] It was also the first political dinner attended by Stevenson since he took the U.N. post three years earlier. Stevenson said of McCarthy, "There is no more eloquent representative of what is good in American life than Senator McCarthy. We all are grateful to him for rehabilitating the phrase, 'Senator McCarthy.' "

Then, on July 30, Johnson unexpectedly went on television to announce what amounted to a final solution to The Bobby Problem — the elimination from vice presidential consideration of all Cabinet members or "those who meet regularly with the Cabinet." His unprecedented decision not only ruled out Kennedy but made Humphrey the runaway choice of party leaders everywhere except the South.[4] But Johnson was still determined to keep his vice presidential options open, if for no other reason than to inject some suspense into the otherwise dull Democratic National Convention scheduled to begin just twenty-four days later in Atlantic City, New Jersey. Thus, he instructed his close friend Jim Rowe to tell Humphrey that unless something personal or political came up, he would get the nomination. At the same time, Johnson told aide Walter Jenkins to encourage McCarthy that he was still very much in the running.

Rowe, who had directed Humphrey's 1960 West Virginia primary campaign, recalls that Johnson called him a few hours before the July 30 announcement and told him to first break the news to Adlai Stevenson — another victim of The Kennedy Solution — and then tell Humphrey. Rowe went to Humphrey's Senate office that night and suggested Humphrey call the president, which he immediately did, saying he understood the rules of the game and assuring Johnson that he could expect his utmost loyalty as vice president.

A few weeks later, in a confidential brief to the president arguing for Humphrey's selection, Rowe elaborated on Humphrey's pledge of loyalty.

> The day you dropped Kennedy, McNamara, etc., you said to tell Humphrey that if you picked him, loyalty to you was essential. I did not then tell you his precise reply:
> "Today the liberals are all for Lyndon Johnson. But I can remember 1959 and 1960 when every New York and most Northern liberals had daggers in their hands which they used with pleasure whenever the name of Lyndon Johnson was mentioned. During those tough years time and time again, both on national television and New York television, I defended Lyndon Johnson as a real liberal. In those days the plains were bleak and the ground dry. Why would I desert him now, be disloyal now when he is fashionable, when I was never disloyal to him when it was unfashionable?"
> I think it was an excellent answer.

Rowe's second bit of advice to Humphrey was that it was now time to go all-out to demonstrate that he had broad public support for the vice presidency. However, remembering Humphrey's disappointment at not being picked as Stevenson's running mate in 1956, Rowe was careful not to give Humphrey the impression that he had the nomination locked up. "I

---

[4] Minnesota almost had a third contender for the vice presidency in 1964. Johnson had fulsomely praised Agriculture Secretary Orville Freeman — along with Humphrey and McCarthy — during a visit to Minnesota in June, and Freeman was among those being mentioned as a possible Johnson running mate. Freeman was personally notified by Johnson of his decision.

was more cautious in talking to Humphrey than Johnson had been in talking to me," Rowe said in a 1971 interview.

A week later, Johnson dispatched Rowe on another, even more delicate mission. Rowe was to interrogate Humphrey on every aspect of his personal and political life that might make him a liability to the ticket. Rowe quizzed Humphrey on his personal finances, his financial or political debts to contributors, his war record, and even the possibility of some hidden scandal in his life. On every count, Rowe reported to the president that there was nothing to cause Johnson embarrassment or concern.[5]

Rowe said in 1971 that he was always convinced Johnson was going to choose Humphrey, "except — and this is a very important exception — that there was a very strong feeling among some of the people around Johnson for McCarthy. John Connally and Walter Jenkins wanted McCarthy and Lady Bird was never too enthusiastic about Hubert. Once he ruled out the Cabinet, it pretty well got down to the Minnesota Twins, and what I call the Texas conservatives and some of the Southerners were pushing hard for McCarthy. Their argument was that Hubert has always been a red flag to the South because of his civil rights stand. They said we know McCarthy has the same views, but the man on the street in the South doesn't know this. Therefore, McCarthy won't antagonize the South and he'll neutralize the Catholic problem. It was made seriously and it was not a bad argument."

As the convention approached, Johnson had clearly not made a final decision, and it was not just because he wanted to maintain the suspense. He and Rowe and two other Johnson intimates, Washington Attorneys Abe Fortas and Clark Clifford, often discussed the relative merits of the two Minnesotans over drinks, and it became clear to the three Johnson friends that he was indeed seriously considering McCarthy. The substance of one of those sessions filtered down to Columnists Rowland Evans and Robert Novak two weeks before the convention, when they declared that "it is now clear that President Johnson's choice for vice president would be Senator Eugene McCarthy of Minnesota — if, that is, the president had a truly free hand." The columnists wrote that Johnson "feels comfortable in the presence of the smooth-as-butter Minnesotan," but that McCarthy's most important qualification was that he probably would be "the kind of vice president that Mr. Johnson was to President Kennedy — unobtrusive, quiet, handling only those duties assigned to him."

[5] In his later memo to the president, Rowe refers to possible Humphrey liabilities Johnson had discussed with him, including his unpopularity in the South, his war record, the fact that he didn't want to lose Humphrey's help in the Senate, and his "ebullience and constant talking." Rowe reassured Johnson on all those points and added, "I am sure you will agree that the Humphrey of 1964 is vastly improved over the Humphrey of 1960. He has become much more mature and much more moderate. . . . From the beginning of your Senate careers it would seem to me you always understood each other. You know his weaknesses, but you also know his strengths and how useful they can be to you. . . ."

Johnson did not, however, have an entirely free hand, mainly because of the overwhelming support for Humphrey from party professionals, civil rights spokesmen and labor leaders. Also, there was almost unanimous agreement among Johnson's official family that Humphrey was the better candidate. A short time after his exclusion of the Cabinet, Johnson called a meeting of his top political advisers, including John Bailey and Richard Maguire, chairman and treasurer of the Democratic National Committee respectively, along with Rowe and aides Jenkins, Jack Valenti, Bill Moyers, Larry O'Brien and Kenny O'Donnell. Johnson opened the meeting by saying that a private survey he'd had taken showed he would have trouble without a Catholic on the ticket, and that this was especially true now that the Republican vice presidential candidate was a Catholic. Johnson went around the room asking each person whether he should put a Catholic — McCarthy — on the ticket. Although almost everyone present was a Catholic, only Jenkins said yes. Every other man recommended that he pick Humphrey. "I think that killed McCarthy right there," says Rowe.

Ironically, some of the strongest pressure for Humphrey came from supporters of Kennedy, the man Johnson had dumped in order to have a free hand. O'Donnell, writing in *Life* magazine in August, 1970, recounted that Kennedy, who had decided to run for the Senate in New York, kept his intentions secret in order to "keep Johnson off balance and enable us to build up support for Humphrey." O'Donnell says he met Humphrey at a Washington hotel on the night Johnson ruled out the Cabinet and warned him that he, too, would be dumped unless he mounted an all-out campaign to generate support for himself. O'Donnell said the Kennedy forces would help Humphrey if there was a floor fight over his nomination. In the next few days, Kennedy publicly announced his support for Humphrey for the vice presidency and helped line up support for Humphrey from United Auto Workers President Walter Reuther, a strong Kennedy supporter. "The Kennedy people really leaned on Johnson after Bobby was out of contention," says Bill Connell. "They trusted Humphrey and didn't want another Catholic in that position."

With Kennedy's backing assured, Humphrey now felt certain he had the nomination if he could avoid any misstep. He personally contacted every Democratic governor and party leader of any consequence, asking for pledges of support (among those who came out early for Humphrey was Governor Harold Hughes of Iowa, who would nominate McCarthy for president four years later), authorized the printing of five thousand campaign biographies (they were stored in the cellar of Bill Connell's Washington home) and the preparation of eight thousand LBJ-HHH campaign buttons and other convention materials (stored in an Atlantic City hotel room). His staff called around the country to collect favorable newspaper clippings, editorials, polls and other studies which were gathered together and sent to the White

House at the end of each day. Favorable polls were also shown the president by O'Donnell and other Kennedy men in the White House.

Humphrey made a special effort to buttress his support in the business community, which still regarded him with some skepticism.[6] Marlin Sandlin, chairman of the Pan American Sulphur Company of Houston and a close friend of President Johnson, helped set up four meetings in July with leading industrialists and business executives in New York, Chicago, and the West Coast at which Humphrey informally discussed his views on the relationship between business and government.

Humphrey also attempted to allay suspicions among businessmen that he was still a flaming radical by publishing a book, *The Cause Is Mankind*, which outlined his political philosophy and offered this tribute to businessmen: "I do not think that we have many real grievances to be urged against bigness in business today. For the most part, big corporations are a source of strength and economic vitality. And certainly big business is here to stay."[7]

Finally, Humphrey sought to smooth over the historical antipathy held for him by the South. In a national television interview in early August, speaking calmly and deliberately in marked contrast to the rapid-fire delivery that was his trademark, he said, "I have a great affection for the South . . . I think I understand a little bit about some of their critical problems and the social tensions that exist there. We have them in the North, I might say, as well." He coupled his courting of the South with the endorsements of several Southern politicians, including Senators George Smathers of Florida and Olin Johnston of South Carolina and Governor Edward Breathitt of Kentucky.

While Humphrey was pulling out all the stops to convince Johnson of his vice presidential support, McCarthy was quietly mounting his own extensive vice presidential campaign. Financed by the late philanthropist Stephen Currier, who became an admirer of McCarthy as the result of his 1960 Stevenson speech, McCarthy supporters opened a secret headquarters in a southwest Washington townhouse. Mayne Miller, then executive secretary of the Wyoming Democratic party, was hired at two thousand dollars a month to run the campaign, and Arthur Michelson, a Twin Cities

---

[6] Minnesota was soon to receive a dividend from Humphrey's friendship with U.S. Steel Chairman Roger Blough. Humphrey and Blough struck a bargain. U.S. Steel would invest at least $100 million in facilities to process low-grade iron ore deposits in depressed northern Minnesota in return for Humphrey's help in passing a state constitutional amendment guaranteeing favorable long-range tax rates to processors. The amendment was passed in November, 1964.

[7] Humphrey did not, however, tone down his commitment to the humanitarian goals of the New Deal and its successors. He called for an all-out war against poverty and for "the triumph of mankind over its traditional enemies — poverty, hunger, disease and ignorance." He also offered Spinoza's words as his own personal credo: "I have made a ceaseless effort not to ridicule, not to bewail, nor to scorn human actions, but to understand them."

television newsman, was hired as a press secretary to serve both the Mc-Carthy Senate office and the vice presidential effort. Among those involved in the meeting to advance McCarthy's cause were Administrative Assistant Jerry Eller; Legislative Counsel Larry Merthan; Real Estate Developer John Safer, a McCarthy neighbor; Maurice Rosenblatt and George Agree of the Committee for a More Effective Congress; Thomas Finney, a Washington lawyer and Johnson political operative, and several other wealthy Stevensonians.

Asked by a television interviewer in July whether he was seeking the vice presidency, McCarthy replied in language inconsistent with the behind-the-scenes campaign on his behalf. The vice presidency, he said, is "an office, a party position for which I cannot run. . . . I'm in the position of really not seeking it but I'm not running away from it." Asked about his view of the functions of the office, he said there were three: presiding over the Senate, acting as an image of the Democratic party, and "first in importance, that of really standing by as an aide to the president. . . ." McCarthy cited the late Alben Barkley as the kind of vice president who represented the image of the party and made a distinctive contribution to his president. He added, "I think people will be watching the kind of man President Johnson chooses."

Two Johnson aides also were involved in the deliberations. Walter Jenkins and Hobart Taylor, Jr., insisted that McCarthy was under serious consideration and should try to generate expressions of support. As a result, McCarthy quietly visited several powerful Democratic leaders to ask for their support. He flew to Los Angeles in July — before Kennedy was eliminated — to confer with Jesse Unruh, speaker of the California State Assembly and a dominant figure in California politics. He came away empty-handed, however, as Unruh made it clear he preferred Kennedy. "That always made me highly suspicious of McCarthy," Unruh said in a 1971 interview, "because I figured he was playing footsie with Lyndon then." After Kennedy was eliminated, Unruh says he and Kenny O'Donnell and other Kennedy people "began to move to cut the ground out from under McCarthy and help Hubert." According to Unruh, Kennedy felt that a Catholic vice president "would present certain obstacles to the [Kennedy] Restoration." After his meeting with Unruh, McCarthy admitted that the Californian hadn't come out for him, but added hopefully, "He hasn't come out against me, either."

McCarthy was more hopeful after meeting with Mayor Richard Daley of Chicago. He said Daley, a fellow Catholic, seemed "partial" to him, and added, "To have an Irishman say he is partial to you . . . well, if he were talking to a girl, it would almost be the same as saying you are engaged." McCarthy was able to extract a promise of support from Frank Smith, boss of the still formidable Philadelphia Democratic machine, but he was the only powerful Democrat other than John Connally and a few other Southern governors he felt he could count on.

Consequently, McCarthy had few illusions about the extent of his support as convention time neared. Participants in vice presidential strategy sessions sensed a growing frustration and lack of interest on his part. McCarthy himself seemed discouraged by his reception by party leaders, and came to feel Johnson wanted him only because of his religion. "He doesn't want my presence," he quipped. "He wants my essence."

Moreover, there were signs that McCarthy's growing rivalry with Humphrey might create problems for his Senate reelection campaign that fall by antagonizing Humphrey supporters in Minnesota. "If anyone would be concerned about it, I should think it would be Senator Humphrey," McCarthy told a Twin Cities news conference in August. "And he's never said anything about it."

McCarthy also disputed the notion that he and Humphrey were the two leading candidates. He listed as still in contention four other people — Senators Fulbright and Edmund Muskie of Maine, Governor Pat Brown of California and Mayor Robert Wagner of New York, none of whom were ever seriously considered. (Asked at the same news conference about reports that Johnson favored him because he felt more comfortable with him, McCarthy responded, "The president hasn't spent much time around me. If he spent more time with me, he might feel less comfortable.")[8]

A central question regarding McCarthy's actions in 1964 — and in subsequent years as well — is how much he wanted to be Johnson's vice president. Some people close to him at the time, such as Maurice Rosenblatt of the National Committee for an Effective Congress, accept McCarthy's later statements to the effect that he was not terribly disappointed when he was passed over. "McCarthy was never slobbering for the vice presidency," says Rosenblatt, who steered thirty thousand dollars in contributions to McCarthy to pay for his convention headquarters at Atlantic City. "I always felt that the possibility of his being picked was much greater than his interest in it."

However, there is even stronger evidence that McCarthy was deeply interested in the vice presidency. A prominent Minnesota Democrat who had been closely associated with both Humphrey and McCarthy since the late 1940's came to Washington — at Humphrey's request — the week before

[8] However, McCarthy was portrayed as a warm admirer of Johnson in an article in the June, 1964, issue of *Harper's* magazine by Marshall Smelser, the man who first got McCarthy involved in politics. "Those now close to him say he has a strong personal affection for President Johnson," Smelser wrote, adding that McCarthy stands "equidistant from his admired friend, President Johnson; from his *beau ideal*, Adlai Stevenson; and from his respected colleague and chief, President Kennedy." Asked about Smelser's comment, McCarthy said, "Well, he said *equidistant*. He didn't attempt to measure the distance."

the convention to try to stave off a confrontation between the two Minnesota senators. "His staff people all told me he had a real good chance to be vice president and that Connally had talked to him and Lady Bird had talked to Abigail and that he'd be crazy to drop out," recalls the man, who asked not to be identified even though his story is common knowledge among Minnesota Democrats. "I told them if Johnson was really afraid of Goldwater and felt he had to have a Catholic on the ticket, then McCarthy might have a chance, but under the circumstances, Gene didn't have the chance of a snowball in hell."

Convinced that there was no chance of changing McCarthy's mind, the man returned to the Statler Hilton Hotel to check out and catch a plane to Minnesota. "Just then, Gene called my hotel room and said he wanted to talk to me. He insisted, so I canceled my reservation and went over the same ground with him, telling him exactly what I'd told his staff. Gene said to me, 'If you were the president, what would you do?' I said, 'I'd ask each of you one question — what would you do when the heat really comes on in Vietnam as I'm sure it's going to?' I said this was going to be the vital issue in the next few years and the president had to be sure his vice president would support his policy." (Congress a week earlier had passed the Gulf of Tonkin Resolution — both McCarthy and Humphrey voted for it — giving the president authority for expanding the Vietnam War.)

McCarthy agreed that Vietnam would be a vital issue and that the vice president had to support the president's stand on it. "He made it clear that he felt we were committed in Vietnam and that we'd have to see it through to the end. Then Gene said that we both know Hubert well enough that if the war becomes very unpopular, he might be inclined to tell the editor of the New York *Times* that he goes along with it because he has to but that we ought to be doing something different."

McCarthy then startled his friend by asking him to talk to the president. "I asked him why in the world Johnson would want to talk to me and he said, 'Why not? He's talking to everybody else.' He said, 'I'd like to call the president and tell him you're very close to both of us and he ought to get an evaluation from you.' I said, 'O.K., I feel so strongly about Vietnam that I'm willing to do it, but the only condition is that I've got to tell Hubert first.' He said that was all right and then he called the White House to set up an appointment. They told him Lyndon had just left for Texas. I went back home and never did see or talk to the president."

The strains that eventually ruptured the friendship between the two Minnesota senators began to show in the weeks preceding the convention. When Humphrey sent an emissary, Minnesota's Democratic National Committeeman Gerald Heaney, to suggest that McCarthy step aside for his senior senator, McCarthy replied, "Where do you want me to step? If I go to the White House and tell Mr. Johnson I'm out of the running, he's going to say,

'Who said you were in the running?' Just explain where and how you want me to step.''

Herb Waters, the former Humphrey aide who was named an assistant administrator of the Agency for International Development in 1961 and who played an important behind-the-scenes role for Humphrey in 1964, recalls that there were few frictions between Humphrey and McCarthy at first. "They'd josh each other about it when they met and there were no problems. McCarthy was riding pretty good with it. Then, somewhere along the line, the vice presidential idea started to catch on and he began to take this thing seriously. But I think Gene always knew in his own mind that the only reason Johnson might take him would be if he thought the Catholic thing was important. And this sort of rankled Gene because he didn't want to be picked just because he was a Catholic; he wanted to be picked as a whole man, because he was as good as anybody else.''

But the real frictions, and the ones that Waters and other people close to both Humphrey and McCarthy think first caused the eventual break between them came not from the two principals but from their staffs. "Humphrey had this goddamned eager-beaver staff," says Waters, "especially Bill Connell, who thought McCarthy was a serious threat and who began pressing the White House with reasons why he shouldn't be the candidate and why Humphrey should be. Connell was the only one saying anything anti-McCarthy — I never heard Humphrey say anything anti-McCarthy. Connell was saying things like, 'Gene's too lazy to make a good vice president,' and these were the things that made the McCarthy people mad." Says another Humphrey staffer, "I don't think there's any question that what happened in 1964 was the beginning of the Humphrey-McCarthy split, but I'm not sure that it was so much a Humphrey-McCarthy split as it was a staff split.''

Humphrey and McCarthy made their last direct appeal for Johnson's blessing on Sunday, August 23, the day before the Democratic National Convention in Atlantic City. They went through their paces on the hour-long nationally-televised program, "Meet the Press," appearing separately for half an hour each. Afterwards, they took a telephone call in tandem from the White House, and each spoke to the president, who gave them both "an A-plus in their trial by television," and to Lady Bird, who told McCarthy "You're my candidate.''

McCarthy, who won a coin toss and appeared first, voiced the reason why few men have been able to resist the tantalizing prospect of living only a heartbeat away from the most powerful political office in the world. The vice presidency, he said, "is the kind of offer which no person who has been a member of the party can really turn down; I think it's a matter of obligation, apart from any personal feelings that one might have either by way of desiring the office or by way of being particularly happy with the . . . United States Senate."

McCarthy did not pass up the opportunity to flatter the president as he defended his right to select a running mate rather than letting the convention do it. "I think in this instance it reflects a confidence in President Johnson and the realization that . . . he will make a choice which will reflect the overall interests of the party and his good judgment in which we have confidence. . . ." McCarthy said he had not discussed the vice presidency with Johnson "in any way" and added that he had tried "not to subject him to any kind of pressure or any kind of special demand" in making the case for his selection as Johnson's running mate. "As far as I've been making a case, it's been to try to be as sure as I could that the president had the knowledge of what kind of limited support I had, and what my qualifications were if he were in any doubt." [9]

Humphrey, like McCarthy, told the panel that there was little he could tell Johnson about himself that he didn't already know. He added that he had not discussed the vice presidency with Johnson even though he had met with him alone for more than an hour the previous Tuesday and again on Thursday. He expressed confidence in Johnson's ability to choose the best qualified running mate and bristled when panelist John Steel of *Time* magazine reminded him of his traumatic experience in 1956 by asking if Humphrey would make a floor fight for the nomination if Johnson threw it open to the convention. "Mr. Steele, why don't you come around to see me if that matter develops and I'll be more than happy to advise you," he said coldly.

Humphrey was even less restrained than McCarthy in his praise of the man who was about to decide his fate. He invoked Johnson's name thirty-two times in the course of his half hour (compared to seven times for McCarthy), calling him a "patriot [who] loves his country . . . a president that seeks a great national consensus, a national unity . . . a president of all of our people . . . a friend not only of the South but every other part of America." Incredibly, he even went so far as to suggest that Johnson's popularity was so great that he could win without a running mate.

Humphrey's praise of Johnson reached a crescendo when he was asked why he would give up his powerful place in the Senate to run for vice president. "Well, I think that was answered in 1960 when the most powerful and influential man in the Congress . . . and one of the most effective leaders of the Senate that America has ever known since the beginning of

[9] As usual, McCarthy got off the brightest line of the day. Asked for his assessment of his potential rival, Republican Vice Presidential Nominee William Miller, McCarthy noted that Miller once served as Republican national chairman and cracked, "There's a period after he leaves office when he's unfit for civilian life. He's like a war dog; it takes him a little while to be reconditioned."

this Republic gave up being majority leader to become vice president with John F. Kennedy. And that man was Lyndon Johnson."

The changes that had occurred in Humphrey's political philosophy during his fifteen years in the Senate, and the attitude that characterized his approach to politics were summarized in his answer to a question about his recent statements criticizing the "all or nothing" approach of uncompromising liberals. "I think it is well for a person to have goals . . . that reach out a long distance and to fight for those goals or those objectives and if you cannot attain them completely at one time you make what progress is available at the moment or at the time. And then you proceed to do what you believe is best sometime later."

Humphrey's talents as a master of compromise were given their ultimate test when Johnson designated him to answer the only major unanswered question — other than the vice presidency — that faced the 1964 convention, how to solve the insurgent Mississippi Freedom Democratic party's demand to be seated instead of the state's all-white regular delegation. That assignment, which in the end would guarantee Humphrey's selection as the vice presidential nominee, was full of irony. Humphrey had begun his climb to political success as the uncompromising "all or nothing" champion of civil rights at another Democratic National Convention sixteen years earlier, and now his future depended on his ability to render a Solomon-like decision that would avoid a nationally-televised racial confrontation and the possible defeat of Johnson in his native region of the South, while at the same time defending the great moral issue that had launched his career.

Humphrey's role in settling the Mississippi imbroglio, which was a prelude to an even more explosive moral issue that would tear apart the next Democratic National Convention, began on Saturday, the day before the convention opened, as Humphrey arrived for the beginning of hearings by the Credentials Committee. The Freedom Democrats' case was being argued by Joe Rauh, the Washington attorney and civil rights activist who had been pushing Humphrey for president or vice president since 1948. However, Rauh's passionate advocacy of the Freedom party's cause and the televised testimony of Negro witnesses who told the committee they were severely beaten when they tried to participate in the regular Mississippi Democratic party's affairs created an explosive situation. "We have a large number of fight promoters," Humphrey said after the hearing. "I think now we need a few people as peacemakers and [to] try to make an accommodation based upon what are the standards of our party."

Humphrey recognized that the Freedom Democrats, composed mostly of Negroes and a few white civil right workers, were basically a protest movement and not a political party, and that the regular party had established a legal right to be seated if it was willing to pledge its support to the Democratic ticket that fall. However, he also understood that the Freedom Democrats had established a moral claim that had to be dealt with by the convention even though it might cause the regular Democrats and other Southern delegations to walk out.

Humphrey's basic strategy in dealing with the Mississippi situation had been developed four days before the convention in the last face-to-face meeting he had with Johnson until becoming his running mate. Johnson, who had not explicitly ordered Humphrey to take charge of the credentials fight but who knew that he would be forced into it because of his deep involvement in civil rights, suggested a three-point compromise plan which called for seating the sixty-eight regular Mississippi delegates, admitting the Freedom Democrats to the floor as honored guests but without votes, and forbidding the next Democratic convention (in 1968) to seat any delegation selected by a process involving discrimination because of race, creed, or color. (The latter proposal would form the basis for subsequent convention challenges by Southern civil rights proponents.)

Johnson sent two highly trusted agents to Atlantic City to help Humphrey carry out the proposed compromise — Walter Jenkins and Thomas Finney, a member of Clark Clifford's Washington law firm and a participant in the McCarthy vice presidential meetings earlier in the year. They kept in constant touch with the White House while working with Humphrey, former Pennsylvania Governor David Lawrence (chairman of the Credentials Committee) and United Auto Workers President Walter Reuther, who broke off contract negotiations with General Motors to come to Atlantic City at Johnson's request.

The job of pushing the delicate compromise through the one hundred member Credentials Committee was given to Humphrey's thirty-six year old protege, Minnesota Attorney General Walter (Fritz) Mondale. Mondale, who would succeed Humphrey in the Senate four months later, recalls the chaotic situation that he found. "The damned committee was really in a mess. Governor Lawrence was an old man and I don't think he sensed that the thing was about to blow up in his face. No one else seemed to know how to get a hold on it either, and I said, 'We're never going to handle this unless we have a subcommittee.' The governor agreed and then he appointed me chairman, right there."

Mondale's five-man committee, meeting with the other principals involved, appeared on the verge of success on Sunday until an Oregon congressman, Al Ullman, offered a substitute motion proposing that both delegations be seated and that the Freedom Democrats be given two of the state's twenty-four convention votes. Ullman correctly saw that the powerful case presented by the Freedom Democrats had made the Johnson-Humphrey compromise wholly inadequate for hundreds of liberal delegates and would make the dreaded floor fight a certainty.

On Monday night, after getting Lawrence to defer the Mississippi issue for a day, an unhappy Humphrey joined Jenkins, Finney, and Reuther to try to work out a settlement. The meeting in Jenkins' hotel room dragged on past midnight, with Humphrey at one point pleading with Jenkins to allow him to call Johnson directly. But Jenkins refused, stressing Johnson's strict orders to avoid involving him directly in the credentials fight. Finally, in the early hours of Tuesday morning, Humphrey suggested that they adopt the Ullman proposal but that the Freedom Democrats vote as members of a special at-large delegation and not as part of any state delegation. The exhausted participants agreed to the plan and made Humphrey and Reuther responsible for selling it to the convention.

The sun was rising over the nearby Atlantic as the meeting broke up, but Humphrey had no time to rest. He called Ullman to his ninth floor suite at the rambling Shelburne Hotel, where he and Reuther extracted a promise of cooperation. They also got Rauh, Civil Rights Leaders Dr. Martin Luther King and Roy Wilkins and others to back the new compromise plan, which was pushed through Mondale's subcommittee and the full Credentials Committee as well.

Although the plan was rejected by both Mississippi parties, the solution was accepted by the delegates who sympathized with the Freedom Democrats and by every Southern state except Mississippi and Alabama, whose delegates walked out. The Freedom Democrats staged a "walk-in" on the floor that evening, but the convention quickly accepted the compromise. Humphrey had survived his test by fire, sparing Johnson the embarrassment of a massive Southern walk-out or a disruptive floor fight, and had helped write a new chapter in the civil rights saga that had begun with his daring advocacy of a strong civil rights plank at the 1948 convention. He had become the symbol of unity for the 1964 convention just as he would become the symbol of disunity at the Democratic convention four years later.

Humphrey later was criticized for his role at the 1964 convention by a member of the Mississippi Freedom party, Miss Ella Baker. In a speech during the May, 1968, Poor People's Campaign in Washington, Miss Baker said Humphrey "blocked the seating of the MFDP" and "used his persuasion on convention liberals to block the MFDP effort to unseat the white Mississippi delegation. . . ." However, Joe Rauh, who by then had deserted Humphrey to work for Eugene McCarthy because of the Vietnam issue, defended Humphrey's role. In a letter to the Washington *Evening Star* on May 17, 1968, Rauh wrote:

> As counsel for the Freedom party, I pleaded publicly and privately for the seating of the entire Freedom delegation. I had several meetings with Senator Humphrey at which no one else was present and where he could have asked me, a longtime supporter, for a concession in the name of gaining the vice presidency. But never once did Senator Humphrey ask for anything based on his own personal interest. We argued on the merits of our case and on what he could get out of the president and out of the convention. (I am

genuinely convinced he got everything he could.) Hubert Humphrey's refusal at any time to apply the slightest personal pressure represented the highest standard of political ethics that I have witnessed in my lifetime.

By late afternoon on Tuesday (August 25) even when it was clear that the Mississippi compromise would be successfully completed, Humphrey was still uncertain about his own fate. His uncertainty was increased by reports that Johnson had approached Senate Majority Leader Mike Mansfield about the vice presidency. But Humphrey's hopes finally were confirmed for him a few hours later by Jim Rowe, who called him from a meeting on the Mississippi problem to his room at the Colony Motel. Humphrey arrived with Muriel and two aides, Connell and Kampelman, and Rowe took Humphrey into the bedroom and closed the door, leaving the others behind. Acting on instructions from Johnson that had been carefully taken down in shorthand and typed by Jenkins, Rowe told Humphrey he would be the nominee and that Johnson wanted him to stand by for a plane trip to Washington, 140 miles away, that night.

There was much more, however. "I remember my instructions very well," Rowe recalls. "I was to find Humphrey and tell him that he was it, but first I was to find a copy of the Washington *Star* [which on Monday had carried a lengthly background interview detailing Johnson's views on what he wanted in a vice president] and have him read the article on the vice presidency. I was to tell Hubert that if he was willing to follow those rules, he would be the nominee."

Rowe couldn't find a copy of the *Star* but he did locate a copy of that morning's Washington *Post,* which carried essentially the same story, and showed it to Humphrey. The article presented an exhaustive list of "do's and don'ts": The vice president above all else must be loyal to the president, he must have no public disputes with the president, he must not do any lobbying for special interests, he must support the president once he has made a decision even though he may have argued against it, and he must sometimes share secrets with the president that he could share with no one else, including his wife. Humphrey read the article and said, "O.K., fine."

Excited and relieved that his long ordeal was finally over, Humphrey started out of the room to break the good news to Muriel and his aides, but Rowe stopped him. The president had given strict orders that Humphrey was not to tell anyone — not even his wife — about his choice as Johnson's running mate. "This is goddam silly," Humphrey protested, but Rowe said, "Those are the rules." The others were told only that Humphrey was to go to Washington to meet with the president and they remained in Rowe's room waiting for word from the White House and watching on television as the Mississippi compromise was accepted. However, the Atlantic City airport was fogged in and no planes were flying. Kampelman suggested they drive to Washington but Rowe said no, the president wanted them to fly.

Humphrey, his nerves strained to the breaking point by the long cat-and-mouse game, finally exploded, but Rowe calmed him down. "I said, 'Hubert, tonight you're just a senator from Minnesota but this time tomorrow night you'll be a candidate for vice president, and then we both can tell Johnson he's a shit.'"

McCarthy, meanwhile, had been observing the unfolding of the civil rights drama from a slightly more remote vantage point, his third floor suite in the Shelburne Hotel. He also had a secret convention headquarters at the Carousel Motel in Brigantine, New Jersey, ten miles north of Atlantic City, which Mayne Miller rented under the pretense that it was for a group of delegates from Indiana.[10] (He signed the motel register as Marshall Smelser, the Notre Dame professor who was McCarthy's former teaching colleague in St. Paul.) McCarthy did not involve himself in the credentials fight, but observed on Tuesday that while it wasn't ideal from a moral standpoint, it was about the best that could be expected under the circumstances.

But the successful conclusion of the civil rights compromise had extinguished McCarthy's last flickering hope for the nomination and he knew it. Near midnight on Tuesday, after watching television and bantering with aides, he and Abigail retired to their bedroom to compose an extraordinary telegram to President Johnson which read in part:

> I have, as you know, during this convention and for several weeks not been indifferent to the choice you must make. The action that I have taken has been to this end and to this purpose: That your choice would be a free one and that those whom you might consult, or who might make recommendations to you, might be well-informed. . . . It is my opinion the qualifications that you have listed or which you are said to have listed as most desirable in the man who would be vice president with you would be met most admirably by Senator Humphrey. . . .

At 6:45 A.M. on Wednesday, McCarthy left his suite, walked across the hall to a room occupied by Eller and Michelson, and woke them up. He instructed Eller to send the telegram to the White House, call Jenkins and read him the text and then to release it to newsmen because he shrewdly anticipated that Johnson would ask him not to release it, which is precisely what happened. Jenkins exploded when he heard Eller read the telegram and angrily demanded that it not be made public. "Too late," said Eller, "it's already done."

---

[10] The Carousel hideaway was populated mostly by McCarthy's associates from St. Paul and a few aides. McCarthy had asked his old friend Bill Carlson to bring his wife and stay there at McCarthy's expense. The Carlsons, who flew from St. Paul with the Minnesota delegation on a chartered plane, were urgently paged at the airport when they arrived and brought immediately to the Carousel. "I thought, oh boy, he's ready to make the big play," Carlson recalls. "When I got to his hideaway, Gene was sitting by the pool in his swimming trunks and I asked him what was going on. He said, 'I thought it would be fun to have you paged.'"

McCarthy, who was at breakfast at a nearby restaurant with several members of the 1958 Senate class, was alerted by Michelson that reporters were waiting outside the restaurant. He excused himself, went into the men's room, climbed out the window and into a waiting car and was driven to his Carousel hideaway where he went swimming and boating with his son Michael for the rest of the day.[11] When he returned from the ocean, McCarthy's secretary told him the White House had called several times. The call was put through at 4:00 P.M. and Johnson came on the line to acknowledge his receipt of McCarthy's telegram.

According to Maurice Rosenblatt, the only person with McCarthy when he talked to Johnson, McCarthy said, "Yes, Mr. President, I thought I'd leave you a little free at the salt lick." Rosenblatt adds, "Evidently, Johnson didn't get it because Gene repeated it. He said, 'I didn't want to crowd you, Mr. President.' "

Johnson told McCarthy the telegram reflected his own thinking and made it a point to say he'd made up his mind before receiving it. Then Lady Bird expressed her regrets, followed by Supreme Court Justice Arthur Goldberg, who exchanged a few desultory comments with McCarthy before the conversation ended. Ten minutes later, Jenkins called back to ask McCarthy to nominate Humphrey. McCarthy, who had just learned that Senator Thomas Dodd of Connecticut was at that moment flying to Washington with Humphrey in the seat intended for McCarthy, coldly suggested that Dodd make the speech. But Jenkins insisted and McCarthy asked for time to think it over. Forty minutes later, he agreed to make the speech.

Reporters who spoke to McCarthy a few hours later thought he did not seem unduly disappointed. He was smiling as he joked with them about his withdrawal from the vice presidential sweepstakes. "It's easy for the horse to move from Churchill Downs to Charles Town [a reference to the famous Kentucky race track and another far less famous track near Washington]. It may be a little harder for his handlers, of course."

Nevertheless, McCarthy was humiliated by his treatment at Atlantic City. He wanted the nomination, although he was enough of a realist to know he did not have the support he needed and that he had only an outside chance for it. But he was deeply offended by Johnson's playing with him like a puppet on a string, and he never forgave Johnson for it. The man who felt Adlai Stevenson was badly treated by John Kennedy now knew from first-hand experience what it was like. Never again would he feel any of his old friendship for Johnson.[12]

[11] Muriel Humphrey was at a women's breakfast when a reporter told her of McCarthy's action. She went first to the Shelburne to see her husband, who had just learned of it from an aide, and then spent half an hour with Mrs. McCarthy, telling her, "I'm glad it's all settled" and that she hoped they could campaign together.

[12] Humphrey said years later that McCarthy told him he "didn't mind not getting the nomination [so much] as the fact that he felt Johnson had used him."

McCarthy's resentment about Johnson's behavior surfaced after he saw newspaper pictures that showed Humphrey at Johnson's Texas ranch the day after the convention astride a horse, wearing a cowboy hat and chasing Johnson's cattle. He told Bill Carlson, "Look at that. I'm glad I didn't get the nomination. He'd have done that to me."

Some people think McCarthy's feelings about Atlantic City involved an older, even more bitter enemy, however. "The thing that really bugged McCarthy about Atlantic City is that he felt that the Kennedys had very shrewdly and subtly maneuvered Lyndon into taking Hubert instead of him," says a person who was with McCarthy throughout the pre-convention and convention period. "Sure, he wanted the nomination. He was already getting bored with the Senate and who wouldn't want to be vice president to a guy who had had a serious heart attack? But he thought Johnson was a coward for letting the Kennedys force him into taking Humphrey. They'd taken Humphrey's measure in 1960 and knew they could handle him later. That's why Gene likes to fight the Kennedys — he feels they're a real match for his mettle."

Said McCarthy several years later, "I was not altogether naive about what this game was all about. I don't quite feel that I was led down the garden path. Yes, there were White House people who said, 'Keep in it.' But it was helping my own Senatorial campaign back home in Minnesota. The kind of publicity I got couldn't be bought." However, McCarthy's smouldering resentment over Johnson's manipulation of him is evident in another retrospective look by him at the 1964 convention: "There was, as I have said before, a point at which they should have given me the scenario for the last act," he said in a 1968 interview. "I didn't mind the second act — that's always confused. But the third act is the point at which you want to know if the end is going to be happy or sad; whether you get out or get killed." McCarthy figured his role was to get killed, that Johnson would have had him and Humphrey fly to the White House and all three would have returned to Atlantic City where Johnson would march up to the podium, crown Humphrey his running mate, and leave McCarthy standing there, an exposed and expendable figure for all the world to see.

Humphrey was awakened by his press secretary, Bob Jensen, with good news Wednesday morning; McCarthy had withdrawn his name from consideration and recommended Humphrey. At breakfast, Humphrey asked his sixteen year old son Douglas, "How would you like your dad to be vice president?"

"That would be swell," said the boy.

"Well," said Humphrey, "he's going to be."

A few hours later, however, Humphrey wasn't so sure. Johnson, still determined to maintain a semblance of surprise in his vice presidential choice, decided to prolong Humphrey's uncertainty for a few more agonizing hours. On Wednesday afternoon, Humphrey was being interviewed by telephone by radio station WCCO in Minneapolis when the announcer broke in with a bulletin from Washington that Johnson had just invited Humphrey to the White House. Humphrey terminated the interview, saying, "Somebody's probably trying to reach me on this telephone; I'd better hang up." A few minutes later, Jenkins called to tell Humphrey that Johnson had told reporters only minutes before that he was calling Humphrey to the White House.

Johnson had one last surprise for Humphrey. He told him that another senator would join him on the flight to Washington. When the other senator turned out to be Tom Dodd, Humphrey was perplexed. But exhausted, he fell asleep during the short flight. The plane arrived in Washington at 4:30 P.M. and because Johnson didn't want Lady Bird's arrival at Atlantic City upstaged on television screens, Presidential Aide Jack Valenti took Humphrey and Dodd on a tour of Washington's monuments for nearly an hour before their limousine entered the White House grounds. There they waited for another half an hour in the car before Johnson knocked on the window and woke the sleeping Humphrey. Humphrey, Dodd, and the president walked across the White House lawn and Johnson took Dodd inside while Humphrey stood outside surrounded by reporters. It began to rain, but Humphrey didn't seem to care. "It's raining?" he said when a reporter suggested they take cover. "I thought we were just getting blessed."

Finally, at 6:05 P.M., Dodd came out and Valenti ushered Humphrey into the Oval Office, where Johnson put his arm around him and said the words the fifty-three year old Humphrey had waited so long to hear. "Hubert, how would you like to be my vice president?" Humphrey said he would be proud and honored.

The two men then sat down and discussed for half an hour Johnson's concept of the vice presidency, what he expected of Humphrey, and all the other points Johnson had detailed in his newspaper interview four days earlier. Humphrey pledged his loyalty and told Johnson he would try to be the kind of vice president he wanted him to be. "The president said, 'If you didn't know you were going to be vice president a month ago, you're too damn dumb to have the office,' " Humphrey recalls.

With that, Johnson picked up the phone and called a half dozen Democratic party leaders at Atlantic City to break the news, then led Humphrey into the Cabinet Room where Defense Secretary McNamara, Secretary Rusk and National Security Assistant McGeorge Bundy were waiting. Johnson paid warm tribute to Humphrey in front of the men and told him they'd all been pushing for his selection. Then he took Humphrey back to the Oval Office where they put in a call to Mrs. Humphrey in Atlantic City. "Hello Muriel," said the president. "You looked very pretty on T.V. this afternoon. We're going to nominate your boy tonight. I want you to put on your best bib and tucker for him." Mrs. Humphrey replied, "Bless your heart, I'm going to put on my best bib and tucker for both of you." All the stunned Humphrey could think of to say to his wife was, "How are you?"

At 7:00 P.M., Johnson called newsmen into his office to announce, "Now I've made up my mind." But he still withheld the news of his decision. Humphrey, addressed by reporters for the first time, as "Mr. Vice President," was closed-mouthed but his beaming face told the story. Johnson announced that he would fly to Atlantic City at 8:30 P.M. to announce his running mate, then took Humphrey and reporters on another two-lap walk around the South Lawn before inviting everyone to his private living quarters for drinks and caviar and cheese sandwiches. A dazed Humphrey accepted congratulations from the newsmen and White House aides, while Johnson dressed in the bedroom with the door open.[13]

Just before the presidential party left Andrews Air Force Base for Atlantic City, Johnson finally disclosed the obvious to reporters, that Humphrey was his running mate."Boys," he said pointing to Humphrey, "meet the next vice president of the United States." He announced the choice to the convention an hour later, calling Humphrey "the best man in America for the job," but still dragging out the suspense to the last possible moment. Only at the end of his final sentence did he bellow out the name, "Senator Hubert Humphrey of Minnesota!" Humphrey supporters finally broke open the boxes of Johnson-Humphrey campaign materials that had been hidden all over Atlantic City and Humphrey and Muriel happily watched the tumultuous demonstration in their honor.

Minutes later, McCarthy stepped to the rostrum and in a restrained speech, nominated Humphrey for vice president. "At no time in the recent history of any political party has a party presented to its convention and beyond that to the people of this country two men who are so alike in energy, in ability, in experience, in dedication, and in compassion as the two men whom the Democratic party will present to this nation for approval in November of 1964," he declared.

McCarthy's speech was shorter and far less eloquent than his convention speech four years earlier. He devoted most of it to denouncing the Republican presidential candidate, Goldwater, saying he lives in a "strange world" in which "the pale horse of death and destruction and the white horse of conquest and of victory are indistinguishable." He ended by calling on Democrats to "dedicate yourselves again in support of Lyndon Johnson as president and to accept my colleague, the friend of the president and my friend, Hubert Humphrey, as vice president."

[13] Ann Terry Pincus, then a Washington correspondent for Ridder Publications, Inc., and the only woman present at the Johnson party, recalls that a fellow reporter called her attention to the president's open bedroom door. "I turned around and looked and, my God, there was the president of the United States standing in his shorts."

But McCarthy's bitterness was evident later that night at a party given for Humphrey by the Minnesota delegation. "He was very sarcastic and very bitter," recalls Mrs. Geri Joseph, a Humphrey adviser and state party officer. "I went up to the McCarthys' suite and urged them to come down to the party. Abigail refused to come. Gene did, but I think he was deeply hurt."

On the last night of the convention — Johnson's fifty-sixth birthday — the president returned to deliver his acceptance speech. Humphrey spoke first and proved that he would be a formidable political antagonist in the coming campaign. Warming up with a long tribute to the president, he offered a scornful litany of indictments against Goldwater's voting record and capped each one with the drum-beat cry that was to become familiar to campaign audiences — "but not Senator Goldwater!" The delegates took up Humphrey's chant and he stole the show from Johnson, who sat in the presidential box looking annoyed and at times bored before he got up and gave a lackluster acceptance speech. He had no more surprises for the convention, which ended with an emotional viewing of a John F. Kennedy memorial film, a burst of fireworks and a $1,000-a-ticket birthday party for Johnson.

The tension and uncertainty of Atlantic City were soon forgotten by Humphrey as he campaigned with euphoric enthusiasm across the country in his aptly-named campaign plane, *The Happy Warrior*. He relieved Johnson of much of the campaign effort, reminding the country of its unprecedented prosperity and promising the flowering of the Great Society in the coming years. He called Lyndon Johnson "the greatest president in the history of the United States," and cautioned against "changing quarterbacks in the middle of a winning game." "We Democrats are a happy lot," he declared at a Chicago rally in October. "We ought to make this campaign not a chore but a happy, joyful effort. The Goldwater party has a sort of patent on booing. But we have a patent on cheering."

Humphrey's campaign reached a sentimental climax when he returned to his hometown of Doland, South Dakota, where his rousing reception moved him to tears and a patriotic exhortation. "We need to set an example in America of how we can reconcile our differences and still be different," he said, "of how we can disagree without being disagreeable to one another. Possibly Main Street in Doland is the best place to talk about building a community of free men. You don't defend freedom in Washington alone. You defend it here by what you do, what you believe, what you say and how you live."

Humphrey's enthusiasm obscured some darkening clouds on the horizon. He gave no major speeches on the subject of Vietnam, limiting himself to defending the president's unilateral military action in Vietnam following the Gulf of Tonkin incident. "Our action in the Gulf of Tonkin is part of the continuing struggle which the American people must be prepared to wage if we are to preserve free civilization as we know it, and resist the expansion of Communist power," Humphrey said in September in one of his rare statements on the war.

And in a bitterly ironic contrast to the reception he would find on college campuses within a few years, Humphrey was greeted by an outpouring of warm affection by young people. Describing Humphrey's visit to the University of Toledo on October 7, where 7,500 students waved signs like "We Love Hubert" and "We Dig Hubert," New York *Times* Reporter John Pomfret wrote:

> The scene was typical of one of the interesting sidelights of the campaign — the unabashed affection that Mr. Humphrey is arousing among the young people. They squeal at him, mob him, steal watches off his wrist, tear cuff-links from his shirtsleeves, delay his tight schedule while the girls insist on kissing him goodbye. And they listen to him.

The 1964 campaign was "like the answer to a political prayer," Humphrey said after he had helped Johnson lead the Democratic party to its greatest victory since 1936 in the November election. "Probably the most heartwarming aspect of the campaign was the interest shown by our own young people," he said in assessing the campaign. "I guess I never have given up the teaching profession. Give me an audience of young folks, and I feel in my element. Their commitment to the Great Society is one of the most dramatic political developments of this generation."

The man who would soon capture the loyalty of the young people Humphrey yearned to teach and influence did not have to work to be reelected to a second term in Minnesota. Aided by the priceless publicity from Atlantic City ("We're going to play the vice presidency soft and run for the Senate hard," he told a friend earlier in the year), the forty-eight year old McCarthy swept to an easy victory over Republican Wheelock Whitney III, mayor of the Minneapolis suburb of Wayzata and head of a Minneapolis securities firm. McCarthy won by the largest popular majority of any Democrat in the state's history (325,420 votes or 60.3 percent of the total).

However, voters never learned about an ironic and tragic incident a month earlier that linked McCarthy and Johnson and threatened their election. Walter Jenkins, the President's closest personal assistant and the man who had most encouraged McCarthy's vice presidential hopes, was arrested in a downtown Washington YMCA on October 7 for what the nation learned a week later was a homosexual incident. Johnson was infuriated because he felt Jenkins, who had been arrested for a similar episode in 1959, had been lured into the YMCA incident by political foes, including a member of Congress. He ordered an FBI investigation of a military reserve unit to which the member belonged, and unexpectedly turned up the fact that a member of McCarthy's staff was implicated in a homosexual ring in the unit. Johnson himself notified McCarthy of the FBI finding, and the aide was fired a short time later, although the incident never came to light and did not noticeably affect the election outcome. Jerry Eller was called to fire the aide, who reminded him that McCarthy had once introduced legislation to protect government employees who were considered security risks (including homosexuals). "I said, 'Yes, but not in the middle of a goddamn campaign,' " Eller recalls.

The campaign was so routine that McCarthy spent part of his time in Oklahoma and Texas helping elect Mike Monroney and Ralph Yarborough, and he even campaigned in New York for Robert Kennedy. After the election, McCarthy had hundreds of illustrated campaign brochures left over. Prominently displayed in the brochure was a photograph of McCarthy standing alone in the Senate's cobblestone courtyard, and a letter written early in the year by President Johnson. The letter read: "Gene McCarthy is the kind of man — as we say in the ranch country of Texas — who will go to the well with you. That's a homely way of saying you can count on him in dark days or bright ones."

CHAPTER XII

SUPER SALESMAN FOR THE GREAT SOCIETY

I did not become vice president with
Lyndon Johnson to cause him trouble.
Hubert Humphrey in a 1965 interview.

Standing at the right hand of the man who could make his lifelong dream of the presidency come true, Hubert Humphrey was sworn in as the thirty-eighth vice president of the United States on January 20, 1965. It was the supreme moment of Humphrey's life, and it was fitting that it should come in conjunction with the ultimate personal triumph of Lyndon Johnson. They had come to the Senate together on another January day sixteen years earlier, had helped each other in their search for political power and now their symbiotic relationship had paid off handsomely for both of them. Johnson had become president in his own right by amassing the largest vote of any American presidential candidate and he had resurrected Humphrey's presidential hopes by placing him on what history had shown to be the most certain path to the White House.

Even though Johnson had told the 1964 Democratic National Convention that he wanted Humphrey to be "an important instrument of the executive branch" who would "connect Congress to the White House," both men were aware of the essentially inconsequential nature of the vice president's role in the American system. Johnson never forgot his own unhappy experiences as vice president under John Kennedy, when he felt he had been kept so busy with insignificant tasks that a rash of "whatever happened to Lyndon?" stories was making the rounds in Washington just before Kennedy's death. But no one had been more loyal to his president than Johnson, and now he demanded the same from his vice president.

Humphrey was confident that he could overcome the built-in frustrations of a job that would impose severe restraints on his bustling energy and soaring ambition and place him under a tough, demanding and egocentric boss. He understood that he was to be strictly the number two man, but he also knew that he started out with an advantage no other vice president had — an intimate personal and political relationship with his president dating back sixteen years — and he felt that advantage would more than make up for the new subservient role he was now expected to play. "I'd rather have the privilege of one hour with the president alongside him, than to have two years on the outside wondering whether I could ever get inside even to talk to him for just a few minutes," he declared shortly after the election.

Humphrey was told in crystal clear terms of the secondary role he would be expected to play on the day Johnson asked him to be his vice president. "We had an understanding," Humphrey later recalled. "I'll never forget that visit in the White House on the day that I flew down from Alantic City. Johnson said he was going to offer me this [the vice presidency] and then he said, 'I just want you to know two or three things: Number one, seldom have the president and vice president ever gotten along. We've had a wonderful friendship, and one reason I've had doubts about this is that I'm afraid that will end. Take a look at Truman and Barkley — they were intimate friends, but a year after the election in 1948, they hardly spoke to one another and Barkley didn't even attend Cabinet meetings. This is true generally of the vice presidency.'

"Secondly, the president said, 'It's got to be like an insoluble marriage. There's no way to back out, and I've got to have loyalty. I gave President Kennedy that and there were real differences between him and me. But we can't have two presidents at once, and we can't have two voices in the White House. I know that you're a real man of conviction and an articulate man, and it's going to be a real test to see if you can discipline yourself to this. If you don't, of course, the relationship gets difficult.'

"Finally, the president told me, 'If this goes through, we have to have an agreement about Cabinet meetings.' He said the reason for it is that 'there are some people around this city who just live on letting out leaks that there is a difference between the president and the vice president. It makes great copy. So if you have something you want to talk to me about that's different from administration policy, come and talk to me privately. Don't put it down on paper. It gets around and causes difficulty. I'm available to you at any hour of the day.' "

Humphrey knew the exact price of becoming Lyndon Johnson's vice president. He would have to recast himself in a role totally different from the free-swinging political activist he had been in the Senate and become instead an energetic salesman for the Great Society and a self-effacing helpmate and confidant to Johnson. It was a price Humphrey was more than willing to pay, as he made clear during a television interview a few days before his meeting with Johnson. "A vice president must be loyal,"

Humphrey said as he summarized his concept of the office he was seeking. "He must have a quality of fidelity, a willingness literally to give himself, to be what the president wants him to be, a loyal, faithful friend and servant."

Humphrey spent the two months between the election and the inauguration assembling a staff, preparing to handle the multitude of chores assigned him by presidential command and, above all, talking things over with the president day and night. Installed in an eight-room suite in the rococo Executive Office Building less than a hundred yards from Johnson's office (he could be at Johnson's side in less than a minute after he called), and operating out of a smaller office just off the Senate floor and another in the New Senate Office Building, Humphrey was prepared to divide his workday between lobbying for the president at one end of Pennsylvania Avenue and counseling with him at the other end.

Johnson decreed that Humphrey, like most vice presidents since the end of World War II, should sit in the highest councils of the government. In addition to being a member of the Cabinet and National Security Council, Humphrey was given the job of coordinating the federal government's civil rights and anti-discrimination programs as chairman of the President's Council on Equal Opportunity; he was ordered to take "a leading role" in the war on poverty as chairman of the Advisory Council to the Office of Economic Opportunity and the President's Council on Youth Opportunity; he was named chairman of the Peace Corps Advisory Council, the National Aeronautics and Space Council, the President's Council on Youth Fitness, the See the U.S.A. program and a host of other advisory and coordinating positions. For good measure, Johnson assigned Humphrey to serve as the White House liaison with the nation's mayors and governors and asked him to help work out, in his spare time, a new Democratic farm policy. Finally, Humphrey was at Johnson's call to perform various ceremonial functions, give speeches and travel the political fundraising dinner circuit.

Above all, Johnson wanted Humphrey to guide the administration's legislative programs through Congress. He felt Humphrey could be an invaluable ally on Capitol Hill with his sophisticated understanding of the legislative process and his excellent relations with many members of Congress, even though both men realized Humphrey's influence would be greatly reduced because of his new role. "I am still in the Club," Humphrey later said of his reception on Capitol Hill, "but no longer a member." Nevertheless, Johnson introduced Humphrey to leaders of the Eighty-ninth Congress on the day after the inauguration as "my man on the Hill," and added, "He has all the information I have and is available to you any time you want to talk to him."[1]

---

[1] Humphrey received duplicate copies of all top-secret intelligence summaries prepared for the president each morning and read them during the forty-minute drive from his suburban home to his office. He was accompanied by a government intelli-

Encouraged by Johnson's attitude and convinced that together they finally would be able to turn the vice presidency into an effective and significant arm of government, Humphrey attacked his new duties with characteristic energy and enthusiasm. But still mindful of Johnson's sensitivity about sharing the limelight, Humphrey never let himself or his staff forget the political umbilical cord that linked him with Johnson. At one of the first staff meetings, an aide remembers that Humphrey walked to the window and pointed across to the White House. "That's how close we are to the president of the United States," he said. "Every word we utter, everything we do, reflects directly on the president and on the White House. Each of us must conduct himself with that in mind. We must dress, act and speak with dignity, wisely and prudently, and when we act, we must be sure it's right. I'd rather have delays than come up wrong."

Humphrey had hardly been sworn into office before he was reminded that he was literally only a heartbeat away from becoming President Humphrey.[2] On January 22, two days after the inauguration, he worked until midnight at the Executive Office Building preparing for a trip to Minnesota and an appearance at the St. Paul Winter Carnival the next day. When he arrived at his suburban Chevy Chase, Maryland, home at about 1:00 A.M., he was exhausted and suffering from a slight cold and went to bed immediately.[3] An hour later he was awakened by the insistent ringing of his bedside "hot line" to the White House and was told by Press Secretary George Reedy that Johnson had been taken to Bethesda Naval Hospital for treatment of an undisclosed illness. Humphrey didn't learn until an hour later that Johnson's trouble was only a severe chest cold.

In the meantime, he pondered the thought that he might be called on to assume the awesome responsibilities of the presidency. Saying nothing to his wife, he went downstairs and walked around the house. Then, he recalls,

---

gence officer who delivered the documents and answered any questions Humphrey had. He also received all other secret foreign policy reports given the president.

[2] There were those who were prepared just in case Humphrey *did* suddenly become president. The *Wall Street Journal,* for instance, had a 2,500-word story set in type and marked "HOLD FOR RELEASE" that began: "Washington — Hubert Horatio Humphrey, who yesterday became the 37th president of the United States as a result of Lyndon Johnson's death, will run an unmistakably activist, liberal administration." The article predicted that Humphrey would push for domestic programs "at least as large" as Johnson's Great Society proposals although his administration would "not be as radical as many conservatives undoubtedly fear." Changes in the Humphrey administration's foreign policy would "be more in style and emphasis than in basic policy," the article said, adding, "The Vietnam War will be prosecuted as vigorously as under Mr. Johnson."

[3] The Humphreys remained in the modest home they had purchased in 1949 until 1966, when they bought a $75,000 townhouse apartment on the Potomac River waterfront in downtown Washington. In 1965, Johnson approved a plan for a government-provided vice presidential residence and Congress authorized $750,000 for the project, but it became another victim of the Vietnam War budgetary squeeze.

"I went back to the bedroom. Muriel was awake. She asked if Winston Churchill had passed away. 'No,' I said, 'the president is sick.' We both went downstairs together and sat and talked."

When the second call came telling Humphrey that the president's illness wasn't serious and that he should go ahead with his planned trip to Minnesota, he understood again how much he was dependent on Johnson for any real chance at the presidency. "I realized my fears and apprehensions were unfounded and I can now smile again," he told reporters in Minnesota later that day.

Humphrey's smile turned to glum silence a few days later when Churchill died and a major flap developed over Johnson's decision not to send him to represent the United States at the British prime minister's funeral.[4] Although Johnson had good reason for his action — he was still not fully recovered from his illness and didn't want his vice president out of the country — he offered no public explanation and it was widely interpreted as a snub to Humphrey when Chief Justice Earl Warren was sent in his place.

Humphrey was embarrassed by the rhubarb over his non-trip, but shrugged it off as another example of Washington's preoccupation with disagreements between the president and vice president. Nevertheless, the Churchill episode was soon to be followed by a far more serious disagreement that had drastic and far-reaching implications for Humphrey's future. That disagreement revolved around the growing U.S. involvement in Vietnam, an involvement that was rapidly becoming Johnson's consuming passion and one that would ultimately drive him from the presidency and help frustrate Humphrey's long-held hopes of becoming president.

Humphrey's basic position on American involvement in Southeast Asia — the issue that later became an unshakeable albatross around his neck — had changed very little during his sixteen years in Washington. Although he later would be criticized for changing his views and compromising his principles to get in line with Johnson's policies, an examination of the *Congressional Record* during his years in the Senate shows that one consistent theme ran through Humphrey's statements on Asia. Whether the immediate focus was Vietnam, Korea, India or Formosa, Humphrey believed that "the greatest risk is Communist aggression, Communist conquest and Communist advance."

For instance, in January, 1950, he told the Senate that "if we lose the south part of Asia . . . we shall have lost every hope that we ever had of being able to maintain free institutions in any part of the Eastern world." In

---

[4] It was not the first time that Humphrey had been disappointed by Johnson's failure to send him abroad. In December, before being sworn in, Humphrey told his aides he had been designated to head the U.S. delegation to the inauguration of Mexican President Gustavo Diaz Ordaz later that month. The day before he was to leave, Johnson decided to send Senate Majority Leader Mike Mansfield as head of the delegation instead.

1951, he called the Indochina war "a war against the same Communism" as that in Korea and compared the loss of the area to Communism to the loss of Korea. In 1953 he declared, "The threat of international Communist aggression is most acute in Southeast Asia." In 1954, as the Senate debated the Southeast Asia Collective Defense Treaty (SEATO), which pledged the U.S. to take action against "armed attack" on any country in Southeast Asia, including South Vietnam, Humphrey warned: "To lose Indochina to the Communists may be to lose all of Southeast Asia. It is unthinkable. It cannot happen. It will not happen." In February, 1955, it was Humphrey who made the motion that led to Senate ratification by an 85–1 vote of the SEATO Treaty, which led to the initial U.S. involvement in Vietnam by the Eisenhower administration.[5] In May of that year, Humphrey criticized the Eisenhower administration for not being sufficiently committed to a free Vietnam and offered an early version of the "domino theory." "If we abandon free Vietnam, we shall have abandoned all of Southeast Asia . . . if free Vietnam falls, or if the Communist elements take over, then every country in the corridor of Southeast Asia will be in more difficulty, and we shall not be able to stop it."

By 1960, Humphrey's words grew even more ominous as he raised the threat of Communist China. "I happen to believe that the most dangerous, aggressive force in the world today is Communist China . . . it is from the Chinese Communists that the free world faces danger." In 1962, he told the Senate that the U.S. should limit its participation in Vietnam to "military assistance, to supplies, and to military training," but he added, "In all of this activity there is a grave risk; but I say most sincerely that the greatest risk is Communist aggression, Communist conquest and Communist advance. That we cannot permit if it is humanly possible to stop it." Finally, during the debate that preceded the August, 1964, Senate passage of the Gulf of Tonkin Resolution, Humphrey said that "the aggressor seeks to bite off piece by piece the areas of freedom . . . our objective is to achieve stability in the area so that we can then go to the conference table. But we ought to make it clear to the world that we do not intend to sit at the conference table with a Communist gun at our heads."

In early 1964, well before he was picked for vice president, Humphrey conducted a private correspondence with Henry Cabot Lodge, the U.S. ambassador to Saigon, whom he had met while serving as a Congressional delegate to the United Nations, and picked the brains of other experts in the government, including his former legislative assistant, Thomas Hughes, then director of the State Department's Bureau of Intelligence and Research. Humphrey became convinced that the best hope for achieving political stability and economic development in South Vietnam lay in counter-insur-

---

[5] Ironically, Johnson was not present when the Senate ratified the SEATO Treaty but was in Humphrey's home state of Minnesota recovering from surgery at the Mayo Clinic.

gency methods similar to those employed by Philippine President Ramon Magsaysay to defeat the Communist-led Huk guerrillas in the early 1950's.

Humphrey was greatly influenced by Edward Lansdale, a retired Air Force major general and counter-guerrilla expert who had been Magsaysay's chief adviser and who became special assistant for pacification to Ambassador Lodge in 1965. Lansdale's theory, which Humphrey enthusiastically supported, was that conventional military techniques were useless against a rural-based Communist insurrection and that the only way to cope with it was to adopt identical guerrilla tactics while at the same time proving to the people that the democratic government could offer them more in protection and social and economic benefits through a "rural reconstruction" program.

Humphrey embellished the Lansdale thesis with some of his own views and presented his argument in a lengthy memorandum to President Johnson in the spring of 1964, even though several of Humphrey's aides disagreed with the memo on the grounds that Lansdale was wrong and that the memo could harm Humphrey's vice presidential prospects. In the memo, Humphrey opposed withdrawal of the sixteen thousand American troops then in Vietnam on the grounds that "it would shake the other Southeast Asian nations." But he argued that "direct U.S. action against North Vietnam, American assumption of command roles, or participation in combat of U.S. troop units, are unnecessary and undesirable." In the memo, Humphrey also urged that "immediate priority" be given to stabilizing Vietnamese leadership and to insuring that "the government is one the population can give their loyalty to. That means there is an immediate need for economic and political reforms."

In August, 1964, shortly after the Tonkin Resolution vote but before the Democratic National Convention, Humphrey offered the most definitive statement of his Vietnam views in a speech — given at Johnson's request — at the Los Angeles Town Hall Forum. His two key policy recommendations were that "we must stay in Vietnam until the security of the South Vietnamese people has been established," and "the primary responsibility for preserving independence and achieving peace in Vietnam remains with the Vietnamese people and their government." On the latter point, Humphrey was emphatic, saying, "May I remind those latter-day prophets of 'total victory' that this is a war for independence — and no lasting independence can be imposed by foreign armies."

Humphrey said little about Vietnam during the 1964 presidential campaign except to reiterate the points of his Town Hall Forum speech and to stress the necessity for political and economic reform in South Vietnam. By the time the Johnson-Humphrey administration prepared to take office, the war was clearly a critical issue inside the councils of government, but was not the overriding national issue it would become by the end of 1965. American forces in South Vietnam at the beginning of the year consisted of 23,300 military personnel, mostly advisers (the figure would climb to 184,300 by the end of the year, with U.S. troops engaged in combat), and public antiwar protests were still unheard of. But as the situation continued to deteriorate in South Vietnam, a majority of Johnson's senior military and civilian advisers was pressing him to make what amounted to a major escalation of the war, and Humphrey, despite his loyalty to Johnson, began to have serious misgivings about the growing pressure for sustained bombing of the North and for large scale troop increases.[6] He expressed those misgivings in several private discussions and secret memos to the president.

However, Humphrey's growing doubts about the course of the war soon caused him to violate his "private disagreement" pact with Johnson, an action that damaged his relationship with Johnson and had untold consequences for his future. His deep reservations first came to the surface at a meeting of the National Security Council on February 10. By then, the U.S. had already conducted two reprisal air strikes in retaliation for a Vietcong attack on February 6 on a U.S. compound at Pleiku and a nearby base that killed nine Americans and wounded more than a hundred, and an attack on an enlisted men's barracks at Qui Nhon earlier that day that killed twenty-three Americans.

At that meeting, Humphrey, like all those present, agreed that some form of response was necessary, but he strongly urged delaying a proposed joint U.S.-South Vietnamese retaliatory air strike against three targest in North Vietnam because of the presence of Soviet Premier Aleksei Kosygin in Hanoi. Those present recall that Humphrey also expressed in emotional language his doubts about the wisdom of bombing North Vietnam to the negotiating table. Humphrey argued that the reprisal attacks be delayed until Kosygin left Hanoi, and was joined in that argument by Undersecretary of State George Ball and by the U.S. ambassador to Moscow, Llewellyn Thompson.

After a long, heated discussion, Johnson agreed to try to meet the Humphrey-Ball-Thompson objections by deleting one of the targets, a key bridge only seventy-five miles south of Hanoi, and hit only the two other targets, military barracks just north of the seventeenth parallel. Humphrey said he had mixed emotions and Thompson still argued for a delay of a few days, but Johnson and the others agreed with Defense Secretary Robert McNamara and the joint chiefs of staff that the air strikes should be carried out the next day, and they were. Two days later, on February 13, Johnson notified U.S. Ambassador Maxwell Taylor and the U.S. military command in Saigon

[6] According to the Pentagon study of the history of the Vietnam War published by the New York *Times* and other newspapers in 1971, Johnson and his advisers had reached a "general consensus" as early as September, 1964, on the necessity for bombing North Vietnam, but delayed taking any action because of "tactical considerations," including a possible adverse effect on the 1964 presidential election and the weakness of the South Vietnam government.

that he had given the order for the first sustained air strikes against targets in North Vietnam below the nineteenth parallel. The attacks, planned under the code name "Operation Rolling Thunder," were set to begin on February 20, but didn't actually begin until March 2. Nevertheless, "Rolling Thunder" represented the first major escalation of the war and opened the door to the later massive American involvement in Vietnam.

Aware that Johnson had not been pleased by his disagreement in front of the others but also afraid that Johnson had been persuaded to step up the war, Humphrey made a last-ditch effort to change the president's mind. He spoke privately to the president on the following night and on February 17, he sent Johnson a lengthy memorandum in which he expressed the fear that Johnson's advisers were urging a policy that "in fact adopted Goldwater's position," a reference to the man Johnson had defeated for the presidency three months earlier.[7]

Humphrey argued in his memo that a full-scale military attack on North Vietnam not only risked the intervention of Communist China and the Soviet Union but that it also would hamper efforts to reach a detente with Russia and would damage U.S. relations with the rest of the world, particularly our Western European allies. He said the U.S. experience in Korea in 1951–52 had demonstrated that we should never again become involved in a land war in Asia, and warned that the fact that the U.S. no longer had a monopoly on nuclear weapons made it even more likely that Red China would intervene.

Humphrey also expressed grave concern that an expansion of the Vietnam War would result in a drain of resources and commitment from the Great Society domestic programs and would not make sense to the American public, which he said was already worried and confused about Vietnam. Finally, he said most Americans, himself included, did not have confidence in the government of South Vietnam, which had been highly unstable since the November, 1963, assassination of President Ngo Dinh Diem.

Johnson's reaction to the memo was predictable. His secretive nature and absolute insistence on avoiding any public display of disagreement between him and his vice president bordered on an obsession, and he upbraided Humphrey for committing his thoughts to paper. "We don't need all those memos, Hubert," Humphrey recalls Johnson telling him. "Frankly, I don't think you should have them lying around your office because there's going to be people coming and going, and as much as we put security controls on them, somebody always makes extra copies. There isn't anything that you

---

[7] Humphrey showed a copy of his memo to Philip Potter, Washington bureau chief of the Baltimore *Sun*, in January, 1970. Potter, a University of Minnesota graduate, a veteran Humphrey watcher and an extremely tough and capable reporter, took notes from the memo for a book he was then planning on Vietnam, but did not complete. However, he wrote an account of the memo for his newspaper in June, 1971.

can put on paper that you can't say to me personally and say it better."
(Humphrey later said of his memo, "I don't think it was very helpful. I don't
think the president thought his vice president needed to do that.")

Humphrey's February, 1965, disagreements with Johnson were a critical
turning point in his vice presidency, although he did not know it at the time.
For almost a year afterwards, he was systematically excluded from Johnson's inner council of advisers — the so-called "Tuesday luncheons" where
critical decisions on the war were made — and forced to concentrate on
strictly domestic matters.

"Humphrey just argued out of political intuition and visceral reaction
against the bombing," says Ted Van Dyk, one of Humphrey's top aides at
the time. "Johnson had talked to him at great length before he took office
saying he didn't want Humphrey disagreeing with him at meetings, and that
they should discuss their differences privately. And right at the start Humphrey breached this. I'm sure this angered the hell out of Johnson — maybe
even more than the fact that Humphrey disagreed with him. Anyway, for
almost a year, we were just plain left out. Humphrey spent most of his time
up at the Capitol working on Great Society legislation, putting all his energies
into the domestic thing because he was just frozen out of foreign affairs."

Other former Humphrey aides agree with Van Dyk's assessment. John
Reilly, Humphrey's foreign affairs specialist, recalls one effect of Humphrey's
outspoken dissent that was immediately apparent. Reilly, a Fulbright scholar
and Harvard Ph.D. who went to work for Humphrey in the Senate when
there were no openings for him on Senator Eugene McCarthy's staff, learned
through an aide to another member of the National Security Council that
an important meeting was scheduled a short time after February 10. Reilly
then discovered that Humphrey had not been invited, apparently on Johnson's orders. "That was the beginning of eleven months in which Humphrey
was kept out of all the important meetings to just an unimaginable extent,"
says Reilly.

George Ball, one of those who sided with Humphrey at the February 10
meeting in urging that the retaliatory raids be delayed at least until Kosygin
left Hanoi, remembers that both he and Humphrey first argued against
bombing the North but that it was clear that Johnson had made up his mind
to do so. "The question then boiled down to a rather narrow issue, whether
we should start the retaliatory action while Kosygin was in Hanoi," Ball said
in a 1971 interview. "As I recall, the vice president and I argued that we
shouldn't be going out of our way to appear to put the Russians in a difficult
position. But we got nowhere because of the extraordinary impatience to
go on with it, particularly on the part of Secretary McNamara, who brushed
aside all political arguments as inconsequential." Humphrey was "forceful
and very frank" in expressing his opposition, Ball recalls. "He left no doubt
as to his own views. On this particular issue, the vice president was in a

singularly difficult position and usually he was very careful not to put himself at cross purposes with the president."

Humphrey had been included in the earlier meetings of the inner circle of Johnson advisers, but after February 10, "he just didn't appear anymore," Ball recounts. "I think the president felt that if the vice president was going to raise any arguments, he didn't want him around. He treated him pretty much in the way the Kennedys treated him when he was vice president. I would have thought that Johnson, having been through this miserable experience himself and being excluded from most things, would have leaned over backwards to treat Humphrey differently, but he didn't. It reminded me of the old system of hazing a college freshman."

Humphrey's exclusion from the Vietnam strategy sessions did not extend to matters relating to the impact of the war on the domestic front, however. Johnson still expected him to help quiet the rising criticism touched off by the escalation of the war, particularly among Humphrey's former colleagues in the Senate, some of whom were beginning to question publicly the president's basic policy in Vietnam in the wake of the "Rolling Thunder" bombings.

Led by the two maverick Democrats who had cast the only votes against the Gulf of Tonkin Resolution, Wayne Morse of Oregon and Ernest Gruening of Alaska, Senate doves were beginning to coo more loudly. Humphrey's next-door neighbor, South Dakota's George McGovern, and Idaho's Frank Church both made speeches on February 17 urging the president to push harder for a negotiated settlement and to rely less on military pressure, while other liberal Democratic senators from the Midwest, including Humphrey's former Minnesota colleague, Eugene McCarthy, Wisconsin's Gaylord Nelson and Ohio's Stephen Young were publicly and privately voicing misgivings about Johnson's Vietnam policy.

Unable to ignore the mounting discontent in the vital liberal wing of his party, Johnson dispatched Humphrey on the first of what would be many futile missions over the next four years to explain and justify to his old liberal friends the growing American commitment in Vietnam. Humphrey's new role as an apologist for Johnson on the war first became clear in mid-February as Johnson sent McGeorge Bundy, his special assistant for national security affairs and one of the principal architects of the Vietnam policy, to Humphrey's private vice presidential office in the Capitol to talk with five key liberal critics who were all good friends of Humphrey — McGovern, Church, McCarthy, Nelson and Young.

While Humphrey sat silently at his desk, Bundy lectured the five senators on the need for unified support for the president's Vietnam policies. "It was a very strange thing and it irritated us all," Nelson later recalled. "Bundy said, 'Now I've gone through the *Congressional Record* and read what you gentlemen have been saying. They're all very reasonable and thoughtful speeches but when this gets in the papers and then gets into the rumor mills over in Vietnam, it gives a totally different impression that the country isn't behind the president.' " Nelson asked Bundy if he was suggesting that "we give up the freedom of speech in this country because some dictator doesn't understand it?" Bundy said that wasn't at all what he meant, but those present felt that it was, and the meeting broke up with the five critics more skeptical than when it began.

Johnson also enlisted Humphrey's help in trying to blunt criticism of his Vietnam policy from the most vocal element of the liberal wing of the Democratic party, the Americans for Democratic Action. Humphrey, who was a founder of the ADA in 1947 and a longtime member of its executive board, helped arrange a meeting at the White House with twenty-two ADA leaders on April 2, while the ADA was holding its annual convention in Washington. The session, scheduled for fifteen minutes, turned into an hour and a half presidential monologue as Johnson offered a preview of his April 7 speech at Johns Hopkins University in Baltimore in which he reaffirmed both the U.S. commitment to South Vietnam and his readiness to begin peace negotiations, and pledged a "billion-dollar investment" for economic development of Southeast Asia.

The session with Johnson neither placated the ADA leaders nor increased their regard for Humphrey. Their grumbling turned to open criticism a few weeks later when he stoutly defended Johnson's April 28 decision to send more than thirty thousand U.S. troops to help quell a rebellion in the Dominican Republic, without first getting the assent of the Organization of American States. Humphrey argued that such a large intervention in Latin America was justified by the need to protect U.S. citizens living in Santo Domingo, but the move was sharply opposed by liberal critics and others. Humphrey, who as a senator only a year earlier had argued against the hardline approach to Latin American affairs advocated by Undersecretary of State Thomas Mann, made it clear he was completely behind Mann and the Dominican intervention.

Despite all of Humphrey's unhappy experiences in foreign policy, he appeared to be thriving in his role as chief promoter of the administration's ambitious domestic programs. Expounding, explaining, exhorting and extolling the virtues of the Great Society at every opportunity, Humphrey established himself as the busiest vice president in history during his first year in office. He helped push dozens of major laws through the first session of the Democratic-controlled Eighty-ninth Congress, including programs which had long been his personal goals such as Medicare, the Voting Rights Act of 1965 — the most comprehensive legislation to assure the right to vote since the Civil War — immigration reform, aid to education, a massive new housing and rent supplements bill and creation of the new Department of Housing and Urban Development.

He also kept up a dizzying pace of speeches and personal appearances (he received as many as a thousand speaking invitations each month and made as many as twenty-five major prepared speeches each month, all cleared by the White House), ranged from coast to coast for political rallies, civic fetes and conventions, and wheeled incessantly from legislative conference to diplomatic reception to cocktail party to labor union dinner in the course of an average sixteen-hour to eighteen-hour day. "Gee whiz," Humphrey exclaimed again and again as he bounded around Washington and the country, "this is a wonderful time to be alive!"

Humphrey's frantic pace impressed many people, but others saw it as evidence that he was still uncertain of his role in the administration and his relationship with his mercurial boss, who would praise Humphrey one day and damn him the next. "It was a sort of a love-hate relationship," recalls John Stewart, one of Humphrey's most able assistants. "There were times when Johnson would call him up every day and have him over for long talks. And then a couple of weeks would go by and he wouldn't hardly see the president . . . . There was an element of uncertainty. On any given day, he didn't know whether Johnson would be ecstatic or furious — he could be both and without any particular warning about what was coming next. Having LBJ breathing down your neck was not a very pleasant way to have to live."

Stewart feels that Humphrey's early opposition to the war "unquestionably damaged his relationship with Johnson — it created a barrier between them that had never been there before." Johnson's preoccupation with the war also hurt Humphrey in another way, Stewart feels. "The war diverted so much of Johnson's attention from domestic things, which was the area Humphrey was supposedly going to have a lot of responsibility in. As a result, the White House staff, which is always kind of suspicious of the vice president, got much more involved in domestic things than they otherwise would have, and they wanted to control everything. And since Johnson was sort of mad at Humphrey about Vietnam, he probably thought that was just what Humphrey deserved."

For example, Stewart points out that Humphrey was given responsibility, with considerable public fanfare, for coordinating civil rights enforcement policies. After consulting numerous civil rights figures, Humphrey proposed a new coordinating council headed by himself and equipped with a high-powered staff to ride herd on individual government agencies. "He got the thing set up and it was just getting going when Joe Califano [Johnson's special assistant for domestic affairs who joined him in July, 1965] came into the White House. By October, the whole thing had been summarily abolished — what was supposed to be a coordinative function was parceled out to various agencies. Humphrey was left standing around looking like a damn fool. I'm sure if Humphrey had been in good favor with Johnson at that point, Johnson would not have let that happen the way it did. Because of the change in their relationship, though, I think the full potential of Humphrey's vice presidency was never realized."

However, Humphrey performed ably in other areas of his job as a civil rights coordinator. For example, in April, Louisiana Governor John McKeithen asked him to help avert a potentially explosive racial situation in Bogalusa, Louisiana. Humphrey persuaded James Farmer, national director of CORE, to go to Bogalusa and mediate the city's racial conflicts. And after racial violence erupted in Selma, Alabama, in March, Johnson called on Humphrey to help calm the situation. Humphrey talked day and night with Negro leaders and after the conflict cooled off, told Johnson, "You're not getting across. You've got to speak again on voting rights." Johnson did, going before a joint session of Congress to urge swift enactment of strong voting rights legislation.

Johnson's reluctance to share the limelight also exacerbated Humphrey's insecurities. He often chided Humphrey when he felt the vice president was getting too much newspaper space, and complained that Humphrey's forty-five member staff was both too large and too publicity conscious. Johnson periodically vented his spleen on Humphrey for tipping his hand, as when Humphrey told a group of labor leaders, off the cuff, that the administration was about to ask Congress for an increased minimum wage. The remark got into the papers and at the next Congressional leadership breakfast, Johnson remarked caustically, "I see by the papers where I have a minimum wage program." When a contrite Humphrey apologized the next day, Johnson put his arm around him and said soothingly, "Well, we all make mistakes."

Humphrey could never be sure when to expect another humiliating broadside from Johnson. In late May, 1965, Humphrey invited a group of Washington journalists for dinner on one of the yachts maintained for White House use. As they cruised down the Potomac River, they met the presidential yacht *Sequoia* going in the other direction. It had barely passed before the captain of Humphrey's boat received a radio telephone call from the captain of the *Sequoia*. "He said the president wanted to know who in the hell had his boat out," a Humphrey aide recalls.

After that, whenever Humphrey wanted a boat, he had to send a request through his military aide, Marine Colonel Herbert Beckington, to Presidential Assistant Marvin Watson, who would put the memo in the president's overnight reading file. The same method was used when Humphrey needed an airplane, the Humphrey aide remembers. "If he had three out-of-town speaking engagements that week, three memos would go from his military aide to Johnson's military aide to Marvin Watson to Lyndon Baines Johnson's overnight reading file, and he would mark them yes or no. That kept up for three-and-a-half years and there were many cases where the memos came back marked 'no.' "

Humphrey was to suffer an even more humiliating experience at Johnson's hands two months later. On the evening of July 27, Humphrey was in Minneapolis, where, in a speech to the annual Governors' Conference, he made an impassioned appeal for support of the president's Vietnam policies and for the pending decision to increase greatly the U.S. combat role, which the president was expected to announce the next day. Humphrey had not yet given the speech but the wire services had reported the substance of it from advance texts when Johnson met with the Cabinet and Congressional leaders of both parties at the White House to appeal for bipartisan support and to tell them what he was going to say the next day. He pulled from his pocket a news ticker account of Humphrey's speech and read it and then, to the amazement of those present, sarcastically and insultingly criticized Humphrey for over-emphasizing the gravity of the troop increase and for hinting that he was going to order a reserve call-up, which he wasn't. At the same time, a Johnson aide was on the phone to Humphrey ordering him to tone down his speech.

Humphrey was fully prepared to play a subsidiary role to Johnson and only rarely complained about his lot. But occasionally, brooding about his treatment at Johnson's hands, he took his frustrations out on his staff. He gave orders to aides to keep scrapbooks of newspaper accounts of his activities on out-of-town trips — after Johnson passed the word that Humphrey was not to take any Washington-based newsmen with him on his domestic travels. One day Ted Van Dyk complained that "we're wasting a hell of a lot of staff time getting the papers from Des Moines or Albuquerque and putting these scrapbooks together. Humphrey said, 'Dammit, after I take a lot of crap all day long from across the street and I'm here alone at night and I want to feel good, I look at those scrapbooks. I don't care how much time it takes.' "

Humphrey finally made his first overseas political mission in June, but even that assignment came in typically Johnsonian spur-of-the-moment fashion. Humphrey was given only a few hours notice that he was to accompany Gemini IV Astronauts James McDevitt and Edward White II to the Paris Air Show. He made the most of his opportunity, meeting with French President Charles de Gaulle for an hour and twenty minutes and making a strong plea for French understanding of the U.S. position on the Dominican Republic and Vietnam.[8] More important, Humphrey was able to assuage the proud de Gaulle's feelings, which had been ruffled when Johnson met

[8] One week before his meeting with de Gaulle, Humphrey answered critics of U.S. policies in the Dominican Republic and Vietnam in a commencement speech at American University in Washington. With his son, Skip, sitting among the graduates, Humphrey called for patience in the handling of America's international commitments and added, "We must recognize that there are times when American power must be used . . . that there is no substitute for power in the face of determined aggression."

him at the White House during President Kennedy's funeral and presumptuously declared that de Gaulle had agreed to return to Washington for another meeting.

The Paris visit was hailed as a public relations success by U.S. and French officials, and Humphrey looked forward to more overseas diplomatic missions. But except for a short and sad trip to London a month later to accompany the body of his old hero Adlai Stevenson back to the U.S., he spent the remainder of the year shepherding Great Society programs through Congress. On October 8, he again stood by while the president went to the hospital, this time for removal of his gall bladder and kidney stones. During Johnson's recuperation, Humphrey was designated to stump for Democratic gubernatorial and mayoral candidates around the country. His campaign forays were largely a series of misadventures as he campaigned for losing machine candidates and confirmed the suspicion of many party leaders that Senator Robert Kennedy of New York was a more potent vote-getter.

Humphrey also continued to lose face among liberals and young people by his effusive praise of Johnson and his sometimes strident salesmanship of the war. Humphrey ran into one of his first groups of Vietnam War protestors in St. Louis in late October. Hearing their shouts outside a hall where he was delivering a moving civil rights speech, Humphrey acknowledged them by saying that "those voices would do more for their country if they were concerned for the people that suffer these indignities rather than proclaiming themselves experts in foreign policy."

Humphrey was stunned in December when he learned how the American public had reacted to his first year as vice president. A Gallup poll showed that a substantial majority (58 percent) of those interviewed didn't want him to become president and that only 23 percent thought he should. The bleak prognosis was made even bleaker by Kennedy's near break-even showing (40 percent "yes" and 46 percent "no"), and precipitated a raging debate among Humphrey intimates over how aggressively he should pursue a new image. Some advisers urged Humphrey to seek more public exposure while others argued that to do so would risk Johnson's wrath.

Humphrey was still mulling over this problem when he went to the LBJ Ranch in early December and found that Johnson had solved his problem for him. The president told Humphrey he was sending him to the December 30 inauguration of President Marcos of the Philippines, with additional stops in Japan, Formosa, and Korea. Although Humphrey was charged with seeking increased commitments from each of the four nations he visited to prevent a Communist takeover of South Vietnam — and, according to the "domino theory," a chain reaction that would imperil other Southeast Asia countries — the trip was also plainly an opportunity to increase Humphrey's visibility and boost his political stature.

At the same time, Johnson, an inveterate poll-watcher, discussed Humphrey's lagging popularity. He indicated that Humphrey should concentrate on being a good vice president and not be concerned about his image. He also pointedly remarked that he hadn't had a press secretary when he was vice president and didn't see why Humphrey needed one. Humphrey got the message and promptly fired his press secretary, Robert Jensen, with whom he was dissatisfied anyway. Jensen, who ironically was one of those urging Humphrey to go slow on seeking publicity, just as promptly leaked a confidential staff memorandum to *Newsweek* magazine telling Humphrey how to bolster his image as a serious presidential prospect.

The image-molding memo, which was symbolic of the policy dispute in the Humphrey camp, advised Humphrey to:

> . . . break the 1966 calendar down into time segments for all facets of your character — making certain that you are spending time in a rich, varied and meaningful life. You will be leading the way into the Great Society. You will also be adding a touch of the harder and sterner side of your make-up which [is] in need of showing to more people. This can be done without losing compassion — God prevent! It can be done by mixing in your concern for the defense of life, people and principle with your love and reverence for them.

Humphrey's diplomatic mission got off to an embarrassing start when the New York *Herald-Tribune* reported that he was going to stop off in Saigon during the trip. The White House denied the story, causing widespread speculation that Johnson was angered by the leak and canceled the Saigon visit or that he just wasn't ready to trust Humphrey in the crucial Vietnam area. But unknown to Humphrey, Johnson received daily critiques of his performance on the trip from Jack Valenti, Johnson's special assistant and confidant who had been sent along to keep an eye on the vice president. Valenti's watchdog role was not confirmed until one of his reports to the president was mistakenly delivered to Humphrey's office. However, Valenti praised Humphrey in glowing terms in his reports describing him as an extremely effective salesman of Johnson's Vietnam policies, and Humphrey returned from the trip to hear a rare presidential compliment for a "job well done."[9]

Humphrey hardly had time to change shirts before he was on his way back to Asia, this time for the funeral of Indian Prime Minister Lal Bahadur Shastri in the second week of January. Again given only a few hours notice, Humphrey and aide David Gartner arrived in New Delhi twenty-seven hours and thirteen thousand miles later. Humphrey and Secretary of State Dean Rusk held an impromptu hour and forty minute meeting with Soviet Pre-

---

[9] Humphrey was angered when he returned home and read an article by the Washington *Post's* Richard Halloran, saying that the trip's main purpose was "to get Humphrey into the public eye on foreign affairs and to enhance his political standing." Even more incensed when Halloran referred to his personal aide David Gartner as a "junior briefcase carrier," he wrote Halloran a letter pointing out that Gartner held a bachelor's degree in economics from Iowa State University.

mier Aleksei Kosygin — the first major face-to-face contact between the new Soviet leader and top American officials. Humphrey and Rusk sounded out Kosygin on the Vietnam War and were able to give Johnson a shrewd analysis of the Soviet reluctance to become directly involved in the war.

The man who had driven the Communists out of the Minnesota Democratic Farmer Labor party and the head of world communism hit it off like long-lost comrades. On the morning of the funeral, Humphrey was taking an early morning walk with Gartner and two Secret Service agents in the garden of the Indian presidential palace when he turned a corner and literally bumped into Kosygin, his English-speaking daughter and two of Kosygin's bodyguards. The chance encounter set a friendly tone for the later top-level conference as Humphrey presented Kosygin with a set of vice presidential cufflinks and told him, "Mr. Chairman, when I see you on television going like this [Humphrey waved his arms in the air and flashed the V-for-victory sign], and I see you're wearing these cufflinks, I'll know that relations between our countries are improving."

Humphrey scored another diplomatic coup before leaving India. On his own initiative, he paid a forty-five minute visit to Mrs. Indira Gandhi, daughter of the late Mahatma Gandhi. Although Mrs. Gandhi was not considered a likely successor to Shastri in Washington, Humphrey's visit proved diplomatically helpful to both countries when Mrs. Gandhi came to power a few days later.[10]

The Indian visit and the earlier Asian trip were crucial turning points for Humphrey. They established his credentials in Johnson's eyes as an able roving ambassador who could hold his own in the high-stakes game of international diplomacy and could effectively present Johnson's Vietnam policies to America's Asian allies and to critics at home. More important, Johnson finally viewed Humphrey as a trusted lieutenant who could be given a far more important and challenging assignment.

In February, Humphrey got that assignment. It was the most important one of his vice presidency and more than anything else irrevocably severed his ties to his old liberal friends and determined his political future. Johnson sent him on a fourteen day, forty-three thousand mile journey to nine Asian nations, including South Vietnam, as a follow-up to the Honolulu conference earlier that month at which U.S. and South Vietnam leaders agreed to the Declaration of Honolulu. Humphrey's mission was to spread the Honolulu Doctrine that henceforth the U.S. approach to South Vietnam and all of Southeast Asia would be based on positive social and economic development goals.

But there were also political reasons for Humphrey's trip. Johnson was

[10] Nevertheless, Mrs. Gandhi later rebuffed Humphrey's personal request for support of the American position in Vietnam, pointing out that India's hands were tied by its official policy of neutrality.

becoming worried about his own growing weakness in the left wing of the Democratic party as the result of the Vietnam War. He also was concerned about the rising popularity of Robert Kennedy, who was stressing civic and humanitarian programs in South Vietnam.[11] Humphrey, with his long association with the liberal wing of the party, his recently demonstrated competence in foreign policy and his position as the most likely heir to the Johnson crown, was the logical choice for the trip.

Several days before the Honolulu conference, Johnson had alerted Humphrey that he might want him to make another Asian trip, but he cautioned Humphrey to tell no one, not even his wife. Humphrey was giving a speech in Chicago on the evening of February 8 — the last day of the Honolulu conference — when word came that the president wanted to meet him in Los Angeles to discuss the results of the conference and then to continue to the Far East.[12] John Reilly took the call at 11:30 P.M. at his Chevy Chase home, and was not surprised to hear a Johnson aide tell him Humphrey was to leave early the next morning. Humphrey was not due back from Chicago until after midnight, so Reilly prepared a lengthy memorandum on the trip, had his wife type it up, and drove the one and half miles to Humphrey's house, where he and Humphrey planned the trip in the early hours of the morning.

Humphrey flew aboard *Air Force Two* to Los Angeles the next day, where he held a ninety-minute airport conference with Johnson. Then he flew to Honolulu, where he picked up South Vietnamese Premier Nguyen Cao Ky, Chief of State Nguyen Van Thieu and other Vietnamese leaders as well as special U.S. Ambassador Averill Harriman, Presidential Aides McGeorge Bundy and Jack Valenti and other U.S. officials, and continued to Saigon to begin his grueling two-week trip to South Vietnam, Laos, Thailand, Pakistan, India, Australia, New Zealand, the Philippines and Korea.

Everywhere he went, Humphrey preached the gospel of the two-war theme enunciated in the Declaration of Honolulu. "Yes, indeed," he declared in South Vietnam as he mingled with American G.I.'s and South Vietnam peasants, "two wars can be won — the war to defeat the aggressors and the war to defeat the ancient and persistent enemies, disease, poverty, ignorance and despair. The people of South Vietnam will have to make their choice. They will choose their government and the opportunity for a decent, finer life for the humblest citizens, and they will reject the Communist system

---

[11] Kennedy was gradually appropriating Humphrey's old liberal constituency as a result of his opposition to the war, but he was not entirely comfortable with all of his new supporters. When he heard that the ultra-liberal California Democratic Council had cheered him and booed Johnson and Humphrey at its February convention, he remarked, "Those are the people with picket signs and beards, aren't they?"

[12] Johnson did not invite Humphrey to the Honolulu conference because he felt both the president and vice president should not be away from the mainland at the same time.

of terror and torture, extortion and fear. And when that choice is finally made, then the Vietcong will wither and fade away." Before he finished his two-day visit to South Vietnam, Humphrey flatly declared both wars were being won.

Humphrey's artesian eloquence charmed, dazzled and at times overwhelmed his Asian hosts, who had been unimpressed with the two previous American vice presidents they had seen, Richard Nixon and Lyndon Johnson. Humphrey wheedled, cajoled, promised and persuaded, criticizing American ignorance of Asian realities, and offering to export the Great Society to Asian countries if they would help the United States stop the Communist menace in South Vietnam. His salesmanship — and showmanship — were demonstrated when he kissed babies in Thailand, called hogs in Vietnam, taught Bangkok school children to say "okay" and "goodbye" in English, compared drought-striken Indian countryside to the dustbowl days of his South Dakota youth and showed the aloof Premier Ky how to campaign in rural rice paddies and Saigon slums.

But above all, Humphrey carried out his own counter-offensive against the Vietcong, denouncing them at every turn and reaching back into his political past to when he battled the Communists in the Minnesota DFL. "I fought those bastards then and I'm going to fight them now," he told a group of reporters in an off-the-cuff talk over drinks one evening. "We licked them then and we can lick them now. They're not the forces of freedom. We are." Humphrey scornfully rejected the idea that the war in Vietnam was a civil war and that the Vietcong were "frustrated social workers and do-gooders. They are hard, disciplined warriors backed by Hanoi and Peking just as Moscow backs East Germany. You can never let the aggressor have his way."

Humphrey's hard-line rhetoric became more pronounced as the trip progressed. By the time he reached Canberra, Australia, for a two-day visit before his last stops in New Zealand, South Korea and the Philippines, he was talking like an out-and-out hawk. He startled and even angered some of his own aides at a late evening staff session at the home of American Ambassador Ed Clark the day he arrived in Canberra. Tired from the trip and letting his hair down after dinner and a few drinks, Humphrey got into a bitter argument with several members of his party about Communist China's role in Southeast Asia. "I think Humphrey used the phrase, 'If we don't stop 'em in South Vietnam they'll be in Honolulu and San Francisco,'" an aide recalls. "The tenor of his comments was that Vietnam was a manifestation of Chinese Communist imperialism and expansion and the only way to stop them was what we were doing in Vietnam." (Humphrey traded some angry words with James C. Thompson, Jr., a Chinese expert and an aide to McGeorge Bundy, who disputed Humphrey's position. The incident rankled

Humphrey and he blew up at Thompson on the plane the next day over the wording of a statement Humphrey was to make later in the trip.)

Humphrey's passionate conviction that the U.S. was on the right course in Vietnam came to the surface at a luncheon given for him the next day by Australia's Prime Minister Harold Holt. He lambasted U.S. critics of the war — including Senator Fulbright — exhorted Australians to send more men and supplies to South Vietnam, and warned that Australia stood only a few falling dominoes away from the threat of a Communist invasion. "It was one of the worst speeches I ever heard Humphrey make," an aide remembers. "It was just a hard-line harangue." Others in the Humphrey party felt that he wanted to prove that he meant what he said the night before and that he was also reacting to the presence of antiwar protestors who picketed the luncheon and called him a "war criminal."

From Australia, Humphrey went to New Zealand, where he called a news conference in Wellington to denounce Robert Kennedy's suggestion that the Vietcong's political arm, the National Liberation Front, should be included in a postwar government in South Vietnam. In typical Humphrey language, he declared that such a concession would be tantamount to putting " a fox in the chicken coop" or "an arsonist in the fire department."

Humphrey returned to Washington on January 24 and was greeted by a warm bear hug from Johnson. To the live television coverage of his homecoming, he proclaimed a condensed version of the message that he would take to the American people for the next two years: "I return, Mr. President, with a deep sense of confidence in our cause — and its ultimate triumph. . . . The tide of battle in Vietnam has turned in our favor."

From that moment on, Humphrey was intimately and inextricably tied to the Vietnam policies that he had expressed strong doubts about only a year earlier. Convinced by his Asian trip of the correctness of the U.S. effort in South Vietnam, he became Johnson's most articulate and indefatigable advocate of the war. After a difficult and painful apprenticeship of more than a year, Humphrey finally had won his spurs from his tough, demanding boss by selling the war in Asia, and now he was being assigned the top-priority mission of selling the war at home.

That mission, which would last until the insoluble problem of the war drove Johnson to declare that he would not run again twenty-five months later, began for Humphrey at 8:00 A.M. the next day. Johnson had invited every member of Congress — half the first day and the other half a day later — to the White House to hear Humphrey report on his trip. Standing before the lawmakers in the East Room, Humphrey assured them that "we have a right to restrained optimism and confidence" in both the military war and the political war. Then, paraphrasing Premier Ky, he declared, "The National Liberation Front is neither national nor liberating, but it is a front. Communism is one thing as a theory for discussion in this country, but it quite another in those small countries of Asia where its teeth are bared and its appetite consuming. Its creed is terror, murder, assassination." At the same time, Humphrey questioned critics who "always suggest what we might give up" to bring about negotiations. "Why not ask what Hanoi might give up?" At the second Congressional briefing, Humphrey said he had been doubtful about the efficacy of U.S. bombing raids, but now he said he was convinced that they were useful.

At each of the Congressional briefing sessions, Johnson introduced Humphrey and then stood by to help him field questions afterwards. At the first session, most of the questions were skeptical or critical, and only two senators, Richard Russell of Georgia and Strom Thurmond of South Carolina, both strong advocates of a military solution to the war, agreed with Humphrey. "I thought, 'My God, is this how far we've come in one year that these are our only friends?' " John Reilly recalls. Senator Wayne Morse of Oregon, an outspoken dove, said, "I never expected my vice president to make this plea for war."

The double-barreled lobbying effort by Humphrey and Johnson was instrumental in beating down a futile attempt by Morse to repeal the 1964 Tonkin Gulf Resolution, which Johnson claimed as one of the basic legal justifications for the growing American participation in the war. That attempt, which came on March 1 on an amendment to a bill authorizing an additional $4.8 billion for U.S. military operations in Vietnam, was defeated by a 92–5 vote. The vote, which marked Johnson's first serious anti-Vietnam test in the Senate, found Morse joined by the only other opponent to the Gulf of Tonkin Resolution, Alaska's Ernest Gruening, as well as three new allies, Fulbright of Arkansas, McCarthy of Minnesota, and Young of Ohio. Two days later, the U.S. troop commitment to South Vietnam increased by another 30,000 to a total of a quarter of a million, a figure that would increase to 380,000 by the end of the year.

Two major factors accounted for Humphrey's new unrestrained support of Johnson's Vietnam policies, those close to him at the time feel. "While he'd had grave doubts about the war up until then," says Ted Van Dyk, "I think he came back from the Asian trip almost startled by the degree to which other Asian leaders said that our presence there was positive. And also he wanted very badly to support the president and I think this kind of gave him the reasons he needed. In this next year particularly, he was most outspoken in defense of the Vietnam policies. That was the point at which he really began defending the administration, and you could see that he began being taken back into the inner councils a little bit."[13]

[13] Tom Wicker of the New York *Times* reported on April 17 that Johnson had rescinded his original directive ordering Humphrey to concentrate on Congressional lobbying, that he no longer required Humphrey to clear his speeches with the White House and that their official relationship had finally "developed some degree of the

Humphrey would make a second trip to Southeast Asia in late 1967 — as well as two other major foreign trips to Europe in early 1967 and Africa at the end of 1967 — but nothing he did as vice president carried as much significance for his future as the February, 1966, Asian odyssey.

"That trip was the most important event of the Humphrey vice presidency," says Reilly. "Having been cut out for a year, he was desperate to get back into Johnson's good graces, and when he got the opportunity, he oversold it. Instead of supporting the president 100 percent, he did it 200 percent. That trip led to some of his most outrageous statements, like the 'fox in the chicken coop' thing. After that trip came the period in which he did the most damage to himself politically because he was now more for Johnson's policies than Johnson."

The severe disenchantment of Humphrey's liberal friends was summarized by New York *Post* Columnist James Wechsler, who wrote in March, after watching Humphrey on television, that "his righteous rhetoric was almost reminiscent of Richard Nixon." But there was no question that Humphrey was an effective evangelist among many other liberals. Appearing before the House Democratic Study Group — the liberal caucus whose members were tortured by doubts about the war — Humphrey drew several bursts of applause with his optimistic appraisal of the course of the war. "He used humor, hard-hitting analysis, appeals to patriotism," said one DSG leader. "The vice president is one hell of a salesman."

Humphrey was acutely pained by the discomfort of his old liberal friends, but he insisted that Vietnam was part of the world struggle for freedom and a better life that he had fought for over the years. "I want to be tolerant but I can't see the difference between containment of Communism in Europe and in Asia," he told Saul Pett of the Associated Press in April in an emotional interview that brought tears to Humphrey's eyes. When Pett asked point-blank whether there was a "new" Humphrey, the answer was "Not at all." Humphrey added, "I've never left the liberals even though some are disappointed in me. Liberals have a great emotional commitment. They're volatile. If you do something to displease them, their respect becomes cynical . . . . I have my own views. I have my own conscience. I wear no man's collar . . . ." Nor should there be any doubt in anyone's mind that he was supporting Johnson's Vietnam policies because he had to, Humphrey declared in another April interview with Emmet John Hughes of *Newsweek* magazine. Cautioning against imagining "that I support some basic administration policies merely because of constricting official involve-

---

rapport that usually has marked their personal acquaintance." Wicker also noted another sure sign that Humphrey's stature had been upgraded — Johnson now frequently invited him to the weekly top-level luncheons at which key foreign policy decisions were made.

ment," Humphrey declared, "I am supporting them out of clear intellectual commitment."

By mid-1966, there were those who were beginning to question whether the vice presidency was taking a costly toll on Humphrey's legendary energy and creativity. "He is running around to every meeting in town as if he were out campaigning again for mayor of Minneapolis," New York *Times* Columnist James Reston, an old Humphrey friend, wrote in May. "His speeches are thin and repetitious." Reston noted that Humphrey, speaking at a recent Associated Press luncheon in New York, still had not overcome his old problem of speaking too long. He had been witty, disarming, impassioned and effective on the subject of Vietnam for the first half hour but went on for over an hour and lost most of his audience. "It was too bad," Reston concluded. "This was the mind that was more creative than almost any other in the Senate in the 1950's, but [it] is scattered now in an endless tangle of little chores, ceremonial greetings and repetitive political arguments."

The optimistic language that characterized Humphrey's Vietnam declaration was as much a part of his personal style as his emotionalism, cheerfulness and loquacity, but it made him appear almost ludicrous at times and further alientated him from his liberal friends. "I am happy to be able to tell you, sir, that out of every one hundred [American soldiers] wounded, ninety-nine live," he responded when asked by a panel of the country's top newspaper publishers about public willingness to tolerate a Vietnam combat death rate that had reached two hundred a week plus several hundred more wounded by the spring of 1966. "This is the highest rate of survival of wounded in the history of warfare."

Humphrey's hyperbolic rhetoric reached new heights when he declared, in a CBS television interview with Eric Sevareid on April 19, that Vietnam is "almost like the first voyage of an explorer into a new land. The ship has almost been storm-tossed on the shore, but we are there." He added, "We are going to be in Asia a long time."

In the same interview Humphrey astounded even some old Vietnam hands by propounding a sweeping new "Johnson Doctrine" for Asia. If studied carefully, Humphrey said, the Honolulu Declaration "has as much significance for the future of Asia as the Atlantic Charter had for the future of Europe." Although there had been nothing in the language of the Honolulu joint statement that spoke of such a broad approach, Humphrey said the statement had pledged the U.S. to "defeat aggression, to defeat social misery, to build viable, free institutions and to achieve peace." He called these "great commitments," and added, "I think there is a tremendous new opening here for realizing the dream of the Great Society in the great area of Asia, not just here at home. And I regret that we haven't been able to dramatize it more."

An incredulous Sevareid sought to make certain that he heard Humphrey correctly, since a debate on the past and future U.S. role in Asia was then raging in Congress. "You seem to me to be saying that the Johnson Doctrine, if we may call it that, is proposing a relationship between this country and Asia, far away as it is, and sprawling and diverse as it is, a relationship as fundamental, as long-lasting, intimate and possibly expensive as our historic associations with Europe. Is it of this scale, of this magnitude?"

"I think so," replied Humphrey, who only a month earlier had reluctantly met with the Senate Foreign Relations Committee and carefully avoided any such statements.[14]

Although the "Johnson Doctrine" statement was broader than many administration officials liked, it drew no rebuke from the president, and oddly received little attention. But Humphrey continued to exploit his new freedom with a vengeance. Ignoring mounting liberal criticism that reached a hysterical pitch when New York literary lion Alfred Kazin called a Washington news conference to charge that Humphrey was trying to "prove his masculinity" by taking a hard line on Vietnam, Humphrey walked into the lions' den of the Americans for Democratic Action annual convention on April 23 and stoutly defended the administration's Vietnam policies. "The Vietcong is not an Asian version of the ADA," he declared. Older members who had helped Humphrey build the anti-Communist liberal organization gave him a warm reception, but younger members were angry and even bitter, and passed a resolution accusing him of making a "false analogy of Munich."

Humphrey made it clear that he was staking his political future on the successful outcome of the Vietnam War, even though the mushrooming U.S. involvement was beginning to increase frustrations across the country, undermine public support of the Johnson administration and generate inflationary pressures that cast serious doubt on the administration's "guns and butter" policies. (He never seemed to tire of emphasizing his close relationship with Johnson, telling the American Newspaper Guild convention in July that "I'm Lyndon Johnson's Eleanor Roosevelt," a self-effacing description that was meant to draw the comparison with Mrs. Roosevelt's role as an extra set of eyes and ears for her husband but which struck many people as a metaphor of questionable taste.)[15]

Humphrey's domestic duties were obscured by Vietnam and by the increasing opposition in Congress to the Great Society programs, but he played a major role in helping pass the administration's Model Cities program and in helping provide jobs for inner-city youths. His excessive

---

[14] Eugene McCarthy, a member of the committee, was unimpressed with Humphrey's testimony, as were most members. "If I had stayed the whole time I would have heard it all before," said McCarthy afterwards.

rhetoric and visceral attachment to the civil rights cause stirred up a controversy of national proportions when, in a compassionate aside in a New Orleans speech about racial violence in the cities, he said he might "lead a mighty good revolt" himself if he lived in a slum. The resulting criticism of his remark led Humphrey to point out later, "But I also said that 'we cannot condone violence, lawlessness and disorder.' "

Nevertheless, the issue of Vietnam never was far from Humphrey's thoughts. Even when he made his only other foreign trip of 1966, a three-day visit to the Dominican Republic to attend the inauguration of President Juan Balaguer and show that the 1965 U.S. intervention had worked, Humphrey linked that intervention with the U.S. commitment to Vietnam. "Our purpose in Vietnam is to provide an opportunity for self-determination to the people of Vietnam, just as you have done here," he told 1,400 U.S. troops in Santo Domingo. "Here it was primarily civil strife, with some interferences from outside, [in Vietnam] it is naked aggression."

Humphrey was confronted with some naked aggression in his home state DFL party at the same time. He tried unscussefully to mediate an endorsement battle between the competent but colorless fifty-three year old governor, Karl Rolvaag, and his openly ambitious thirty-seven year old lieutenant governor, A. M. (Sandy) Keith. Humphrey was doubly embarrassed when Keith challenged Rolvaag for the DFL gubernatorial endorsement and, in a marathon twenty ballot state convention, defeated him. Rolvaag won the gubernatorial nomination in the primary election but was defeated in the November election by Republican Harold LeVander, and the extremely bitter political fight, which was exacerbated by the clumsy handling of some Humphrey operatives, did not enhance Humphrey's national stature. It also left deep wounds in the party that would be reopened in 1968 between Humphrey and Eugene McCarthy over the Democratic presidential nomination.[16]

Humphrey's experience as the administration's chief spear carrier in the 1966 fall elections was scarcely any more rewarding. Confronted by an

---

[15] Humphrey's self-deprecating humor almost invariably included a reference in his speeches to the dissimilar eagles portrayed on the presidential and vice presidential seals. Noting that the president's eagle was powerful, fleet of wing and clutching numerous arrows, he said, "Mine looks emaciated and the wings droop down as if it's getting set for a crash landing. On one side, there's only a teeny and scrawny-looking olive branch. And on the other side, why, the eagle is holding just one little arrow. But I want you to know, I'm saving that arrow for the right time."

[16] Humphrey tried unsuccessfully to get Rolvaag appointed U.S. ambassador to Sweden or Norway, where Rolvaag's late father, Author Ole Rolvaag, is a revered figure, but had to settle for less prestigious Iceland. Rolvaag, who served as ambassador from 1967–69, said of his relationship with Keith five years after the 1966 defeat, "He's not one of the guys I would want on a desert island with me." His remark illustrates the political divisions that still exist in Humphrey's home party, even though Rolvaag is no longer politically powerful.

August Gallup poll which showed Robert Kennedy more popular than either he or Johnson, and bothered by speculation that Kennedy would replace him in 1968, Humphrey was moved to tell a St. Louis audience he was certain Johnson wanted him as his running mate. He was promptly dressed down by Johnson for doing so. "The realities of politics require that a president have many options," a chastened Humphrey said a few days later. "I don't predict whom he will want in 1968."

Nevertheless, Humphrey campaigned in twenty-six states on a "run on Vietnam" theme. Calling it not only politically but morally right to support the president's war policies, Humphrey declared, "I happen to believe that the only danger at the polls for Democrats is if they weasel — or wobble — if they spread a canopy of doubt or confusion." But the electoral pendulum was beginning to swing back and Republicans gave it a push by concentrating their fire on the issues of Vietnam, inflation, crime in the streets and the "credibility gap" between what Johnson said and what he actually did.

Johnson himself widened the credibility gap at the height of the campaign by scheduling a conference of Asian leaders on the Vietnam War in Manila from October 17 to November 2, and then on his return, by announcing that he was going to have minor throat and abdominal surgery and therefore would not become involved in the campaign. Humphrey, who had been campaigning for almost a month, announced he would suspend his campaigning to remain in Washington during the president's absence from the country.

In November, the Republican party scored a dramatic come-back from its devastating 1964 defeat by electing eight new governors, three new senators, and forty-seven new House members, thus clearly suggesting the possibility of a Republican victory in the 1968 presidential election.

For once, Humphrey probably wasn't sorry that his campaigning had been curtailed. The heavy burden of the president's declining popularity, the war, and evidence of Kennedy's usurpation of his liberal constituency were reflected in a Humphrey who bore little resemblance to the "Happy Warrior" of 1964. Particularly painful to Humphrey was the defection of college students, many of whom now turned up chanting, "Hubert Humphrey, LBJ, How many kids did you kill today?" Humphrey seemed almost desperate to regain his standing among the young, declaring in one campaign interview that he was "happiest among young people" and that he hoped to spend one day a week on a college campus in 1967 talking to and studying with students. "Poor Hubert," a Senate colleague remarked in October, "He has no enemies, but more ex-friends than any man I know."

But "poor Hubert" wasn't feeling sorry for himself as he reached the halfway point in his vice presidency. The personal and political transformation that had taken place over the first two years was evident in the fatalistic attitude expressed by one of his closest advisers in a January, 1967, interview. "He's a fatalist who tries to maximize his opportunities," said Max Kampelman. "I think he feels if you do everything you're capable of, virtue will triumph. He gives the president eighteen hours a day, he doesn't play golf, he's working all the time and when he's not working, he's thinking. So, while he would be disappointed if history decided he's not to be president, he wouldn't be a beaten, depressed man. He's service-oriented and he would want to serve in some other way."

Humphrey's equanimity was sorely tested at the beginning of the new year, however. For some inexplicable reason — some said it was the election results while others said it was because he talked too much — he again found himself in Johnson's doghouse. Johnson gave firm orders that Humphrey was not to be given any prior knowledge of the contents of the 1967 State of the Union message, and he was never consulted during its preparation nor was he given a copy — again on Johnson's specific orders — until after White House reporters had been briefed on its contents. "Thus it was that the relationship between Johnson and Humphrey in mid-January was such that every newspaper reporter in Washington knew the contents of the State of the Union message before the vice president of the United States did," Douglas Kiker wrote in *Atlantic* magazine.

However, the tortuous path between the Scylla of Johnson's anger and the Charybdis of his indifference was taking a psychological toll on Humphrey. "If I could just find a way to convince this man of my loyalty," Humphrey told a sympathetic presidential aide at one point. The hot-and-cold Johnson treatment turned hot again as the dogwood and azaleas bloomed in the nation's capital. In March, the New York *Times*' James Reston was writing, "President Johnson seems to have liberated Vice President Hubert Humphrey from his opulent doghouse." Reston's comment was prompted by Johnson's reply when asked at a news conference about speculation that he planned to drop Humphrey as his running mate. "I've never known a public servant I've worked better with or one for whom I've had more admiration or one that the public can trust more. . . . I feel even stronger about him today."

At the same time, Johnson announced that Humphrey was being given the task of rebuilding the Democratic party — which had fallen into disuse due to Johnson's neglect — and that he was sending him and Muriel on a fourteen day tour of seven major West European capitals aimed at reassuring Europeans the U.S. was not wholly preoccupied with Vietnam. Humphrey, taking advantage of old friendships with British Prime Minister Harold Wilson, West German Foreign Affairs Minister Willy Brandt and Italian President Guiseppe Saragat, pushed the nuclear non-proliferation treaty, East-West trade negotiations and international monetary reform as well as pleading for European understanding of the U.S. role in Vietnam.[17] He also paid a return visit to French President de Gaulle and, throwing away a stiffly worded prepared toast, brought tears to the haughty de Gaulle's eyes by ad-libbing an eloquent tribute to the memory of the French soldiers and statesmen who helped win the American Revolution.

Humphrey was greeted by antiwar demonstrations — many of them violent — in almost every one of his European stops, but he was welcomed as a returning hero by Johnson on the White House lawn, and clearly was back in the president's good graces. Still, he continued to be cruelly torn between his loyalty to Johnson and his old liberal friends, the people whom, he told an aide, "I really care about."

The excruciating agonies that Humphrey had endured for the past year would be vastly accelerated as the country waded deeper and deeper into the Vietnam quagmire. They came to a head on the balmy spring evening of April 17, 1967, at the Washington home of Joseph Rauh, Jr. Humphrey had asked Rauh to invite some of Humphrey's old liberal friends who had been critical of him to sit down with him at dinner and talk over their differences. Humphrey arrived shortly before 8:00 P.M., and was greeted warmly by the nine men present, including Presidential Assistant Arthur Schlesinger, Columnists James Wechsler and Clayton Fritchey, Editor Gil Harrison of the *New Republic* magazine, and Harvard Economist and former Ambassador John Kenneth Galbraith. Before Humphrey arrived, Schlesinger reminded everyone that even though they all felt very strongly about the war, Humphrey was an old friend and they owed him a polite reception.

"It was very pleasant for a while," Rauh recalled later. "Everyone seemed to be trying to avoid the hard issue of Vietnam." As a result, the discussion during dinner centered on Humphrey's account of the farm problem, Minnesota politics, his just-completed European trip, and sentimental reminiscences about earlier, happier days in the ADA as Mrs. Rauh and two Secret Service agents waited in the kitchen. But after dinner, the conversation finally turned to the grim subject that everyone knew was the reason for the meeting.

It was first mentioned as Humphrey, discussing his audience with Pope Paul, said that the pope repeatedly expressed great personal sympathy for Johnson and great concern for the American image. But when Wechsler asked Humphrey whether the pope had expressed his opposition to the

---

[17] While in Rome, Humphrey also had an audience with Pope Paul VI, who gave him an envelope addressed to Johnson. A week after Humphrey returned to Washington, an aide discovered the forgotten letter, which contained a personal message urging peace negotiations in Vietnam, and quickly delivered it to the White House, expecting the presidential wrath to follow. However, Johnson never said anything about the delayed letter.

U.S. bombing of North Vietnam, Humphrey paused briefly and said, "Yes, he did."

Then Schlesinger, depressed because he had just come from a meeting with Robert Kennedy and felt Kennedy was trapped between his opposition to the war and his reluctance to openly challenge Johnson, gratuitously suggested that the group understood Humphrey could not speak freely because of his loyalty to Johnson. Humphrey assured everyone present that he would speak candidly and wanted them to, an assurance that touched off forty-five minutes of continuous and acrimonious exchange on the subject of Vietnam, mostly between Humphrey and Schlesinger, with Rauh trying unsuccessfully to act as moderator.

The intensity of the discussion that night and the total disillusionment of Humphrey's former liberal supporters with him are evident in a detailed memorandum of the meeting prepared a few days later by one of those present:

> The bitterest debate centered on Arthur's charge that the administration stupidly failed to understand that there had been tremendous changes in the Communist world and was still basically clinging to the view that Communism was a monolithic structure. Humphrey took sharp issue with this, insisting that they did understand what the conflicts were about. He said at one point that there has been less "demogogic Russian baiting" under Johnson than at any time in our modern presidential history and that there were clear gains beginning to be made in the progress toward detente. However, he did acknowledge and even volunteered the point that this progress was jeopardized by the Vietnamese War.
>
> It was when Humphrey referred to the Indonesian situation that the biggest explosion occurred. He said almost parenthetically that he thought our stand in Vietnam had been a key factor in the anti-Communist resistance in Indonesia. Arthur blew up and said, "You know damn well those generals were just fighting for their lives and would have done so whether we were in Vietnam or not." When Humphrey rather defensively reaffirmed his own view, Arthur exclaimed: "Hubert, that's shit, and you know it."
>
> They went back and forth on this point somewhat in the fashion of two bar room brawlers who keep repeating themselves for many moments, but Humphrey seemed determined not to explode. The other biggest blowup came when Humphrey said he thought we had to take seriously the counsel of the military with respect to the bombings. Arthur responded with some derision that the joint chiefs of staff had been catastrophically wrong about the Bay of Pigs among other things; when Humphrey asked him whether he felt he was better equipped than the generals to evaluate these matters, Arthur said rather heatedly that, "I damn well do." It really looked for a while as if things were getting out of hand and that there wouldn't be any real chance for serious dialogue. But gradually Arthur subsided and others took the floor.
>
> In the ensuing discussion the thing I remember most vividly is Humphrey looking at us at one point and saying in effect: "Now suppose I were president and you were my advisers, what would you tell me to do to get us out of this morass?" I remember that he used the word "morass" at least twice

thereafter and I thought it reflected his own deepening despair about the entrapment.

After numerous exchanges in which Ken Galbraith and Clayton Fritchey spoke at some length, and in which I took part in lesser degree, he looked at us finally and said: "I gather that all of you in this room think that we should stop the bombing." The vote was unanimous and then Humphrey said very quietly: "On balance, I think you are right that the risks of stopping the bombings are less significant than the other factors. But the president's advisers obviously don't agree." He then went on to emphasize that he had only periodic, fragmentary participation in the foreign policy discussions.

In discussing his own view of the war, Humphrey seemed far less optimistic and self-righteous than he has on other occasions. He made the concession on the bombings; he was obviously moved when Clayton Fritchey delivered a quietly eloquent sermon on the cruelly divisive effects of the war. Clayton said that never in his lifetime had he seen this country — families, business partners, law firms, universities — so divided into hostile camps. He and Galbraith, in response to Humphrey's invitation to offer recommendations, both stressed the point that a halt in the bombings would not be enough. It was generally agreed that if this were the only step taken and it failed to produce negotiations, there might be an adverse and dangerous reaction. Both of them earnestly stressed the point — and Humphrey listened very intently as they spoke — that the real question was whether we could reverse the whole momentum of our propaganda and put the Vietnam War in a different perspective. Galbraith expressed doubt that we could and at one point someone — I think Gil Harrison — said to Humphrey: "Do you think that the president is capable of even implying that he has made a mistake in our escalation and, like Kennedy after the Bay of Pigs, publicly acknowledging error?" Humphrey was silent for about twenty seconds and then he said: "I don't know."

Galbraith and Fritchey both contended vigorously that a decisive change in the climate of opinion, as well as in our strategy, could only be achieved if there was a drastic overhauling of the State Department. At no point did Humphrey defend Rusk. But when Schlesinger said with some feverishness that "everybody in the State Dept. identified with Dean Rusk has to be thrown out" if there was to be a real new direction in our policy, Humphrey, for one of the few times in the evening, raised his voice and responded angrily: "Arthur, these were your guys. You were in the White House when they took over. Don't blame them on us." Arthur did not answer back.

It was after midnight when the Vietnam discussion petered out and it appeared that the meeting was about to break up, but Humphrey insisted on bringing up the subject of his much-publicized trip to Georgia in February, where his picture was taken arm-in-arm with segregationist Governor Lester Maddox. The picture was subsequently printed in most of the nation's papers, much to the dismay of his liberal friends.

Describing it as another "journalistic disaster," Humphrey said the real story behind the picture was totally different from the public story. He said he had warned Maddox that he had to comply with federal civil rights laws or face federal legal action and that Maddox had assured him he would choose compliance. He explained the picture was taken as they were walking down some steps and "the old fellow started to stumble and I grabbed his arm."

After four and a half hours, the meeting finally broke up, with Humphrey going out of his way to put his arm around Schlesinger and Schlesinger apologizing for the vigor of his arguments. But despite the friendly conclusion, it was the last serious attempt by Humphrey's old liberal friends to change his mind on the war. He had convinced them that if he had to choose between his old liberal constituency and supporting the president, he would do the latter. As one of the participants in the meeting later noted, "Most of us were struck by the sense that he was increasingly conscious of the dead end into which his own political life might be headed as a result of the war."

For Humphrey, the ensuing months had a nightmare quality about them. He watched helplessly as major racial violence flared in Detroit and Newark and other cities whose mayors he had worked with to prevent such tragedies; he agonized over the steadily worsening situation in Vietnam and his desertion by liberals and the mounting opposition he met on college campuses; he grieved over the death of his only brother Ralph, a cancer victim; and he worried about the specter of another Kennedy dashing his hopes for the presidency once again. (He paid little notice, however to reports from friends that Eugene McCarthy was giving serious thought to challenging Johnson in several presidential primaries in 1968.)

On October 27 — the day after McCarthy hinted in a speech at Berkeley, California, that he would challenge Johnson — Humphrey left for his second trip to Southeast Asia. It was a ten-day mini-tour that took him to South Vietnam for the inauguration of President-elect Nguyen Van Thieu, and then to Indonesia and Malaysia. In the two weeks before he left for Saigon, he had delivered six major speeches defending U.S. policies in Vietnam, and he was now prepared to live or die politically on that issue. "The future of mankind may hang on the outcome of the war in Vietnam," Humphrey declared in the exotic setting of Kuala Lumpur, Malaysia. "If it's a colossal failure, I know what happens to me."

CHAPTER XIII

THE GREYING OF GENE MC CARTHY

I think I've always been the one to do some-
thing when no one else would do it. . . .
Eugene McCarthy in a 1967 interview.

The tantalizing taste of the vice presidency had turned into the dregs of rejection for Eugene McCarthy when he returned to the Senate in January, 1965, to begin his second six year term. Contrary to his public utterances after Lyndon Johnson picked Hubert Humphrey instead of him for vice president at Atlantic City, McCarthy didn't relish the idea of being put out to pasture at age forty-eight in a Senate and a party where there was little room for advancement. Although he was now Minnesota's senior senator, McCarthy still found himself in Humphrey's shadow. He had little seniority or influence in the Senate and less inclination to ask any favors of the man who had humiliated him at Atlantic City. "People never really understood how much he wanted to be vice president," McCarthy's brother-in-law Stephen Quigley later remarked. "He really felt he was led down the primrose path."

McCarthy's disenchantment with the prospect of a secure but unexciting future in the Senate was evident in his reelection campaign, a desultory affair in which he was more concerned with outpolling the Johnson-Humphrey ticket than with beating his Republican opponent, Wheelock Whitney III. He handily defeated Whitney, a political neophyte for whom he had so little regard that he sent aide Larry Merthan to debate him, but ran behind the Johnson-Humphrey ticket in Minnesota by 106,000 votes. "In previous years, McCarthy loved campaigning in Minnesota, but in 1964, he hated it," Merthan later recalled. "He'd been in the national limelight and there was a real letdown. I felt it myself. Here he was going all over the country seeing guys like Dick Daley and Jesse Unruh and all the power brokers and he comes

256

back to Minnesota and who does he see? Wheelock Whitney and a bunch of guys who want to be postmaster."

McCarthy's longtime friend, Minnesota Congressman John Blatnik, also sensed the change in McCarthy. "He was making wisecracks that were just plain cynical and I'd say, 'Now Gene, you're just getting plain mean,' " Blatnik recalls. "And he'd say 'Yeah, I know,' and just kind of smile. Some were about Hubert but mostly they were about Johnson. I noticed a real change in him because his comments used to be a beautiful blend of cleverness and meaning with a little nip to them, but now they had a mean thrust. They were delivered with a cynical meanness that just wasn't characteristic of Gene before." [1]

McCarthy briefly considered capitalizing on Humphrey's departure from the Senate by trying to succeed him as assistant majority leader. He sounded out a number of his colleagues and seriously discussed it with friends. However, he could find few senators willing to back him, and Louisiana's Russell Long was elected to the post, leaving McCarthy more convinced than ever that there was no future for him in the Senate. Nevertheless, McCarthy received a consolation prize that would prove to be far more important — the seat on the Foreign Relations Committee vacated by Humphrey. McCarthy had long wanted a greater voice in shaping U.S. foreign policy and in fact had asked to be assigned to the comparable House committee, Foreign Affairs, when he first came to Congress in 1949.[2]

McCarthy's new committee assignment would become an important factor in his later emergence as the foremost challenger of Johnson's Vietnam policies. The committee post gave McCarthy an official entree to administration foreign policy testimony and other "inside" information which would lead to his first significant break with the administration, and also provide a highly visible forum from which to launch his presidential candidacy less than three years later. McCarthy was far from ready to become an all-out critic of the Vietnam War in 1965, however. Like all but two other senators, he had voted for the August, 1964, Gulf of Tonkin Resolution that provided Johnson with the legal basis for beginning the massive American involvement in Vietnam, and he did not make his first public criticism of the administration's Vietnam policy until January, 1966.

[1] McCarthy supported Blatnik to fill the Senate seat vacated by Humphrey but Governor Karl Rolvaag appointed Humphrey's protege, Attorney General Walter F. Mondale, instead, in December, 1964. His new junior colleague did not escape McCarthy's biting wit. "Fritz is the new brand of Senate liberal," he told friends a short time later. "He's like that toothpaste that comes in a plastic bag with a brush — you get it all at once."

[2] McCarthy, who was named to the Democratic Steering Committee and remained on the Finance Committee, won a miniature test of strength with one of the men he would battle in the 1968 presidential primaries, Senator Robert Kennedy, who also wanted a seat on the Foreign Relations Committee.

(The *Congressional Record Index* shows no statements by McCarthy about Vietnam during 1965.)

McCarthy began to have his first serious doubts about the accuracy of administration statements on Vietnam in February, 1965, shortly after the U.S. began heavy and sustained bombing of North Vietnam. He had attended a private briefing with four other key Democratic senators by Presidential Assistant McGeorge Bundy in Vice President Humphrey's private office shortly after Bundy returned from a visit to South Vietnam, and was offended, as were the other senators, by what they regarded as Bundy's arrogant manner. A few days later, on the evening of February 18, McCarthy attended an elaborate White House briefing with about twenty other senators and listened as Johnson, Defense Secretary Robert McNamara, Secretary of State Dean Rusk, CIA Director John McCone and other members of the Johnson High Command gave a glowing report on the military and political situation in Saigon. McCarthy later recalled that the senators were told at about nine o'clock that the Saigon government, then headed by General Nguyen Khanh, "looked like a pretty stable, acceptable government." The next morning's newspapers disclosed that the Khanh government had been overthrown at the same time the White House briefing was going on. "After an experience or two of this kind, I think you inevitably begin to raise some questions and have some doubts," McCarthy said.[3]

The steady escalation of the war may have made the ultimate rupture of McCarthy's tenuous relationship with Johnson inevitable, but an event in the summer of 1965 accelerated it. On July 14, five years and one day after McCarthy paid tribute to him in a famous nomination speech, Adlai Stevenson dropped dead on a London street.[4] Stevenson's death came as a shock to McCarthy, who respected him more than any other man in public life for his historical awareness and understanding of the limitations of governmental power. To McCarthy, Stevenson's approach to power was the antithesis of Johnson's or John F. Kennedy's, and he felt a need, which would become evident in the next few years, to perpetuate the ideas and influence of Stevenson. "We must speak, as he would speak," McCarthy said in a eulogy on his political idol, "of the strength of our nation, but at the same time, acknowledge the limits of that strength and, even more importantly, the limits on the use of the strength which we do possess." Stevenson,

[3] After the briefing, as the other senators waited for Johnson to finish a private meeting with Idaho's Frank Church, who had criticized the president's Vietnam policy in a Senate speech a few days earlier, McCarthy joked, "If Church had just surrendered, we could have gone home thirty minutes ago."

[4] McCarthy was having lunch with Maurice Rosenblatt of the Committee for a More Effective Congress when he received the telephone call notifying him of Stevenson's death. Rosenblatt, with whom McCarthy was having lunch when President Kennedy was assassinated in 1963, recalls that McCarthy put down the telephone and said, "Maurice, I'm not going to have lunch with you anymore."

McCarthy said, had accepted the role of the statesman, "which is never to attempt to write the third and final act of the play of history, but rather to continue to direct the action of the second act so that none in our own time may be moved or given the opportunity to write the final act, which, on the record of history, has generally ended in tragedy." [5]

McCarthy soon had reason to believe that he would not live long enough to preserve the Stevenson legacy. A few weeks later, he entered Georgetown Hospital in Washington for treatment of a urinary tract infection, and was so ill that he thought he was near death. "He called me in and said, 'Promise me if I die, you'll take care of Abigail and the children,' " recalls Larry Merthan. "He really thought he was going to die." After extensive tests, McCarthy underwent prostate surgery. It was followed by a prolonged period of convalescence that left him weak and pale looking for months and touched off a rumor campaign in Minnesota that he had cancer or some other serious illness. Jerry Eller, his administrative assistant, helped the rumors along by refusing to disclose the nature of his illness and in fact, misled reporters by telling them McCarthy had undergone an operation for a back ailment. Returning from his first visit to Minnesota following his recovery, McCarthy said of his constituents, "They didn't want to shake my hand — they wanted to feel my pulse."

Even before his illness, McCarthy was moving toward his first open break with the administration over its foreign policy.[6] At issue was the U.S. military intervention in the Dominican Republic following the outbreak of a civil war earlier in the year. Johnson had sent four hundred Marines to Santa Domingo on April 28 to carry out the evacuation of Americans and other foreign nationals after Donald Reid Cabal's pro-U.S. government was overthrown and the capital was caught in an armed struggle between supporters of former President Juan Bosch and a military junta headed by the militant anti-Communist General Wessin y Wessin. It was the first U.S. military intervention in Latin America since 1927, and it grew well beyond the needs of protecting American citizens as more than thirty thousand troops were sent there in the ensuing months. But even more disturbing to McCarthy and other members of the Foreign Relations Committee were the administration's exaggerated claims of Communist influence in the rebel Bosch camp. Johnson

[5] McCarthy commemorated Stevenson's death by offering visitors to his office cards bearing the inscription "In Memory of Adlai Ewing Stevenson: February 5, 1900–July 14, 1965," and a passage from a marked page found on Stevenson's bedside table after his death. The passage taken from the essay "Desiderata" by Max Ehrmann, begins, "Go placidly amid the noise and the haste, and remember what peace there may be in silence . . . ."

[6] McCarthy had differed with the administration's foreign policy on one previous occasion. In June, he called for a Foreign Relations Committee investigation of "Project Camelot," a U.S. Army-sponsored research project aimed at analyzing potential insurgent groups in several nations, including Chile. He charged then that the Army "has intruded itself into the field of foreign policy without authority."

himself raised the spectre of a Castro-type takeover in the Dominican Republic when he went on T.V. on May 2 to announce that more troops were being sent to Santo Domingo. "The American nation cannot, and must not, and will not permit the establishment of another Communist government in the Western Hemisphere . . . ," he declared. "Our goal in keeping with the great principles of the inter-American system is to help prevent another Communist state in this hemisphere."

As criticism of the Dominican intervention mounted in the U.S. press and in Congress, Johnson went to extraordinary lengths to justify his actions. He told a news conference in his office in June that "some 1,500 innocent people were murdered and shot, and their heads cut off," in Santo Domingo. He said that the American ambassador had asked for help while he was hiding under his desk and bullets were flying through his windows. McCarthy thought Johnson's claims were preposterous and urged Foreign Relations Committee Chairman J. William Fulbright to conduct an intensive secret investigation of the entire Dominican crisis. Fullbright, equally disturbed by Johnson's assertions, agreed to hold the hearings to find out, as McCarthy expressed it, "why the administration found it necessary to dispatch a strong force of Marines and paratroopers to the Dominican Republic to protect lives."

The hearings opened on July 14 — the same day as Stevenson's death — and continued for nine days, with administration witnesses, headed by hardline Undersecretary of State Thomas Mann, indicating that they preferred a military dictatorship friendly to the U.S. rather than an anti-American Communist regime.[7] McCarthy was incensed by Mann's testimony, particularly by his characterization of the ex-teacher Bosch as "a poet-professor type" who was a puppet of the Communists. McCarthy said after the hearings that he was not convinced that the crisis was Communist-inspired, but he refrained from making any major statement on the matter until two weeks after Fulbright, in a bitter speech that caused an irreparable break with Johnson, attacked the administration for its overreaction, lack of candor and exaggerated estimates of Communist influence.

McCarthy formalized his first significant break with Johnson over a foreign policy matter on September 30 when he took the Senate floor to speak in support of Fulbright. He called for an examination of the role of the U.S. in the Organization of American States, and questioned, as he had so many times in the past, whether the administration was taking into account the constitutional role of the Senate in shaping foreign policy. "Our function in the Senate is not merely to find out what the administration policy is and then

---

[7] McCarthy was late for the opening of the hearings, as he almost always was. "You never knew whether he was coming, even when he had something to push," a committee staffer recalls. "When he did show up, he was always late and he had some droll comment on the news of the day."

say yes or no to it — and oftentimes too late. We have a definite responsibility to develop policy ourselves. . . . The Senate would be remiss in its duty if it denied itself that prerogative."

At the same time, McCarthy criticized the administration for injecting "the distracting and confusing issue of who is pro-Communist and who is not pro-Communist" into the discussion of Fulbright's speech, saying that it prevented the speech from serving as the starting point for a "thorough discussion of Latin American policy." Noting that no report of the committee's secret hearings had been issued and that lists of Communists or alleged Communists involved in the Dominican revolt had been inserted into the *Congressional Record* by administration supporters, McCarthy said, "It is always dangerous to publish a portion of a record. . . . If a portion of the record is published, then it may be necessary to publish the entire record with the exception of those portions of it which may have bearing on national security." Other committee members recalled McCarthy's remarks in early November when the secret document was leaked to the New York *Times*, and blamed him for it. They were at least half right. Jerry Eller showed portions of the secret testimony to several reporters including Ann Terry Pincus, Washington correspondent for Ridder Publications, Inc., who wrote stories saying that the testimony confirmed the criticisms of Fulbright, McCarthy and other critics of the intervention.

McCarthy escalated his criticism of the administration's Dominican policy on November 17, bluntly warning in a detailed statement that the U.S. must "determine what we want to achieve and we must be willing to take what action is necessary to achieve it." Although falling short of Fulbright's harshly-worded criticism that questioned the justification of the intervention, McCarthy's statement was considered significant, the Washington *Post* noted, "because McCarthy is regarded as a close friend of the president . . . ." McCarthy argued that the Dominican intervention had caused Latin Americans to question the sincerity of the U.S. commitment to the Alliance for Progress, which he called the "high water mark of our relations with Latin America." He recommended a long-range aid program for the Dominican Republic, including massive development assistance and preferential trade treatment for Dominican goods. "Whatever may be history's ultimate judgment as to the wisdom and necessity of the intervention — and I believe there are still many areas where the facts are not clear — examination of our policy can be profitable if it gives some guidance for the future," he declared.

McCarthy's public opposition to the Dominican intervention did not cause any noticeable change in the administration's actions, but it marked a turning point in his relationship with Johnson. In the past, he had refrained from all but the mildest criticism of Johnson's Vietnam policy and had been a willing member of his Great Society consensus, but now, like Fulbright and other liberal Democratic senators who had been for the most part loyal Johnson allies, he began to move toward an open break with the president over the far more important issue of Vietnam.

McCarthy made that break — and clearly aligned himself in the Vietnam debate for the first time — on January 27, 1966, when he joined Indiana's Vance Hartke and thirteen other Democratic senators in signing a public letter urging Johnson not to resume the bombing of North Vietnam, which had been halted during the holiday truce period.

On the same day, McCarthy made his first formal statement in the Senate in opposition to Johnson's Vietnam policy as he joined a chorus of senators urging that the bombing halt be extended. Asserting that the bombing of North Vietnam had initially been justified on both military and political grounds, McCarthy challenged the administration "to prove, if it can, that the bombings in the past have had any significant military effect" – or that they have had a "beneficial political or diplomatic effect." He said the bombing had not had these effects in the past and he was not convinced resumption of bombing "would advance the military objectives, or . . . our political objectives." McCarthy tried to ease the shock to Johnson of the Hartke letter by saying that "it would be of no help to him if we were to say nothing to indicate our judgment."

In addition, as he had during the Dominican intervention, McCarthy suggested that the public debate over the resumption of the bombing could serve as "a proper point for the beginning of a much deeper and much more extensive discussion not only of Vietnam, but also of the whole function of America in history during this second half of the twentieth century." McCarthy said the war in Vietnam was unlike the war in Korea because in the case of Korea, U.S. objectives were "easily defensible" and the nation was able to make "a quite full moral commitment to the achievement of those objectives." [8] The war in Vietnam, he said, "calls for a national debate, a national discussion, and a real searching of the mind and the soul of America." (McCarthy also made another suggestion on January 27 that went unnoticed in Washington but would cause a controversy of major proportions when Senator Robert Kennedy made an almost identical proposal a month later. In an interview with his hometown newspaper, the St. Paul *Pioneer Press*, McCarthy said that the Vietcong should be included in any new coalition government in Saigon. When Kennedy made the same suggestion on February 19, he was denounced by top administration officials, including Vice President Humphrey, who was touring in Southeast Asia and compared the idea with "putting foxes in the henhouse.")

Johnson immediately sent a pair of emissaries, McGeorge Bundy and General Maxwell Taylor — who had just completed his tour as ambassador to

---

[8] McCarthy supported the Korean War because he felt it was a relatively clear case of aggression against a nation willing to defend itself with the support of the U.S. and other members of the United Nations.

Saigon — to Capitol Hill to try to change McCarthy's mind and that of another key signer of the Hartke letter, Gaylord Nelson of Wisconsin, but both senators were unmoved. The next day, Johnson sent a curt, two-paragraph reply to Hartke that merely acknowledged his letter and referred to a longer, more complete letter concerning his efforts to end the war which he had sent to a group of House members a week earlier.

On January 31, after conceding that his "peace offensive" had failed, Johnson ordered a resumption of the bombing after a thirty-seven day pause. It caused McCarthy to again express concern over the constitutional role of the Senate in making foreign policy. He told the Senate it was essential "that there be a sharing of that responsibility between the Senate and the president." He also warned against accepting the advice of "hawks" who wanted an even greater military effort. "To ask the Senate to trust the military, as some have asked us to do, is to ask the Senate to repudiate its duties under the constitution and its responsibilities under the constitution. I and many other senators do not intend to give up those responsibilities."

But McCarthy's concerns about the Vietnam war were going well beyond the question of the senate's role in foreign policy. He felt the administration was misleading the public about its real goals in Vietnam much as it had done during the Dominican crisis. "The public and private testimony of the administration has not been realistic," he told the Minneapolis *Tribune* on February 27. "This war is not simply an extension of North Vietnamese or Chinese communism. There is a much stronger element of a South Vietnamese civil war to it than the administration states." He said the administration "has not been proving its case for steady escalation of the war. The burden of proof for expanding the war rests with the administration and they haven't proved it. In 1961, they talked about saving it with $50 million in aid with U.S. advisers. Last year, the story was we would win if we could get through the monsoon. Then we were told that bombing the North would do it. There is justification for asking explanations of why we have failed and why we haven't negotiated."

Three days later, on March 1, McCarthy formally aligned himself for the first time with the Senate's embryonic peace bloc by voting against a motion to kill an amendment by Oregon Democrat Wayne Morse that would have rescinded the Gulf of Tonkin Resolution. The vote, which came during Senate consideration of the 1966 supplemental authorizations for military procurement, placed McCarthy in the conspicuous company of four of the Senate's most strident anti-Vietnam voices – Morse, Fulbright, Alaska's Ernest Gruening and Ohio's Stephen Young — as the Senate killed the Morse amendment by a 92-5 vote. McCarthy's vote came as a surprise to many of his colleagues, who recalled his comments two weeks earlier after Dean Rusk and other administration witnesses testified at the Foreign Relations Committee's televised hearings on Vietnam. "I believe that there is reason to be encouraged by the intensive efforts to work out some kind of peaceful settlement and by the renewed emphasis upon economic and social reconstruction in South Vietnam," McCarthy said on February 13. But President Johnson's sweeping commitment to South Vietnam and Vice President Humphrey's zealous defense of the U.S. war effort after returning from his Asian trip raised new doubts in McCarthy's mind about the long-range course of the Vietnam conflict.

Although McCarthy's vote had the effect of lumping him with those war critics whom Johnson later contemptuously referred to as "nervous Nellies," it did not mean that McCarthy felt he belonged there. Displaying a fine if somewhat confusing concern for constitutional propriety, McCarthy told the Senate that he voted against the motion to kill Morse's amendment because of parliamentary procedural questions, but that he would have voted against the Morse amendment itself, and against another proposed amendment to reaffirm the Tonkin Resolution. McCarthy said both amendments showed that "too much emphasis has been placed on resolutions like the Tonkin Gulf Resolution" and declared that they "tend to undermine the constitutional authority of the president and may be used to restrict and impede the Senate in the fulfillment of its constitutional responsibility." It was not necessary to either rescind or reaffirm the Tonkin Resolution, he said, because "I believe that the actions of the president in Vietnam are constitutional and legal without the resolution." McCarthy, who voted for the original Tonkin Resolution in August, 1964, when he was still under consideration as Johnson's running mate, also expressed concern that the resolution had "taken on a meaning and a significance which had not been attributed to it at the time it was before the Senate." He also charged that it was being used "as a means of suppressing criticism and challenge to the administration's policies in Vietnam."

McCarthy's stand drew editorial criticism back home in Minnesota. The St. Paul *Pioneer Press* accused him of "walking both sides of the street" on the Vietnam issue, and described his convoluted explanation of his vote as "a lot of parliamentary gobbledygook." The newspaper said that about the only thing McCarthy had done was

> to completely confuse the public as to his real views on Vietnam. He didn't offend the hawks by voting for the military authorization bill. He didn't offend the doves by opposing the Morse amendment. He now owes the public a much clearer picture of just how he does view President Johnson's Vietnam policy and what the future policy of the United States in Southeast Asia should be. He can't remain an "ambivalent" bird forever.

McCarthy didn't offer that explanation, but as the Foreign Relations Committee hearings continued and the war steadily escalated, he became convinced it was necessary to obtain a better moral and historical perspective of the U.S. position in Vietnam. Perhaps recalling his words to the graduating class of Trinity College in Washington the previous May when he said, "Politicians today are calling up the moralists for guidance and for direction and for clarification," McCarthy suggested an unprecedented step — inviting prominent theologians and historians to testify at the hearings on the moral and historical aspects of the Vietnam War. "It was pretty easy to justify our position in World War II," McCarthy said on March 18, "but that's not the case now." He said he and several other committee members favored the idea, although he conceded that the theologians "might present a . . . delicate situation. I wouldn't expect them to condemn our position, but they certainly would raise some moral questions." McCarthy felt that the hearings, which were being televised live, in color, and were attracting nationwide attention, could be a vehicle for helping the country make a moral judgment on the war. However, unable to persuade Fulbright to call in the theologians and historians, McCarthy now moved inevitably toward the next step of his dissent in which he himself would become that vehicle.

McCarthy's role as the nation's leading antiwar dissenter was still in the distant future in the spring of 1966, however. In fact, he was far less critical of the administration on the subject of Vietnam than Fulbright or any of a dozen other senators, at least in his public statements. Speaking on Producer Theodore Granik's television show, "Youth Wants to Know," on March 19, McCarthy was asked by a panel of young people if he felt the war in Vietnam should be escalated "so far that we [would] have to draft college students?" His reply illustrates how far McCarthy would move in his thinking on the war in the ensuing months:

> I don't know that I'd make that the absolute standard at which we might stop the escalation. I think the decision as to whether we ought to have more troops should be made on some other basis. . . . I think that the kind of escalation we now have, in which we're sending in more troops, is defensible on the part of the administration. Certainly, I don't feel that members of the Senate and of the Congress can very well challenge it since it is primarily a military decision. If we move from this kind of escalation to, let us say, bombing civilian areas in North Vietnam, this is a change of substance and it's a kind of escalation which is a concern to me and one which I think should be challenged. That doesn't mean we would stop it, but one which, if it does occur, we must challenge the administration to justify and to explain.

Appearing on the CBS television program "Face the Nation" on May 1, just after a large anti-American demonstration in Saigon, McCarthy challenged a statement by Senator John Stennis of Mississippi that Americans should consider getting out of South Vietnam if they couldn't walk the streets safely in Saigon. "I would not agree with the absoluteness of the senator's statement," McCarthy replied. "I think that the situation is very bad in South Vietnam, but that we have to anticipate, I think, demonstrations and protests against the American position there as a part of the problem over the foreseeable future." When he was asked what would happen if the coming national elections in South Vietnam produced a government that openly opposed the U.S. presence, McCarthy indicated he felt the U.S. should stay, even if it had to make "some kind of adjustment." Asked if he was saying "Maybe we could stay there even if there were a government asking us to leave," McCarthy said, "Well, it would depend upon how stable that government was and with what kind of authority it spoke. It's my opinion that the administration would then look at it in terms of a lot of other considerations in addition to the protest from a government which was holding what appeared to be the power in South Vietnam."

McCarthy's role as a Vietnam dissenter was sublimated in other activities until early 1967, but he was not unaware of the growing criticism of the war on the homefront and the political implications of the mounting casualty rate. Back in Minneapolis in June for the Democratic Farmer Labor Party state convention, McCarthy told friends that the war would have an impact on the 1966 elections. "He said when they start bringing the bodies home to small towns in Minnesota, that's when people are going to start turning against the war," recalls a DFL official. "And he was right. I think there was a lot of anti-war feeling that just didn't show up in the polls."

Nothing typified McCarthy's tenuous relationship to the party that had launched his political career better than his actions at the DFL convention, where he made an attempt to produce a compromise candidate when the convention was unable to settle a fight between Governor Karl Rolvaag and Lieutenant Governor A. M. Keith over the gubernatorial endorsement. His heart really wasn't in it, however. David Broder of the Washington *Post*, one of the national political reporters covering the convention because of Humphrey's involvement in it, recalls going to McCarthy's hotel suite while the battle raged among the delegates fourteen floors below. "When you knocked at the door, Jerry Eller would peek out the next door down the hall and if he knew you, he'd let you in," says Broder. "His explantion was that 'McCarthy doesn't want to see any of those goddamn delegates.' Anyway, there was McCarthy, sitting there discoursing on a speech he'd made about the NATO Treaty and the Spanish ambassador coming to see him and wondering whether he might be able to enlist his support in reviving the Treaty of Utrecht. It was typical of McCarthy — the elegant dilettante talking about a four hundred year old treaty while his party was tearing itself apart downstairs."

The twelve year old campaign by McCarthy to loosen the cloak of secrecy in which the CIA wraps itself finally began to bear fruit in the latter part of 1966. He felt that the CIA's clandestine operations played a major role in the formulation of U.S. foreign policy, and he had sought every year since 1954 to bring the huge intelligence branch under closer Congressional scrutiny.

Although McCarthy's relationship with Johnson had been strained by the events of Atlantic City, his criticism of the CIA caused Johnson to invite him to dinner at the LBJ Ranch after McCarthy completed a speaking engagement in nearby Austin in April, 1965. A third guest was Richard Helms, whose appointment as deputy director of the CIA was to be announced the next day. Johnson called on Helms to buttress his argument that the administration was pursuing the wisest possible course in Vietnam, but McCarthy was unimpressed and decided to have fun at Helms' expense. Pointing to some yellow flowers on the table, McCarthy asked Helms to identify them. Helms couldn't, nor could he identify several other varieties. McCarthy then asked Helms if he could tell him the vintage of the wine they had drunk at dinner. Again, Helms could not. "James Bond would have known the answer," McCarthy told the embarrassed Helms, who was named head of the CIA the following year and later opposed McCarthy's efforts to bring it under closer Congressional supervision.

McCarthy had called in November, 1965, for "a full and complete investigation" of the CIA, whose role in the Dominican Republic, Vietnam, Cuba and other areas he said "raised serious questions about the relationship of the agency to the process of making and directing foreign policy." Six months later, the Foreign Relations Committee approved, by a 14-5 vote, McCarthy's proposal to create a formal CIA oversight committee composed of three members from the Armed Services, Appropriations and Foreign Relations Committees, which would replace an informal six-member watchdog committee drawn from the Armed Services and Appropriations Committees.

The proposal touched off an acrimonious floor debate in which Georgia's Richard Russell, chairman of the Armed Services Committee and chief of the informal CIA watchdog committee, denounced the resolution as an attempt to "muscle in" on his group's role in formulating foreign policy. Recalling the secret hearing report of the Dominican intervention which escaped from the Foreign Relations Committee files, he warned that expanding the watchdog committee could cause dangerous leaks of secret information. "That's ridiculous," said McCarthy. "There are probably thirty or forty people right now who are fully informed about CIA operations. It's just nonsense to say that making the Senate watchdog committee a formal group and adding three members will cause leaks. The important thing is that we make them face up to our own principle of government instead of all this crazy stuff about leaks." McCarthy also accused Russell and his supporters of having what he called "a psychosis of the inner ring — they feel they have to be more and more exclusive. . . . This ties in the general disposition you get in the Pentagon to be as secret as possible."

The Senate rejected the McCarthy watchdog proposal by a 61-28 vote on July 14, after a three hour and forty-one minute secret debate that was only the second held by the Senate since World War II. McCarthy called a news conference the next day to take a verbal swipe at the Senate "establishment" for working to sidetrack his proposal. He said Vice President Humphrey, the Senate's presiding officer, had helped his opponents by an advisory ruling that permitted the Senate to vote on referring his proposal to the Armed Services Committee rather than voting on the proposal itself. McCarthy caustically compared his Senate elders with the buffalo bull — "He can't eat all the grass but he won't let anybody else into the pasture either."

The defeat fed McCarthy's growing frustration with the slow pace of the Senate — even though he achieved his original objective in early 1967 when Russell announced that he would ask three members of the Foreign Relations Committee to attend the meetings of his CIA oversight panel (McCarthy was not one of those asked). His strong feelings were evident on July 28 when he called the Senate's attention to a letter written by CIA Director Helms to the St. Louis *Globe-Democrat* lauding the paper for an editorial critical of Fulbright. Helms, who had flunked McCarthy's flowers-and-wine quiz at the LBJ Ranch a year earlier, was forced by the resultant Senate outcry to apologize to Fulbright. Said McCarthy, his voice dripping with sarcasm, "This is one of the risks you run into when you promote career men. It's a little like the trouble you run into with armed slaves — it takes a little while for them to adjust."

During the Helms letter episode, McCarthy also raised a question that would be answered the following February in the sensational disclosures of the CIA's secret financing of the National Student Organization and other private voluntary organizations. McCarthy's concern about possible CIA involvement in domestic politics caused Fulbright to suggest that Helms should be questioned about "whether or not his agency takes part in domestic affairs, for example, in the elections in our labor unions and whether or not the CIA was using the exchange program."

Another longtime McCarthy crusade that soon came to fruition was the restriction of sales of arms to militarily weak and underdeveloped nations. Writing in the July 9 issue of *Saturday Review* magazine, McCarthy charged that huge exports of arms by the U.S. — an estimated $35 billion worth in the last fifteen years — was undermining U.S. foreign policy and increasing world tensions. He zeroed in on a now-familiar adversary, Defense Secretary McNamara, by pointing out that the Pentagon encouraged defense manufacturers to sell arms overseas because it allegedly helped strengthen recipient countries against Communist subversion and aggression and improved the U.S. balance of payments situation. McCarthy's article, which was based on a study prepared by the Foreign Relations Committee staff, was the latest of many warnings he had sounded of the dangers of promoting the militarization of small nations through uncontrolled arms sales, and it helped lay the groundwork for Congressional passage of a number of provisions restricting credit sales of U.S. military equipment to foreign nations in 1967 and 1968.

Personal feelings had always been an important factor in McCarthy's actions as his political opponents were well aware. Few incidents better illustrated this or had more meaning for his future than a run-in with Attorney General Nicholas Katzenbach in September, 1966. The tall, balding, Katzenbach incurred McCarthy's wrath while the committee was considering his nomination for undersecretary of state. McCarthy angrily delayed approval of the nomination after tracing the origin of an erroneous newspaper report about him to a casual comment by Katzenbach at a Washington cocktail party. Katzenbach told Columnist Howard K. Smith that McCarthy had been absent because of a paid speaking engagement in St. Louis when the Senate fell ten votes short of invoking cloture (forcibly ending debate) on the 1966 Civil Rights Act on September 19, and cited him as one of those responsible for the death of the bill.

When Smith's syndicated column singled out McCarthy's behavior as an example of the "dereliction" of Congress on civil rights legislation, an angry McCarthy collared Smith and pointed out that he had indeed been present and had supported the administration, as he always had, by voting for cloture. When Smith identified Katzenbach as the source of his erroneous column, McCarthy became livid. He remembered all too well that it was the attorney general who only a year earlier had asked him to help assure a court test of the poll tax by voting against a controversial amendment to the 1965 Voting Rights Act. The amendment, sponsored by Senator Edward Kennedy, prohibited poll taxes in state and local elections, but Katzenbach advised the Senate that if it were passed, it would confuse a pending Supreme Court test of a Virginia poll tax case. He asked McCarthy and several other liberal senators to vote against it, pointing out they had good civil rights records and could afford a vote that might be interpreted as anti-civil rights. McCarthy voted against the amendment, which was defeated by a 45-49 vote, and the court subsequently declared state poll taxes unconstitutional when it ruled on the Virginia case in March, 1966. But McCarthy was widely criticized for his vote — as he would be again by Robert Kennedy's supporters during the 1968 election. He later termed the Kennedy criticisms about the poll tax vote "the worst inaccuracy of all" in distortions of his voting record.[9]

Katzenbach's nomination for undersecretary came before the Foreign Relations Committee on September 27, but McCarthy requested a delay so he could ask him an "important question," which he did when a contrite Katzenbach came to his Senate office that evening. Katzenbach explained that he

---

[9] Nothing angered McCarthy as much during the 1968 campaign as attempts by Robert Kennedy's supporters to distort his voting record, particularly the poll tax vote. He told a news conference in Philadelphia on April 18, 1968, that Katzenbach had told him and other senators that "those of you who are responsible and are interested in civil rights and not in publicity, please vote against this amendment and this bill." McCarthy added plaintively, "I did it at Mr. Katzenbach's request, who was a Kennedy appointment."

did not know that McCarthy had been present for the cloture vote and apologized for having mentioned McCarthy's name while discussing the matter with Smith. McCarthy withdrew his objection the next day, and Katzenbach was confirmed after cooling his heels for a few days. "He didn't offer much of an explanation, but the case was not sufficient to use for holding up the appointment," McCarthy said. "I don't think any cabinet member ought to tell anybody what a member of the Senate is going to do before he does it."

The Katzenbach incident would have cataclysmic reverberations when he and McCarthy disagreed over the meaning of the Gulf of Tonkin Resolution in August, 1967, but McCarthy was clearly anticipating a test of the administration's foreign and domestic policies long before his second confrontation with Katzenbach. In a position paper entitled "My Hopes for Democrats" which he wrote for the November 5, 1966, *Saturday Review* magazine, McCarthy offered a prophetic analysis of likely trouble spots for Lyndon Johnson and the Democratic party in the next two years. Asserting that "the appearance of consensus is much greater than its reality," McCarthy warned that the party had developed internal strains and weaknesses and that Democrats in the 1966 election would have to face the challenge of inflation and prove the workability of Great Society programs. But foreign policy would not become a critical issue until the 1968 elections, he predicted.

The real challenge to the Democratic party in the field of foreign affairs, McCarthy wrote, in what was to be a self-fulfilling prophecy, "will come in 1968, at which time the presidential candidate of each party will be called upon to present his proposals for this country within the current of history. Generalizations about the speed of change and how the world has grown smaller, replays of our triumphs, and appeals to our treaties and declarations will then not be acceptable. Both old and new myths which are irrelevant or deceptive will then have to be challenged."

The time when McCarthy himself would make that challenge was still almost a year away when he wrote these words, but the idea of that challenge was already formed in his mind and in the minds of several of those close to him. Larry Merthan and Martin Haley, an international businessman who had worked on McCarthy's 1948 House campaign, sat down at Merthan's Georgetown house on a snowy Christmas Eve in 1966 to work out a plan which McCarthy could use to run for president. The six page plan, dubbed "Operation Casa Blanca" (White House), basically involved building "core groups" of McCarthy supporters in each state, a stepped up speaking schedule for McCarthy and opening a Washington office to coordinate the various activities.

"It was not as much of a McCarthy-for-President plan as it was a McCarthy 'structure' plan," Haley later recalled. "There's a difference — certainly, McCarthy might use such a structure to run for president in 1968, but he might use it for other purposes as well, such as running in 1972 or 1976 or to become a national figure. We thought he should have a rational plan for any and all national purposes, but we had no indication he was going to do what he did." When Merthan showed the plan to McCarthy a short time later, he expressed interest in it, but never gave the order to implement it, and Operation Casa Blanca never got off the ground.

Ever since signing the January, 1966, letter urging the president not to resume the bombing of North Vietnam, McCarthy had held strong doubts about the military and political objectives of the war in Vietnam. But by the beginning of 1967, with the escalation of the war climbing inexorably — U.S. troop strength was nearing 400,000 — and with growing discord at home accompanied by spiraling inflation that threatened unmet domestic needs, McCarthy was convinced that the nation was ready to make a harsh moral judgment on the war as well. McCarthy made his first public call for that judgment on the evening of February 1, when he spoke at a Washington conference of Clergy and Laymen Concerned About Vietnam.

An estimated two thousand clergymen and laymen from forty-five states had come to the Capital for the two-day "peace mobilization" sponsored by the coalition of Christian and Jewish leaders, and at least half of that number was jammed into the New York Avenue Presbyterian Church two blocks from the White House when McCarthy stood at the pulpit to speak.[10] McCarthy's speech was flat and dispassionate compared to the angry rhetoric of two Democratic senators who preceded him, Wayne Morse and Ernest Gruening. Morse and Gruening, who had led Congressional opposition to the war, assailed it in fiery language as morally and legally unjustified and needlessly prolonged. But McCarthy, speaking in the unemotional tones that would become the hallmark of his later campaign speeches, began by commending the religious leaders for calling attention to the "moral dilemma" of the war. He followed with a lengthy historical analysis, in which he compared Vietnam to other major wars the U.S. had been involved in. "In every other war, we've had the support of what is generally accepted as the decent opinion of mankind," he said. "We do not have that today. . . . We're called upon to justify if we can our objectives and purposes and the methods which we're using in the conduct of the war."

Three questions must be considered in seeking to justify U.S. objectives in Vietnam, McCarthy declared. "First, we must ask if there is a possibility for victory? Second, will the cost of that victory be proportionate to what is gained? And finally, will a better life emerge following our victory?" McCarthy concluded that "the answers must be quite positive on each of the

[10] Among the organization's leaders was the Reverend Robert McAfee Brown of Stanford University, who had worked in McCarthy's 1952 House campaign and would work for him in 1968 as well. One of the founders of Clergy and Laymen Concerned About Vietnam was the radical Catholic priest, Daniel Berrigan, who like McCarthy grew up in Minnesota but chose a far more unorthodox mode of dissent against his government's foreign and domestic policies.

counts if we are to proceed." He drew prolonged applause from his audience as he declared, "I do not believe any of the answers are positive and since they are not, we must be prepared to pass harsh and severe judgment on our position in this war."

The speech represented the strongest antiwar statement McCarthy had made, and signaled his arrival at a point that many in his audience had passed months and years earlier. He had been moving toward outright opposition to the war for many months, but it was accelerated by the persistent and passionate arguments of his eighteen year old daughter Mary. An undergraduate at Radcliffe College and a leading campus peace activist, Mary had crystallized her father's instinctive and intellectual opposition to the war in numerous dialogues with him. The essence of her argument was a plea that her father take an unequivocal stand in 1968 on the most critical issue facing the country, even though that stand undoubtedly would place him on a collision course with the incumbent president of his own party. His daughter's urging was hardly out of line with his own thinking, but it did impress upon the fifty-one year old McCarthy more than ever before the deep sense of anguish and hopelessness that the war instilled in young people. It also made the next step of his dissent inevitable.

McCarthy now began moving around the country, speaking on college campuses, to church women's groups and at community forums, plumbing the depth of antiwar sentiment and confirming his instinctive feeling that the country was ready to pass a moral judgment on the war. His own pronouncements on the administration's conduct of the war became steadily bolder, although he still remained in the shadow of more famous dissenters such as Morse, Fulbright and Robert Kennedy. He seemed to feel a need to test his views first in the familiar surroundings of his home state, returning to Minnesota repeatedly in the first part of the year.

On February 28, McCarthy told a student gathering at the University of Minnesota that the war was "morally unjustifiable" and called on Johnson to "look at what we are doing in Vietnam." On March 5, speaking to a community forum in the Minneapolis suburb of Edina, McCarthy proposed for the first time that the U.S. give up its fruitless effort to begin negotiations and try a disengagement "to see what happens." It might not work, he said, but it was better than "more violence and destruction on both sides." On March 18, he told a DFL fundraiser in Minneapolis that "as the war has dragged on, the moral component has become more important and the need for more judgment more essential." In April, when President Johnson called General William Westmoreland back from Vietnam to defend the U.S. war policy before a joint session of Congress, McCarthy said it was a "dangerous practice" to have a military field commander "make a case which is not only military but also political" and denounced the move as an "escalation of language, method and emotions." In May, he defended dissent as more of a duty than a right, saying, "What we are really asking today from the people of this country is heroic virtue and no one has the right to ask for heroic virtue unless he has done everything to prevent conditions from developing in which that kind of virtue is called upon." Finally, speaking at Hamline University in St. Paul in June, he said Americans are being called upon "for the first time in the history of our country, certainly in this century . . . to question seriously the rightness of our involvement in a war." [11]

McCarthy's conviction that the war was a paramount moral issue was coupled with a growing sense of Johnson's political vulnerability, a feeling shared by some supporters who viewed him as Adlai Stevenson's heir apparent. McCarthy met with several of those supporters on March 22 in the luxurious New York City apartment of Thomas Finletter, a former Secretary of the Air Force and a leader of the New York Democratic reform movement. The purpose of the meeting was to try to persuade McCarthy to position himself so he could run for president if the opportunity presented itself. McCarthy was receptive to the idea, according to Russell Hemenway, director of the National Committee for an Effective Congress, who along with Wall Street Lawyer John Shea had gotten financial pledges from other wealthy Stevensonians to bankroll McCarthy's build-up. "McCarthy said that night that the only way to get Johnson to change would be for someone to run against him, and that he just might do it if no one else would," Hemenway later recalled. "No matter how much the Senate might do, Lyndon Johnson would not be moved unless someone challenged him electorally. Gene felt that was the only thing he would understand."

Hemenway and his friends thought they had a potential candidate who would run if Johnson decided not to and later in the evening they called a young lawyer who agreed to go to work for McCarthy. However, two days later, McCarthy told them he had changed his mind. "He was saying, 'Well, maybe the time isn't right; play it by ear; live off the land; let's see what happens,'" Hemenway recalls.

McCarthy may have had second thoughts about Johnson's vulnerability or about the likelihood that Robert Kennedy would run against Johnson as an antiwar candidate. He had told James Wechsler of the New York *Post* in March that he thought Kennedy should run and that he would support him if he did. Soon afterwards, however, he told his brother Austin's daughter, Patricia, in an interview for her high school newspaper in Willmar, Minnesota, that he thought Johnson would run again and win reelection.

[11] Strangley, McCarthy's own staff seemed unaware that the Vietnam war was the most important issue before the country. A twelve-page news release summing up McCarthy's accomplishments in the first six months of 1967 led off with the declaration that McCarthy "has led the way . . . toward a better break for Minnesota farmers," and quoted him as saying, "Low farm income continues to be a serious national problem."

"On the Democratic ticket, it's most likely that President Johnson will run again for reelection," McCarthy said. "If he decides to run, if he does not withdraw, it would seem to me that he would certainly receive the nomination of the party, and in my judgment, once the people are given the choice between two candidates in 1968, that his strength in the polls would rise high enough that he would be reelected."

In the same interview, McCarthy offered a concise view of his reasons for opposing the war in Vietnam:

> The difficulty with the war, as I see it, is on two major points: One, it begins to appear that whatever good we may possibly achieve in Vietnam is nothing compared to the destruction of life and property, the loss of diplomatic and moral position on the part of the U.S. in the rest of the world; and secondly, we continue to spend at the rate of two to two and a half billion dollars a month in support of this war. If we continue to spend at this rate, we are distracted from doing the things that we ought to be doing in other parts of the world. . . . We drain off our military and our economic and our moral strength, and neglect problems both at home and abroad.

Despite his growing opposition, McCarthy carefully avoided becoming too closely identified with the growing flock of doves in the Senate. He was conspicuously absent among the sixteen signers of a "plea for realism" statement drafted by Idaho's Frank Church urging Hanoi to come to the conference table because the great majority of Americans opposed a unilateral withdrawal from Vietnam. McCarthy decided against signing it for several reasons. First, he said by emphasizing that dissenting Americans are a distinct minority, the statement appeared to be "responsive to administration assertions that dissenters give encouragement to the enemy and are discouraging to our own effort." Second, he said he hadn't advocated unilateral withdrawal of the troops in the past and didn't see any point in asserting that he was now against it. Finally, he questioned whether the statement could be of any value. "I think the way has to be kept open for criticism and questioning of our Vietnam war policies, and signing a statement of this kind would have a tendency to set limitations and restrictions on this discussion and questioning."

Most of McCarthy's statements and speeches in mid-1967 were concerned with Vietnam and foreign policy (he was named chairman of the Foreign Relations Subcommittee on African Affairs earlier in the year), and even though he occasionally discussed domestic problems, they were often tied into the war. In a Senate speech on August 8, after racial violence broke out in Detroit and Newark and other large Northern cities, McCarthy warned against ignoring the root causes of racial violence or hoping that it will "go away with a change of weather." He offered an eight-point program aimed at eliminating the causes of racial inequality and economic deprivation of minority groups, and related the disturbances to the Vietnam War by questioning whether the nation can afford both "guns and butter." "We must set some priorities even though the secretary of defense recently was quoted as saying we are capable of fighting another war of the magnitude of Vietnam. We can put off our pursuits of the supersonic transport and slow down our efforts to reach the moon if need be. It will not go away and we now know what it is made of."

McCarthy's preoccupation with foreign policy was evident during the fourteen-month long investigation by the Senate Ethics Committee into Senator Thomas Dodd's financial affairs that ended with Dodd's censure in June, 1967. McCarthy, one of six members of the committee that recommended Dodd be censured for diverting political campaign funds to his personal use, complained that the nine day Senate debate on Dodd's censure "has distracted us from representing our own states and from carrying on the official business of the Senate in the fields of foreign policy and finance and other important areas." Obviously displeased by the unconventional tactics of Dodd's self-appointed defender, Senator Russell Long of Louisiana, McCarthy at one point threatened to resign from the committee if the Senate failed to censure Dodd, and he predicted that the debate "indicates that it would be very difficult to develop a workable code of ethics for the Senate." [12]

McCarthy provided his foes with an excuse to criticize his own code of ethics a few months later when he voted in the Finance Committee to table an amendment by Long to require the federal government to purchase drugs by their generic names rather than buying them under their more expensive brand names for the Medicare program. McCarthy felt more study was needed of the complex administrative problems involved, an approach welcomed by the drug industry and by his former legislative counsel, Larry Merthan, who was then lobbying on Capitol Hill for Charles Pfizer & Company, one of the largest drug manufacturers in the country. The tabling motion, taken up in a closed session, failed, and McCarthy voted with the majority as the generic drug amendment was passed on the floor. However, House-Senate conferees later agreed to hold the legislation in abeyance until the studies favored by McCarthy were completed. McCarthy's defenders pointed out that he had voted for an unsuccessful amendment directed against drug monopoly prices in 1962 — when Merthan was still on the staff — but he never offered a convincing explanation for the later vote.

In mid-August, McCarthy returned to Washington from a visit to Minnesota, where, despite criticism of the president's newest decision to expand the bombing of North Vietnam and of his proposal for a 10 percent surtax on federal income taxes, he had described himself as a "reasonably good

---

[12] While the Ethics Committee was trying to decide whether to recommend that Dodd be "censured" or "condemned," McCarthy offered the tongue-in-cheek suggestion that the committee settle for the word "objurgate."

supporter" of the administration. Two days later, on August 17, he no longer could make that claim.

On that day, Undersecretary of State Nicholas Katzenbach, the man whose confirmation McCarthy had held up a year earlier, testified before the Foreign Relations Committee on U.S. commitments and declared that Congress was "compelled" to support administration foreign policy and that the Gulf of Tonkin Resolution amounted to the "functional equivalent" of a declaration of war. In the middle of Katzenbach's testimony McCarthy stalked from the hearing room, visibly angry. When Reporter E. W. (Ned) Kenworthy of the New York *Times* caught up with him in the hallway, McCarthy declared, "This is the wildest testimony I have ever heard. There is no limit to what he says the president can do. There is only one thing to do — take it to the country."

McCarthy's resolve to do just that was reinforced on October 12, when Secretary of State Dean Rusk held a news conference in which he depicted Vietnam as the key to a larger strategy for containment of Communist China. "Within the next decade or two," said Rusk, "there will be a billion Chinese on the mainland, armed with nuclear weapons, with no certainty about what their attitude toward the rest of Asia will be . . . ."[13] Three days later, McCarthy rose on the Senate floor and in a major speech, charged that Rusk's "careless or intentional abuse of the language can serve only to raise the emotional level of the debate, obscure the issues . . . and cause further frustration and division within the country as well as between Congress and the Executive branch . . . ." He said it was clear from Rusk's remarks that the administration had decided on an overall strategy of containing China through encirclement and declared that such a strategy reflects "the ancient fear of the yellow peril." To carry out such a strategy, McCarthy said, would require the U.S. to maintain 100,000 to 200,000 troops in South Vietnam for 15 to 20 years after the fighting stops. He added, "The process must be reversed before the temporary recommitment assumes the character of a permanent establishment. . . ."

The Rusk and Katzenbach statements were very much on McCarthy's mind as he headed for Los Angeles for a meeting on October 20 that would irrevocably commit him to challenging Johnson.

The meeting had its genesis in late July, when McCarthy received a letter from Gerald Hill, a San Francisco attorney and chairman of the 33,000-member ultra-liberal California Democratic Council. The CDC had voted in March, 1967, to run a slate of delegates against Johnson in the June,

---

[13] A day earlier, Vice President Humphrey declared in a speech in Doylestown, Pennsylvania, that America's future was at stake in Southeast Asia. He called Red China the center of "militant aggressive Asian communism," and warned that if the Communists won in Vietnam, "the entire power structure of the world would be destroyed."

1968, California primary if nothing had been done in six months to wind down the war. Hill had written to a number of other prominent Democrats besides McCarthy — Robert Kennedy, Senator Frank Church of Idaho, Senator George McGovern of South Dakota and oddly, Mayor Jerome Cavanaugh of Detroit — telling them of the peace slate and asking if he could discuss it with them. The others merely acknowledge his letter but a few days after the Katzenbach testimony, Hill received a letter from McCarthy, saying he would be in Los Angeles in October and that he would be glad to meet with him.

At the same time, Allard Lowenstein, an intense, thirty-eight year old activist for liberal causes who had once worked on Hubert Humphrey's Senate staff and who was now dedicated to stopping the war by challenging Johnson's renomination, was scurrying about the country trying to recruit a candidate to lead that challenge. On August 5, he and Hill met in Hill's house and agreed to raise $1,500 apiece and hire Lowenstein's friend, Curtis Gans, a member of the Washington staff of the ADA, to set up an office in Washington to organize peace groups around the country under the aegis of the Conference of Concerned Democrats. Lowenstein then set out to find a candidate to challenge Johnson for the Democratic nomination. He put together a list of people, including Kennedy, McGovern, Church, McCarthy, Congressman Don Edwards of California, Harvard Economist John Kenneth Galbraith, retired Army General James Gavin and even several governors and university presidents. "It was a list of people on the right side of the issue, people with credibility and credentials," Lowenstein said later.

Lowenstein went first to see Kennedy, bceause it was clear that if Kennedy would go, his job would be over. "The notion of getting involved in an arduous organizational task around the country was lunacy if Kennedy ran," says Lowenstein. But Kennedy said no. Lowenstein then talked to Edwards, then to Church, but both said no. He approached Galbraith, who was willing but declined because he was Canadian-born. He talked to Gavin, whose theory of holding onto strategic strong points or "enclaves" in South Vietnam and allowing the U.S. to continue an effective but limited presence in Vietnam had attracted considerable attention. But Gavin was willing to run only as a Republican. Kennedy had been enthusiastic about McGovern, and Lowenstein went to see him. "His enthusiasm dovetailed with what I felt about McGovern," says Lowenstein, "but there was no conscious decision to put McGovern before McCarthy on the list. Several factors caused me to go to him first. One was that I knew him and could get to see him — in those days I didn't have easy access to senators. Very often after hearing what you wanted to talk about, they thought you should be committed.

"McGovern's own comment which astonished me and made me feel very warm about him — most people took the position that it was almost irresponsible to talk about it — was that yes, this should be done. It was enormously encouraging. But he said he was up for reelection and he thought it would be impossible for him to do this. I said I didn't think it was and he asked me to spend some time in South Dakota and tell him what I thought. I spent three or four days there and saw a great many people, and I concluded that it was not impossible, but it would be very difficult. I felt rhetoric would be the problem because there was such a totally different situation in South Dakota. People in the East were talking about the unraveling of the cities — can you picture Sioux Falls unraveling? There just wasn't the sense of apocalypse there was in other parts of the country.

"At that point — and let's be very clear about this, McGovern never said he wouldn't do it — I said since we agree it will be very difficult for you to do it, let's talk to someone else." McGovern got out a copy of the *Congressional Record* to see which of the Senate doves were up for reelection in 1968, and found only two he felt were worth considering — McCarthy and Lee Metcalf of Montana. "Have you talked to Gene yet?" McGovern asked. "I know he's feeling very frustrated about the war."

Lowenstein didn't need to be directed to McCarthy. "He'd been something of a hero to me," says Lowenstein, whose ties to Minnesota included his service on Humphrey's staff, as well as the fact that he was a law school classmate of Lieutenant Governor A. M. Keith at Yale and had been elected president of the National Student Association at Minneapolis in 1951. In early October, Lowenstein talked to McCarthy. "At first, he was rather Hamlet-like," Lowenstein recalls. "He said 'Bobby should do it' — he always called him 'Bobby.' But the conversations became progressively more encouraging. They went from being discussions in philosophical terms to political terms and it became clear that he was becoming more interested.

"I don't know to what extent I affected his thinking because he never says how anyone affects his thinking. I never felt right saying I persuaded him. I think that's arrogant. My part was very, very minor. If I had any part in persuading him, it was in bringing him information for assessment of reality. It was a marginal part, but what wasn't marginal was the organizing going on around the country. If it weren't for all the things that had been done to give him a base, no matter what he thought, he wouldn't have been in a position to run. It's demeaning to him to suggest that one person persuaded him to run, but later, when things weren't going right during the campaign, he used to say, 'You people talked me into this and all I said was that I'd give you my name.' "

On October 20, McCarthy went to Los Angeles for his meeting with Hill. They met for breakfast in McCarthy's suite at the Ambassador Hotel, the same hotel where Robert Kennedy was to meet a tragic end eight months later. Lowenstein was not invited but he found out about the meeting and flew out to attend.[14] Also present were Jerry Eller and Maury Weiner — an aide to Los Angeles City Councilman Tom Bradley, and a friend of Hill's. Hill, who had never met McCarthy before, recalls that he was "bigger, greyer, and much funnier than I expected. He kidded during the whole conversation, but he was also asking technical questions about money and labor and how many people we had — all Jim Farley-type nuts and bolts questions. Most of the conversation was between him and me. He was surprised to see Lowenstein there and later told me he didn't remember him being there. After about an hour and a quarter, he stood up and he had a big grin on his face. He said, 'You guys have been talking about three or four names. I think you can cut the list down to one now.' "

[14] When McCarthy later told Eller he didn't remember Lowenstein being present at the meeting, Eller said, "That's easy to remember. He's the guy who had corned beef on rye for breakfast."

BOOK FOUR
CROSSROADS
1968

CHAPTER XIV

THE POLITICS OF PRINCIPLE — MC CARTHY vs. JOHNSON

> *We're going to make a lot of people honest*
> *before this is over.*
> Eugene McCarthy in a 1968 interview.

Seven minutes after ten o'clock on the morning of November 30, 1967, Eugene McCarthy stepped before a podium in the Caucus Room of the Old Senate Office Building and in dry, matter-of-fact tones, announced the decision that would change American history. Donning a pair of horn-rimmed glasses to read from a two-page statement, McCarthy said he intended to enter four presidential primaries, but that he was still undecided about two others, including the first one in the nation on March 12 in New Hampshire.

McCarthy, who had never been to New Hampshire or Vietnam, went on to say his decision to challenge President Johnson on "Vietnam and other related issues" in the primaries had been strengthened by the continued escalation of the war and the absence of any signs of a negotiated settlement. "I am concerned that the administration seems to have set no limits on the price that it is willing to pay for military victory," he said as he summarized the cost of the war in terms of the physical destruction and human suffering inflicted on South Vietnam and the casualties and expenditures incurred by the United States.

Then the fifty-one year old McCarthy offered his vision of the campaign he was about to undertake and, at the same time, gave a prophetic assessment of the historic impact of that campaign.

> I am hopeful that this challenge I am making, which I hope will be supported by other members of the Senate and other politicians, may alleviate the sense of political helplessness and restore to many people a belief in

the processes of American politics and of American government. On college campuses especially, but among adult thoughtful Americans it may counter the growing sense of alienation from politics which I think is currently reflected in a tendency to withdraw from political action, and talk of non-partisan efforts; to become cynical and make threats of support for third parties or other irregular political movements.

Even though he was challenging the renomination of an incumbent president of his own party, McCarthy was careful to portray himself as a loyal Democrat. He was also more than a one-issue candidate, he claimed. "The issue of the war in Vietnam is not really a separate issue but one which must be dealt with in the configuration of other problems in which it is related," he said in a slightly nasal voice. "And it is within this broader context that I intend to take the case to the people of the United States."

It had been an unconventional announcement of a presidential candidacy (McCarthy never once said he was seeking the presidency itself), but the re-strained language of his announcement was consistent with the carefully planned strategy that McCarthy had developed over the past few months.

Before making up his mind in late October to challenge Johnson, he had discussed with a number of his colleagues the possibility of having them run as favorite sons in their own states in hopes of forcing a change in Johnson's Vietnam policies. "It might have worked out differently," Mc-Carthy explained in an interview in early November, "but unfortunately, most of those who would have been joining me in this — McGovern, Church, Ful-bright, Nelson, Morse, Clark — were all running for reelection to the Sen-ate. We had thought of having each of these men seek support as a favorite son, then pooling our strength. But they had reelection campaigns. That put the burden on me."

McCarthy was particularly careful to try to ascertain Robert Kennedy's plans before committing himself. He had private conversations with him and sounded out several of his associates before buttonholing Kennedy in the Senate cloakroom in October. McCarthy said he was considering enter-ing the primaries himself since it didn't appear likely that Kennedy would. "I didn't ask him what he was going to do," McCarthy said later. "I just said, 'I'm not worried as to whether I'm a stalking horse for you,' meaning if Bobby were to enter later on I would not say I'd been tricked. I left it open to him. He didn't give me any encouragement or discouragement. He just accepted what I'd said." [1]

At the same time, McCarthy carefully refrained from attacking Johnson personally, always stressing that it was the issue of Vietnam and its effect on the country that he was concerned about and not denying Johnson the

[1] McCarthy was still trying to goad Kennedy into challenging Johnson as late as his October 26 Berkeley speech when he said, "There come certain times in politics when the individual I do not think really has the right to anticipate how things are going to be better for him in 1972."

nomination. "The word 'dump Johnson' has never been one of my words," he told John Herbers of the New York *Times* on November 2. "I think it is a bad word. I think it is inexcusable. I think it is one of the things that the press does that tends to interfere with a proper discussion of problems. The first question you get is 'do you want to dump Johnson?' Well, I don't want to dump Johnson." [2]

Instead, McCarthy called for efforts to obtain an antiwar plank in the 1968 party platform, to instruct delegates to oppose the administration's Vietnam policy and to send to the convention favorite son candidates to challenge Johnson on the war. Finally, he spoke of the possibility of running against Johnson in several state primaries. All of these steps, he insisted, constituted an entirely proper use of the party's political machinery. In fact, he compared it to the raising of the civil rights issue by Humphrey at the 1948 Democratic National Convention, and without naming him, even criticized Humphrey for not recognizing that he was trying to force an open discussion of the Vietnam issue just as Humphrey had forced the party to fight out its deep-seated differences over civil rights in 1948. "Some of those today who are calling for unity in the party were most active in the civil rights effort in 1948, which was a thoroughly divisive proposition to bring before a Democratic convention," said McCarthy, "and although there is no direct comparison between this issue and civil rights, the basic principle of facing up to it within the framework of the political party, I think, still is entirely valid." [3]

Despite his now-open revolt against Johnson, McCarthy offered the conditions under which he would consider abandoning his challenge of the administration's conduct of the war. He told a November 3 news conference in the Twin Cities that Johnson would first have to call an unconditional halt to the bombing of North Vietnam and then offer "realistic negotiations" which would include a coalition government in South Vietnam. He said the administration's recent offer to quit bombing if North Vietnam would quit supplying its troops in the South was not a true peace proposal. "It's like saying we'll stop eating for twenty-four hours if you will stop breathing. It's not negotiable."

McCarthy tested the themes of his candidacy during a five-day speaking tour in mid-November that concentrated on college audiences. The trip, which began at the school where Humphrey once taught, Macalester College in St. Paul, reinforced McCarthy's conviction that tremendous dormant political energies were waiting to be tapped. "There is a deep anxiety and alienation among a large number of people," McCarthy said at the time, "so we have demonstrations and draft card burning and all the rest. Someone

---

[2] A month and a half earlier in Denver, McCarthy said "dump Johnson" talk was nothing but "newspaper talk."

[3] "He is my friend," Humphrey said shortly after McCarthy announced his candidacy, "and no matter what happens, we will continue to have lunch together."

must give these groups entrance back into the political processes. We may lose, but at least in the process of fighting within the political framework, we'll have reduced the alienation. This is absolutely vital."

At Macalester on November 9, in the heart of the Congressional district he once represented in the House, McCarthy raised the basic question that he said must be faced in 1968 — whether "what is called our commitment in South Vietnam is morally defensible," and not simply whether it was legally, militarily and politically defensible. "We must raise the essential moral question," he said in a statement he would repeat in endless variations in the coming months, "as to whether or not there is a proper balance in what we may gain in what is projected as victory, in contrast with the loss of life, the loss of material goods, the loss of moral integrity and moral energy which goes with the effort. The answer, I think, is that it is not."

At the same time, just as he had done in his first political campaign in St. Paul in 1948, McCarthy was trying to expand the appeal of those groups most sympathetic to him — young people, intellectuals and clergymen — and break into the stronghold of traditional party loyalists. "Party unity is not a sufficient excuse for silence," he declared two nights later at the Young Democrats' convention in Cambridge. (He was met at the Boston airport by "McCarthy for President" placards and a demonstration led by his nineteen year old daughter Mary, a sophomore at Radcliffe.) He called Vietnam too important an issue to place "the burden of criticism and dissent — as it now is — on the academic community, religious leaders and on the young people of America," and in words that soon would look strangely out of place, proclaimed, "This is not the kind of political controversy which should be left to a children's crusade or to those not directly involved in politics. It should rather be taken up by adult political leaders and activists in America." [4]

Behind the shrewd political judgment by McCarthy that much of the nation shared his frustration over Vietnam was a growing conviction that Johnson was a man who corrupted people and eroded the institutions of government. McCarthy felt Johnson's appetite for power had destroyed the Democratic National Committee, turned the once-independent Senate into "another House of Representatives," diminished the stature of the Supreme Court (by assigning members nonjudicial chores) and in general, resulted in a dangerous interference with the constitutional processes. "The Senate Foreign Relations Committee was turned into sort of a stockpen," McCarthy told an old friend, the late Edwin Lahey of the Knight Newspapers' Washington bureau in a mid-November interview. "Odd lots of senators were

---

[4] Not everyone on the campuses was convinced that McCarthy really intended to challenge Johnson. After McCarthy's Cambridge speech, a young man expressed his skepticism about it to McCarthy's aide, Jerry Eller. "He said, 'Bullshit! McCarthy's just a front for Lyndon and he's just trying to keep the campuses quiet,'" Eller recalls. "He said, 'When McCarthy betrays us at Chicago, we'll burn the place down!'"

assigned, the way you assemble odd lots of cattle at stockyards."

Because of his long friendship with Lahey, McCarthy agreed to sit down to a tape recorded interview — something he rarely did — with Publisher John S. Knight and editors of the Miami *Herald* during a visit to Miami in early December. In the interview, McCarthy made it clear he felt that Johnson was a manipulator of men and institutions. "Truman wouldn't send up a Korean Resolution. But Johnson sends one up on Southeast Asia. Harry said, 'To hell with it, it's my responsibility and I'll do it.' Johnson brings [General William] Westmoreland back to give a political speech. Truman fired MacArthur for giving a political speech. Truman said, 'We'll take over the steel mills. . . .' Johnson calls the steel guys into the White House and says, 'Now look, if you fellows want to fix prices, it's illegal. But it's all right as long as you do it in my presence.' It's like the king calling in the barons and saying, 'Now look, fellows, we have laws for the people, but they don't apply to you and me.' "

McCarthy also charged that Johnson misled the Senate on the Gulf of Tonkin Resolution. "If the Foreign Relations Committee has the nerve to really investigate that resolution, it seems to me the confidence of the public in the administration will be severely shaken." His political instincts, McCarthy said, told him that it wouldn't take much to change people's minds on the war. "They don't have to take any giant strides. They're very close to the fulcrum. . . . Their disposition, in the name of patriotism or loyalty or because they're in doubt, is to stay with the government, which is not a bad disposition. But they could change very quantitatively without much of a change on their position or judgment on the war."

McCarthy explained his case against Johnson in more formal language in an article written for *Look* magazine in December. In the article, in which he incorrectly forecast that he "would anticipate more support from Senator Kennedy as time goes on," McCarthy reiterated his arguments against the war and then stated an equally important factor in his decision to challenge Johnson. "What we have is a personalized presidency, somewhat independent of the government and somewhat independent of the political party from which the president has come. . . . Sometimes, I think it is a mistake not to limit the presidency to one term. If we did, the party position and the institutional approach would predominate. Instead, as it is now, the tendency for the man in the White House is to say, 'This is MY presidency, MY White House, MY vice president,' and so on, whatever it might be. We are getting a reflection of this in the administration's shocked and angry reaction to the challenge within the party in a presidential year."

McCarthy also acknowledged the political risks he was taking, saying, "The right of dissent is a kind of protection to ensure us and to encourage us to exercise what is a fundamental human obligation: the duty to speak one's mind, to tell the truth, to make one's best moral judgment whenever the conditions and the demands of the time require it." However heroic such dissent might be, McCarthy wasn't ready to become a hero himself. "What we are really asking today from the people of this country is heroic virtue. And no one really has the right to ask for heroic virtue unless he has done everything in his power to prevent conditions in which heroic virtue is required."

A sign that McCarthy saw himself as an anti-hero came in the first major speech of the campaign, at the December 2 national Conference of Concerned Democrats at the Conrad Hilton Hotel in Chicago — where the death knell for his candidacy would be sounded eight months later. The conference was organized by Allard Lowenstein, who hoped that McCarthy would use the occasion to announce his candidacy, but McCarthy had purposely announced two days earlier to avoid having his candidacy linked too closely with the Conference and its vociferous anti-Johnson, end-the-war membership. At least 2,500 people, many of them students from nearby Chicago colleges, were jammed into the Hilton ballroom and another 3,500 people listened on loudspeakers in adjacent rooms as they waited for McCarthy, who was late. After Congressman Don Edwards, a liberal California Democrat who was the first member of Congress to publicly endorse McCarthy, finished his introduction, Lowenstein attempted to build up the crowd's enthusiasm by delivering a blistering denunciation of Johnson that lasted almost twenty minutes.

As Lowenstein brought the crowd to a fever pitch, McCarthy arrived and stood at the back of the room, unnoticed by Lowenstein. People standing near McCarthy saw the blood drain from his face, then watched as he paced back and forth like a caged animal, muttering and angrily kicking a paper cup against the wall. Finally, Lowenstein was through and McCarthy walked grim-faced through a sea of waving banners and cheering supporters. The audience was looking for exciting oratory but McCarthy gave them none. He read his speech quickly and quietly, evoking the memory of Adlai Stevenson by noting that Stevenson was first nominated for president in Chicago in 1952, and recalling John F. Kennedy, who he said had revived Stevenson's ideas "in a new language and a new spirit." McCarthy devoted most of his speech to the Vietnam war, declaring that the United States had lost "the support of the decent opinion of mankind," and drawing an analogy between Vietnam and the Dreyfus affair in France by citing Charles Péguy's warning that ". . . the acceptance of a single dishonorable act will bring about the loss of one's honor, the dishonor of a whole people."

Although McCarthy was widely criticized for the rather pedantic content and unexciting delivery of his speech, it was one of the most important of his campaign. First, it expanded on the basic reasons for his campaign that he had stated two days earlier in his announcement and proclaimed his intention to "test the mood and spirit" of America. Second, by his restrained understatement, McCarthy established the fundamental tone and spirit that would characterize his campaign and would prove a source of bewilderment and fascination to critics and supporters alike. It was not, McCarthy later said, "a time for storming the walls, but for beginning a long march."

One of the steps in that long march was the April 30 Massachusetts primary. McCarthy had held off committing himself because he was uncertain whether Johnson would allow his name to be entered or whether he would persuade Senator Edward Kennedy or some other popular figure to stand in for him as a favorite son candidate. Yet at the same time, McCarthy felt Massachusetts would provide an important test of his strength in the Northeast, and that he would run better there than in hawkish, unpredictable New Hampshire, which had the only other major early primary in that region of the country. McCarthy also was coming under intense pressure from his Massachusetts supporters, particularly at Chicago, to run in Massachusetts to demonstrate his independence and to prove that he was not a "stalking horse" for Robert Kennedy, as many people believed. In fact, Jerome Grossman, a wealthy envelope manufacturer and peace activist who subsidized the Massachusetts delegation's trip to Chicago, went so far as to present McCarthy with an ultimatum — either he announce his intention to enter the Massachusetts primary or the Massachusetts delegation would leave Chicago and withdraw all its considerable support.

On the day of his Chicago speech, McCarthy was weighing Grossman's ultimatum when he received word that the Massachusetts State Democratic Committee that afternoon had overwhelmingly approved, by a 44–4 vote, a resolution supporting President Johnson and his Vietnam policy. Even though the resolution had been watered down by State Chairman Lester Hyman — a key Kennedy ally — so as not to force McCarthy's hand, McCarthy felt the vote was clear evidence that he would not receive a fair share of the delegates as Edward Kennedy had assured him only two days earlier. Therefore, in a news conference following his speech, McCarthy announced he was going to run in Massachusetts.

One of the people present when McCarthy reached that decision was Joseph Holsinger, chairman of the California Eleventh Congressional District Democratic party and later the head of McCarthy's northern California campaign. Holsinger was in McCarthy's room at the Sheraton Blackstone Hotel — the same hotel where Warren Harding's nomination was assured in the original "smoke-filled room" forty-eight years earlier — when Jerry Eller brought McCarthy the news of the Massachusetts State Democratic Committee's action. "This means Massachusetts isn't going to have a favorite son — Kennedy's failed to do it," Eller told McCarthy. Holsinger recalls that "McCarthy then got up and made a fist and shook it at Eller and me and he said, 'We've got them, we've got them!' I could tell from the conversations we had that day that McCarthy knew all along he was going to have to fight the Kennedys. But he figured he could get far enough in front so Kennedy couldn't catch him."

There was an even more important result of the Chicago conference, however. The most far-reaching decision of the McCarthy campaign and indeed of the entire 1968 presidential campaign, had its genesis in the Chicago meeting when two peace activists from New Hampshire, David Hoeh and Gerry Studds, urged McCarthy to reconsider his early judgment that the March 12 New Hampshire primary was not an important factor in his campaign strategy. Hoeh, a Dartmouth College faculty member long active in state politics, and Studds, a teacher at the exclusive St. Paul's Boys' School near Concord, both felt that McCarthy could do well in their state despite discouraging polls and the conventional wisdom that the predominantly Republican New Hampshire voters would support the war because of the large number of defense contractors in the state.

In response to their pleadings, McCarthy agreed to meet with a group of potential supporters after delivering a previously scheduled lecture on the country's housing problems in Bedford, New Hampshire, on December 14. About fifty people gathered in the living room of one of Hoeh's friends afterwards to beg McCarthy — or, as his name was pronounced in the local accent, "McCahty" — to enter their primary. Someone asked if taking a poll would help persuade him. "No, I don't think so," said McCarthy, "I think it would be very discouraging." The New Hampshire supporters insisted McCarthy could wage an effective campaign in their state in just fourteen days, but he still refused to give them a commitment. Although impressed by the deep feelings expressed at the meeting against the war and Johnson, McCarthy still fully intended to bypass New Hampshire and concentrate on the Massachusetts primary a week later. On the way back to the airport that night, McCarthy told writer David Halberstam of *Harper's* magazine that he probably would not run in New Hampshire. A despondent Hoeh sat listening in the back seat, but refused to give up. After McCarthy left, Hoeh sat down with Studds and drew up an optimistic memorandum which summarized their arguments for McCarthy's entry into New Hampshire and laid out a twelve day schedule that would give McCarthy maximum exposure in the state.

Although the Hoeh-Studds memorandum badly underestimated the cost of McCarthy's campaign ($55,000 as opposed to the more than $175,000 actually spent), it effectively made the point that McCarthy had much to gain and nothing to lose by coming into New Hampshire. "Given the general impression that it is a 'hawkish' state and a 'conservative' state — plus Senator McIntyre's [Democratic Senator Thomas McIntyre] extraordinary prediction that McCarthy would get 3,000 to 5,000 votes [i.e., less than 10 per cent], anything better than that can be hailed as a stunning performance (and we can do considerably better than that)." But Hoeh and Studds had set their sights high. Arguing that McCarthy could "reaffirm the seriousness of his national candidacy" by entering New Hampshire, they said a victory was now "within the realm of possibility" and declared, with ironic understatement, that such a victory "would have major national reprecussions." Wrapping up their memo with a plea for a prompt go-ahead, they sent it to Blair Clark, a fifty-year-old former New York newspaper publisher and broadcasting executive who had been appointed McCarthy's campaign manager on December 12 after writing McCarthy from London to offer a small donation and his services.

Clark, a mild-mannered, pipe-smoking man who fit perfectly into the historic pattern of unexciting and unexcitable McCarthy aides, was impressed by the Hoeh-Studds arguments. A Harvard classmate and friend of John F. Kennedy's, he had little experience in politics but had once published a paper in New Hampshire and was familiar with the state. He also had good contacts in wealthy Eastern social circles and was certain there would be no trouble financing a New Hampshire effort.

A few weeks later, when bad weather forced McCarthy to take a train to New York instead of flying, Clark went along and presented the Hoeh-Studds arguments to him in the dining car. Although many people later credited Clark with persuading McCarthy to take the step that would cause a revolution in American politics, he is modest about his role. "Some of the history books will say that I persuaded McCarthy to go into New Hampshire on a train journey from Washington to New York just before Christmas," Clark later said, "and they'll be wrong. I made the journey and put the case, but you don't persuade McCarthy to do things like that; he decides himself."

Still, it took McCarthy almost two more weeks of weighing the advantages and disadvantages to come to that decision. On January 2, just when his New Hampshire backers had given up hope, McCarthy sent Clark to meet with Hoeh at the Sheraton Wayfarer Motel on the outskirts of Manchester and alert him that McCarthy soon would announce his intention to enter New Hampshire. They were having dinner when Hoeh was paged for a phone call. He returned and jubilantly told Clark that McCarthy himself had authorized him to go ahead and announce his decision the next morning. Hoeh immediately passed the word to McCarthy supporters around the state and opened up a state headquarters in Concord in a dingy electrical supply store. The total McCarthy-for-President bankroll at the time was four hundred dollars, two hundred and fifty of which was donated by an uncle of Hoeh's wife.

McCarthy didn't return to New Hampshire until January 25, three weeks after his official entry, despite pleas from his New Hampshire supporters to come in earlier. In the meantime, the first faint signs appeared that his candidacy was not quite the impossible dream it seemed to be. A Gallup poll showed that if the election were held then, he would draw about twelve percent of the total, an impressive figure for a man still confused in much of the nation with the late Senator Joseph McCarthy. Evidence of concern about McCarthy's challenge of the president came from Democratic National Chairman John Bailey, who refused to even answer McCarthy's request to appear at the committee's convention planning session in Chicago on January 7 to explain why "many loyal Democrats believe as I do that the administration's course in Vietnam is dangerous and wrong." Bailey said there was no need for him to answer McCarthy because the committee didn't plan to discuss Vietnam, and added, "the Democratic National Convention is as good as over. It will be Lyndon Johnson again, and that's that."

Vice President Humphrey, who denied that he had been designated as the administration's chief stop-McCarthy spokesman, appeared at the California State Democratic Convention on January 13, in the middle of a six-day visit to the state by McCarthy, and spoke for more than an hour in an emotional defense of Johnson's Vietnam policy. The next day, McCarthy stood at the same podium and quietly accused Johnson — as he had accused Barry Goldwater in 1964 — of being unable to distinguish between "the pale horse of victory and the pale horse of death," and of allowing the "dead hand of John Foster Dulles" to guide his foreign policy. McCarthy's low-key speech, capped by the modest battle cry, "I ask you to stand with me in this reexamination and this attempt to rewrite Democratic foreign policy in 1968," caused dismay among would-be supporters. "I respect his intelligence," said one woman after hearing him talk, "but couldn't he pound the table a little?" When complaints about his phlegmatic style reached him, McCarthy cracked, "What did they expect me to do — tear down the wall around the White House?"

By mid-January, a loosely structured campaign organization was beginning to take shape, even though McCarthy had given little thought to the building of one. His standard reply when asked what he would do for for campaign finances and workers in the other primary states was, "We'll live off the land." McCarthy had run his past campaigns in Minnesota more or less out of his hip pocket in an outwardly disorganized manner but with such consistent success that a Minnesota party figure once remarked that "McCarthy's campaigns are run by the Holy Ghost." It was a way of saying that McCarthy made the basic strategy and policy decisions and let whoever wanted to take care of the essential organizational details. "The real problem," he declared in New Hampshire "is to get a good man to drive your car during the campaign."

The McCarthy campaign organization eventually became an administrative monstrosity, with no one ever really mastering its freewheeling development and byzantine intrigues. But at first, it was relatively simple and well-organized with Blair Clark setting up a national McCarthy-for-President headquarters — which McCarthy never visited — on the fifth floor of an office building two blocks from the White House. "We have sort of an ad hoc system here," Clark explained at the time in a comment that summarized the McCarthy organizational approach. "We don't have titles for anybody."

Although the McCarthy-for-President staff was young (five of Clark's seven top assistants were under thirty-three years old) and inexperienced (almost none of them had been on the inside of a national political campaign before), it had an oversupply of self confidence and dedication. Asked what his duties were, Sandy Frucher, Clark's twenty-three year old assistant, replied in all seriousness, "To help spark a revolution." The most important figure next to Clark was thirty year old Curtis Gans, a gaunt and competent political organizer who had worked with Lowenstein in organizing the Concerned Democrats and who was placed in charge of the search for delegates. Other key members of the national campaign staff were Press Secretary Seymour Hersh, thirty, an ex-Associated Press reporter who later broke the story of the My Lai massacre; Peter Barnes, twenty-five, an ex-*Newsweek* reporter who quit the staff of Senator Walter Mondale of Minnesota to do research and writing for McCarthy; and Sam Brown, twenty-four, a Harvard divinity student hired at the suggestion of McCarthy's daughter Mary as national coordinator of McCarthy's student army. Abigail McCarthy organized a women's volunteer mail-answering operation centered in the attic of the McCarthy home and later established in a nearby apartment building.

The first of many financial angels attracted to the McCarthy campaign was a wealthy San Francisco divorcee, June Degnan, who gave one of the first sizeable contributions ($5,000) to McCarthy and became chairman of his national finance committee. She would later make other substantial contributions, along with Clark; Martin Peretz, a wealthy young Harvard professor; Arnold Hiatt, a Boston shoe manufacturer and Howard Stein, president of the $2.1 billion Dreyfus Fund. Stein, onetime "boy wonder of Wall Street" who headed one of the most successful mutual funds in the country, promised to pay all the media costs in New Hampshire, and along with Hiatt, was ultimately responsible for raising several million dollars for McCarthy.[5]

McCarthy's first campaign visit to New Hampshire was a dismal flop by the usual political standards. He started off by posing uncomfortably in front of a bust of John F. Kennedy outside Nashua City Hall, where Kennedy had begun his campaign eight years earlier, and then went on a walking tour of Nashua's nearly deserted Main Street. Later in the day, an advance man who was to have arranged a stop outside a Manchester textile mill dis-

---

[5] McCarthy received an average of $1,000 a day in campaign contributions in the mail in December. The figure rose steadily until after the New Hampshire primary, when it leveled off at about $14,000 a day, according to Mrs. Degnan.

appeared and McCarthy had to stand around in the cold for half an hour waiting for the shift to change. When it did, only a handful of women walked by. Finally, someone pointed out it was a nonunion plant, and McCarthy muttered, "Well, that's enough of that," and left.

Nevertheless, McCarthy was almost ebullient when he spoke to seven hundred people at St. Anselm's College in Goffstown that evening. In full possession of his audience, which included black-robed Benedictine monks from the college, he told of his opposition to the war and how he had come to challenge Johnson. But he said he was "not so much challenging as suggesting, really, a change of course for America. . . . This can be, I think, an America again which is singing, an America which is full of confidence, which is full of trust, and which is full of hope. Not just an example to the world, but a genuine help to the world."

Slowly, imperceptibly, McCarthy's campaign began to gather momentum in the following weeks. "You fight from a low crouch," he said in the face of anxious advisers' criticism of his pedantic speeches and his refusal to attack Johnson more vigorously. "You wait for events. You let it come to you."

McCarthy didn't have to wait long for the first in a string of unexpected events that would transform him from a long-shot darkhorse into a bona fide contender. It happened far from the snow-covered granite hills of New Hampshire on January 31 as Communist troops launched a savage offensive during the Lunar New Year period called Tet. The seriousness of the Tet offensive soon became clear as Vietcong sappers briefly invaded the U.S. embassy compound in Saigon and bloody battles raged in the capitals of almost all of South Vietnam's forty-four provinces. Suddenly, millions of Americans began to question the efficacy of U.S. policy in Vietnam and the credibility of government statements about the progress of the war, the same questions McCarthy was raising.

Whatever the final military assessment of Tet — and it may never be clear who won — there was no question about its political impact. The Johnson administration had clearly lost the confidence of the people and McCarthy deftly exploited that loss of confidence. In early February, he reminded his listeners that the administration's repeated "hollow claims of programs and victories" in Vietnam had not proven accurate. "For the fact is that the enemy is bolder than ever, while we must steadily enlarge our own commitment. . . . Only a few months ago we were told that sixty-five percent of the population was secure. Now we know that even the American Embassy is not secure." (Asked whether the Tet offensive would win votes for him, McCarthy said, "Give it three weeks, time to sink in. By then it could make a difference.")

The Tet offensive and subsequent developments such as the leaked story that the administration was considering sending another 206,000 men to

Vietnam and the announcement that the draft had been increased and graduate deferments ended, changed McCarthy's New Hampshire campaign in a fundamental way. He had felt the sense of hopelessness and outrage at the war on college campuses over the past few months, and he was sure he could enlist students in his campaign just as he had done in his Senate campaigns when they helped with get-out-the-vote drives and other work. But only a handful of students had arrived in January, most of them from the Ivy League colleges and exclusive private schools in the Boston area who came on weekends out of curiosity or conviction to help the only man openly challenging a president whom they distrusted and disliked. The Tet offensive changed all that. Underscoring despair over the war, it sent first hundreds and then thousands of young people streaming into New Hampshire from as far away as the Carolinas and the Midwest until, in the first week of March, an estimated two thousand students were campaigning fulltime and as many as five thousand were present on weekends.[6]

McCarthy's student crusade was one of the most significant developments of the 1968 presidential campaign. It demolished the conventional political wisdom that a highly organized, efficient campaign could be put together only by professional planners. It made the country suddenly aware that alienated and uncommitted young people desperately wanted to revitalize political processes and were willing to give up long hair, unconventional dress and unorthodox behavior to do it. It proved to taciturn New Hampshirites and to millions of other Americans that young people in the words of a McCarthy campaign ad, had indeed "come back into the mainstream of American life," and that it was possible to bridge the generation gap after all.

Thanks to his unpaid volunteers, McCarthy's staff was able to mount a door-to-door canvassing operation that provided a personal McCarthy contact with more than half the homes in New Hampshire, including most of the state's 90,000 registered Democrats and 100,000 independent voters. The canvassers were turned loose only after rigorous inspection by their peers to make certain that the slogan "Neat and Clean for Gene" was adhered to. Some of the most brilliant young minds in the country were working sixteen hour days putting together a complex, well-organized canvassing and logistical operation that was so specialized it was able to translate McCarthy literature into French for New Hampshire's French-speaking population, or provide babysitting for voters while they went to the polls. "My campaign may not be organized at the top," said McCarthy, "but it is certainly tightly organized at the bottom."

While McCarthy benefited from the immense publicity given to a campaign that could harness the idealism and energy of young people, his own air of calm reason and lack of standard political rhetoric were helping him

---

[6] On the final weekend, McCarthy's headquarters had to turn away 2,500 volunteers, including a group ready to charter a plane from California.

portray an image of decency, integrity and good sense. He played ice hockey — a favorite New Hampshire sport — for twenty minutes with a group of Concord semipros, which New Hampshire voters were reminded of when his supporters distributed thousands of windshield ice scrapers showing him on skates and saying, "McCarthy Cuts the Ice." Actor Paul Newman led a phalanx of celebrities into the state to stump for McCarthy, winning at least a few converts among women voters by fixing his deep blue eyes on them and declaring, "I didn't come here to help Gene McCarthy. I need Gene McCarthy's help. The country needs it." McCarthy, whether traversing the state with Poet Robert Lowell at his side or staring down from billboards bearing the slogan, "New Hampshire Can Bring America Back To Its Senses," was becoming a familiar figure to New Hampshire voters.

Still, without the ineptness of the local Democratic organization — an ineptness bred by the lack of any firm direction from the White House — McCarthy might have been forced to go back to being just the senior senator from Minnesota after March 12. The New Hampshire Johnson-for-President organization, headed by Governor John King, Senator Thomas McIntyre and Johnson's campaign manager, Bernard Boutin, was well financed and seemed a formidable political organization. But because of McCarthy's underdog status in both private and public polls (an Elmo Roper poll published in *Time* magazine in the last week of February showed McCarthy getting only 11 percent of the vote while a White House poll taken about the same time showed him getting 18 percent), the King-Boutin-McIntyre forces made several serious tactical errors. First, they permitted forty-five names to be placed on the ballot as pro-Johnson candidates for the state's twenty-four national convention delegate positions, while McCarthy strategists limited their candidates to exactly twenty-four, enabling McCarthy supporters to win all but four of the delegates seats.

A much more serious blunder was Boutin's ill-advised plan — carried out with consent of White House Aide Marvin Watson — to send numbered pledge cards to registered Democrats asking for a pledge of support for Johnson. They were asked to fill out the three-part cards, keep one part as a reminder and send the other two parts back to the state committee, which would forward one part to the White House. McCarthy promptly denounced the cards as an infringement on the right of a secret ballot, saying, "It's not at all inconsistent with administration policy to kind of put a brand on people." McCarthy's advisers kept the issue alive throughout the campaign — even though the cards mysteriously disappeared in the face of public opposition — by reproducing the pledge cards on a campaign poster under the slogan, "You Don't Have to Sign Anything to Vote for Gene McCarthy." The pledge cards also gave McCarthy the perfect opportunity to expand his campaign from its antiwar base to the broader question of

Johnson's concept of the presidency, particularly the issue of the credibility gap.

Finally, in the closing days of the campaign as it became apparent McCarthy was running much stronger than expected (Michigan Governor George Romney dropped out of the Republican primary on February 28, leaving McCarthy the only remaining underdog in the primary), the Johnson loyalists began to show signs of panic. King publicly labeled McCarthy "a champion of appeasement and surrender" and predicted in newspaper and radio ads that any significant vote for him "would be greeted by cheers in Hanoi." On the day before the election, McIntyre attacked McCarthy's proposal for selective conscientious objection to the draft and amnesty for persons fleeing the country to avoid the draft as a plan that would "honor draft dodgers and deserters." The crudity of the attacks, coupled with radio spots urging people not to vote for "fuzzy thinking and surrender," offended many voters' sense of fairness and caused a small wave of sympathy for McCarthy.[7]

On March 5, one week before the New Hampshire primary, two important out-of-state political events added to McCarthy's momentum. In his home state of Minnesota, McCarthy's followers, using tactics similar to those that helped him take over the Ramsey County Democratic Farmer Labor party twenty years earlier, packed precinct caucuses and wrestled control from Johnson-Humphrey regulars in three of the state's five Congressional districts in what was actually the nation's first significant expression of anti-administration sentiment.[8]

At the same time in next-door Massachusetts, McCarthy picked up his first convention delegates as President Johnson waited until the last minute before refusing to permit his name to be placed on the ballot for the April 30 primary. Since Massachusetts Democrats also refused to file anyone as a stand-in for Johnson and the law provided that all delegates elected in the primary were bound to cast a first ballot vote for the presidential candidate with the highest vote in the primary, it gave McCarthy seventy-two first ballot votes. It also provided a tremendous psychological boost to his New Hampshire campaign by showing that his candidacy was having an effect on Johnson's actions.[9]

[7] William Loeb's militantly right-wing newspaper, the Manchester *Union-Leader*, apparently recognized a kindred spirit in King. It editorially applauded him for indulging in the "the right brand of McCarthyism." But on the Senate floor, South Dakota Democrat George McGovern charged that the King ads were the "tactics of Hitler's Germany and Stalin's Russia."

[8] Among those ousted from precinct offices were Humphrey's son and his son-in-law Bruce Solomonson.

[9] A third important development took place late on the evening of March 5 in California, where nearly five hundred parties had been organized to get the 13,746 signatures necessary for placing McCarthy's name on the ballot for the June 4 primary. Since the candidate who first filed the necessary number of signatures had his name

For the last two days before the election every major radio station in New Hampshire played a spot each half hour in which a calm voice said, "Think how you would feel to wake up Wednesday morning to find out that Gene McCarthy had won the New Hampshire primary — to find out that New Hampshire had changed the course of American politics." When the election returns were in on the snowy election day, the first thing had not happened but the second had. McCarthy got 42 percent of the Democratic vote compared to Johnson's 49, and when the Republican write-in vote for both men was counted, McCarthy came within 230 votes of defeating Johnson. The vote was not, however, so much a repudiation of the war as it was of Johnson himself. An NBC poll taken just after the primary showed that more than half of the Democrats questioned did not even know where McCarthy stood on the war issue.

Nevertheless, New Hampshire had indeed demonstrated Johnson's vulnerability and had instantly transformed McCarthy from a hopeless underdog into a serious challenger of the president. It was a triumphant moment for McCarthy and the students who had been a central feature of his campaign and he acknowledged their contribution in an impromptu midnight victory speech at the Sheraton-Wayfarer Motel.

"People have remarked that this campaign has brought young people back into the system," he said as his glowing face reflected the electric fervor of his cheering supporters. "But it's the other way around: The young people have brought the country back into the system."

---

placed at the top of the ballot, McCarthy supporters held the parties late in the evening, and began collecting signatures in the first minutes of March 6, the earliest date allowed under the law. By the next morning, McCarthy had 28,000 signatures and won the top spot on the ballot.

CHAPTER XV

THE POLITICS OF PERSONALITY —
MC CARTHY vs. KENNEDY

*Bobby's campaign is like a grass
fire — it will just burn off the surface. Mine
is like a fire in a peat bog. It will hold on
for six months.*
Eugene McCarthy in a 1968 interview.

Eugene McCarthy was a happy man as his Northeast Airlines Boeing 727 sliced through the cold, clear New England sky on the morning after the New Hampshire primary. Still elated from his stunning show of strength and savoring the headline in the Boston *Globe* that lay in his lap ("McCarthy's N.H. Dream Becomes LBJ Nightmare"), he accepted the congratulations of newsmen and other passengers with a satisfied grin. "Well, I guess I've finally established my identity," he told one well-wisher. "That's really what I was doing up there." [1]

McCarthy hardly seemed to notice that the plane was buffeted by turbulence as it neared the end of its Boston-to-Washington run and prepared to land at Washington's National Airport. But his euphoric mood quickly vanished as the plane taxied to a halt and aide Jerry Eller bounded up the steps past the descending passengers and said urgently, "Let's talk." The two men sat down and Eller said, "Bobby wants to see you — he's going to tell you he's going." Then Eller handed McCarthy a hastily torn carbon copy from a news ticker. McCarthy's jaw muscles tightened as he read that Kennedy was "reassessing my position as to whether I'll run against President Johnson."

[1] One of the passengers was Senator Thomas McIntyre, the New Hampshire Democrat who had attacked McCarthy's patriotism during the closing days of the primary campaign. When he offered his congratulations, McCarthy replied in an icy voice, "Thanks, Tom . . . I'm surprised to see you riding first class this morning."

McCarthy walked off the plane into a herd of clamoring newsmen. Most of the questions were about Kennedy's imminent candidacy and McCarthy bit off his answers. What did he think of Kennedy's reassessment? "Well, that's something you should ask him." Would he voluntarily step aside if Kennedy came in? "It might not be voluntary." Would he welcome Kennedy into the race? "Well, I don't know. It's a little bit crowded now." On the ride to his Senate office, McCarthy noticed that the stories of Kennedy's "reassessment" had already replaced the New Hampshire primary outcome as the number one story in the early editions of the Washington afternoon papers, and he commented bitterly, "He wouldn't even let me have my day of celebration, would he?"

Shortly after McCarthy arrived at his office, Kennedy called again, and McCarthy arranged to meet him on the fourth floor of the Old Senate Office Building late that afternoon in Edward Kennedy's office on the same floor as McCarthy's. To avoid the reporters clustered outside his door, McCarthy ducked into the Senate gymnasium in the basement of the building, then went out a back door and doubled back to Edward Kennedy's office where Robert Kennedy was waiting. The two men talked alone for about twenty minutes, the longest conversation they'd ever had, but it was a strange, strained visit punctuated by periods of cool silence. "What was not said at the meeting was more important that what was said," McCarthy later commented, referring to the fact that Kennedy never specifically stated his intention to run. However, Kennedy left little doubt about his intentions, and spent most of the session talking about the reasons for his "reassessment." He explained that he had held back before for fear of splitting the party, but that New Hampshire had shown the party was already badly split. McCarthy said Kennedy could do what he wanted but that it would have no effect on his own plans. He added that while he did not think he could win the nomination, just in case he did and was elected president, he only wanted to serve one term, and hinted that Kennedy might be wise to wait until 1972. The meeting ended as uncomfortably as it began, and McCarthy emerged with another sardonic quip: "Now, at least three people in Washington are reconsidering their candidacy."

McCarthy was determined not to let Kennedy shoulder him aside. On the following day, he announced that he was entering two more primaries — Indiana and South Dakota — and then flew off to Wisconsin to begin the final push for that state's April 2 primary. He had refused Kennedy's offer of help in Wisconsin, where it was too late for Kennedy to file, and had rejected out of hand all suggestions of a possible accommodation with him.[2] However, unknown to McCarthy, several of his advisers were ex-

___

[2] McCarthy also dropped the references to John F. Kennedy that had dotted his speeches before Robert Kennedy entered the race.

ploring a scheme to divide up the primaries — in order to register the largest possible combined vote against Johnson and the war — and have the two contenders meet in a winner-take-all confrontation in the June 4 California primary.

The plan, developed in the best tradition of the old politics that McCarthy regarded with such disdain, was the brainchild of Richard Goodwin and McCarthy National Organizer Curtis Gans, who felt a greater loyalty to the antiwar cause than to any candidate. They put their plan into effect on Friday, March 15, the day before Kennedy was scheduled to announce his candidacy. Goodwin, traveling with McCarthy in Wisconsin, talked to Edward Kennedy, who was anxious to secure a statement of cooperation with McCarthy that could be used in his brother's announcement.

Gans talked to Blair Clark, who reached McCarthy by phone in Sheyboygan and arranged a secret meeting between him and Edward Kennedy that evening in Green Bay. Kennedy, Gans and Clark then flew by commercial airliner to Chicago but missed their connecting flight to Green Bay and had to charter a Lear jet — using Clark's personal credit card. They arrived in Green Bay well after midnight, but McCarthy, tired of waiting for his visitors, had gone to bed. He was awakened sometime after one o'clock by his daughter Mary, who told him Kennedy was at a nearby hotel and wanted to see him.

Kennedy arrived at McCarthy's suite at 2:30 A.M. and the two men spent thirty-five minutes in a conversation in which Kennedy did most of the talking. A roomful of witnesses, including Abigail and Mary McCarthy, Jerry Eller, Goodwin, Gans, Clark, and Sam Brown looked on. Kennedy had brought along a reconciliation statement that he hoped McCarthy would agree to, but he never got a chance to take it out of his briefcase. The meeting ended with Kennedy telling McCarthy that his brother planned to announce the next morning and McCarthy reiterating that the announcement would cause no change in his own plans. A weary Kennedy flew back to Washington and arrived at his brother's home at daybreak to announce that the Green Bay summit meeting had turned out to be nothing more than a "courtesy call," because the compromise plan had been vetoed by Mrs. McCarthy. "Abigail said no," Kennedy declared.

Mrs. McCarthy doesn't accept Kennedy's version. "I couldn't kill it because I didn't know what they were doing," she later explained. "The only reason Mary and I were there was because Gene wouldn't get up. . . . Mary and I were in Green Bay campaigning and Gene showed up and we thought he had come to have dinner with us. Then he went to bed and we were still up when someone said that Teddy was here to see Gene. I got worried because I thought our whole staff had gone over to Bobby, but I didn't say that to anybody. . . . Mary finally got Gene to get up — he wouldn't at first. I kept asking people what was going on and Curtis Gans just kept saying, 'The common enemy is Johnson!' "

Less than six hours after Kennedy left his room, McCarthy was sitting in a Green Bay television studio watching on a TV set as Robert Kennedy announced his candidacy in the same spot where McCarthy had announced 106 days earlier. It was a defensive speech, designed to blunt criticism that his candidacy was the result of a personal struggle with Johnson or a ruthless attempt to push McCarthy aside. Kennedy said his brother had made it clear to McCarthy "that my candidacy would not be in opposition to his, but in harmony." A cynical smile flickered over McCarthy's taut face as Kennedy lauded him for his "remarkable victory" in New Hampshire and again as Kennedy assured skeptical reporters that his candidacy would "broaden" rather than narrow the protest against Johnson's policies.

As soon as Kennedy was through, McCarthy went on the air himself. He was tough, almost openly aggressive, as David Schoumacher of CBS quizzed him about a possible "deal" with Kennedy. "I'm not really prepared to deal with anybody . . .," said McCarthy. "I committed myself to a group of young people and, I thought, a rather idealistic group of adults in American society . . . I'll run as hard as I can in every primary and stand as firm as I can at the convention and then, if I find that I can't win, I will say to my delegates: You're free people, go wherever you want and make the best judgment that you can make."

McCarthy drew a scornful comparison between Kennedy and himself as he reminded viewers that he had raised "this challenge against the Johnson administration at a time when it seemed to me a lot of other politicians were afraid to come down onto the playing field. They were willing to stay up on the mountains and light signal fires and bonfires and dance in the light of the moon, but none of them came down. They weren't even coming in from outside, just throwing a message over the fence." Even with Kennedy in the race, McCarthy boasted, "I'm still the best potential president in the field." At a news conference later that day, he was even more pugnacious: "I don't need a stalking horse at this point. We don't need money. We don't need organization. I just need running room."

McCarthy was justified in not being worried about money or organization in Wisconsin. By the time he made his first campaign trip to the state, an army of nearly three thousand adults led by Donald Peterson, an Eau Claire frozen pizza company executive, and Ted Warshafsky, a Milwaukee attorney, and others had been busy for weeks raising money and organizing McCarthy-for-President offices around the state. Almost $200,000 had been raised, and student and women's groups — soon to be headed by Abigail McCarthy — had been established as McCarthy's Wisconsin supporters, unable to obtain financial and organizational help from Blair Clark or Mc-

Carthy himself in the first months of his candidacy, went ahead on their own.

The Wisconsin people were so well organized, in fact, that frictions developed when the national staff, cocky and flushed with victory after New Hampshire, moved in and acted as though the Wisconsin organization didn't exist. Still, the two factions were able to absorb and effectively use the thousands of students who flocked to Wisconsin in the closing weeks of the primary campaign.

McCarthy's performance in New Hampshire and Kennedy's announcement triggered a quantum jump in campaign contributions. The first mail delivery to the McCarthy-for-President headquarters on the Monday after Kennedy's announcement brought 917 individual donations totaling $19,943, and small contributions for the rest of March continued to pour in at about twice the $8,000 daily average just before New Hampshire. In addition to the money raised by McCarthy supporters at the local level, Howard Stein and other key McCarthy moneymen raised major sums in the business community.[3] By the end of the Wisconsin campaign, the McCarthy forces had spent $600,000, or more than six times the pro-Johnson camp.

Mrs. June Oppen Degnan, the chairman of McCarthy's national finance committee, whose $5,000 check was his first major contribution, remembers the fantastic growth in individual donations as the campaign progressed. "The flow charts were fascinating to watch. The contributions went up by a geometrical progression from about $30,000 in December to $64,000 in January and so on, doubling each month, and of course the states were taking in money too." She recalls that before New Hampshire, "money was very hard to get and people gave out of desperation, but after New Hampshire, people thought they might have a winner and they gave in increasing amounts. Once a person gave, you could count on him to give three or four times more." Interestingly, Mrs. Degnan, estimates that about a third of the mail contributions came from Republicans and independents, many of whom voted for Barry Goldwater in 1964. "You could tell from the letters that the response to McCarthy was a very special one. The key words were always 'honest' and 'courageous.' "[4]

Although a January Gallup Poll showed McCarthy getting only twelve

[3] McCarthy fund raisers were greatly helped by an article in *Fortune* magazine ("Business Versus Bobby Kennedy") that appeared at the time of Kennedy's announcement. The article probed the attitude of the U.S. business community and found "agreement that Kennedy is the one public figure who could produce an almost united front of business opposition."

[4] Mrs. Degnan's most profitable list of potential contributions was that of the President's Club, the $1,000-a-year fund raising gimmick started by President Kennedy and continued by Johnson. "It was a beautiful list," says Mrs. Degnan. "There were really angry people on it." Another rewarding source of contributions was the 145,000-name subscription list of *Ramparts* magazine which Mrs. Degnan obtained because she was director of the magazine.

percent of the Wisconsin vote, he considered the state tailor-made for his candidacy and fully expected it to provide him with his first primary victory. In fact, until Kennedy entered, McCarthy felt that the state that had been a graveyard for Hubert Humphrey's presidential hopes in 1960 could give him the momentum to sweep most of the remaining primaries and to go to the Democratic National Convention as the leading candidate. In addition to having a name familiar to Wisconsin voters, McCarthy knew that the state's independent, progressive tradition, which was similar to Minnesota's, and the existence of strong antiwar sentiment, particularly among the liberal academic community at the University of Wisconsin in Madison, would work to his advantage. Finally, an important technical point in his favor was the fact that Wisconsin law allowed Republicans to "cross over" and vote in the Democratic primary. The prospect of liberal Republicans crossing over in large numbers to embarrass Johnson or express opposition to the war increased greatly when George Romney dropped out of the race and New York Governor Nelson Rockefeller announced he would not enter.

There had been virtually no pro-Johnson activity in Wisconsin before the New Hampshire primary as state party officials badly misread McCarthy's growing strength. "The only question is whether he can produce more than a hundred and fifty thousand votes," State Democratic Chairman Richard Cudahy declared in February. However, after New Hampshire, five top administration officials, including McCarthy's two fellow Minnesotans, Vice President Humphrey and Agriculture Secretary Orville Freeman, made repeated visits to Wisconsin to combat McCarthy's surging primary campaign. Freeman, who a few months earlier had predicted that McCarthy's candidacy "will be a very small footnote if a footnote at all, in history," was loudly heckled during an appearance at the University of Wisconsin, while Humphrey was greeted by disappointingly small crowds in the working class neighborhoods on Milwaukee's South Side where Johnson was considered strongest.

While Humphrey and other administration loyalists were feeling the sting of Johnson's unpopularity, McCarthy for the first time showed that he considered himself a serious contender for the presidency. In a speech in Milwaukee on March 23, and again at a tumultuous rally before 18,000 persons at Madison two days later, he made clear that the presidency was no longer an impossible dream in his mind:

> This movement of which you are a part, and which I, in a limited way, personify now by interaction of many circumstances, is not a movement which is carrying on a simple educational program in this country, as it was suggested we were going to do when we started. We are not really out trying to raise an issue for the attention of the people of this nation, because the issue has been raised and the people of this nation are aware of what that issue is. What we are doing is laying down a challenge to control the presidency of the United States of America.

McCarthy, who later said he felt the spirit of the campaign at this time "as I had never felt it before," stressed his view of the presidency as an office men should not aspire to because of personal ambition, the urging of party leaders or by "succession" — a reference to Kennedy. Instead, echoing his nominating speech for Adlai Stevenson eight years earlier, McCarthy said he preferred leaders sought out by the people over those who seek power for themselves. "The seeking of me as a candidate came like the dew in the night," said McCarthy. "It was rather gentle, I must say, soft, but there were signs in the morning that something had happened during the night, and so here I am."

Finally, he offered a view of the presidency radically different from that of any other presidential candidate in modern American history. A president, said McCarthy, should not only be able to sense the needs and aspirations of the country and accept the limitations of his power, but he also "should understand that this country does not so much need leadership, because the potential for leadership in a free country must exist in every man and every woman. He must be prepared to be a kind of channel for those desires and those aspirations, perhaps giving some direction to the movement of the country largely by the way of setting people free." [5] McCarthy expanded on the same idea of individual accountability and responsibility in a speech in Milwaukee a few days later. "If there is one central theme to my campaign, it is the president's duty to liberate individuals so they may determine their own lives, to restore that mastery and power over individual life and social enterprise which has been so seriously eroded by the growing impersonality of our society and by the misuse of central power."

McCarthy's unorthodox view of the presidency as an office that should be used not for exercising power but for sharing it so people could control their own destinies may have run counter to conventional thinking, but it fit perfectly into the scheme of things as far as his followers were concerned. When reporters asked Parker Donham, a twenty-three year old Harvard student who dropped out of school to work on the campaign, whether he wanted a Cabinet post if McCarthy was elected president, he replied, "Hell no, I just want to be chairman of my local draft board."

Not all of McCarthy's aides were as pleased with their leader as Donham, however. On March 25, at the beginning of the final week of the Wisconsin campaign, about forty young staff people gathered in the Milwaukee hotel room of Curtis Gans and held an angry discussion that centered around the lack of a special effort by McCarthy in Milwaukee's black ghetto. Although

---

[5] In the Milwaukee speech, McCarthy also publicly referred to his fondness for poetry for the first time in the campaign. He introduced his friend, Poet Robert Lowell, and concluded with the Walt Whitman passage that was to become a familiar theme during the campaign: "Poets to come, and orators to come, and singers, all of you who are to come . . . arouse, arouse, for you must justify me; you must answer."

the meeting was a rather trivial incident in an otherwise smoothly running operation, it became a well-publicized turning point in the campaign when McCarthy's press secretary, Seymour Hersh, and his assistant, Mary Lou Oates, resigned the next day for what they said were "personal reasons." Details of the meeting were leaked to the New York *Times* and the resulting story that the two aides resigned because of dissatisfaction with McCarthy's position on civil rights plagued him throughout the rest of the primaries.

The staff dispute centered around the contention that McCarthy should speak more forcefully on civil rights matters and specifically, that he should make an appeal for the Negro vote in Milwaukee, a city weary of long open housing demonstrations led by the militant white priest, Father James Groppi. Gans and Richard Goodwin argued at the meeting that this would cost McCarthy votes among Milwaukee's heavy working class population. Besides, they pointed out, McCarthy had adequately defined his civil rights position in other speeches and in his campaign advertising. But other aides argued that it was important to lay the groundwork to compete for the black vote with Kennedy in the coming primaries. Gans' pragmatic view won out as the meeting broke up amid cries of "white racist" and "back to the Resistance!" Press questions about the meeting drew a testy response from McCarthy. He said he felt that he had made a strong enough case for civil rights and that "if there is some dispute with how they want me to campaign, they know this [approach] has characterized my campaign from the beginning." McCarthy was piqued when reporters suggested that the resignations might indicate deeper staff problems. "Most of you fellows are frustrated campaign managers," McCarthy said snappishly. "I don't think we have problems of organization. This is one of the things the press has built up. . . . We have one of the best organized campaigns in the history of the country at the lower level, which is where it is important."

Nevertheless, McCarthy was troubled by the tempest stirred up by the Hersh-Oates resignations. " I couldn't . . . say anything that would do as much damage as that story has done," he lamented privately. He responded to the growing criticism by delivering a civil rights speech, essentially unchanged from one he had given in New Hampshire — a state with no black ghettos — and which he was to give throughout the 1968 campaign. And he went for a five-mile walking tour through Milwaukee's black and Polish neighborhoods, mostly for the benefit of his staff and the press.

It was the press, in fact that McCarthy blamed — along with Kennedy's entry — for making an issue out of the infrequency of his visits to the ghetto. The press, he told the Boston *Globe* after the campaign was over, "has kind of set patterns they follow in politics, and they keep trying to put you into it. Like walking in the ghettos, which was all press stuff. It didn't make any difference. . . . This was the kind of thing that was entirely irrelevant to the campaign against Johnson, the question of who could get the biggest crowd in the ghetto. . . . About once a week . . . a guy didn't know what to write, he'd say Senator McCarthy was in Chicago, he went through Chicago today and he didn't go into the ghetto area. . . . Well, it was pointless . . . I couldn't get the Negro votes away from Bobby Kennedy. I could have moved into the ghettos and stayed in them the whole campaign."

The internal problems of the campaign had little effect on Wisconsin voters, however. On March 30, three days before the election, a McCarthy canvass showed him getting sixty-three percent of the vote, enough, he was certain, that his candidacy would acquire plausibility in Wisconsin. On the next day, Sunday, March 31, McCarthy went to church with his family and then started out on his last full day of campaigning before the primary two days later. "I don't wish to sound overconfident," he said at the first of three college campuses he appeared at that day, "but I think the test is pretty much between me and Nixon now."

Despite his confident words, McCarthy possessed a nagging feeling that President Johnson might try to precipitate a last-minute shift of votes by a dramatic announcement in his nationally televised broadcast that evening. When McCarthy arrived at Carroll College, just outside of Milwaukee, for his last speech of the Wisconsin campaign, he watched the beginning of Johnson's speech before starting his own. Twenty minutes later, reporters and students were swarming over the stage and voices were shouting at McCarthy, "He quit! Johnson quit! He's not running!"

McCarthy, looking stunned, responded with classic understatement. "It changes the political picture in the United States for 1968."

After his own speech, McCarthy left immediately for his Milwaukee hotel while his wife, Abigail, who remained at the hotel to watch the president's speech, called the White House a few minutes after the speech ended and reached the president. She assured Johnson that her husband's campaign, which she had opposed at first because of her friendship with Mrs. Johnson, had been based on principle and not personal feeling and she expressed the hope that they could remain friends. Johnson was gracious and told her, "No man can stand in the way of history," but when he put Lady Bird on the phone, the conversation turned cool. When McCarthy arrived, he was composed and relaxed, and was in no hurry to talk to the television correspondents clamoring outside his door. "Just tell the TV stations to put on a little music until I get there. Or maybe they should read a little poetry. This is a night for reading poetry — maybe a little Yeats." Although elated by Johnson's action, McCarthy had some reservations as well. "I feel as if I've been tracking a tiger through long jungle grass, and all of a sudden he rolls over and he's stuffed," he quipped.

When he finally did talk to newsmen, McCarthy was generous in his judgment of the President's action. He said Johnson "now has cleared the way for the reconciliation of our people . . . and for a redefinition of the purpose of the American nation." But McCarthy emphasized that Johnson's decision would not cause any change in his plans, nor would it change his attitude toward Robert Kennedy. "I have not been seeking a knock-down, drag-out battle with him up to this point; on the other hand, I have not been seeking an accommodation . . . I really had just begun to adjust to the entrance of Senator Kennedy. Now I think I will remain quiet for a while until we see whether there are any other entries. Then we will reassess our position." [6]

With Johnson's withdrawal, the result of the Wisconsin vote was anticlimactic and its meaning blurred. A McCarthy telephone poll on Monday showed a seven percent dropoff from the sixty-three percent predicted in the poll taken two days earlier, and the final count coincided with those figures. In the last election of Lyndon Johnson's thirty-seven years in public office, he was defeated by McCarthy, 412,160 votes to 252,696, or 56.2 percent to 34.6 percent of the Democratic vote. The man who had helped smooth McCarthy's way in the Senate and who had humiliated him at Atlantic City in 1964 was now free to devote all his time and energy to ending the war that had destroyed him politically.

From the outset of his campaign, McCarthy had looked to Wisconsin to give him his first clear-cut victory over Johnson. But just as he had not expected Kennedy to enter the race when he did, neither did he expect Johnson to pull out so early. "McCarthy had an absolute scenario but it kept getting upset," says Gerald Hill, the San Francisco attorney who was instrumental in getting McCarthy to run. "He counted on Johnson staying in through the California primary and beating him in Oregon and California. California was the key. Johnson would quit and try to throw it to Humphrey. At that point, Bobby would get in. McCarthy figured Bobby wouldn't get in until Johnson got out and Johnson would get out after he lost California. The last line of McCarthy's scenario had the convention deadlocked over him, Hubert and Bobby. Hubert wouldn't be able to make it and he would be taken out by Johnson and Daley and the boys who say it's all over, and then Johnson would have to decide, who does he hate more, Bobby or Gene? That's one of the reasons McCarthy got so upset with Al Lowenstein's speech at Chicago. He wanted to sneak up on Johnson and not attack him personally."

Even before Johnson's withdrawal, McCarthy sensed the fundamental change that Kennedy's entry would cause in his carefully planned scenario. In an interview with *U.S. News and World Report* published the week before the Wisconsin primary, McCarthy said Kennedy's candidacy prob-

[6] As for the likelihood that Vice President Humphrey would now become a candidate, McCarthy said he wasn't certain, "but I think if you look closely, you might see a slight cloud on the horizon tomorrow morning."

ably would result in a more divisive campaign centering on personality rather than issues:

> I'm of the opinion that our being in the same primary is not really a particularly helpful way to make the case. It could be divisive. The split that would have developed in the Johnson-McCarthy contest was on issues and I think could pretty well have been healed. But in the case of the Kennedy-McCarthy contest, a division on personality may take place, which may cause people to leave us and not come back. Senator Kennedy's challenge to me gets down to two questions: Can he win more easily than I can? Or is he a better man somehow — unrelated to the issue. Usually that kind of contest becomes somewhat personal.

McCarthy had correctly forecast the tone of the campaign that he and Kennedy would wage against each other. Johnson's withdrawal and the simultaneous announcement of a bombing halt and new peace negotiations took away McCarthy's two most compelling issues and left him engaged in an increasingly bitter personality contest with an opponent he neither liked nor respected. At the same time, McCarthy was certain that Hubert Humphrey now would stake his claim as Johnson's political heir, leaving McCarthy, as he put it, like a race horse that finds a fresh rival waiting after each lap. In fact, the day after the Wisconsin primary, McCarthy spent most of his time telephoning Democratic party leaders around the country asking them to hold off on committing themselves to Kennedy or Humphrey. It was the first and only time he would make such an appeal during the entire campaign, but it was an indication that his campaign was beginning to change as he prepared for his first head-to-head battle with Kennedy in the Indiana primary.

The three pivotal events in the McCarthy campaign had been the Tet offensive, his own surprising showing in New Hampshire, and Lyndon Johnson's withdrawal. On April 4, it was marked by a fourth event — Martin Luther King's assassination. McCarthy was in California when he received the news. Meeting with a group of labor leaders at the San Francisco Hilton Hotel, he asked for a minute of silence and then went to his room and drafted a statement saying that "all people, especially Americans, have lost a man of peace."[7] Although he initially planned not to attend the funeral because he did not know King well, McCarthy was persuaded by advisers that it would be politically unwise for him not to attend and he did, taking a seat directly behind Robert Kennedy.

[7] Abigail McCarthy was sitting in the living room of the McCarthy home across the street from the Washington Cathedral when she heard the Cathedral bells tolling. Although she had not heard of King's death, she sensed intuitively that something had happened to him. "It's the only time in my life I really had ESP," she later recalled. A longtime friend of Mrs. King's, Mrs. McCarthy stopped in Atlanta to see her while flying to Florida to recuperate from a virus infection acquired during the Indiana primary. The visit was never made public because Mrs. McCarthy felt it would look like she was doing it for political purposes.

McCarthy's reluctance to attend the King funeral was consistent with his cerebral approach to emotional issues and events, but it highlighted his lack of identification with blacks and other minority groups and his stubborn refusal to make a special appeal to minority groups. McCarthy's unemotional sytle contrasted sharply and almost always unfavorably in the eyes of blacks with Kennedy's passionately stated feelings about racial injustice, and caused many blacks to feel he was indifferent to their plight. "Bobby had all the moves, talked their language," says Gerald Hill, "but McCarthy still talked the lingo of the 1940's liberal. It's a wonder he didn't call them 'colored.' " McCarthy compounded the problem by adopting an uncompromising attitude when challenged on his civil rights record, which was solid but unspectacular. The gap between McCarthy and the black community was never better illustrated than when he appeared at predominantly-black Howard University and suggested that blacks could examine his record if they wanted to know what he had done for them. "Record hell," shouted a man in the audience. "Tell us what you *feel*."

McCarthy seemed determined to continue his experiment of running a presidential campaign that completely rejected the element of emotion. However, he reiterated his views on civil rights in a speech at Boston University on April 11, after resuming his campaign following King's death. Although the speech was billed as a major civil rights address, a shift in his campaign strategy and a tacit admission that he had not devoted enough attention to the subject, he had expressed the central thesis of the speech, that black Americans were kind of domestic colonial people, in a speech at Hartford, Connecticut, only the day before King's death. In his Boston University speech, McCarthy made a remarkable statement for a liberal Democratic presidential candidate — that all the landmark civil rights legislation passed by Congress in recent years had done little to alleviate the social and economic conditions at the root of the ghetto dweller's plight. He called for "a whole new set of civil rights" that included the right to a decent job, home, medical care and education.[8]

But his proposals to realize these goals were hardly remarkable — a guaranteed annual income and major new federally subsidized health insurance, education and housing programs. McCarthy later expanded his "domestic colony" theme while criticizing Kennedy's emphasis on rebuilding ghettos through private enterprise, declaring that such privately financed programs amount to a kind of apartheid and "can easily become paternalism."

Despite the somber mood of the country in the wake of King's death and the widespread civil disorders triggered by it, McCarthy was suprisingly

[8] McCarthy's four civil rights were not a new idea. He patterned them after similar points in Franklin Roosevelt's 1944 State of the Union address and had used variations of the idea in speeches since his early days in Congress.

sanguine. "I sense a new flow of confidence in America, a new sense of understanding and of common purpose," he declared in Boston. McCarthy's sense of optimism reflected his buoyant state of mind after McCarthy supporters did surprisingly well the day before in Connecticut when they uncovered an election law provision that allowed them to force primaries in thirty cities and towns to elect delegates to the state convention. The McCarthy forces got forty-four percent of the vote and dealt an embarrassing setback to State Democratic Chairman John Bailey, who was also National Democratic Chairman.

A second and even more significant test of the party processes that raised McCarthy's hopes for the coming primary battles with Kennedy came on April 23, when McCarthy received 428,259 or 71.6 percent of the vote in the Pennsylvania primary. McCarthy had hesitated to enter Pennsylvania because the primary was a non-binding "popularity contest" in which the presidential preference vote had no bearing on the selection of delegates. But his supporters flooded the ballot with McCarthy pledged delegates who agreed to support the top McCarthy candidates for the four delegate seats elected in each Congressional district. They won nearly a fifth of the total delegate seats.

The events in Connecticut and Pennsylvania boosted McCarthy's spirits as he prepared for his first head-on confrontation with Kennedy in the May 7 Indiana primary. He hoped Indiana would provide convincing proof that the phrase which had become the theme of his campaign — "the new politics" — was indeed an important new fact of American political life. He defined the phrase in the context of his campaign when he said, on one of his first visits to Indiana, that 1968 was destined to be a year "of the people of this country so far as politics is concerned, not of political leadership, not of organized politics, but a politics of participation and a politics of personal response on the part of the citizens of this country." It was, he said, a politics "which indicates a basic confidence in American democracy, a genuine hope in the future, and fundamental to all this a willingness to use reason and knowledge which are the only instruments we have by which we can give direction to life and history; to use these also as instruments to make important political decisions."

At the same time, however, McCarthy made it clear that the new politics wasn't really new but actually had its roots in the American Revolution. Using language virtually identical to that which would be ridiculed as inappropriate when Hubert Humphrey used it in announcing his candidacy five days later, McCarthy said on April 22 in Cleveland:

> It is a politics as old as the history of the country, because it's clearly consistent with what [John] Adams described as the spirit of this country at the time of the American Revolution. He said that at that time there was abroad in the colonies what he called "a spirit of public happiness . . ."

And he said that that spirit was manifest among the people who lived in
this country back in 1776 in this way: they were willing to take on responsibilities of self-government, willing to participate in public discussion,
willing to make decisions about what should be done to the common-
wealth; and having made those decisions, to take responsibility for them
and then to take whatever action was necessary or possible in order to
carry out those decisions. He said this spirit was so strong then that in fact
the Revolution was won before it was fought. . . .

The popular image of the McCarthy campaign was that of a Children's
Crusade and a dedicated band of amateurs taking on the corrupt machine,
but the image bore little relationship to reality in Indiana. The internal
stresses of a campaign well-organized at the bottom but not at the top
began coming to the surface, causing a factionalization from which the
campaign never fully recovered. In addition, an ugly new element was introduced into the campaign as Kennedy supporters launched an attack on Mc-
Carthy's record in Congress and McCarthy responded with increasingly
bitter personal sallies at Kennedy.

One of McCarthy's most chilling comments about Kennedy was based
on several lines from a poem entitled "Lament of an Aging Politician," which
McCarthy wrote in 1967:

> I have left Act I, for involution
> and Act II. There mired in complexity
> I cannot write Act III.

Explaining the poem to *Life* magazine's Shana Alexander, McCarthy pointed
out that the rules of classical Greek drama call for stating the problem in
Act I, presenting the complications in Act II and resolving everything in
Act III. "I'm an Act II man," he said. "That's where I live — involution
and complexity. In politics, I think you must stay in Act II. You can't draw
lines under things, or add up scores; the complications just go on in different forms. . . . When you get into Act III, you have to write a tragedy."

McCarthy classified Kennedy as an Act I man. "He says here's a problem.
Here's another problem. Here's another. He never really deals with Act II,
but I think maybe Bobby's beginning to write Act III now. Bobby's tragedy
is that to beat me, he's going to have to destroy his brother. Today I occupy
most of Jack's positions on the board. That's kind of Greek, isn't it?"

The attack against his voting record, which McCarthy blamed on Kennedy's aide Pierre Salinger, was "the most disappointing part of the entire
campaign," McCarthy later declared. The principal vehicle of the attack
was a widely circulated "fact sheet" issued in April by the Citizens for
Kennedy office in New York, which charged McCarthy with illiberal, hypo-
critical votes on a number of issues, including the oil depletion allowance,
housing, social security and similar legislation. After examining the charges
and comparing McCarthy's and Kennedy's voting records, the New York

Times concluded on May 5 that the "fact sheet" had distorted and in some cases falsified McCarthy's votes. Even though Kennedy disavowed the "fact sheet," McCarthy held him accountable for it and the dispute dominated their relationship during the last month of Kennedy's life.

In Indiana, it became clear that McCarthy no longer had the running room he needed. With Indiana Governor Roger Branigin standing in for Humphrey as a favorite son candidate and Kennedy mounting a well-organized, well-financed effort aimed at finishing him off, McCarthy was forced on the defensive for the first time in the campaign. As he told the Boston *Globe* in December, 1968, "You see, once he (Kennedy) came in it was old politics, pretty much. It wasn't really the challenge to the Johnson position, it got into the question of what's your record on civil rights, and why is your attendance record bad? And all these other side issues that Bobby introduced. The question of my being for a guaranteed annual wage, stuff like that, that changed the whole context of it . . . changed it significantly." [9]

The campaign was changing in other ways as well. It was breaking into bitterly feuding spheres of influence whose members fought for control of everything from the candidate's time to the kind of advertising he would use.[10] McCarthy's personal staff, dominated by his coldly efficient personal secretary, Miss Jean Stack, and by brusque Jerry Eller, went to great lengths to shield the candidate from the demands of the national staff, even to the extent of refusing to take telephone calls or give out McCarthy's itinerary. Curtis Gans and the national staff, on the other hand, fought with the local McCarthy organizers and especially with the Washington finance office, which was now headed by Abigail's brother, Stephen Quigley, on leave from his job as commissioner of administration in Minnesota. Quigley quarrelled with McCarthy's top fund raisers and just about everyone else over the skyrocketing expenses of the campaign which reached the astronomical sum of $800,000 in Indiana, including $78,000 for telephone calls alone.

McCarthy wasted much of his time in Indiana through poor scheduling

[9] Either because he was being virtually ignored by the news media in Indiana or because he was trying to stake out a more radical position than Kennedy, McCarthy began to talk more and more of the need to oust officials like Dean Rusk, FBI Director J. Edgar Hoover, and even Indiana-born Lewis Hershey, head of the Selective Service.

[10] McCarthy had been unhappy with the efforts of several high-powered New York advertising people who volunteered their services in New Hampshire because he felt their work was in the traditional mold. Several ad agencies were tried and found wanting before McCarthy called in Bill and Kay Nee, whose Minneapolis agency had handled his Senate campaign advertising. The Nees, whose emphasis on homey, low key advertising caused some campaign workers to refer to them as "Ma and Pa Kettle," took control of the local advertising effort in Indiana and continued through the remaining primaries while most of the national advertising was prepared by volunteers from the New York agency of Doyle, Dane, and Bernbach, who prepared some of the most original and effective political advertising of the year.

and a "rural strategy" designed by Gans that had him concentrating on small towns. He summed up his Indiana experience by writing an aptly-named poem, "Three Bad Signs," which parodied small town provincialism ("This is a clean, safe town No one can just come round With ribbons and bright threads Or new books to be read.") Without the corps of effective local organizers that had helped him so much in New Hampshire and Wisconsin, and almost ignored by the Indiana news media, McCarthy was surprised and relieved when he did better in the May 7 primary than the poll had predicted. Two days before the primary, voter surveys showed McCarthy getting between 19 and 24 percent, but on election day, he polled 27 percent, compared to 42.3 percent for Kennedy and 30.7 percent for Branigin. McCarthy had been damaged, but not eliminated, and Kennedy had been kept from claiming an overwhelming mandate. "We have tested the enemy," McCarthy declared on election night. "We know his techniques, we know his weaknesses."

If McCarthy had found Kennedy's weaknesses, he didn't do anything with them in Nebraska, a rural state with a liberal tradition in which McCarthy originally expected to win. His campaign was an even greater disaster than in Indiana, with little money, virtually no local organization or support and a discouraged candidate. On May 14, McCarthy took his second consecutive drubbing as Kennedy got 51.7 percent and he got only 31.2 percent. Although it was again better than the polls had predicted Pierre Salinger proclaimed that Nebraska had "finished Gene McCarthy as a credible candidate," and there were many in the McCarthy camp who wondered if he was right.[11]

McCarthy wasn't finished, as he was soon to demonstrate in Oregon and California, but only a major shake-up in the McCarthy organization saved the foundering campaign. That shake-up began the day after the Nebraska primary as Thomas Finney and four other men flew from Washington to Minneapolis to meet McCarthy, who was staying there overnight before leaving on a two day campaign trip to Florida. The five men, all longtime friends of McCarthy, were determined to get him to turn over active supervision of his campaign to Finney, a forty-three year old partner in the law firm of Defense Secretary Clark Clifford and a participant in McCarthy's

[11] The decisive defeat in Nebraska did nothing to soften McCarthy's biting wit. On the morning after the primary, he offered Shana Alexander of *Life* magazine some animal images for his two chief Democratic rivals. Hubert Humphrey, he said, was like a dog that barks and sits up without being asked — "He wants the office so bad, you want to give it to him." Kennedy was in some ways like the wolverine — "kind of a torn animal. It doesn't really know its identity. It fouls up traps, or destroys what's in a trap, and its frightening snarl scares trappers in lonely camps." He even extended the imagery to himself. Pointing out that Nebraska was the fourth in what he calculated were nine steps to the presidency — seven primaries, the convention and the November election — McCarthy said, "Look up the ancient Chinese poem about cranes. The crane was sacred to poetry and to peace. They take nine steps before they fly. A pigeon just jumps up. Like Bobby."

short-lived vice presidential campaign in 1964. The others included Maurice Rosenblatt, the Washington representative of the Committee for a More Effective Congress; Washington Lobbyist Larry Merthan; John Safer, the Washington real estate man who had been McCarthy's finance chairman, and Thomas McCoy, an ex-CIA official.

When Finney and his companions arrived at McCarthy's hotel they found him in bed, so they flew to Florida with him the next day. On the flight, they presented their argument: that McCarthy could beat Kennedy in Oregon and California and win the nomination as a compromise candidate if his campaign organization and finances were professionally managed. By the time they reached Florida, McCarthy had agreed that Finney would take charge of the campaign in Oregon and California, replacing Gans as field campaign coordinator, and that McCoy would travel with McCarthy in both states. McCarthy summoned Gans and Blair Clark to Florida and told them of his decision, then called a general strategy meeting for the following Saturday in his Senate office. Gans, distrustful of Finney's ties to the CIA and Johnson, and convinced that the accession to power of Finney and McCoy meant the "new politics" was about to be replaced by the old, conventional politics, walked into McCarthy's office before the meeting and told him he was leaving the campaign for "personal reasons."

Fifteen men who represented the nucleus of his campaign team crowded into McCarthy's small Senate office to hear him explain why he was placing Finney in charge. McCarthy spoke briefly, acknowledging the fact that he needed better organization to beat Kennedy, and told them to work out the details. The meeting ended with Finney outlining his plans and everyone pledging to cooperate. The next day, May 19, Finney, McCoy and Norval Reece, a Pennsylvania ADA official who was placed in charge of scheduling, departed for California to set up a communications center from which the Oregon and California campaigns would be coordinated, and ran into Gans on the plane. Finney talked him into rejoining the campaign and agreed to place him in charge of Southern California operations. They announced the appointment in a San Francisco press conference in an attempt to knock down rumors of dissension in the McCarthy ranks.

The Finney-Gans affair illustrated a fundamental weakness of the McCarthy campaign which, while greatly improved in Oregon and California, would never be completely corrected and would return to plague McCarthy at the Democratic convention. McCarthy pinpointed that weakness when he later observed that "Our problem was too much help and too much financial support. . . . People moved in, you know, who wanted to raise money. It's pretty hard to say 'no.' They'll do it on their own anyway. Run kind of separate efforts."

The dimensions of the organization problem were later defined by Steve Quigley who, more than anyone else including McCarthy, tried to solve it. "There must have been ten different campaigns going on, all under the umbrella of the overall McCarthy campaign," Quigley said in a 1971 interview. "Basically, every week there was some conspiracy by a new group to take over the campaign. It was just impossible to get control of it because every time you would set something up, somebody would set something else up. We got control of all the bank accounts, and then Gans and his people would set up their own finance committee and open bank accounts all over the country. We never did get hold of all the travel and telephone credit cards. We did get some control on the spending, but because everyone had been given free reign in the early months, we were unable to get total control. Gene has great distaste for personal confrontations and rather than say anything, he just let things drift along. This was the central weakness in the McCarthy campaign — no one ever knew who was boss, even McCarthy didn't know — it certainly wasn't him."

Quigley, brought into the campaign at the urging of Abigail McCarthy, who feared her husband would be saddled with an enormous campaign debt, found the campaign lurching toward insolvency. The free-spending habits and grandiose plans of the national staff, whose lifestyle on the road did not include the peanut butter and jelly fare of McCarthy's student volunteers, had left the McCarthy campaign deeply in debt even before Indiana. Quigley was appalled to find unpaid bills from New Hampshire and Wisconsin which would total over $100,000 still pouring in. More than a dozen "Q" air travel cards which could be used by anyone were in circulation, while almost anyone was free to obligate the campaign by renting cars, ordering campaign material, making long distance calls and signing hotel bills. One national staffer in Indiana chartered an airplane to bring students from the East while another ordered $10,000 worth of campaign material after national campaign headquarters vetoed it. "These people just went out and charged things and after the campaign was over, we were deluged with unpaid bills," says Quigley. "People would rent cars and when they ran out of gas, they'd leave them by the side of the road. Dick Goodwin was one of the worst offenders. He rented a car in Washington one day, parked it in the Madison Hotel garage and weeks later we found out about it. I refused to pay it — I don't know who did."

Quigley has scant sympathy for Gans' difficulties, proving that the generation gap bridged by McCarthy still existed within his campaign organization:

> After New Hampshire, the stories about the thousands of idealistic young volunteers being bussed in were a myth. There were guys in Nebraska calling for help and Gans was drying those places up because the operation wasn't being run by people who were loyal to him. Gans felt I was part of the old establishment that didn't know anthing about the new politics — I told him that what he called new politics we were practicing twenty years ago. Doorbell ringing put McCarthy in Congress.

While Finney whipped the national staff into shape, McCarthy had a much more effective organization at work for him in Oregon. The depth of antiwar sentiment in the state was so strong that dissident Democrats had sounded out McCarthy about running against Johnson a month before he announced. By the time he arrived on May 20 for the final push to the primary eight days later, they were better organized than in any other state, and when he heard on May 21 that Kennedy had publicly stated that he would not be "a very viable candidate" if he lost in Oregon, McCarthy smelled victory. However, the Oregon campaign almost blew up in his face that same day when he told reporters aboard a plane from Klamath Falls to Coos Bay that there could be circumstances in which he would support Humphrey but only, he insisted, if Humphrey changed his Vietnam position.

The story was aired nationally immediately after the plane landed and brought an instantly unfavorable reaction from McCarthy's supporters. To many of them, it sounded like he was quitting while others considered it a sign that Finney had talked McCarthy into making a deal with Humphrey. McCarthy first said he'd been misquoted — he hadn't — then tried to clarify his statement, made when he was very tired, by explaining that he had no preference between Humphrey and Kennedy. But the statement sent shudders through the McCarthy camp and some top aides threatened to resign unless McCarthy made a tough speech clearly disassociating himself with Humphrey as well as Kennedy.

They didn't have to wait long for him to make that speech. On the following night, May 22, in San Francisco's Cow Palace, in what was the toughest speech of his campaign, McCarthy attacked Humphrey and Kennedy alike. Essentially, McCarthy argued that the war in Vietnam had grown out of a "systematic misconception" of America's role in the world and that anyone who failed to combat that misconception should be held accountable. The thrust of the speech, which was actually an assault on all U.S. postwar foreign policy, is contained in two key passages:

> I am not convinced that the senator from New York has entirely renounced those misconceptions; nor is the vice president prepared to say that the process is wrong as well as what it produces. If they did — in the case of the senator from New York — I would find it difficult to explain why he would use an endorsement from the former secretary of defense, who was one of the principal engineers of those policies. I have not yet heard him criticize . . . the role of the military in this nation, nor the Department of State nor the Central Intelligence Agency . . . .
>
> At the very time when American foreign policy was growing more disastrous, the vice president became its most ardent apologist . . . . Not merely did he defend the war but he defended the assumptions which produced it — America's moral mission in the world; the great threat from China; the theory of monolithic Communist conspiracy; the susceptibility of political problems to military solutions; the duty to impose American idealism upon foreign cultures, especially in Asia — all of these myths and

misconceptions, so damaging in their consequences, have had, I must say, the enthusiastic support of the vice president. And those who thought, in the best American tradition, to question those policies have been subject, all to often, to ridicule and to scorn.

McCarthy's Cow Palace speech took him off the hook that he'd gotten on in Coos Bay by making it clear he wasn't about to sell out to Humphrey, but his delivery showed that he found it difficult to personally attack his old Minnesota colleague. He spoke the words pertaining to Humphrey in a rapid, subdued manner that lessened their impact and preserved his original intention, which was to make it easier for Humphrey supporters in Oregon and California — particularly organized labor — to support him in the two key primaries.

With Kennedy, however, McCarthy's personal feelings coincided with the political realities that demanded he go after his major opponent, and he did so with ever-increasing wit and bitterness in the closing days of the Oregon campaign. "Bobby threatened to hold his breath unless the people of Oregon voted for him," went one of McCarthy's favorite lines. Better educated people would vote for him, not Kennedy, he said. Kennedy was trying to beat him with "a dog and an astronaut," McCarthy jibed after Kennedy campaigned with his dog Freckles and Astronaut John Glenn. The campaign reached a symbolic climax in the Portland zoo the Sunday before the primary as Kennedy, in full view of television cameras, fled a chance confrontation with McCarthy amid McCarthy aides' taunts of "chicken" and "coward!"

By primary day, there was little doubt in either Kennedy's or McCarthy's minds what the outcome would be. Kennedy's private poll showed him two percentage points ahead, but the Kennedy professionals knew that McCarthy almost always ran better than the polls and they flatly told Kennedy to be prepared to accept defeat. Fifteen minutes after the polls closed, McCarthy knew that he had won his second great victory of 1968. Even more satisfying to him, he had dealt the Kennedy family its first defeat in twenty-eight elections. Only the final figures were in doubt (McCarthy 43.9 percent, Kennedy 37 percent, Johnson 12.4 percent and Humphrey less than one percent in write-ins) when McCarthy joined his deliriously happy supporters at a victory celebration in the Portland Elks Temple. "In Nebraska, I said that many wagons got to the Missouri, but the real test began when they crossed and started up the Oregon Trail," he said when the cheering died down. "Here we have shown who had the staying power, who had the strength and the commitment. We had the best horses, the best wagons, and the best men and women." Then, like a priest blessing his congregation, he raised him arm and gave the V sign as he declared, "California, here we come."

Kennedy was gracious in defeat, sending a congratulatory telegram to McCarthy that emphasized the massive anti-administration vote they had won between them, but declared Humphrey the leading candidate for the nomination. But the harsh reality of his defeat and the memory that Mc-Carthy had never sent a traditional congratulatory message in Indiana or Nebraska only served to increase the bitterness toward McCarthy in the Kennedy camp as the two antagonists headed into the state where the emotional roots of their campaigns for the presidency were planted and where the tragic finale of their intense rivalry would occur one week later.

The June 4 California primary that was so crucial to the hopes of both Kennedy and McCarthy ultimately hinged on one event — an hour-long televised joint appearance by the two candidates three days before the primary. Although it was not precisely a debate — they would be quizzed by three reporters and given an opportunity to rebut each other's questions — both men understood that the outcome of the primary and thus their fate at the national convention was resting on this, their first and only direct confrontation of the campaign. Kennedy had exercised the frontrunner's prerogative of refusing McCarthy's challenge to a debate. But Oregon made it impossible for him to let it be said he was afraid to debate, particularly since it looked as if McCarthy was coming on strong in California's vote-heavy suburban areas.

The television confrontation came off in San Francisco on Saturday afternoon, June 1, but it was hardly the decisive showdown that both sides expected. McCarthy spent the final hour or so before the debate joking, reading poetry and singing Irish songs with Poet Robert Lowell, Blair Clark, and two women reporters who had covered his campaign closely since before New Hampshire — Mary McGrory of the Washington *Star* and Shana Alexander of *Life* magazine. He arrived at the television studio, smiling and looking unconcerned. Some McCarthy people, Tom Finney in particular, feared McCarthy had lost his fighting edge, and his fears were confirmed as he watched the debate proceed to an inconclusive finish.

McCarthy started out strong, plainly showing Kennedy was wrong in accusing him of "forcing a coalition government on Saigon." But McCarthy was put on the defensive by Kennedy's complaint about a McCarthy newspaper ad that incorrectly linked him to the U.S. decision to intervene in the Dominican Republic (when Kennedy was not even in the administration), and McCarthy's countercharge that Kennedy aides had distorted his own voting record was weak and unconvincing. He hardly bothered to fight back when Kennedy, in a thinly disguised appeal to white suburban prejudices, twisted a McCarthy public housing proposal to make it look as though he were proposing a large scale movement of blacks into the suburbs. McCarthy finished with a strong sum-up, but overall, his performance was not impressive and it effectively ended the momentum of his Oregon victory. McCarthy described the debate as a fight "with three referees and the contestants wearing sixteen-ounce gloves," but Finney had no doubt that his candidate had lost his chance for a knockout. "He flubbed it!" Finney said as he rode back to his hotel, "Blew it! Threw it away. How can you get him elected?" Afterwards, McCarthy joined a few friends at a swank San Francisco restaurant and told Gerald Hill, "I don't want to talk about politics. I want to talk about Dante's Sixth Canto," and he proceeded to do so with Robert Lowell. "He had obviously not done as well as he hoped," says Hill.

McCarthy hit back the next day at what he called Kennedy's "scare tactics" and "crude distortion" of his suburban housing proposals, but it was too late. Polls showed most people believed Kennedy had won the debate and probably the primary with it. On election night, a CBS computer projection showed Kennedy winning by fourteen percent, and McCarthy was downplaying the importance of the primary he had considered crucial all along. "This has gone about as we expected," he told David Schoumacher of CBS shortly after the network projected Kennedy's victory. "We've made our real test in Oregon, where there were no bloc votes, and we made the case as clear as we could there, neglecting California in order to run in Oregon, and expected it would go about like this."

McCarthy knew he had lost California, but he was almost certain that the vote would be closer than CBS had projected. (He was right — Kennedy's final count was 46.3 percent, while McCarthy got 41.8 percent and the pro-Humphrey slate headed by California Attorney General Thomas Lynch got 11.9 percent.) Shortly after midnight, he was sitting in his seventh floor suite at the Beverly Hilton Hotel several miles from Kennedy's Ambassador Hotel headquarters in downtown Los Angeles with Tom Finney and Blair Clark drafting a congratulatory telegram to Kennedy. The draft referred to Kennedy's "splendid" victory, but McCarthy suggested the word be changed to "fine" instead "because I don't think the percentage will go that high."

Suddenly Schoumacher burst into the room and shouted, "Senator Kennedy has been shot."

"You're kidding," someone said as McCarthy and the others stared in disbelief.

"I'm not," Schoumacher replied. "I'll go back and get more."

Minutes later, Schoumacher returned and said Kennedy had been shot in the head. An ashen-faced McCarthy, sitting in a corner chair and watching the television screen, put his hands to his head, then looked up. "Maybe we should do it in a different way," he said quietly. "Maybe we should have the English system of having the cabinet choose the president. There must be some other way." Abigail McCarthy sat on the edge of a bed murmuring "Oh my God," while Mary McCarthy, who had urged her father to run and had campaigned for him in each of the primaries, clenched her fists and said, "This country. . . ."

In the morning, after three hours' sleep, McCarthy was told Kennedy wasn't expected to live, and he decided it would be best if he returned to Washington. He also decided he should go to the hospital where Kennedy lay. Before leaving the hotel, he read a statement to the press expressing his sympathy to the Kennedy family and calling a halt to his campaign. "The nation, I think, bears too great a burden of the kind of neglect which has allowed the disposition of violence to grow here in our own land, or the reflection of the violence which we have visited upon the rest of the world, or at least part of the world," he declared.

On the way to the airport, McCarthy stopped at the hospital briefly, but even that act produced more of the bitterness that plagued the McCarthy-Kennedy rivalry as his police escort unthinkingly kept its sirens on right to the hospital door. "I heard they complained that when I did come to the hospital, I came with the sirens on," he said later. "Well, when you get into that kind of response, why, you just figure it is best not to try to prove anything anymore." He spoke briefly with Dick Goodwin and Pierre Salinger, then went to the airport and boarded his plane for Washington.

During the flight back, Finney raised the subject of what McCarthy should do in the two months before the Democratic convention but McCarthy cut him off. "It's not going to make any difference. What we have to do now is cut down and just see what influence we can bring to bear on the situation between now and August. It's all over."

CHAPTER XVI

THE POLITICS OF HAPPINESS —
HUMPHREY vs. MC CARTHY

I'm not going to be an aggressive, self-esteemed, grasping candidate. I don't think the public needs that. I don't think they need anybody to stir them up anymore.

Hubert Humphrey in an April, 1968, interview.

Muriel Humphrey was the first person to make her husband fully aware that the tragedy that made him certain to win the Democratic nomination might also keep him from becoming president.

"Daddy, the shot that killed Bobby has wounded you, maybe very seriously," she told Humphrey when he returned to the Triple H Ranch at Waverly the week Robert Kennedy died.

"Why do you say that?" Humphrey asked.

"Because people are just going to be so sick of politics, so sick of Democrats, that it's just going to be impossible to do anything," she replied.

Humphrey had weighed the probable consequences of Kennedy's abrupt removal from the three-way battle for the nomination before hearing his wife's ominous prediction, but he was too shaken by Kennedy's death to consider its deeper meaning for his own future. It was the second time in slightly more than two months that his long dream of the presidency had been dramatically affected by events beyond his control.

That dream first seemed on the verge of becoming a reality on the morning of Sunday, March 31, when President Johnson called Humphrey as he and Muriel were preparing to leave on an official trip to Mexico City. Humphrey had despaired of his political future so many times in the past three years that Muriel found it hard to be sympathetic. "I'll never run for president," Humphrey had told her only a few weeks earlier for perhaps the hundredth time. "I'll be sixty-one in 1972. There'll be nearly ten years of the Johnson administration behind us. People will want a change."

When Johnson arrived at the Humphrey's Potomac waterfront apartment after attending Mass at nearby St. Dominic's Catholic Church with his daughter Luci and her husband Patrick Nugent, he took Humphrey into the study, and handed him a copy of his Vietnam speech. Humphrey was pleased to see that Johnson was calling for a limited bombing pause as part of an effort to bring peace negotiations, and he complimented the president, "That's just great, the best thing I ever heard you say."

Then Johnson handed Humphrey another piece of paper, telling him it was an alternative ending to the Vietnam speech and commanding him to read it aloud. Humphrey began reading, scarcely believing his eyes as he reached the final words: "Accordingly, I shall not seek, and I will not accept, the nomination of my party for another term as your president . . . ."

"Mr. President, you're kidding, you can't do that," Humphrey protested, tears welling in his eyes. "You can't just resign from office. You're going to be reelected."

Johnson cautioned Humphrey that he had not finally made up his mind, but he indicated that he felt there was no other way he could lead the country to peace. "He said, 'Hubert, nobody will believe that I'm trying to end this war unless I do that,' " Humphrey recalled in a 1971 interview. " 'I just can't get them to believe that I want peace. And I don't think I can get any cooperation in this battle against inflation unless I do this. I've got to become totally non-political. I just don't see any way out of it.' He also told me, 'This is a terrible strain, and men in my family have died early from heart trouble. I'd like to live a little bit longer.' "

Johnson cautioned Humphrey, as he always did on matters of importance, not to tell anyone because he hadn't decided whether he would use the second ending. He said he would let Humphrey know ahead of time which of the endings he was going to use. Then he embraced both the Humphreys warmly and told them goodbye, putting a finger to his lips in a private gesture to Humphrey. After he left, Mrs. Humphrey wondered if something was wrong with the president. "Is he ill?" she asked. "No, Momma," said Humphrey. "It's just the speech. It's a very important speech and there was a lot of trouble about it among his advisers." En route to the airport for the flight to Mexico City, Muriel again voiced her feeling about the president: "Something's bothering him. The way he held me, and the way he looked — there's something wrong. You're not telling me what he told you." Humphrey explained that the president had sworn him to secrecy. "I don't think that's very nice," Muriel replied angrily. "There's something wrong and we're a team too, you know."

"I'm not going to tell anyone, so forget it," Humphrey retorted. And he didn't. "I didn't used to tell her any of these things," Humphrey later explained. "When the president told me not to tell, I didn't tell *anybody* about *anything*. Despite what he used to think sometimes about leaks, most of it was right out of the White House, not out of our shop over there."

That night in Mexico City, the Humphreys joined Mexican President Gustavo Diaz Ordaz and U.S. Ambassador Fulton Freeman for dinner. It was a special occasion since it was the first time a Mexican president had dined in the American ambassador's residence, and when Humphrey suggested that Diaz Ordaz "will want to hear what his good friend, President Johnson, has to say," several of the guests thought it was an unusual request. Nevertheless, Humphrey, Diaz Ordaz, Freeman and Sol Linowitz, the U.S. ambassador to the Organization of American States, went into the library to listen to the speech on shortwave radio. About fifteen minutes before the speech was over, Humphrey was called into an adjoining room for a phone call from Johnson's special assistant, Marvin Watson. "Mr. Vice President, the president says to tell you it will be the second ending." Humphrey replied, "Oh my God, he shouldn't do that." "We told him that," said Watson, "but he's made up his mind."

Humphrey returned to the library, stunned by the final realization that the presidency was now finally within his grasp. "What is it, Hubert?" Mrs. Humphrey asked. "Nothing Muriel, just wait." The radio was crackling with static throughout Johnson's thirty-five minute speech, and when it appeared he was almost through, Freeman impatiently suggested they rejoin the waiting guests. Humphrey told him to wait. "Everybody be quiet, now. Listen to this."

As Johnson began to read the surprise ending, Humphrey muttered, "You shouldn't do this." The shocked silence that greeted Johnson's announcement was broken by the sound of Muriel's sobbing voice. "Why didn't you tell me?" she demanded. Before Humphrey could answer, an aide, Ted Van Dyk, burst into the room to congratulate the man he thought had just become president. "We were listening on another radio and there was a bad transmission," Van Dyk recalls. "I thought Johnson had quit and turned the presidency over to Humphrey." Assuring Van Dyk that wasn't the case, Humphrey led Muriel into an adjoining room to regain her composure, then joined the other guests at dinner.

It wasn't until later, after the long dinner and reception, that Humphrey had a chance to consider the implications of Johnson's political bombshell. Back at his hotel with the handful of aides who had accompanied him — Van Dyk, Norman Sherman, John Reilly and Dr. Edgar Berman (his personal physician) — Humphrey said it was too early to make any decisions. "Let's cool it," he said. "I have to talk this over with Muriel and think it through myself. Don't do anything." He called Johnson to say that he was sorry he had withdrawn, but spoke very briefly since he had been warned that any telephone calls might be monitored. There were more than fifty telephone calls for him, but Humphrey, for reasons he doesn't recall, returned only two — to Margaret Truman Daniels, daughter of the former president, in New York, and Patrick O'Connor, a Minneapolis lawyer and friend, in Tucson, Arizona. Both urged him to run, but he merely thanked them and said he would make his decision later.

The next day, April 1, after attending the signing of a nuclear non-proliferation treaty that was the main purpose of the trip, Humphrey boarded his plane for the flight back to Washington. He seemed troubled as he pondered the events of the day before, telling an aide that it was entirely possible that Kennedy might have moved into the power vacuum already and sewed up the nomination. "I don't want to be destroyed again in a fight with the Kennedys," said Humphrey, remembering his humiliating experience in the 1960 primaries. "He was brooding, very quiet," recalls Sol Linowitz. "At one point, he indicated he wanted to talk and I asked what he was going to do. He said he didn't want to get into it, but that he just didn't know what he would do. I urged him to reserve judgment and said I didn't see how he could not get into it, and that he would have to face the fact that his candidacy would be launched anyway. In that conversation, what emerged was that he would just wait and see."

It was evening when the silver-and-blue Air Force 707 touched down at Andrews Air Force Base outside Washington. As the plane taxied to a stop, Humphrey peered out of the window and saw a crowd of supporters, many of them waving "Humphrey for President" signs, waiting for him. "I remember him shaking his head and saying, 'Oh no, oh no,' like it was too soon for that," says Linowitz. Mrs. Humphrey said simply, "Well, Daddy, there they are once again."

However, Humphrey disappointed his reception committee by going directly home without making the announcement they all hoped to hear. The ghost of past campaigns that had been launched without adequate assurances of support still haunted him as he stepped off the plane and was greeted by William Connell, his closest and most trusted aide. "Has Bobby got it locked up yet?" Humphrey asked. Connell, who had taken it upon himself to call about fifty Democratic leaders around the country and tell them he was certain Humphrey would run after he was unable to get through to Humphrey the night of Johnson's speech, assured Humphrey that the Kennedy bandwagon was stalled. "Sometimes I was just minutes behind one of the Kennedys," Connell later recalled, "but everybody said they would hold." [1]

---

[1] There was no doubt in Connell's mind that he was right in predicting Humphrey would run, even though Humphrey had told numerous people he'd be too old to run for president in 1972. "We had been thinking and talking about 1972 all the time," Connell later said. "We had a better organization around the country than Johnson did — lots of labor people, governors, mayors, somebody in every state. It was really geared to the 1968 Johnson campaign, but it was our guys, we picked them. Johnson didn't really know about them."

Connell's assessment of the situation was backed up by a group of men who had gathered at his house for dinner earlier in the evening and concluded that Humphrey must immediately make it clear he would run. The guest list included Humphrey's two longtime confidants, Max Kampelman and Dr. Evron Kirkpatrick; William Welsh of Humphrey's staff; Gus Tyler of the Ladies Garment Workers Union; Richard Maguire, a former treasurer of the Democratic National Committee, and Eugene Foley, a Humphrey protege and former government official related by marriage to Eugene McCarthy's wife. All had agreed that Kennedy would not be able to take the party by storm and that Humphrey would be the only candidate who could capture the Democratic party center — where the decisive political strength of the party historically lay.

Most of Connell's dinner guests were present the next day as Humphrey huddled with his top aides in his vice presidential office to plan his strategy. Although everyone present automatically assumed Humphrey would run, he seemed genuinely undecided. "Should I run, and if I do, will I get the nomination?" Humphrey asked over and over again. "I think he half-expected Bobby to wrap it up and if he did, he wasn't about to plunge into all that again," says Van Dyk. "We must have had ten meetings before he was convinced the votes were waiting for him and there would be enough money, and he gave the go-ahead."

Humphrey's consuming passion to be president made it a virtual certainty that he would run, but it did not blind him to the obstacles he faced. "The first thing I had to do before I made any decision — or before I announced any decision — was to sort of get my ducks in a line," Humphrey said later. "You don't just get up the next morning and say, 'I'm going to run for president.' That would look like you're too anxious. In my own mind, I felt that I had a chance and that I ought to go, but I thought we ought to touch base with certain people and that I ought to be sure of what support I would have."

He spent most of the day telephoning the same Democratic leaders Connell had contacted — including each of the twenty-four Democratic governors — telling them that although he couldn't yet announce that he was running, he could promise them they wouldn't be sorry if they'd just hold fast for a few more days. Humphrey was encouraged by the response of most of those he called. Governors Richard Hughes of New Jersey, Warren Hearnes of Missouri, John McKeithen of Louisiana, Mayors James Tate of Philadelphia, Joseph Barr of Pittsburgh, Richard Daley of Chicago and Joseph Alioto of San Francisco, labor leaders George Meany of the AFL-CIO and I. W. Abel of the Steelworkers — all said he should get into the race. The seventy-four year old Meany traversed the two blocks between his office and Humphrey's to jab his ever-present cigar in Humphrey's face and urge him in the strongest possible terms to announce immediately. "I think I'll wait and see what we've got, George," said Humphrey, still careful and prudent. "I want to see how certain key governors and state chairmen feel about it."

Equally encouraging to Humphrey was the fact that his years of faithful service in the Democratic party vineyards were finally paying off. He flew to New York that night for a dinner at the Waldorf Astoria Hotel arranged by publishing magnate Gardner Cowles, whose family owns the Minneapolis *Star* and *Tribune,* and Dwayne Andreas, a wealthy Minneapolis businessman and one of Humphrey's closest friends. At the dinner and afterwards at the Andreas' apartment, some of the wealthiest men in America — including Henry Ford II, Jacob Blaustein of the American Oil Company, financier Sydney Weinberg and industrialist Marvin Rosenberg — pledged to support Humphrey against Kennedy, whom many of them feared, or McCarthy, whom they were uncertain of. "I never thought I'd see the day that Hubert Humphrey is the most conservative candidate we've got," one of the dinner guests commented afterwards.

McCarthy's solid victory in the Wisconsin primary came as welcome news to Humphrey the same evening. He was now even more certain that McCarthy and Kennedy would weaken each other in head-on primary confrontations in Indiana, Nebraska, Oregon and California, and that it would be unwise for him to enter any primaries.[2] "I saw no reason to go into any of the primaries," Humphrey said later. "I didn't have time to raise the money, to get organized for them. I thought it would be kind of foolish to do so."

Humphrey also hoped that Johnson, who had said in his March 31 speech that he would have a hands-off policy in the selection of his successor, would at least give him a private assurance of support, but he soon learned that was not to be. Johnson summoned Humphrey to the White House after spending more than an hour with Kennedy, who had requested a meeting with the president. Johnson told Humphrey essentially the same thing he had told Kennedy, that he would remain neutral in order to devote all his time to ending the war. When Humphrey said he planned to run if the support was there, Johnson said he was not surprised and that he had expected Humphrey to run, but he did not offer any advice or encouragement to him. Humphrey did not ask directly for his help. He accepted Johnson's public attitude of non-involvement as necessary to avoid upsetting his peace negotiations, but he was not happy at the lack of private encouragement from the man he had served so faithfully. "Lyndon Johnson did not renounce the presidency in order to be succeeded by Robert Kennedy," Humphrey said defensively when a friend expressed surprise at Johnson's seeming neutrality.[3]

[2] Filing deadlines were past for all primaries except South Dakota and New Jersey.
[3] Humphrey felt better the next day when Johnson heaped praise on him during a Cabinet meeting and then followed up with a forty-five minute telephone call to bring him up to date on the Vietnam peace negotiations and other foreign policy

Humphrey's disappointment was forgotten the next day when he went to Pittsburgh to talk to the Pennsylvania AFL-CIO convention. Introduced as "the next president," Humphrey almost let himself be drafted then and there as three thousand union members jumped up and down in the aisles in a six-minute demonstration and interrupted his speech with cries of "Tell us what we want to hear." "I know what you want," Humphrey told the wildly cheering audience. "I'm not one to walk away from a decision."

Humphrey sounded like a candidate and his advisers were pressing him to become one, but the possibility of an immediate announcement was precluded by the assassination of Martin Luther King that evening. Humphrey learned of King's death as he returned to Washington, which was beginning to erupt in looting and burning that would reach within two blocks of the White House. "The criminal act that took his life brings shame to our country," he said in a hastily-written statement in which he gave expression to the goals of his own lifelong involvement in civil rights struggles: "The blight of discrimination, poverty and neglect must be erased from America . . . an America full of freedom, full and equal opportunity shall be his living memorial." King's death and the civil disorders that followed provoked a mood of national uneasiness that Humphrey responded to by placing himself in the role of reconciler and healer. In the week after returning from King's funeral, Humphrey told audiences in Louisiana, Virginia and North Carolina that it was time for an end to divisiveness, time for "maturity of judgment."[4] It was an attempt to present himself as a mature leader offering a calming influence in troubled times, and he drew a sharp contrast between himself and his two opponents for the nomination, who were widely regarded as symbols of unrest and the demand for change. "America doesn't need emotion, frenzy, demagoguery or false promises," Humphrey told an audience in Jackson, Tennessee, a short time later. "I'm going to ask Americans to think positively, affirmatively, creatively. I'm going to ask them to stand proud and stop carping about America. I think that's what the American people want. I know that's what they need."

Whatever doubts there were in Humphrey's mind about running were resolved by Easter Sunday, April 14. On that day, at a conference on Key Largo, Florida, he worked out the final details of his candidacy. He and Muriel had gone there for a few days of rest with Dwayne Andreas and his wife on the Andreas' cabin cruiser. The Humphreys walked the beach and

---

issues. At the Cabinet meeting, Johnson said, "When I look back at what I did when I was vice president, I'd have to give myself a grade of B or B—. But when I think of how Hubert Humphrey has performed, I'd have to give him a triple A+."

[4] Unlike earlier years, Humphrey found warm receptions throughout the South. In Baton Rouge, after he gave one of the strongest civil rights speeches of his life, Governor John McKeithen said, "We've changed a lot and he's changed a little. He doesn't compromise on civil rights, but he has an understanding heart. He doesn't treat the South like some stepchild."

swam and talked from Friday night through Sunday before Humphrey finally decided to run. On Sunday night, they were joined by the two senators who would serve as Humphrey's pre-convention campaign managers, Walter Mondale and Fred Harris, as well as their wives and several Humphrey aides. The group had dinner at a private club on the waterfront, then adjourned to the boat and stayed up until 3 A.M. plotting the campaign. Mondale, Humphrey's forty year old successor in the Senate, and Harris, a thirty-seven year old Oklahoman, agreed to serve as co-chairmen of his campaign, and April 27 was picked as the date of Humphrey's announcement.

Only two weeks earlier, Mondale had been certain Humphrey wouldn't get the nomination. After watching the president's withdrawal speech on T.V. with Senator Henry Jackson of Washington, Mondale told Jackson, "Bobby's nominated. Hubert shouldn't even get in the race." But it soon became clear that Kennedy wasn't going to walk away with it, and Mondale was receptive when Humphrey's old friend James Rowe, Jr., suggested he run the campaign after Humphrey's first choice, Postmaster General Larry O'Brien, declined the offer and managed Kennedy's campaign instead. Mondale was disturbed by press reports that Humphrey was thinking of picking conservative Governor John Connally of Texas as his running mate, and after getting assurances that he wasn't, Mondale accepted. However, he suggested that to avoid an all-Minnesota campaign team, his good friend Harris, be named co-chairman. Humphrey was at first dubious about a two-headed campaign, but decided at the Key Largo conference to place them in charge of the official campaign organization, United Democrats for Humphrey. With his delegate hunting apparatus in good hands, Humphrey returned to Washington to prepare for his long-awaited announcement of candidacy.

Early on the evening of April 26, Humphrey sat in his office reworking the speech he was to deliver the next day and reflecting on the reasons for his decision to run. "I've been in public life for more than twenty years," he told a reporter-friend. "When you have a career, you tend to follow it to its ultimate destiny." Then, looking out the window at the White House fifty yards away through eyes accentuated by dark lines of fatigue, Humphrey pointed out that his fifty-seventh birthday was only a month away and that this probably would be his last chance for the presidency. "I just think I ought to do it," he declared.

Eighteen hours later, his spirits revived by a crowd of two thousand roaring supporters, Humphrey stood on a platform in the jammed main ballroom of Washington's Shoreham Hotel and announced his candidacy. Although he depicted himself in his carefully prepared statement as the man who could unify his party and country with "maturity, restraint and responsibility," the mood of the moment caused him to add extemporaneously the words that provided an unfortunate campaign theme that would be the first of many handicaps he and his campaign would bear in the months ahead. "Here we are," he enthused, rubbing his hands gleefully as he surveyed his audience, "just as we ought to be, the people, here we are, in a spirit of dedication, here we are, the way politics ought to be in America, the politics of happiness, the politics of purpose, and the politics of joy. And that's the way it's going to be, all the way, from here on in!"

To many people, Humphrey's attempt to interject joy and happiness into one of the most divisive presidential campaign years in American history had a hollow ring, but it reflected the kind of hopeful cast he sought to give his candidacy. Again and again during the speech, in ironic counterpoint to the events of the coming months, Humphrey emphasized the need for national unity, tolerance, understanding, mutual trust. "What concerns me is not just winning the nomination, but how it is to be won," he declared. "The man who wins the nomination must be able first to unite his party . . . and his nation. You can rest assured that I . . . do not intend to and will not divide either my party or my country." At the end of his speech, Humphrey responded to shouts of "We want Hubert" with a happy grin. "You've got me," he said, clasping his hands over his head like a winning prize fighter.

Humphrey's announcement, described by *Newsweek* magazine as "an effervescent outburst of balm, blarney and brotherhood," was quickly followed by evidence that the delegate harvesting operation engineered by Mondale and Harris was an effective one. Two days after Humphrey announced, he won control of Maryland's forty-nine member delegation when the state Democratic convention voted for the unit rule in Chicago. The action prompted his scorekeepers to predict confidently that 1,200 of the 1,312 delegates votes needed for the nomination were already committed or leaning toward Humphrey. At the same time, Humphrey climbed dramatically in the public opinion polls. A week after his announcement, the Louis Harris survey showed him leading Kennedy — who had promised to "chase Hubert's ass around the country" — among Democratic voters 38 to 27 percent, almost an exact reversal of a Harris survey a month earlier, while McCarthy climbed from 22 to 25 percent.

Naturally, since he wasn't entered in any primaries, Humphrey downplayed their importance. In an interview with his favorite magazine, *U.S. News and World Report,* on May 27, he said, "This nomination will not be decided by the primaries, even though primaries are important psychologically. The nomination will be decided by the convention delegates, and better than three fourths of those delegates are selected in non-primary states." Humphrey ventured a guess that Richard Nixon would win the Republican nomination over New York Governor Nelson Rockefeller, and in the process described almost perfectly his own strategy of relying on party organization and public opinion polls instead of primaries:

I think that because the nomination is made by delegates at a convention, because Mr. Rockefeller is not in any primaries, and because he also is not an organization man, he has less chance of getting the nomination than Mr. Nixon . . . . I think on that basis — of strength in the party organization — Mr. Nixon is far ahead of Mr. Rockefeller, and will most likely be able to sustain that lead unless he drops in the polls so significantly that the Republican party would see his nomination would lead to defeat . . . . I think that the polls in this instance are much more significant than the primaries.

While others trumpeted the virtues of the New Politics, Humphrey was perfectly happy with the Old. On the eve of the Oregon primary, Humphrey was back in Minnesota celebrating his fifty-seventh birthday at a series of parties that added $300,000 to his campaign coffers when he made his first important breakthrough. Fittingly, he had just finished carving up a cake decorated like a map of the United States when Mondale and Harris called from Harrisburg, Pennsylvania, with the news of the Humphrey campaign's biggest coup yet. The state Democratic Committee had given him two-thirds of its 130-vote delegation despite the fact that McCarthy had outpolled Humphrey by an 8 to 1 margin in the state's non-binding April 23 primary — 4 days before Humphrey was even a candidate. The dispirited McCarthy camp labeled it "the Pennsylvania railroad," but Humphrey's strategists recognized that it was a major step on the road to Chicago. "Humphrey was nominated in Pennsylvania," Harris would declare after the Pennsylvania delegation assured Humphrey's first-ballot victory at Chicago.[5]

Early on the evening of the California primary, Humphrey arrived at the U.S. Air Force Academy in Colorado Springs, where he was to deliver the commencement address the next day. Riding in from the airport, he confided to Ted Van Dyk that he hoped Kennedy would win handily in California so as to eliminate McCarthy from the race. There was little chance Kennedy could win the nomination, he mused, because too many party leaders opposed him, but he was enough of a party regular that he would support Humphrey after the convention. Humphrey knew he couldn't expect the same orthodox behavior from McCarthy. "Gene's my friend," he said quietly. "I've known him for twenty years. But if he wins tonight, he'll plague Bobby and me all the way to the convention."

Humphrey had been asleep for about half an hour in his room in the Air Force Academy's VIP quarters when Dave Gartner woke him up to tell him Kennedy had been shot. "You've got to be kidding," said Humphrey, "and if you are, get the hell out of here!" Unable to believe the tragic news

---

[5] Harris later described the technique he and Mondale used in foraging for convention votes in the non-primary states. "If there was a Democratic governor or lieutenant governor who might be for us, we started with him. If there was no one in the statehouse, we tried the mayors, and if there was no one in City Hall, we tried the union halls."

until he got up and looked at the television set in the next room, Humphrey immediately placed a call to Edward Kennedy at the Fairmont Hotel in San Francisco and offered to do what he could to help. Kennedy asked if Humphrey could arrange to have a prominent Boston brain surgeon, Dr. James Poppen, flown to Los Angeles and Humphrey said he could. He called Air Force Chief of Staff General John McConnell, who was in a nearby room, and ordered him, in the name of the president, to have Dr. Poppen flown to Los Angeles. Later, Pierre Salinger called and asked if another plane could be made available to fly several of Robert Kennedy's children and friends from Washington to Los Angeles, and Humphrey again ordered McConnell to provide it.[6] When Humphrey said he would return to Washington the next morning, McConnell protested, insisting that he had to make the commencement speech. "I said, 'General, I don't have to do anything,'" Humphrey recalls. "I said, 'I'll do what I think is right and I don't think it's right for me to be making a speech tomorrow morning at the Air Force Academy that some people will interpret as politics. Get yourself another commencement speaker!'"

With Kennedy's death early on the morning of June 6, Humphrey's drive for the nomination became almost mechanical. The same revulsion and disorientation among the electorate that Muriel Humphrey sensed was felt by the Democratic regulars, who now banded together more tightly than ever behind the one candidate who offered them a reassuring link to the party they were familiar with. No one understood better than McCarthy what Kennedy's death meant to his own hopes for the nomination. "I think if I had won in California against Bobby that that would have eliminated him as a candidate at the convention," McCarthy said after the 1968 election. "It would have put them in a hard way not to pick me, but his people would have gone over to Humphrey at that point. And then, of course, when he was killed, why at that point, why, I knew that we didn't have a chance. . . . Once Bobby was killed, why it was bound to be Humphrey."

Humphrey saw that his task had now become not winning the nomination but making certain the nomination was worth winning. By the middle of June, with only five weeks to go before the Chicago convention, a New York *Times* poll gave him 1,600 delegates, comfortably ahead of the 1,312 he needed for the nomination. Humphrey was anything but comfortable, however, and the reason was obvious. "What I think the Kennedy assassination did was to sour the whole public, and particularly the Democratic party, on the election and on the political process," he reflected later. "We'd had the

[6] Humphrey was quickly reminded that he was not yet in a position to give orders. When he returned to Washington, Presidential Assistant Marvin Watson demanded to know why he hadn't cleared his request for the planes with the White House. "Watson really raised hell with him," says a Humphrey aide. Humphrey's explanation was "I did it because I knew that's what the president would have wanted."

Tet offensive — which was a political disaster in this country — and then you get McCarthy on the road, you get Bobby in the primaries and you get Martin Luther King's assassination, and the party is now torn in many ways, in disarray. And then Bobby, on the night of the election in California, is assassinated. I think this was just too much. It was like a mental break-down for the American political community."

The summer of 1968 was not a good one for Humphrey despite his belief that he was almost certain to win the Democratic nomination. Caught in a dilemma between remaining loyal to President Johnson and asserting his in-dependence, Humphrey tried to stake out his own position on the crucial issue of Vietnam without repudiating the administration or upsetting the Paris peace talks, which had begun in May. He retired to his lakeside home in Waverly after Robert Kennedy's funeral to prepare the speech that would mark the resumption of his campaign. But even as Humphrey labored over that speech, there were signs that the stubborn war which had given him his chance to run for the presidency also would be an unshakable albatross around his neck.

First, there was the prediction by Bill Moyers, Johnson's former press secretary and publisher of the Long Island newspaper *Newsday*, that Hum-phrey was about to publicly dissociate himself from the administration's Vietnam policy. In a New York radio interview on June 14, Moyers implied that Humphrey's private position on the war was different from his public position. A day later, Moyers predicted that Humphrey would "emerge on his own within the next week or so." Humphrey reacted strongly when asked about Moyers' comments. "I may be wrong or stupid," said Humphrey, "but I'm not a hypocrite."

Humphrey was reminded of the potency of the peace issue on June 18, the day he returned to Washington from Waverly. McCarthy, who had re-sumed his campaign a few days earlier by calling on the United States to take "our steel out of the land of thatched huts," and his New York sup-porters demonstrated the power of the new politics as they out-organized the Democratic machine with a grassroots campaign that gave him 62 of the 123 delegates in New York's statewide primary, compared to 30 for Ken-nedy, 19 uncommitted and only 12 for Humphrey. In addition, Paul O'Dwyer, an outspoken McCarthyite who flatly refused to support Hum-phrey because of the war, upset strong Humphrey and Kennedy men in the Senatorial primary.

McCarthy's victory, which the New York *Times* said had shown that "whatever the nation wants, it does not want more of the same," under-lined the necessity for Humphrey to adopt a posture of political independ-ence. Humphrey attempted to do that in a carefully structured National Press Club speech on June 20 that illustrated the sharply defined limits of his freedom. In his formal speech, Humphrey completely avoided Vietnam. He concentrated instead on domestic policies and called for both "law and order" and "social justice." He urged stronger gun control laws than those contained in an administration bill, warmly approved the report of the President's National Advisory Commission on Civil Disorders — which he had criticized when it was released in March — and renewed his call for a "Marshall Plan" for the cities — which Johnson had slapped down when Humphrey suggested it earlier.[7] The issue of Vietnam was quickly raised in the traditional question and answer period following his speech and the first question was about Moyers' statement. Humphrey was evasive, declaring that Moyers was simply pointing out what he had always said, that the war should be ended by a political rather than a military settlement. Humphrey refused to discuss Vietnam at length, however, saying only that the Paris peace talks offered "the best hope" for a settlement.

He turned the day's hardest question to his advantage by emphasizing his newly declared independence. Asked "To what extent you are committed to the policies of the administration that you have been defending?" Humphrey answered with an allegorical reference to his son, Skip, who was in the audience. "I don't ask him to live his father's life. I ask him to live his life. The president of the United States has not asked me to live his administration when I am privileged to have the Humphrey administration. And there will be, if I have anything to say about it . . . a Humphrey administration with its own program, its own nuances, its own sense of direction, its own perspective, its own objectives."

Newspaper accounts of Humphrey's Press Club appearance ignored his prepared remarks and stressed his vows of political independence (the Washington *Post* headlined its story, "HHH Sees Himself a 'Man of Change' "), but he soon learned that it would take more than vaguely worded promises to break the chains linking him to Johnson and to Vietnam. His campaign swings around the country during the rest of June and July were near disasters, with angry demonstrations, small and unenthusiastic crowds and, as one reporter wrote, "an unmistakable whiff of mediocrity" shrouding the Humphrey operation. Humphrey tried to leapfrog the Vietnam issue by emphasizing how the nation would be able to satisfy its unmet needs once the peace negotiations were successfully concluded, and by depicting Vietnam and Southeast Asia as less important than overall East-West relations. Forced to cancel an appearance at a rally in Los An-

[7] President Johnson greeted the report of the Commission (popularly known as the Kerner Commission after its chairman, Governor Otto Kerner of Illinois) with noticeable coolness, presumably because it ignored his administration's efforts in the antipoverty field and called for "unprecedented levels of funding and performance" to remove the causes of violence. While McCarthy and Kennedy attacked Johnson for not speaking out in favor of the commission's proposals, Humphrey said the report's conclusion that the nation is moving toward two societies, "one black, one white — separate and unequal," is "open to some challenge."

geles in early July because he had the flu (2,000 antiwar demonstrators showed up anyway), Humphrey returned to Los Angeles later in the month to meet with the 173-member California delegation and was greeted by 5,000 demonstrators outside the posh Century Plaza Hotel. The demonstrators combined tastelessness and ingenuity to produce such signs as "Hitler, Hubert, and Hirohito" and "Help Hubert Hibernate," but Humphrey seemed unpreturbed by the omnipresent protestors. "You know, a lot of the so-called pickets aren't really hostile," he told reporters on the plane back to Washington. "They'd have a sign saying, 'Peace in Vietnam,' and I'd say 'That's for me,' and stick out my hand and they'd shake it. I was for peace before they could spell it."

Humphrey could shake the hand of every antiwar demonstrator in the country, however, and still not solve his basic problem, which was that too many Americans regarded him as a Lyndon Johnson without the Texas accent. "Vice President Tries, But Can't Shed Image As the President's Boy," the *Wall Street Journal* proclaimed in a headline over an account of his Western trip that accurately pinpointed the difficulties Humphrey was having. Humphrey's problems were illustrated on July 20 by a Harris poll that caused a near panic among some of his advisers. Released prematurely during a stop in Louisville by McCarthy — who had consistently downgraded the meaning of such polls — the poll showed Humphrey barely beating Nixon, 37 percent to 35 percent, while McCarthy ran far ahead of Nixon, 42 percent to 34 percent. And if New York Governor Nelson Rockefeller were the Republican candidate, the poll had Humphrey trailing by three points while McCarthy led Rockefeller by four.

"I could just sense all sorts of things were going amiss in that whole period," Humphrey said later. "It wasn't because we were doing anything wrong, we weren't. In fact, we were doing more things right, at least we were locking up delegations in the latter part of July and early part of August [Humphrey's private delegate count had reached 1,642 by the first week of August]. But I sensed that the public felt politics was a dirty word, a dirty disease, and they didn't want any part of it."

The unfavorable poll reinforced Humphrey's own feeling that he had to make a fundamental break with Johnson on Vietnam in order to establish his political independence, win over supporters of the late Robert Kennedy and bring McCarthy and his followers back into the fold after Chicago. Humphrey himself had tipped off several journalists that a major Vietnam policy statement was forthcoming, and on July 17, told Theodore Sorenson and Stephen Smith in New York that he would make a "very significant" statement on Vietnam within a few days. On Thursday morning, July 25, a fifteen-member task force headed by Harvard Professor Samuel P. Huntington, which had been working on a Vietnam white paper for more than a month, assembled in Humphrey's office in the Executive Office Building to prepare a final draft of that statement. The Huntington task force, one of two foreign policy advisory groups organized by Humphrey aide John Reilly, was joined by four members of Humphrey's staff — Reilly, Ted Van Dyk, William Welsh, and John Stewart — and by Agriculture Secretary Orville Freeman and Washington Attorney David Ginsburg, who was designated by Humphrey as his representative in the negotiations over the convention plank on Vietnam.[8]

Humphrey's foreign policy advisers started with the assumption that the cornerstone of his statement had to be a call for an immediate halt in the bombing of North Vietnam. Anything less, they reasoned, would not be considered a significant departure from the administration position or a clear enough signal to Humphrey's critics that he intended to change Vietnam policy if elected. Reilly had prepared a draft statement based on the Vietnam white paper, and the group labored over it, coming up with a thirteen-page final draft which was retyped while they went to lunch. In the afternoon, Humphrey joined them, read over the final draft and pronounced it satisfactory. Although the president had told him that he should clear any major policy statements on Vietnam with Secretary of State Dean Rusk, Humphrey decided this one was too sensitive and should be shown to the president. After some discussion, his advisers agreed.

That evening, Humphrey went next door to the White House and handed the statement, entitled "Vietnam: Toward a Political Settlement and Peace in Southeast Asia," to Johnson. "The president was very much opposed to it," Humphrey remembers. "I showed it to him, went all over it with him. His reaction was, in substance, 'Hubert, if you do this, I'll just have to be opposed to it, and say so. Secondly, Hubert, you ought not to do this because we have some things underway [in Paris] now that can lead to very important developments. Thirdly, Hubert, I have two sons-in-law over there, and I consider this proposal to be a direct slap at their safety and at what they are trying to do.' "

A dejected Humphrey returned to his office to break the news to his staff. "He said Johnson was mad as hell about it," Ted Van Dyk recalls, "that it would threaten the negotiations, that he would have to denounce Humphrey as being harmful to peace and that he'd have the blood of Johnson's sons-in-law on his hands. I told the people who were expecting the statement that there had been a lot of people with Johnson when Humphrey went over and that he never got a chance to show it to him, but that wasn't true, even though the story came out that way in the papers the next day."

Humphrey gave the draft back to Reilly and Ginsburg and asked them to rewrite it. Then he took their version with him to Waverly and reworked

[8] The other task force organized by Reilly was concerned with Asia as a whole and was headed by Columbia Professor Doak Barnett.

it himself. On August 9, the day after Richard Nixon was nominated by the Republican Convention in Miami Beach, Humphrey flew to the LBJ Ranch with draft number eleven. The draft contained Humphrey's promise to "not do or say anything that might jeopardize the Paris peace talks." Its key passage called for stopping all bombing of North Vietnam "when reciprocity is obtained from North Vietnam." [9] Even though "reciprocity" was essential to the administration's position, Johnson again denounced the draft in emotional terms that still remain fresh in Humphrey's memory:

> The main point he raised on the two occasions that I came to talk to him about Vietnam was, "You can get a headline with this, Hubert, and it will please you and some of your friends. But if you just let me work for peace, you'll have a better chance for election than by any speech you're going to make. I think I can pull it off. I think that I possibly can get negotiations going, and possibly get the beginnings of peace. If I do, that would be the greatest thing that ever happened to this country, and it would be the greatest thing that ever happened to you." This was a very sensible position that the president was taking and it put me very definitely on the spot with a lot of my people over what to do. [10]

Johnson's hint of an imminent breakthrough in the peace negotiations left Humphrey with no choice but to sit on his Vietnam statement and hope that Ginsburg would be able to engineer some sort of Vietnam plank which would be acceptable to Johnson, yet would mollify McCarthy and the liberal, peace-minded wing of the party at the convention, now only two and a half weeks away. Still, Humphrey was haunted by the feeling that Johnson, who was then seriously exploring plans for a summit conference with Soviet Premier Aleksei Kosygin, might be reconsidering his retirement. A curious incident on the day following Humphrey's visit to the LBJ Ranch did nothing to quiet those fears. Humphrey had been instructed by the White House not to bring any newsmen to the ranch with him, and Johnson ordered him not to reveal the substance of their discussion, which he didn't. But on the next day Johnson invited Nixon and his newly-selected running mate, Maryland Governor Spiro Agnew, to stop at the ranch on their way to San Diego for their campaign strategy planning session. The visit was widely publicized by a large contingent of newsmen accompanying Nixon and Agnew to the ranch. "I don't know why he did that," Humphrey later complained. "That bothered me and it still does."

In fact, Humphrey is convinced that Johnson was having second thoughts

[9] The draft was essentially unchanged from the one Humphrey had shown Johnson at the White House on July 25, except that it contained an added section on "Future Policies" in Southeast Asia, which it said should be based on three guidelines: self-help, regional and multilateral responsibility, and selective U.S. assistance. The draft also anticipated a strategy successfully pursued by Richard Nixon as it called on the U.S. to "help break the Chinese people out of their self-imposed isolation" and widen diplomatic contact with them.

[10] From an interview with the author on August 20, 1971.

about his decision not to run again. "I feel that the president, during this period, was in the throes of feeling that he maybe shouldn't have resigned," Humphrey said in the 1971 interview. "There are some people who think that he was looking forward to dropping in on the convention in Chicago and being renominated by acclamation. . . . I didn't feel that was much of a possibility . . . but there were people who thought it was a possibility and I think there was a move on for that with [Mayor Richard] Daley and some of them."

Humphrey's explanation of Johnson's behavior from then until the end of the campaign clearly reflects Humphrey's belief that Johnson was finding it very difficult to loosen his grip on the reins of power. As Humphrey said in the same interview:

> What I think happened all through this period was that the president couldn't help feel that here he was, a man that had given up the presidency, and here was his vice president, a man that was maybe going to get the presidency, and how could that vice president not endorse everything that the president had been for? . . . He was absolutely, totally involved [in Vietnam]. That was his major consideration. He had put so much into it and gone through so much pain and suffering for it, that there was just no way that he could disengage himself from it. And any retreat from his position that he didn't make himself looked like it was sabotaging his efforts. He changed his position, obviously, when he went into the Paris peace talks and stopped the bombing north of the DMZ. These were all policy changes on the part of Johnson. But for anybody else to recommend those changes, that was something that he couldn't take.

If Humphrey was haunted by Johnson's motives in the two and a half months between Kennedy's death and the convention, a different kind of ghost haunted McCarthy. The day after he returned from California — the day of Kennedy's death — he had lunch with Mrs. Geri Joseph, the DFL national committeewoman from Minnesota and a vice chairman of the United Democrats for Humphrey. Mrs. Joseph, who had known McCarthy ever since she interviewed him as a cub reporter after his first election victory in 1948, was shocked by his reaction to the assassination. "That's the only time in my life that I've ever seen him really incoherent," she recalls. "One sentence didn't have anything to do with the next. . . . I think that he honestly thought that Bobby had brought some of this on himself. And this troubled him terribly, the whole violence of it. I think that he was upset that he had set himself against the Kennedys and now this Kennedy had been killed. It wasn't really clear at all. He was just violently upset."

McCarthy's dark mood reflected his feeling that his only hope for the nomination, a stalemate between Kennedy and Humphrey, was now gone. "It's like someone gave you the football," he told the New York *Times* a few days after the assassination, "and the field never ends. There's no goal line. No opponent. You just run." His deep melancholy was equally apparent to his close friend, *Life*'s Shana Alexander, at about the same time. "I feel like the Black Knight out in the center of the field," he said. "I turn my horse round and round, but there is no one to fight. I go to their tents to strike their shields with my lance, but not even a shield hangs there now. Only flapping rags."

On the afternoon of June 7, McCarthy came to Humphrey's vice presidential office in the Executive Office Building for a meeting that might have prevented the beatings and bitterness of Chicago. McCarthy, who asked for the meeting, spent about an hour alone with Humphrey. Ted Van Dyk, whom Humphrey called into his office immediately after McCarthy left, recalls Humphrey's impression of the meeting: "It was clear that what Gene was doing was trying to find a reason to drop out — he wanted Humphrey to do something which would give him such a reason. He just had no more heart for it and quit campaigning, although at that time, it seemed to Humphrey that Gene was trying to dictate conditions which Humphrey just couldn't accept. I think that Gene was truly trying to help, that he was honestly and honorably trying to find some way to support Humphrey if Humphrey would just make some changes on Vietnam which don't look so major now, but they did then. There was no animus, they just agreed to disagree."

Four days later, McCarthy met for the last time with the man he'd forced from the presidency. Lyndon Johnson sat across a large conference table and briefed McCarthy on the military situation in Vietnam and the Paris peace talks as well as domestic policies. After the forty-minute session, McCarthy left as he came — by a rear entrance to avoid reporters. "He told me the Vietcong are getting desperate — making a last-ditch stand," McCarthy told an aide afterwards. "We're going to negotiate from strength. The same old stuff."

McCarthy's formal resumption of his campaign on June 12 was marked by the same kind of enigmatic behavior that would characterize his actions for the rest of the summer and the rest of his Senate career as well. At the last minute, he discarded a prepared statement emphasizing the need for a change of policies and leadership to meet the crisis of discontent in America, and also switched the news conference from the Senate Caucus Room — where he and both John and Robert Kennedy had announced their candidacies — to a much smaller room. He said he would continue a "limited campaign" and that the issues remained the same — Vietnam and "the militaristic thrust of American foreign policy" that he would remind people of unmet domestic needs and ask them "to continue to test the American political process." McCarthy mentioned Kennedy's name only in passing, said he would find it difficult to support Humphrey if his position on the war remained the same, and said he would not ask undecided delegates to vote for him rather than Humphrey. "I simply will ask them to be responsible delegates and to make the judgment that has to be made in August, which is a question of what issues the Democratic party is going to support at that time; and then to ask the question as to which candidate is likely best to carry those issues to the country."

It was clear, even to McCarthy's staunchest supporters, that he no longer had any stomach for campaigning. "McCarthy did not resign his candidacy," McCarthy Speechwriter Jeremy Larner later wrote in *Harpers* magazine, "he left his lottery ticket in the big barrel to await the hand of God. But he never again addressed himself to the moment. He stood all summer passive and self-absorbed in the winding-down of his campaign. . . . Now in the heat of a lost, hot, vacant summer, while millions hoped for him and waited, Gene McCarthy regressed to his balanced presentation of self, to the sacred ceremony of his personality." [11] Larner is one of those who feel that McCarthy was in a unique position for a brief period after the assassination to bring together the two halves of the Democratic party, but could not or would not do it. "If McCarthy had stepped forward at that moment with full presence and power, no one would have looked larger beside him," wrote Larner.

McCarthy's behavior grew more and more puzzling as the convention drew near. He spoke publicly about going to Paris for a first-hand look at the peace negotiations but dropped the idea because of its political and diplomatic sensitivity, he alienated Kennedy people by saying he didn't think a strong federal gun control measure ought to be passed "under panic conditions," and he hinted that he could support Rockefeller for president under certain conditions. When McCarthy's daughter Mary was asked by a reporter how her father was at this point, she replied, "Oh, he's feeling alienated."

McCarthy flaunted his alienation by refusing to make the slightest concession to political etiquette. He refused the entreaties of supporters to campaign in the New York primary, causing one of his New York organizers, Harold Ickes, Jr., to comment later, "McCarthy didn't throw cold water on the New York primary — he pissed on it." McCarthy also failed to return phone calls to several governors who had sent word to him that they were considering supporting him if only he would ask. (One of these was Harold Hughes who would nominate McCarthy at Chicago.) On two occasions, he canceled appointments with Mayor Daley that had been arranged by Patrick Crowley, a wealthy Catholic attorney in Chicago. UAW President Walter Reuther sent word through his top lieutenant, Leonard Woodcock — himself a McCarthy backer — that the UAW was considering endorsing McCarthy and that McCarthy should call Reuther to discuss the matter.

[11] Larner's article was condensed from his novelistic portrait of the McCarthy campaign, *Nobody Knows* (The Macmillan Co., New York). McCarthy called the book "a political *Portnoy's Complaint*," although he later said some of Larner's critical judgments about his personality were "acceptable to me."

McCarthy called Reuther once, but Reuther was out, and even though Reuther returned McCarthy's call five times in the next three days, Mc-Carthy's staff couldn't locate him. Finally, Senator George McGovern of South Dakota passed word that he might give his endorsement if asked. McCarthy never asked, and McGovern announced his candidacy a short time later, drawing off a considerable number of convention delegates who might have gone for McCarthy.

Although McCarthy continued a heavy speaking schedule, mostly in the non-primary states in the weeks preceding the convention, he was, as he later said, "speaking more about the Democratic party than about my own candidacy." In July, he took a break in his campaign, returning to his alma mater, St. John's University at Collegeville, Minnesota, for three days of relaxation. While the nine Secret Service men who had been assigned to him after Kennedy's assassination played softball with the monks and nuns, McCarthy sunbathed, went for long walks in the woods, read his poetry at a local coffeehouse, and mingled with the members of the monastic community he had once belonged to as a Benedictine novice.[12] "It is a great joy to me in the Lord that at last you have shown some concern for me again," he said, quoting St. Paul's letter to the Phillippians as he read the epistle at a private mass one night. ". . . I am not talking about shortage of money; I have learned to manage on whatever I have. I know how to be poor and how to be rich too. I have been through my initiation and now I am ready for anything anywhere; full stomach or empty stomach, poverty or plenty . . . ."

Nonetheless, McCarthy was blessed with political riches. A Harris survey of 1,524 voters in early July showed McCarthy with an impressively strong personal appeal. "Two facts emerge sharp and clear," Pollster Louis Harris wrote, "first, that in a clear-cut test today, McCarthy is a more appealing candidate personally than Humphrey; second, that the vice president has yet to project himself as a decisively positive presidential figure." McCarthy's drawing power was spectacularly demonstrated at a series of rallies in the month before the convention. He drew large crowds and warm receptions during a trip through the South. An estimated 50,000 people turned out for a fundraiser at Boston's Fenway Park — the largest crowd of the year at that point for any political event — on July 25, with many paying the same price to see the former Great Soo League first baseman that they would have paid to watch the Boston Red Sox baseball team. Two days later, an estimated 25,000 showed up at Detroit's Tiger Stadium, while a capacity crowd in St. Louis' mammoth Kiel Auditorium gave McCarthy a full 10 minute ovation on August 13. Madison Square Garden in New York was

[12] The Secret Service code name for McCarthy reflected both the popular image of his native state and the confused nature of his campaign. It was "Snowstorm."

sold out for McCarthy on August 15, the same day McCarthy rallies were held in thirty cities around the country.

Despite the encouraging public response, McCarthy felt there was little chance he would get the nomination but wanted to make certain enough pressure could be exerted on Humphrey to ensure that the two cardinal issues which had compelled him to challenge Johnson in the first place — Vietnam and party reform — were given their fullest possible expression in the convention. However, McCarthy had offered no leadership to accomplish this and, as a result, the campaign that had inspired so much hope in New Hampshire had now degenerated into three bitterly feuding factions, each more convinced than McCarthy was that he had a chance to win the nomination and each with a different strategy for doing so.

One faction represented the vestigial remains of the Children's Crusade. Led by Blair Clark, Curt Gans, and Sam Brown, it favored "people power," a national grass-roots organizing drive carried out by young volunteers to mobilize the pro-McCarthy sentiment around the country and to intimidate delegates into supporting McCarthy. A second group, headed by former Democratic National Committee Chairman Stephen Mitchell, who had joined the campaign in May, adopted the approach of "confrontation politics." Mitchell's strategy was to mount an all-out assault on the convention machinery — credentials, rules, platform — that would force Humphrey to choose sides among the various segments of his support. Mitchell's complex plan was succinctly expressed by Jerry Eller: "Achieve panic — then win." [13] Finally, there was the quieter, more traditional approach of Tom Finney, who felt that a small corps of seasoned political operatives, heavy use of television and selective polls, and pragmatic alliances at the convention represented McCarthy's best chance. But McCarthy, who turned to Finney in desperation for a strong man to bring the badly disorganized campaign together as he had in the Oregon and California primaries, refused to give him overall control and the Mitchell strategy prevailed. The disintegration of the command structure led to some incredibly wasteful ventures, including the ordering of 1,000,000 post cards for a pre-convention propaganda drive (850,000 of which were unused because time ran out) and the duplication of secret polls costing $25,000 apiece, one set of which was returned to Pollster Oliver Quayle in October unopened.

Humphrey had publicly stated during the summer that the selection of McCarthy as his running mate was "not an impossibility," and several of

[13] McCarthy leaned toward the Mitchell strategy, he indicated during an interview on "Face the Nation" on August 25, the day before the convention opened. He said he would win when delegates decided "that they have to have me to win," and then added, in what would prove to be an accurate description of the convention, "That's why you run a three-day convention, you've got to get people tired and worried and anxious, and Chicago is a big place, they get worn down to the point where they make a decision. It's a kind of trial by ordeal; it's not a logical process at all."

Humphrey's supporters, including Miles Lord, a former Minnesota attorney general who had been made a U.S. district judge on McCarthy's recommendation, had sounded out McCarthy about his interest in the vice presidency.[14] McCarthy said he was not interested and suggested that it would be better if he wasn't even asked. For him to join Humphrey on the ticket, he said, would be like "the captain of a ship getting in the first lifeboat and waving to those on board saying, ' I hope it doesn't sink.' " He instructed Tom Finney to set up a meeting with Humphrey and, early in the week before the convention, the two old friends from Minnesota who had come to Washington together twenty years earlier and now represented the forces of conflict in the Democratic party, sat down to breakfast at Humphrey's southwest Washington apartment.

McCarthy knew that Humphrey had the nomination all but locked up. But he was obsessed with keeping faith with his supporters and with exercising maximum influence on the position of Humphrey on Vietnam and party reform. He emphasized that he would not accept the vice presidency and Humphrey assured him there would be no more talk of offering it to him. Humphrey, on the other hand, explained his dilemma over the Vietnam plank, adding that it would be impossible for him to break with the president's hard line policy but that he would gladly accept a dovish plank if the convention voted it. Humphrey knew that McCarthy's proud and uncompromising nature could make him a major obstacle to post-convention party unity if he withheld his support or if, as Humphrey had been told, McCarthy was considering a fourth party challenge in the fall. But McCarthy assured Humphrey he did not intend to form a fourth party and, when the hour-long meeting ended, Humphrey felt he had an agreement that would prevent a disastrous party split from developing at Chicago.

"Gene and I had an understanding before Chicago," Humphrey said in a 1971 interview. "We met in my apartment just before the convention and I told him that if he got the nomination, he'd have my support, and that if I got the nomination, I hoped that he would support me. He said it would be impossible for him to come up to the platform on the night of the nomination and pledge his support right away, but that if I gave him a couple of weeks for a turn-around, he could do it. I said, 'Gene, can you be sure you can do it sometime in mid-September?' and he said, yes, he could."

[14] Lord's role as a self-appointed emissary between Humphrey and McCarthy was one of the more intriguing aspects of the Humphrey-McCarthy relationship. He frequently turned up on the candidates' planes and was, according to one Humphrey aide, "forever trying to get them together." His efforts were largely unnecessary as the two candidates were in frequent direct contact on their own. On one occasion, informed by Lord that McCarthy was willing to see him, Humphrey retorted, "Miles, I just talked to Gene last night and we both agree that you're the cause of all the trouble between us."

CHAPTER XVII

CATASTROPHE — CHICAGO 1968.

*Well, it looks like all my friends have come
to witness the execution.*
> Eugene McCarthy, arriving at the Democratic
> National Convention: August 25, 1968.

I proudly accept the nomination of our party.
> Hubert Humphrey: August 29, 1968.

Despite the efforts of Hubert Humphrey and Eugene McCarthy to avoid a confrontation at Chicago, other forces were at work to frustrate those efforts and propel them into a savage clash that would rupture their long friendship, hamstring Humphrey's presidential hopes and shake the Democratic party to its foundations. Nowhere were the forces that thrust Humphrey and McCarthy together more evident than in the drafting of the platform plank on Vietnam, the critical issue that had divided them and the Democratic party from the first months of the Johnson-Humphrey administration.

By the time the Platform Committee began hearings at the Statler Hilton Hotel in Washington on Monday, August 19, one week before the convention opened, a coalition of antiwar factions comprised of McCarthy, Kennedy and McGovern supporters had been working behind the scenes for weeks trying to fashion a unified minority plank. David Ginsburg, Humphrey's chief negotiator on the Vietnam plank, had been working quietly with the coalition, and he felt that it was not impossible that Humphrey could endorse the minority plank. Also, Senator Edmund Muskie on the same day presented to the Platform Committee the outlines of a compromise plank which had Humphrey's tacit approval. However, President Johnson, in a hard-line speech in Detroit that day, made it clear that he regarded anything but a plank that strongly supported the administration's Vietnam policy a personal affront to him.

Whatever slim chance existed that Humphrey might be able to support a peace plank, no matter how carefully worded, vanished on August 20 when Soviet troops invaded Czechoslovakia. The invasion gave the Platform Committee, which was heavily weighted with Johnson supporters, a perfect rationale for approving a hard-line Vietnam plank. Johnson called a late night session of the National Security Council at the White House to discuss the invasion and, afterwards, sternly warned Humphrey against going too far to placate the doves.

Czechoslovakia also gave McCarthy a chance to exercise his penchant for saying the wrong thing at the wrong time. Disturbed because he felt Johnson was trying to make political hay out of the invasion, he issued a statement criticizing the president for overreacting. "I do not see this as a major world crisis," he declared. "It is likely to have more serious consequences for the Communist party in Russia than in Czechoslovakia. I saw no need for a midnight meeting of the U.S. National Security Council." Nowhere in his statement was there a condemnation of Russia, and McCarthy's horrified aides persuaded him to issue another statement and to hold a news conference to clarify his position. "Of course I condemn this cruel and violent action," McCarthy said in his second statement. "It should not really be necessary for me to say this, but to make clear my attitude, I do." Asked why he had not expressed the same sentiments in his original statement, McCarthy replied in an irritated voice, "That goes without saying. Do I have to say it every time?"

By Friday night, August 24, the McCarthy-Kennedy-McGovern coalition, meeting in Chicago, had come up with a minority plank acceptable to all the antiwar factions. The strongly worded plank, which was based largely on a speech given by Edward Kennedy in Massachusetts three days earlier, contained four principal proposals. First and most important to the peace forces because it was the touchstone of their position, the plank called for "an unconditional end to all bombing of North Vietnam." Second, it asked for negotiation of a mutual phased withdrawal from South Vietnam of all American and North Vietnamese troops. Third, it encouraged the Saigon regime to negotiate a coalition government with the National Liberation Front, and finally, it recommended lowering the level of violence and reducing offensive operations to enable early withdrawal of foreign forces from South Vietnam.

Richard Goodwin, who had helped write the Kennedy speech, had returned to the McCarthy campaign and was his principal agent in the peace plank negotiations, successfully opposing efforts by Ted Sorenson, Kenny O'Donnell and others to water down the plank so Humphrey could run on it. Goodwin read the final draft over the phone to McCarthy back in Washington and, when McCarthy gave his approval, the plank was released late that night.

Although a strong plank, it was still essentially a compromise document. Of its four principal points, only the first, the call for an unconditional end to the bombing of North Vietnam, reflected the intransigence of the peace forces. As soon as the minority plank was released, Ginsburg and William Welsh, Humphrey's administrative assistant who had been in Chicago working for Ginsburg since Wednesday, went over it word by word with Congressman John Gilligan of Ohio, one of those trying to work out a minority plank acceptable to Humphrey. Ginsburg was optimistic when he finished reading the plank. "There's not ten cents of difference between this and the vice president's policy," he declared.

Ginsburg's optimism was misplaced, however. Immediately calling Humphrey, who was still at his office next door to the White House, he read the minority plank to him. Humphrey agreed that there was not that much difference between the minority plank and one drafted for him by Ginsburg. Humphrey, who had been told by the president to clear all statements on Vietnam with Dean Rusk or Presidential Adviser Walt Rostow, called both of them that evening and read the Ginsburg draft to them. They indicated they saw no problems with it, and Humphrey left for Waverly the next day for a short rest before going to Chicago, convinced that he could successfully negotiate the perilous Vietnam issue at the convention. However, just as Harry Truman had been unaware that Humphrey would cause the civil rights issue to blow up in his face at the 1948 Democratic convention, Humphrey did not know that his efforts to avoid a divisive floor fight on Vietnam were about to be wrecked by Lyndon Johnson.

On Friday night, Johnson had summoned the chairman of the Platform Committee, Congressman Hale Boggs of Louisiana, back to the White House for a briefing on the Czechoslovakian crisis, and had shown him intelligence reports warning of the dire effect a bombing halt would have on the American military situation. Boggs returned to Chicago more determined than ever to defeat the minority plank. On Saturday night, Charles Murphy, a former chairman of the Civil Aeronautics Board and one of Johnson's personal representatives at Chicago, called at Humphrey's headquarters on the twenty-fifth floor of the Conrad Hilton Hotel and asked for a copy of Ginsburg's plank draft. The next night he was back and, in a private meeting with Ginsburg, Welsh and Boggs, announced that the draft plank was utterly unacceptable to the president. The president objected to much of the language in the draft, Murphy said, particularly the call for a halt in the bombing. (Ginsburg had written, "Stop the bombing of North Vietnam. This action and its timing shall take into account the security of our troops and the likelihood of a response from Hanoi." Johnson insisted that the language should read,

"Stop all bombing of North Vietnam when this action would not endanger the lives of our troops in the field; this action should take into account the response from Hanoi.")

On Monday morning, August 26, as Boggs prepared to ram the majority plank through the hundred-member committee, Humphrey found out just how completely Johnson intended to make this his convention. Postmaster General Marvin Watson, who was closeted with Murphy and a few other trusted Johnson lieutenants in a secret communications center just two floors below Humphrey's headquarters, arrived at Humphrey's suite and told him Johnson absolutely refused to accept Humphrey's draft plank.

Humphrey, astounded because he had cleared the plank with Rusk and Rostow, immediately called Johnson at the LBJ Ranch. "He told me that the plank did not meet with the policies of this government," Humphrey recalled in a 1971 interview. "I said, 'Mr. President, this is what I feel we ought to be doing for the future.' He made it clear that we were not discussing these things. He said, 'I can't go for this and I don't think that the platform committee is going to go for it either.' I said, 'But Mr. President, this has been cleared with Rusk and Rostow.' He said, 'Well, it hasn't been cleared with me.' "

At almost the same moment that Humphrey and Johnson were speaking, the Platform Committee, in a 65-35 vote, emphatically endorsed the majority plank and Johnson's Vietnam policy. The action set the stage for the bitter floor fight Humphrey feared. But McCarthy welcomed the committee's action as an opportunity to settle finally one of the issues on which he'd based his candidacy. "Now the lines are clearly drawn between those who want more of the same and those who think it necessary to change our course in Vietnam," he said. "The convention as a whole will decide."

The now-certain prospect of a divisive fight over Vietnam compounded Humphrey's uncertainty as he waited to take his place alongside the other men of history who had been nominated for president of the United States. He had arrived in Chicago the day before after the four hundred mile flight from Waverly, a few hours after McCarthy, to be greeted by a wailing bagpipe band that provided a fitting accompaniment for his harrassed state of mind.

One of Humphrey's first concerns as he checked into Suite 2525A in the Conrad Hilton was the atmosphere of excessive security and control clamped on the convention and the city of Chicago by Mayor Daley and President Johnson. Humphrey had appealed privately to Johnson and Democratic National Chairman John Bailey to move the convention to Miami Beach — where the Republicans had held their convention without any major disruptions — but Johnson had decided on Chicago. In early August, Humphrey had written to Daley urging him to provide a hall for the thousands of youthful antiwar demonstrators expected to descend on the city during the convention, but Daley didn't answer.[1] The unprecedented security arrangements, which included barbed wire ringing the convention hall and some 30,000 police, firemen, National Guardsmen, regular army troops, FBI and Secret Service agents on duty or on call, caused Humphrey to fear that his candidacy would be tainted with the aura of bossism at best and bloody repression at worst.

Even more grating to Humphrey at the time was the fact that he had no control over convention logistics. Johnson's control of convention machinery was so thorough that Humphrey had to send his son-in-law, Bruce Solomonson, to stand in line each morning outside a Johnson functionary's room to plead for extra tickets to the convention hall for his family and friends. Humphrey railed against his predicament his first day in Chicago when an aide told him that McCarthy was complaining about accommodations for his staff. "What the hell's he complaining for?" Humphrey retorted. "I'm the vice president of the United States and I'm being treated like a Yugoslavian peasant!"

Humphrey's frayed nerves were not soothed by an embarrassing situation he found himself in soon after he arrived in Chicago. His chief delegate counters, Bill Connell and Larry O'Brien (O'Brien had become Humphrey's chief of staff after Kennedy's death), assured him he had between 1,400 and 1,500 delegate votes, many more than the 1,312 needed for nomination, but there was an unstable element in their count.[2] The South, with 527 delegates, was unhappy about Humphrey's stand on the unit rule. Connell, a native Texan, earlier in the summer had privately assured Governor John Connally of Texas, Governor John McKeithen of Louisiana and other Southern leaders that Humphrey would oppose abolishing the unit rule — a device giving the majority view on a delegation control of the entire delegation— at the 1968 convention. But on Wednesday, August 21, the day before the Rules Committee began hearings on convention procedure, Humphrey released the text of a letter to the committee chairman, Governor Sam Shapiro of Illinois, urging abolition of the unit rule "at this convention" and in the call to the 1972 convention. Connally, who was also unhappy with Humphrey's wooing of the McCarthy-Kennedy doves, and with credentials challenges aimed at Texas and other Southern states, denounced Humphrey and began talking about starting a "draft Johnson" movement. Humphrey offered profuse apologies to Connally on Monday, assuring him he would fight to keep the unit rule for the 1968 convention, that he would not waver from Johnson's Vietnam

---

[1] McCarthy also was concerned about the possibility of violent demonstrations and telephoned Daley before the convention to offer his help. Daley did not offer any suggestions nor did he ask for any. However, McCarthy asked his student supporters to stay away from the convention.

[2] The 3,099 delegates at Chicago had a total of 2,622 votes.

policy and that he would oppose the credentials challenge to the Texas delegation.

Humphrey's obeisance to Connally did not come, however, in time to prevent a McCarthy operative from approaching Connally about the possibility of becoming McCarthy's running mate. Dick Goodwin, who recalled that Connally had favored McCarthy instead of Humphrey for vice president in 1964, spent two hours with Connally on Saturday night — pointedly reminding him Humphrey would not dare to take a Texan on his ticket — and came away from the meeting ready to bet that Connally would take it. Patrick Lucey, the former Wisconsin lieutenant governor and Kennedy aide who became a key figure on McCarthy's convention team and who had arranged the Goodwin-Connally meeting, now had to find out if McCarthy was amenable.

"I'm going to pose a question," said Lucey as he rode in from the airport on Sunday afternoon with McCarthy. "You can take twenty-four hours to answer it. Do you want to be president bad enough to have John Connally as a running mate?" McCarthy didn't need twenty-four hours. "The answer is no," he quickly replied.

McCarthy had good reason for his unhesitating rejection of Lucey's feeler. He had been introduced at the airport to the more than ten thousand supporters who met him by Senator Ralph Yarborough, a leader of the liberal wing of the Texas Democratic party and a mortal political enemy of Connally. McCarthy, in turn, referred to Yarborough as "a man who has stood up to Allan Shivers [a former Texas governor], John Connally and Lyndon Johnson." Calling for just a "modest use of intelligence" by the delegates, McCarthy said he was "not interested in compromising the cause at any point in the platform or on the slate itself. And with the mixture of the new politics of ideas and of sound judgment, we are prepared to mix a little bit of the old politics in trying to persuade them that, not only is McCarthy the best man, but he is the man with whom the Democrats can win in 1968."

McCarthy began mixing old and new politics shortly after arriving in Chicago. That afternoon, he paid an obligatory call on Mayor Daley and the Illinois caucus. McCarthy spent about twenty minutes exchanging pleasantries and emerged without any encouragement from his fellow Irish Catholic. "He didn't say much," McCarthy explained in language virtually identical to that which he had used to describe his strained meeting with Robert Kennedy five months earlier. "It was what he didn't say, really."

What Daley didn't say was that he had made up his mind that he could not support McCarthy under any circumstances and that Humphrey could not win in November. In fact, Daley had had breakfast that morning with Jesse Unruh, the leader of the big California delegation, and agreed that Humphrey wasn't a winner and that they should look for another candidate. Unruh, still grieving over the death of Robert Kennedy and deeply committed to seeing that Kennedy's antiwar position was reflected in the party's candidate and platform, arranged the breakfast with the idea of asking Daley to hold off so they could search for another candidate. But before he could suggest it, Daley beat him to it. "Humphrey's a lousy candidate," Unruh recalls Daley saying. "If we're going to have another Lyndon Johnson, let's draft the real thing." Unruh said Johnson was unacceptable to him and Daley said McCarthy was unacceptable to him. The man both Daley and Unruh really wanted as the presidential nominee, they quickly agreed, was Edward Kennedy.

The Daley-Unruh breakfast touched off a "draft Kennedy" movement that finally proved abortive, but it represented a very real threat to Humphrey's nomination and greatly increased his insecurity. Once again, he faced the possibility that a Kennedy would snatch away the prize he had sought so long, and he was stunned when Daley announced after the Sunday caucus that he had decided to hold off committing the Illinois delegation "to see if something develops." The unprecedented move by Daley didn't go unnoticed by McCarthy who, after a staff meeting in his twenty-third floor suite at the Conrad Hilton on Monday morning, asked Goodwin, "What about this Teddy thing?"

McCarthy's inquiry was the beginning of an intriguing subplot that made him a central figure in the most important backroom meeting of the year, brought to an end the challenge he had begun in New Hampshire and paved the way for Humphrey's nomination. Goodwin later described that subplot and meeting in a *Look* magazine article that McCarthy said was "just about the way it was."

> I replied that I had not talked with Kennedy but I was sure he was not a candidate and did not want the nomination. I did not believe he would allow himself to be drafted in opposition to McCarthy. Furthermore, he might not allow his name to go before the convention under any circumstances.
>
> "Well," McCarthy replied, "we might do it together. After all, experience isn't really important in a president as long as he has the right advisers. Character and judgment are the real thing."
>
> I was still unsure of his meaning until he continued: "Of course, he's young, but then, those fellows in the Revolution were young too — Jefferson and Hamilton. But Jefferson had to wait a little while to be president. Still, that's not important. Let's see how things develop."

Goodwin immediately called Stephen Smith, Kennedy's brother-in-law and his principal agent at Chicago, and suggested that he and McCarthy get together. Smith said he needed time to think it over and continued canvassing the delegates to see if there were enough votes to stop Humphrey. In the meantime, Humphrey and his top aides were frantically trying to shore up their support. By late in the day, his pledges to stand fast on the unit rule and Johnson's Vietnam policies had paid off. In order to stop

Kennedy, Johnson had ordered Watson to get Connally and other Southern leaders back into line behind Humphrey and the Southern revolt collapsed. "It became apparent to some of us," Goodwin wrote, "that the last miracle was not to be. Humphrey would be nominated."

On Tuesday morning, McCarthy again asked Goodwin about Kennedy's position. Goodwin repeated what he had said the day before and suggested that McCarthy speak directly with Smith, using the Vietnam plank debate that was scheduled that night as a cover for the meeting. McCarthy agreed and the meeting was held late that afternoon in McCarthy's suite. Again, Goodwin describes what went on:

> As he and Smith sat facing each other, the talk began with pleasantries and a quick agreement by Smith to cooperate on Vietnam.
>
> Smith then said he wanted McCarthy to know that Senator Kennedy was not a candidate, and that neither he nor anyone else had lifted a finger on his behalf. Nor would they do so. His only role was to listen and observe, making sure that no one did anything that might be misinterpreted as a Kennedy desire for the nomination.
>
> McCarthy listened calmly and then proceeded. "I can't make it," he said. "Teddy and I have the same views, and I'm willing to ask all my delegates to vote for him. I'd like to have my name placed in nomination, and even have a run on the first ballot. But if that's not possible, I'll act as soon as it's necessary to be effective."
>
> That was it, McCarthy had not been asked for support, and he had asked nothing in return. Both Smith and I walked from the room deeply moved. I thought of the snows of New Hampshire, the endless months of campaigning, the dedicated movement that had gathered around McCarthy banners—all now graciously and austerely offered to the Massachusetts Senator.[3]

The Kennedy boom collapsed that night in confusion and mutual distrust between the McCarthy and Kennedy forces. Steve Smith was conferring by phone with Kennedy, who remained at his Hyannisport, Massachusetts, home throughout the convention, when CBS erroneously reported that Smith had spent two hours with McCarthy (the meeting lasted only about ten minutes) seeking his support for Kennedy. An infuriated Smith demanded a retraction from Goodwin, and Goodwin put out a statement confirming the meeting but denying that Smith sought McCarthy's support. However, the situation was too muddied now, and early the next morning (Wednesday), Kennedy telephoned Humphrey, Daley and Jesse Unruh to tell them he would withdraw his name even if nominated and would put out a public statement to the same effect. Only then was Humphrey finally certain he would be the Democratic nominee.

[3] A slightly different account of the McCarthy-Smith meeting was later provided by Smith in *New York* magazine. Smith said that McCarthy made his offer to support Kennedy and then added gratuitously, "While I'm doing this for Teddy, I never could have done it for Bobby." When *Time* magazine reported that the offer brought tears of gratitude to Smith's eyes, he said, "Somebody mistook it for all the spit in them."

McCarthy's role in the chain of events that assured Humphrey's nomination is fairly clear but his motives are not, unless viewed in the context of two events that happened earlier on Tuesday. One was his appearance with Humphrey and McGovern before the California delegation — the only face to face confrontation of the convention between Humphrey, McCarthy and McGovern.[4] The other was an interview McCarthy gave to the Knight newspapers shortly before his meeting with Steve Smith.

At no time during the convention did McCarthy's undisguised feeling that his position was hopeless come through more distinctly than in his appearance before the California delegation. As the lone survivor of the two candidates who had won eighty-eight percent of the vote in the California primary, McCarthy ordinarily would have been expected to control the delegation. But his refusal to invoke the slain Kennedy's name during an appearance before the delegation at the California state Democratic convention on August 10 had alienated many delegates. "Everybody was looking for an excuse to go with him and if he'd said anything at all about Bobby, they would have been up cheering him wildly," recalls Richard Kline, an Unruh aide and later chief fund raiser for Senator Edmund Muskie's presidential campaign.

Nevertheless, the California delegation was still dispirited and hungry for a candidate other than Humphrey when it arrived in Chicago. "We knew in our hearts that the Kennedy boomlet wasn't real and that he wasn't going to and shouldn't run," Frank Burns, the delegation vice chairman and Unruh's top political agent said later. "It was just total frustration and a feeling of doom and inevitability." Just before McCarthy, Humphrey and McGovern showed up in the Grand Ballroom of the LaSalle Hotel on Tuesday morning, Unruh told McCarthy that he could win over the delegation if he would only say a kind word about Robert Kennedy but McCarthy refused. In fact, he had attempted to get out of the three-way confrontation, protesting that he had spent so much time in California the past nine months that there was little more he could say that the delegates hadn't already heard from him. But he finally agreed to come and led off by saying, "I suppose that this delegation needs to hear me less than it needs to hear any candidate in history." He mentioned Kennedy but only as part of the historical record. "You know my stand on the issues," he said. "Senator Kennedy and I went up and down and across the state; and the results of that election are known to you and what happened. . . . I do not intend to restate my case."

Instead of paying homage to Kennedy or restating his case, McCarthy launched a verbal attack on McGovern, with whom he was furious for a comment he had made about McCarthy the day before. "He has taken

---

[4] Humphrey and McCarthy had agreed to a television debate before the convention but called it off by mutual consent.

the view that a passive and inactive presidency is in order," said McGovern, "and that disturbs me. Solving our domestic problems will be much more difficult and that will require an active and compassionate president." Mc-Carthy coldly responded to McGovern's comment: "I am surprised to find that yesterday I was said to have no domestic program. Well, I have had a domestic program since 1948, when I first ran for Congress. . . . They suggest that I would be a passive president. Well, I think a little passivity in that office is all right — a kind of balance, I think." Passive or not, Mc-Carthy said he had been "the most active candidate in this party this year." However, he declined to answer a question about his views on Vietnam because he said they were well known, and when it came his turn to give a closing summary, he said: "I suppose it must come to this — that one explain nine months in three minutes. But we expect to be put to rather severe tests. It is a little like building boats in a bottle. . . ."

McGovern stole the show and some delegates with a brilliant performance, while Humphrey gave a typically rambling speech that cited his belief in "the politics of hope and of faith," his civil rights stand at the 1948 Democratic convention and his lifelong dedication to peace.[5] However, he did not say what McCarthy and many of the delegates were waiting to hear — that he had moved toward a break with Johnson on Vietnam. "I did not come here to repudiate the president of the United States," Humphrey declared in response to a question. "I want that made quite clear."

He made a familiar defense of U.S. policy in Vietnam: "We have not sought to impose a military solution. Regrettably, wars have their built-in escalation. No one sought to escalate it on our side. . . . I believe that it is about time that we recognize that some things have happened that are within what we would call our hopes and aspirations. . . . The roadblock to peace, my dear friends, is not in Washington, D.C. It is in Hanoi. And we ought to recognize it as such."

Humphrey had convinced McCarthy he was still locked in the embrace of Lyndon Johnson and was not prepared to pay McCarthy's price for party unity, McCarthy indicated in an interview with the author the next day. He said he felt Humphrey's position "was not simply a question of his loyalty to the administration but reflects his own thinking. I felt that he doesn't offer a real alternative and I think he'd carry on pretty much the same way as Johnson did. It was not just a question of his doing it because he was the vice president but because I think he believes in it."

However, it was another interview that McCarthy gave on Tuesday afternoon, an hour before his meeting with Steve Smith, that finally sounded the

[5] The California delegation gave McGovern fifty-one votes, compared to ninety-one for McCarthy, seventeen for the Reverend Channing Phillips, a favorite son candidate from the District of Columbia, and only fourteen for Humphrey. There was one abstention.

death knell for his long campaign and signaled his abandonment of hope that Humphrey would change on the war. With his legs propped up on a coffee table in his suite, McCarthy told Publisher John Knight and several reporters from the Knight newspapers that, "I think it was probably settled more than twenty-four hours ago." Asked if he meant the nomination was wrapped up for Humphrey, McCarthy replied, "I think so." Did he think Humphrey would now have to take a different position on Vietnam, Knight asked. "Well, it looks as though he's going to try to say that Nixon's position and [his] on the war are the same, and try to neutralize that issue, and run on domestic issues. That was his pitch today. It looks to me that that's the way Humphrey's going to try to play it."[6]

Although McCarthy later claimed he understood that the interview would not be published until after the nomination, he had in fact placed no restrictions on its use. Word that McCarthy had given up spread through the convention hall along with rumors of his meeting with Smith as McCarthy went to dinner with Robert Lowell and a few friends and recited poetry.

In the convention hall, meanwhile — after unenthusiastic delegates listened to Anita Bryant sing "Happy Birthday" to an absent Lyndon Johnson — the Democratic party was taking the last of several momentous steps of self reform. On Monday night and early Tuesday morning, following hours of argument, the convention disposed of the most important of the fifteen credentials challenges that represented the basis of the McCarthy forces' strategy of disruption. "Yell foul at every turn of the screw" and "get the delegates in the habit of voting against Humphrey" was the way Steve Mitchell had described his basic plan of attack the week before the convention. However, it was apparent that that strategy was failing when the convention early Tuesday morning defeated an attempt to split the Texas delegation by seating part of a racially mixed slate headed by Ralph Yarborough and turned back a motion to give all of Georgia's seats to a reform slate headed by black activist Julian Bond instead of dividing the delegation between Bond and Georgia Governor Lester Maddox as the Credentials Committee had recommended.[7]

On Tuesday night, the convention accepted the Credentials Committee compromise on Georgia and settled the remaining credentials contests,

___

[6] McCarthy said several other things in the interview: that he would not form another party and that he'd probably support Humphrey "after a couple of weeks"; that Nixon probably would beat Humphrey in November; that he might retire from the Senate after his term ended in 1970; that he might run for president again, and that he doubted that Edward Kennedy could win the nomination.

[7] Another major credentials challenge and an exception to the Mitchell strategy was over the seating of the Mississippi delegation, where Humphrey and McCarthy forces worked together to sustain a challenge of the regular Mississippi Democratic party on the basis of racial exclusion in the selection of delegates.

mostly to the benefit of the regulars. But in one of the most significant actions in the party's modern history, the convention approved, by a 1,350-1,206 vote, a minority report from the Rules Committee barring the unit rule at all levels of the party. Reform of the party processes had been one of the principal themes of the McCarthy campaign, and indeed, was the issue which led to his first involvement in politics twenty years earlier, so it was ironic that the death of his candidacy coincided with the lone major triumph of his supporters at the 1968 convention.[8] The credentials challenges and the abolition of the unit rule for the 1972 convention (delegates had done the same for the 1968 convention by a voice vote the night before) provided the foundation for reforms that would drastically change the nature of the party and the make-up of the next convention. Specifically, the convention ordered the party to set up a special committee to reexamine the entire delegate selection process, with all delegates to the 1972 convention to be elected through "procedures open to public participation," to be chosen "within the calendar year of the convention" and ruled that the unit rule was to be eliminated clear down to the lowest level of the party.[9]

Hubert Humphrey awoke shortly before 8:00 on Wednesday, August 28, and saw that the sun was sparkling off the blue waters of Lake Michigan twenty-five stories below the Conrad Hilton Hotel. He had been up late the night before, attending a wedding anniversary party for his son Robert, and he had gone to bed just after 1:00 A.M., as demonstrators in Grant Park across the street chanted "Dump the Hump" and "Stop the War" and other slogans. But now the sun was shining and it looked like a good beginning for the biggest day of his life. Humphrey dressed quickly in the blue ensemble that Muriel liked — dark suit, pastel shirt and dark tie — and hurried out into the living room of his spacious suite to greet Mayor Daley, who had come for breakfast, and finally to pledge his support. As they ate, Edward Kennedy telephoned, assuring Humphrey that he would not accept a draft. Now Humphrey was certain that he would be nominated for president that night, and his certainty was reinforced when Governor John McKeithen of Louisiana arrived a short while later for a second breakfast with a pledge of support from the Southern governors.

Still, Humphrey did not allow himself the luxury of behaving like the nominee. "I have been in politics long enough to know its uncertainties," he cautioned a caucus of Connecticut delegates later that morning in a

[8] On Monday night, McCarthy worked on a party reform speech which he was considering delivering in a dramatic appearance before the convention on Tuesday, but he dropped the plan in light of Tuesday's events.

[9] Over six hundred delegate votes — almost one-fourth of those at the convention — were cast by delegates elected between two and four years before the convention, according to the Ad Hoc Commission on the Democratic Selection of Presidential Nominees organized earlier in the year by McCarthy supporters and headed by Iowa Governor Harold Hughes.

jammed, sweaty room at the nearby Pick-Congress Hotel. Then, in a voice already hoarse from too many similar speeches, he added, "I've won a lot of elections and I don't intend to lose this one to Richard Nixon."

Returning to the Hilton, Humphrey walked through a packed lobby that was still reeking from the stench of stinkbombs placed there the night before. Smiling broadly as he pumped outstretched hands, he looked startled when a man wearing a McCarthy button shouted, "You used to be our hero!" Seconds later, a boy who appeared to be in his late teens called to Humphrey. "Mr. Vice President, you're a warmonger." Humphrey stopped, looked the boy in the eye and said calmly, "You know better than that, son." A Secret Service agent pushed the boy back and another teenage boy shouted, "Dump the Hump!" touching off a chorus of "Dump the Hump! Dump the Hump!" as Humphrey disappeared into the elevator.

Humphrey spent the rest of the day in his suite, but he had virtually no time to relax or reflect. He had decided that Mayor Joseph Alioto of San Francisco should give his nominating speech and now Humphrey's speechwriters labored over it and his acceptance speech in an adjacent conference room. He lunched with black athletes Jackie Robinson and Elgin Baylor, watched the Vietnam plank debate on the two color television sets in the living room of the suite, greeted politicians and old friends who moved in and out, gave interviews and posed for photographers, and conferred with key staff members about various problems. Periodically, Humphrey directed bitter comments toward the television sets as they showed the angry floor debate on Vietnam or scenes of the demonstrations the night before. "If that instrument would stop playing up the kooks and rioters, they put them on only when the cops are fighting with them; that instrument just recruits trouble." Humphrey bristled when Sander Vanocur of NBC referred to the "Kennedy boom" of the day before. "Hell," he snapped "that wasn't a Kennedy boom, it was a Vanocur boom." As the convention prepared to vote on the Vietnam plank, and delegates from his native South Dakota passed out black arm bands, Humphrey sat down for an interview with *Time* — which was planning a cover story on him — and *Life* and complained about press misinterpretation of his stand on the Vietnam plank. " 'Hubert hardens his line,' say the papers, but how can they say I'm hardening my line, when all I'm saying is that you shouldn't sell anybody out?"

Meanwhile, two floors below Humphrey in Suite 2320, as the voting began on the issue that had compelled him to lay his political life on the line nine months earlier, McCarthy played mock baseball in his suite with his brother Austin, using an orange for a ball. Goodwin, Mitchell and Finney had pressed McCarthy to ignore the traditional ban against a candidate going to the floor before the nomination so he could make an impassioned speech in favor of the minority plank on Vietnam. He briefly considered their suggestions, including one by Finney that he agree to support the ticket if the convention adopted the peace plank, but he decided against it, even though Mitchell called him three times from the floor and urged him to come. McCarthy replied: "I've always been running against Johnson; if he shows up I will." Although McCarthy had authorized Goodwin to accept the compromise wording of the Vietnam minority plank, he now complained that it left out essential points of his position and was poorly drafted.

By 5:00 P.M., the voting was over. The majority plank on Vietnam had prevailed by a vote of 1,567-1,041, and the McCarthy-Kennedy-McGovern delegates donned black arm bands and joined in a mournful chorus of "We Shall Overcome" as the convention recessed until evening for the nomination itself. In Grant Park, where ten thousand demonstrators had gathered, the first of the day's two violent clashes with police occurred, but it was mild compared to what was to come.

At 8:00 P.M., as the nominating process began at the amphitheatre, blue-helmeted police clashed with demonstrators in the streets outside the Hilton. McCarthy watched from his twenty-third floor vantage point as the police attacked the demonstrators who had taunted them for days. Onlookers were pushed through the plate glass windows of the Hilton. He watched with shocked fascination, comparing the double envelopment of the demonstrators by the police and National Guardsmen to an ancient battle between Hannibal and the Romans. "It looks like the battle of Dannae," he said. He searched for an adequate phrase to describe the scene below. Finally he found one. "A battle of purgatory," he said, turning from the window in disgust.

As tear gas wafted through the open windows of his suite, McCarthy hurried to the fifteenth floor where a campaign poster proclaiming "Gene McCarthy — A Breath of Fresh Air" marked an improvised emergency first-aid room set up to treat the injured. He helped his brother Austin, a surgeon, and Psychiatrist William Davidson, who had traveled with McCarthy throughout the campaign, comfort the bruised and bleeding, and in a rare loss of composure, exploded at newsmen, "Get out of the way, fellows. You don't have to see anything. Get the hell out of the way."

Shaken and angry, McCarthy returned to his suite, muttering "It didn't have to be this way." He watched silently with Abigail and their three daughters — Michael, seventeen, had gone to the amphitheatre — while Governor Harold Hughes gave McCarthy's nominating speech. The McCarthy campaign, Hughes said, had "caused a clean wind of hope to blow across this land. . . . The people found Gene McCarthy for us. They found him; they followed him; they have urged him on us. He is more accurately the people's candidate than any other man in recent history." Then, as Julian Bond and John Kenneth Galbraith seconded the nomination, McCarthy made a final gesture to end the violence. Calling Blair

Clark and Dick Goodwin, his convention floor managers, he asked if they agreed it would reduce tensions if he had his name withdrawn from the nominations. He told them to think it over and call him back in ten minutes. "It looked like the convention might break up in chaos," he later said. "I thought this might stabilize it." But McCarthy didn't wait for his aides to call back. "Hell, I think we ought to get out of this thing," he said and put in an urgent call to Hughes. But it was too late. The balloting had already begun, and McCarthy could see he was losing badly. Someone made a derogatory comment about Humphrey and McCarthy said wearily, "It's no use being bitter about Hubert. He's too dumb to understand bitterness."

Humphrey, however, did understand that the violence was damaging his chance to be president. His eyes still watering from the tear gas, he held a news conference at 10:00 P.M. in his suite. His aides told him of the violence below, he said, but he had been too busy to spend much time watching. He said he was dismayed by the violence, and he castigated the demonstrators. "They don't represent the people of Chicago. They've been brought in from all over the country. We knew this was going to happen. It's a separate act to itself," he said of the violence. "A kind of side show." Later, as he watched the delayed scenes of the street violence intermingled with coverage of the nominating speeches, Humphrey's anger grew. "I'm going to be president someday," he snapped at the television set as film clips erroneously indicated that violence was breaking out anew. "I'm going to appoint the FCC — we're going to look into all this!" Then, a final blow. After Alioto's nominating speech, Carl Stokes, the black mayor of Cleveland, rose to give the seconding speech and signal Humphrey's civil rights commitment. But NBC aired its film of the violence and Stoke's speech was replaced by scenes of bloody rioting.

Finally, at 11:19 P.M., the balloting began. Humphrey, sitting in an easy chair with a pad of paper marked "Office of the Vice President of the United States," marked off the actual vote against his projected votes. There were no surprises and he grinned with satisfaction as he got 38½ votes from Minnesota compared to 13½ for McCarthy. He had 61 votes projected for New Jersey — he got 62. "Ninety-six," he said when New York came up. The vote for him was 96½. When Pennsylvania's turn came at 11:47 P.M., Humphrey leaned forward in anticipation. This would put him over the top. "Ah," he said happily as Pennsylvania — a state McCarthy had carried in a non-binding primary by more than a half million votes — gave him 103¾ votes for a 1,317½ total. "I feel like jumping," Humphrey declared, and he leaped into the air just as he had when the 1948 convention passed his minority civil rights plank.[10] As a smiling Muriel Humphrey, who

[10] The final count was Humphrey 1760¼, McCarthy 601, McGovern 146½, The Reverend Channing Phillips (favorite son of the District of Columbia and the first

was at the amphitheatre, appeared on the T.V. screen, Humphrey enthused happily, "There she is. I wish Momma were really here. See how pretty she looks." With that, he patted the screen and bent down and kissed her image.[11]

A few minutes later, two calls arrived for Humphrey. He went to an anteroom and spoke first to President Johnson, calling from his ranch. "Bless your heart, thank you," Humphrey said to the man whose shadow he thought he finally had escaped. The second call was from Richard Nixon, returning the courtesy call Humphrey had made to him at Miami Beach three weeks earlier.

Even as Humphrey celebrated his nomination, his thought turned to his next urgent task — choosing a running mate. Throughout the summer, Edward Kennedy had been his first choice for vice president, but despite repeated entreaties by Humphrey and some of his aides, Kennedy, who was still recovering from the trauma of his brother's assassination, refused to go on the ticket.[12] McCarthy was clearly out of the question, and Humphrey had ruled out Governor Richard Hughes of New Jersey a few days earlier because he felt he would not help the ticket. After one final, futile phone call to Kennedy on Wednesday, Humphrey pondered the only two remaining serious contenders, Oklahoma's brash young Senator Fred Harris, and Maine's Senator Edmund Muskie, a slow-moving, straight-talking moose of a man who had been one of Eugene McCarthy's closest friends until lining up with the Johnson supporters in the Vietnam plank battle.[13]

Negro ever to have his name placed in nomination for the presidency) 67½, Governor Dan Moore of North Carolina 17½, Edward Kennedy 12¾, and others 16½.

[11] The mixed reaction to Humphrey's nomination was evident in the Minnesota delegation. Thomas Kelm, a big, ruddy-faced man whose father had helped launch Humphrey's political career in 1944, was one of the happiest Minnesota delegates. "I guess my first thought when the vote was announced was about my father," said Kelm, with tears in his eyes. "He put Humphrey on the 1944 campaign as a state manager for Roosevelt and Truman." A few feet away sat Howard Kaibel, a twenty-three year old law student who had helped organize the first group of McCarthy supporters in the state in late 1967. "Hubert Humphrey will go down to overwhelming defeat in November," he said, adding a prediction that Humphrey's nomination would mean "the death of the Democratic party."

[12] Two examples serve to illustrate Humphrey's desire to persuade Kennedy to accept the vice presidential nomination. He had Robert Short keep his private jet ready to fly to Cape Cod on a moment's notice to pick up Kennedy and return him to Chicago to be dramatically unveiled as his running mate. Even more intriguing was a plan proposed by several advisers and endorsed by Larry O'Brien that called for Humphrey to announce in his acceptance speech that he was going to resign as vice president and fly to Massachusetts to ask Kennedy to become his running mate. "He gave it serious consideration for about a half an hour," says Max Kampelman.

[13] The only other persons given serious consideration by Humphrey were Kennedy's brother-in-law Sargent Shriver and former North Carolina Governor Terry Sanford. Shriver was rejected mostly because of objections from Kennedy supporters, and Sanford was rejected because Humphrey felt he could not take a Southerner on the ticket. Earlier in the year, Humphrey also discussed the possibility of asking New York

Humphrey gave the first indication of his choice at a 1:30 A.M. meeting in his suite with a group of Southern governors led by Tennessee's Buford Ellington — but dominated by John Connally — who came to extract their pound of political flesh for helping make Humphrey the nominee and for their continued support in the coming campaign. "Humphrey began the meeting by saying, 'I'm thinking of Ed Muskie — what do you think of that?' " recalls Ted Van Dyk. "They clearly were there as Strom Thurmond and the Southerners had come to Nixon [after Nixon's nomination at Miami Beach a few weeks earlier] and they were damn well going to dictate something, but Humphrey knew what they were trying to do and that took the edge off of them." [14]

Humphrey obviously still hadn't made up his mind between Harris and Muskie, however, as he discussed the matter with Van Dyk and Connell while relaxing on a rubdown table getting a massage at 3:00 A.M. He went to bed with the matter still apparently undecided, but was no longer indecisive when Van Dyk went to wake him up a few hours later. "He was always tough to get up in the morning," Van Dyk recalls, "and, God, much to my surprise, he was sitting up wide awake and said, 'Well, what do you think now?' I said, 'Well, overnight I was thinking what about Gene?' and he said, 'No, the job's too important,' and just dismissed it. I said 'Then it's still between Muskie and Harris?' and he said, 'It's Muskie. Why don't you go phone him.' "

For ten minutes, Van Dyk tried to call Muskie's room on another floor of the Hilton, but the line was busy. Finally, Van Dyk went to get him. "Knowing Humphrey, I was afraid somebody else would walk in and make an argument for Harris and there might not ever be a nominee," says Van Dyk, who told Muskie that Humphrey wanted to see him. "He was a little nervous, but the funny thing was that when I came into his room, everybody knew what it must be and they started shaking hands and slapping each other on the back without anything ever being said." Mrs. Muskie, he recalls, was still on the phone.

Humphrey first called in Harris and broke the news to him. He explained that he felt Muskie, as an older, more experienced man who was an ex-governor and a Catholic, would strengthen the ticket more than Harris. Then Humphrey brought in Muskie, had him and Harris shake hands, and said, "Ed, I think you knew all the time I was for you."

Governor Nelson Rockefeller, a Republican, to join him on a coalition ticket. Massachusetts Governor Endicott Peabody approached Rockefeller on Humphrey's behalf, but Rockefeller said he did not think he could run as a Democrat.

[14] Connally also expressed the Southerners' discontent with Richard Hughes, whom they disliked because they felt he had shortchanged the South as chairman of the Credentials Committee. Hughes later said the Southern governors were responsible for his not being on the ticket, but Humphrey had ruled him out well before the convention.

Humphery explained in a 1971 interview with the author why he picked Muskie:

Because I thought that Muskie was a stable man, a decent man. I thought that we would make a good team. I could see that he would make a good vice president in some of the plans that I had for coordinating domestic policy. I thought also that he was an honest man, that he would bring a sense of integrity to the government. I felt that there was a need for a kind of stabilizing force in the government. And my politics had always been a little more strident than his, more evangelical. I guess what I was really looking for was somebody who would complement me on the ticket. Plus the fact that I don't think the vice presidency ought to be handled by incompetents. I think my judgment was damn good.

While Humphrey chose a vice president and prepared his acceptance speech, McCarthy was looking beyond the November election. He told a post-midnight press conference that his defeat was only a "temporary setback to our cause. . . . I think we opened up a new kind of politics for America. I think it will manifest itself after the convention and make itself even more strongly felt in the next four years." His support of Humphrey would depend upon "his interpretation of what the platform means," McCarthy said, but he would not lead a fourth party and expressed doubt that such a party would be a "substantial force" in the election.

McCarthy did not appear embittered by his defeat, and he spoke with wry humor Thursday afternoon in a Hilton ballroom as he thanked cheering supporters for their efforts in the long campaign. Smiling, he waited for the chants of "We want Gene" to die down, and then tried to put his campaign and his defeat into perspective. It was a protest movement, McCarthy said, but like most protest movements, it had been swallowed up by those in power and the protest would be incorporated into the Democratic party and would change it. But it would not end there he predicted:

I think that the country has passed a judgment on the war. Our failure here was not with the people, not with reference to our not having accomplished our purpose — because we did accomplish that. It was only that the judgment of the people could somehow not be put through the procedures of politics in 1968. And I don't say that we have altogether failed as yet. But in any case, we have tested the process and we have found its weaknesses.

He called for "one man, one vote" at the next convention and when someone yelled, "Forget the convention!" he answered, "We've forgotten the convention. We've forgotten the vice presidency. We've forgotten the platform. And we've forgotten the national chairman of the Democratic party."

Then McCarthy explained why he still believed in the system he had challenged for so long.

We have had a great victory to this point, one which should reassure us about the system itself. But more important than that . . . I think we are on the way in 1968 to preparing the way for the judgments that need to be made, perhaps somewhat less clearly, perhaps with our getting less credit than we might have liked if we had the White House. But we are willing to share that, and to forgo it, if we can accomplish these things for the country. I think that the outlook is one that must be reassuring; one of confidence and one of optimism — not really of our own making, but by virtue of our having discovered it to exist in the minds and in the hearts of the people of this country. . . . But I think that we can say that we were willing to open the box and to see what America was. We had that kind of trust and that kind of confidence. And when we opened it, we found that the people of this nation were not wanting.

Minutes later, at almost the same time that Humphrey was introducing his new running mate to a press conference, McCarthy walked with his Secret Service escort across Michigan Avenue through the lines of National Guardsmen with their sheathed bayonets and into Grant Park, where he stood under an elm tree with a red balloon in its branches and spoke to the dispirited band of demonstrators. "I am happy to be here to address the government of the people in exile," he said, describing his own future condition. And in language reminiscent of St. Paul writing to his brethren in far-off Galatia, McCarthy expressed the determination that would sustain him until the next Democratic convention: "So that is the message on this late afternoon. I will not compromise. All the way, I say! I have not departed from my commitments to you, nor have you departed from your commitments to me. . . . So we go on in this same spirit."

A few hours later, Humphrey stepped to the podium of the convention hall and tried to repair the deep wounds caused by the old foreign war that had divided his country and the new domestic war that had divided his party. As hundreds of green and white "Humphrey and Muskie" signs blossomed on the floor and huge banners saying "We Love Mayor Daley" unfurled from the galleries, Humphrey declared, "I proudly accept the nomination of our party." Then he referred to the violence that had made this, the long-anticipated moment in his life, a searing disappointment, he deplored ". . . the troubles and the violence which have erupted, regrettably and tragically, in the streets of this great city, and for the personal injuries which have occurred. Surely we have now learned the lesson that violence breeds counterviolence and it cannot be condoned, whatever the sources."

Humphrey's speechwriters had argued with him over the next passage, and when the argument went unresolved, they simply omitted it from the final copy of his speech. But Humphrey wrote it back in with his black felt tip pen during the ride to the amphitheatre and he now invoked St. Francis of Assisi to help him find peace amidst all the turmoil: "Where there is hatred, let me sow love. Where there is injury, pardon. Where there is doubt, faith. Where there is despair, hope. Where there is darkness, light."

He reviewed the convention's accomplishments and paid tribute to the great figures of the Democratic party who had stood where he now stood: Franklin Roosevelt, Harry Truman, Adlai Stevenson, John Kennedy . . . "and Lyndon Johnson." The hall exploded with cheers and boos at the mention of Johnson's name, but Humphrey continued, ignoring the derisive catcalls: "I truly believe that history will surely record the greatness of his contribution to the people of this land, and tonight to you, Mr. President, I say thank you. Thank you, Mr. President." Then Humphrey spoke eloquently and emotionally of the three "new realities" that faced the nation — "the necessity for peace in Vietnam and the world . . . the necessity for the peace and justice in our cities and in our nation . . . and the paramount necessity for unity in our country."

He tried once more, as he had since the day he became a candidate, to break loose from Lyndon Johnson on the great issue of Vietnam:

> If there is any one lesson that we should have learned, it is that the policies of tomorrow need not be limited by the policies of yesterday. My fellow Americans, if it becomes my high honor to serve as president . . . I shall apply that lesson to search for peace in Vietnam as well as to all other areas of national policy.

Then, asking for the unity that would never come, Humphrey asked for the help of his defeated rivals:

> To my friends — and they are my friends, and they're your friends, and they're fellow Democrats — to my friends Gene McCarthy and George McGovern, who have given new hope to a new generation of Americans that there can be greater meaning in our lives . . . to these two good Americans: I ask your help for our America, and I ask you to help me in the difficult campaign that lies ahead.

Finally, Humphrey ended his forty minute speech with a plea that would fall on ears deafened by the bedlam that surrounded his nomination:

> I say to America: put aside recrimination and dissension. Turn away from violence and hatred. Believe — believe in what America can do, and believe in what America can be. And with the help of that vast, unfrightened, dedicated, faithful majority of Americans, I say to this great convention tonight, and to this great nation of ours, I am ready to lead our country!

Flanked by his newly nominated running mate, Edmund Muskie, and one of his defeated opponents, George McGovern, Humphrey accepted the convention's acclamation. But McCarthy was conspicuously absent. He had declined Humphrey's last minute request to appear on the platform with him.

However, while Humphrey never rejected McCarthy as a potential ally, the Chicago police still looked upon McCarthy as an enemy. Shortly after 5:00 A.M., police and National Guardsmen raided the McCarthy staff head-quarters on the fifteenth floor of the Conrad Hilton. Their excuse was that objects had been thrown at them from the windows of Suite 1505A, and although it was never proven that the McCarthy workers threw any of the objects, the police broke open rooms, beat McCarthy workers with billy clubs and herded them roughly into elevators to the main lobby. McCarthy, who had arisen early with the intention of going to Grant Park again, was leaving his suite when he ran into a campaign worker, whose head was swathed in a bloody bandage. The worker told of the trouble in the fifteenth floor and McCarthy went there to find his young campaign helpers in a state of panic and a number of girls, including his niece, Marybeth McCarthy, crying hysterically. He demanded to know who was in charge, but the police could not tell him. "Just what I thought," said McCarthy, "nobody's in charge."

Word was sent to Humphrey's suite, asking that he come at once and help quell the latest violence, but his press secretary, Norman Sherman, not realizing the seriousness of the situation, refused to waken the sleep-ing nominee. Humphrey's failure to condemn the beatings was later cited repeatedly by McCarthy as a significant reason for his long delay in en-dorsing Humphrey for president. Humphrey, in a 1971 interview, gave these reasons for his failure to respond:

> Frankly, I was so involved with the things that we were doing, and actually — I regret to say — so isolated from the things that were happening there, and so angry with some of the activities of those that were there, that it was difficult, maybe, to make a valid or a good judgment.
>
> I had gone through several months of this unbelievable harrassment. It's not very pleasant to be invited to a place to speak, as a guest, and have people spit on your wife, and call her every filthy name in the book when you're going into a place, to have people throw urine on you, human excreta, to have them tear your wife's coat practically off her back and call her a whore. How do you think you would like that, day after day, month after month? By people who say they believe in peace and brotherly love. I just couldn't quite take that.
>
> After a while, I got to looking at these people and saying: "Well, they're just not decent people." When they throw stink-bombs in the lobby of the hotel, and when they stand down under your window and utter the most foul profanity all night long — I don't consider that peace-making . . . I really don't . . . I think it was a terrible thing.

McCarthy delayed his departure from Chicago from Friday morning until late that afternoon to assure that police did not take further action against his young campaign workers. As his chartered airplane left the city that had witnessed the destruction of McCarthy's hopes and Hum-phrey's Democratic party, the pilot announced over the intercom, "We are leaving Prague."

CHAPTER XVIII

THE UNHAPPY WARRIOR

*After Chicago, I was like the victim of a
hurricane, having to pick up the debris and rebuild
but with too little time to do the job.*
                              Hubert Humphrey in a 1969 interview.

Not even Hubert Humphrey's legendary optimism could hide the reality
of his desperate condition as he flew to his Waverly home with his running
mate, Senator Edmund Muskie, on the evening after his acceptance speech
at Chicago. The convention that nominated Humphrey had been a disaster,
leaving the Democratic party in ruins and Humphrey still tied to Lyndon
Johnson and the war. After the violence at Chicago, there was talk of a
splinter party on the left, while Alabama Governor George Wallace threatened to make heavy inroads among blue-collar voters and Southerners on the
Democratic right. With the traditional Labor Day opener just three days
away and the election only eight weeks away, the Humphrey campaign was
bankrupt and beset by severe organizational difficulties, with polls showing
that only about 30 percent of the voters favored him. Meanwhile, Richard
Nixon relaxed at Key Biscayne, Florida, secure in the knowledge that the
Republican party was united behind him and that his well-financed campaign was functioning with smooth efficiency.

Humphrey never came to grips until after the convention with the tough
question of what kind of a campaign he would run against Nixon. He failed
to delegate clear authority to anyone to plan the details of the campaign
until shortly before the convention, and he was unable to do anything about
the savage infighting going on among a half dozen of his top advisers for
control of the campaign. The two young senators who had conducted his
delegate search, Walter Mondale and Fred Harris, left Chicago with a sour
taste in their mouths and were only marginally involved in the campaign

365

after the convention.[1] Humphrey's loose chain of command allowed Bill Connell to exercise partial control of post-convention planning while Agriculture Secretary Orville Freeman, who had been asked by Humphrey to draft an overall campaign strategy, was told that he would be running the post-convention effort. (Humphrey originally had asked former White House aide Kenny O'Donnell to run the campaign, but O'Donnell declined shortly before the convention because he felt it would damage his chances to run for governor in Massachusetts in 1970).

Humphrey had told Freeman in early August to "think about what I should be doing the day after the convention." Freeman drew up a plan that called for Humphrey to take his running mate and top advisers to the Greenbriar Hotel in White Sulphur Springs, West Virginia, for several days immediately after the convention to work out his schedule, his positions on the key issues and other major details of the campaign just as Nixon had done. Freeman showed Humphrey the plan, which included a massive media effort, about a week before the convention, but Humphrey felt it was unrealistically expensive. He turned in desperation to Larry O'Brien, who had agreed to run Humphrey's campaign only through the convention. O'Brien reiterated his intention to quit after the convention but said he would revise the Freeman plan first. He and two aides from the Democratic National Committee, Ira Kapenstein and Joseph Napolitan, drafted a rough, thirty-five page plan that wasn't completed until August 28, the day Humphrey was nominated. A few hours before the balloting, O'Brien and Humphrey went over the plan and Humphrey approved everything in it. At 3:00 A.M. on August 30, the last day of the convention, Humphrey called O'Brien to his suite and pleaded with him to change his mind and take over the campaign. "Larry, I've just got to have you," Humphrey said as he offered to make O'Brien both campaign manager and chairman of the Democratic National Committee. O'Brien gave in, although as he later recalled, "Frankly, it looked like a hopeless task. I only took it because of a great sympathy for Humphrey and the problems he faced, and his ability to convince me it was only for a brief period and that I had a responsibility to the party to see it through."[2]

[1] Mondale's disenchantment stemmed from personal battles with several of Humphrey's more conservative advisers. His bitterest fights were with Bill Connell and Max Kampelman over efforts to push Humphrey toward an open break with Johnson on the war. Mondale, who like Harris virtually disappeared after the convention, later said, "I didn't leave Chicago, I escaped it." The reason for Harris' departure from the campaign leadership was later described by Humphrey: "Fred wanted to be vice president. He was terribly disappointed when I didn't pick him."

[2] Freeman was so unhappy over Humphrey's decision not to turn over the campaign to him that he threatened to quit the campaign until Humphrey placated him by personally asking him to stay on as a top adviser. Humphrey felt Freeman, who had run three campaigns for him in Minnesota, lacked national campaign experience and would give his campaign too much of a Minnesota coloration.

With his campaign finally in the hands of a competent professional, Humphrey headed for Waverly with the Muskies. The homecoming for the first Minnesotan ever nominated for president by a major party was a quiet one, with only about three hundred persons waiting at Twin Cities International Airport to greet the new Democratic nominee. Although the crowd was friendly, there were reminders of the unpleasantness of Chicago. One young man carried a crudely lettered sign that read, "Go back to Chicago and Daley's fascist cops, Humphrey," prompting a member of Humphrey's party to reach across the fence and angrily rip up the sign.

Humphrey was still smouldering about the violence that had besmirched his nomination when, in the first public statement of his campaign the next day, he denounced the riots and defended Mayor Daley. He said the riots were "planned" and "premeditated," and added, "We ought to quit pretending that Mayor Daley did something that was wrong. He didn't condone a thing that was wrong. He tried to protect lives." On Sunday, September 1, after more than two thousand friends and neighbors turned out in front of the Waverly Village Hall to pay tribute to the Humphreys and Muskies — and to hear eighteen year old Krista Elsenpeter sing "The Hubert Humphrey March" — Humphrey again deplored the action of the Chicago demonstrators. "If there is any one thing that the American people need to rise up and protest about, it is this tendency of some to take to the streets to settle their problems," he told the cheering crowd.

That evening, Humphrey flew to New York to open his campaign formally by marching in the city's Labor Day parade the next day — he passed up the traditional Democratic campaign kickoff in Detroit's Cadillac Square because of the prospect of slim crowds — and was forced to enter his hotel by a side entrance to avoid several hundred shouting demonstrators. Humphrey had tried out the phrase "a New Day" in his acceptance speech and again at Waverly for use as his campaign theme, but the demonstrators provided the only theme of his first month of campaigning as they chanted "Dump the Hump" over and over again. On Monday, after a twenty-five block march up Fifth Avenue, Humphrey backtracked on his initial stand on the Chicago disorders. In an interview on a local educational television station in which he proposed a blue-ribbon committee to study the Chicago violence, he said four times that Chicago police had "overreacted" He said he was certain that Mayor Daley "didn't want to condone the beating of those people with clubs," and added, "I didn't condone it."

Humphrey's ambivalent stand on the Chicago violence would hurt him with Eugene McCarthy's supporters and with the Daley organization, but he had more critical problems to worry about at the time. Picking up O'Brien and his two helpers, Kapenstein and Napolitan, in New York, Humphrey flew back to Waverly Monday night to fill in the details of his campaign plan. The work began on the plane as Napolitan, a specialist in the use of political advertising, typed up a three-page plan that Humphrey marked "O.K. — HHH — go."

O'Brien had enjoyed two full weeks to plan John F. Kennedy's campaign against Nixon in 1960, but now he didn't even have time to sleep. He and his two aides went straight to a guest cabin when they arrived at Humphrey's lakeside home, and sitting down with yellow legal pads and a big pot of coffee, stayed up all night plotting the campaign that had already begun. At 6:00 A.M., as the braying of Humphrey's Abyssinian jackass greeted the Minnesota sunrise, the trio finally got a few hours of sleep. At 11:00 A.M., O'Brien called in Humphrey, Mrs. Humphrey, Orville Freeman, campaign treasurer Robert Short, fund raisers Dwayne Andreas, Patrick O'Connor and Jeno Paulucci, Humphrey's longtime confidant Fred Gates, and several other Humphrey advisers to go over O'Brien's plan. "It was a very basic plan, nothing very fancy," O'Brien later recalled. "It was sort of flying by the seat of your pants. The first element of it was simply where is the candidate going to go? It was a matter of just getting on the telephone and seeing where we could send him to kick off the campaign."

The group went on to talk about an even more pressing problem which was familiar to Humphrey — the lack of campaign funds. An estimated four million dollars had been spent in the pre-convention effort, much of it for extravagant purposes such as flying delegates to Washington on chartered airplanes to be wined and dined, and the campaign already was deeply in debt.[3] Napolitan's media plan called for concentrating the advertising effort in the final weeks of the campaign and Short said he was confident he could raise two million dollars by then, but everyone present knew the campaign finances were in dismal shape.

As the Waverly planning session broke up, Richard Nixon was completing a triumphal tour through downtown Chicago, the first stop of a lavishly financed campaign. An estimated 400,000 persons greeted Nixon as he drove through the Loop during the lunch hour before retiring to his hotel to prepare for a carefully staged $35,000 regional television panel show that evening. Nixon's highly successful Chicago visit presented such an obvious contrast with the Democratic disaster of only a week before that Humphrey and all his strategists knew they were starting with a terrible handicap. "I felt when we were done that we had at least put something together so we could start the ballgame, but God, it was just an unbelievable nightmare and it stayed that way throughout the campaign," O'Brien later recalled. "I frankly feel that of all the other matters that people discuss about why Hubert Humphrey lost the election, the most significant element,

[3] Humphrey's pre-convention spending fell far short of the other major candidates of both parties, according to figures compiled by Dr. Herbert Alexander of the Citizens Research Foundation. Eugene McCarthy's pre-convention campaign cost $11 million; Robert Kennedy's $9 million; Richard Nixon's between $10 million and $12 million, and Nelson Rockefeller's $8 million.

the basic problem, was the extremely limited time we had to put together a campaign organization under perhaps the most difficult circumstances that the party has faced in a long, long time."

Humphrey's handicaps were all too evident when he began his formal campaign on Monday, September 9, with a single day cross-country trip that took him from Philadelphia to Denver to Los Angeles. Humphrey was subjected to unmerciful heckling from antiwar demonstrators among a disappointing crowd which Mayor James Tate estimated at 100,000 but which less partisan observers pegged at only one-tenth that size. Pressed by reporters to spell out his stand on the war, Humphrey said, "I think I can safely predict that unless there are any unusual developments . . . we'll be able to start to remove some of our troops. . . . I would think that negotiations or no negotiations, we would start to be able to remove some of the forces in early 1969 or late 1968."

Later that day in Denver, where he was again plagued by poor advance work and angry hecklers, Humphrey startled reporters by declaring that he would have "no trouble at all " accepting the defeated minority plank on Vietnam that called for an unconditional halt to the bombing of North Vietnam. Although he qualified his remarks by telling newsmen on the flight to Los Angeles that a bombing halt would have to include a reasonable response from North Vietnam, the qualifier didn't prevent him from being undercut in Washington. The next day, Secretary of State Rusk repudiated Humphrey at a news conference, saying "No one should suppose that a bombing halt is going to produce peace in a few days."

At the same time, President Johnson sternly cuffed his vice president into line when at an American Legion convention in New Orleans, he flatly dismissed a bombing halt and declared, in an obvious reference to Humphrey's prediction of more troop withdrawals, "No man can predict when that day will come." Humphrey, meanwhile, continued to grasp at straws. Arriving in Houston a few hours later, Humphrey waved a copy of the Houston *Post* with a headline that reported the withdrawal of a Marine regiment from Vietnam and said the story "verified" his prediction and was a forerunner of more troop withdrawals. Minutes later, however, aides pointed out what Humphrey had failed to see, that the Marine regiment had only been on temporary assignment and had already been replaced by an equal number of troops. Later that day, still in Houston, Humphrey changed his "prediction" of a troop withdrawal to a "hope," and released a statement saying that the return of the Marines "in no way indicates any general withdrawal of American troops." A dispirited Humphrey returned to Washington that night, only to receive a 1:00 A.M. telephone call from Defense Secretary Clark Clifford, who bluntly pointed out he had gotten his facts wrong on the troop withdrawal statement.[4]

---

[4] Muskie also angered Johnson on September 10 when he told questioners in St.

While Humphrey was trying to disentangle himself from his own rhetoric on Vietnam, he received more depressing reports from Larry O'Brien about the sad state of his campaign machinery. Humphrey himself had seen signs of serious Democratic disunity on his cross-country tour. Texas Governor John Connally and California Assembly Speaker Jesse Unruh were conspicuously absent when he visited their states. Nor was there any evidence that Eugene McCarthy soon would return to the fold. "It is inconceivable to me," Humphrey had told a Houston rally in a direct appeal for McCarthy's support, "that we wouldn't be together when the choice is between Nixon and Wallace and myself."

As Humphrey waited for party wounds to heal, he sought the support of less intransigent doves like Senators Edward Kennedy and George McGovern. In the second major trip of his campaign, a fifteen-day tour of fourteen states beginning in Boston on September 19, Humphrey joined Kennedy, who was making his first political appearance since the assassination of his brother Robert. But even Kennedy's presence on the same platform failed to quiet the raucous noise of antiwar demonstrators that was now becoming a regular feature of Humphrey's campaign appearances. Hundreds of angry college students confronted Humphrey with the most vicious heckling he had yet faced as he tried to speak before an estimated ten thousand persons jammed into a downtown intersection. They booed and shouted "Shame on Teddy!" and "Sellout!" as Kennedy introduced Humphrey and declared his support for him. Much of Humphrey's twenty-minute speech was drowned out by the angry protestors. Finally, as Kennedy sat grim faced and Muriel Humphrey studiously tried to ignore the screaming, placard-waving students, Humphrey spoke directly to his antagonists: "We will not move this country forward if it is plagued by those who deny freedom of speech, and who deny freedom of assembly to those who offer appeals to reason!" The demonstrators were unmoved by Humphrey's appeal to reason. "Bullshit! Bullshit!" they shouted over and over again.

Humphrey was bitter about his rough treatment in Boston as he flew to Sioux Falls, South Dakota, to accept McGovern's public pledge of support. Calling the pickets "intentionally mean anarchists . . . who are determined not to let anyone speak," Humphrey told reporters he would not be intimidated. "They have met a tough guy . . . I have no intention of being shouted down. . . . Take a look at them — filled with hatred, bitterness, bigotry. Look at their faces, filled with violence. They will never live long enough to run us off the platform because basically they are just cowards."

Even more frustrating to Humphrey than the hecklers who wouldn't let him speak was an opponent who wouldn't debate him. Using all the oratori-

Louis that "I think stopping the bombing can be a valuable step toward peace and that it would be a valuable risk we should take."

cal weapons at his command, Humphrey attempted to portray Nixon as a man of unsure convictions, unsettled philosophies and untested mettle. In Springfield, Illinois, standing on the steps of Abraham Lincoln's home, Humphrey declared, "I think it's time we stopped passing like ships in the night . . . I think it's time we discussed our differences . . . openly, forthrightly, face-to-face — in Peoria, in Springfield, or on a television network." He charged Nixon with equivocating on important issues such as the nuclear non-proliferation treaty, order and justice, (Humphrey's phrase for "law and order"), civil rights and farm problems. Ticking them off one by one, he asked after each, as if he were actually debating him, "Mr. Nixon, where do you stand?" In Louisville, Kentucky, he heaped sarcasm on Nixon: "Every day you read about that cool, that confident, that composed and that smiling Mr. Nixon — the man who campaigns without running, the man who takes it easy and never makes a mistake . . . who either evades or straddles every major issue. . . . Is it confidence when he refuses to join me in a direct television debate on the issues or is it something else?"

Humphrey kept up his barrage of criticism of Nixon, but he wasn't ignoring the threat of George Wallace's appeal to the masses of blue-collar voters who traditionally voted Democratic. After paying a visit to his political idol, Harry Truman, in Independence, Missouri, ("He told me to give 'em you know what, and that's just what I'm going to do," Humphrey said as he emerged from Truman's white-frame house), Humphrey began aiming more of his barbs at Wallace. He took note of Wallace's steady climb in the polls while speaking to an enthusiastic noon-hour crowd in downtown Toledo, Ohio, on September 2: "They tell me he's got a following. And if he got it on the basis of law and order, then it's the greatest hoax that's ever been perpetrated on the American people — because then he ought to start at home. . . ." In Minneapolis the next day, where he stopped to visit his seven year old retarded granddaughter, Vicki Solomonson, who was hospitalized with pneumonia, Humphrey reminded delegates to a statewide AFL-CIO convention that in Wallace's Alabama, "the worker finds low wages, low unemployment benefits, the lowest workman's compensation in the country, unemployment rates above the national average and the highest sales tax in the country" along with one of the highest crime rates. And at a news conference in Robert Short's Leamington Hotel, Humphrey castigated what he called "the racist crowd — those who believe this country can be two countries, separate and unequal. . . . I'm going to remind them that my purpose is to heal this nation, to reconcile the differences between the vast majority of people." [5]

[5] Humphrey correctly assessed the Wallace threat early in the campaign. During the flight from Louisville, Kentucky, to Independence, Missouri, on September 21, he told reporters that "I believe Wallace is hurting us in the North now, but as we get closer

But Humphrey was unable to solve the problem that lay at the heart of all his other political difficulties — his inability to break out of Lyndon Johnson's fatal embrace. Humphrey himself described his quandary during a background session with reporters aboard his campaign plane a few days earlier. "My most serious dilemma, the thing that is at the core of our whole campaign is how on the one hand do you chart an independent course and yet at the same time not repudiate the course of which you've been a part. . . . I don't think any vice president is going to be able to fundamentally alter the policy of this country between now and January 20. Our advice and counsel may be sought, but we are not in charge, any of us. Comes January 20, high noon, 12:01 in the afternoon, then I will be in charge. And I will set the policy. And I will determine what we are going to do about our foreign relations and our national security, including Vietnam. And I have some rather strong ideas about it."

The twenty-four hour pit stop in Minnesota temporarily recharged Humphrey's batteries, but the next few days showed that the Humphrey campaign vehicle was indeed sputtering toward disaster. He made a forlorn visit to Los Angeles that drew sparse and unenthusiastic crowds and ended in a men's room of the Los Angeles International Airport, where Humphrey unsuccessfully pleaded with U.S. Senate candidate Alan Cranston just to mention the Humphrey-Muskie ticket in his speeches. At Sacramento, there weren't even any microphones available at the airport for Humphrey. At the birthplace of the United Nations in San Francisco the next day, in what was intended as the major foreign policy kickoff speech of his campaign, a small, quiet crowd was on hand as Humphrey took his boldest step away from the administration by suggesting that United Nations peacekeeping forces move into Vietnam "to administer free elections and verify the withdrawal of foreign troops."

The San Francisco speech was addressed to those Democrats who still found it impossible to support Humphrey because of the war, but the one Democrat whose support Humphrey was most anxious to claim clearly wasn't ready to oblige him. Eugene McCarthy returned from a ten-day vacation on the French Riviera on September 27 to declare that he had no intention of endorsing Humphrey. Looking tanned and rested, McCarthy told reporters in New York that he would campaign for candidates, particularly Senate candidates, who shared his views on the war and party reform, but that he still saw no sign that Humphrey had changed his basic position on the war.[6]

---

to the election, his support, especially in the North, will peel away as people come to understand that this is not the way to select a president. I'm betting on that."

[6] Earlier, stretched out in the sun on a beach at Nice, France, McCarthy fashioned one of his colorful and typically obscure similies to express his contempt for the two major-party presidential nominees. "Nixon doesn't have woof. Humphrey has lots of

McCarthy's stubborn stance was followed the same day by even worse news for Humphrey. Preparing to leave San Francisco for Portland, Oregon, he received advance word of the latest Gallup poll, which showed that he now trailed Nixon by 15 percentage points and led Wallace by only 7. Later that day, Humphrey was subjected to another humiliating display of antiwar sentiment when several hundred students from Reed College and Portland State University walked out during a speech, shouting "Stop the War!" and then picketed his hotel that night. Humphrey's campaign was collapsing around him and he knew he had to do something drastic to save it. The rhythmic chanting of the demonstrators outside his hotel was ringing in his ears as Humphrey spoke by telephone to Larry O'Brien, who agreed that he somehow had to cut the Gordian knot that tied him to Johnson. There was only one way to do that and that was by clearly delineating his position on Vietnam. O'Brien said he would scrape together $100,000 for a half-hour national television broadcast on Monday, when Humphrey would be in Salt Lake City at the end of his Western swing, and he could give his definitive speech on Vietnam then.

Humphrey also telephoned George Ball, the former undersecretary of state whose resignation as U.S. ambassador to the United Nations had been announced on Thursday, and asked him to meet him in Seattle, where Humphrey was to speak the next day. Ball had offered his services after watching Humphrey's precipitous decline in the polls, and now Humphrey sought his help in making certain that his Vietnam speech would not raise havoc with the Paris peace talks. "I thought it was catastrophic for the Democratic party that Humphrey should be beaten as badly as it appeared he was going to be," Ball said later. "I didn't have the faintest hope that he could win, but I was most concerned that he make a fair showing because I thought the consequences for the party and for the political future of the United States would be seriously impaired otherwise." Humphrey had his Washington office deliver to Ball a copy of a draft speech on Vietnam just completed by Ted Van Dyk and based on the Vietnam white paper produced in August by Professor Samuel Huntington's task force. Ball read the speech during the flight to Seattle and was so unhappy with it that he rewrote it completely, but found still another version waiting at Seattle. "When I got there, I found that they had a totally different draft ready," Ball recalled in a 1971 interview.

Meanwhile, back in Washington, O'Brien was reading the same draft Ball had and was even less happy with it. "I thought there had to be a clarification once and for all of the Humphrey position [on the war], but it was clear to me that this was an attempt to evade and avoid the issue. I felt,

woof but no warp," said McCarthy, referring to the lengthwise threads in the weaver's loom (warp) and the crosswise threads (woof).

my God, we've been living with this thing for weeks and it's just causing us tremendous problems and here's this speech which utterly failed to meet the basic objectives of clarity, decisiveness, specificity and the rest of it." In the anger of the moment, O'Brien fired off a memo to Humphrey, telling him the speech wasn't worth $100,000 to televise nationally, and that unless he came up with something better, he could kiss the election goodbye. Humphrey, troubled by the normally even-tempered O'Brien's outburst, called back a few hours later and explained that Ball and others were now helping him prepare a new speech and suggested O'Brien also join them.

While his advisers gathered to hammer out the details of what was shaping up as his most critical campaign speech, Humphrey ran into the most vicious heckling he had ever faced. Appearing before an estimated ten thousand people who jammed the Seattle Center Arena while several thousand more people waited outside, Humphrey was baited by a group of two hundred young demonstrators who shrieked electronically amplified epithets as he was introduced by Senator Warren Magnuson. Humphrey's exchange with the protestors, who were finally ejected from the auditorium by police and Secret Service men, exemplified the cruel handicaps he labored under through the first half of his campaign:

> Humphrey: Thank you, ladies and gentlemen. Thank you, Senator Magnuson. . . . Now you'll have equal time. Shut up. Distinguished guests, Senator. . . . Ladies and gentlemen, there's a man that wants to make a speech. Let's listen to him. All right, go ahead. Make your speech.
> Bullhorn: Mr. Humphrey, Mr. Humphrey, in Vietnam there is a scream that does not end.
> Humphrey: Yes, yes, I'm listening. [Loud booing from the audience.]
> Humphrey: One set of bad manners is enough. We'll keep quiet. We're going to let this fellow talk. Go ahead.
> Bullhorn: In Vietnam, there is a scream that does not end. There is a wound that does not cease its bleeding. I'm talking about the scream of death and the wound of war. Why is the scream being heard in Vietnam by our soldiers and innocent Vietnamese people? Why is there this wound because of war — not a war for democracy but a war which supports a puppet government, a government where the now number-two man said his hero is Adolph Hitler? You have supported this man. You have supported Johnson. You have supported this war, this needless waste, this murder. We have not come to talk with you, Mr. Humphrey, we have come to arrest you.
> Humphrey: Proceed. Be sure there's no police brutality, that's all. Proceed.
> Bullhorn: What about democracy in Chicago?
> Humphrey: This is Seattle. Shut up.
> Bullhorn: Mr. Humphrey, you are being accused now of complicity in the deaths of tens of thousands of Americans and hundreds of thousands of Vietnamese. This is not a joke to us, it is not a ploy. This is serious.
>
> We charge you with crimes against humanity. They did not escape. You shall not escape. Will you come to stand trial before the world, before the United Nations? Do you dare to do that? Do you dare to stand forth before the nations of the world at the United Nations and let them try you?

Humphrey: Are you through, sir?
Bullhorn: I have only begun, but for the moment I'll be quiet.

Humphrey began again, deploring the "danger of the tyranny of an organized minority," and pleading with the hecklers "in the name of freedom and peace, for which they say they stand, to please be ladies and gentlemen and permit this meeting to go on or get out." But the youth with the bullhorn and his friends continued their harrassment until a red-faced Humphrey, now completely out of patience and his voice quivering with anger, declared, "I shall not be driven from this platform by a handful of people who believe in nothing!" Finally, in exasperation, Humphrey implored his antagonists to "please now — knock it off, will you, please?" but they continued until a scuffle broke out and the ringleaders of the group were ejected, with the others following as they chorused, "Dump the Hump!" The disruption lasted almost a half an hour, and Humphrey responded with an emotional declaration of his personal credo that summed up better than anything else he said during the campaign his approach to public leadership and his total commitment to the democratic processes of government:

> Ladies and gentlemen, I must say to you in all the seriousness of my heart that . . . there is not a single grievance in this country that cannot be settled reasonably. And there is not a single problem in this country that is not subject to reason and negotiation and at least some form of conciliation . . . . We shall never settle our problems if we take them to the street in violence. We have a better way. We have the way of dialogue, of debate, of discussion, yes, even of open and honest dissent. Dissent in America, yes, but disorder in America, no. . . .

Humphrey was able to finish uninterrupted by hecklers and, encouraged by the rousing ovations from the sympathetic crowd, he cast himself in the mold of Harry Truman's underdog candidacy of 1948. "According to the polls and surveys, I guess I can say in some truth and some jest, my campaign has not peaked too soon." He was an underdog, just as Truman had been twenty years earlier, Humphrey recalled, and was threatened on the left and the right just as Truman had been. "Harry Truman had on the one side the Dixiecrats — you know who I mean — Strom Thurmond, the next partner of the Republican nominee," said Humphrey. "He had on the other side what they call the peace party or the progressive party. . . . He had as his Republican opponent the former governor of the state of New York, Thomas Dewey. . . . Then Mr. Truman went out to do just what I am going to do. He went out to tell the American people the truth and he went out to give them you know what, and that is what we are going to do."

The analogy with Truman was an apt one. Baxter Omohundro, Washington correspondent for the Ridder newspapers, recalled in a story the next day that Truman turned the corner in his campaign and went on to defeat Dewey after a rousing St. Paul rally attended by sixteen thousand persons —

including Humphrey — the month before the election. Omohundro predicted that "Seattle could be the St. Paul of two decades ago" for Humphrey. It was an accurate assessment, Humphrey said later. "In many ways, Seattle was the low point of the campaign, but all it did for me was to make me more determined than ever that we were going to conduct our kind of campaign and not let a militant, noisy minority drive us off platforms. I think the outrage over that kind of thing may have helped us too, because people just decided that was too damned much. It definitely was the turning point for me." [7]

Coming on the heels of the Gallup poll that showed him trailing Nixon by 15 points, the disrupted Seattle rally made Humphrey more determined than ever to do what he must to become his own man. He stayed up most of the night with George Ball, Fred Harris, and a handful of aides working over the text of his new position on Vietnam. The next day, Sunday, he canceled a planned salmon fishing trip on Puget Sound to work some more on it before leaving for Salt Lake City later that day.

That evening, sitting in his bathrobe in his suite at the Hotel Utah in Salt Lake City, Humphrey held a final strategy session to go over the speech he was to deliver the next night. About a dozen of his closest aides and political advisers were present, with the lines drawn between those who wanted him to come out flatly for a bombing halt and those who insisted that nothing should be done that might harm the American position at the Paris peace talks and incur Lyndon Johnson's wrath. The doves were led by O'Brien, Harris and Van Dyk, while Bill Connell and Humphrey's old friend Jim Rowe — who had flown out after being alerted by Connell — took the hawkish position.

The debate raged until almost 4:00 A.M. with the central point of dispute the problem of what Humphrey would say about a bombing halt and what kind of qualifications he would place on it. The heart of the speech was contained in three brief paragraphs: the first paragraph stated Humphrey's willingness to stop the bombing "as an acceptable risk for peace"; the second paragraph contained an important qualifier — there must be evidence of Communist willingness to restore the DMZ before stopping the bombing and, finally, the third paragraph left the door open to resuming the bombing if the North Vietnamese showed "bad faith."

O'Brien, Harris and Van Dyk argued vehemently for a firm, unequivocal statement that would attract the support of the McCarthy-Kennedy-Mc-Govern followers, and said Humphrey should remove the qualification on

---

[7] Humphrey still blames the news media for paying too much attention to the demonstrations that plagued the first part of his campaign. "May I say that your profession never gave us a fair shake of the dice?" he said in a 1971 interview with the author. "And I'm never going to forgive them for it. They were caught up in the same emotionalism that other people were caught up in. They ought to have been more objective."

the DMZ. Connell and Rowe were just as adamantly opposed to making any concessions to the doves and, in fact, argued that Humphrey should not even make the speech.

"Connell and Van Dyk represented the polarization," Humphrey later recalled. "They were always at odds and would argue with each other on these trips. Connell's reasoning was, 'If you get the president down on you, plus everything else you have against you, you haven't got a chance. You've been a part of the administration, so stick with it.' Van Dyk's position was, 'You have to make the break.' "

Finally, Humphrey's patience snapped, and with it, the chains that had bound him to Johnson. "I told everybody to get out," Humphrey said later. "I got very angry and just kicked them out of the room. I said, 'Get out, I'm tired of listening to all this argument.' I said, 'This is my life and it's going to be my speech, not yours. I'm the man who's running for president, not you.' I told them to get me a couple of secretaries in there and I dictated the basic outline of the speech and I said, 'This is the way it's going to be. You fellows fill it in.' "

Humphrey finished dictating the key elements of the speech shortly after 5:00 A.M. After a few hours sleep, he went to breakfast with Utah Democrats and candidly told them, "If the election were held today, we wouldn't have a prayer. You know it and I know it." Then, after a noon speech at the Mormon Tabernacle, he went back to his hotel to polish the Vietnam statement with George Ball.[8] Ball, who had been assured by Averill Harriman, chief U.S. negotiator at Paris, that Harriman would not repudiate Humphrey's speech, finally finished the speech as Humphrey left for the television studio.

Fifteen minutes before Humphrey was to go on the air, he placed a call to the White House. He waited until the last minute, when the text of the speech was already in the hands of reporters. "I'd met with Johnson at the White House two or three times in September," Humphrey later recalled. "I never told anybody about those meetings. Each time, I would tell him I wasn't going to rock the boat, but now I'd decided that I just had to make the move. I said, 'Mr. President, we've gone over this material before and I think I have sufficient protection in the language of this speech so that in no way will it jeopardize what you are trying to do.' " Then Humphrey read the key passages concerning the bombing halt.

Johnson's reaction was, as expected, not favorable. As Humphrey later told friends in private, Johnson's first words were "Hubert, you give that

---

[8] In his Mormon Tabernacle speech, Humphrey used a phrase that would later become a theme of the Nixon administration. He warned that extremists of the right and left are trying to destroy the moderate middle, which he characterized as "the silent majority."

speech and you'll be screwed." Publicly, Humphrey has a different recollection of Johnson's reaction: "He said to me, in substance, 'Hubert, you're not asking for my advice, I gather. You're just informing me.' I said, 'Mr. President, I guess that's about right.' "

The vice presidential seal had been removed from the lectern, and for the first time, Humphrey was not introduced as vice president when he began the speech that finally liberated him from the man who had dominated him for so long: "Tonight I want to share with you my thoughts as a citizen and as a candidate for president of the United States," Humphrey said, looking grimly into the camera. He had tried in the first month of his campaign, he said, to tell the nation "what was in my heart and on my mind," but he had been unable to because his message had often been drowned out by angry voices. But now, he declared, "I shall not let the violence of a noisy few deny me the right to speak or . . . destroy the orderly democratic processes. I have paid for this television time this evening to tell you my story uninterrupted by noise . . . by protest . . . or by second-hand interpretation."

Humphrey walked his tightrope with consummate skill, taking two steps forward and one backward as he approached the critical portion of the speech. He had supported President Johnson's decisions on the war and would continue to support them until the new president was elected, he said. But recalling the words of his acceptance speech, he boldly declared, "The policies of tomorrow need not be limited by the policies of yesterday." Then, he uttered the three paragraphs over which he and his advisers had anguished so long:

> As president, I would stop the bombing of the North as an acceptable risk for peace because I believe it could lead to success in the negotiations and a shorter war. This would be the best protection for our troops.[9]
>
> In weighing that risk — and before taking action — I would place key importance on evidence — direct or indirect, by deed or word — of Communist willingness to restore the Demilitarized Zone between North and South Vietnam.
>
> If the government of North Vietnam were to show bad faith, I would reserve the right to resume the bombing.

Humphrey went on to summarize the other "risks I would take for peace":

> Careful, systematic reduction of American troops in South Vietnam — a de-Americanization of the war — turning over to the South Vietnamese army a greater share of the defense of its own country.
>
> An internationally supervised cease-fire — and supervised withdrawal of all foreign forces from South Vietnam.
>
> Free elections, including all people in South Vietnam willing to follow the peaceful process.

[9] Despite the extreme care with which the speech had been constructed, Humphrey made one more last-second change. The language contained in the speech text given reporters read, "As president, I would be willing to stop the bombing," etc.

The speech was not a radical departure from the president's position. What it gave to the doves with one hand (the long-delayed call for a bombing halt), it took away with the other (the qualifier on the bombing halt and the prospect of resuming the bombing). "It was just enough to give a little light between the president's position and mine, but without jeopardizing his," Humphrey later explained.[10] But for the beleaguered candidate, it was the Magna Charta and Declaration of Independence rolled into one. "It was the turning point of the campaign, not because of what he said, but because saying it liberated him internally," says Ted Van Dyk, one of the architects of the speech. "The American voter watching the screen that night finally saw that Humphrey was for peace, that he was sincere, and that he meant it. On that night, the onus of the war shifted to Nixon." Larry O'Brien agrees that the speech lifted a tremendous psychological burden from Humphrey's shoulders. "He felt good about it, he was his own man," says O'Brien.

Humphrey's campaign had hit bottom in Seattle, but Salt Lake City started it on an upswing that would continue until the election five weeks later. "I feel good inside for the first time," Humphrey enthused afterwards. The change in Humphrey and in the campaign was apparent the next night in Knoxville, where he spoke at the University of Tennessee. For the first time since Chicago, there were no hecklers. Instead of antiwar demonstrations, Humphrey saw signs that said, "If You Mean It, We're With You," and "Stop the War — Humphrey We Trust You," and he was able to dismiss the issue that had caused him such anguish in a single paragraph:

> Last night I expressed my own views on that war and need not repeat them here except to say that if I am elected president and the war has not ended, the first priority of the Humphrey-Muskie administration will be to bring the war to an honorable conclusion.

Finally free of his defensive posture on the war and confident that dovish Democrats would soon return to the fold (three days later, the executive board of the Americans for Democratic Action endorsed Humphrey by a vote of 71-16), Humphrey went on the attack. His Knoxville speech revealed the strategy he would follow with ever-increasing effectiveness in the closing weeks of the campaign. First, he would try to blunt Wallace's appeal to the workingman by painting him as a dangerous extremist and enemy of organized labor; second, he would keep Nixon on the defensive by continuing to challenge him to a debate and by forcing him to cripple his own Southern strategy by taking a stand against Wallace; finally, Humphrey would try to infuse into his own campaign the overall theme of trust by his

[10] Nixon was quick to try to exploit Humphrey's break with Johnson. Speaking in Detroit the next day, he suggested there was disagreement over what Humphrey had said and hinted he had undercut the American peace negotiations. "I hope that Vice President Humphrey would clarify his position and not pull the rug out from under the negotiators and take away the trump card [the bombing halt] the negotiators have."

forthright stand on civil rights and by constantly contrasting his choice of Muskie as his running mate with Nixon's choice of Agnew and Wallace's choice of superhawk Air Force General Curtis LeMay.

Humphrey launched his frontal attack on Wallace with the harshest language he had ever used against a political opponent. Calling him a "political plunger who is gambling everything on a campaign of organized hate," "an apostle of hate and racism," and "the creature of the most reactionary, underground forces in American life," he reminded his Knoxville audience that Wallace's Alabama had both the highest murder rate and one of the lowest wage scales in the nation. Humphrey compared Wallace's appeal and potential threat to that of Hitler during the 1930's, and declared, "If in this campaign I make no other contribution to America's national life than to expose this threat — personified in George Corley Wallace and expressed in his odious appeal — I will rest content on November 6."

Humphrey coupled his assault on Wallace with words that were designed to link the Alabaman with Nixon: "I know that in his speeches, my Republican opponent appeals to the same fears . . . the same passions . . . the same frustrations which can unleash in this country a torrent of unreasoning hate and repression." Only the Democratic team of Humphrey and Muskie, Humphrey declared in what would soon become a constant refrain, offered "a reasoned and forthright accounting of where we — the American people — find ourselves today, and where we must move in the months and years ahead."

Another important factor in Humphrey's dramatically improved situation was the outpouring of small, individual contributions triggered by the Salt Lake City speech. An appeal for funds tagged onto the broadcast at the last minute by Larry O'Brien brought more than a quarter of a million dollars into the Humphrey treasury within a week in contributions that averaged fourteen dollars each. At the same time, Bill Connell was engineering an ingenious behind-the-scenes maneuver designed to repair Humphrey's discouragingly low standing in the public opinion polls and to convince would-be contributors that Humphrey's cause was not as hopeless as it seemed. Stung by the September 22 Gallup poll that showed Humphrey 15 percent points behind Nixon, Connell came up with a bold plan to manipulate the polls and the news media in a way that would give important added momentum to Humphrey's campaign. Connell outlined this plan in a memorandum prepared on October 2, two days after the Salt Lake City speech that he had so vigorously opposed.

Connell argued that there were 14 "probable" states with a total of 194 electoral votes that Humphrey could count on carrying, that 9 other states with 82 electoral votes were "real possibilities," and that if he could carry all 23, he would have more than the required 260 electoral votes needed to make him president. Connell's proposition was simply to use private polls commissioned by the Democratic National Committee and by Humphrey to discredit unfavorable polls and publicity and turn the psychological tide in Humphrey's favor. "We should prepare a full-scale orchestration on the theme, 'The swing is on to Humphrey,'" he wrote. "We should hit key columnists, writers and financial people with the news that we were already in the ballgame at the time the bad Gallup poll was taken, and with this new national upsurge, we have strengthened ourselves . . . in enough states to win the election in the electoral college."

With the blessing of Humphrey and Larry O'Brien, Connell's plan was put into effect and the results were quickly apparent. On October 9, the New York *Times,* under an eight-column headline reading, "Democratic Leaders, Calling Polls Misleading, Say Humphrey Can Win," reported that Humphrey's advisers had taken an extensive state-by-state survey costing $250,000 that convinced them he had a "fair chance to win the presidency." Connell quickly pulled together the results of the private polls commissioned by Humphrey and the national committee that served as the basis for the *Times* article and distributed them to selected reporters and columnists under the title, "Humphrey on the Upswing, Gallup or Not!" At the same time, Connell sent telegrams to all state Democratic chairmen and Humphrey leaders around the country calling attention to the favorable private polls and urging that they be used to influence potential contributors to the Humphrey campaign.

By mid-October, the public polls were beginning to reflect the Humphrey strength that Connell claimed his private polls showed. On October 10, a Louis Harris survey, the first national poll taken after Salt Lake City, showed Humphrey had moved to within 5 points of Nixon (40 percent to 35 percent, with Wallace at 18 percent), while the Gallup poll narrowed Nixon's lead from the 15 points it had been at the end of September to 12 points on October 12 (43–31) and only 8 points (44–36) by October 21. The climbing polls also were influencing the weathly contributors who constituted the heart of the Humphrey fund-raising apparatus. The first million dollars in contributions had not been received until October 10, but by October 21, Bob Short was able to tell a relieved Humphrey that he had raised another two million in contributions and loans.

One place where Short wasn't raising any money, however, was Texas, and he places the blame for that deficiency squarely on Lyndon Johnson's doorstep. "Johnson could have elected Humphrey if he wanted to," Short said in a 1970 interview with the author. "He never used the power of his office to help us. We got damn little money from Texas. I don't think the word had been passed on from on high." Short recalls that he made three trips to Texas, but each time received little cooperation and less money. On the first occasion, in early September, Short and two other top Humphrey fund raisers, Minnesota businessmen Dwayne Andreas and Jeno

Paulucci, met with a group of oil millionaires in Houston's plush Petroleum Club. "We asked them to underwrite [loan] a million dollars" to start Humphrey off with a big national television advertising push," Short recalls. "As near as I can remember, we got nothing." Just before Humphrey's Salt Lake City speech, Short went to Austin to meet with Governor John Connally, who had been so obviously absent when Humphrey visited Texas earlier that month, and asked for his help in putting on a fund-raising dinner, one of a series of such dinners Short was planning. "We decided it wouldn't do any good to have a dinner in Texas because we just couldn't get any cooperation from Connally." [11]

Short, who would later buy the Washington Senators baseball team and move it to Texas, is also critical of Johnson for refusing to release an estimated $700,000 raised through a 1965 party advertising book. Because of criticism over the way the money was raised — by selling corporations space in the book at $15,000 a page — it had not been released, and there were reports in the press that Johnson was withholding the money to keep Humphrey in line on Vietnam.

Whether that was Johnson's intention in withholding the money isn't clear, but there is little doubt that he was unhappy with Humphrey's Salt Lake City speech. That was abundantly clear to two Humphrey advisers, former North Carolina Governor Terry Sanford and Jim Rowe, when they paid a call on Johnson in early October to ask him to campaign in New Jersey, Texas, and several key border states. Rowe recalls that Johnson refused their request with the comment, "You know that Nixon is following my policies more closely than Humphrey." When Rowe protested that the Salt Lake City speech did not deviate from Johnson's policy, the president brought up a background briefing given the press afterwards by George Ball in which he portrayed the speech as a sharp break with administration policy. "It was all very pleasant," says Rowe, "but we didn't get a thing out of Johnson." [12]

The Salt Lake City speech may have been too much for Johnson, but it wasn't enough for Eugene McCarthy, who declined to comment publicly on it but said privately after watching it in Washington, "It's good openers

[11] Short hoped to raise six million dollars through a series of fundraisers in Houston, New York, Chicago, Los Angeles, Washington, San Francisco and Minneapolis-St. Paul, but because of Humphrey's poor prospects in September, he was able to stage only four of them and raised less than half the amount he was aiming at. Of the $11.6 million eventually spent by the Humphrey campaign after Chicago, more than half was raised by borrowing. By contrast, Nixon's post-convention campaign cost an estimated $25.4 million and Wallace's $9 million.

[12] Johnson made only one campaign speech for Humphrey, until their November 2 joint appearance in Houston, an October 10 nationwide radio broadcast sponsored by the International Ladies Garment Workers Union, in which he attacked Nixon and Wallace and said, "When you vote for Hubert Humphrey and Edmund Muskie, you will be voting . . . for progressive Democratic leadership in America."

for twenty-five cent poker." He added that he did not consider it a "significant" move away from the president's position. McCarthy observed Humphrey's dilemma from, of all places, the baseball stadiums in St. Louis and Detroit, where he was covering the World Series for *Life* magazine. McCarthy seemed more concerned about the outcome of the World Series than the presidential election, according to *Life's* Loudon Wainwright, who recorded McCarthy's musings on the Series. "It is the *game* that interests McCarthy, not the outcome," Wainwright wrote in words that had more meaning for politics than sports. McCarthy's attitude towards Humphrey was revealed in other ways as well. Asked by a sportswriter what he thought of Humphrey, McCarthy said he was like the kid who was permitted to join the sandlot game only because he offered the use of his school bag as second base. Some of Humphrey's supporters thought McCarthy was describing his own behavior when he commented, after watching a Detroit batter hand St. Louis Cardinal Catcher Tim McCarver his discarded mask, "I don't believe in that sort of thing. It ruins the game. He should give that mask a kick and make the catcher walk after it."

Before leaving Washington to cover the Series, McCarthy had received a letter from Gerald Hill, chairman of the California Democratic Council, urging him not to support Humphrey unless he made a distinct break with Johnson on the war. On the day after Humphrey's Salt Lake City speech, McCarthy tried to telephone Hill at his San Francisco law office to tell him that on the basis of the speech, he had no intention of supporting Humphrey, but was unable to reach him. Instead, McCarthy wrote out on the envelope of Hill's letter four conditions Humphrey would have to meet to win his support, and asked aide Jerry Eller to telephone them to Hill, which Eller did.[13]

The following weekend, October 5 and 6, while McCarthy was at the Series, supporters of McCarthy, McGovern and Robert Kennedy met in Minneapolis to organize the New Democratic Coalition, which they conceived as the germ of a new liberal Democratic party. Hill and Eller were both there, and Hill recalls that Eller told him, "The boss says it's O.K. if you want to release those points he gave you." Eller even suggested that Hill call a press conference, but Hill pointed out that all the participants had agreed no one would hold separate press conferences. "How about talking to a reporter if I sic one on you?" asked Eller. Hill was agreeable, and when Eller sent Bernie Shellum of the Minneapolis *Tribune* to see him, Hill gave

[13] Earlier, McCarthy had discouraged efforts to put his name on the ballot in several key states where he had shown strength in the primaries — California and New York particularly — lest it throw the election into the House of Representatives. He had briefly considered a fourth-party candidacy and had authorized supporters in California to allow his name to go on the ballot if they could collect the 330,000 signatures required by law, but then he left for his vacation and the drive fell short of its goal. In all, he blocked moves by his supporters to place his name on the ballot in twenty-five states, including Minnesota.

him what he understood to be the terms under which McCarthy would support Humphrey. Hill, figuring the cat was out of the bag, wanted to make certain the story got national coverage so he also gave the story to Robert Walters of the Washington *Star*. Walters, who confirmed the details with Eller, wrote a story that ran that afternoon under the headline, "McCarthy Sets Terms for Aid to Humphrey."

The terms were stiff, according to Walters' story. In order to win McCarthy's support, Humphrey would have to publicly support an immediate and unconditional halt to all U.S. bombing of North Vietnam; free elections in Vietnam, with participation by the National Liberation Front — the political arm of the Vietcong; reform of the U.S. Selective Service laws, including provision for conscientious objection to specific wars, and restructuring of the Democratic party.

Three days later, on October 8 in New York City where he was to give his first major political speech since the convention, McCarthy was asked about the veracity of Hill's disclosures. His fuzzy answer was both a confirmation and a denial: "I never drew up a list," said McCarthy, "and if I had, the demands would not be four but probably two and a half."

Nevertheless, in his speech that night at a fund-raising dinner for Senate candidate Paul O'Dwyer, McCarthy enumerated "the three basic issues we have raised in this country and those upon which we must continue to stand in what remains of this campaign." The issues were essentially the same as those he had given Hill. The first issue was Vietnam, he said, using an oblique reference to Humphrey's Salt Lake City speech to make his point: "We are not really satisfied by the grand intentions of free elections at sometime in the future or qualified statements with reference to stopping the bombing, but rather . . . that we have to be willing to accept a new government in South Vietnam, because that is what the war has been about." Second, McCarthy called for changing the draft laws so as to allow conscientious objectors to "accept other responsibilities to prove the genuiness of their action" and to relieve "the burden of moral responsibility and . . . sense of guilt that rests upon the young people of this country . . . ." Finally, McCarthy said the political processes must be reformed "so that we shall not have another Chicago" and so that the Democratic party "does not run behind the nation in terms of its acceptance of democracy and its trust in people's judgment. . . ."

There had been speculation that McCarthy would use the occasion of the speech to endorse Humphrey, but his intransigent words made it look as though he might not endorse him at all: "The call goes up now for party unity, but this is the same thing that was urged upon us a year ago when we first began to question programs and policies of our government," he declared.

We judged that it was a time for dissent and division — a time to test the unity of the party on what we considered to be rather vital matters. I see no reason why if the cry for unity then was not acceptable, it is any more acceptable today. We did not raise the issues a year ago or eight months ago in order to save the party. We took up issues which we thought had to be raised in order to give meaning and significance to American politics in 1968. And these issues are still with us.

We did not raise these issues to gain control of the Democratic party eight months or a year ago, but rather we thought that by raising issues and giving the people of this country a chance to act on them that we could give the party back to the Democrats. We are still concerned to do that, and we will continue to be concerned to do that.

Humphrey was naturally disappointed that McCarthy still withheld his support, but was so absorbed in his frantic efforts to overtake Nixon that he told associates there was no use worrying about McCarthy — if he decided to come around, he would, and if he didn't want to, there was no way to persuade him. Humphrey's hopes were not lifted any by the bellicose pronouncements of some McCarthy supporters after the O'Dwyer speech. Martin Peretz, the wealthy Harvard professor who had been one of McCarthy's principal contributors and fund raisers, expressed the feelings of many McCarthyites when he wrote in the October 19 *New Republic* magazine that "we must demonstrate a conscientious withholding of our support from the national ticket, lest acquiescence be taken as a sign that we are yet to be taken again. . . . Whatever the particular method, we should participate in Humphrey's defeat." Nor was Humphrey encouraged by the arrogant attitude of other antiwar liberals like Stewart Mott, the General Motors heir who gave more than $200,000 to the McCarthy campaign. Mott wrote Humphrey on October 13 to say he and a group of other McCarthy financial backers had decided to give Humphrey "a personal, private interview of one hour's length — in order to question you about our own view of the nation's future and what it ought to be. . . . If we become 'turned on' and enthusiastic towards your candidacy, we have the capacity to give one million dollars or more to your campaign — and raise twice or three times that amount." Humphrey, who earlier in his campaign had turned down an offer of several million dollars from oil industry representatives if he would promise to oppose as president reduction of the 27½ percent oil depletion allowance, dismissed the idea out of hand.

Humphrey's uncertain mood was reflected in an interview published in *Time* magazine on October 25, in which he sounded like Richard Nixon after his 1960 presidential defeat. "You may not believe this, but in some ways, I'm a loner," Humphrey confided to Correspondent Hays Gorey. "I'm a loner particularly when things go bad. I retreat within myself. Well, one of my problems in this campaign has been that I have been in trouble and I have become more and more of a loner. Even after all my years in public life, I don't really feel I understand the press. Sometimes I think if I make myself too available, you fellows will think I'm trying to do a snow job. This surprises you, doesn't it? Well, Humphrey isn't quite the cocky guy everybody thinks."

Humphrey had all but given up hope of winning McCarthy's support when he arrived in Pittsburgh on the night of October 28, eight days before the election, and was told by aide Norman Sherman that Jerry Eller had called to tell him McCarthy was going to declare his support for Humphrey the next night. When Sherman also said McCarthy would announce that he was not going to run for reelection to the Senate in 1970, Humphrey, whose own election prospects still looked uncertain at best, startled his aides by his reaction. "Somebody in the room said that if McCarthy wasn't going to run for the Senate, then Humphrey could," recalls D. J. Leary, who was handling Humphrey's media campaign. "And Humphrey said, 'By God, that's exactly what I'm going to do! I'll go back to Minnesota and run for the Senate!' And that is almost his exact quote."

Later that evening, McCarthy himself told Humphrey of his decision. As Humphrey recounted the telephone conversation to his aides, McCarthy seemed uncertain about what he would say in his announcement. Leary recalls that Humphrey told McCarthy, "Well, Gene, you can say just what I've been saying all along, that we've been friends for twenty years and our families have been friends and we'll be friends long after this is all over. You're my friend and I've never said anything other than that you are." Afterwards, shaking his head, Humphrey used a word none of his aides had ever heard him use before to describe the behavior of his longtime friend. "You know," said Humphrey, "I think Gene's flaky."

Despite his puzzlement, Humphrey welcomed McCarthy's last-minute declaration of support, even though it was lukewarm and late, exactly one week before the election. McCarthy issued a prepared statement from his Senate office on the morning of October 29, and then went to the television studios in the Capitol to tape the statement for broadcast. He said he would vote for Humphrey and speak on his behalf in Los Angeles the next day, and recommended that supporters of his who had been waiting for his announcement also vote for Humphrey. He said Humphrey's position on the major issues "falls far short of what I think it should be," but said he felt that Humphrey had shown "a better understanding of our domestic needs and a stronger will to act." Also, McCarthy said Humphrey seemed more likely than Nixon to scale down the arms race and reduce military tensions in the world. Devoting the rest of his statement to his own political future, McCarthy promised to continue to "test the established political processes of the Democratic party" and "to discuss the substantive issues of American politics." Then he added the words that he hoped would prove he had kept faith with his supporters:

In order to make it clear that this endorsement is in no way intended to reinstate me in the good graces of the Democratic party leaders, nor in any way to suggest my having forgotten or condoned the things that happened both before Chicago and at Chicago, I announce at this time that I will not be a candidate of my party for reelection to the Senate from the state of Minnesota in 1970. Nor will I seek the presidential nomination of the Democratic party in 1972.

Humphrey greeted the news of McCarthy's grudging endorsement as a major boost to his underdog campaign. "I am a happy man this morning," he enthused as he began the final week of his campaign. Humphrey was a much happier man the next night when President Johnson, in his last major effort to end the war that had perverted his dream of a Great Society, announced that the bombing of North Vietnam would cease the next day and that peace negotiations would begin the following day in Paris. An elated Humphrey went on television following the president with his own paid broadcast and hailed the president's decision, which he clearly regarded as an affirmation of the step he had suggested at Salt Lake City and the critical step that could win the election. The surge of hope that went through the Humphrey camp was dashed, however, on Saturday, November 1, by the shattering news that the South Vietnamese were refusing to take part in the peace talks.

Then, in the space of two frantic days, an ugly episode of behind-the-scenes meddling by a wealthy Nixon supporter, Mrs. Anna Chennault, came to light, confronting Humphrey with the decision of whether or not to exploit the politically explosive situation by linking her efforts with Nixon. Mrs. Chennault, the Chinese-born widow of Flying Tigers General Claire Chennault, had been using her Vietnamese contacts to try to short-circuit the peace talks so Humphrey could not capitalize on them. Her activities had been under surveillance by the American government, and when White House aides passed the knowledge on to Humphrey, several advisers pressed him to charge Nixon with trying to wreck the peace talks for political gain. But Humphrey, who was convinced that Nixon had been unaware of Mrs. Chennault's machinations, refused to use the political ammunition he had been handed because he agreed with some of his advisers that it would remove any slim chance of getting the South Vietnamese to the peace table and also would make it difficult for Nixon to govern if elected.[14]

The decision not to exploit the Chennault affair was not an easy one for Humphrey. His campaign had picked up considerable steam in the weeks since Salt Lake City and he knew he was within striking distance of pulling off a political upset of an even greater magnitude than Harry Truman's

[14] "I know of no more essentially decent story in American politics than Humphrey's refusal to do so," Author Theodore White wrote in *The Making of the President — 1968.* "His instinct was that Richard Nixon, personally, had no knowledge of Mrs. Chennault's activities; had no hand in them; and would have forbidden them had he known."

famous 1948 victory. But there were still painful reminders of the agony of the Democratic convention. On Saturday, the same day that Thieu threw cold water on the peace talks, Humphrey returned for the first time to the city where he had won the nomination. Earlier, he had boasted that he would make Nixon's triumphal visit to Chicago on September 3 look "like he held it in a telephone booth," but he drew only about 200,000 people, half of what Nixon had drawn, during a two-mile parade through the Loop. At Chicago Stadium, the scene of Democratic election eve rallies since 1936, only about 14,000 people greeted Humphrey at an event that had attracted 26,000 just 4 years earlier. Daley was on hand for the parade and rally, but he did not hide his pessimistic view of Humphrey's chances in Illinois. In fact, Daley had given up hope for Democrats in statewide contests and was concentrating on the Cook County ticket, where a Democratic victory was vital to his organization.

Humphrey returned to Washington on Saturday night before the final campaign swing. Appearing on ABC's "Issues and Answers" show the next morning before leaving for Houston, he attempted to place the confused peace negotiations in the best possible light by asserting that the U.S. had "every right to expect" that the Saigon regime would ultimately agree to take part in the Paris talks. "After all, the American people have paid a very heavy price in men and material and in many other ways for the defense of South Vietnam," he declared, "and I think it is fair to expect that that government will recognize the sacrifices that we have made and will respond to what is an honorable effort to bring about the cessation of hostilities."

Only a few hours earlier, Humphrey had received cheering word of a final Gallup poll which showed he had pulled to within only 2 points of Nixon, 42–40 (Louis Harris reported Nixon leading by only 3 points on Friday), but he sounded like a man preparing himself psychologically for defeat as he spoke to the television panel. Conceding that he didn't know if he could win, Humphrey said, "I will tell you one thing. We have no regrets. We think we have done the best we could have, given it all we have, and what is more, we have said what is in our hearts as well as in our minds. We have made some mistakes, but we think we've done a pretty good job."

Humphrey's natural exuberance returned when he arrived at Washington's National Airport for the flight to Houston. Spotting several hundred supporters waiting to give him a send-off on the final leg of his campaign, he shouted over the roar of jet engines, "There's going to be a happy time in the Humphrey ranks next Tuesday night." The man they had once called the "Happy Warrior" was just that again when he appeared that evening at the Houston Astrodome with President and Mrs. Johnson at his side for the first time since the campaign began. While a crowd of 58,000 frenzied partisans shouted its approval and the Astrodome scoreboard spelled out

"HHH" in four-story high letters and exploded in imitation fireworks, Humphrey gratefully accepted Johnson's belated anointment.

"In this election, a progressive and compassionate American is seeking the office of president . . ." Johnson said of the man he had virtually ignored during the campaign. "That man, my friend and co-worker for twenty years, is a healer and a builder and will represent all the people all the time." Then, pointing to the beaming Humphrey, he said, "Hubert Humphrey has worked all his life not to generate suspicion and not to generate fear among people, but to inspire them with confidence in their ability to live together." Johnson motioned Muriel Humphrey to his side, and putting his arm around her, told the crowd, "You'll never find a better first lady than this one and I hope you'll put her there Tuesday."

Unlike the Texas-style welcome he had received, Humphrey's speech was calm and reflective. He praised the man whom he had been so loyal to for so long, calling Johnson "one of the truly great men of our country for all times." He spoke of his gratitude for all that his country had given him, saying he was now asking only for the chance to return some of those blessings. And he summarized what he had tried to do in his campaign: "I have told you the hard truths about our nation's problems at home and abroad. I have told you exactly where I stand, so if you vote for me, you will know not only whom but what you're voting for."

Then, as the crowd trickled out of the huge domed stadium, Humphrey gave an eloquent testimonial to the liberal faith that had dominated his political philosophy during a quarter of a century in public office:

> I have always believed that freedom was possible. I have always believed that the basic decency within this nation would one day enable us to lift the veil from our eyes and see each other for what we are as people — not black or white, not rich or poor, not attending one church or another — but as people standing equally together, free of hate or suspicion.
>
> I have always believed that within the sharecropper, the son of the immigrant, the grandson of the slave, lay such human potential that America need only call it forth to see its full realization.

Returning to the central theme of the campaign that had taken him from an almost certain defeat to the point where pollsters now said the election was too close to call, Humphrey declared: "No one man can alone lead this country out of crisis and into a certain, happier future. But if you will trust me, I will tell you that I shall call forth from America the best that lies within it."

Humphrey ended his long quest for the presidency in California, the home state of Richard Nixon, the state that had provided the earliest and strongest support for Eugene McCarthy, and the state where Robert Kennedy had met his death. But the sweet smell of Democratic victory was in the air as Humphrey made a last-minute bid for the peace vote in a televised statement in which he prodded the reluctant South Vietnamese leaders. "The foreign policy of the United States and the fate of young Americans in Vietnam should and will be determined by the U.S. and not by any foreign government," he said. "That policy and those young Americans should not be placed at the mercy of domestic political considerations in another country."

After making the statement, Humphrey climbed into a convertible with Senator Muskie and drove past the neighboring Century Plaza Hotel where Richard Nixon, shaken by the evidence of Humphrey's dramatic comeback, was in seclusion, and began a triumphal lunch-hour motorcade through downtown Los Angeles. As Secret Service men clung to his legs to keep him from being pulled out of the car by the cheering mobs, Humphrey was treated to an uproarious reception equal to that which Robert Kennedy had received in the same streets on the day after the Oregon primary. Secure in the knowledge that his campaign had hit its zenith on election eve and thrilled by the most genuine display of emotionalism of his campaign, Humphrey leaned over and told Muskie, "I feel great, just great, because this is the best it can be." An old woman standing in a doorway captured the mood of the moment when she shouted at Humphrey, "I wish I could vote for you a thousand times!"[15]

California had been all but written off after Chicago as impossible for Humphrey to carry, but now a statewide poll showed that Nixon's lead had shrunk from 14 points to 1 point, and Humphrey began to believe that his impossible dream was no longer impossible as he began a 4-hour $300,000 telethon in ABC's Los Angeles television studio just 12 miles from the studio where Nixon was holding a similar telethon. Humphrey was in top form as he fielded callers' questions with Muskie and a bevy of big-name Hollywood stars that included McCarthyites Paul Newman and his wife, Joanne Woodward. While Nixon — with Agnew pointedly absent — took carefully screened calls that were fed to him by ex-Minnesota football star Bud Wilkinson, Humphrey answered many of the calls himself, including an unexpected one from McCarthy, who expressed approval of Humphrey's Vietnam statement earlier in the day. "I hope I've cleared the way so my friends are free to vote for you," McCarthy said, "not only free but a little moved by what I've said."

Humphrey's television extravaganza was capped by a filmed tribute from Edward Kennedy and ended with a sentimental documentary of Humphrey's life that showed him playing with his mentally retarded granddaughter, tearfully explaining how he and Muriel had learned the power of human love through her affliction. With his long campaign finally over after traveling more than 98,000 miles and visiting 136 cities in 36 states, Humphrey relaxed at a boisterous post-midnight party at the Beverly Hills home of

---

[15] Muskie took a dim view of Humphrey's eleventh hour activity, and only reluctantly consented to fly to California from Maine for the telethon and then back to Maine for the election.

a supporter, former U.S. Protocol Chief Lloyd Hand. While a band played the obligatory "Happy Days are Here Again," Humphrey immersed himself in the noisy crowd of three hundred friends, aides, politicians, movie stars, newsmen and hangers-on and even danced the Charleston at one point. At 2:30 A.M. he boarded his chartered Boeing 727 jet to return to the place where his public life had begun to wait the verdict of the American people in an election that the pollsters now agreed would be very close.

"We've done the best job we could," Humphrey told reporters as he stepped off his plane into a cold drizzle at Twin Cities International Airport shortly before 8:00 A.M. "The American jury is out now. We hope things come out well. We shall see." Humphrey drove directly from the airport to the Marysville Township Hall, a tiny white-frame building about a mile from his Waverly home, where he and Muriel marked their paper ballots and dropped them into a green ballot box.[16] Then they went home to have breakfast and to get some much needed sleep. In the afternoon, while Muriel went to the hairdresser, Humphrey drove to the nearby village of Buffalo to drop off a blue suit at the cleaners and sip hot chocolate at a local restaurant. Early in the evening, he and Muriel drove through a snow flurry to Dwayne Andreas' home in a Minneapolis suburb for a quiet dinner, and then to the Leamington Hotel in downtown Minneapolis where he pushed through a mob of admirers and made his way to a fourteenth-floor suite to watch the returns on three television sets.

By the time Humphrey arrived in his suite, which was now crowded with aides, campaign workers and friends, CBS reported that he had carried Connecticut and had swept New York. The News Election Service computers had Humphrey actually surpassing Nixon in the popular vote with 36 percent of the returns counted. By 11:30 P.M., with half the votes counted, NBC reported that Humphrey was 600,000 votes ahead, had carried New York, Pennsylvania and Michigan, and was catching up with Nixon in electoral votes.[17] Briefly allowing himself to believe that he might pull off one of the greatest political upsets in history, Humphrey blurted out, "By golly, we might do it!" But in the next hour and a half, Larry O'Brien's intelligence system brought in the gloomy reports from a handful of key states that were soon confirmed on the television screen. Humphrey was falling behind in all but 1 of 6 key states with a total of 146 electoral votes: California (40), Illinois and Ohio (26 each), Texas (25), New Jersey (17) and Missouri (12). His only hope now, it was clear to Humphrey and his staff, was that

[16] Humphrey's home precinct gave him 385 votes to Nixon's 128 and Wallace's 15.

[17] The early returns from the industrial Northeast states reflected the massive and unprecedented effort made by organized labor on Humphrey's behalf during the closing weeks of the campaign. According to the AFL-CIO, labor registered 4.6 million new voters, handed out personally and mailed 115 million pieces of literature, and manned more than 8,000 telephones in 638 cities with an estimated 25,000 volunteers. Labor also spent an estimated $10 million in an overall effort to boost Humphrey and to lure the blue-collar vote away from George Wallace.

George Wallace would help prevent Nixon from winning a majority of 270 votes in the electoral college and throw the election into the Democratic-controlled House of Representatives.

But even that slim hope vanished in the next hour as Nixon moved steadily in front in all of the six undecided key states except Texas. Larry O'Brien knew Humphrey was in deep trouble when he called Governor Richard Hughes of New Jersey shortly after 1:00 A.M. to ask if the network projection showing Nixon winning New Jersey was correct. "Are you *sure* you have everything in and there aren't any errors in the computers?" O'Brien asked anxiously. Hughes said he would check again to make certain and called back a few minutes later to tell O'Brien, "Larry, that's it." Having lost New Jersey, which he later described as "one of the most surprising setbacks on election night" (Missouri was lost by now too), O'Brien knew Humphrey's only chance lay in winning Ohio, Illinois and California, all of which were doubtful.

A little after 2:00 A.M., when it became clear that the Democratic machines in Chicago and Cleveland had not provided a large enough vote to stop Nixon from carrying Illinois and Ohio, O'Brien told Humphrey what he already sensed, that Nixon's lead looked insurmountable. "When word finally came that Chicago and Cleveland weren't coming through and it was clear that he had lost," recalls Ted Van Dyk, "Humphrey stood up, hitched up his pants and said, 'Well, sir, the American people will find that they have just elected a paper-mache man.' "

Humphrey knew he had lost, but he wasn't quite ready to concede defeat. Descending to the main ballroom of the Leamington at 2:30 A.M., he thanked his campaign workers and told them to be of good cheer because several important states were still undecided. "As you know, this is at best, as we put it, a donnybrook. Anything can happen." Smiling grimly, Humphrey said he felt "sufficiently at ease so that I want to get a good night's rest," and urged his glum followers to do likewise. "I feel that by the time that the turn of the day comes tomorrow, that you and I are going to be a lot happier and much more cheerful than we are now."

Humphrey went to sleep shortly before 4:00 A.M., and when he awoke at 8:45 A.M., it was clear that there had been no last-minute miracles. Illinois and California were incontestably lost and Richard Nixon would be the next president of the United States. As Muriel and a few aides and close friends slipped into the suite and began expressing regrets, Humphrey gently chided them. "I don't want any sympathy from any of you," he said.

Humphrey had come close enough to justify a lifetime of second-guessing and far closer than he or anyone else dared believe only a few days earlier. The dimensions of his loss were agonizingly narrow: Nixon had won 31,770,000 votes or 43.4 percent of the vote, compared to Humphrey's

31,270,000 or 42.7 percent, while 9,906,000 voters or 13.5 percent had chosen Wallace. Humphrey accepted his crushing defeat gracefully but his face could not hide the anguish he felt. Smiling bravely as he walked to the stage of the Leamington ballroom with Muriel at his side shortly after 11:00 A.M., Humphrey told several hundred cheering, tearful supporters that he had just called Nixon at his Waldorf Astoria Hotel headquarters in New York and offered his congratulations.

Then he read the concession statement in which he promised Nixon his support in healing the wounds caused by one of the most unpleasant presidential campaigns in American history. Continuing to read from his prepared statement, Humphrey thanked his supporters on behalf of himself and Senator Muskie, and made it clear this wouldn't be the last hurrah for Hubert Humphrey: "I intend to continue my dedication to public service, and to the building of a responsive and vital Democratic party," he declared as his listeners burst into applause. "I shall continue my personal commitment to the cause of human rights, of peace, and to the betterment of man. If I have helped in my campaign to move these causes forward, I feel rewarded. I have done my best. I have lost. Mr. Nixon has won. The democratic process has worked its will, so now let's get on with the urgent task of uniting our country. Thank you."

Humphrey had finished his prepared statement and was about to leave the stage, but his supporters wouldn't let him. Returning to the microphones, his spirits lifted by the applause, Humphrey said, "Now go have some fun." Then his eyes brimming with tears, he added, "It has been a lot of hard work. I don't want anybody to have any extra sympathy. As a matter of fact, what I would like to have you do is just redouble your efforts to do what you thought you were doing and what I thought I was doing, and maybe we can make an even greater contribution to the things that are important to this country." Humphrey confessed that he felt a "great sense of release and relief," and said he hoped his supporters felt the same way. "I want you to be of good cheer," said the man whose name had become synonymous with cheerfulness in the face of adversity. "I would like for you to feel a little happy. It is not easy, but quite frankly, this was an uphill fight all the way."

There was nothing cheerful about Eugene McCarthy's reaction to the outcome of the election, however. Sitting in his black-walled Senate office on a cold, grey afternoon with a volume of Yeats' poetry in his hand, he told Reporter E. W. (Ned) Kenworthy of the New York *Times* that it was "a day for visiting the sick and burying the dead. It's grey everywhere — all over the land." The man who had waited until a week before the election to give Humphrey a lukewarm endorsement now became one of the first to second-guess him. "If he'd said a month ago what he said last week," McCarthy declared, "he would have won."

BOOK FIVE
TWO TRANSITIONAL MEN
1969–1972

CHAPTER XIX

ALONE IN THE LAND OF THE AARDVARKS

I know what I want to do. Whether I'll do
what I want to do is another question.
Eugene McCarthy in a 1969 interview.

The capacity audience at the Poetry Center of the Ninety-second Street Young Men's and Young Women's Hebrew Association in New York gave Eugene McCarthy a standing ovation as he introduced Greek Poet George Seferis on the evening of December 3, 1968. "This is a somewhat new role for me," said McCarthy, acknowledging that he frequently was inspired by Seferis, a Nobel Laureate and former Greek diplomat whose works expressed the paradox of the private man in public office. One of McCarthy's favorite Seferis poems was based on the troubled hero of Greek mythology, Orestes, who avenged his father's murder by killing his mother and her lover and then spent his life trying to win expiation for the crime. It was Seferis' first American reading and McCarthy listened appreciatively as he recited the poem in Greek and then as it was translated into English:

> Again, again into the track, once more into the track!
> How many turns, how many laps of blood, how many black
> Circles of faces watching; the people watching me
> Who watched me when, upright in the chariot,
> I raised my hand, brilliant, and they roared applause.

Afterwards, as McCarthy led a discussion period, he used the Orestes poem to hint that he intended to avenge wrongs he felt had been inflicted upon him during his unsuccessful campaign for the Democratic presidential nomination. "We haven't given up — Orestes didn't," McCarthy said as the crowd roared its applause. "We may have to go back on the track again." [1]

---

[1] Seferis, who died in Greece in 1971, sounded a McCarthyian protest against the policies of his government in March, 1969, when he accused the military regime that

McCarthy's enigmatic behavior, which had manifested itself with his late and limp endorsement of Hubert Humphrey a week before the election, was becoming conspicuous as he showed more interest in poetry than politics and refused to take a leadership role in the Senate or the Democratic party. In December, he toyed with the idea of accepting President-elect Nixon's offer of the United States ambassadorship to the United Nations, but turned it down when Minnesota's Republican governor, Harold LeVander, refused to appoint a Democrat to McCarthy's Senate seat. Then, as the Ninety-first Congress convened in January, 1969, McCarthy took two more steps into political limbo.

First, he supported Louisiana's Russell Long against Edward Kennedy in Long's unsuccessful bid for reelection as assistant majority leader of the Senate. The vote appalled many of McCarthy's supporters who, recalling Long's record as a strong supporter of Lyndon Johnson's Vietnam policy and a friend of the oil and gas industries, agreed with the assessment of McCarthy's friend, Mary McGrory of the Washington *Star,* that "last year's shining knight" was suddenly transformed into "this year's old politician." McCarthy explained his vote by saying that the substitution of Kennedy for Long as Senate whip would provide only "the shadow but not the substance of reform." McCarthy compared the Senate whip's job to that of a waterboy, and said it was so "unimportant that reporters shouldn't even bother to ask how you voted." Nevertheless, McCarthy was hard pressed to explain how he could offer Kennedy his support for the presidency at Chicago and then oppose him for Senate whip or, as Miss McGrory put it, how he could favor Kennedy for pope but not for parish priest. Most people attributed the vote at least partially to McCarthy's old feud with the Kennedy family, but he considered it a tempest in the Senate's snuffbox. "I went against Lyndon Johnson last year because I thought there was a great issue at stake," he explained. "I would have voted against Russell Long, too, if I thought there was some issue or principle involved. But what was it? You come back in two years and show me how the Senate is changed or improved by having Teddy as whip instead of Russell Long." [2]

While McCarthy's vote for Long could be explained in terms of personal and political motives, there seemed to be no adequate explanation for McCarthy's second puzzler, his abrupt decision to resign from the Foreign Relations Committee so that Wyoming's Gale McGee, one of the Senate's most consistent hawks on the Vietnam War, could take his place. Again,

---

had taken power in Greece two years earlier of infringing on personal and political freedoms. Seferis' criticism put him in official disfavor with the Greek government.

[2] Long later said he "had every right to expect" McCarthy's vote since he was chairman of the Finance Committee and had helped McCarthy pass tax legislation helpful to Minnesota industry. Long offered similar reasons of friendship for the support of four other non-Southern senators — Wisconsin's Gaylord Nelson, Wyoming's Gale McGee, and New Mexico's Clinton Anderson and Joseph Montoya.

McCarthy's explanation was less than convincing. He said he supported Chairman J. William Fulbright's desire to reduce the size of the committee to make it more effective. However, this would mean that McGee, who had been knocked off the committee two years earlier because of Republican election gains but promised the next opening by the Democratic Steering Committee, could not be seated. McCarthy, a member of the steering committee, contended that it was bound to "honor its commitment" to McGee and volunteered to step down, choosing as his new assignment the Government Operations Committee. He said that this would allow him to "review how operations affect policy," a reference to his campaign theme that the operations of the executive branch often tended to assume a life of their own and determine policy rather than the other way around.

However, there were simpler reasons for McCarthy's actions, and they had little to do with upholding the honor of the Democratic Steering Committee or improving the effectiveness of the Foreign Relations Committee. "The thing that really triggered his decision was that he got sick and tired of listening to the steering committee arguing about taking care of Gale McGee," recalls McCarthy's former aide, Larry Merthan. "Here he was, after everything he'd been through in 1968, listening to Mike Mansfield and everybody else worrying about taking care of a guy who was a superhawk and an apologist for President Johnson. He just said 'the hell with it, let McGee have my seat.' " A second and perhaps equally important reason for McCarthy's decision was that he no longer needed the forum that the committee provided after using it to launch the attack on U.S. foreign policy that drove Lyndon Johnson into retirement. "Four years ago, everybody said I couldn't be vice president because I didn't have any foreign affairs experience," he told the New York *Times'* William Shannon. "So I went on the committee so people would understand that I am an expert. Now that I've established that, you don't have to stay on the committee to talk about foreign affairs." [3]

If McCarthy's actions were puzzling to his colleagues, they were even more inexplicable to many of the young people who once supported him. The Harvard *Crimson*, in an editorial entitled "Not So Clean," said McCarthy's resignation strengthened the impression that he "has gone over the political deep end." Even Allard Lowenstein, the antiwar organizer who had helped McCarthy make an ex-president out of Johnson and had been elected to Congress himself in 1968, publicly criticized McCarthy's vote for Long. Lowenstein made it a point to praise Kennedy's election as whip while sharing a platform with McCarthy in Brooklyn in January, prompting

---

[3] McCarthy, who was low-ranking Democrat on the committee, also disliked having to wait until more senior senators ran out of questions at committee hearings so he could ask his. Noting that the pedantic Claiborne Pell of Rhode Island was next in line above him, McCarthy cracked, "Any committee with Claiborne Pell on it that Gale McGee wants to get on can't be all that important."

McCarthy to retort that Lowenstein "can tell you exactly what the whip election in the Senate meant after being in the House for five days. . . . If I had just known how important the whip was we would not have had to go to New Hampshire last year." (Lowenstein, never one to let anybody have the last word, said later, "I didn't need five days to tell the difference between a Long and a Kennedy.")

A Midwestern Democratic Senate colleague subsequently took note of the changes he observed in McCarthy in the year since the New Hampshire primary: "He was Clean Gene last spring and summer, he was Mean Gene last fall, and he's Unseen Gene now." But McCarthy saw little need to explain his inactivity in the early months of 1969. He told one reporter that when he was a hockey player, "I used to spend a lot of time cruising around near the net just waiting for a loose puck." To another reporter, he said, "The ball is in the other fellow's court. This is a time for watching and waiting. When the time comes to move, when there's something to do worth doing, I'll do it." One of the few things McCarthy found worth doing in early 1969 was to write his campaign memoirs under a generous contract from Doubleday & Company, Inc., a task which occupied him until mid-year as he attempted to explain "what my intentions were, which I think I knew better than some of the people who are telling what they were."

McCarthy was not uncomfortable with Richard Nixon in the White House, and agreed with his inaugural plea that Americans "lower our voices so we can speak to each other." He rated Secretary of State William Rogers, an old friend, far above his predecessor, Dean Rusk. "I found out where the Secretary of State's office was in six weeks in this administration," McCarthy said in March. "I was never there when Rusk was secretary." McCarthy also gave high marks to Secretary of Defense Melvin Laird, whom he'd known in Congress, again comparing him to his predecessor. "We know where Laird stands and he won't give us all that double-talk that [Robert] McNamara did." McCarthy did label Nixon's decision in March to seek deployment of the Safeguard antiballistic missile system as "the president's first serious mistake," but the criticism didn't prevent Nixon from inviting him to the White House for a half-hour chat on April 22. Referring to widespread antiwar dissent among young people, McCarthy said he and Nixon talked about "what's been happening on the campuses." But he rebuffed a questioner who asked if he'd offered Nixon any solutions to campus disorders. "We really haven't thought about the role of the university in a hundred and fifty years." Nor was McCarthy critical of Nixon's deliberate pace in winding down the Vietnam War. "I never was a unilateral withdrawal man," he declared as he emerged from the White House meeting.

Although McCarthy refused a formal role in helping rebuild the Democratic party, and downgraded the importance of the newly-created Commission on Delegate Selection and Party Structure headed by South Dakota

Senator George McGovern ("They had all the facts they needed for party reform at Chicago," McCarthy remarked at one point), he agreed to testify at the commission's opening hearings in Washington on April 25. In his first statement on party reform since the election, McCarthy suggested annual conventions which he said "would have less the aspect of carnivals and circuses and would concern themselves more with the serious business of directing the organization in determining the policies of the party." He reiterated that he would not ask those who had supported him in 1968 to work within the party unless it adopted fundamental reform and implied that he would not come to the 1972 convention unless all possible steps were taken to make certain that it "is truly representative of the people who choose the Democratic party as their instrument for political action."

In the Senate, McCarthy showed up for votes he considered important, such as the confirmation of his fellow Minnesotan and former political foe, Chief Justice Warren Burger. McCarthy, one of only three senators to oppose Burger's confirmation, was paying off an old grudge. He told the Senate that Burger was "a most active participant" in his bitter 1952 House campaign which had overtones of a Communist "smear" attempt. McCarthy admitted that his reasons for the vote were "somewhat personal and political," and asserted that Burger had helped distort his position on issues in a way "designed to elicit an emotional if not prejudiced response."[4]

McCarthy concentrated on the Finance Committee, where he introduced a bill to give single taxpayers the same treatment as married couples, and spoke out on several issues he felt were critical. In May, he told the Senate that U.S. policy on the Nigerian-Biafran civil war was much like that on Vietnam: "It began with misconception, was followed by self-justification and is ending in tragedy." McCarthy urged that the U.S. aid starving Biafrans and recognize their independence from Nigeria.[5] He also pushed for reform of draft laws, which he said were full of "injustices and irrationality," and called for a new selective conscientious objection law that would allow a person to be exempted from military service in a particular war on non-religious grounds. McCarthy's position was in conflict with that of his eighteen year old son, Michael, who asked for conscientious objector status in May on the grounds that he was a Catholic pacifist. McCarthy felt that granting exemptions on religious grounds was unconstitutional and that the only proper basis for draft exemption was a non-religious, reasoned objection. Nevertheless, he did not challenge his son's action. "He may be right," said McCarthy, "he just says that modern war is likely to be nuclear war,

---

[4] See chapter 7.
[5] Nigeria's government-controlled *Morning Post* newspaper bluntly told McCarthy to keep his nose out of Nigeria's internal affairs. In an editorial entitled "Shut Up McCarthy," the paper said McCarthy's statement had "proved that he was only a little better than a semi-illiterate from the backwoods of America."

and . . . they're not going to let you decide which you think is bad so you'd better object to all of them, and it's a logical position."

McCarthy paved the way for Hubert Humphrey's return to the Senate when he told a Minneapolis news conference on July 24 that he felt it was necessary to reiterate his decision not to run for reelection to the Senate under any banner.[6] His reasons for leaving the Senate were, like his vote against Burger's confirmation, both personal and political. As he explained in an interview with television personality David Frost a few months later, his principal reason for not seeking the Senate or the presidency again as a Democrat was that he would not do anything "that might lead the young people to think that I had somehow . . . led them down the trail and then had, myself, taken to the high ground and sent them on ahead." But McCarthy had decided even before 1968 that this probably would be his last term in the Senate, and had in fact told several people this shortly after his reelection in 1964. Pressed by Frost to give his private reasons, McCarthy pointed out that he'd been in the House ten years and the Senate twelve and said he felt "there are some changes taking place . . . in the manner in which you deal with the problems in America." Then he explained his new view about the exercise of political power:

> When I went to the House, the real problems were legislative — to pass certain laws that needed to be passed, and I think in the Senate, the last ten or twelve years, the question's been more one of how power's brought to bear — not really through the legislative process but outside of it, in confirmations, for example, in treaties . . . and I'm not sure now but that you can have more influence, probably by coming at some of these problems from outside either the Senate or the House.

The reaffirmation of McCarthy's self-imposed exile from his party and the Senate was followed a month later by the disclosure that he and his wife Abigail had separated after twenty-four years of marriage. In August, McCarthy confirmed rumors of marital troubles that had been circulating for months. He said he had moved out of their large three-story home across the street from Washington's National Cathedral and into a $450 a month apartment in a nearby hotel.[7] The breakup of the marriage stunned the McCarthys' friends even though some had sensed difficulties caused by the pressures of the 1968 campaign. "It was evident at Chicago that they were not getting along," recalls Bill Carlson, who with his wife was among the McCarthys' oldest and closest St. Paul friends. "It was very strained and very different from what it had been before." Raphael Thuente, another longtime

---

[6] Some McCarthy supporters also urged him to start an independent campaign for the presidency by seeking reelection to the Senate as an independent in a major state such as New York or California, but McCarthy did not seriously pursue that possibility.

[7] Rumors about the McCarthys' marital difficulties first cropped up during the Indiana primary in April, 1968, when Mrs. McCarthy suddenly quit her husband's campaign and flew to Florida to recuperate from a virus infection.

friend and former colleague of McCarthy's on the College of St. Thomas faculty in St. Paul, had a different reaction. Thuente, referring to a former president of St. Thomas and prominent Catholic bishop who was also a friend of the McCarthys', said, "There's about as much chance of Gene and Abigail separating as there is of Jim Shannon leaving the Church and getting married." Fifteen months later, James Shannon became the first American Catholic bishop to quit the priesthood and marry.

The agony of the McCarthys' marital crisis was compounded by their public prominence and by the fact that both were devout Catholics who had been deeply involved in Church activities. Washington social circles, where the McCarthys were familiar figures and where a politician's private life is often more closely analyzed than his public life, buzzed with gossip and speculation about the reasons for the breakup. Some people, recalling that McCarthy often was seen having dinner with attractive women reporters who covered his campaign, asserted that he was romantically involved with them. One of the women linked with McCarthy in print was Shana Alexander, the *Life* magazine columnist who wrote admiringly of him during the 1968 campaign and persuaded him to write a monthly column for *McCall's* magazine when she became editor in early 1969. Other women were publicly and privately named in the continuing speculation about the breakup of the marriage, but most people who know McCarthy well discount such speculation, even though Mrs. McCarthy told several people she believed there was another woman. "Jerry Eller has sworn to me that there's nothing to the talk about another woman, and I don't think he would lie to me," a person close to both the McCarthys told the author. "And Larry Merthan has said to me, 'I've been up and down the country with McCarthy and he could have had any woman he wanted, but there's never been even a hint of anything like that.' "

A more plausible explanation for McCarthy's separation from his wife, most of the couple's close friends and associates agree, is simply a clash between two strong-willed, highly intelligent and very independent people. Mrs. McCarthy, like most Minnesota political wives, was always deeply involved in her husband's campaigns, and although initially opposed to his decision to run for president, she took an active role in his campaign. However, partly because of the antagonisms between her and the McCarthy staff and partly because of the unorthodox nature of the campaign, she was prevented from playing a central role. "I think it was very difficult for Abigail to play second fiddle to Gene," says Mrs. Geri Joseph, the former Minnesota Democratic national committeewoman and ex-vice chairman of the Democratic National Committee. "She's really a brilliant person and I think she's been very competitive with Gene in her writings and her thinking. That's not unusual for Minnesota political wives, because many of them, like Abigail and Jane Freeman and Arvonne Fraser, could easily have been political leaders in their own right. But, unlike Muriel Humphrey, I think Abigail found it much more difficult to mesh her personality with that of her husband, and I don't think Gene found it easy to look on her as an individual."

Mrs. McCarthy, who made it clear from the beginning that her religion prevented her from granting her husband a divorce, remains reluctant to discuss the reasons for the breakup of their marriage. "There's been enough written that's been injurious to everyone concerned," she told the author in an 1971 interview. "I've never said anything to harm Gene or affect his political future and I don't like being put in the position of having to defend myself. I don't think people should discuss it — it's just a simple fact and it has no bearing on what he's done or what he stands for. Since no one can really know, it seems to me this kind of gossipy speculation is not really even honest. All this probing will just drive people to talk about things I don't want my children to have to hear or have talked about. I see no reason why people should build a case for him or against him. I just want everybody to come through able to keep their dignity and keep things in perspective. I mean, here's a man who's going to run for president, and in the meantime, I have my children to think of and my own life to lead." [8]

The painful reordering of McCarthy's personal life coincided with his reemergence into the public spotlight for the first time since 1968. On October 2, after returning from an eleven-day trip to three South American countries to meet with government, business, and academic leaders, McCarthy ended his eight-month silence on the Vietnam War. Speaking so softly that many reporters had trouble hearing him, McCarthy told a press conference in the Caucus Room of the Old Senate Office Building — the same room where he announced for president almost two years earlier — that President Nixon was following the same policy on Vietnam as that of the Johnson administration. "All the old lines are coming back," McCarthy said as he characterized Senate Minority Leader Hugh Scott's request for a sixty-day freeze on criticism of Vietnam policy as an attempt to stifle the national student-led moratorium on the war scheduled for October 15. "If the president does have a new policy, he should tell us what it is," McCarthy declared. "If he has a secret policy that he can't tell us about, as in the campaign, then he must run the risk of criticism while carrying it out." At the same time, McCarthy announced his support of the Vietnam Moratorium, noting with wry satisfaction "the conversion of

[8] The McCarthys' four children continue to live with their mother when not away at school. Mrs. McCarthy is actively involved in Church Women United and other ecumenical movements, serves on the board of directors of the Dreyfus Corporation that is headed by one of her husband's principal financial supporters, and completed her own memoirs in 1972.

many who were strong supporters of the war . . . to . . . a position of challenge and opposition."

Appearing before some four thousand persons at Rutgers University in New Brunswick, New Jersey, on the day of the Vietnam Moratorium, McCarthy criticized Nixon for saying he would not be the first president to preside over the military defeat of America. "None of us feel history would be badly served if Richard Nixon did preside over the first military defeat of this country," he said after receiving a sixty-second standing ovation. "I don't think history would call it that, but would call it a sign of great statesmanship." McCarthy received an even warmer welcome in his second speech of the day when he was introduced to an estimated 25,000 persons in Manhattan's Bryant Park by Actress Shirley MacLaine as "the man who started it all." Sharing the same platform with Mayor John Lindsay, whom he endorsed for reelection, and New York Republican Senator Charles Goodell, who succeeded Robert Kennedy and who was sponsoring a measure in Congress to put a time limit on the U.S. commitment in Vietnam, McCarthy urged his listeners to "somehow develop another process by which the president will sense the will of the people."

McCarthy's long-awaited book on his 1968 campaign was published in late October, and while it shed little new light on his campaign or on the man himself, its dispassionate prose contained a warning for fellow Democrats that they would be called to give an accounting of their progress toward party reform in 1972. Without the "perfection of procedures so that the position of a strong minority is sure to be reflected in the party platform and the position of its candidates," McCarthy wrote, "I doubt very much whether anyone could persuade the young people or the relatively independent practitioners of politics to test the processes within the Democratic party again in 1972." McCarthy also hinted at his own intentions in 1972. "If party procedures are not reformed, both in the Democratic and Republican party, I anticipate that a third party or a fourth party will develop on the liberal side with the same strength and thrust that the George Wallace party had on the conservative side in 1968." [9] At the same time, McCarthy was trying to define his relationship to the Democratic party after having raised the issue that had split the party in 1968. He told a television interviewer on November 4 that he was questioning whether he could be "particularly useful either to the party or useful in the party after that — a little like they say with Lazarus when he came back from the dead, they didn't want to deal him into the card game. They said, 'Look, we don't play with you any more, and we don't know what you're up to.' "

McCarthy saw ominous overtones in President Nixon's November 3 speech announcing an accelerated schedule for withdrawal of troops from Vietnam, calling it "a very hard speech" which, by asking Americans to sup-

[9] *The Year of the People,* Doubleday & Company, Inc., Garden City.

port the war for patriotic reasons, amounted to "a kind of escalation, I think, even beyond anything President Johnson had done. . . . The tone and the thrust of it was a kind of threatening speech, I think, and a disturbing one." McCarthy also was disturbed by Vice President Spiro Agnew's attack on the news media in his November 14 speech in Des Moines. "I think maybe we've been a little too ready to laugh at Agnew," he said. However, McCarthy did not see the alleged massacre of Vietnamese civilians by U. S. soldiers at My Lai as important in the overall context of the war. "My reaction to it is no different than my reaction to the rest of the war," he said in Philadelphia on December 1. "My opposition is not based simply on atrocities. I don't think it will affect policy." [10]

McCarthy began his final year in the Senate with a ten-day trip to Moscow and Paris in January, 1970. He met with Soviet, French and North Vietnamese leaders but was unable to accomplish a major purpose of the trip, which was to speed the release of U.S. prisoners of war held by North Vietnam. However, he told the Senate Foreign Relations Committee in February that his talks with North Vietnamese and Vietcong diplomats in Paris had convinced him that a negotiated political settlement of the war was a "real possibility" if the United States would agree to withdraw its forces and allow the formation of a coalition government in Saigon. McCarthy disputed the optimistic assessment of U.S. policy in Vietnam given the committee earlier by administration officials. Accusing Nixon of misleading the nation with talk of gradual troop withdrawals, he said Vietnamization — Nixon's policy of gradually transferring combat responsibility from United States to South Vietnamese forces — was neither workable nor desireable and would only lead to "Asians killing Asians with American arms." McCarthy, who was making his first appearance before the committee he had so abruptly left a year earlier, also scoffed at Nixon's repeated references to the need for an "honorable settlement" and a "just peace." "One must ask what, if any, honor has been gained by the death and destruction and social chaos that has gone along with our overwhelming military power and massive physical presence in Vietnam over the past five years — and what will be gained from the continuation of the war," he said.

While McCarthy's testimony helped draw the lines between the Nixon administration and the Foreign Relations Committee on Vietnam, it appeared that there was little of the moral indignation over the war that made it such a potent issue in 1968. Nevertheless, McCarthy seemed to feel that the war was still a critical issue. In fact, he praised the new Democratic Policy Council for passing a resolution a week earlier calling for total U.S.

[10] Ironically, McCarthy's office ignored a registered letter from Ronald Ridenhour, a Vietnam veteran, detailing five eyewitness accounts of the My Lai massacre, which were later disclosed by Seymour Hersh, a freelance reporter who had been McCarthy's press secretary during the early part of the 1968 campaign.

withdrawal from Vietnam within eighteen months and indicated he felt it was close to the view he fought for at the 1968 convention. "The party is beginning to look pretty good," said McCarthy, who had told American students in Paris that he might help form a new political party in 1972. "It is beginning to look like the party I was describing back in 1968."

In March, McCarthy paid his first return visit to the state where he scored his greatest political triumph and proved the depth of public opposition to the war. Speaking to a group of his earliest supporters at Dartmouth College in Hanover, New Hampshire, on the second anniversary of the 1968 New Hampshire primary, McCarthy said the mood of the country was little different from what it was when he first campaigned in the state. "The issues are the same, the policies are the same and the personalities haven't changed much," McCarthy said after attending a premier of a documentary film on his campaign. "The people are prepared to make the same kind of moral judgment they made in 1968." The New Hampshire visit had cheered him, but he was even more cheered on the following night by the repeated ovations given him by four thousand students who came to hear him give a poetry reading at the University of Massachusetts. Swamped by well-wishers as he left the building where eighteen days earlier Hubert Humphrey had been razzed so badly that he was unable to give a prepared speech, McCarthy said, "It's harder to stop running than it is to get started." [11]

McCarthy may indeed still have been running, but he made it clear in May that he was not yet interested in leading the opposition to the Indochina war again. He condemned the Nixon administration decision to send America combat troops into Cambodia on April 30, saying it proved that Nixon had no clear policy for ending the war and that he did not have the war "under control." But he did not offer himself as a focal point for the antiwar dissent that exploded following the Cambodian incursion and the fatal shootings of four students by Ohio National Guardsmen at Kent State University on May 4. As others in the Senate planned antiwar strategy and thousands of angry student demonstrators protested on Capitol Hill and elsewhere around the country, McCarthy refused to assume the antiwar leadership that many of his old supporters urged on him. Even though he received a hero's welcome from most of the students who descended on Congress to protest the Cambodian involvement and the Kent State shootings, he disappointed many of them by declining a larger role in the Congressional attack on the president's Indochina policies.[12] On May 5, after

[11] Two years after New Hampshire, McCarthy still owed about two-thirds of the $1.4 million debt from his 1968 campaign. He refused to pool his deficit with that of other candidates to be handled by the Democratic National Committee, and paid off the larger creditors at the rate of about twenty-five cents on the dollar. However, in February, 1972, American Airlines filed a law suit against McCarthy for $135,000 in bills left over from the 1968 campaign.

[12] A short time later, McCarthy offered an amendment to a military procurement

meeting in his office with a group of despairing students from Macalester College in St. Paul — where Hubert Humphrey was teaching — McCarthy was challenged by eighteen year old Thomas France of Duluth, Minnesota. "I don't sense any kind of commitment from you, sir," France said after McCarthy told the students they would have to follow their own consciences in deciding whether to engage in civil disobedience actions such as draft resistance and refusing to pay taxes. "Well, I'm sorry, man," McCarthy shot back. "I was around in 1967 and 1968 and it was a long lonely road. . . . You're asking others what you should do. . . . I'm not ready to say don't pay your taxes or resist the draft."

McCarthy's former supporters saw his willingness to let others carry the antiwar ball as another sign that he was dropping out. When Sam Brown, one of his student organizers in 1968 and a leader of the new antiwar lobbying drive, called McCarthy several weeks before the Cambodian incursion and asked if he would join several other senators in leading the fight to cut off appropriations for the war, he replied, "There are plenty of leaders now. Call me sometime when there's no one else to call on." Brown was disappointed, but he understood why McCarthy had turned him down. "He wants to be, needs to be, the loner who stands up when no one else will," said Brown. McCarthy's sense of historical futility was apparent to others who urged him to speak out and do more against the war. Other senators were doing an adequate job, he told Jules Witcover of the Los Angeles *Times* on May 24, adding that he saw no reason to remind everyone that "I said it first. . . . I really don't want to compete with others."

Although McCarthy insisted that he had made no plans for the future except to "try to be a political force in 1972," he indicated in an interview with the author in June that he was eyeing another presidential race. "I've always been active in presidential years because I think there's a pretty heavy obligation on everybody that holds office to get involved then whether they're running for office or not," he said. "Presidential years are the years of decision." In the same month, McCarthy hinted that he might try to run as the martyred hero of the excluded left as he discussed the possibilities of a liberal third-party movement in an article for the New York *Times* magazine. He argued that even without an issue comparable to Vietnam, the growing dissatisfaction with major political parties and candidates could "make a third [Liberal] party not only possible, but potentially a real force in determining the outcome of the election in 1972." But whether there would be such a third party, he told Paul Hope of the Washington *Star* in August, depended largely on the Democratic party's stand on the critical issues, its candidates and the reform of party procedures. As for who might

---

bill that would have required a presidential order for the use of live ammunition by National Guard troops in a civil disturbance. The amendment was defeated by an 87–2 vote on August 19, with only Edward Kennedy joining McCarthy in support of the amendment.

lead a third party, McCarthy neither offered nor ruled himself out. "There isn't much I can do about it," he declared. "Circumstances will decide."

While Hubert Humphrey campaigned in Minnesota for the Senate seat he was vacating, McCarthy spent his final months in the Senate stumping for carefully selected candidates for the House and Senate.[13] McCarthy had no difficulty selecting the candidates he wanted to campaign for. "I'm trying to help the people who went out of their way to help me and I'm trying to hurt the ones who went out of their way to hurt me two years ago," he said at one point. One candidate McCarthy tried to hurt was Senator Henry Jackson of Washington, whose solid support of the military, hawkish stance on Vietnam and strict party regularity had caused frequent clashes with McCarthy in the Senate. In a September speech in Seattle for Jackson's Democratic primary opponent, black antiwar lawyer Carl Maxey, McCarthy said Jackson favored the militarization of American politics. "Henry Jackson and some others in the Senate would not feel safe if the sky was black with strategic bombers, if there were so many nuclear submarines in the ocean that they were running into each other. . . ." Jackson retorted that he was proud he had "opposed both McCarthys" during his time in the Senate. (Jackson brushed aside the latest McCarthy challenge, overwhelming Maxey in the primary with 87 percent of the vote.) McCarthy's other campaign apearances, which usually took the form of poetry readings in which he combined political messages with his own poetry, were not much more effective. Of a dozen House, Senate and gubernatorial candidates he campaigned for in nine states, only Ronald Dellums, a black city councilman elected to Congress from Berkeley, California, was successful in the November election.[14]

While he waited for his Congressional career to expire, McCarthy called two days of unofficial "people's hearings" on the Nixon administration's major welfare reform proposal, the Family Assistance Plan. McCarthy, who had introduced legislation a year earlier asking for a guaranteed income for all Americans, called the hearings at the urging of the National Welfare Rights Organization, a group representing 125,000 welfare recipients strongly opposed to the plan but not permitted to testify against it at the Finance Committee hearings. More than five hundred welfare recipients from seventeen states came to Washington for the hearings in late November and told McCarthy and ten other senators who attended the hearings that the plan,

[13] From January to September, McCarthy voted in only 37 percent of the Senate's 243 roll call votes. In 1969, he voted in 61 percent of the roll call votes. During his 10 previous years in the Senate, he voted in between 80 and 85 percent of the roll call votes except for 1965, when he was sick part of the year, and 1968, when he ran for president.

[14] McCarthy made single appearances for two other successful candidates — Hubert Humphrey, who was elected to succeed him in the Senate, and Patrick Lucey, elected governor of Wisconsin. However, he had supported Lucey's primary opponent earlier in the year.

which guaranteed federal payments of $1,600 a year to a family of four with no income, actually would result in reduced benefits for most families on welfare. McCarthy regarded welfare reform as a potent social issue which could help develop a new constituency among the poor and urged that the minimum guaranteed annual payments for a family of four be raised to $5,500. The administration bill was rejected by the Finance Committee and a compromise bill was killed by the Senate in December. But McCarthy had found a loyal and potentially powerful following because of his leadership on the welfare reform issue, according to George Wiley, executive director of the NWRO. "He's hooked up with a constituency that could help make him a contender in 1972," Wiley said. "That's just what he did with the peace issue and he's developing the same deep-seated relationship to these people."

The Senate bid a fond farewell to its best-known poet on December 21 as thirty-eight of his colleagues paid tribute to McCarthy. The plaudits ranged from emotional expressions of gratitude to statements of regret at his departure, and centered around the single theme of respect for the catalytic role he played in galvanizing antiwar dissent into a political force in 1968. Walter Mondale, McCarthy's junior Democratic colleague from Minnesota, led off the tributes while McCarthy sat in a far corner of the Senate chamber looking slightly embarrassed. "I think every American owes him an enormous debt," said Mondale. "He brought this country to its senses on Vietnam." Mondale's remarks set the tone for an hour and a half of effusive praise for the departing McCarthy, whose acid wit was etched in the minds of most of his colleagues as deeply as his accomplishments.[15] McCarthy, in a brief response, acknowledged his reputation as the Senate's one-man Greek chorus and offered an uncharacteristic apology for the criticisms he'd made of his fellow senators. "I have been given publicity, and I will not say justly or unjustly, for having criticized the Senate and senators; the positive things I have said have often been ignored." McCarthy ended his Senate career on a postive note, however, as he summed up his view of how the Senate had functioned and should function:

> What the Senate is doing and has been doing through the years, perhaps at a pace that might have been somewhat different, is in accordance with the constitutional intent and purpose and also, in the best tradition of the Senate, to stand in judgment for the country over the judicial system of this country, to judge how national policy, particularly foreign policy, should be

[15] Wisconsin's William Proxmire, whose verbal battles with Oregon's ex-Senator Wayne Morse once were characterized by McCarthy as "trouble in the leper colony," noted McCarthy's sharp, "sometimes cutting wit" and recalled that "some of us have been victims of it." Warren Magnuson of Washington gave the least eloquent tribute as he compared McCarthy to a Minnesota pike — "a fish that swims into a shallow, sluggish area and nudges the inhabitants there, to come alive and think, come out of their lethargy, if they are to survive. . . ." Magnuson originally used the word "carp" but later revised the word to "pike."

conducted, to judge the personnel of the government, and also to stand in reserve judgment over the action of the House of Representatives.

McCarthy's voluntary retirement from the Senate did not mean he was retiring from presidential politics, however. He told a panel of newsmen on NBC's "Meet the Press" television show on December 27 that while he had no firm plans, he hoped to remain in Washington and "be as active and effective as I can" through 1972 in regard to issues and presidential candidates. McCarthy spelled out four critical issues which he said might induce him to run for president again, including the Indochina war, the "militarization of American life," the handling of the economy, and the reform of the political processes. He saw no problem in his loss of the Senate forum and, in fact, said he probably could be more effective outside the Congressional and political party structures. He did not eliminate the possibility of joining or leading a new political party and said only that he would not be a candidate on the Republican ticket. He was willing to accept the possibility that "there may be no need for me and maybe nobody will want me [in 1972]. That is all right too. I will accept that. All I am saying is I am willing and I am going to make some preliminary moves. I will set up a small office. I expect that as I go around the country speaking that I will meet with some of the people who were in my campaign. We hope to give support to some of the good things that are going on now."

McCarthy gave a clearer indication of what kind of role he saw himself playing in 1971 and 1972 when he flew to Santa Barbara, California, on the day after leaving the Senate in early January and spoke at the Center for the Study of Democratic Institutions. Asserting that regular political party channels "are pretty well clogged up now," McCarthy said a "third party is beginning to look like a good risk, especially as it now appears that the Democrats and the Republicans are again going to come to the people, as they did in 1968, without offering any real choice, and without raising the important issues for public examination." It would not be difficult to mount a third-party challenge on the presidential level, even after the 1972 Democratic National Convention, McCarthy said. Such a party would be built "around the principles and around the public concern over the political process itself," although it could result in dividing Democratic votes and allowing Richard Nixon to win reelection. McCarthy was not frightened by that prospect: ". . . there comes a point when you simply have to run that risk. You say, 'All right, so the wrong people won because of us, but we told you that was the risk you were running.' It becomes a kind of poker game."

McCarthy began his new role as a poet, politician and private citizen on January 21, 1971, the day Hubert Humphrey moved into his Senate seat and office. While Humphrey celebrated his return to the Senate at a gala party at the Shoreham Hotel, McCarthy marked his exit at an Irish wake in his small, sparsely furnished townhouse in the capital's exclusive Georgetown section less than a mile away. McCarthy, who bought the townhouse in 1970 after moving out of his hotel apartment, shared passages of his bittersweet poetry and reminiscences of days gone by with a few friends and fellow alumni of St. John's University in Minnesota who gathered to mark the death of Father Walter Reger, a well-known St. John's priest. (McCarthy also reminded newspaper reporters who telephoned for a comment on Senator Edward Kennedy's defeat for reelection as Senate whip earlier in the day that he had predicted when he voted against Kennedy in 1969 that Kennedy's election would not improve the Senate.) One of the poems McCarthy read for his guests was from a new volume of poetry — his second — published in November and called, *Others Things and the Aardvark*. The opening lines of the book's title poem provided an apt description of McCarthy's current political and personal state:

> I am alone
> in the land of the aardvarks.
> I am walking west
> all the aardvarks are going east.

McCarthy believed that if he walked west far enough, eventually he would meet the eastbound aardvarks, and he set out at a brisk pace. Operating out of a two-room suite in a hotel directly behind the Senate Office Building — the same hotel that Lyndon Johnson's disgraced protege Bobby Baker once made his headquarters — he began testing the water for another presidential race. He held poetry readings, made speeches, gave interviews, held press conferences and wrote articles for *Life, New Republic, McCall's, Business Week,* New York *Times, National Catholic Reporter,* and other publications. In the first four months of the year, for example, he made twenty-one speeches in eighteen cities and college campuses from New York to California; spent a week in Israel where he met with Prime Minister Golda Meir; conferred with President Nixon's national security adviser, Henry Kissinger, at the White House, and opened a series of university teach-ins intended to rekindle opposition to the war.

Spurred by the antiwar candidacy of South Dakota Senator George McGovern that threatened to leave him in the middle of the liberal Democratic spectrum, McCarthy toughened his criticism of the Nixon administration's Indochina policies and of all those who bore any responsibility for the war. He told a February 21 antiwar rally in Boston that the U.S.-supported invasion of Laos by South Vietnamese troops earlier that month showed that "barbarism is almost instinctual with President Nixon." On March 26, McCarthy charged in a guest column in the New York *Times* that there was less constitutional justification for the war than in 1967. "It is a war which is more open-ended and less subject to political or policy direction and which is, therefore, more dangerous," McCarthy wrote as he called on Americans to hold everyone responsible for the war and "to leave no one an easy way out as we did in 1967 and 1968." And on April 4, McCarthy returned to Washington's New York Avenue Presbyterian Church where he first publicly called on Americans to make a harsh moral judgment against the war in February, 1967, and launched a Holy Week clergymen's "fast for peace" by declaring that the Americans were suffering from the same moral blindness in regard to Vietnam that white South Africans do in regard to apartheid.[16]

On April 8, the day before the Pentagon announced that the death toll of American soldiers in Vietnam had exceeded the Korean War total (54,000 U.S. military personnel killed in Vietnam since 1961, including an estimated 15,000 since Nixon took office), McCarthy showed the frustration he felt over the way the public debate on the war was moving. "It's not really a debate anymore," he said during an interview in his Washington office. "The president is advocating military action and the other people [supporters of a proposed withdrawal deadline] non-military action and nobody's talking about a negotiated settlement. It's the same proposition we've been raising since 1967 — that negotiated settlement is still the right way to proceed instead of a military effort. In each case, there's a refusal to take political responsibility. Neither side is talking about a negotiated settlement. If we tried for a negotiated settlement and it didn't work, then we could say we're going to withdraw." The war almost certainly would be an issue in 1972, McCarthy said, "but the question is how to present it. Trying to make an issue out of a scheduled troop reduction or whether we should have a date for having everybody out is like choosing between eight times two or two times eight."[17]

The tide of antiwar dissent reached a peak on April 24 when a crowd estimated at between 250,000 and 300,000 marched on the U.S. Capitol to culminate a week of antiwar lobbying by the Vietnam Veterans Against the War, and again, in the first week in May, when an estimated 10,000 persons were arrested when they attempted to disrupt traffic and close down government offices in Washington.[18] But for McCarthy, the highwater mark of the long, lonely struggle to vindicate his 1968 defeat came on May 23

[16] McCarthy shared the platform with Congressman Paul McCloskey, the California Republican who was about to mount a similar but far less effective challenge to President Nixon on the war than McCarthy carried out against Lyndon Johnson in 1968.

[17] McCarthy also decided to return to a part-time teaching career in April, as the University of Maryland announced that he had agreed to teach an undergraduate poetry course one day a week during the 1971-72 school year. Dr. Morris Freedman, chairman of Maryland's English Department, said in announcing the appointment that McCarthy "was reluctant to teach government, politics or sociology. He wanted to talk about poetry."

[18] Among those arrested in the Mayday demonstrations was McCarthy's son Michael, a junior at Harvard University. He was charged with disorderly conduct but his case was thrown out of court a month later after prosecutors were unable to find out why he had been charged.

in his home state of Minnesota. Appearing before an estimated 25,000 persons jammed into the Metropolitan Sports Center in the Twin Cities suburb of Bloomington, he told a nonpartisan "dump the war" rally arranged by Allard Lowenstein that he hoped that both the Democratic and Republican parties would succeed in nominating presidential candidates in 1972 who were committed to ending the war, reforming American politics and reordering national priorities. "Let us say that it is our design and our hope that we can accomplish all of these good things within both political parties or possibly within one of them," he said as the crowd came to its feet and cheered, "but that if we cannot, let us have a new party and a new policy and a true America."

The Bloomington speech, which McCarthy called "the most moving experience of my political life," earned him his greatest visibility since 1968 and convinced many people that he had unofficially launched his candidacy. McCarthy denied that this was his purpose, however. "I don't think so," he told Mike Wallace on the CBS program "Sixty Minutes" two days later. "I think it was more of an effort to suggest the need for a third-party movement, and I've been rather careful since '68 to try and discount or discourage what might develop into a McCarthy movement. I don't think it should be that." McCarthy agreed that a third party could result in President Nixon's reelection, but he saw that as a secondary consideration. "The point is that you can't go on forever letting the parties say, 'Look, if you do this, bad things will happen.' There comes a point at which you say to the parties, 'When are you going to be responsible?' "

McCarthy understood that a third–party candidacy could be attempted only after he first made an effort to win the Democratic nomination, as was evident on June 10 when he met with fifty New York Democratic leaders in the Park Avenue penthouse of New York City Democratic Chairman Jerry Finkelstein. McCarthy said he might enter some of the 1972 Democratic presidential primaries, particularly those like New York and Pennsylvania where he felt he had been unfairly treated by party leaders in 1968, and added: "The Democratic party would rather take a chance on Nixon winning than have a McCarthy." [19]

In July, after defending the publication of the Pentagon study of American involvement in Vietnam and charging that the Pentagon papers proved the Johnson administration was even "more devious and more deceptive than was suspected," McCarthy tried to deal himself back into the Democratic presidential card game. He called together a group of twelve of his most

[19] The beatings of his campaign helpers in Chicago in 1968 was a festering sore that never healed for McCarthy. On March 17, the day after his fifty-fifth birthday, he told William Shannon of the New York *Times*, "I never got so much as an apology from anyone on how my people were treated at Chicago. No leader of the party said to me even in private, 'Gene, I'm sorry.' not to mention publicly condemning as wrong what happened at the Hilton."

loyal supporters from 1968 for a six-hour strategy session at the luxurious St. Regis Sheraton Hotel in New York City. It was clear to those present that McCarthy had already crossed his Rubicon.[20] "He started the meeting off by saying, 'What primaries shall we run in?' " recalls Jerome Grossman, the Massachusetts businessman who had been responsible for getting McCarthy to enter his state's 1968 primary. "There was a gasp in the room and a void of utter silence, which I ultimately filled by saying, 'Gene, I thought the purpose of this meeting was not to decide *how* to go but *whether* to go.' He said, 'Well, let's talk about that then.' " Those at the meeting joined in the criticism. "We don't need any more educational campaigns," said Sterling Black, a New Mexico attorney and the son of Supreme Court Justice Hugo Black. "Almost everyone raised questions with McCarthy about the kind of campaign he would run, the kind of personal commitment that he would bring to the campaign, and demanded certain personality changes, organization changes and attitudinal changes on McCarthy's part," Grossman said later. "They complained about his failure as a campaigner in 1968, his failure in the last few years to hold on to the constituency he had." McCarthy was angered by the criticism. "He said he hadn't dropped out," recalls Martin Peretz, the wealthy Harvard professor who bankrolled McCarthy in 1968 to the tune of at least $100,000 and was prepared to do so again. "He ticked off the list of primaries around the country where he'd intervened [in 1970] where no other Democrat dared to tread on behalf of peace candidates running against war candidates, how he'd spoken for Biafran relief, for the Vietnam moratorium and the mobilization against the war, how he'd pushed for party reform and for reform of the welfare system. He said he hadn't dropped out but that he'd been as active as anybody else and we just hadn't noticed."

McCarthy also assured his supporters that he was prepared to wage a serious campaign for the Democratic nomination and the meeting ended with McCarthy agreeing to test his support in anticipation of a candidacy announcement later in the year. He then left immediately for a week-long European trip while Jerry Eller leaked the story of the meeting to the newspapers. However, McCarthy disputed the resulting stories that he had all but decided to make another presidential race. "I haven't made any plans," McCarthy said when contacted in Rome where he was attending an international youth conference. "I'll have to get back and see who said that."

McCarthy cut short his European trip to return home for the funeral of his longtime aide and close personal friend, Emerson Hynes, on August 3, and then began seriously probing for signs of support around the country.

[20] Only the day before, he received pledges totaling $1.5 million from a group of financial supporters organized by Howard Stein, head of the Dreyfus Corporation. At the same time, he met with Richard Goodwin, the brilliant ex-White House aide who had been a key aide in his 1968 campaign and who was willing to help him again in 1972.

He opened his unofficial campaign for the presidency on August 12 by telling the Southern Christian Leadership Conference in New Orleans that "the question is not the defeat of Richard Nixon in 1972 — that is almost certain. The question is not who will be elected president, but rather the principles, the policies and the programs to which the next president is committed before the election." McCarthy, who joined in a six-mile "poor people's" march and met privately with SCLC leaders during the visit, was making a special effort to find a new constituency among blacks and other minorities. One could start with the assumption, he said repeatedly during 1971, that approximately eighty million Americans would vote in the 1972 presidential election, that Nixon would be the Republican candidate, that Humphrey or Senator Edmund Muskie would be the Democratic nominee and that George Wallace would run again as an independent. Wallace could be expected to draw off about ten million votes equally from the two major parties, leaving 70 million votes to be divided among Republicans, Democrats and a new liberal fourth party. It was therefore possible, McCarthy said, that the next president could be elected by only twenty-five million votes.

The minority vote was the keystone of McCarthy's plan to win those twenty-five million votes, he indicated in an interview with Saul Pett of the Associated Press shortly before the New Orleans speech. Twenty-five million young people would be eligible to vote for the first time in 1972 because of the constitutional amendment lowering the voting age to eighteen, McCarthy said. If only fifteen million of these actually voted, ten million would be likely to go for a new liberal party candidate. This would leave another fifteen million voters to be picked up among older voters "who want change but feel politically impotent," he added. "The only real question would be what share of the minority vote can a new party candidate get. That's the only uncertainty. If not for that, a fourth party with a good candidate could win just on the record of 1968."

On August 18, in a follow-up to the St. Regis meeting in Washington, McCarthy agreed to "go operational" by opening a full–scale national campaign headquarters in Washington. "I don't know whether we're clinging to a ghost or not," Martin Peretz told the author the morning after Peretz and several other McCarthy supporters planned the mechanical details of his campaign during dinner at a Georgetown restaurant. "The real question is whether McCarthy can get a good staff together and round up enough workers around the country like George Wallace has done."

In September, McCarthy returned to the college classroom for the first time since he left St. Paul to come to Congress in 1949. He began his new one-day-a-week job as visiting professor of English at the University of Maryland by telling two hundred and fifty students who showed up for his first class on September 14, "I want to have you understand most clearly that I really am serious about poetry, as I am about politics." McCarthy's seriousness about politics had been open to question since 1968, but it would not be in the next four months as he crisscrossed the country, preaching the gospel of party reform, personal responsibility and political action in over eighty personal appearances. "Woodrow Wilson said that a political party could never be an organization," he told an independent Democrats' forum in Oak Park, Illinois, on October 8. "It had to be an organism, he said, which was open to all of the movement and spirit of the nation, taking in new ideas . . . new energy . . . new persons and personalities." McCarthy continued to insist that he was not yet a candidate, but he left little doubt that the quality of other Democrats would soon make him one. "If the other candidates," he said during a five-day visit to California in early October, "were raising the right issues, talking about party reform and gaining [in] popularity, there would be no reason to intrude and become an active candidate. But they seem to be falling short on all three points."

On October 29, McCarthy sent out 150,000 letters soliciting support for "The Politics of 1972." In his letters, McCarthy announced his intention to strengthen his staff, establish a campaign committee and pursue "an active and positive effort to secure convention delegates with views similar to ours" through involvement in all primary and non-primary states. McCarthy listed three "principal purposes" to which he would dedicate himself in the coming year. First, he called for an immediate end to the war in Vietnam and to American military involvement in Southeast Asia, and for a political settlement. Second, he asked for a vast array of new approaches to domestic problems, condemning the proposals of fellow Democratic candidates as "little more than warmed over New Deal programs or quantitative increases in Nixon proposals." Finally, he again urged party reform and bitterly criticized the Democratic National Committee and Chairman Larry O'Brien, declaring that "the same people who mishandled the Chicago convention of 1968, who mismanaged the campaign of 1968, and who have mismanaged the party since then are still in control and obviously intend to remain there."

There was one candidate McCarthy could not fault for raising the wrong issues, however, and that was George McGovern. McCarthy had seen many of his former supporters join McGovern, who had been an announced candidate for a year, and the two men had maintained an uneasy truce, with McCarthy even suggesting that they form a coalition to avoid splitting the vote of the Democratic left. McCarthy seemed unconcerned about the possibility that McGovern would walk away with most of McCarthy's old constituency of the young and the disaffected. "George is trying to do 1968 all over again," McCarthy said during a two-day trip to Minnesota in early December to prepare for the state's February precinct caucuses, "and it won't work. He hasn't added anything new. But I guess we'll have to let him brazen it out, then see where we stand when he fails." In the meantime, McCarthy continued to try to recapture the stubborn loyalties he had found on the college campuses in 1968, stressing the issues of the "arrogance of technology" in America, the need for "equal justice" for young people and minorities, and the need to "challenge every American institution" — corporations, labor unions and political parties — to demand they live up to their responsibilities.

On December 17, McCarthy casually placed himself in the running for the 1972 presidential race. At a news conference in Boston to announce the opening of a "McCarthy for President" headquarters in Massachusetts, McCarthy was asked by reporters if this meant he was announcing his candidacy for the Democratic presidential nomination. "It's kind of an announcement, yes," he replied. "I am running now in the Democratic party as I did in 1968. But whether or not I support the ultimate candidate of the party depends on what issues that candidate supports." McCarthy's new strategy and his assessment of the changed political situation were evident in his decision to forego the primary that had been the catalyst of his 1968 campaign. He would not enter New Hampshire, he said, because it is "too time consuming, too expensive and too cluttered" with other candidates.

McCarthy followed up with what he called "Phase Two" of his announcement of candidacy on January 5, 1972. Standing in a small, crowded room next to his office in the Capitol Hill Hotel, his face showing the strain of a man who had been running hard much longer than most people were aware, McCarthy made it clear that his goal was the purification of his party and the political processes as much as it was achieving the presidency. "The issues are not overriding [now] in the way they were in 1968, and the measure of personal responsibility for programs and for policy is much greater," he said. "And therefore, in the primaries and beyond, I will talk about where people stood in 1968 and what they did in 1968 and what they have done and not done since that time." McCarthy promised to hold other Democratic candidates "accountable" for past policies, and immediately zeroed in on Senator Edmund Muskie, the then-acknowledged frontrunner who had announced his candidacy the night before and would be McCarthy's major opponent in the March 21 Illinois presidential preference primary. Muskie, said McCarthy, "was the most active representative of Johnson administration Vietnam policy at Chicago."

Many people failed to share McCarthy's conviction that he was destined to play a major role in the 1972 presidential campaign. "There are moments when one wonders whether he is aware that his own legions have fragmented and that it is not easy to turn on all the old emotions after an absence from the national stage since he capriciously left the Senate," New York *Post* Columnist James Wechsler, a leading voice of the liberal community, wrote shortly after McCarthy's announcement. "He may be understandably reluctant to let the history books close on him with the 1968 chapter . . . [but] . . . a return engagement that had only the quality of self-righteousness, self-deception and self-pity would be a sad anti-climax." McCarthy responded that he had proved the columnists wrong before and mounted an all-out campaign in the Illinois primary, which he said would give Illinois voters "a chance to show the Democratic party which way it should go" and prove that he still retained popular appeal. But after a month of intensive campaigning and the expenditure of an estimated $300,000, McCarthy received 37 percent of the vote to Muskie's 63 percent.

McCarthy continued his attack on his fellow Democrats in the Wisconsin primary. His chief target was McGovern, but it was evident throughout the campaign that McCarthy now had his sights firmly fixed on a third–party candidacy. Four days before the April 4 primary, McCarthy made his final appearance of the Wisconsin campaign and issued a statement criticizing McGovern and New York Mayor John Lindsay. When he was asked by a reporter whether a third-party candidacy simply wouldn't wind up reelecting President Nixon, McCarthy shot back: "You can't go on forever making choices between Nixon and Humphrey if you want the country to progress." He underscored his point by issuing a nine-point program he said the Democratic party would have to accept unless it was prepared to face a third-party challenge in the fall, and declared, "Unless these nine basic issues are included in the Democratic platform, one would have to give serious thought to a political movement that would realize their importance and carry them to the people for judgment." [21]

McCarthy received only 15,652 votes, or less than 1 percent of the total, and finished seventh among 11 Democratic contenders in the Wisconsin primary that established McGovern as the new leader of the Democratic left. The Wisconsin primary had shown that McCarthy had become, as he said of Adlai Stevenson in 1960, a prophet without honor in his own party. He was now prepared to carry out the strategy of disenchantment that he had been planning since 1968.

[21] The nine-point program included an immediate end to the Vietnam War and U.S. withdrawal of support to the Thieu government, amnesty for all draft evaders who left the country, an income support program for the poor, a shorter work week and curbing of corporate power. Other provisions included a redirection of national resources away from military expenditure and highways, reorganization of American medical practice, prison reform and "a firm and unequivocal commitment" to a single system of justice for everyone.

CHAPTER XX

THE RETURN OF HUBERT HUMPHREY

> *A man in Washington without political power is a museum*
> *piece. I like museums, but I don't want to be in one.*
> Hubert Humphrey in a 1971 interview.

Hubert Humphrey watched, grim and unsmiling, as Richard Nixon was sworn in as the thirty-seventh president of the United States on the grey, chilly afternoon of January 20, 1969. "I sat there and couldn't help but think, well, we came mighty close," Humphrey said in a voice heavy with the emotion of defeat.

The burden of Humphrey's defeat was not made any easier by Lyndon Johnson. Humphrey's administrative assistant, William Welsh, recalls that a few nights before the inauguration, he found Humphrey sitting at his desk in the Executive Office Building in glum silence, and asked what was wrong. "He shook his head and said, 'I can't believe what I've just been through,' " Welsh remembers. "He said he'd just been over in the residency, upstairs at the White House, listening to an hour and a half lecture as to why he personally lost the election, why it was all his fault, and all that he did wrong in the campaign."

The trauma of Humphrey's defeat was severe and slow to heal. In the period between the election and the inauguration, he frequently lapsed into self-pity as he confronted the reality of his defeat by a man who personified much that was alien to his personal and political nature. "I'm sorry I let you down," Humphrey quietly told dozens of his friends and supporters in the days following the election. "I let so many people down."[1]

---

[1] Humphrey still blamed others for his defeat, however. He reserved his harshest feelings for Jesse Unruh, the California Democratic leader who lost his bid for governor in 1970. "Jesse Unruh was a double-crosser all the time, he never worked for us," Humphrey later told the author. "He did not play the kind of politics that a

Humphrey returned to Minnesota the next day to plot a new course for his life as a private citizen. He had hinted at what that course would be in his first public speech after the election, a November 22 appearance before the Farmers Union Grain Terminal Association in St. Paul, when he spoke longingly of a desire to mingle with young people and to visit the university campuses where he had been so unwelcome as a presidential candidate. He said he wanted to study and teach about the structure of government in the United States and to "talk to people who dream big dreams." Humphrey's wish soon was granted. In December, he accepted a $30,000 a year professorship requiring him to divide his time between Macalester College in St. Paul, the school where he taught political science twenty-five years earlier, and the University of Minnesota, where he first formally studied political science more than thirty years earlier. "I return not primarily to teach — but I come back to learn and to have my mind and senses stretched once again," the new holder of Macalester's Hubert Humphrey Professorship of International Relations declared.[2] Recalling that he had visited 130 college campuses as vice president, Humphrey said he was convinced that many answers to questions of "fundamental human relationships" that were once satisfactory to young people "are no longer acceptable. They are speaking out with a sense of honesty and morality which, on occasion, produces more heat than light," he said, already sounding very much like a professor. "But they are rightly questioning the assumptions and institutions which they see as irrelevant to the contemporary human condition." Humphrey indicated he might produce a little heat himself as he warned that he would not be a non-controversial professor. "I have a lot of things bottled up inside me that may explode," he declared.

Humphrey found plenty of other ways to help him follow his late father's advice that one should never dwell on his past failures. In addition to his teaching posts, Humphrey accepted the offer of his old friend, former Connecticut Senator William Benton, to become a consultant and member of the board of directors for Encyclopedia Britannica, Inc., and a subsidiary firm at a salary of $75,000 a year. He also became chairman of the board of trustees for several universities and non-profit educational institutions; wrote a $200 a week syndicated newspaper column on political affairs and signed a fat publishing contract to write his memoirs and a book on American foreign policy. ("Boy, it will be great to be anti-junta again," he said as he

good Democrat ought to play — and he got his comeuppance for it. He was out there bad-mouthing me up and down the state when he should have been helping us. Politics isn't a matter of making love — it's a matter of making choices." Humphrey is more charitable towards Eugene McCarthy: "I thing Gene should have helped us more too. What he did at the end wasn't much help, but I'm not angry about it. I have a kind of simple philosophy: The chickens come home to roost and you get what you plant."

[2] Humphrey's title at the University of Minnesota was visiting professor of social sciences.

looked forward to writing the book on foreign policy.) With his $17,000 a year Senate pension, a fully furnished house provided by Macalester, and dozens of $2,500 speaking fees, he soon was making more money — an estimated $200,000 a year — than at any time in his life.

At his first formal lecture, a two-hour session with twenty-six political science students at Macalester on the subject, "Decision-making in the Executive Branch of the Federal Government," Humphrey appeared uncomfortable and slightly defensive. "Don't worry about taking any notes," he told his attentive but critical students on February 27. "If what I say is worth anything, you'll remember it." Humphrey then launched into a rambling discourse about government and politics, peppering his remarks with facts, insights, opinions and frequent allusions to his friendships with famous people and his former proximity to power. The reaction to Humphrey's first lecture was mixed. Jeff Stillings, a nineteen year old sophomore, praised him: "It was really inside information. It made me think that maybe I should go to law school and then get into politics." But others were less impressed. "I was a little disgusted," said Marnie Hammer, another nineteen year old sophomore. "All we got were homilies." Her classmate, Martha Moore, added, "I think we were all a little turned off. He just sounded out of touch."

While many of his new students looked on Humphrey as a figure out of the past, others could not forget his association with the war. "He had a terrible time at the beginning," recalls Mrs. Geri Joseph, the former vice chairman of the Democratic National Committee and a longtime Humphrey confidante. "The kids were very rough on him and you could see he was struggling and wasn't confident that he could get across to young people or that they would like him. I can understand a little of what he went through because even coming back from that silly little job as vice-chairman, and trying to re-orient myself in my own small world was very difficult. But to go from being vice president to being a teacher, particularly when he knew how the kids felt about him, that must have been a fantastic change. I think he had to swallow his pride every morning with his coffee, because that's how insulting some of the kids were. They didn't accept his experience and they constantly questioned him, sometimes in very cruel ways. But he stuck it out and he did win many of them over."

Humphrey later said that the turning point of his resumed teaching career came soon after he arrived at Macalester when one of his students approached him after class and said, "Why don't you forget the past and just teach? You're so defensive about the past that we can't think about the future. Why don't you just relax and go on from here?" Humphrey took the advice and gradually became comfortable in his new role.[3]

[3] Humphrey was given a sharp reminder that he was still tied to the Vietnam War during a business trip to London in May when a group of about forty British students

While Humphrey was slowly learning to bridge the generation gap, he also was beginning to think seriously about his political future again for the first time. At first, Humphrey recoiled from politics and things political. "He just sort of withdrew," recalls Bill Connell, the ex-aide who managed Humphrey's Encyclopedia Britannica office in Washington and remained one of his closest political advisers. "You couldn't get him to talk about politics. He didn't want to even think about it. He'd been actively involved in politics since his first mayor's campaign in 1943 and he needed a sabbatical. But gradually he started to cock his ear again toward national issues. He was very disturbed with what Nixon was doing with the economy and he began to say, 'We've got to get this guy out of there — he'll wreck us, economically and socially.' "

Humphrey had been urged by some friends and advisers to run for governor in 1970 against incumbent Republican Harold LeVander, but decided against it because it would not give him a national forum. "Contemplation of another presidential race was one of the considerations for not going for governor," Connell later said. "He felt it would remove him from the national scene and give him no options for 1972." Humphrey's first choice was to return to the Senate, but he was not willing to commit himself until learning of the intentions of Eugene McCarthy, who had announced that he would not run for the Senate again as a Democrat but had not ruled out running as an independent.

Even though Humphrey still had one eye on the presidency, he was fatalistic about it. Sitting in his Danish modern office on Macalester's tree-lined campus before leaving on a month-long trip to several European countries and the Soviet Union in July, 1969, Humphrey reminded a reporter that some Democratic leaders were saying that Senator Edward Kennedy was a shoo-in for the party's 1972 presidential nomination. Then he told the reporter the lesson he had learned so painfully and so well in 1968: "Events are going to affect elections more than personalities."

Subsequent events gave those words a prophetic ring. On July 19, Kennedy drove his car off a bridge on Chappaquiddick Island and a young woman companion was drowned under questionable circumstances, and then a few days later McCarthy reaffirmed his intention not to seek reelection to the Senate. Humphrey immediately issued a statement after returning from Europe saying he was giving "serious consideration" to running for McCarthy's seat, but added that he would make no decision for at least several months. Humphrey made his statement after meeting with McCarthy for what Humphrey said was "just a general discussion about our respective political activities." But Humphrey left no doubt that his presidential hopes were revived once again. Asked by a reporter if the new turn of events might lead to another try

---

invaded a pub where he was eating and forced him to leave. The students kicked and pounded his car, shouting antiwar slogans at him.

for the presidency in 1972, Humphrey replied, "I just don't think anybody can predict. But I do know what I have to do between now and then. I've got to keep myself mentally and intellectually active, and keep in touch with the political forces in the world." [4]

Abandoning the sideline role he had played since the election, Humphrey agreed to become chairman of the new seventy-six member Democratic Policy Council, created by the Democratic National Committee in September to act as a watchdog over the Nixon administration's programs and to present Democratic alternatives to those programs. One week later, on September 24, he launched his first strongly partisan attack on the Nixon administration in a speech at the Minnesota AFL-CIO convention in St. Paul. Encouraged by three standing ovations and a brass band that played the obligatory "Happy Days Are Here Again," Humphrey sounded very much like a candidate. However, he confined his criticism of the administration almost entirely to domestic and economic policy except for accusing the administration of vacillating on the issue of arms control negotiations with Russia. On October 6, he repeated his attack in a similarly worded speech before the AFL-CIO national convention in Atlantic City, again being careful not to criticize Nixon's Vietnam policies.

It soon became clear why Humphrey was holding his fire on Vietnam. On October 10, he emerged from an hour-long meeting with Nixon at the White House and announced that the president was "proceeding on the right path" for ending the war. "We have only one president at a time," said Humphrey, who was making his first visit to the executive mansion since Nixon was sworn in, "and I think the worst thing we could do is to undermine the position of the president. . . . We simply have to accept the man's good faith. . . . I don't think we should set deadlines . . . or restrict his freedom."

Humphrey's decision to throw his full support behind Nixon's Vietnam policy enraged many liberal Democrats, who felt he had played into Nixon's hands by echoing his appeals for public support for what they regarded as little more than a warmed-over version of Lyndon Johnson's policy. But Humphrey, who arranged the meeting on the pretext of having breakfast with Nixon's foreign policy adviser, Henry Kissinger, had made a different reading of the Vietnam issue and was persuaded that Democrats could only lose by trying to play politics with it. "I'm convinced that he wants to get out," Humphrey said a short time later, "just as soon as he can and a lot sooner than a lot of people think. I keep telling my liberal friends who

[4] During his trip to Europe, Humphrey spent thirteen days in the Soviet Union and met with numerous Soviet leaders, including Premier Aleksei Kosygin. He said he advised Kosygin that President Nixon would be receptive to negotiations to reduce the nuclear arms race and dissolve the cold war.

attack him for not getting out faster, 'You're gonna lose — he's gonna get out.' But they won't listen."

During his meeting with Nixon and Kissinger, Humphrey strongly recommended that the president go before the nation to explain his Vietnam policy. He told Nixon that the war was having a more divisive effect on the country than either of them realized and warned him that any broadening of the conflict would provoke more mass protests such as those planned for a Vietnam Moratorium Day on October 15.[5] Humphrey pledged to defend Nixon if he mounted a "peace offensive," and did so when Nixon went on nationwide television on November 3 to announce a program of accelerated, systematic withdrawals. Humphrey said it was the same policy he would have followed if he had been elected. The Humphrey-Nixon honeymoon on Vietnam was disturbed by Nixon's attitude toward antiwar dissenters, however. In the harshest criticism he had yet made of Nixon, Humphrey charged the administration, during a November 17 press conference in Washington with "a calculated, premeditated attack" on the right of dissent and free speech. He accused Nixon of fostering Vice President Agnew's attack against the television industry and the news media in a Des Moines speech four days earlier, and said the speech, along with Attorney General John Mitchell's denunciation of the generally peaceful Vietnam Moratorium Day demonstrations, represented an effort to "create an atmosphere of suppression and call it patriotism."

Defending the administration's position on Vietnam was a familiar role for Humphrey, and provided an appropriate backdrop for his first meeting with former President Johnson since the two men left office. Humphrey and his wife Muriel spent three hours at the LBJ Ranch in Texas on December 1 in a visit that Humphrey said was "primarily social." However, Humphrey's social call did not prevent Johnson from publicly criticizing him a few weeks later. In a CBS television interview, Johnson made it clear he felt Humphrey would have been president if he had not made his "stop the bombing" speech at Salt Lake City in September, 1968. The interview and other public and private comments by Johnson as well as his revealing neglect of Humphrey in his 1971 memoirs have left Humphrey with an agonizing uncertainty about whether Johnson wanted Humphrey to succeed him in the presidency. "I think he wanted me to win, but I think that he constantly felt that in order to win, I had to do it his way," Humphrey

---

[5] In a confidential memo to Kissinger dated October 11, Humphrey summarized his conversation with the president. "Vietnam is sapping the spirit of the country," Humphrey wrote. He also called for "American initiative in seeking a cease-fire and so-called stand-still of all combat forces. I know this is difficult, but we should press it. The military doesn't like it, but our options are not very many or very good." Humphrey said he was offering his views "in confidence and in a spirit of helpfulness," and added, "I want to help the president, and I am prepared to defend him as he moves on his peace offensive, but it must be a peace offensive."

told the author in a 1971 interview. "I think he had mixed emotions. It's hard for me to give you an honest answer on that because I have mixed emotions too." Humphrey feels he may have offended Johnson by not involving him more in the campaign. "I think that if I had gone to Johnson earlier and really put it on the line and said, 'Mr. President, you have to help me,' then he would have done more. I think he felt — with some justification — that he was not being asked to do enough . . . that once I was out on my own, I was running away from him rather than coming to him. And he resented it."

Humphrey was convinced that Vietnam would not be the pivotal issue in 1970, when he planned to begin his political comeback by running for McCarthy's Senate seat. "The issue that is going to determine the elections in 1970 is the economy, not Vietnam," Humphrey told reporters on February 9 as the Democratic Policy Council met in Washington to approve a resolution calling for "a firm and unequivocal commitment" for the withdrawal of all American troops from Vietnam within eighteen months. Humphrey, who backed an unsuccessful effort by several supporters of former President Johnson to soften the language of the resolution and helped defeat several stronger substitute versions, hailed the action as the key to Democratic unity. He predicted that it would finally heal the wounds the war had inflicted on the party, and said, "I think this has defused Vietnam as a political issue."

The Vietnam resolution may have defused the war issue in the Democratic party, but it didn't remove the lingering suspicion of Humphrey on college campuses. For the first time in his life, he allowed vocal opposition to prevent him from giving a speech when about two hundred jeering students forced him from the speaker's platform at the University of Massachusetts on February 24. The disruption, which came as Humphrey began a foreign policy speech before about 4,500 persons, was in protest of the sentencing of 5 of the 7 defendants charged with inciting to riot during the 1968 Democratic National Convention. Humphrey waited for about fifteen minutes, and even offered to discuss the Chicago trials, but the heckling continued. "Well, that's it," he said, and left the stage, telling his tormentors, "I got paid already. This speech is written out, so anybody who wants can read it. Frankly, I'm not vice president any more and I don't have to be nice to you or anyone." Humphrey then went to a nearby inn where he gave the speech to a group of fifty students and faculty members.

Humphrey's comeback road became bumpy again a few days later when he became involved in an imbroglio over finding a replacement for Oklahoma Senator Fred Harris as chairman of the Democratic National Committee. Humphrey had given Harris the job a year earlier as a consolation prize for having passed him over as his vice presidential running mate, but had become disenchanted with Harris' failure to reduce the party's staggering $9.3

million debt, his ill-concealed ambition and his courting of the party's left wing — particularly on the issue of party reform. Convinced that the party needed a full-time chairman who was a nuts and bolts technician and not an ideologue, Humphrey pushed for Harris' resignation and then offered the job to Terry Sanford, the former North Carolina governor who was serving as president of Duke University. Sanford wasn't interested and suggested Larry O'Brien, who had managed Humphrey's and two previous Democratic presidential campaigns and had opened a political consulting firm in New York, and he tentatively agreed to accept. However, he turned it down after finding that the solid support from all segments of the party that Humphrey had promised him was missing. O'Brien was also discouraged when he found out the party was deeper in debt than he suspected. Humphrey then convinced a reluctant Matthew Welsh, a former governor of Indiana, to accept the post, but the party's Executive Committee, in a clear rebuff to Humphrey, turned him down on March 2 and pleaded with O'Brien to take the job on his own terms.[6]

Humphrey's handling of the matter exploded the myth that the party's titular leader had any real power, and exposed him to charges of "bungling" and "ineptitude" at a time when he hoped to project an image of strong leadership. "The 1968 presidential nominee and the 1969 titular leader appears to have become a 1970 paper tiger," Ted Knap, Washington correspondent for the Scripps-Howard Newspapers, wrote in a judgment that reflected the feelings of many party leaders at the time. Knap called the O'Brien affair "a monument to inept political management" by Humphrey that "may mark his finish as a presidential prospect."

Humphrey's presidential hopes may have been dimmed, but they certainly weren't extinguished as far as he was concerned. He made that clear on March 30 when he sat down with a group of Washington political reporters for an off-the-record dinner at the home of Jack Germond of the Gannett News Service. Basically, Humphrey had only one message — that he was tired of the academic life and yearned to be back in Washington and the political arena. In fact, he left little doubt that he was not only off and running for the Senate but also was seriously thinking of another bid for the White House in 1972 and would like to have Senator Edward Kennedy as his running mate. Comparing his thirst for political office to that of an alcoholic for drink, Humphrey complained that Minnesota was an inadequate base for national campaigning and that it was virtually impossible for a public figure to attract national attention unless he operated in New York or Washington where the news media is concentrated. Humphrey admitted that he probably would be charged with using the Senate as a stepping

---

[6] The Executive Committee's action came twenty years to the day after Humphrey's famous confrontation with the late Senator Harry Byrd, Sr., on the Senate floor, and many Democrats felt it was a political blunder of equal magnitude.

stone to another try for the presidency but he brushed it aside by saying he was certain Minnesotans would be happy to have one of their native sons running for the White House again.

Humphrey didn't share with the reporters his thinking about what direction he wanted the Democratic party to move under its new chairman, but his closest advisers were arguing that the party must avoid being pulled away from the center if it seriously hoped to challenge Republicans in the 1970 and 1972 elections. "The heart of the Democratic party still has a strong blue-collar, labor orientation," Bill Connell told the author as O'Brien took office. "Nixon's middle America has got a lot more than just small businessmen and farmers in it." Connell noted that in 1968, Humphrey lost six Deep South states won by John Kennedy in 1960, and commented, "That's the real problem we have as a national party in electing a president — we get wiped out in the South." Connell said one of the first things he hoped O'Brien would do would be "to sit down with the Southern moderates, who feel they're being left out and that the party is listening to people like McCarthy and McGovern and John Kenneth Galbraith and Gloria Steinem — the Peter Pan Brigade." Connell analyzed the party as consisting of a "moderate middle" that represents about 65 percent of the membership, as "ideological peace-oriented left wing" of about 15 percent and an "all-out Vietnam hawk" right wing of about 15 percent. "The economic issues unite all three wings but the racial issue and Vietnam — that's where we've got the divisions in the party."

Humphrey had warned his fellow Democrats against playing politics with the war, but he ignored his own advice when Nixon ordered U.S. troops to support an incursion by South Vietnamese troops into Cambodia on April 30. "No amount of explanation can erase the fact that the level of combat and casualties has been increased," he said after returning from a business trip to Japan. "The war has been expanded and the hope for peace seriously damaged." In addition, Humphrey said the wave of public protest stirred up by the move showed for the first time that Nixon was politically vulnerable and predicted that the Cambodia action could compound the problems of the United States' uncertain economy.[7]

Humphrey formalized his bid for political resurrection on June 13. In a five-page statement in which he announced his candidacy for the Senate seat being relinquished by McCarthy, Humphrey said he had no intention of seeking the Democratic presidential nomination in 1972, but carefully avoided ruling it out: "I would be less than candid if I tried to pretend that

[7] Two days later, in Israel to receive an honorary fellowship from the Weizman Institute in recognition of his fund-raising activities on behalf of the United Jewish Appeal, Humphrey called on the U.S. to supply Israel with more war planes and other weapons to defend itself against Soviet-equipped Egyptian forces. He called the Middle East the most dangerous area in the world, even more so than Southeast Asia.

I would turn away from the nomination if it came my way," the fifty-nine year old Humphrey declared. Humphrey, who said he looked on the period since his defeat by Nixon as one of "renewal and learning," touched only briefly in his statement on matters of concern to Minnesota voters. Most of the statement dealt with national issues as Humphrey accused Nixon of failing to provide sound leadership on the war and the economy, and described the nation as "torn and divided because of it."

Humphrey, who described himself as a "recycled" candidate, faced two obstacles to a fourth term in the Senate. The first was Earl Craig, a thirty-one year old black instructor at the University of Minnesota who had been active in Eugene McCarthy's 1968 campaign and served as a national officer of the New Democratic Coalition. An eloquently soft-spoken and self-professed radical, Craig agreed to run after he was unable to find anyone else to challenge Humphrey in Minnesota's September DFL primary. Craig became the focus of anti-Humphrey feeling among many former McCarthy supporters who agreed with his judgment that Humphrey represented "a kind of stale and unresponsive liberalism." However, Humphrey easily disposed of Craig by 250,000 votes (the final margin was 338,996–88,709) and then faced what at first appeared to be a stiff challenge from five-term Republican Congressman Clark MacGregor, an able and articulate Nixon-style centrist.

Humphrey's 1970 Senate campaign would serve as a prototype for his campaign for the 1972 presidential nomination that he said he had no intention of waging. In MacGregor, he had a Nixon substitute on whom he could test his political skills while preparing for another chance to run against the real thing, and he welcomed the invasion of Minnesota by more than a dozen top Republican officials — including Nixon. More important, Humphrey found himself a skilled political manager in Jack Chestnut, a thirty-seven year old successful Minneapolis attorney who had proven his ability as an organizer and expert advance man in Humphrey's 1968 campaign. Chestnut, who was to return to Humphrey's side as manager of his 1972 presidential campaign, engineered what would be the best organized campaign Humphrey ever ran, utilizing highly sophisticated computer mailing and get-out-the-vote techniques that augmented Humphrey's 99 percent recognition among Minnesotans and his indefatigable personal campaigning.[8]

It didn't take long for the image of a "New Humphrey" to emerge. Glorying in his freedom from Lyndon Johnson's tight rein and the organizational and financial difficulties that plagued him in 1968, Humphrey bore little re-

[8] The computer mailing and telephone bank operations, which provided a personal Humphrey contact with every registered Democrat in the state, was conducted by Valentine, Sherman & Associates, a political consulting firm headed by Humphrey's press secretary, Norman Sherman.

semblance to the harried candidate of two years earlier. Outfitted with a spiffy new wardrobe, his modishly long hair dyed black, and twelve pounds lighter than he was in 1968, Humphrey oozed self-confidence. He was ferried around the state in a plane and helicopter that made his comings and goings events in themselves, was seldom late and kept his speeches mercifully short. (More than once, when he reminded his audiences that if he'd gotten a few more votes in 1968, they could have joined him at a party in the White House Rose Garden, Humphrey heard the reassuring reply, "That's all right, Hubert — we'll get you there yet.")

Humphrey's campaign slogan, "You Know He Cares," reflected the traditional liberal concern for generous federal spending on social programs, and he zeroed in early on Nixon's handling of the economy. But the Humphrey campaign also showed the deficiency, as it was shown in many states, of the Republican party's "law and order" rhetoric and Vice President Agnew's fulminations about the dangers of "radical-liberal" permissiveness. Humphrey refused to stand still and be tarred as soft on law and order. Again and again, he returned to the theme of a speech he gave to the American Bar Association in St. Louis on August 11. The speech was written by aide Ben Wattenberg, who with another longtime Humphrey adviser, Richard Scammon, authored the newly-published political book, *The Real Majority*. In the speech entitled, " 'Liberalism' and 'Law and Order' — Must There Be a Conflict?" Humphrey proclaimed the doctrine of the book, which advised liberals to temper their preoccupation with youth, the poor and blacks, and pay more attention to the concerns of Middle America about "disruptive social change" if they wanted to rebuild a winning Democratic coalition and push for historic liberal programs. In the central passage of his speech, Humphrey appealed to "true liberals" to "let Mr. and Mrs. Middle America know that they understand what is bugging them, and . . . that they too condemn crime and riots and violence and extreme social turbulence, and they scorn extremists of the left as well as the right. . . ." [9]

Although Humphrey intended the speech as an effort to separate liberalism from extremism and to help the party recover the balance it lost in Chicago, many liberals saw it as evidence that he was determined not to let Republicans usurp the law and order issue. Humphrey was angered by the resulting criticism of his speech, particularly when the state's largest newspaper, the Minneapolis *Tribune*, asked editorially whether the speech "suggests a rightward drift to reflect the conservative temper of the times and

[9] Humphrey's St. Louis speech did not represent a newly arrived at position. He gave several tough "law and order" speeches during the 1968 campaign, including one on September 11 in which he said, "Rioting, burning, sniping, mugging, traffic in narcotics and disrespect for the law are the advance guard of anarchy. They must — and will — be stopped."

the nature of Humphrey's Republican opposition." "I don't think I have
to reestablish my liberal credentials," he retorted. "I've spent a lifetime trying
to point out you can't have civil order without civil justice. . . . This
wasn't a speech backing away from any conviction. This was a speech of
common sense and everybody who wants to have a better society knows so."

Minnesota voters apparently agreed with Humphrey. After a rather
routine campaign that amounted to a battle for the political center, he
swamped MacGregor in November by 220,000 votes or nearly 59 percent
of the vote.[10] The victory had clearly allowed Humphrey to keep his place
in line among the Democratic party's presidential contenders as his coattails helped the DFL elect the nation's youngest governor (thirty-seven
year old Wendell Anderson), take over most of the other major state offices,
pick up a Congressional seat and give the DFL-allied Liberals greatly increased strength in both houses of the legislature that had long been dominated by Republican-oriented Conservatives.

Humphrey recognized that he returned to the Senate under unusual circumstances. Never before had a former majority whip, vice president, and
presidential candidate returned as a freshman senator. He also realized
he had lost his seniority and the power that went with it.[11] "It will be a
rather delicate operation . . ." he told a group of Washington newsmen
on December 10, as he recalled the lesson of his disastrous Senate debut
twenty years earlier. "When I go back I've got to exemplify the qualities
of leadership but have humility. I'm not going back seeking any titles. I'm
not going to tell the boys, 'You've done it all wrong.' I have to go back and
work." At the same time, Humphrey intended to make his presence felt
again in the nation's capital. "The Democratic party is going to hear from
me. I'm going to have a hand in the Democratic party. I'm not a boss . . .
but I'm a little firmer now; I'm not so interested in whether people don't
like me."

Humphrey's colleagues broke into applause as he was sworn in as the
new junior senator from Minnesota — and the oldest of ten freshmen — by
his successor, Vice President Agnew, on January 21, 1971, exactly two years
and a day after Humphrey's unhappy inaugural day. Eight hours later, some
six hundred of Humphrey's friends, supporters and political associates helped
erase the disappointment of that day by throwing a big "Welcome Hubert Humphrey" dinner in Washington's mammoth Shoreham Hotel.

---

[10] The campaign was enlivened by memorable quotes by each candidate. Early in
the campaign, MacGregor remarked that "if Humphrey was a girl, he'd be pregnant
all the time because he can't say 'no.' " The Humphrey camp accused him of "border-
line obscenity." In October, Humphrey was quoted by the New York *Times* as calling
former President Johnson "paranoid" about the war in 1968. Humphrey apologized
to Johnson, but not before Vice President Agnew branded him a "turncoat."

[11] Humphrey was seventeenth on the Senate seniority list when he left to become
vice president but was ninety-second when he returned to the Senate.

Humphrey's beaming face told how happy he was to be back from the edge of political oblivion among the merchants of power whom he had lived and worked with for more than two decades. But even the party that celebrated Humphrey's return was dominated by talk of an event which reminded him that the dream he held for so long was still not dead. Senator Edward Kennedy's defeat by Senator Robert Byrd of West Virginia for reelection as assistant majority leader, a job once held by Humphrey, was another political setback that most of those at the party agreed further reduced the slim chance that Kennedy would be a presidential candidate in 1972. Humphrey understood the lesson of Kennedy's defeat as only a man could who had endured crushing defeat himself and learned that in American politics, few defeats are ever final. "This decision only shows the unpredictability of politics," Humphrey said afterwards. "It also shows how events can affect the ultimate outcome of things. Sometimes you're the beneficiary of events or accidents, and sometimes you're the victim."

Settling into Eugene McCarthy's former suite on the fourth floor of the Old Senate Office Building — after ordering the grey walls painted an off-white — Humphrey temporarily pushed aside the tantalizing thought of the presidency and prepared to focus his attention on the Senate. "I happen to think that is the best politics," he said a few days later. "People watch the Senate and what goes on here and who the participants are." Humphrey appeared more energetic and more relaxed than he had been during sixteen years in the Senate and four in the vice presidency. "He's no less active in terms of what he wants to do," explained his new administrative assistant, Kenneth Gray, "but everything doesn't have to be done today or tomorrow." Gray — who agreed to join Humphrey's staff only after Humphrey assured him he had no plans to run for president again — also recalls that Humphrey wanted to make certain he was not isolated from young people. "His first instruction to us was that when students and young people come in and want to see him that we send them in. He said he didn't care if he was meeting with a Cabinet officer. He wants to see young people."

Humphrey came back to the Senate hoping to play an important role in the Ninety-second Congress as a legislative craftsman. He had prepared proposals in the fields of national health insurance, federal revenue sharing, rural development and urban planning, and disarmament and arms control. But he quickly discovered that the Senate had changed as much as he had, and that the levers of power he was once able to push so adroitly were no longer available to him. The death of Georgia's gaunt, patrician Richard Russell, the dean of the Senate, on the day Humphrey was sworn in was a sign of the changing nature of the Senate, which had added twenty-six new members — a fourth of its total — since the 1968 election. As majority whip and even as vice president, Humphrey had known every senator, his weaknesses and strengths and what he wanted out of life, but now there were senators he'd never met before and he'd lost touch with many of those he did know. There were new committee and subcommittee chairmen and most of the issues that Humphrey had pioneered as the Senate's most respected liberal activist had been staked out by others. Humphrey chafed under the constraints of his new role. He was unhappy that he wasn't given his first choice of a committee assignment — Appropriations — and had to settle for Government Operations, Agriculture and Joint Economics instead. He complained about the paucity of his Senate staff allowance that gave him a staff only a fourth as large as he'd had as vice president. He bridled against the parliamentary discipline imposed by the new majority whip, Robert Byrd, and even engaged in an acrimonious exchange with him on the floor one day over Byrd's refusal to extend the fifteen-minute period for morning business. Finally, Humphrey missed the open door at the White House and the presidential calls asking him to perform important political chores.

The difficulties Humphrey faced were compounded by the death of his closest friend, Minneapolis Businessman Fred Gates, on February 1. The sixty-two year old Gates, who had held the Bible on the day Humphrey was sworn in as vice president, was one of the few people Humphrey trusted without reservation and he was shaken by his death.[12]

Humphrey's reentry problems were apparent to his staff. "He often expressed his frustration in staff meetings," Ken Gray recalls. "He'd try to do something with an issue that his name had been attached to over the years and he'd find out it was somebody else's issue now. He'd come up with a Humphrey amendment or a Humphrey bill and we'd tell him 'So and so's already got a bill like that,' and he'd say, 'Dammit, I want my own bill.' " Even when Humphrey broke new legislative ground by coming up with a bill that would create a National Domestic Development Bank patterned after the World Bank to help provide a new source of funds to state and local governments — and similar legislation to create a rural development bank to help arrest the decline of small-town America — his proposals received little attention in the news media.[13]

[12] A bizarre sequel to Gates' death occurred three days later when his home was burglarized and a secret safe robbed during his funeral services. Although there were rumors that the safe contained a large amount of cash — Gates was comptroller of Humphrey's 1968 campaign — Gates' associates believe it is unlikely since he was not in the habit of keeping more than a few thousand dollars on hand at any time. Still, police never determined the amount of the loss or the identity of the burglars.
[13] Humphrey called his bill to establish a National Domestic Development Bank "one of the most important pieces of legislation I've ever presented," and expressed amazement at the scanty coverage given the press conference at which he announced it. "Really, this is what's so discouraging," he said afterwards. "I get up here and condemn Mr. Nixon about something and I get a headline. If I go out on some crazy ridiculous statement that isn't supported by fact or even good opinion, it makes news. But when you get down to talking about priorities and goals and ways to achieve them, it just doesn't hit."

Humphrey teamed up with Democratic Congressman Henry Reuss of Wisconsin on his first day back in the Senate to push a compromise revenue sharing plan that included many of the Nixon administration's welfare reform goals, but the two were unable to deliver the necessary Democratic votes to persuade the administration to back the compromise. Humphrey's call for a national health insurance program, an idea he'd first suggested twenty years earlier, was largely ignored when a bipartisan group of senators and House members announced its support for a similar bill introduced by Edward Kennedy.

Although stymied in his initial legislative ambitions, Humphrey began breaking out of his slump in late March. A major turning point came on March 24 when he supported a successful Senate move to cut off further federal spending for the proposed $1.3 billion supersonic transport airplane (SST). The vote represented a cruel dilemma for Humphrey. It forced him to choose between his longtime supporter George Meany and the AFL-CIO, who were among the strongest advocates of the SST, and a coalition of liberals, environmentalists and others — including many of his Minnesota constituents — who regarded the plane as a symbol of environmental degradation and misplaced national priorities. Although Humphrey said his decision was based on the economic, technological and environmental arguments made against the plane, some saw it as a sign that he was trying to reestablish his credentials with the liberal wing of the Democratic party — a sure tipoff that he intended to run again. Humphrey maintained that his vote wasn't presidentially motivated. "I had to make up my mind whether I was running for president or whether I was a senator from Minnesota," he later explained.[14]

Nevertheless, Humphrey was clearly removing some of the suspicions about his liberal instincts that had been planted during his vice presidency. On the same day as the SST vote, Humphrey presided over a session of the Democratic Policy Council that reached unanimous agreement on a resolution condemning President Nixon's Vietnam policy and urging the withdrawal of all American forces by the end of 1971. Humphrey strongly supported the resolution, which represented a turnaround from the platform position on Vietnam demanded by former President Johnson at the 1968 convention. When the final vote was recorded, Humphrey indicated his relief that Johnson's hold on the party and on him had finally been broken. "My God," said Humphrey, clapping his hand to his forehead, "it finally happened."[15]

[14] Humphrey disputed reports that he had given his word to Meany that he would support the SST. He acknowledged that he had told Meany several weeks before the vote that "I would do what I could to help him," but he called Meany two nights before the vote and informed him he was going to oppose the project. "I didn't doublecross Mr. Meany," Humphrey insists.

[15] Humphrey earlier had become a co-sponsor of a proposed amendment by Senators George McGovern and Mark Hatfield that endorsed the same principle of total

A day later, Humphrey took the Senate floor to make his first major policy speech since returning to Congress. The subject of his "maiden" speech was one on which he could speak with more knowledge and experience than almost anyone in Washington — disarmament and arms control. Humphrey had made his first formal statement on the subject in 1950, and his Disarmament Subcommittee had paved the way for creation of the U.S. Arms Control and Disarmament Agency in 1961 and the successful negotiation of the first partial nuclear test ban treaty in 1963. Speaking against the backdrop of the resumption of the U.S.-Soviet strategic arms limitation talks (SALT) in Vienna that began in 1969, Humphrey expressed the feeling that leaders of the Nixon administration were too much the "prisoners of fear" to successfully conclude the SALT negotiations. He offered a practical suggestion in the form of "a guideline to the administration" to break that cycle of fear, calling on the United States to accept a Soviet offer to ban or limit deployment of the principal defensive nuclear weapon — the antiballistic missile — for a temporary period that would be extended only if the Soviets responded positively to American proposals for a freeze on the testing and deployment of offensive weapons.

Humphrey's arms control speech and his SST vote projected him into the spotlight for the first time since he returned to the Senate, and coincided with a sudden rise in public opinion polls which now showed him running third — just behind frontrunner Edmund Muskie and non-candidate Edward Kennedy. Humphrey had carefully kept the door open to another presidential race from the moment of his 1970 election ("Listen, the minute you rule yourself out completely, you have no power in Washington," he declared shortly afterwards), and now his dormant presidential sap was beginning to rise. He told a group of students at Georgetown University on March 31 that he would make a decision on whether he would run for president towards the end of 1971 after seeing how other Democratic contenders were doing. If by the end of the year, it appeared that no other Democrat had emerged strongly, Humphrey declared, "then I will take a good look" at running again.

At the same time, Humphrey was moving to promote party unity. He helped Larry O'Brien negotiate an agreement among the eight presidential hopefuls — himself, Muskie, Kennedy, McGovern, Henry Jackson, Fred Harris, Harold Hughes and Birch Bayh — to help pay off the party's debt and to refrain from carving each other up too badly in the 1972 primaries.[16] Humphrey repeated the harmony theme in late March at a Washington con-

---

withdrawal from Vietnam by the end of 1971, and was a strong backer of Majority Leader Mike Mansfield's resolution calling for total withdrawal of U.S. forces from Indochina at a "time certain" within two years.

[16] Eugene McCarthy was not invited to the meeting at which the agreement was made because, according to O'Brien, he was not considered a serious contender.

ference of Democratic state chairmen, telling them, "We cannot afford the wasteful luxury of destructive disunity." Humphrey offered his own state party as an example of how warring Democratic factions could be brought together. "If the state of Eugene McCarthy and Hubert Humphrey can do what Minnesota did in 1970, you can do it in your states." The unity pitch paid off in the form of a successful fundraiser held by the party in Washington on April 21. More than two thousand persons paid five hundred dollars apiece to see the eleven new Democratic governors and almost as many presidential hopefuls put on display, but the crowd saved its warmest response for Humphrey, who drew the only standing ovation of the evening.

In each of his first three months back in the Senate, Humphrey had made an average of ten out-of-town speaking trips, partly to raise money to hire additional staff but also for the purpose of testing public response to him. Almost invariably, he came back encouraged by that response. "As I travel around the country now, I find that people are very warm, very friendly to me," he told an old reporter-friend, Godfrey Sperling, Jr., of the *Christian Science Monitor,* in late April. "Three years ago and two years ago, as I traveled around the country, people treated me respectfully in some instances. . . . But today it is very different. People go out of their way to come up and talk. . . . I think that when I get around this country and get to see people again, I have a message for them. I have something to offer them. Whether it is enough or not, they will have to decide."

The "I'm getting a tremendous reception everywhere I go" syndrome was a sure sign that Humphrey's presidential fever had returned, and those around him knew it. "I'd say it was around April that he began to give serious thought to it for the first time," recalls Bill Connell, who with Max Kampelman and several other Humphrey confidants had been making plans since late 1969 to help Humphrey if he decided to run again. "As he traveled around, he began to sense that there was a reservoir of good will towards him, and that the hostility he felt in 1968 had worn off. In January and February and March, people would talk to him about running and he'd just say he didn't know, but by April he began to get interested and he'd say, 'Well you better stay loose because I'm giving some thought to it.' "

On his sixtieth birthday — May 27 — Humphrey let his presidential cat out of its loosely tied bag. Meeting with a group of Washington reporters for a breakfast interview at the National Press Club, he doused his ham omelet with catsup and declared exuberantly: "I've got the sails up. I'm testing the water. I'm not salivating but I'm occasionally licking my chops."

Humphrey's candid admission that he was indeed eyeing the presidency again was made in the afterglow of a birthday party that would have swayed even a less reluctant candidate. Some two hundred invited guests representing several hundred million dollars in collective wealth attended the party the night before at Washington's posh Madison Hotel. The party, which included the most generous contributors to Humphrey's 1968 campaign, was officially designated as non-political, but none of the guests missed the meaning when Actress-Singer Edie Adams toasted Humphrey on his "sixtieth birthday going on '72." The party may have been technically non-political, but the reasons behind it were not. "It was sort of raising the flag and saying Humphrey was now a major national figure again," recalls Connell, who understood as well as Humphrey did that the guest list represented a solid core of financial support that would make it much easier for Humphrey to commit himself firmly to the decision he was approaching.

Whatever lingering doubts Humphrey still had about another bid for the presidency were resolved for him by his wife. Muriel Humphrey long ago had accepted her husband's ambition to be president, and while her gentle nature was repelled by the thought of seeing him subjected to another and possibly even more devastating defeat than he had suffered in 1968, she understood that there was only one way that he could put to rest the ghost of 1968. "Daddy, your whole life has been a preparation for the presidency," she told him shortly before his sixtieth birthday, "and you just owe it to yourself and to everything you've accomplished and to everything we've done together to run again. You came so close the last time and if you don't try it this time, we'll never know."

Humphrey had been dipping his toe into the waters of the Rubicon all spring, and in July he crossed it. He spent the Fourth of July weekend at Waverly with Jack Chestnut, the coolly efficient Minneapolis attorney who had engineered his 1970 Senate victory and decided then to "make a run to see if I ought to run." Chestnut, who had been pushing hard for Humphrey to run, told him, "If you've got any worries about a campaign organization, you can forget them because we're going to put together a vigorous organization with new people and young blood. There won't be any talk about a tired old Humphrey team this time. We did it for you in Minnesota in 1970 and we can do it nationally in 1972."

On July 6, Chestnut and John Morrison, a thirty-four year old self-made Minneapolis millionaire who would serve as Chestnut's right-hand man, met in Washington with a select group of Humphrey advisers that included Connell, Kampelman, Humphrey's former press secretary Norman Sherman, and H. Harrison (Sonny) Dogole, a wealthy Philadelphia businessman who was one of Humphrey's chief financial supporters. The meeting lasted until 3:00 A.M., with Humphrey telling those present what they had wanted to hear since early 1969 — that he was throwing his battered hat into the ring once again. Humphrey said he was convinced he had "50-50 chance" for the nomination because Muskie wasn't catching on. He told the group that he planned to travel extensively around the country in the coming months, speaking to political gatherings and to as many party leaders as possible. He said he would avoid entering the early primaries, hopefully allowing the other candidates to knock each other out while he demonstrated his appeal in the last big primaries in New York and California and won the nomination at the July convention. Humphrey also emphasized that he had given Chestnut control of his embryonic campaign and told everyone that, from now on, they were to "clear it with Jack." (Humphrey's high regard for the thirty-nine year old Chestnut was apparent when he told an aide a few days after the death of Fred Gates, "Jack Chestnut is my new Freddie Gates.") Finally, it was agreed at the meeting that an in-depth national poll would be commissioned in the fall to gauge more accurately the public response to Humphrey and to discern the current mood of Democratic voters.

In August, during the Congressional recess, Humphrey spent two weeks in Minnesota, touching bases with state party leaders, telephoning supporters all over the country and laying plans for a preliminary campaign that could suddenly expand into a full-scale presidential effort. "He clearly had a head of steam up at that point and was set to go," recalls DFL State Chairman Richard Moe, one of those who met at length with Humphrey at the time. "He said he was surprised that Muskie hadn't wrapped it up and it was clear to me that that was the thing that convinced him that he should run." [18]

After Labor Day, Humphrey began a travel schedule that would take him into twenty-six states in the next three months. His travels merely reaffirmed his conviction that he still had a solid base of support in all regions of the country — he even spoke in Alaska — but he also found that many party leaders didn't think he could win the nomination. "He got this negative sounding everywhere he went, that people would say, 'You've done so much for the party and we love you but we don't think you can win,' " Humphrey's press secretary, Jack MacDonald, recalls. "This made a deep impression on him and made him feel that he had to demonstrate to people who were friendly but doubted his vote-getting ability that he could win." As a result, by late November Humphrey had abandoned his strategy of bypassing most of the primaries. "Whoever gets the nomination will have to be in the primaries — a representative sampling of them," he declared on November 19 as he approved plans to open a Washington Humphrey-for-President headquarters in a suite of offices vacated by Indiana Senator Birch Bayh when he abandoned his candidacy a month earlier.

Humphrey decided to make an all-out effort in two early primaries where

[18] The new generation of DFL leaders that came to power in 1970 was reminiscent of the earlier era that produced Humphrey, McCarthy, Orville Freeman and so many other national figures. In addition to the thirty-five year old Moe, who was the nation's youngest Democratic state chairman, the party boasted the nation's youngest governor in Wendell Anderson (thirty-seven); the nation's youngest legislative leader in House Minority Leader Martin Sabo (thirty-three), and the nation's youngest state Democratic chairwoman in Koryne Horbal (thirty-five).

he was automatically entered — Florida on March 14 and Wisconsin on April 4 — to prove that he could shake off his loser's image. "A lot of people around the country are basically for me," he said in early December as he described his major political handicap, "but they're not sure I can win, so they're hanging back. Well, there's one simple remedy for that — win a few [primaries]." The decision was a strategic one that committed him to a full-scale campaign in the later primaries as well. Humphrey first disclosed that decision on December 4 at a private dinner party at the elegant Miami Beach home of Banker-Attorney Arthur Courshon, a veteran Humphrey supporter.

Humphrey's decision was facilitated by two key private polls commissioned by his campaign staff. The first, an in-depth nationwide survey of 760 registered Democrats taken by International Research Associates of New York City in October and November and completed on December 1, showed that much of the negative feeling toward Humphrey stemming from 1968 had dissipated and that voters perceived him as the most experienced candidate in the party.[19] More significantly in the eyes of Humphrey's advisers, the poll showed him leading every Democratic contender except Kennedy. It gave Humphrey a 6 percentage point lead over Muskie with Kennedy out of the race, and showed him ahead of Muskie among Catholics, blacks, the young and the blue-collar voters. "He really didn't make a full-scale decision to go ahead until the results of that poll were in," says Connell, who was pleased when a December 26 Gallup poll found that, with Kennedy out of the race, Humphrey had a 3 percentage point lead over Muskie. The second private Humphrey poll was taken in December among 450 Florida voters and showed him running second — by only 4 percentage points — to Alabama Governor George Wallace, while edging out Muskie and running well ahead of all other contenders. Humphrey had tentatively planned to announce his candidacy formally in Florida in late January, but as he and the top lieutenants of his national and Florida campaign teams gathered for a secret strategy session in the Miami Beach suburb of Bal Harbour on December 29, they agreed that Humphrey had to make an even earlier official start to head off Muskie in Florida and subsequent primaries as well as in the non-primary states.

Humphrey suggested for sentimental and practical reasons that he make his announcement in Philadelphia on January 10. He picked the date because it was the deadline for entering the crucial April 25 Pennsylvania primary, with its 182 delegate votes. He picked the city because of the importance of the Pennsylvania primary in his long-range strategy for stopping Muskie, but also because of its symbolic meaning for his own remark-

[19] The poll was not entirely positive, however. It showed that many voters still regarded Humphrey as too talkative, too willing to take both sides of an issue and too much a figure of the past.

ably long and checkered career. He had first burst upon the national scene in Philadelphia at the 1948 Democratic National Convention, he had begun his ill-fated 1968 campaign there, and now he would return to that city to open the campaign that he hoped would allow him to go to Philadelphia as president in 1976 to lead the nation in celebrating its two hundredth birthday.

At 11:00 A.M. on Monday, January 10, 1972, Hubert Humphrey announced for the third time in twelve years that he was seeking the presidential nomination. Standing in front of a large reproduction of the first three words of the Preamble to the Constitution — "We the People" — that provided the theme of his declaration of candidacy, Humphrey told the three hundred newsmen and cheering supporters who were jammed into a small room in the Poor Richard Club why he was seeking the presidency again.

"As I see it, my task is reconciliation, rebuilding, and rebirth," Humphrey said in a serious low-key speech that evoked none of the "politics of joy" of his 1968 announcement. "America is not sick. What we lack is leadership and vision. Our nation was founded on the principle of faith and trust in the people. The 'We, the People . . .' of our Constitution's Preamble has too often been forgotten by those who govern. But it is in the people that our strength, my strength lies."

He dismissed his past defeats as preludes to victory. "In my years of government experience, I have learned an essential fact: We may suffer an occasional defeat. We all do. But with determination and faith, a man or a nation can grow from defeat."

Then the man whose career had paralleled the ups and downs of the Democratic party for more than a quarter of a century, summed up the attitude that had made his life a testimonial to the human spirit's refusal to accept defeat: "Persistence and tenacity are old American virtues," he declared. "I was defeated for mayor the first time I ran for office, but I was elected the second time. I was defeated for the vice presidental nomination the first time I sought it — but I was later nominated and elected. I was defeated, as you know, for the presidential nomination in 1960 — but I was nominated in 1968. I was defeated in the presidential election of 1968. But I return to the battle determined to do my best to achieve victory in 1972."

CHAPTER XXI

NEW DEAL AND NEW POLITICS

*There is this built-in momentum in politics. It's like a
magnet drawing you if you're involved at this level
of political life. You sort of feel that this is what you
are moving toward. This is the ultimate, the climax,
the center of your political life.*

Hubert Humphrey talking about the presidency.

*If you're in politics fifteen or twenty years, you kind
of respond to circumstances. And then you're willing to
have a try at it. Do I want it for myself? No. There's
no personal need driving me toward it. But if the
situation compels you and you're in politics, you go.*

Eugene McCarthy talking about the presidency.

Hubert Humphrey had always found his greatest strengths in adversity
and defeat, and it was only natural that he began his final campaign for
the presidency by drawing encouragement from a primary in which he
had finished a distant second. Humphrey's assessment of the result of the
Florida primary in March, 1972, was accurate. Even though he won only
19 percent of the vote and finished far behind George Wallace, who received
42 percent, Humphrey had begun to reestablish himself as the authentic
spokesman for the historic center of the Democratic party. Senator Edmund
Muskie, who a week before had won the New Hampshire primary but displayed serious weaknesses as a campaigner, won only 9 percent of the
Florida vote and came in a faraway fourth behind Senator Henry Jackson. Three weeks later, after Muskie defeated Eugene McCarthy in Illinois,
he finished fourth again in the Wisconsin primary, winning only 10 percent
of the vote and failing even to carry the heavily Polish wards in South Mil-

waukee. Humphrey, meanwhile, came in third in Wisconsin with 21 percent, behind Wallace, who received 22 percent, and Humphrey would have been in a virtual tie with George McGovern for first place had it not been for the large Republican crossover vote.

Humphrey's campaign managers agreed both before and after the Wisconsin primary that the central purpose of their campaign in that state was to make Humphrey appear more attractive to prospective Democratic contributors than Muskie, who was already financially over extended after his disappointing showing in the early primaries. "The man who looks like he's going to win gets the money," said San Francisco Mayor Joseph Alioto, who nominated Humphrey for president in 1968 and campaigned strenuously for him throughout the country in 1972. Alioto told Lou Cannon of the Ridder newspapers just before the Wisconsin vote, "Contributors are bettors and they bet on the man they think will win."

At the same time, the Wisconsin primary symbolized McCarthy's precipitous fall from political grace. In 1968 he had won Wisconsin with 56 percent of the total after Johnson unexpectedly announced that he would not run again, but now he received less than 1 percent of the vote and ran seventh among 11 Democratic candidates. It was clear that McCarthy was finished as a political force except for a possible third–party effort that could help return Richard Nixon to the White House. McCarthy himself acknowledged the almost impossible odds against winning the Democratic nomination when he decided, the week after the Wisconsin primary, not to make an all-out campaign effort in subsequent primaries.

*　*　*　*　*　*　*

The apparent revival of Humphrey as a presidential contender in early 1972 emphasized the perseverance that has made him one of the most durable figures on the American political scene. His ability to overcome past defeats and to adapt to the changing social and political currents of the ages in which he has lived is matched only by Richard Nixon among modern American politicians. That Humphrey has remained a viable political figure throughout the four tumultuous decades spanned by his public career is in itself convincing testimony that he touches a common chord among the American people. Humphrey described his fundamental appoach to political leadership shortly before the 1968 Democratic National Convention in a memorandum to aides who were preparing his presidential nomination acceptance speech. The theme of his speech, he emphasized, must be that "there is a basic reservoir of good will and decency in Americans; if we can harness this reservoir and make it work we can yet control our own destiny." Humphrey's theme was obscured by the violence of Chicago and by the dissonance of the ensuing presidential campaign, but he remains as determined to "touch the hearts and minds of Americans" in 1972 as he was in 1968 or when he first ran for the presidency in 1960.

Any search for a common denominator that explains Hubert Humphrey must begin with his idolatry of Franklin Delano Roosevelt and the New Deal. Humphrey is, above all, a child of the Depression who still sees and deplores, as Roosevelt did in his second inaugural address, "one third of a nation ill-housed, ill-clad, ill-nourished." Unlike many of his fellow liberals, however, Humphrey has never lost faith in the New Deal doctrine that the test of national progress is not whether more is added to the abundance of those who have much but whether enough is provided for those who have too little. He believes that more federal spending can alleviate and eventually cure the nation's social problems and can, as he wrote in his 1964 book, *The Cause is Mankind*, lead to "the triumph of mankind over its traditional enemies — poverty, hunger, disease and ignorance." Humphrey's commitment to the humanitarian goals of the New Deal and to the historic thrust of liberalism is nowhere more evident than in his enduring popularity among low and middle–income Americans, particularly blacks. His strong support among blacks and other minorities in the 1972 Florida and Wisconsin primaries bears witness to the fact that he still speaks to that segment of the American population living in conditions more akin to the Depression than to an affluent society.

Yet while Humphrey is the symbol of the American dream to many of those who have not yet realized it, his obsession with seeing that the nation shares her bounty with all her citizens has also been one of his greatest weakness. He was too absorbed in the visions of the Great Society and in his own unfulfilled yearning for the presidency to recognize that the Vietnam War was a great moral evil that could destroy everything he dreamed of.

The man who did recognize that evil and who stood up at a critical moment in American history to warn the nation of it was Eugene McCarthy. Just as Humphrey had forced the nation to confront the civil rights issue in 1948, McCarthy's stand against the Vietnam War in 1968 was a singular act of courage that grows larger in retrospect and guarantees him a secure place in the history of his country. The consequences of his opposition to the war have been obscured by his own unorthodox behavior since 1968, but regardless of future events and whatever one thinks of McCarthy the man or whatever becomes of him, the steady withdrawal of U.S. combat troops from Vietnam during most of the Nixon administration was a direct result of his challenge and remains his most fitting monument.

McCarthy showed that it is possible for one man to make a difference in a democratic society, and that not even the immense power of the presidency can withstand the pressure of opposition from a public aroused by a man who speaks out against what he sees as an immoral action by his government. It is unlikely that any American president will ever again assume that he is safe from challenge by a member of his own party, as Richard Nixon found out in 1972 and as future presidents undoubtedly will realize. McCarthy's challenge also brought with it the emergence of what was called the "new politics," which, while not new in its techniques, drew thousands of young people and adults into active participation in politics for the first time. Finally, McCarthy forced the Democratic party to institute fundamental reforms which have drastically altered the nature of the party and which will strengthen the Democrats' claim to be the party of the people.

Whether McCarthy is destined to be remembered as the midwife of a new day in American politics or merely as a brilliant gadfly of the old, it is clear that American politics in the 1970's will reflect the dedication to reforming political processes and limiting executive power that is the common denominator of his public career. At the same time, McCarthy is obsessed with doing all he can in 1972 to elect a president who comes closest to meeting the three principles he feels were exemplified by his political hero, Adlai Stevenson: "First, a decent respect for the opinions of mankind in world affairs; second, a willingness to accept the judgment of the majority and the popular will in domestic politics, as manifest in party conventions or in general elections; and third, an unselfish surrender of his own personal reputation and image for the good of the common effort if, in his judgment, that surrender would advance the cause of justice and order and civility."

Regardless of the respective roles of Hubert Humphrey and Eugene McCarthy in 1972, however, they remain important symbols of the forces of conflict that have brought the Democratic party and American liberalism to major crossroads in the 1970's. Humphrey represents the politics of consensus which manifests itself in the two-party system and in the traditional liberal belief that man's problems are subject to temporal solutions. McCarthy represents the politics of change which threatens to realign permanently traditional voting patterns and which holds that government should not promise solutions but only promise to seek solutions.

Different approaches to the pursuit and exercise of political power were, in the end, what set Hubert Humphrey and Eugene McCarthy on the collision course that prevented either of them from being elected president of the United States in 1968 and could prevent Humphrey from being elected president in 1972. Their differences also damaged the causes for which they had fought so long. "It's not a question of whether Hubert lost or Gene lost," Congressman John Blatnik of Minnesota, who came to Washington two years before Humphrey and McCarthy, said in late 1971 shortly after his two old friends began moving toward another confrontation. "They both knocked each other out of the ring in 1968 and the loss was for the whole liberal philosophy, the liberal cause itself, all the things that so many of us have struggled for all the way back to Franklin Roosevelt. How little time we liberals have had to do the things we believe in and believe ought to be done, and could have been done and would have been done if somehow Hubert and Gene hadn't had that split. If only they'd pulled together, one of them would have been president, not Richard Nixon, and we'd have been out of the war by now. I say it now with sadness because we're all approaching the late afternoon of our lives, but we really could have solved some of the monumental problems that confront us both at home and abroad. We always talked about that, Hubert and Gene and the rest of us, and here we had a chance to finally do something about it and we never did. It's a real tragedy."

INDEX

A Note About The Author

ALBERT EISELE is a Washington correspondent for Ridder Publications, Inc., and a winner of the 1971 American Political Science Association Award for distinguished reporting of public affairs.

A native Minnesotan, he graduated from Saint John's University in Collegeville, Minnesota, in 1958, and spent two additional years at the University of Minnesota. After serving in the U.S. Army and playing professional baseball in the Cleveland Indians organization, he was editor of the Mankato (Minnesota) *Free Press* from 1962–64, and worker as a reporter for the St. Paul *Dispatch* and *Pioneer Press* from 1964–65. Since 1965, he has been a member of Ridder Publications, Inc., which publishes fifteen daily newspapers in eight states.

Eisele's articles have appeared in the *New Republic*, the *Washingtonian* and other publications. He and his wife, Moira, and two daughters live in Falls Church, Virginia.

Printed and bound by The Book Press, Brattleboro, Vermont.